FORENSIC PATHOLOGY OF FRACTURES AND MECHANISMS OF INJURY

Postmortem CT Scanning

FORENSIC PATHOLOGY OF FRACTURES AND MECHANISMS OF INJURY

Postmortem CT Scanning

Michael P. Burke

CRC Press
Taylor & Francis Group
Boca Raton London New York

CRC Press is an imprint of the
Taylor & Francis Group, an **informa** business

CRC Press
Taylor & Francis Group
6000 Broken Sound Parkway NW, Suite 300
Boca Raton, FL 33487-2742

First issued in paperback 2021

Version Date: 2011926

ISBN 13: 978-0-367-77819-4 (pbk)
ISBN 13: 978-1-4398-8148-4 (hbk)

Library of Congress Cataloging-in-Publication Data

Burke, Michael P.
Forensic pathology of fractures and mechanisms of injury : postmortem CT scanning / Michael P. Burke.
p. ; cm.
"A CRC title."
Includes bibliographical references and index.
ISBN 978-1-4398-8148-4 (hardcover : alk. paper)
I. Title.
[DNLM: 1. Fractures, Bone--pathology--Case Reports. 2. Autopsy--methods--Case Reports. 3. Forensic Pathology--methods--Case Reports. 4. Fractures, Bone--radiography--Case Reports. 5. Tomography, X-Ray Computed--methods--Case Reports. WE 180]

614'.1--dc23 2011039356

Visit the Taylor & Francis Web site at
http://www.taylorandfrancis.com

and the CRC Press Web site at
http://www.crcpress.com

Monash University

"Ancora imparo"

"I am still learning"

Table of Contents

List of Illustrations

Chapter 1

Chapter 2

Chapter 3

Chapter 5

Chapter 7

Chapter 9

Preface

At the Victorian Institute of Forensic Medicine (VIFM), forensic pathologists routinely interpret computed tomography (CT) images and provide opinions to coroners that are at least partly based on this interpretation. The purpose of this book is to provide forensic pathologists with an overview of our experience with CT in routine casework, an appraisal of the literature with respect to fractures, and suggestions for the evaluation of CT images by pathologists. I then suggest what reasonable conclusions can be drawn in cases of trauma, where the medicolegal investigation is limited to an assessment of the circumstances surrounding the death, an external examination of the deceased, and the CT images.

This book in no way intends to suggest that forensic pathologists can become competent in interpreting CT images without additional formal training under the tutorage and guidance of a radiologist.

Acknowledgments

I would like to thank the state coroner for making her files available, Kerry Johannes, Jill Roberts, Ruby Haouchar, Caroline Rosenberg, Ron Rose, and the pathologists at the Victorian Institute of Forensic Medicine (VIFM).

On behalf of the forensic pathologists at the VIFM, I would like to acknowledge and thank Dr. Chris O'Donnell, consultant forensic radiologist, whose enthusiasm and generous teaching has made the introduction of routine CT scanning an interesting and welcome part of our practice.

The Author

Michael Burke, M.D., is a forensic pathologist who has worked at the Victorian Institute of Forensic Medicine (VIFM) in Melbourne, Australia since 1993.

In 1996, he was a member of the forensic team involved in the criminal investigation in the aftermath of the Port Arthur incident in Tasmania, Australia, in which 35 people were murdered by a single gunman. In 1999, he was part of the British forensic team in Kosovo as part of the United Nations War Crimes Investigation.

Dr. Burke has published a number of papers in forensic and medical literature and a book touching on forensic pathology and motor vehicle incidents.

In 2005, the VIFM was one of the first forensic pathology centers in the world to acquire a computed tomography (CT) scanner. As one of the specialist forensic pathologists at the VIFM, Dr. Burke has practical experience with the introduction of multidetector CT (MDCT) scanning into the routine work of a busy mortuary.

Introduction

The *Webster's New International Dictionary with Reference History* (circa 1930s) defined an *autopsy*, in the medical sense, as the "dissection of a dead body for the purpose of ascertaining the cause, seat, or nature of a disease; a post-mortem examination." This definition has stood the test of time for a considerable period. However, the rapid evolution of imaging technology now means that one does not necessarily have to conduct a formal dissection of the deceased in order to address the medicolegal issues involved in each particular case of death investigation.

The dictionary also has a more general definition of autopsy, which is derived from the Greek words for *self* and *seen*. The general definition states that an autopsy is a "personal observation or examination; seeing with one's own eyes; an ocular view."

Perhaps it is time for forensic pathologists to be more flexible in deciding what type of "autopsy" is indicated for each individual case. To "see with one's own eyes" can just as easily signify a computed tomography (CT) image on a computer screen as it has traditionally meant the direct observation of the macroscopic findings during a conventional autopsy.

What is vitally important in the medicolegal system is for the forensic pathologist to understand, "to see," what is illustrated on the CT images. This issue may well be the limiting factor for the widespread incorporation of postmortem CT into routine practice.

It may be suggested that the introduction of routine CT scanning to death investigation has reduced the importance of the forensic pathologist. This view is folly. The introduction of CT scanning into a forensic institute will most likely decrease the proportion of cases undergoing full, conventional internal examination. The consequence of the lack of an internal examination means the expertise of the forensic pathologist to assess the circumstances of the death and the external examination findings is more valuable than ever before.

Last, it is also important to state that by simply reading this book forensic pathologists cannot consider themselves competent in the use of postmortem CT. The process of educating ourselves is an ongoing one that should include formal education by radiologists, correlation of the CT findings with conventional autopsy, sharing and discussing cases with colleagues, and attendance at targeted CT conferences.

1 Introduction of Computed Tomography (CT) into Routine Forensic Pathology Practice

Introduction

In many jurisdictions around the world, the practice of forensic pathology is in the process of change. For many years the autopsy rates in hospitals have been declining. In many major teaching hospitals a full conventional autopsy examination with dissection of each organ system and formal neuropathological examination of the brain is uncommon. The reasons for this change are diverse. In most hospital pathology departments the autopsy is seen as less important than providing the routine surgical pathology service. The deceased's next of kin are given more information about the autopsy and are more active in the decision-making process. Some reasons for objection to autopsy are emotive, some due to religious concerns, whereas others are purely logistical (i.e., wanting timely organization of the funeral).

Alternatives to full autopsy examination have been proposed. These include partial and targeted autopsies and the use of CT and magnetic resonance imaging (MRI), with integration of ultrasonography guided 12-gauge biopsies of the heart, the lungs, liver, spleen, and kidneys. The use of biopsies is an integral part of the "minimally invasive autopsy" [1].

A study of 30 deceased hospital patients showed that in 23 (77%) cases there was agreement in the anatomical cause of death between the conventional and minimally invasive procedures. The technique was reported as correctly diagnosing common hospital-associated causes of death such as sepsis and pneumonia. Important though, the major false-negative results in minimally invasive autopsy included acute myocardial infarction, obstructive coronary artery atherosclerosis, and gastrointestinal hemorrhage [1].

The autopsy in the coronial or medicolegal system has been somewhat exempt from these changes as the deceased's body is under the control of a coroner or similar authority. An autopsy has always been considered desirable in the eyes of the law. Forensic pathology had become "the last bastion of the autopsy." However, following a number of highly publicized incidents involving mortuary practice in a number of centers around the world and a swing of the pendulum toward more autonomy for the deceased's family, the usual practice of scheduling a full autopsy examination for each routine forensic case has changed. Certainly this has been the situation at our place of work, the Victorian Institute of Forensic Medicine (VIFM), and it is very likely to occur in many other institutions.

The introduction of the CT scanner into the practice of forensic pathology allows an alternative to routine "conventional" full autopsy examination. The challenge is to use this alternative wisely and appropriately. It is a change in practice that is not without its challenges.

The forensic pathology community has a responsibility to provide objective leadership in educating the public, coroners, and the medicolegal system in the advantages and disadvantages of performing conventional or alternative medicolegal postmortem examinations.

The Victorian Model

In the State of Victoria, Australia, there is a coronial system of death investigation. The deceased's body is under the legal control of the coroner. The forensic pathologist is employed by the VIFM, a department of the Faculty of Medicine of Monash University, Victoria, Australia. The forensic pathologist provides expert advice to the coroner with respect to medical and forensic issues. The coroner may order a full autopsy examination or an "inspection and report" examination based, at least in part, from the recommendation provided by the pathologist. In the latter examination, the pathologist performs an external inspection of the deceased's body, reviews the available medical records, and provides the coroner with a reasonable cause of death.

In the Victorian system, prior to late 2009 when the latest Coroner's Act was introduced, the senior next of kin had the legal right to object to conventional autopsy examination. The coroner had to weigh the wishes of the grieving family, the medicolegal opinion provided by the forensic pathologist, the interests of other parties such as hospital medical staff or police officers, and the good of the wider community.

The Introduction of Postmortem CT

In July 2005, the VIFM had a multidetector computed tomography (MDCT) scanner installed in its mortuary. As part of the routine admission process to the institute each body undergoes a full (head-to-toe) MDCT scan before removal of the deceased from the body bag. At the end of 2009, the institute had scanned just under 20,000 cases.

As has been documented by Thali and his colleagues from the Virtopsy group, and an ever-increasing number of other workers, MDCT has the potential to provide a wealth of information for medicolegal death investigation [2]. The Virtopsy approach utilizes three-dimensional surface scanning of the body surfaces, MDCT, and magnetic resonance imaging as a possible alternative to conventional autopsy.

The VIFM took a slightly different path. The CT scanner was introduced as an adjunct to autopsy examination. In 2008, the institute performed 2404 full autopsy examinations. There were 841 cases where the senior next of kin objected to autopsy and 714 cases where an external examination of the body was performed as part of an inspection and report examination. A smaller number of cases were admitted which subsequently had a death certificate provided by their general practitioner. In all, 3959 cases had a full body CT scan performed. All bodies admitted to the institute also have a set of routine external photographs with further photographs taken of specific injuries or matters of interest.

The introduction of CT into the routine practice of the institute was associated with a small reduction in the relative number of cases that underwent full autopsy examination. The CT was able to demonstrate a number of common fatal pathologies that could be easily diagnosed by the forensic pathologist. These included pericardial tamponade, massive hemothorax, and large intracerebral hemorrhages. A selection of the typical types of cases assessed primarily by CT examination by the forensic pathologists will be presented in a series of case studies at the end of this chapter.

At the time of the initial incorporation of the CT into routine practice, the institute had an expert radiologist in house for one session per week. Although the radiologist was able to be contacted for an expert opinion at other times, one could not be guaranteed of an immediate response as he was otherwise engaged in full-time clinical work. Radiology education of the pathology staff was provided by the radiologist at weekly case meetings.

Current Victorian Institute of Forensic Medicine (VIFM) System

A significant change in practice resulted from the introduction of the new Coroner's Act in 2008. The practical consequence of the Act for pathology services was that the deceased's family assumed a more active role in the decision-making process with respect to the "need" for autopsy. The VIFM introduced duty pathologists whose role was to review the known information on every case admitted to the institute, review every CT, perform an external examination of the deceased's body, and subsequently discuss the need for autopsy for each case with the duty coroner.

A form summarizing the circumstances of the case, the known past medical history, the relevant findings on provisional external examination, and the results of the CT analysis is completed by the duty pathologist for each case and presented to the coroner. The form becomes part of the coroner's and institute's case files. When the medicolegal investigation is limited to an external examination, the duty pathologist then performs a formal external examination that is recorded in the institute's case system and forms part of the official autopsy report. If a full conventional autopsy is performed, the case is referred to a second pathologist who then completes the full autopsy.

Pathologists tend to have a wider view of what the medicolegal autopsy entails. Whereas the coroner is primarily concerned with determining a reasonable cause of death, the pathologist views the autopsy as providing additional medical information for the deceased's immediate family and targeted information for allied death investigators. Thus, built into our system is a fundamental discrepancy between the objectives of the coroner's system and that of the forensic pathologists.

Decision-Making Process

Two key elements in the traditional decision-making process of the medicolegal investigation are the availability of appropriate clinical or scene information pertaining to the death, and the associated findings on external examination of the deceased's body. CT scans provide a third important source of information. This information may include the presence of collections of blood and other fluids, the presence of gases, gross enlargement of organs, and whether there is injury to the skeleton.

The appropriate information required to make a decision concerning the need for autopsy can of course vary considerably depending upon the particular case. A relatively straightforward decision is presented by the death of an elderly man with a history of hypertension who collapsed and fell to the ground at a family function. The presence of injuries in a single plane to the deceased's face is readily explained by a simple fall from a standing height. In these circumstances, the postmortem CT scan could reveal an intracerebral hemorrhage centered on the basal ganglia. The case could reasonably be completed as death from intracerebral hemorrhage associated with hypertension.

An extra level of complexity is added if the elderly man had not been seen collapsing. In these circumstances the pathologist may still be comfortable in providing the same cause of death. When there is no past medical history available and the episode of collapse is not witnessed, the pathologist could reasonably take a conservative view and recommend a full autopsy examination. Similarly when there is a small intracerebral hemorrhage, the deceased may have an initial period of survival, producing additional injuries on the deceased's body from semipurposeful movements. These injuries are usually over bony prominences and extensor surfaces of the body and are familiar to forensic pathologists. However, these injuries may persuade the pathologist to take a more conservative stance and recommend a full autopsy examination.

The next level of complexity occurs when the individual had been on anticoagulant therapy. The death may then present to a pathologist with considerable bruising related to the initial fall and subsequent semipurposeful antemortem movement. It is likely that in such cases the pathologist will recommend a full autopsy to exclude foul play. The full autopsy examination could also be seen as a safeguard for the pathologist from later criticism that the case should not have been treated as an inspection only investigation.

It is here where the experience of the forensic pathologist is vital. To laypersons, and a good number of medical practitioners, the described case with multiple abrasions and bruises could appear suspicious. It does not necessarily follow, however, that a full conventional autopsy needs to be performed if the pathologist is satisfied with the overall findings in the case.

On the other hand, a completely unremarkable external examination may be irrelevant to the decision-making process for full autopsy in cases where there are highly suspicious scene circumstances. Evidence of a break-in, threats made against the deceased during life, and reports of a disturbance are situations where a full autopsy is mandatory. As is well known by forensic pathologists, there are times when significant force can be applied to a victim with no external evidence of trauma.

In cases of death from intentional medication overdose, the CT has been very useful. When there is a history of depression, empty medication containers and a suicide note at the scene, no injuries on external examination or CT scanning, and a layer of radiopaque material seen within the stomach on the CT images, a full postmortem examination is not necessarily indicated. As one sequentially removes each of these positive features of the death, individual forensic pathologists will reach a point where they believe an autopsy is required to safely manage the case.

It is important that there is consistency between the recommendations for complete autopsy examination by different pathologists at any particular institution. Individual practitioner decision-making practices should not deviate substantially from immediate or distant colleagues, and review mechanisms must be in place to monitor these practices.

Cause of Death

Fundamental requirements of a coroner's system include the provision of a reasonable cause of death, the manner of death, and whether a person or persons contributed to the death. Deaths reported to the coroner for medicolegal investigation include natural deaths where the treating medical practitioner is unable to determine a cause of death; and nonnatural deaths including cases of suicide, accident, and homicide.

The most common cause of natural death in our community is coronary artery atherosclerosis (ischemic heart disease). Whereas calcification of coronary arteries due to atherosclerosis is easily visualized on the CT images, stenosis or occlusion of those arteries cannot be seen using routine postmortem CT. In these cases the recommendation provided to the coroner in relation to the need for autopsy takes into account the past medical history, risk factors for heart disease, a clinical history around the time of death, and the absence of injuries on external examination. CT provides further assurance to the pathologist and coroner by excluding obvious skeletal injury and intracranial hemorrhage.

Minimally invasive autopsy, as described previously, is currently not a suitable method for the routine investigation of deaths in forensic cases. The technique would appear to have potential in specific forensic issues such as obtaining a core biopsy of the pulmonary artery and contents when the sole concern in the case is whether pulmonary thromboembolism is the cause of death. Further studies, which include conventional autopsy confirmation of the core biopsy diagnosis, would certainly be useful.

A reasonable cause of death as provided by the pathologist following a full conventional autopsy is not necessarily a definitive declaration of the actual cause of death. In cases of myocardial free wall rupture from a recent acute myocardial infarction, the cause of death is definitive. An unwitnessed death from a cardiac arrhythmia associated with coronary artery atherosclerosis when an acute coronary lesion is not identified is less authoritative. There is always the possibility that the death could have resulted from an arrhythmia associated with a profound metabolic disturbance, undiagnosed channelopathy, or subtle neurological disorder. The degree of certainty is obviously diminished when a conventional autopsy is not performed.

Postmortem CT scanning is not a substitute for the full medicolegal autopsy. A good example of this is hemopericardium causing pericardial tamponade. The common causes are ruptured acute myocardial infarction and rupture of thoracic aortic dissection. Our experience has been that only some cases of dissection can be detected with confidence using postmortem CT (noncontrast). We have also seen a number of instances of hemopericardium from rupture of the right ventricular free wall secondary to attempted cardiopulmonary resuscitation in cases of massive pulmonary thromboembolism. In these cases the CT could not differentiate between these pathological processes.

Family Contact Program

The VIFM had introduced a family contact program prior to the introduction of CT. The family contact program was developed to ensure that important medical information would be given to the deceased's family in a coordinated manner. An electronic message is sent from the pathologist to a liaison nurse indicating a disease process discovered at autopsy that may have significant health implications for the family members. The liaison nurse organizes the family to meet with one or more of a selected group of interested clinicians.

For example, following the autopsy diagnosis of a condition such as coronary artery atherosclerosis in an individual younger than 50 years of age, Marfan's syndrome, or hemochromatosis, the family is referred to a group of interested clinicians, which include physicians, cardiologists, and geneticists.

The previous example of pericardial tamponade illustrates the educative role forensic pathologists can play for the coroner and the deceased's family. Although the CT may provide the coroner with a cause of death in such a case, it is the responsibility of the pathologist to inform the coroner and the family of the importance of diagnosing the underlying pathology such as dissecting aneurysm and inheritable conditions such as Marfan's syndrome.

Marfan's syndrome has typical phenotypic features which can suggest the diagnosis and CT images can be used to demonstrate an abnormal metacarpal index (arachnodactyly) [3]. Other phenotypic features such as a high arched palate do not appear to have well-defined radiological or morphological criteria. Cases of forme fruste of Marfan's syndrome with aortic dissection but without the other usual phenotypic features are also known to occur. We believe that deaths in individuals under 50 years of age without a history of hypertension from pericardial tamponade, even though it can be diagnosed on CT, should still undergo full autopsy examination with appropriate ancillary investigations.

CT in Trauma

CT is a remarkable imaging modality for the demonstration of fractures. CT image analysis can document and display complex fractures in a far more succinct manner than a lengthy autopsy report. Furthermore, CT images may be seen by the courts as less emotive to members of a jury than forensic photographs of the actual injury.

CT images can also facilitate an understanding of injury causation of individual fractures or of the entire skeleton. CT analysis of bones and associated soft tissues can be interpreted in relation to the known circumstances of a death to provide a better understanding of injury mechanism.

CT in Tissue Donation

The Donor Tissue Bank of Victoria is the largest tissue bank in Australia. The facility is housed within the same building as the VIFM and the Coroner's Court. The Donor Tissue Bank processes and distributes various tissues including skin, tendons, bone, and heart valves.

One of the duties of the forensic pathologists is to examine the bodies of suitable potential donors who are selected by liaison nurses from cases reported to the coroner. There are strict selection criteria, which exclude the deceased from being a potential donor. CT has streamlined the selection process by allowing early diagnosis of fractures to long bones, thus excluding them from the potential donation pool. The CT examination of the chest can reveal the presence of multiple fractured ribs, fractured sternum or hemothorax indicating thoracic trauma, and excludes those cases from potential heart valve donation.

The practical consequence of the CT is that the deceased's relatives are spared the distress of agreeing to donation, but then being informed that the tissue was not suitable. Furthermore, the time of Donor Tissue Bank and mortuary staff is not wasted in retrieving tissue that is subsequently discarded.

Errors in CT Diagnosis by Forensic Pathologists

It is inevitable that the forensic pathologist will make errors in the interpretation of CT images. Expert radiologists are known to make errors in clinical diagnosis [4]. It has been reported that the most common errors made by radiologists in clinical practice are errors in perception [5]. Perception errors are believed to account for about one-half of errors in radiology. The lesion is present on the CT images but the abnormality is missed.

The nonexpert will be prone to making recognition and decision-making errors [6]. These are errors in interpretation. Recognition errors occur when an abnormality is seen but is not recognized as being abnormal. A decision-making error occurs when an abnormality is recognized but is believed to be an artifact. The pathologist may also make a false-positive error in diagnosis, where a diagnosis is made when the diagnostic features are not present in the images.

A further issue is allied to the use of routine full body CT scans. Due to the substantial workload, the "duty pathologist" is often primarily concerned with the cause of death. Naturally, if one sees an obvious cause of death in the initial survey of the axial views such as a large intracerebral hemorrhage, then one may not appreciate a subtle abnormality in the pelvis. This has been termed "framing bias" [7]. Thus potentially important medical information that would have been detected at autopsy is lost.

Proficiency Standard of Forensic Pathologists in Analysis of CT Images

It is impractical for the vast majority of forensic pathology centers to have the complete set of CT scans on every case reported by a radiologist. Furthermore, as reported by Filograna and colleagues [6], consultant radiologists without forensic experience may well make errors simply due to a lack of forensic training. As such, when CT is incorporated into routine service provision, assessing the vast majority of the CT images will be the pathologists' responsibility.

It will be important for forensic pathologists to demonstrate their proficiency in reading the images or confidence in the system will surely diminish. In diagnostic imaging some methods to reduce the frequency of error includes dual or multiple reporting of images and institution of protocols [6]. Depending upon the pathologists' caseload, dual reporting of CT images would satisfy the first suggestion and provide immediate feedback to the pathologist from a colleague.

The introduction of a duty pathologist to triage every death that is admitted to the VIFM means that in practice two pathologists review every case. The duty pathologist can be appraised of the relevant positive and negative findings, and correlate the autopsy findings with the CT images.

CT Education for Forensic Pathologists

The VIFM has been fortunate that its radiologist has a keen interest in forensic medicine and has completed a diploma in forensic medicine through Monash University. This situation will most probably prove to be highly unusual. The radiologist attends twice-weekly case meetings where interesting CT scans are regularly presented to the forensic pathology group.

The institute's pathologists have also been encouraged to attend radiology conferences concentrating on emergency and trauma CT. It would seem a *fait accompli* that, as the use of CT as a tool in forensic decision making becomes a routine and expected process in any institution, a formal teaching program and associated qualification in forensic radiology has to evolve [8].

At the VIFM the radiologist has established a targeted education program focused on death investigation.

Deficiencies of CT in Routine Forensic Practice

Locard's principle is an important rule in forensic casework. Locard's principle states that when there is contact between two objects there will be an exchange between the objects, that is, so-called trace evidence. The recovery of trace evidence requires an active examination of the surface and depths of an injury. This practice is unlikely to occur in the majority of cases that are limited to an external examination of the deceased and CT. However, one must concede that in the vast majority of cases undergoing conventional autopsy, trace evidence is either not deemed necessary or is not actively sought.

It is considered best practice to perform a conventional autopsy examination with associated forensic science assessment, including collection of trace evidence, in all cases of suspicious deaths and hit-and-run pedestrian deaths. Postmortem CT alone does not provide the mechanism for detection of this material.

In nonsuspicious circumstances, the case of a death with a single scalp laceration and associated skull fracture demonstrated on CT could conceivably be misdiagnosed when a conventional autopsy is not performed. A full autopsy examination might reveal unusual foreign matter adherent to the periosteum. This in turn might lead to a more thorough investigation by police and could prove to be a case of concealed homicide. It must be said that such cases are rare and the identification of unusual trace evidence in such a case is exceedingly rare. The remote possibility of such a scenario is not a valid argument against the use of CT and external examination for routine casework. In fact it is far more likely that the CT will reveal an unexpected finding such as a subdural hemorrhage or the external examination will show unanticipated injuries that will stimulate further police inquiries.

In clinical practice contrast enhanced CT is used to identify visceral and vascular injury. Routine postmortem CT can identify collections of blood within body cavities. The location of the blood within these cavities can provide a reasonable probability of the origin of the hemorrhage, that is, so-called sentinel hemorrhage. However, this does not equate with definitive evidence of the source of hemorrhage in a particular case.

The conventional autopsy can allow the pathologist to identify the source of hemorrhage in victims of trauma and postsurgical deaths, though in practice it is often difficult to be certain of the source of hemorrhage in a death where there is substantial blood and the vessel involved is relatively small. In deaths associated with bleeding from injured pelvic vessels, the complex anatomy and difficult access are further challenges in dissection.

We have examined a case of death secondary to blunt force pelvic trauma in a middle-aged man who was struck by a train. The victim died as a consequence of hypovolemic shock while being prepared for interventional angiography in the radiology suite. As a major issue in the case was the source of the hemorrhage we performed postmortem CT angiography by canulating the distal descending aorta and injecting contrast agent. The CT images showed extravasations of contrast material in a position consistent with an origin from the superior gluteal artery. This case will be presented later in a case study.

The disadvantage with this approach of CT angiography is the need for a routine autopsy incision, which may not be acceptable for some families. The Virtopsy group has successfully used peripheral venous canulation and a heart lung machine to define the arterial and venous anatomy in a small series of cases [9].

MDCT has poor soft tissue discrimination. MRI is a far superior technique in demonstrating soft tissue pathology. MRI is used in the Virtopsy project. The Virtopsy team and other workers around the world have published case reports and small series of cases describing the usefulness of MRI in forensic investigations by demonstrating subcutaneous bruises. The medicolegal investigation into the deaths of four pedestrians and a cyclist was clearly assisted by demonstrating the presence of hemorrhage in subcortical bone marrow. Such hemorrhages have been termed “bone bruises” [10]. The cost of a MRI machine and the time taken to acquire images currently limit the usefulness of MRI in routine forensic work.

An attractive alternative for busy forensic institutions is dual source, dual energy CT (DECT) [11]. With this technique, the images produced by CT are not limited to differences in x-ray attenuation but also allow elements of functional and tissue characterization [11]. DECT is said to have the potential to demonstrate bruises in subcutaneous fat and muscle.

An important component of the conventional autopsy performed on suspicious deaths in children is to date skin injuries and fractures. The histological evaluation of callous obtained during the postmortem examination can give a time range for the infliction of the injury. Preliminary studies have been performed using CT to quantify fracture callus volume. An experimental study using sheep showed CT was superior to conventional radiology in assessing the healing of fractures, though the authors conceded that correlation with histology is required to determine the accuracy of the technique [12].

Audit

The VIFM has had an audit program for routine autopsy cases since 2000 [13]. This process entails the random selection of 100 cases per year that are reviewed by a second pathologist. The review includes an inspection of the autopsy report, examination of the histological slides, and the cause of death that was issued on the case. A prescribed form is completed on each case. The audit program now includes a mandatory review of the CT scans from the case.

Audit of CT interpretation by forensic pathologists has been a difficult issue. The result of the CT analysis is universally incorporated into the initial report for the coroner but not always into the full autopsy report. Recently a formal audit process has been instituted by the radiologist. Each month, 10% of admissions assessed by the duty pathologist are randomly selected, CT scans retrospectively analyzed by the radiologist, and any substantial errors discussed at an internal radiological/pathological meeting.

Practical Issues in the Use of CT in Routine Forensic Practice

The introduction of CT into routine practice introduces a number of challenges for a medicolegal death investigation system. In most busy forensic institutes one is not going to have the luxury of a full-time radiologist providing a report on each case. In fact, it is likely the majority of institutions may only have access to a radiologist for a few sessions per week. The radiologist may be available for an urgent opinion via telephone or e-mail, but it is our experience that one cannot assume there will be immediate access to an expert radiological opinion for some cases. The system has to be flexible enough to accommodate a turnaround time of around 24 hours or more for an expert opinion on such cases.

The pathologist, by necessity, must only refer such cases that genuinely require expert opinion lest the system be ground to a halt by the radiologist being swamped with straightforward cases. During the initial implementation of the CT into the daily practice of the institute, the pathologists referred a wide range of cases. Within a relatively short period of time we found that we became far more selective in the number and types of cases that were referred.

The key to this process is education. There are a comparatively small number of pathologies that lead to the great majority of deaths in both natural and non-natural cases. A great many of these pathologies show gross changes on CT. The pathologists can be taught to recognize these CT changes reasonably quickly through their regular case meetings, through one-on-one sessions with the radiologist, by correlating the CT findings and the autopsy examination in their individual cases, and by disseminating interesting and classical cases with each other via e-mail.

Nevertheless, the problem will remain of not knowing what you do not know. Inevitably there will be cases where the pathologist will be accessing a routine case that appears to be relatively clear-cut, yet there are important CT changes that are not recognized. It is a matter of fact that unless the system is prepared to provide the resources for a full-time radiologist to review every CT on every deceased person, then these errors are going to occur. The aim of the system is to minimize such errors.

The following cases will endeavor to show some typical and interesting CT diagnoses that we dealt with in the daily routine forensic pathology caseload. In our previous coronial system, the cases that were initially limited to external examination and CT were those that had a formal objection to autopsy lodged by the senior next of kin. With the later introduction of a new coronial system, a duty pathologist initially evaluates each case with an external examination and CT.

Illustrative Case Studies

It is important to emphasize that although illustrative images are selected to show some important findings in these case studies, in practice the assessment of the CT images is performed using multiple images and multiple views.

Case Study 1: Coronary Artery Disease

A 65-year-old man with a past history of ischemic heart disease was found deceased at his home. There were no suspicious circumstances. The deceased appeared to have fallen forward to the ground and sustained a laceration to his right eyebrow. The deceased's general practitioner declined to provide a death certificate and the case was referred to the coroner. The senior next of kin lodged a formal objection to autopsy.

The external examination showed a lacerated injury to the right eyebrow and a bruise to the right cheek in the same plane. These injuries were deemed to be consistent with a simple fall. There were no injuries seen to the buccal mucosa or to the neck. There was no suggestion of assault. The CT examination showed no subdural or other intracranial hemorrhage. There were no fractures seen and no evidence of cervical spine injury. There was marked calcification of the coronary arteries (Figure 1.1).

The coroner was informed that there was no suggestion of any injury that would have contributed to the death. There was calcification of the coronary arteries. The coroner was informed it was likely the death occurred as a result of a sudden cardiac arrhythmia secondary to myocardial ischemia caused by coronary artery atherosclerosis.

Forensic Issues

This case illustrates the most common type of death investigation at the VIFM. The death of an individual with a history of heart disease may be referred to the coroner because the treating doctor wants to make sure an injury that occurred during an episode of collapse is not associated with intracranial hemorrhage or perhaps a cervical spine injury. Some general practitioners

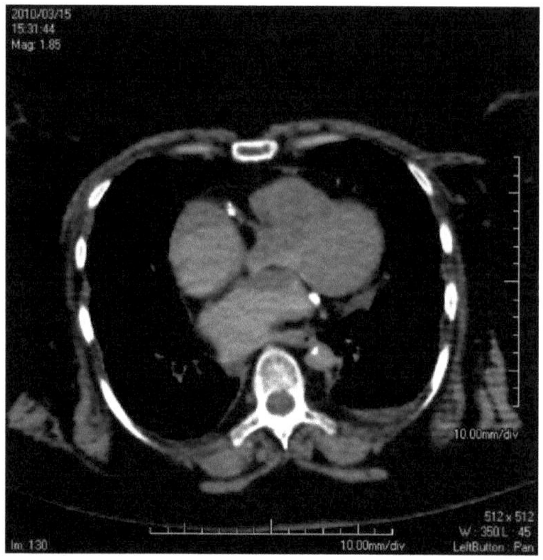

Figure 1.1 Coronary artery calcification. Axial postmortem CT showing calcification within the left and right main coronary arteries. One cannot stipulate a degree of stenosis based on the images.

do not issue a death certificate if they had not seen the deceased for some time prior to the death.

The absence of injury on external examination and CT is reassuring to the coroner that the death is a straightforward natural event.

The issue of coronary artery disease is challenging for the pathologist. On a postmortem CT scan one is only seeing calcification of the coronary artery and does not confirm either severe stenosis or a complication to an atheromatous plaque. One is required to integrate the available clinical past history, the reported scene findings and circumstances of death, and the external examination findings with the coronary artery calcification.

In deaths where there is a history of heart disease or significant risk factors for heart disease the coronary artery calcification may be deemed to be important. However, in the death of a young individual, or where there are few or no risk factors for heart disease, it has been our usual practice to recommend a full internal examination. There will, of course, be varying conclusions where one pathologist is comfortable with providing the coroner with the diagnosis of coronary artery disease, whereas a colleague given the identical information may recommend an autopsy.

Although it is important to maintain a high degree of uniformity in such decision-making processes, one must allow a level of professional autonomy between forensic pathologists.

Case Study 2: Hemopericardium and Aortic Dissection

An 80-year-old resident of a retirement village who had a past history of emphysema was found deceased in her bed. The deceased's general practitioner was contacted but declined to issue a death certificate as she had been well when he last saw her a month before her death. The death was reported to the coroner. The deceased's senior next of kin lodged a formal objection to autopsy.

The external examination showed no evidence of injury. The CT examination revealed a hemopericardium (Figure 1.2a,b). The coroner was informed of the diagnosis and the body was released without autopsy. The pathologist referred the images to the radiologist as he felt there may be an underlying dissection of the aorta. The radiologist confirmed a type A aortic dissection.

Forensic Issues

A hemopericardium is easily seen on a postmortem CT. The blood within the pericardial sac typically has Hounsfield units of ~40 (see Chapter 3) and usually displays a hematocrit effect, with "settling" of cells to the dependant aspect of the collection.

The vast majority of cases of hemopericardium result from either a ruptured acute myocardial infarct or from rupture of an aortic dissection into the pericardial sac. Sometimes the deceased's immediate clinical history may provide a clue to the underlying pathology. A recent history of chest pain radiating to the jaw or arm may suggest a myocardial infarct as the underlying cause of death. Aortic dissection may be suggested by a history of pain radiating to the back or "spine."

In some cases the postmortem CT shows the aortic dissection (Figure 1.2c,d). In noncontrast postmortem CT scans the pathologists have found this diagnosis to be difficult and referred most of the cases to the radiologist for an expert opinion. In elderly persons it may not be as important to determine the exact underlying

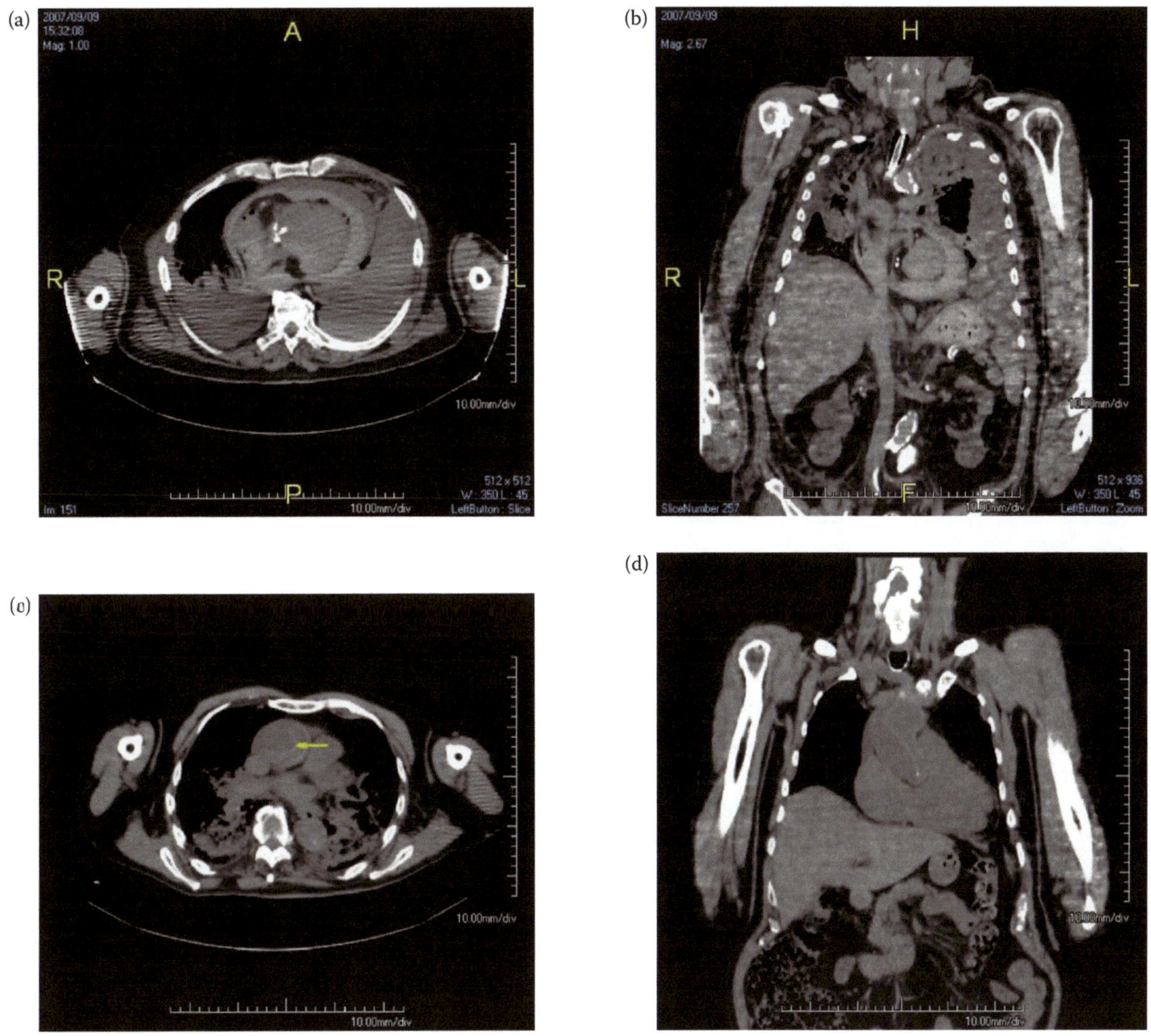

Figure 1.2 Hemopericardium. (a) Axial postmortem CT showing blood within the pericardial sac. The axial images often show a hematocrit effect with settling of erythrocytes to the dependent aspect of the sac. (b) Coronal postmortem CT showing blood within the pericardial sac. Blood typically has Hounsfield units of ~40. (c) Axial postmortem CT that does show an intimal flap. In our experience it is not common to see the intimal flap on the noncontrast postmortem CT. (d) Coronal CT showing false lumen in aortic dissection. In this case the dissection had not ruptured into the pericardial sac or pleural space. Presumably the deceased's chest pain and collapse related to the dissection involving the coronary artery.

cause of death. Although there may be occasional cases of undiagnosed Marfan's syndrome among the deaths, the majority of the cases will be related to the effects of long-standing hypertension.

In younger individuals it is vital to establish the nature of the fundamental pathology. Whether there is a disease such as Marfan's syndrome causing the dissection or early onset coronary artery disease leading to a ruptured myocardial infarct, the presence of such significant cardiovascular disease in a younger individual has considerable implications for the deceased's family. In such cases we have recommended a full autopsy examination.

A further issue in deaths where hemopericardium is identified on CT imaging is the possibility of resuscitation artifact. Virtually all of these cases have been associated with massive pulmonary thromboembolism. We have seen this phenomenon prior to the introduction of the CT machine, but its presence in cases that would have been designated as probable ruptured myocardial infarction has made us more cautious in our recommendations to the coroner. Massive thromboembolism can cause complete obstruction to blood flow through the pulmonary artery. This can then lead to considerable pressures within the right side of the heart during external cardiac compression and then lead to free wall rupture.

Case Study 3: Ruptured Abdominal Aortic Aneurysm

An 86-year-old woman collapsed at home in the company of her husband. The deceased was a Christian Scientist and did not have a general medical practitioner.

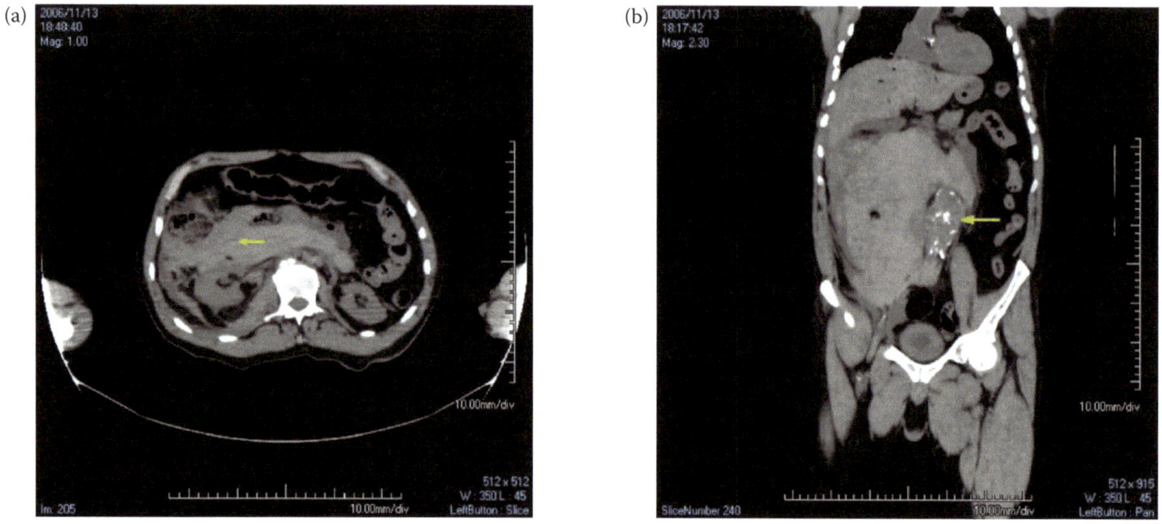

Figure 1.3 Rupture of abdominal aortic aneurysm into retroperitoneum. (a) Axial postmortem CT showing typical expansion of retroperitoneum by blood. (b) Coronal postmortem CT scan showing the calcified wall of an abdominal aortic aneurysm with bleeding into the right retroperitoneum.

The death was reported to the coroner and her husband lodged a formal objection to autopsy.

The external examination was unremarkable. The CT scan showed an abdominal aortic aneurysm with rupture into the retroperitoneum (Figure 1.3a,b). The diagnosis was conveyed to the coroner and the deceased's body was then released from the institute.

Forensic Issues

A ruptured abdominal aortic aneurysm is a CT diagnosis that is quickly recognized by the pathologist. The axial CT scans show expansion of the retroperitoneum by blood. There may be rupture into the peritoneum. The aorta is usually calcified and hence its dilated nature may be readily identified.

The diagnosis is particularly straightforward if there is a history of severe abdominal pain prior to collapse. When the death is not witnessed or the history is unclear, the diagnosis relies on a methodical approach to the CT scans. As will be discussed further in Chapter 3, many pathologists often commence their examination of the CT scans with a preliminary screening of the axial images. Such an approach will usually reveal a ruptured abdominal aortic aneurysm in the majority of cases.

Case Study 4: Pericardial Effusion

An 85-year-old woman with severe aortic stenosis, breast carcinoma, chronic renal failure, and atrial fibrillation was admitted to the hospital for elective aortic valve replacement and coronary bypass grafts because of increasing shortness of breath and orthopnea. Following the surgery she was admitted to the intensive care unit. She developed multiple organ dysfunction followed by multiple organ failure.

Despite maximum support she continued to deteriorate. An echocardiogram showed the presence of pericardial and pleural effusions, which were clinically thought not to be significant. She was reviewed by the cardiologists and intensive care team prior to a recommendation of withdrawing support. The patient died within an hour of withdrawing inotropic support. Because the death was temporally related to a medical procedure the case was referred to the coroner. The deceased's senior next of kin lodged a formal objection to autopsy.

The external examination was unremarkable. The postmortem CT scan showed a pericardial effusion, bilateral pleural effusions, right pneumothorax, ascites, and peripheral edema (Figure 1.4a,b). The radiologist was asked to provide an opinion on the significance of these CT findings. The radiologist stated the pericardial effusion was of "moderate" severity. The coroner was informed of this finding. The coroner accepted a reasonable cause of death of cardiogenic shock, postaortic valve replacement, and coronary artery bypass surgery.

Forensic Issues

There is a poor correlation between the volume of a pericardial effusion and its functional effects. A large amount of fluid may be accommodated by a patient if the fluid accumulates slowly, whereas the presence of a relatively small amount of fluid may have major hemodynamic effects if it accumulates rapidly.

Clinicians and radiologists use echocardiograms to determine the pressure effects on the cardiac chambers

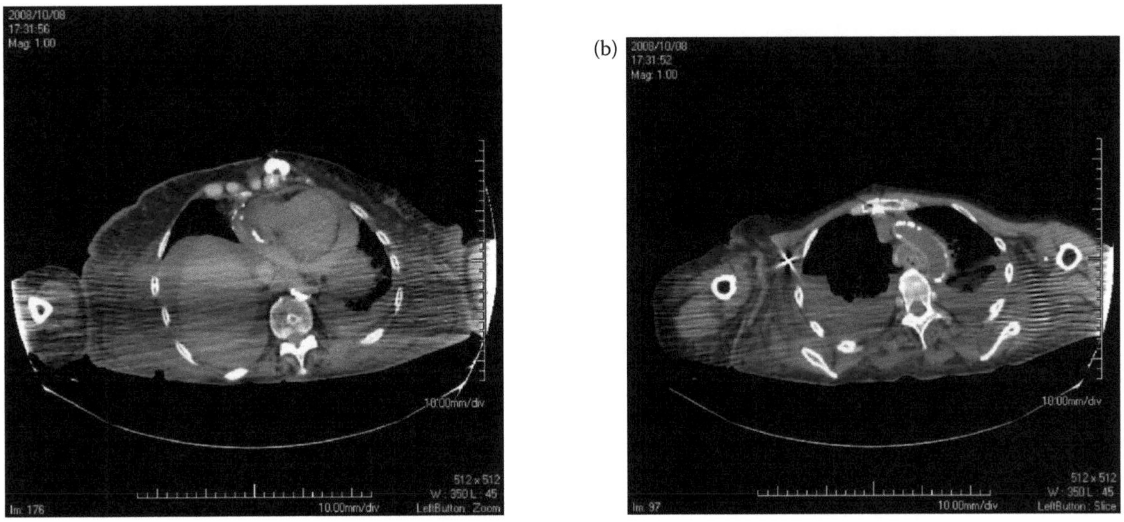

Figure 1.4 (a) Axial postmortem CT showing pericardial and pleural effusions. One notes the presence of calcified coronary arteries. (b) Axial postmortem CT image detailing bilateral pleural effusions. Metal flare from sternal wires indicating prior cardiothoracic surgery. The second metallic flare in the soft tissues of the right chest suggests the presence of a pacemaker wire.

by the fluid rather than estimating its volume. It has been suggested that the description of a pericardial effusion on CT should be in broad terms such as a small, medium, or large volume of fluid. It must also be remembered that the amount of pericardial and pleural fluid may well have substantially increased during the period between withdrawal of supportive treatment and the subsequent death.

The deceased was a known poor surgical candidate with severe symptomatic aortic stenosis, coronary artery atherosclerosis, and chronic renal impairment. She was thoroughly reviewed by the cardiology and intensive care teams prior to the surgery and during her admission. She had appropriate investigations including complete microbiological workup and received broad spectrum antibiotics. An infarct had been excluded using serial troponin analysis and electrocardiograms. A reasonable cause of death could be issued from an examination of the medical record.

Because an echocardiogram had been performed during life, an interested party could review this investigation. Although the microbiological cultures had not revealed any organisms, this cannot be taken as proof that an occult focus of sepsis was not present. This issue could be addressed by the conventional autopsy. The autopsy could have excluded pericardial and pleural involvement by breast carcinoma as the cause of effusion.

The postmortem CT can reasonably exclude hemorrhage into the pericardial sac by simply measuring the Hounsfield units of the fluid. A conventional autopsy examination would confirm the correct function of the valve and the absence of thrombus.

Case Study 5: Cardiomegaly

A 41-year-old woman was running a bath for her grandson. She was discovered face down in the bath by her daughter. The woman's husband removed her from the water and attempted cardiopulmonary resuscitation. She passed away at the scene.

Review of the deceased's medical history showed her to be chronically obese and a heavy smoker. She had a history of diabetes mellitus, asthma, and a long history of hypertension. A full conventional autopsy was performed. The cause of death was a massive basal subarachnoid hemorrhage arising from a ruptured berry aneurysm. She was also found to have marked cardiomegaly (heart weight, 1065 g; body weight, 140 kg; body length, 174 cm) (Figure 1.5a,b). There was no macroscopic or microscopic evidence of hypertrophic cardiomyopathy. There was no evidence of valve disease. There was an incidental papillary carcinoma of the thyroid gland.

The deceased's family was referred to the VIFM's Family Contact Program in relation to the marked cardiomegaly and thyroid carcinoma.

Forensic Issues

This death occurred in 2009, just before the introduction of the new Coroner's Act and current model of case management. It is interesting to ponder how such a death would be managed now. The cause of death was clearly apparent on the postmortem CT scans. However, a significant issue in this death is the marked cardiomegaly.

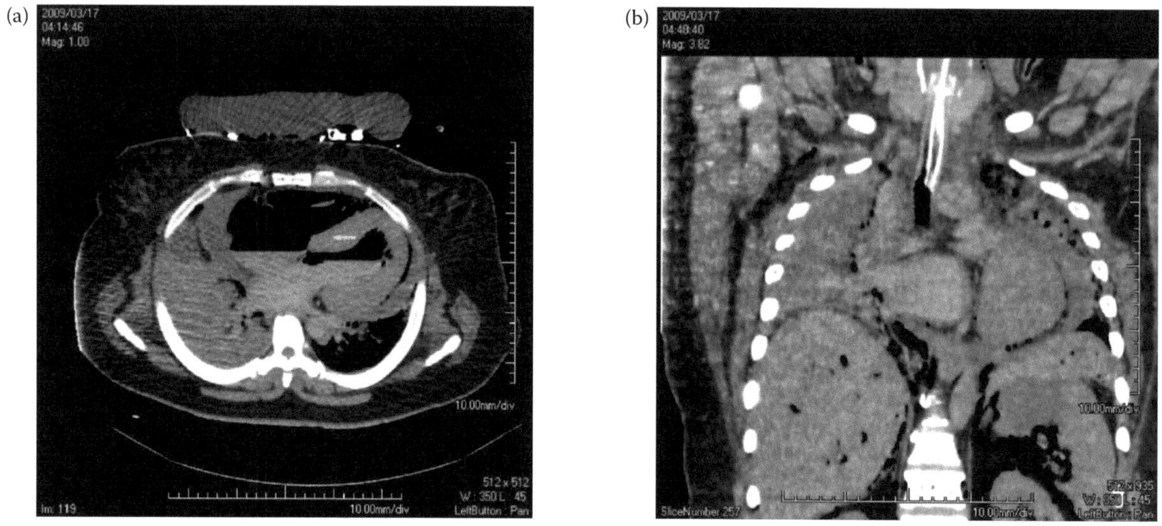

Figure 1.5 (a) Axial CT showing florid cardiomegaly. (b) Coronal CT showing florid cardiomegaly.

The enlarged heart was readily apparent on the postmortem CT scans when seen by the pathologist. The issue was discussed with the radiologist. He agreed the heart appeared "massive," especially for a 41-year-old woman. The radiological literature confirms clinical CT as a means to assess left ventricular mass [13]. We could not find any large series comparing heart size as documented at autopsy with postmortem CT examination.

The weight of the heart was well in excess of accepted normal limits for a woman of the deceased's height and weight. It could be argued that the deceased's longstanding hypertension may have been the cause of the marked cardiomegaly, though anecdotally we had not seen such left ventricular enlargement in pure hypertensive heart disease. Interestingly, we have seen a series of cases of confirmed death from hypertrophic cardiomyopathy in two brothers where the first brother's heart did not display either septal or apical asymmetric hypertrophy, nor was there myocardial fiber disarray on histology. The second brother's heart showed classical macroscopic and microscopic features of hypertrophic cardiomyopathy.

It would appear highly likely that forensic pathologists will identify such cases of massive cardiomegaly on CT. A case of undiagnosed hypertrophic cardiomyopathy (heart weight, 570 g) has been diagnosed at autopsy in a man in his 30s, where the pathologist believed the heart appeared large on CT and recommended a full autopsy examination. Lesser degrees of cardiomegaly may well go unrecognized. There is an urgent need for correlation between heart weights and specified measurements at autopsy and postmortem CT. In the meantime we believe the pathologist should err on the conservative side and recommend a full autopsy if there is a suspicion of cardiomegaly in a young individual.

Case Study 6: Hemothorax

Case 6.1

A 24-year-old man was riding a motorcycle when, for no apparent reason, his bike left the road and he crashed into an embankment. He was thrown from the motorcycle and his head impacted directly with a tree. From the police examination of the scene, there did not appear to be speed or alcohol involved in the collision. The death was reported to the coroner. The deceased's senior next of kin lodged an objection to autopsy. The reason for the objection was that the cause of death was obvious.

The external examination showed multiple abraded and bruised injuries in keeping with the circumstances of death. The CT scans showed a massive left hemothorax and multiple skull fractures (Figure 1.6a,b,c). The radiologist was consulted to confirm that no aortic dissection was evident on the CT images.

The coroner was informed that there was sufficient information on the CT to provide a cause of death, however one could not address the issue of possible underlying natural disease contributing to the crash without an autopsy examination. A full autopsy was recommended.

A full autopsy was performed. A typical deceleration-induced rupture of the descending thoracic aorta was identified in addition to a complex skull fracture with brain injury. No anatomical cause for loss of control of the motorcycle was found. Cannabis was later identified within the deceased's blood at levels consistent with recent use.

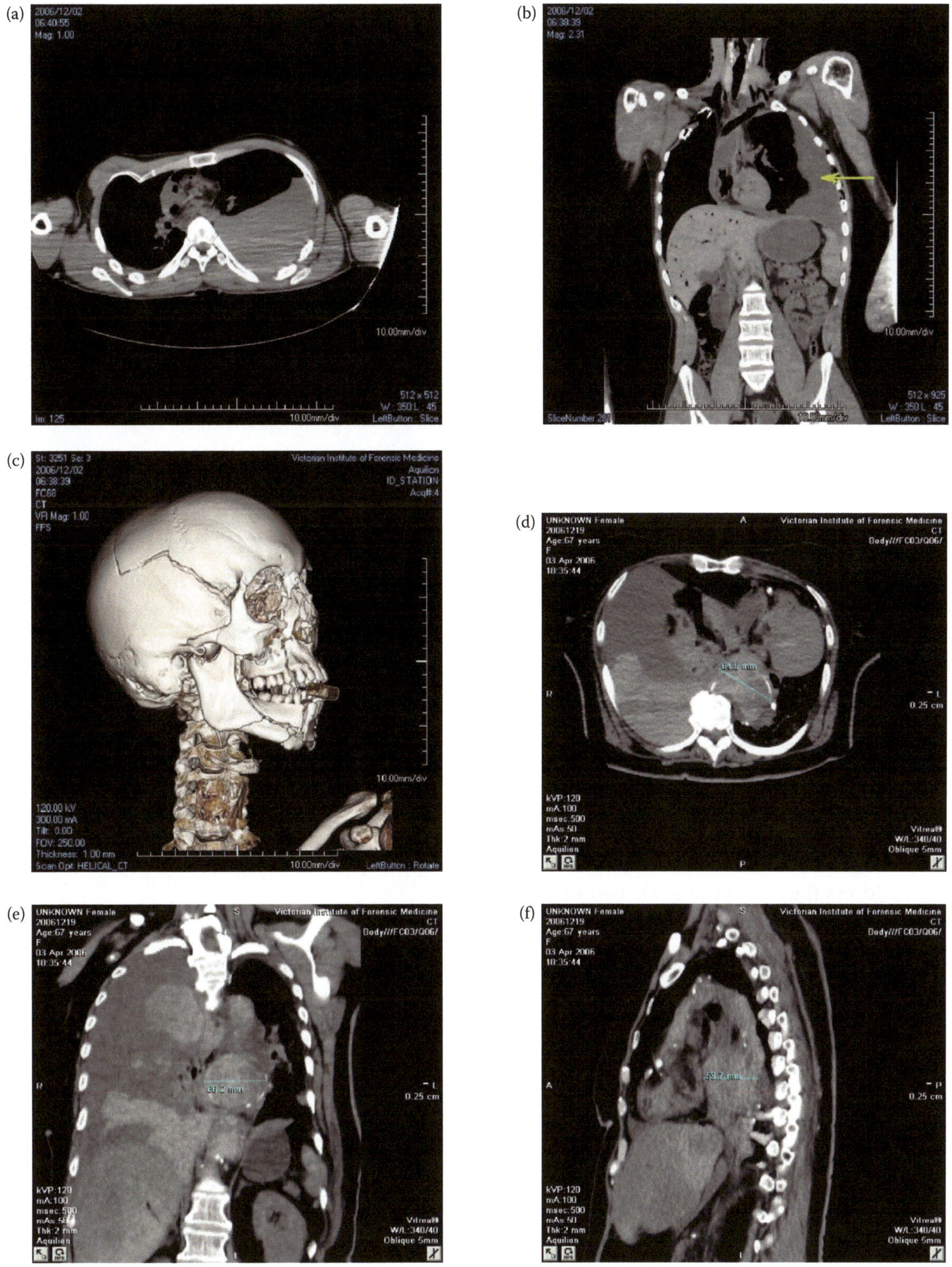

Figure 1.6 (a) Axial postmortem CT showing massive left hemothorax. Note the fractured rib on the right. (b) Coronal postmortem CT showing left hemothorax with mediastinal shift to the right. (c) Three-dimensional reconstruction showing multiple skull and facial fractures to the right of the head. Figure 1.6a had also shown a right-sided fractured rib suggesting the major impact was to the right side of the deceased's body. (d) Axial postmortem CT scan showing massive right hemothorax. (e) Coronal postmortem CT showing massive right hemothorax. (f) Sagittal postmortem CT demonstrating the dimensions of the saccular aneurysm arising from the descending thoracic aorta.

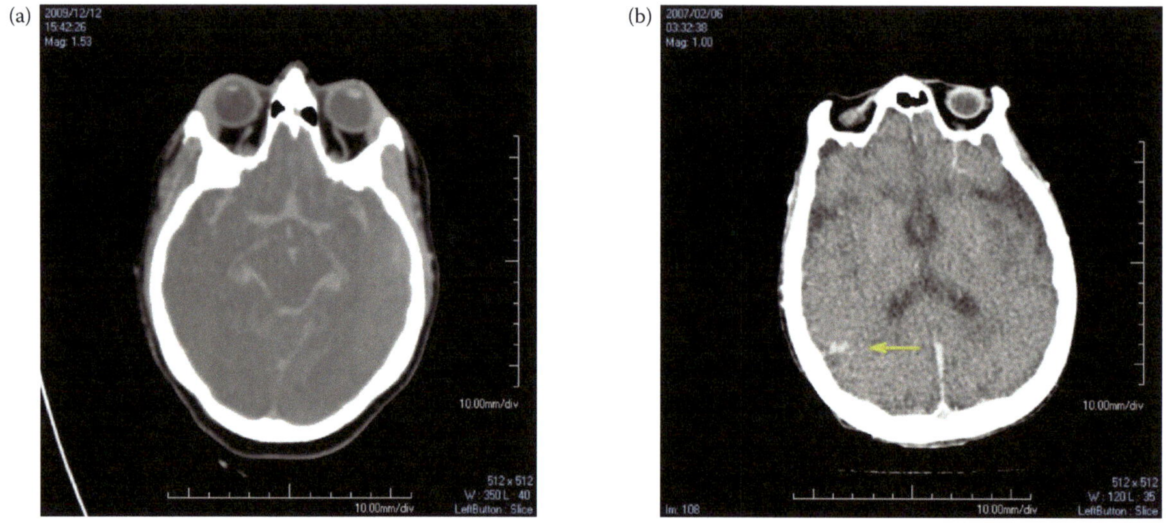

Figure 1.7 (a) Axial postmortem CT showing typical features of massive basal subarachnoid hemorrhage. There is blood within the basal cisterns and between cerebral gyri. (b) Axial postmortem CT showing a potential mimic of basal subarachnoid hemorrhage. The images show marked congestion within cerebral veins with minimal true subarachnoid blood.

Forensic Issues Hemothorax is readily identified on postmortem CT scans. The blood shows Hounsfield units of ~40. In circumstances of a motor vehicle incident, the most common underlying cause of the hemothorax is rupture of the descending thoracic aorta. Although trauma to the chest can lead to ruptures of the heart or any of the other great vessels, we have found that, for the purposes of the routine forensic case, it is generally sufficient for the coroner that the presence of a massive hemothorax is established.

In the case in question, an autopsy was recommended to address the issue of possible natural disease contributing to the incident.

Case 6.2

A 67-year-old woman with a past history of metastatic carcinoma of the bowel was presented to hospital with back pain, which was believed to be caused by metastatic disease. She also had a past medical history of ischemic heart disease and hypertension. She was admitted to the general ward and was later discovered deceased by nursing staff. As there was no cause of death apparent to the treating medical staff, the death was reported to the coroner. The deceased's family lodged an objection to autopsy, as they believed the cancer caused her death.

The external examination showed a mildly cachectic woman but was otherwise unremarkable. The pathologist inspected the CT scan. A massive hemothorax was identified. Given the history of hypertension and history of back pain it was believed the cause of the hemothorax was rupture of a dissecting aortic aneurysm. The CT scans confirmed multiple liver metastases. The coroner was informed of the diagnosis, and the deceased's body was released from the institute. The CT scans were referred to the radiologist for review.

The radiologist confirmed the pathologist's diagnosis of a massive hemothorax as the ultimate cause of death. However, the expert review showed that the underlying aortic disease was rupture of a midthoracic saccular aneurysm, which measured approximately 6 cm, rather than dissection (Figure 1.6d,e,f).

Forensic Issues The pathologist identified the massive hemothorax, which was the ultimate cause of the death. The coroner was satisfied with the cause of death. The deceased's family was informed of the cause of death and understood that it was not related to her malignancy. However, the pathologist had not appreciated that the aortic disease was a saccular aneurysm and not dissection. Such cases serve as a reminder to us that the forensic pathology staff must undergo ongoing education in the interpretation of the CT images.

Case Study 7: Basal Subarachnoid Hemorrhage

Case 7.1

The 41-year-old woman described in Case Study 5 was shown to have suffered a massive basal subarachnoid hemorrhage (Figure 1.7a).

Case 7.2

A 100-year-old woman with a past history of congestive cardiac failure and permanent pacemaker had a fall at her residential care facility. She struck the back of her head and required sutures to an occipital laceration. She was discharged to her residence but refused to take her medications and food. She rapidly deteriorated and died a week following the fall. As the deceased's general practitioner believed the death could be related to the fall, the death was reported to the coroner. The senior next of kin lodged a formal objection to autopsy.

The external examination revealed a large bruise that appeared to have "tracked" down from the occipital region consistent with the original fall. A green-colored bruise was also noted to the posterior aspect of the left elbow. There were no other injuries. There were no pressure areas or other changes to suggest neglect.

The postmortem CT scan showed no skull or cervical spine fracture and no evidence of extradural or subdural hemorrhage. There was no evidence of fractured pelvis, fracture neck of femur, and no fractured ribs. The heart appeared markedly enlarged and there was florid calcification of the coronary arteries. The pathologist thought there may be some subarachnoid blood and requested a formal radiology opinion (Figure 1.7b).

The radiologist reported a little subarachnoid blood over the right temporal lobe. The rest of the blood was in dilated cerebral veins. The coroner was informed of these findings. The coroner accepted the objection to conventional autopsy and the deceased's body was released from the institute.

Forensic Issues A substantial basal subarachnoid hemorrhage is a relatively straightforward diagnosis that can be reasonably expected of the forensic pathologist. The scans show blood (Hounsfield units of ~40) within the basal cisterns, within the Sylvian fissure, and between cerebral gyri.

Clinical experience with CT has shown that some patients with diffuse cerebral edema may show increased attenuation within the basal cisterns and mimic a basal subarachnoid hemorrhage [15]. We have found that congested cerebral vessels can certainly mimic subarachnoid blood in the postmortem setting.

Traumatic subarachnoid hemorrhage shows a thin film of blood over the cerebral hemispheres, whereas basal subarachnoid hemorrhage usually results from rupture of a berry aneurysm within the circle of Willis. Basal subarachnoid hemorrhage may also arise from traumatic rupture of the basilar or vertebral arteries. In cases of significant trauma where a basal subarachnoid hemorrhage is diagnosed on postmortem CT, examination of the CT images may show a fracture to the cervical vertebrae or atlantooccipital dissociation. Until the forensic pathologist is experienced with such cases there should be a formal radiology review or conventional autopsy.

Case Study 8: Intracerebral Hemorrhage

Case 8.1

A 62-year-old man had a past history of alcohol abuse, hypertension, diabetes mellitus complicated by nephropathy, renal failure, and a kidney transplant. He was discovered deceased on the kitchen floor by members of his family. His death was reported to the coroner and a full autopsy examination was performed.

The autopsy revealed a large intracerebral hemorrhage. The bleed appeared centered on the right basal ganglia and had ruptured into the ventricular system. A secondary Duret hemorrhage was noted in the midbrain (Figure 1.8a,b). The radiologist was requested to review the CT images as an educational exercise for the pathologists.

Review of the postmortem CT scans by the radiologist confirmed a right basal ganglia hemorrhage with rupture into the third and fourth ventricles. There was an extension of the hemorrhage into the upper midbrain.

Case 8.2

A 67-year-old woman with arthritis developed sudden onset of shortness of breath and being acutely unwell. Her husband called an ambulance, however, his wife was deceased before its arrival. The death was reported to the coroner. The deceased's husband lodged a formal objection to autopsy.

The external examination was unremarkable with no injuries seen. The postmortem CT scan showed a radiopaque mass within the brain. The images were referred to the radiologist for expert opinion. The radiologist reported that there was a 2 cm hyperdense mass within the lateral wall of the left lateral ventricle (Figure 1.8c). Blood was noted within the lateral ventricle with a distinct fluid level seen. The appearances suggested a parenchymal hemorrhage with rupture into the ventricle. A possible underlying cause was a vascular malformation such as a cavernous hemangioma. The presence of the bleeding suggested it was a recent event and may well be related to the cause of death.

The coroner ordered that no further examination of the deceased's body was required and the body was released from the institute.

Case 8.3

A 63-year-old woman with a history of hypertension collapsed at her home. Her body was taken to the VIFM for medicolegal examination.

External examination showed no evidence of any injury. The postmortem CT showed a large left intracranial hemorrhage (Figure 1.8d). There was considerable mass effect. The pathologist thought the hemorrhage

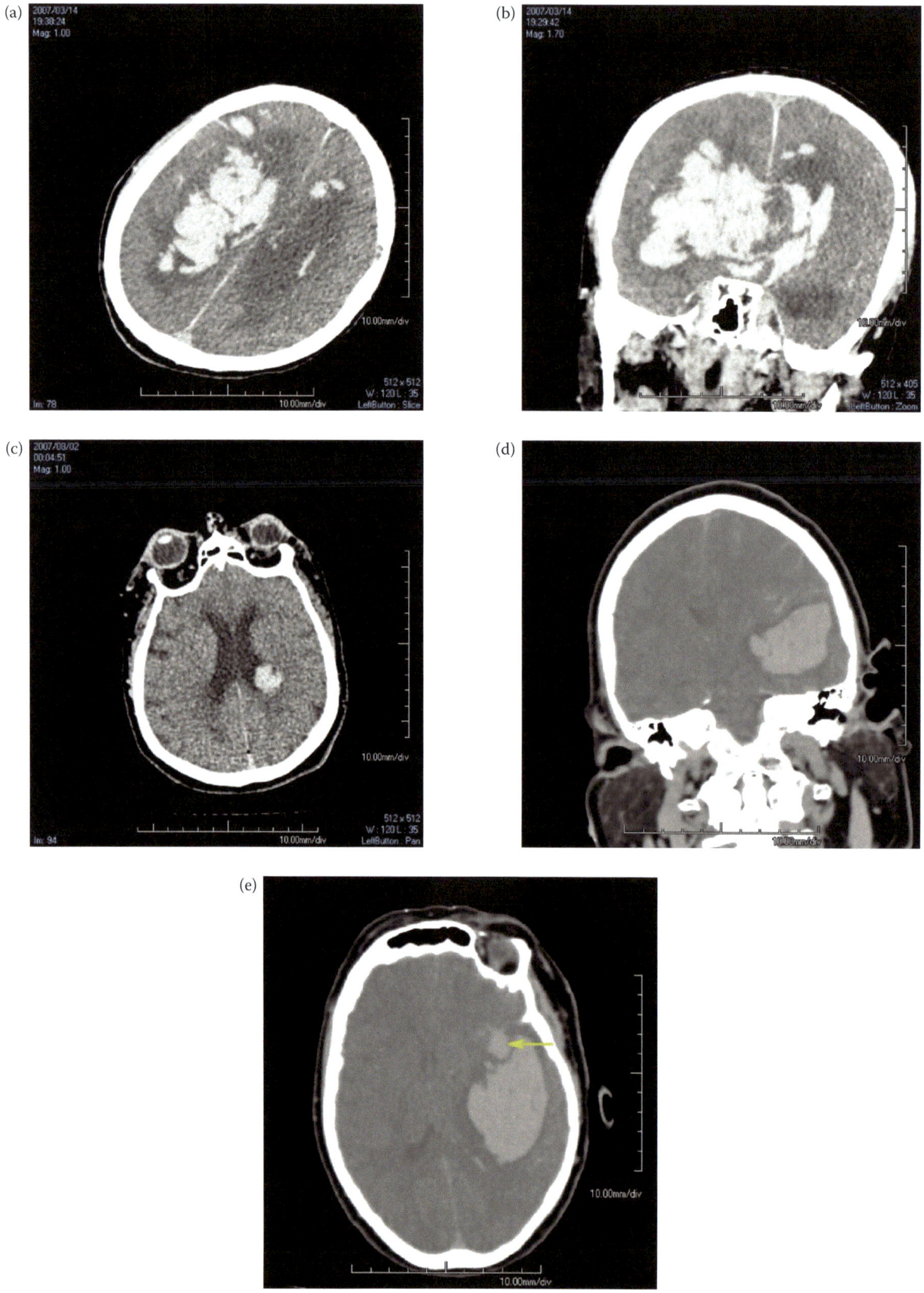

Figure 1.8 (a) Axial postmortem CT showing a right intracerebral hemorrhage centered on the basal ganglia suggesting a hypertensive hemorrhage. (b) Coronal postmortem CT showing a right intracerebral hemorrhage. (c) Axial postmortem CT showing a localized intracerebral hemorrhage. (d) Coronal post mortem CT showing a left intracerebral hemorrhage. (e) Axial postmortem CT showing left intracerebral hemorrhage.

appeared too lateral for a typical hypertensive hemorrhage. The images were referred to the radiologist for an expert opinion.

The radiologist agreed the site of the hemorrhage was not typical for a primary hypertensive bleed. The axial images showed a smaller, well-defined collection of blood with an adjacent large hematoma (Figure 1.8e). It was unclear whether the larger hemorrhage was intraparenchymal or was within the Sylvian fissure. It was thought that the hemorrhage most likely originated from an aneurysm of the left middle cerebral artery rather than a basal ganglia hemorrhage.

An autopsy was performed. There was a 1 cm aneurysm adjacent to the left middle cerebral artery and an adjacent hemorrhage confined to the left Sylvian fissure.

Forensic Issues Hypertensive brain hemorrhages usually involve the basal ganglia, thalamus, cerebellar hemispheres, or pons. The postmortem CT scan shows hemorrhage that is centered on the origin of the bleed. Hypertension is the cause of around one-half of all intracerebral hemorrhages.

The postmortem CT is not definitive with respect to the pathological cause of the hemorrhage. An intracerebral hemorrhage can result from a large number of pathologies including amyloid angiopathy, berry aneurysm, vasculitis, trauma, arteriovenous malformation, and bleeding disorders. The designation of hypertension as the most probable cause of an intracerebral hemorrhage is a function of the deceased's medical history and the radiological anatomical site of the hemorrhage. Clearly each death is evaluated on its own terms. The assessment of an intracerebral hemorrhage in an 80-year-old hypertensive individual is entirely different to a 35-year-old person with no relevant medical history.

In the first case, the radiological review corrected an error in the pathological examination of the brain. At the VIFM we do not routinely fix brains for formal neuropathological examination. For a formal neuropathological examination to occur, one must obtain permission from the deceased's family through the coronial system. Thus the majority of brains are cut fresh. In this case there appeared to be a separate secondary hemorrhage within the midbrain. The radiological examination showed the hemorrhage was in fact continuous with the basal ganglia bleed.

In the second case the radiology demonstrated a recent hemorrhage within the brain. We were unable to determine the exact neuropathological process as the coroner was satisfied with an intracerebral hemorrhage as the reasonable cause of death.

The third case showed an intracranial collection of blood that appeared too lateral to the basal ganglia to allow one to be comfortable with the diagnosis of primary hypertensive hemorrhage. Although the CT images in isolation would be consistent with a hemorrhage associated with amyloid angiopathy secondary to a fall, the deceased's age was considered to be far too young for this to be a reasonable possibility. The radiologist identified a separate well-demarcated opacity adjacent to the large collection and suggested a ruptured berry aneurysm with either rupture into the cerebral hemisphere or hemorrhage contained in the Sylvian fissure. The autopsy showed the latter pathology.

The case demonstrated the advantage of having an expert radiologist available to consult on the images.

Case Study 9: Subdural Hemorrhage

Case 9.1: Acute Subdural Hemorrhage

A 50-year-old man with hepatitis C and severe chronic liver disease had been drinking with friends. He arrived home and told his partner he had been assaulted by an unknown male in the street. The deceased's partner stated that the deceased had a swollen lower lip when he returned home. The deceased went to bed and his partner left to go to work. When the partner arrived home later that evening he found the victim dead in bed. The death was reported to the coroner. The deceased's senior next of kin lodged an objection to autopsy.

The external examination showed a transverse laceration to the lower lip in the middle with associated bruising. The postmortem CT scan showed a large subdural hemorrhage with midline shift (Figure 1.9a,b). The coroner and homicide squad of the Victorian police force were informed and a full postmortem examination was performed.

The postmortem examination showed no other evidence of injury. There were no facial fractures. A forensic dental examination showed no damage to the teeth. Reflection of the scalp showed no further bruises. There was an established micronodular cirrhosis with moderate fatty change. No other bruises or evidence of spontaneous hemorrhage was seen. A formal neuropathological examination showed a large left subdural hemorrhage with herniation of the left cingulate gyrus, uncal herniation, and minor traumatic subarachnoid hemorrhage.

The manner of death was issued as homicide.

Forensic Issues The postmortem CT scan allowed an early appreciation of the suspicious nature of the death. As will be detailed later, an acute subdural hemorrhage is a diagnosis that can be readily recognized by the forensic pathologist on a noncontrast postmortem CT scan. The blood extends over the entire surface of the cerebral hemisphere, as opposed to the extradural hemorrhage, which has a biconvex localized appearance.

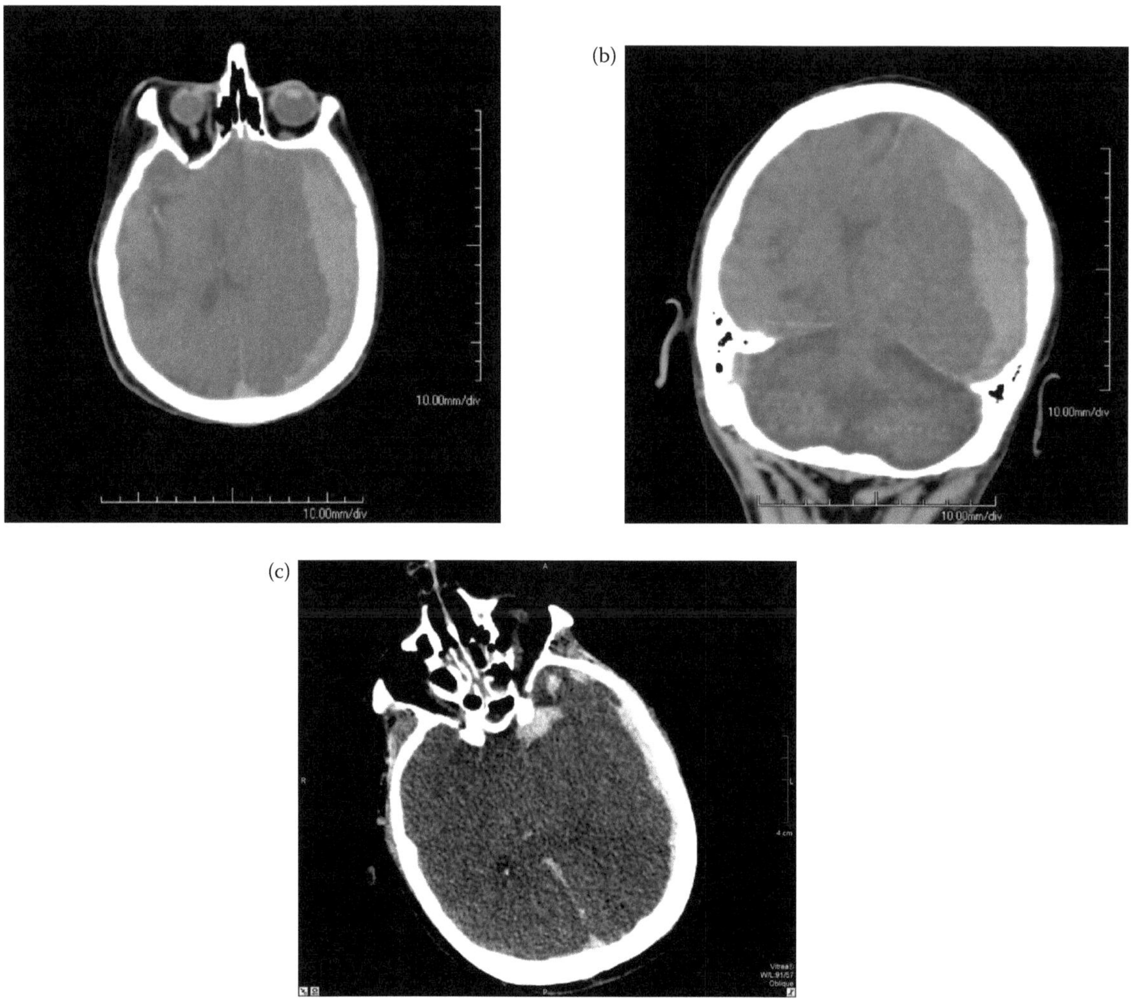

Figure 1.9 (a) Axial postmortem CT showing acute left subdural hemorrhage. (b) Coronal postmortem CT showing acute subdural hemorrhage with significant mass effect with left uncal herniation. (c) Axial postmortem CT showing an acute subdural hemorrhage with a focal left frontal hemorrhage.

The presence of raised intracranial pressure is revealed by compression of the ipsilateral lateral ventricle and midline shift. There may be settling of cells within the dependent part of the hematoma (hematocrit effect). Organization of the hematoma can lead to a variegated quality to the hematoma and a well-established chronic subdural hemorrhage can show a radiopaque membrane on the scans.

Case 9.2: Acute Subdural Hemorrhage Arising from an Arachnoid Cyst

A middle-aged woman had a verbal argument with her teenage son during which she was witnessed to collapse to the ground. It was unclear if she had struck her head. She could not be resuscitated and her death was referred to the coroner for medicolegal death investigation. The deceased's senior next of kin lodged a formal objection to autopsy.

An external examination of the deceased showed no evidence of any injury. The CT images showed a subdural hemorrhage. As the vast majority of subdural hemorrhages are associated with trauma, and the fact the deceased's family did not want a conventional autopsy with neuropathological examination, the radiologist was requested to review the images.

The radiologist confirmed the presence of a subdural hemorrhage, but importantly was also able to identify hemorrhage into an arachnoid cyst (Figure 1.9c). About this time the VIFM liaison service was able to access the deceased's medical history. She was found to have a history of headache.

Review of the literature showed that hemorrhage into an arachnoid cyst with subsequent subdural hemorrhage is an uncommon but recognized complication of an arachnoid cyst. The coroner and the deceased's family were informed of the CT findings. The coroner was satisfied with the cause of death that was issued as acute subdural hemorrhage complicating an arachnoid cyst. No further autopsy examination was directed by the coroner.

Sometime following the death, the deceased's family lodged a formal complaint to the coroner in regard to the deceased's general practitioner's management of her headaches, given the possible complication of fatal hemorrhage. The family was educated in regard to the rarity of the complication and the issue was referred for mediation.

Forensic Issues The majority of subdural hemorrhages result from rupture of bridging veins secondary to rotational forces applied to the head from blunt force trauma. Less commonly a subdural hemorrhage can occur via bleeding from an arteriovenous malformation, the effects of anticoagulants, or other uncommon pathologies such as hemorrhage from an arachnoid cyst.

The fact that the episode of collapse in the second case was witnessed provides the pathologist with some confidence that the death has occurred from a natural disease process. The radiologist was consulted to ensure that the pathologist had not missed an underlying lesion.

The radiologist recognized the underlying arachnoid cyst. The death was clearly from natural disease and the family's formal objection to conventional autopsy examination was upheld by the coroner.

Some months following finalizing the report, the deceased's family made a complaint that the treating general practitioner should have investigated the deceased's history of headache. The family opined that if a CT had been performed and the arachnoid cyst diagnosed, then the deceased may have chosen neurosurgical intervention.

The case raises an issue that is quite familiar to forensic pathologists. It is not uncommon for questions to be raised by interested parties long after the deceased has been released from the mortuary. In such cases the performance of a full autopsy would be advantageous. It is advisable that the pathologist has a brief summary of the known information on the case incorporated into the medicolegal report. This ensures that any criticism relating to the pathologist's recommendation for autopsy is viewed fairly.

In the absence of a full autopsy with formal neuropathological examination of the brain (with consent of the deceased's senior next of kin), it is highly likely the arachnoid cyst would have been overlooked. It would seem unlikely that the pathologist would appreciate the hemorrhage into an arachnoid cyst when the brain is cut in the fresh state.

In these instances the CT provides a permanent objective record of the brain pathology.

Case Study 10: Cerebral Infarction

An 80-year-old man with a past history of atrial fibrillation and cerebrovascular accident had recently undergone nasopharyngeal biopsy. He was on anticoagulation therapy. The biopsy subsequently showed a large B cell lymphoma. The anticoagulation therapy had been ceased during the hospital admission for the biopsy.

The patient was presented to the hospital by his family when he developed right-sided limb weakness. A CT scan showed ischemic changes within the frontal region of the brain. The situation was discussed with the deceased's family. He rapidly deteriorated and palliative care was instituted. The death was reported to the coroner. The death was believed to be related to the cessation of anticoagulant therapy. The deceased's family lodged a formal objection to autopsy.

The forensic pathologist performed the initial assessment of the scans. The postmortem CT scan showed obliteration of the left lateral ventricle and loss of gyral markings in the left cerebral hemisphere (Figure 1.10a). The images were referred to the radiologist.

The radiologist diagnosed a huge left hemispheric cerebral infarct from involvement of the anterior, middle, and posterior cerebral artery territories (Figure 1.10b). Focal hemorrhagic changes were seen in the right cerebrum. There were increased markings within the lungs consistent with the clinical picture of bronchopneumonia.

The cause of death was issued as bronchopneumonia secondary to massive cerebral infarction. The deceased's body was released from the institute without further examination.

Forensic Issues

The diagnosis of cerebral infarction is particularly difficult for the forensic pathologist on the noncontrast postmortem CT scans. The forensic pathologist may identify the radiological changes in cases of established large cerebral infarcts and especially where there is a suggestive clinical history.

In general, death occurring from cerebral infarction is not a common type of forensic case. The degree of brain swelling required to cause death takes time to develop so that most affected individuals will be brought to medical care and, if death does occur, a certificate is subsequently issued. Of course there are many elderly citizens in our community who live a reclusive or unsupported life, and are often the same individuals who do not have a primary care physician. Such deaths may well be reported to the coroner or medical examiner.

Massive cerebral infarcts are often associated with florid edema. Cerebral edema has lower attenuation values than normal brain parenchyma and can be seen on postmortem CT scans. Cerebral edema of sufficient severity to cause death usually takes approximately 24 to 48 hours to evolve.

CT does not show posterior fossa structures particularly well because of the robust nature of the adjacent

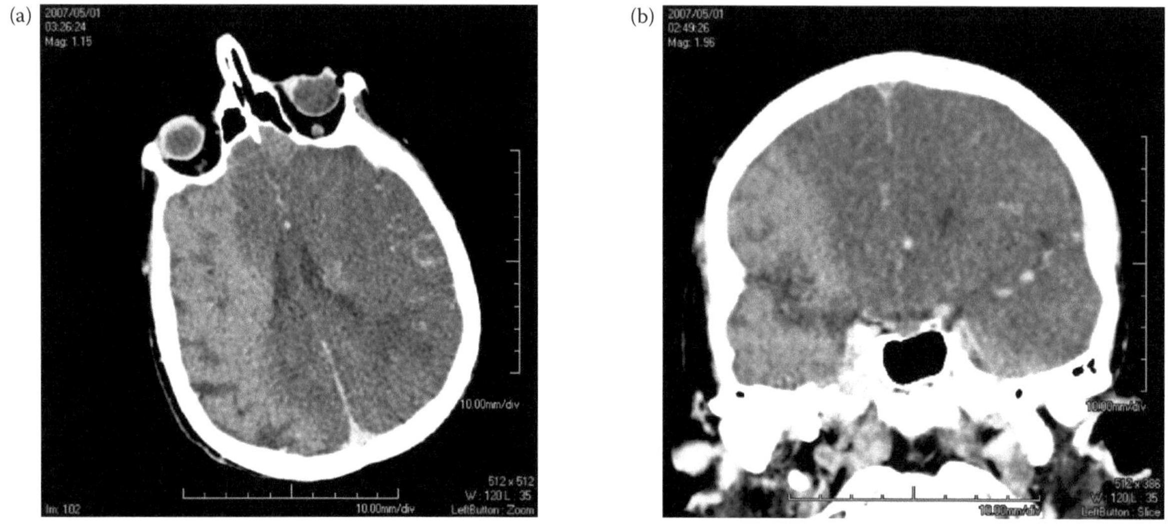

Figure 1.10 (a) Axial postmortem CT scan showing left cerebral infarction. Note the darker (less attenuation) color within the edematous left cerebral hemisphere. (b) Coronal postmortem CT scan showing midline shift to the right by mass effect of edematous infarcted parenchyma.

base of skull. Thus posterior fossa infarcts are exceptionally difficult to see on postmortem scans.

Case Study 11: Hydrocephalus

At the VIFM, as in many centers around the world, the routine practice of fixing brains for formal neuropathological examination has been replaced by a more targeted approach following the acquisition of formal consent from the senior next of kin. The introduction of postmortem CT scanning has facilitated the diagnosis of hydrocephalus. The CT images may reveal the diagnosis in cases where the pathology was not previously known or confirm the diagnosis in those cases with a detailed clinical history. In the former type of case, the family and coroner may be approached with objective evidence of the presence of neuropathology and an informed decision as to the need for keeping the brain is subsequently made.

The postmortem images of a man with neurofibromatosis and hydrocephalus are shown in Figure 1.11. The scans of the brain show dilated lateral, third and fourth ventricles (Figure 1.11a,b). In addition, the images of the lumbosacral spine revealed a mass expanding and destroying bone (Figure 1.11c,d). The clinical history would suggest a malignant schwannoma. Confirmation of this diagnosis would require internal examination or punch biopsy. In this case a conventional autopsy was not performed.

Case Study 12: Pneumoperitoneum

A 79-year-old man with a history of ischemic heart disease and gastrointestinal bleeding had rapid development of severe abdominal pain. He was taken to the hospital by ambulance where investigations showed gas under the diaphragm and a coagulopathy. While he was being medically stabilized he suffered a cardiac arrest and died. The death was reported to the coroner. The deceased's senior next of kin lodged an objection to autopsy.

Review of the postmortem CT scans by the pathologist revealed gas under the diaphragm (Figure 1.12a,b,c). The case was referred to the radiologist. The radiologist identified sigmoid diverticula (Figure 1.12d). The coroner was informed of the diagnosis of a perforated viscus, with the possible site of origin being a sigmoid diverticulum. It was stated that an autopsy was required to confirm the diagnosis. The coroner accepted that the death had occurred secondary to a perforation in the bowel. He ordered that no further examination of the body was required. The deceased's body was released from the institute.

Forensic Issues

CT is exquisitely sensitive in demonstrating gas. Free intraperitoneal gas is best seen on axial and coronal views. Pneumoperitoneum is best seen using soft tissue windows such as lung windows. The lung window allows better differentiation between gas and fat.

When dealing with postmortem remains there is always the possibility that gas could have arisen from the effects of decomposition. Pathologists are well acquainted with the external features of decomposition to a corpse. The early features include green discoloration to the right lower abdominal wall over the region of the cecum. Experience with routine CT scanning of the deceased has shown that there can be significant gas

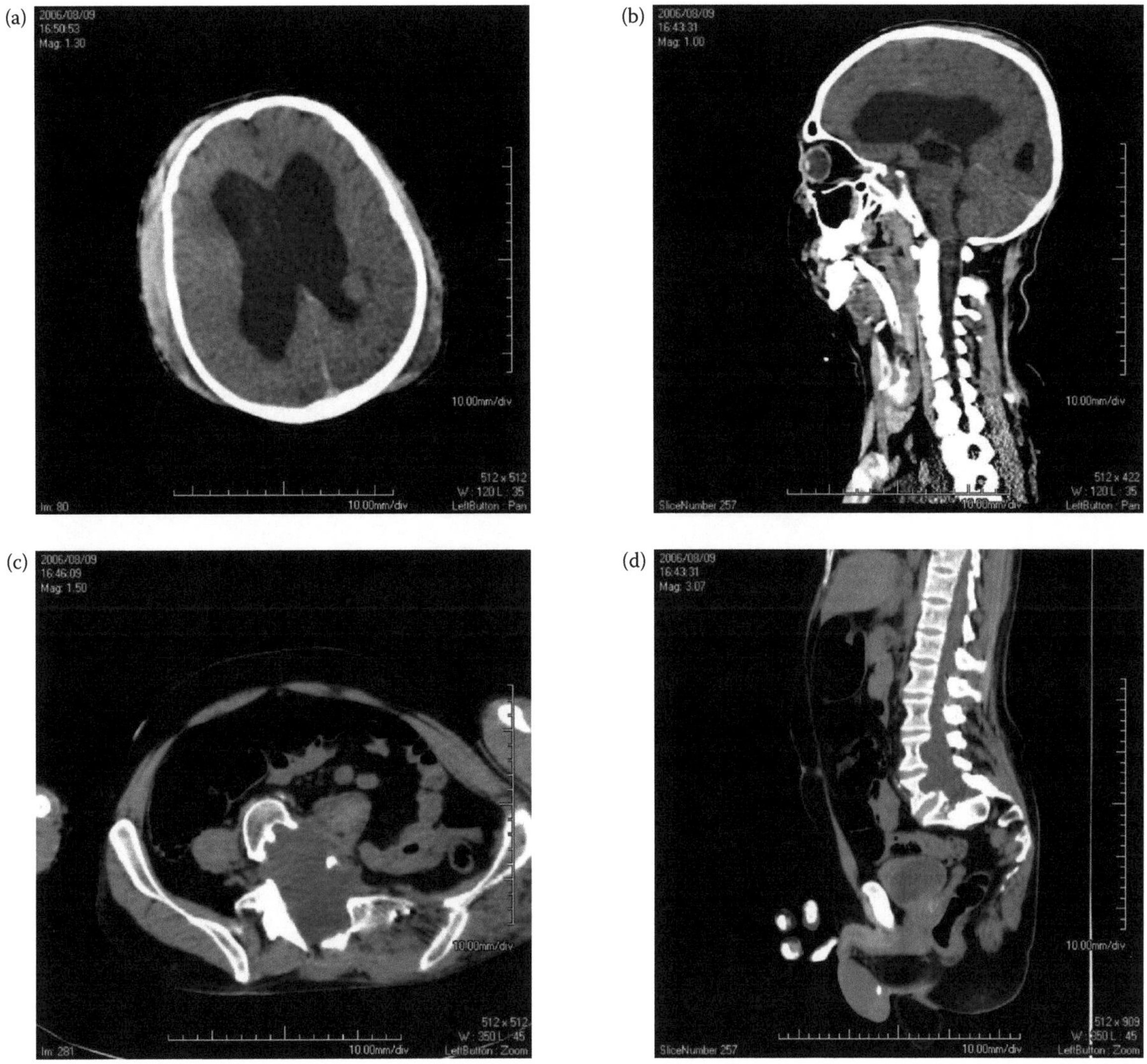

Figure 1.11 (a) Axial CT showing dilated lateral ventricles. (b) Sagittal CT showing dilated lateral, third and fourth ventricles. (c) Axial CT showing a mass expanding and destroying the lumbar vertebra. There is no calcification to suggest a chordoma. (d) Sagittal CT of the abdomen and pelvis showing a soft tissue mass within the spinal canal resulting in destruction and distortion of the vertebra.

production by decomposition within the deceased's body without any overt external signs of decomposition.

One may assess the CT images for evidence of decomposition by looking for gas in the portal veins, right side of the heart, or abdominal wall. The progressive accumulation of intracardiac and intrahepatic gas has been documented in a recently deceased person who died from a head injury using serial postmortem CT scans [16].

The site of the underlying pathology within the abdomen is aided by the presence of stranding of mesenteric fat. Stranding refers to increased attenuation within the mesenteric fat and reflects the presence of an inflammatory process. Sigmoid diverticula are relatively easy to recognize but are also very common in the community.

Ischemic bowel can show nonspecific bowel wall thickening and may reveal alternating layers of high and low attenuation. Intramural gas is a more specific finding but is relatively uncommon, and in the postmortem setting the diagnosis is complicated by the possibility of decomposition. In clinical practice absent or poor enhancement of the bowel wall following injection of contrast is seen.

We have found that a full autopsy examination is warranted in the majority of cases where free intraperitoneal gas is identified.

Case Study 13: Bowel Obstruction

A 92-year-old woman was found dead on the floor in her bedroom. She had a history of aortic stenosis, coronary artery disease, hypertension, and anemia. Her general practitioner would not issue a death certificate and the death was reported to the coroner. The deceased's senior next of kin lodged an objection to autopsy.

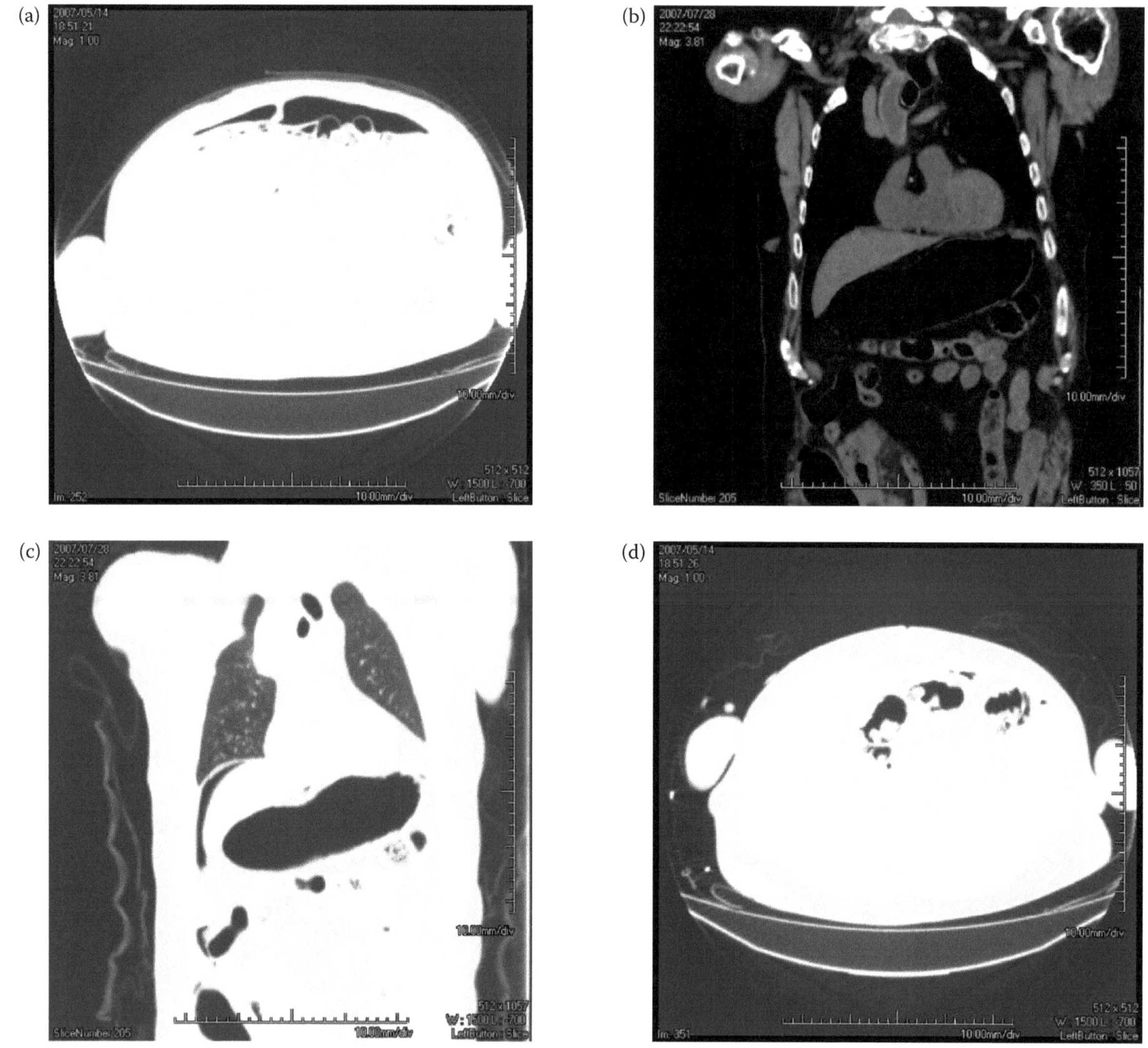

Figure 1.12 (a) Axial CT using a lung window to highlight the presence of gas. The image shows the presence of free gas within the peritoneum. The gas is noted at the highest point of the abdomen. (b) Coronal CT showing typical gas under the diaphragm analogous to conventional radiography films. (c) Coronal CT using lung window to highlight the presence of gas. (d) Coronal CT using lung window showing diverticulum within the sigmoid colon.

The external examination showed no suggestion of any injury. The postmortem CT scans showed no skull fracture or intracranial hemorrhage. The hyoid and thyroid cartilages appeared intact. There was calcification of the coronary arteries and aortic valve consistent with the known medical history. There were dilated loops of bowel (Figure 1.13a,b). The images were referred to the radiologist for expert review.

The radiologist diagnosed an obstructed right inguinal hernia (Figure 1.13c). The hernia contained a loop of small bowel. There were dilated loops of bowel entering the hernia and collapsed loops exiting the hernia. There was gross small bowel obstruction with fluid levels in small bowel, and dilatation of the small bowel, stomach, and esophagus (Figure 1.13d).

The diagnosis was reported to the coroner. No further examination was deemed necessary and the deceased's body was released from the institute.

Forensic Issues

The postmortem CT examination of the bowel is difficult for pathologists. Basic changes such as multiple fluid levels are readily identified, though subtle changes such as bowel wall thickening and intramural gas require input from an expert radiologist (Figure 1.13e). Once the forensic pathologist has seen a few cases of hernia it is surprising how quickly one is able to recognize them even on a scanning examination of the images. In rare cases gross fecal loading may lead to bowel obstruction. This finding is well seen on postmortem CT (Figure 1.13f).

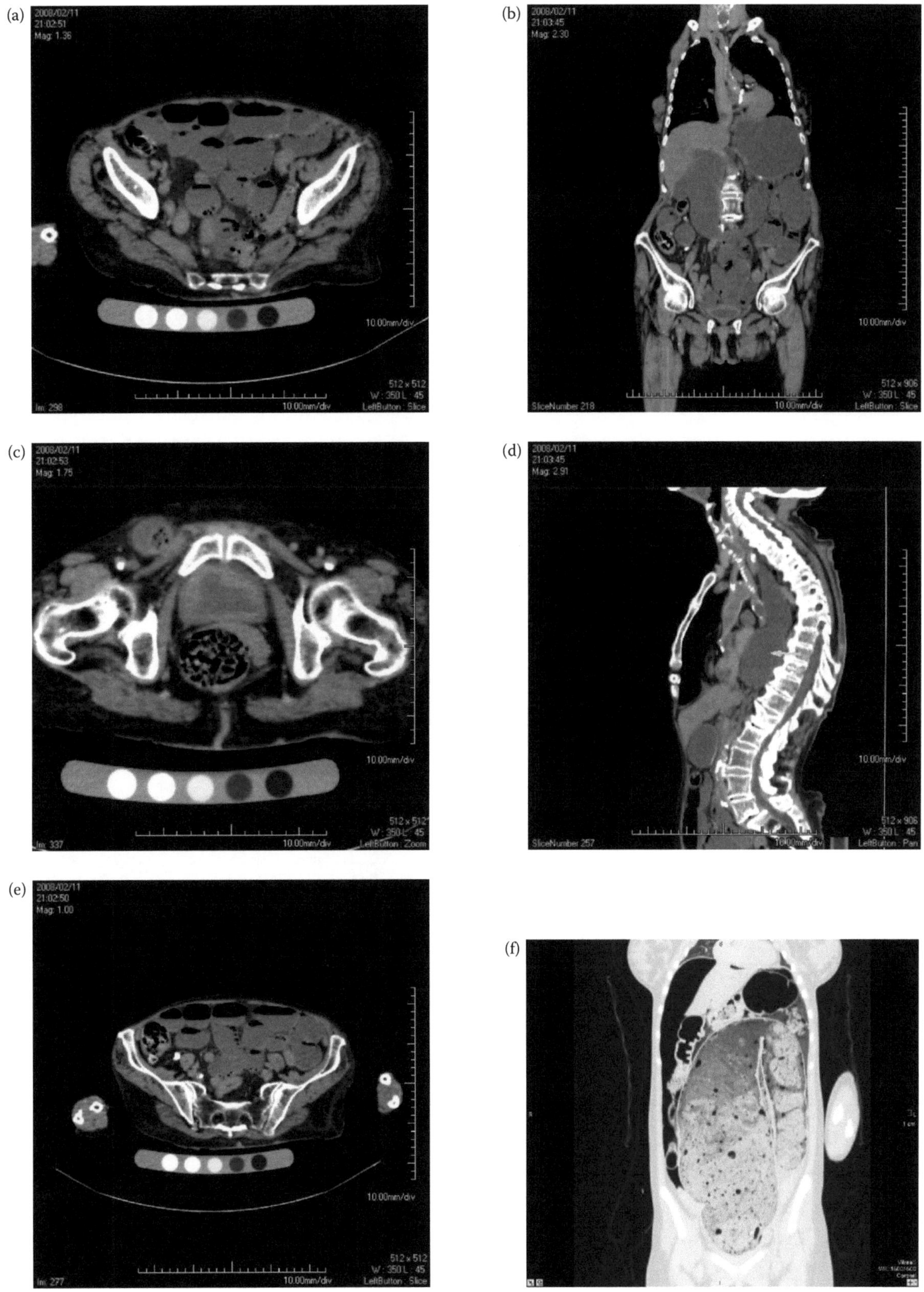

Figure 1.13 (a) Axial CT of the abdomen showing multiple fluid levels. (b) Coronal CT showing dilated fluid-filled small bowel. (c) Axial CT showing a hernia within the right inguinal canal. (d) Sagittal CT showing marked dilation of the stomach and esophagus. (e) Axial CT showing typical multiple fluid levels consistent with a small bowel obstruction. (f) Coronal CT showing gross fecal loading within the colon resulting in megacolon. There is a pneumoperitoneum.

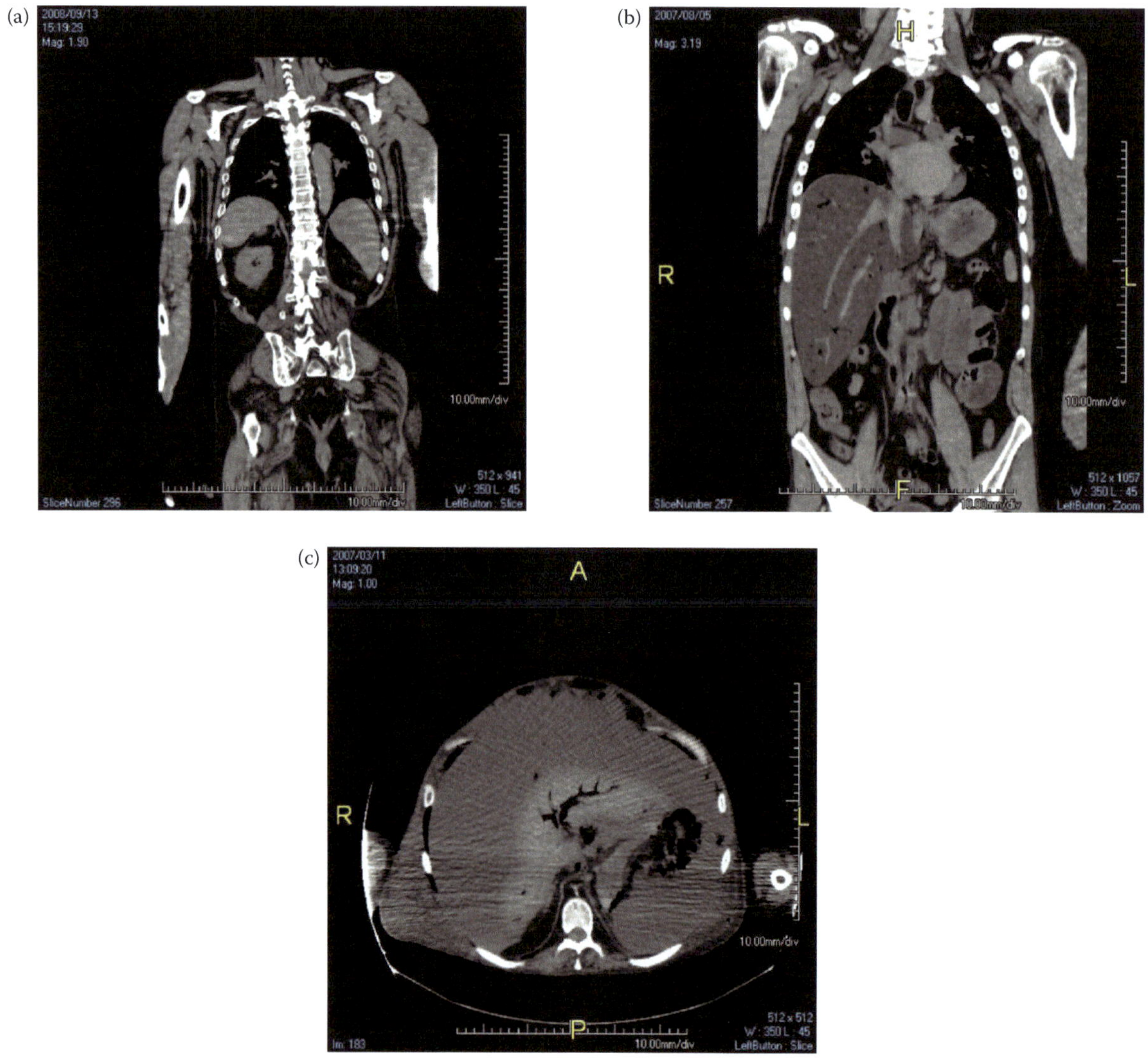

Figure 1.14 (a) Coronal CT scan showing liver cirrhosis and ascites. (b) Coronal CT scan showing decreased attenuation within the liver parenchyma resulting in a darker color. (c) Postmortem CT scan of the abdomen showing a large volume of low attenuation (dark) fluid around the liver. The fluid had Hounsfield units of 0.

Abdominal pathology is probably the most likely body region where the forensic pathologist is going to overlook important radiological changes. One's experience suggests that in cases where intra-abdominal pathology is the major factor in the death of a person whose investigation is reported to the coroner, a very low threshold for recommending a full autopsy is probably safe practice.

Case Study 14: Liver Disease and Ascites

Case 14.1

A 78-year-old man with a past history of alcohol abuse was found deceased on the floor in his bedroom. The death was reported to the coroner. A full autopsy was performed. The autopsy showed widespread bronchopneumonia, focal coronary artery atherosclerosis, and an established cirrhosis. There was no evidence of gastrointestinal hemorrhage. No Alzheimer type 2 cells were seen within the brain to suggest an encephalopathy.

Review of the postmortem CT scan showed a shrunken, irregular liver with splenomegaly (Figure 1.14a).

Case 14.2

A 45-year-old man with a history of alcohol abuse died committing suicide by hanging. The postmortem examination showed a markedly fatty liver. Review of the CT scan showed a darker color within the liver parenchyma typical of diffuse moderate to severe fatty liver (Figure 1.14b).

Forensic Issues In cases of established liver cirrhosis the noncontrast postmortem CT scans may reveal a shrunken, irregular liver. The noncontrast postmortem CT can show the changes of a fatty liver. Fatty liver as a cause of death is somewhat controversial. Many forensic pathologists accept that a severe fatty liver can potentially cause death from metabolic disturbances such as profound hypoglycemia or hypophosphatemia. However, this determination is made in the setting of an otherwise negative full autopsy examination with full toxicology.

Fatty liver leads to decreased attenuation within the liver. The normal liver has approximately 40 to 60 Hounsfield units. In a CT scan of a normal healthy individual the liver is normally lighter in color than the spleen. When there is severe fatty change to the liver the attenuation is about 20 Hounsfield units and the liver appears darker than the spleen.

Metastatic disease in the liver may not be seen on noncontrast CT scans if the attenuation values of the tumor and the liver parenchyma are similar. In cases where the metastases are necrotic they may be seen as lighter in color than the surrounding normal liver. When there are viable metastases in a fatty liver, the differences in electron density between the necrotic tumor and the fatty liver parenchyma allow detection in a noncontrast scan.

Ascites is common in deaths in those with liver failure. Ascitic fluid within the peritoneum is readily identified on postmortem CT scans (Figure 1.14c). Ascites usually has Hounsfield units of 0 but may occasionally be slightly higher. The fluid is visualized particularly around the liver in axial and coronal views.

Case Study 15: Hemoperitoneum

A 66-year-old man with a medical history of depression, alcohol abuse, and chronic liver disease was found deceased in his room in a boarding house. The death was reported to the coroner. The deceased's senior next of kin lodged an objection to autopsy.

An external examination showed no suggestion of an injury. The postmortem CT scan showed no skull fracture or intracranial hemorrhage. There was no evidence of hyoid bone or thyroid cartilage fracture. The images of the abdomen showed a hemoperitoneum (Figure 1.15). The coroner was informed that without a full postmortem examination the cause of the hemoperitoneum could not be ascertained. An autopsy was ordered by the coroner.

At autopsy the hemoperitoneum was confirmed. There was a tear to the capsule of the spleen. There was no evidence of an assault. No bruises were seen to the face or neck. No bruises were seen to the abdomen.

The police informant was contacted to clarify the circumstances surrounding the death. The informant stated that in fact the deceased had been located within a locked bathroom.

Forensic Issues

A hemoperitoneum is readily identified on postmortem CT scans. The blood is often first recognized around the liver on axial or coronal CT images. Intraperitoneal fluid has Hounsfield units of about 30 to 45. There may be some variation in the attenuation reflecting the lines of Zahn seen macroscopically in established clots. The origin of a hemoperitoneum on CT may be suggested by localization of the blood (sentinel clot). The CT images suggested the origin of the bleeding was in the left hypochondrium.

In selected cases, following an initial examination of the peritoneum cavity to exclude major organ rupture,

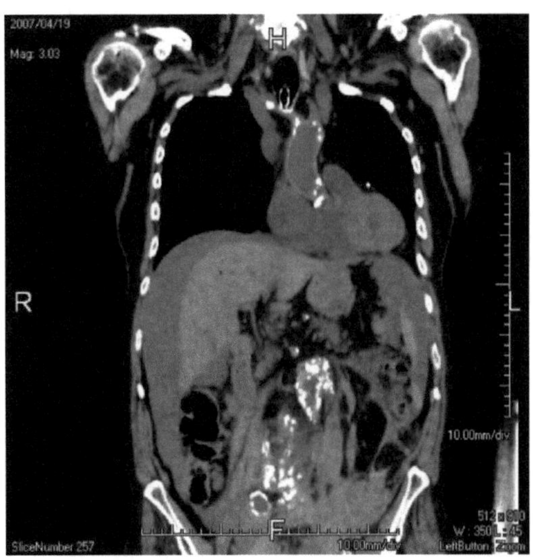

Figure 1.15 Postmortem coronal CT showing hemoperitoneum. There is fluid around the liver and spleen with Hounsfield units of between 30 and 40. There is a suggestion of an increased volume of blood in the region of the spleen (sentinel) clot.

one may cannulate the specific vascular tree suggested by the sentinel clot and perform CT angiography.

The postmortem CT scans allowed the pathologist to inform the coroner of the diagnosis in a timely manner and that a full autopsy examination was required.

Case Study 16: CT in Medication Overdose

A 25-year-old woman with a history of depression and prior suicide attempts was found deceased by her sister in the bathroom of her residence. Three empty boxes of mexiletine were found in the kitchen trash can and a suicide note was located in the bedroom. Mexiletine is a therapeutic drug used in the treatment of certain cardiac arrhythmias.

A full postmortem examination was performed. There was no evidence of injury and no anatomical disease process was identified. Examination of the stomach showed a small amount of pinkish-tan sludge. The stomach contents and routine toxicology specimens were recovered for toxicological examination. The toxicology result showed a mexiletine level of ~11 mg/L. Deaths have been described with mexiletine levels >2 mg/L. The death was issued as being due to toxicity to mexiletine.

The postmortem CT scan showed significant changes within the stomach. There was fluid within the stomach that contained radiopaque material with Hounsfield units of 124 to 145. Importantly there was a dependent layer of very opaque material with Hounsfield units of 200 to 234 (Figure 1.16a).

Forensic Issues

We have found that CT is useful in cases of intentional therapeutic medication overdose. A case report in the forensic literature has described the presence of radiopaque material within the stomach in a case of suicide [17]. In our unpublished experience we compared the findings on postmortem CT in 65 cases of confirmed death from intentional medication overdose with 65 control cases. There were many cases where the postmortem CT was unremarkable. However, many cases demonstrated the presence of radiopaque material within the basal aspect of the stomach with Hounsfield units consistently over 100. No control cases were seen with material having Hounsfield units of 100 or more.

The high radiodensity of therapeutic drugs is related to excipients in the tablets rather than the active pharmacological component. The marked radiodensity is of course not specific for tablets and must be interpreted in context with the circumstances surrounding death and the results of the toxicological analysis. To illustrate this point we have seen a case where quite radiopaque material within the stomach seen on the CT images prior to full autopsy was subsequently shown to be large potato chips (Figure 1.16b,c).

The VIFM has introduced a preliminary overnight toxicology service. A toxicology screen is performed on a sample of femoral blood taken from the deceased following admission to the institute. Although this adds further information in determining whether an autopsy is required it must be remembered that the result has not been validated and confirmed with a second method of analysis.

The amount of radiopaque material can vary quite a deal between cases of overdose (Figure 1.16d,e).

The introduction of the CT scanner and the concurrent change in decision making regarding the need for full internal postmortem examination has meant that the aforementioned CT changes can be very important in deciding whether an autopsy is required. It would appear reasonable to suggest that, in cases where there are classical scene findings suggesting intentional overdose, where there are no injuries seen on external examination of the body and on CT scans, and where a layer of radiopaque material is seen within the stomach with Hounsfield units >100, then it would be reasonable to suggest that a full postmortem examination is not essential. Otherwise it is safer to perform a full autopsy examination to determine the presence and contribution of natural disease to the death, and collect stomach contents to confirm an unusual amount of drugs.

Case Study 17: CT in Pulmonary Thromboembolism

A 59-year-old woman with a past history of stomach cancer collapsed at her home. Upon arrival of the ambulance personnel she was found to be hypotensive, pale, and short of breath. She died at the scene. Her local medical practitioner suspected the cause of death was a massive pulmonary thromboembolism, however he refused to issue a death certificate. The death was reported to the coroner. The deceased's husband lodged an objection to autopsy.

The postmortem CT showed subtle expansion of the main pulmonary trunk with the suggestion of a "coil" of thromboembolism (Figure 1.17a,b).

Forensic Issues

The CT scan showed subtle expansion of the main pulmonary trunk. There were "blunted" ends to the embolus reflecting the ends of the segments of thrombus that had dislodged from the peripheral veins. These are different to the attenuated picture seen with typical postmortem clot ("chicken fat"). Though the diagnosis of pulmonary thromboembolism is made clinically using contrast CT or echocardiography, a clinical report has suggested the diagnosis can be made using noncontrast CT [18].

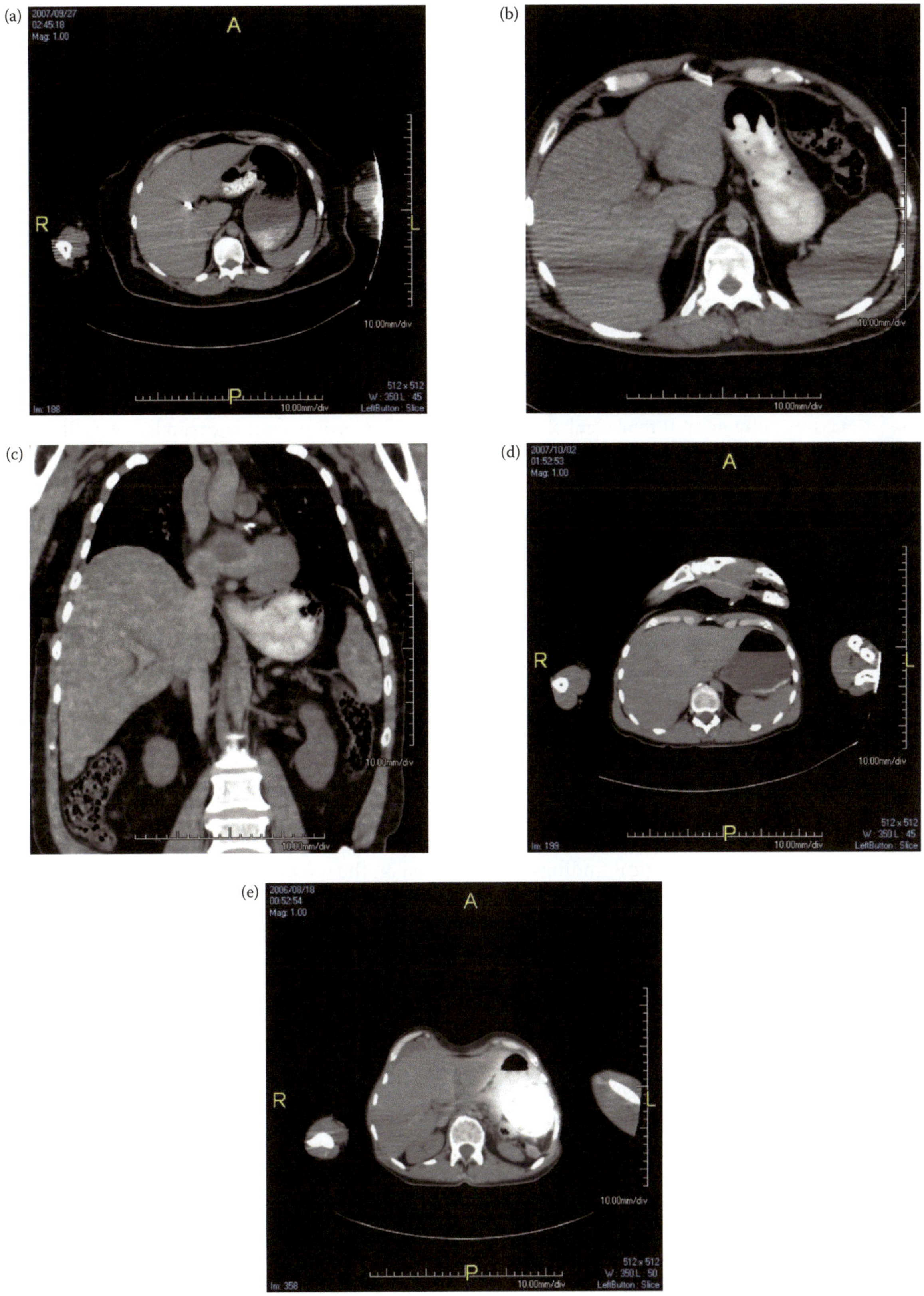

Figure 1.16 (a) CT in medication overdose. Axial CT of the abdomen showing basal radiopaque material within the stomach. The material had Hounsfield units >100. (b) Axial CT showing variegated and structured radiopaque material within the stomach. The material was shown to be potato chips at the autopsy examination. (c) Coronal CT showing radiopaque material within the stomach, which was later shown to be potato chips. (d) Axial CT of the abdomen. There is a thin layer of radiopaque material lining the dependent gastric mucosa. (e) Axial postmortem CT showing gross radiopaque material in the stomach.

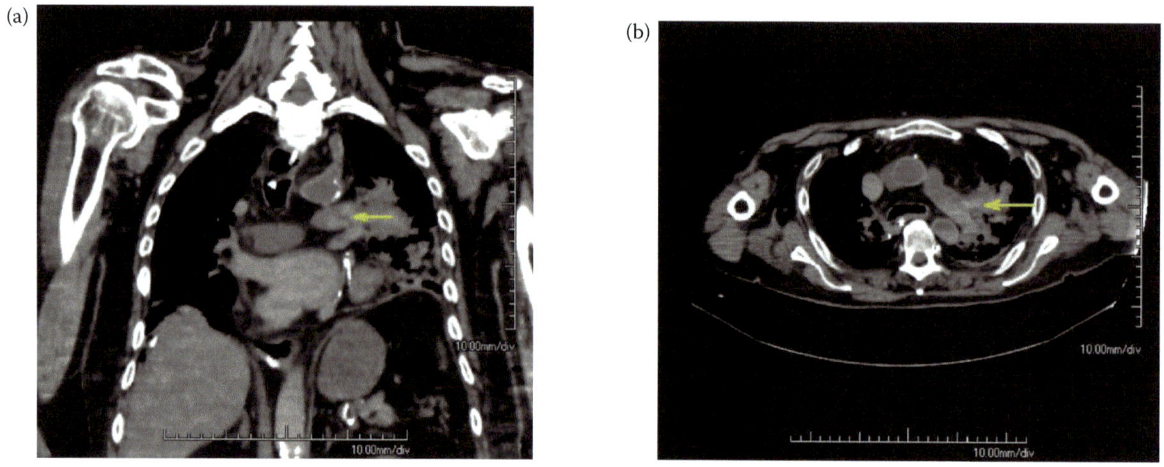

Figure 1.17 (a) Postmortem coronal CT scan showing coils of material within the pulmonary artery. (b) Axial CT image in a case of massive pulmonary thromboembolism. The pulmonary artery appears expanded. A well-defined opaque cylinder is seen.

Although the diagnosis does appear quite subjective in noncontrast CT scans, there are cases where a coil of variable attenuation can be recognized in the main pulmonary trunk. In our experience in the majority of cases the diagnosis is not clear. In the future a targeted punch biopsy of the pulmonary artery may be performed to confirm the diagnosis when raised by postmortem CT.

In forensic cases with a typical history of pulmonary thromboembolism, clinical laboratory studies, or clinical imaging findings that are highly suggestive of thromboembolism, it may be argued that a full postmortem examination is not necessarily indicated. In cases where the clinical or radiological findings are not clear-cut then a conventional autopsy is required to provide a reasonable cause of death.

Case Study 18: Pneumonia

A 94-year-old woman who had not seen a doctor for over 50 years had a gradual decline in general health over the previous year and recent loss of weight. She had stated to her family that she no longer wanted to live. She died peacefully in the presence of family members. As she did not have a regular doctor to issue a death certificate, her death was reported to the coroner. The senior next of kin lodged an objection to autopsy.

The external examination showed no evidence of injury. The postmortem CT scan showed no fractures or other injuries. Examination of the CT images by the pathologist showed a right-sided lobar pneumonia (Figure 1.18a,b). The images were referred to the radiologist for expert review. The radiologist confirmed the presence of a lobar pneumonia but also identified a right hilar mass. There were no other significant findings.

Overnight toxicological examination was performed and showed no drugs. These findings were presented to the coroner who indicated that no further examination should be carried out. The deceased's body was released from the institute.

Forensic Issues

In this case the cause of death, without an autopsy examination, is open to discussion. The external examination and CT scans showed no evidence of any injury. At the time of this recent case the institute had introduced overnight screening toxicology. No drugs were identified on the screening tests.

The pneumonia may have lead to death from the systemic effects of inflammation and sepsis. The radiological appearance of the lungs did not suggest any significant underlying parenchymal changes that would indicate a purely respiratory mode of death. As is often the case in the early stages of a forensic investigation, there was scant information available on the deceased's symptoms prior to her death.

The radiologist identified a hilar lung mass and suggested that the pneumonia was a postobstructive infective process. Although it appeared highly likely that the hilar mass was a malignant lesion, we were unable to confirm this radiological impression. The deceased's senior next of kin was informed of the potential health benefits to the family members from diagnosing the true nature of the lung mass. This opportunity was declined.

Lung CT is best assessed using "lung windows" where gas (air) is shown as black, aerated lung parenchyma as gray, and other structures white (Figure 1.18c,d). Consolidation on CT scans is seen as a lung opacity without volume loss. Volume loss occurs with collapse.

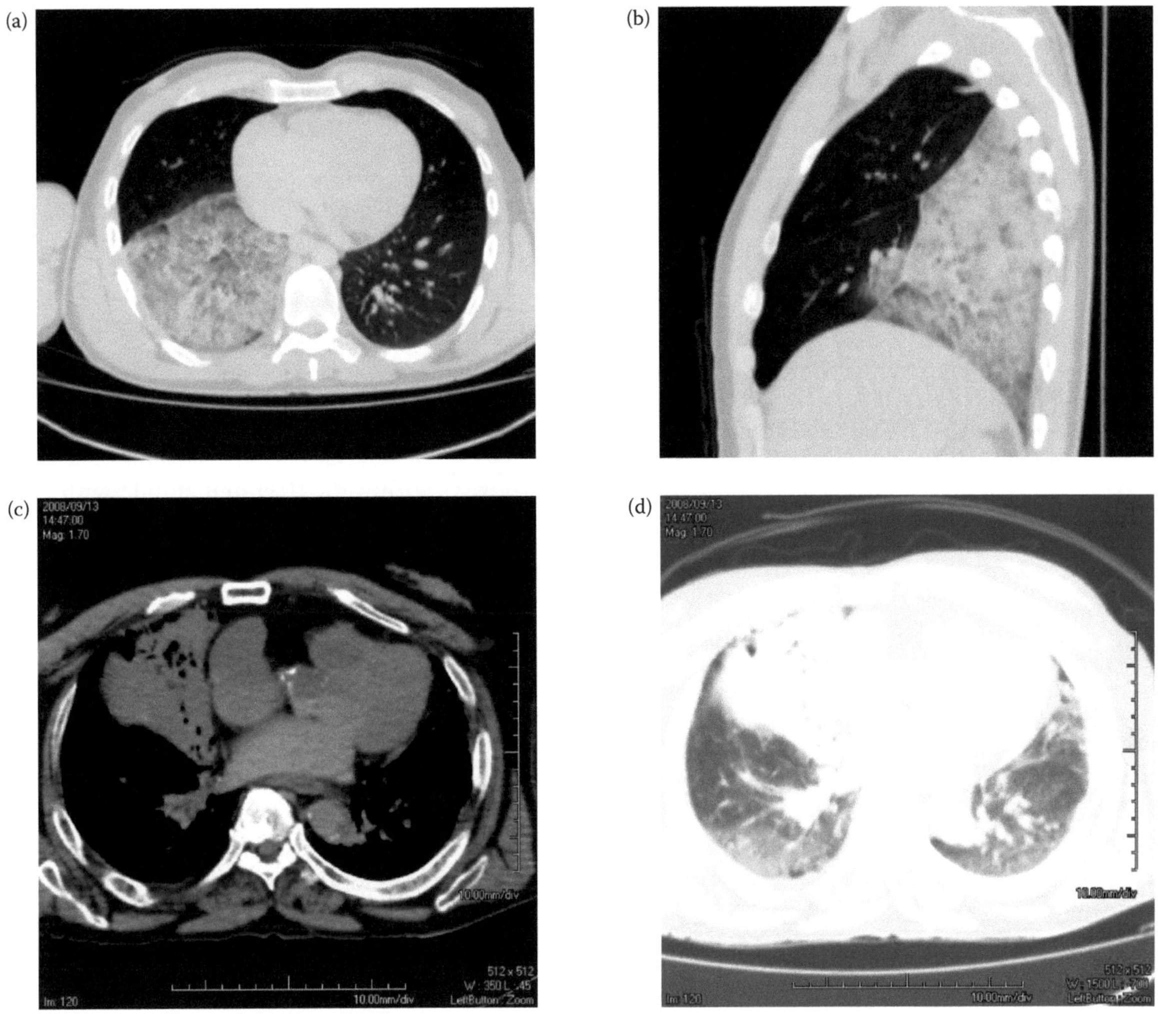

Figure 1.18 (a) Axial postmortem CT showing demarcated lung opacity consistent with lobar pneumonia. (b) Sagittal postmortem CT showing a well-demarcated lung opacity. (c) Axial postmortem CT showing air bronchograms within consolidated lung. (d) Axial postmortem CT using lung windows to highlight air bronchograms.

The most likely diagnosis is lobar pneumonia. The CT images showed consolidation of the lung parenchyma with air bronchograms. While this appearance is entirely consistent with infection, one certainly cannot entirely exclude the possibility of some other disease process. The differential diagnosis includes consolidative bronchioloalveolar carcinoma, alveolar proteinosis, lymphoma, and other inflammatory conditions. The presence of a hilar mass would increase the likelihood of an underlying malignancy.

Postmortem pulmonary CT is a particularly difficult area for the forensic pathologist. It is wise to remember that recognized patterns of CT abnormalities reflect pathological processes occurring in particular anatomical and regional parts of the lung parenchyma, but these patterns can have many different causes.

When death appears to have been caused primarily by lung disease, without good supporting clinical or laboratory evidence the pathologist should have a low threshold for recommending a full autopsy examination.

Case Study 19: Peritonitis and Appendicitis

A 50-year-old man with a past history of alcoholism, duodenal adenocarcinoma treated by Whipple's procedure, and hydatid disease was found deceased on his couch at his home. The death was reported to the coroner and a conventional autopsy was ordered.

At autopsy peritonitis was identified. All surgical anastomoses appeared intact. There was no evidence of recurrent tumor. No perforation was evident. Examination of the liver showed cirrhosis and cysts with focal calcification and a laminar membrane. Frank pus was most prominent to the diaphragmatic region of the liver. Swabs from the hydatid cyst and the peritoneum both grew *Bacteroides fragilis*.

(a) (b)

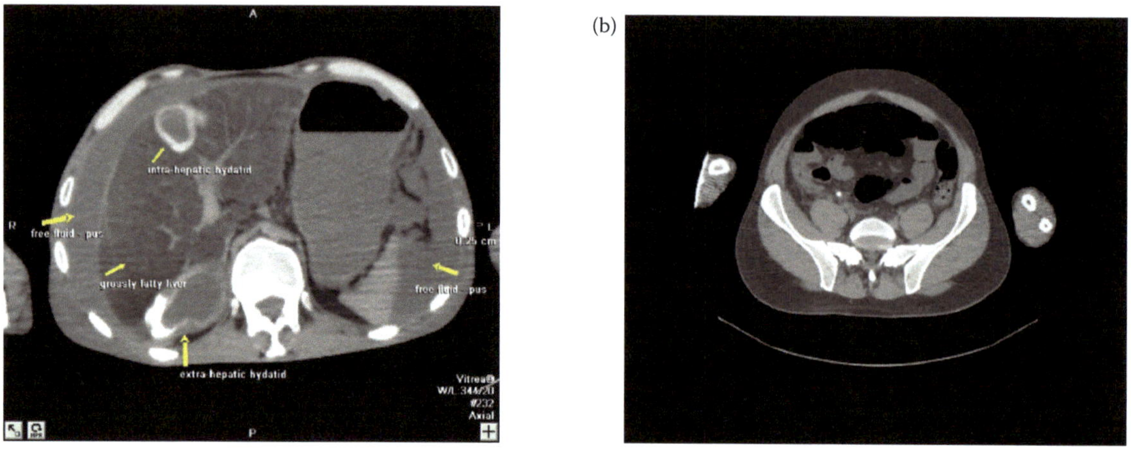

Figure 1.19 (a) Axial postmortem CT showing well-demarcated cysts within the liver and "fluid" within the peritoneum. The fluid had Hounsfield units of ~20. (b) Axial CT showing an appendicolith with adjacent fat stranding indicating acute inflammation.

Review of the CT scan with the radiologist confirmed liver cysts and fluid within the peritoneum (Figure 1.19a).

Forensic Issues

The CT scan had clearly shown fluid within the peritoneum. The differentiation between ascites, bile, and pus is difficult.

Pus and ascitic fluid have Hounsfield units considerably less than that seen with blood. Pus in the peritoneum can have a range of Hounsfield units typically from 10 to 20. Although peritonitis is usually associated with perforation of a viscus and may thus show gas within the peritoneum, primary bacterial peritonitis may occur in association with chronic liver disease and ascites. This rare and unusual case of peritonitis appeared to result from rupture of an infected hydatid cyst within the liver.

CT is a routine clinical investigation in cases of suspected acute appendicitis. Postmortem CT may suggest the diagnosis (Figure 1.19b). Cases of suspected acute appendicitis that culminate in peritonitis and death should undergo full autopsy examination.

Case Study 20: Air Embolism

A 20-year-old male unrestrained driver of an older model motor vehicle crashed into a light pole. The deceased's head went through the windscreen resulting in a large gaping incised injury to the neck. The victim died at the scene. The death was referred to the coroner. The deceased's next of kin lodged an objection to autopsy.

The external examination showed a large incised injury to the neck with large caliber vessels easily seen within the depths of the wound. The postmortem CT scan showed no skull or cervical spine fracture. There was no evidence of hemothorax or hemoperitoneum. The pathologist identified extensive intracranial air. There was a large volume of air within the heart (Figure 1.20a,b). The images were referred to the radiologist for an expert opinion.

The radiologist reported that the incised injury extended from the anterior aspect of the neck to the oropharynx (Figure 1.20c). It was also indicated that the injury extended to the region of the vertebral artery with glass fragments noted within the foramen transversarium. There was extensive intracranial gas. Gas was present within the heart and hepatic artery, but no gas was seen within the hepatic vein.

The coroner was informed that a reasonable cause of death was air embolism secondary to incised neck injury in the motor vehicle incident. The deceased's body was released from the institute.

Forensic Issues

CT is an excellent tool for demonstrating gas. The traditional autopsy technique of opening the heart in the water-filled pericardial sac is not always a successful procedure. Conventional radiology is not nearly as sensitive as CT.

The postmortem CT provides a permanent record in cases of air embolism. Furthermore, the total body CT can also confirm the absence of gas in the portal veins thus virtually excluding decomposition as a cause of gas production.

The diagnosis of massive air embolism can provide an explanation of sudden collapse and death in a victim of penetrating head and neck trauma who had previously appeared clinically stable.

Case Study 21: Hyoid Bone in Hanging and Neck Compression

A stocky 35-year-old man was found hanging by a cord that was attached to a rafter in the garage at his home. The

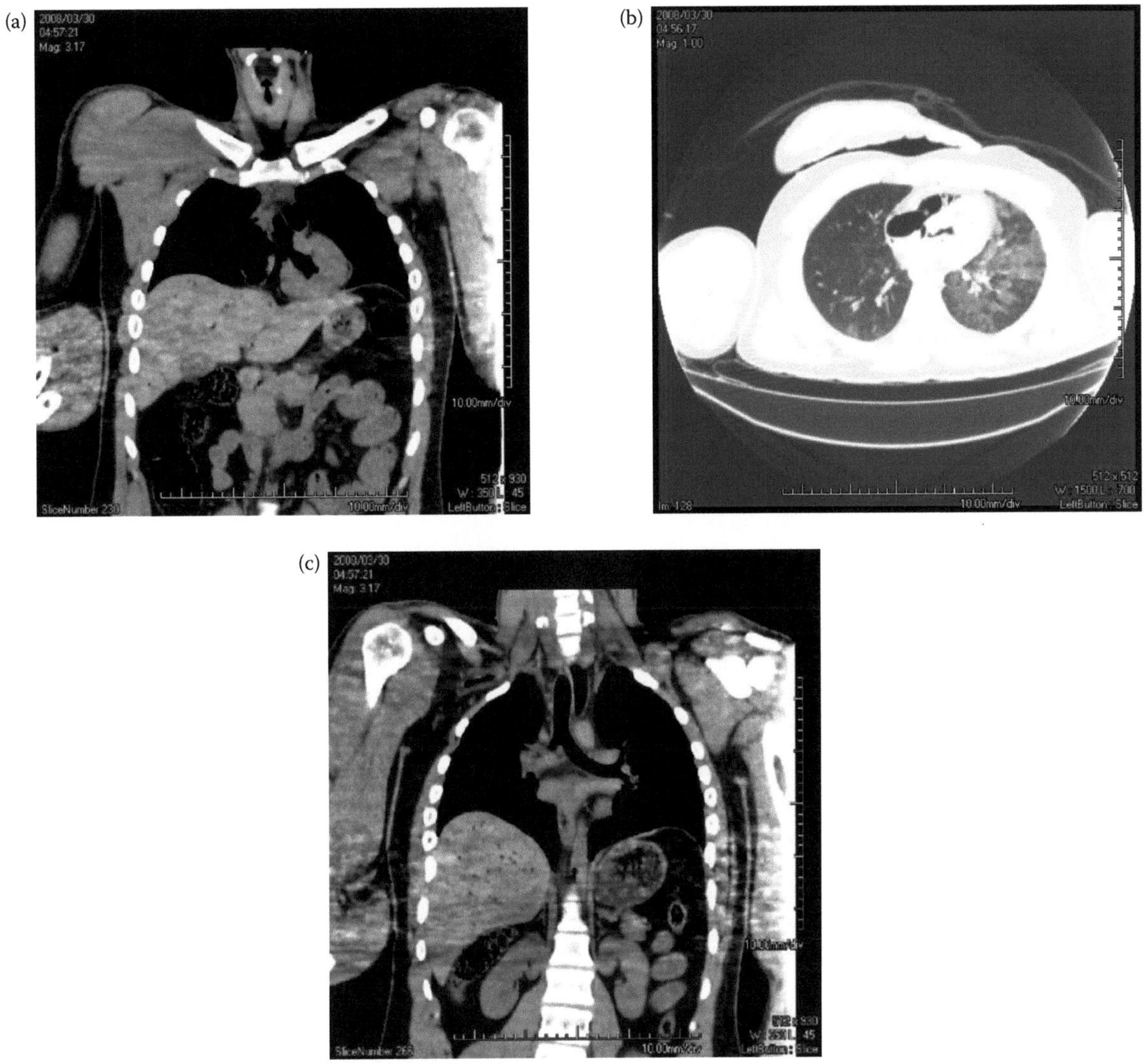

Figure 1.20 (a) Coronal postmortem CT showing air within the heart. (b) Axial CT with lung window showing dilated right heart from presence of air. (c) Coronal CT showing anatomical proximity of air within large veins in the neck adjacent to the soft tissue injury to the neck.

deceased had a past history of depression and had been under the care of a psychiatrist. A suicide note was present at the scene when the deceased was found by his father.

The deceased's body was taken to the institute for medicolegal autopsy. The senior next of kin lodged a formal objection to autopsy. The external examination showed a furrow and abrasion to the neck in association with the ligature. The skin of the upper neck and face was markedly plethoric, and there were petechial hemorrhages within the conjunctivae. There were no other injuries seen.

The postmortem CT scan showed no evidence of skull fracture or intracranial hemorrhage. The hyoid bone was fractured (Figure 1.21a,b).

The coroner was informed of these findings. He ordered that no further examination of the deceased's body was required and the deceased was released from the institute.

Forensic Issues

Hanging is a common cause of suicide in Victoria, Australia. The death is related to obstruction to the airway, major blood vessels in the neck, and may be associated with carotid body stimulation in some cases. The presence of a fracture reflects the application of force to the neck, but it does not, of itself, directly cause death.

In our current system the diagnosis is reached by a combination of the typical scene findings, absence of external injuries and "negative" CT. Some unusual skin injuries may be explained by the position of the deceased during the incident or when they are cut down from the suspension point. In these cases close cooperation with the police investigators at the scene and evaluation of any photographs taken *in situ* are often crucial in making the correct diagnosis.

The inspection of the hyoid bone and calcified thyroid cartilages becomes part of the routine assessment

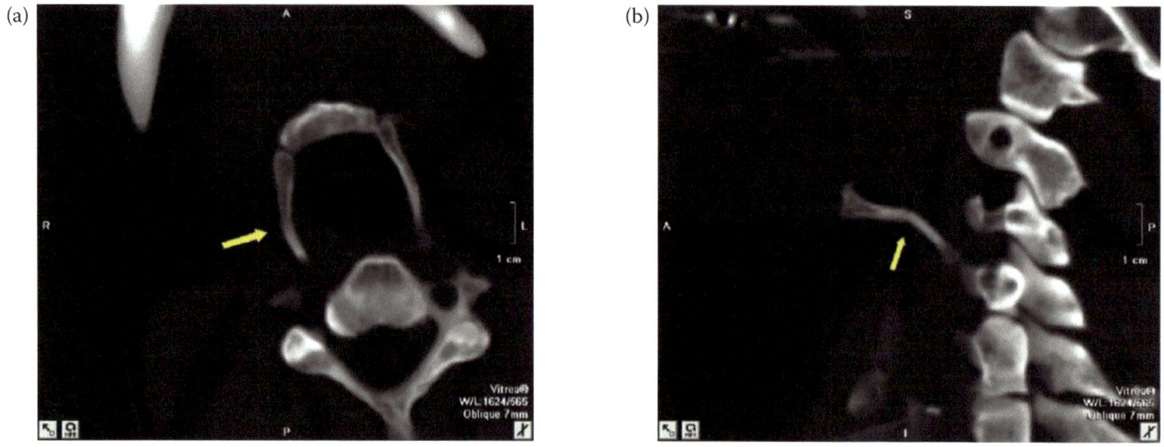

Figure 1.21 (a) Axial CT showing recent fracture to the hyoid. (b) Sagittal CT showing fractured hyoid.

of the CT images analogous to direct inspection of the larynx during the conventional autopsy. In young individuals the absence of a fracture does not exclude the application of significant force to the neck because the pliable nature of the laryngeal structures often precludes a fracture.

In cases with any unusual features that are not readily explained through discussions with the scene police investigators, a full internal examination with formal neck dissection is mandatory.

Case Study 22: Postmortem Angiography

A 62-year-old man was said to have suffered a seizure, following which he commenced coughing up blood, had a cardiac arrest, and died. The case was discussed with the coroner and a postmortem angiogram was performed, and a full autopsy examination was ordered.

The postmortem angiogram showed a "cast" of contrast within the small bowel (Figure 1.22). The contrast was most prominent within the duodenum with a small amount of contrast seen within the stomach. There was no contrast seen within the trachea or bronchi.

The autopsy revealed a 2.5 cm chronic peptic ulcer within the first part of the duodenum with a large artery at the base.

Forensic Issues

At the VFMI we have successfully performed a number of postmortem angiograms to examine the vertebral arteries in cases of traumatic basal subarachnoid hemorrhage, to identify possible sites of operative and postoperative hemorrhage, and to identify damaged vessels in anatomically difficult locations such as the pelvis. The procedure is performed by the forensic technician using a simple infusion pump that is attached to the femoral artery and vein. Approximately 150 ml of radiographic contrast (Ultravist 370 solution) is mixed with 1700 ml of PEG200 solution.

In the case described the angiogram clearly demonstrated continuity between the arterial circulation and proximal small bowel. The autopsy confirmed the presence of a large artery in the base of a chronic gastric ulcer.

Case Study 23: Cautionary Cases

Case 23.1

A 24-year-old man was discovered deceased in a suburban street. It was alleged there had been an altercation earlier in the evening. His body was taken to the VFMI for medicolegal examination.

At autopsy a depressed fracture was found to the skull. There was a severe brain injury. Loosely adherent to the periosteum were numerous small fragments of hard grayish-black material (Figure 1.23a). After stripping away the periosteum an unusual patterned quality to the skull fracture. The depressed region of the skull was somewhat ovoid in shape and a second curved indentation to the skull was noted immediately below the depression (Figure 1.23b). Furthermore, at the lower edge of the region of depressed bone was a distinctly right-angled component.

A dark-colored metallic car lock was found and compared to the injury. There were a number of projections to the area of the key mechanism that provided a close match to the bony injury. A male was charged and convicted of inflicting fatal head injuries with the car lock.

Case 23.2

An intoxicated 21-year-old man was involved in a witnessed altercation in which he was struck to the nose. The blow resulted in the man falling backward and striking the back of his head. He had a brief period of loss of consciousness after which he was helped back to his

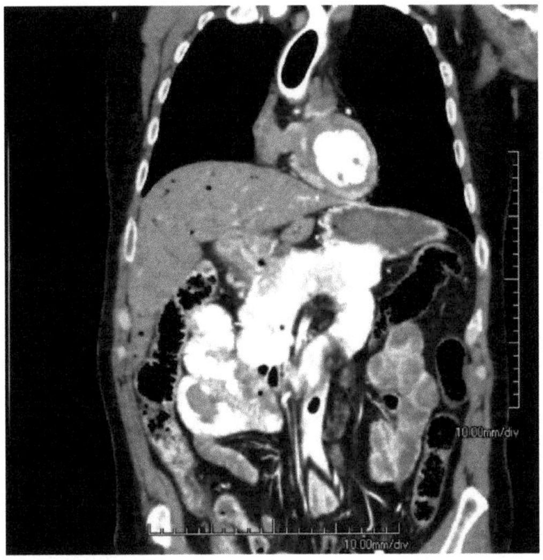

Figure 1.22 Coronal CT angiogram image showing extravasations of contrast into the duodenum.

residence where he went to bed. He was found deceased in the morning. His body was taken to the VFMI for medicolegal examination.

The external examination showed a bruise involving the mouth and nose. There was a large bruise to the occiput noted on reflection of the scalp. Examination of the brain showed typical contusions to the base of the frontal lobes and temporal poles resulting from a fall to the back of the head (contrecoup contusions) (Figure 1.23c). There was a large volume of extradural blood in the posterior cranial fossa associated with a longitudinal fracture of the occipital bone (Figure 1.23d,e). The cause of death was a posterior fossa extradural hematoma. The assailant was charged and found guilty of manslaughter.

Forensic Issues It is not particularly difficult to find examples where the CT cannot resolve important issues in a case. In the first case the foreign material and the patterned skull injury require direct inspection by a pathologist during an internal examination of the body. CT analysis of posterior fossa structures is difficult. In the second case it is quite likely the pathologist might not identify the posterior fossa extradural hematoma, which ultimately caused the death. This could become an issue if the cause of death, other than simply "head injury," was contested in court. As these cases were suspicious deaths, these findings would not be missed as the case would go to conventional autopsy. However, they do highlight the potential for important information to go undetected.

The CT is an important tool used by the pathologist in a medicolegal investigation. A far more important factor in the investigation is information on the case. The information leads the pathologist to manage some cases with external examination and CT, whereas others must be managed with external and internal examination.

Conclusions

The transition from routine conventional autopsy in the majority of cases to the use of external examination and CT scanning can be problematic.

Forensic pathologists are at ease in the concrete nature of observing pathologies in the mortuary and subsequently under histological examination. By working in the medicolegal area we are aware of the importance of hard evidence when formulating reports for the various courts. We are also acutely aware of the importance of experts keeping to their field of expertise. Herein lies the problem for forensic pathologists who incorporate CT diagnosis into their decision-making process in the medicolegal investigation of a death.

Is the forensic pathologist an "expert" in interpreting CT scans? One clearly cannot reasonably expect a forensic pathologist to approach the expertise of a consultant radiologist. However, because of financial and manpower restraints, the plain truth is that in a busy forensic institution the pathologist will have to at least screen the CT scans of routine cases.

It is reassuring to remember that, especially in fit, young adults, disease processes and changes associated with trauma are likely to show quite marked changes on CT. On the other hand, elderly trauma victims or those with significant underlying disease processes can succumb to relatively small amounts of blood loss or a relatively small pneumothorax. In these cases, subtle

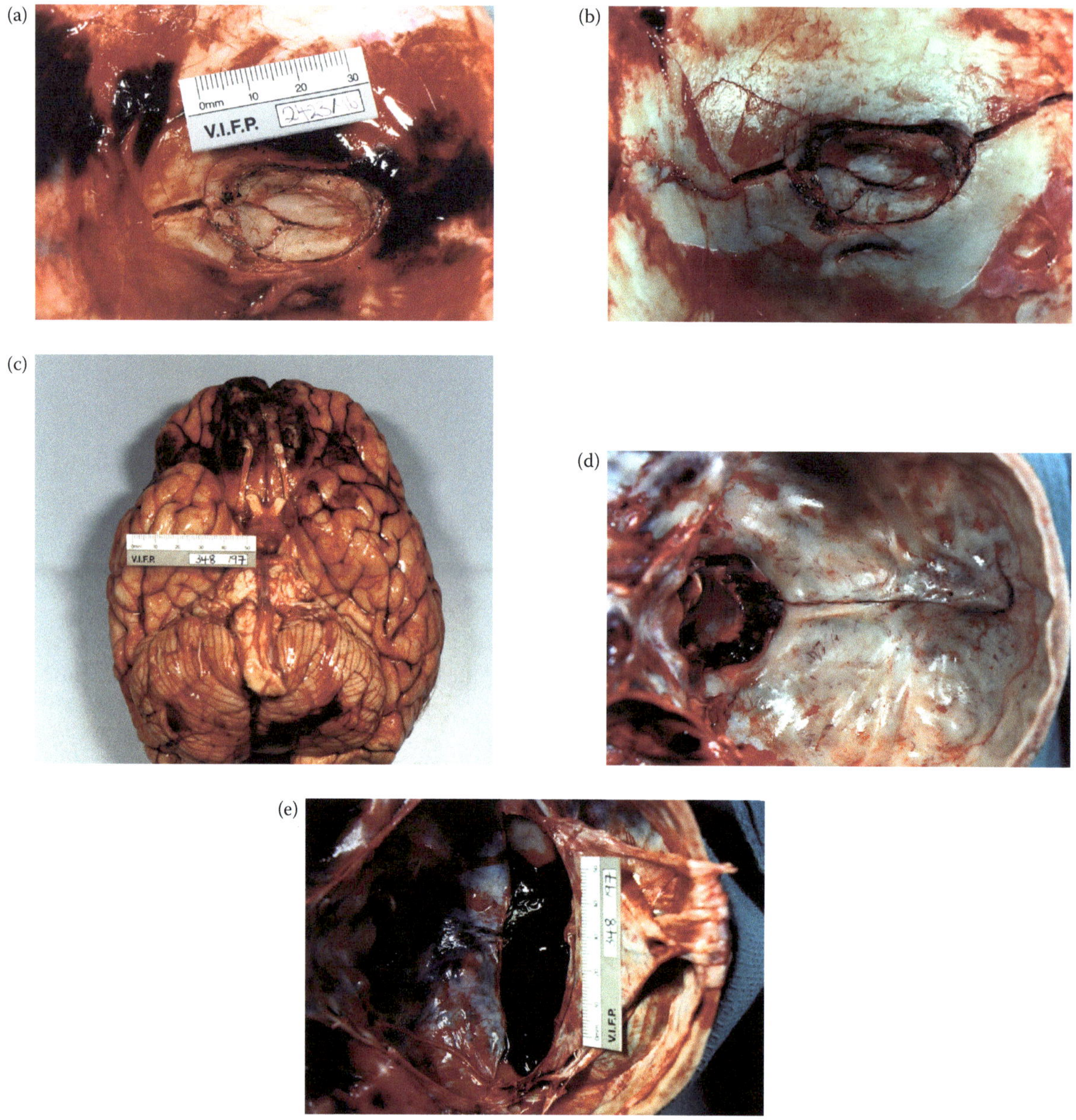

Figure 1.23 (a) Photograph of a depressed fracture of the skull with foreign material loosely adherent to the periosteum. (b) Photograph of depressed skull fracture with periosteum removed. There is a patterned quality to the bony injury. (c) Photograph showing typical contrecoup contusions to the base of the brain. (d) Photograph of longitudinal linear fracture to the occipital bone consistent with a fall to the back of the head from a standing position. (e) Photograph of associated extradural hematoma within the posterior fossa.

changes on the postmortem CT scans may indeed be important from a medicolegal point of view.

Undoubtedly each of the pathologists at the VIFM has probably overlooked collections of blood within the abdomen in cases of multiple trauma with massive hemothoraces associated with a ruptured aorta. It would be unlikely that following a relatively small amount of time using the CT and with some basic education that a hemoperitoneum or hemothorax of sufficient volume to cause death in a fit healthy individual would be overlooked. Furthermore, in the cases where the pathologist does not identify the collections of blood that are in fact present on the scans, then the pathologist is likely to conclude the death is unascertained and thus recommend a conventional autopsy.

It is naïve to think that issues will not arise because of this change in practice. At least at the VIFM, we have found that if pathologists embrace the technology and have expert radiologist support, then the system can provide the various stakeholders with a quality medicolegal investigation process.

References

1. Weustink AC, Hunink MG, van Dijke CF, Renken NS, Krestin GP, Oosterhuis JW. Minimally invasive autopsy: An alternative to conventional autopsy? *Radiology* 2009; 250(3):897–904.
2. Bolliger SA, Thali MJ, Ross S, Buck U, Naether S, Vock P. Virtual autopsy using imaging: Bridging radiologic and forensic sciences. A review of the Virtopsy and similar projects. *Eur. Radiol.* 2008; 18(2):273–282.
3. Reid A, Schneider-Kolsky ME, O'Donnell CJ. Comparison of computed radiography and multidetector computed tomography in the detection of post mortem metacarpal index. *Forensic Sci. Int.* 2008; 177(2-3):192–198.
4. Berlin L. Accuracy of diagnostic procedures: Has it improved over the past five years? *Am. J. Roentgenol.* 2007; 188:1173–1178.
5. Berlin L. Malpractice issues in radiology. Perceptual errors. *Am. J. Roentgenol.* 1996; 167:587–590.
6. Filograna L, Tartaglione T, Filograna E, Cittadini F, Oliva A, Pascali VL. Computed tomography (CT) virtual autopsy and classical autopsy discrepancies: Radiologist's error or a demonstration of post-mortem multi-detector computed tomography (MDCT) limitation? *Forensic Sci. Int.* 2010; 195:e13–e17.
7. Pescarini L, Inches I. Systematic approach to human error in radiology. *Radiol. Med. (Torino)* 2006; 111:252–267.
8. O'Donnell C, Woodford N. Post-mortem radiology—A new sub-specialty? *Clin Radiol.* 2008; 63(11):1189–1194.
9. Grabherr S, Gygax E, Sollberger B, Osterhelweg L, Bolliger S, Christe A, Djonov V, Thali MJ, Dirnhofer R. Two-step postmortem angiography with a modified heart lung machine: Preliminary results. *AJR* 2008; 190(2):345–351.
10. Buck U, Christe A, Naether S, Ross S, Thali MJ. Virtopsy—Noninvasive detection of occult bone lesions in postmortem MRI: Additional information for traffic accident reconstruction. *Int. J. Legal Med.* 2009; 123(3):221–226.
11. Persson A, Jackowski C, Engstrom E, Zachrisson H. Advances of dual source, dual-energy imaging in postmortem CT. *Eur. J. Radiol.* 2008; 68:446–455.
12. Klaus AJ, Schmutz B, Wullschleger ME, Schuetz MA, Steck R. Quantification of fracture callus volume from CT scans. *J. Bone Joint Surg. BR.* 2009; 91-B,SII:353.
13. Burke MP, Opeskin K. Audit in forensic pathology. *Am. J. Forensic Pathol.* 2000; 21(3):230–236.
14. Budoff MJ, Ahmadi N, Sarraf G, Gao Y, Chow D, Flores F, Mao SJ. Determination of left ventricular mass on cardiac computed tomographic angiography. *Acad. Radiol.* 2009; 16(6):726–736.
15. Given CA III, Burdette JH, Elster AD, Williams DW III. Pseudo-subarachnoid hemorrhage: A potential imaging pitfall associated with diffuse cerebral edema. *AJNR* 2003; 24(2):254–256.
16. Singh MK, O'Donnell C, Woodford NW. Progressive gas formation in a deceased person during mortuary storage demonstrated on computed tomography. *Forensic Sci. Med. Pathol.* 2009; 5(3):236–242.
17. Leth PM, Worm-Leonhard M. Tablet residues in stomach content found by routine post-mortem CT. *Forensic Sci. Int.* 2008; 179(1):e16–e17.
18. Kanne JP, Gotway MB, Thoongsuwan N, Stern EJ. Six cases of acute central pulmonary embolism revealed on unenhanced multidetector CT of the chest. *AJR* 2003; 180:1661–1664.

Classification of Injuries

2

Introduction

As the assessment of purely skeletal remains is a relatively uncommon occurrence in routine forensic practice, it is fundamental for the forensic pathologist to interpret a fracture with respect to the associated soft tissue injuries. An understanding of skin and soft tissue injuries is essential to the forensic evaluation of a fracture.

Reconstruction of computed tomography (CT) data can provide a three-dimensional surface shaded depiction of the skin. This can be used to document cutaneous injuries and other changes. Although these CT images are a reasonable representation of the surface of the body and are less confronting for lay persons than actual forensic photographs, it is the author's opinion that such images are not suitable for proper review of the case by an independent expert forensic pathologist.

It would appear a reasonable basic principle that if one is relying on CT for the diagnosis of fractures and other significant internal body changes, then it is essential that an expert forensic pathologist carries out the external examination of the body. Furthermore, it is advisable that forensic photographs are taken of any important injury or feature of interest. The importance of a thorough and knowledgeable external examination cannot be overemphasized.

Types of Skin Injury

In the context of blunt force trauma, the most important types of skin injury are abrasions, lacerations, and bruises. The presence of abrasions, lacerations, and bruises indicate the application of blunt force, usually indicate the site of the application of blunt force, and may signify the site of an associated fracture. In general, the larger the degree of inflicting force, the greater the skin injury. Nonetheless numerous other factors may contribute to the size of an injury including the anatomical site of the injury, the presence of preexisting disease processes, and the physical qualities of the offending implement.

Abrasions

An abrasion may be defined as the loss of the epidermis. Abrasions result from the application of blunt force. Abrasions are usually an indicator of the primary site of the application of blunt force.

Abrasions can display directionality. As a hard object moves forcefully across the surface of the skin small portions of skin are often raised above the surface of the surrounding skin. These raised portions of skin are usually referred to as "skin tags." The presence of the skin tags does not indicate whether the injured body part is moving across a fixed hard object or whether a moving hard object has struck the victim's stationary body.

Directionality can also be determined by the presence of linear abrasions forming part of the abrasion. Linear abrasions are often within a larger diffuse abrasion and are orientated along the longitudinal axis of the injury (Figure 2.1).

At the point of initial contact between a hard object and the skin the abrasion tends to be more prominent. The abrasion then becomes less well defined as the forceful contact between the skin and the object decreases. Sometimes when a heavy hard object strikes the skin at a more obtuse angle the initial contact may not be so forceful, yet as the object decelerates the abrasion can then become more pronounced.

In the acute situation abrasions are usually a dark red color, but with the passage of time the injury often undergoes drying, resulting in a parchment-like appearance to the injury.

The presence of abrasions in particular regions of the body is consistently seen in certain situations. Classical examples include abrasions over the bony prominences of the face, that is, the forehead, tip of the nose, zygomatic regions, cheeks, and chin in cases of sudden unconscious collapse resulting in a fall onto the face. Depending upon the orientation of the body at the moment of collapse one may see the injuries in the midline or on either side of the face. In any event the injuries tend to occur in a single plane.

In cases of sudden unconscious collapse with a fall backward, there may be an abrasion to the occiput, over the scapular regions, and the point of the elbow(s) (Figure 2.2). These injuries may be masked or altered by the presence of hair and clothing.

Abrasions may also have patterned qualities. These may range from a distinct, well-defined linear edge seen when forceful contact occurs between the skin and the

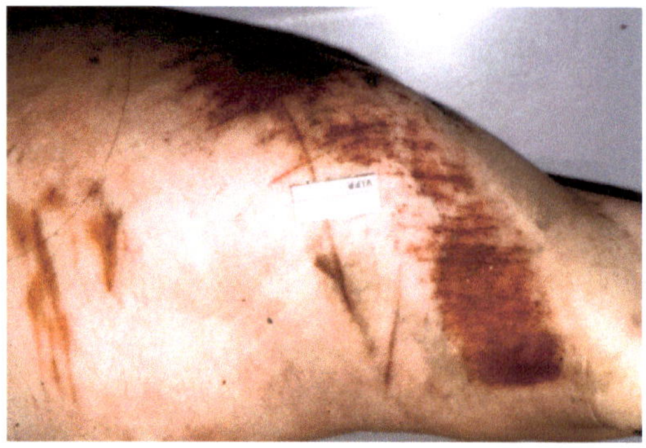

Figure 2.1 An abrasion to the left thigh of a young female occupant of a motor vehicle that sideswiped a concrete barrier. There was significant intrusion into the passenger side of the vehicle. There is an underlying fracture to the femur. The other occupant of the vehicle (the driver) had no significant injuries. The presence of the leg injury indicated her position in the vehicle.

straight edge of a hard object, to right-angled, curved, and various other shapes. The patterned shape of the abrasion will tend to be more obvious when the forceful contact was in a perpendicular orientation.

Patterned abrasions are relatively uncommon but important injuries (Figure 2.3). Generally the patterned quality of the injury is easier to recognize than it is to match the abrasion to a causal object (Figure 2.4a,b). A significant exception to this rule is the seatbelt abrasion. This classic example of a recognizable patterned abraded injury is characterized by an oblique linear abraded injury that extends from the anterior shoulder across the chest.

Punctate abraded/incised injuries result from contact with fragmented tempered glass in motor vehicle incidents. Although in isolation these injuries may not be diagnostic of an individual's seating position in a motor vehicle, they can be used in conjunction with other information to provide an opinion on such matters. In general, the individual who is closest to the broken tempered glass has the greater concentration of punctuate abraded and incised injuries (Figure 2.5).

In addition to external direct blunt force, another cause of an abrasion is "internal stretching" of the skin. Severe stretching of the skin well beyond the normal range of movement may cause superficial tearing to the epidermis. Common examples include changes to the inguinal skin in association with extreme hyperextension around the hip joint or suprapubic abrasions associated with gross separation of the symphysis pubis.

Lacerations

A laceration is a splitting or crushing injury to the skin. A laceration results from the application of blunt force. As such, the injury is often seen in association with an abrasion or bruise (Figure 2.6a,b).

The differential diagnosis of a laceration is an incised injury. Incised injuries are due to the application of sharp force as may occur from a razor, knife, or machete (Figure 2.7a,b). The correct diagnosis is reached from a careful examination of the wound.

The edges of lacerations tend to be irregular. Because lacerations result from blunt force injury, the nerves, vessels, and other connective tissues in the depths of the wound may be crushed but tend to remain intact.

A laceration may be caused when the sharp end of a fractured bone extends through the skin. In these cases there are generally no abrasions surrounding the laceration. An exception to this rule is the shored injury.

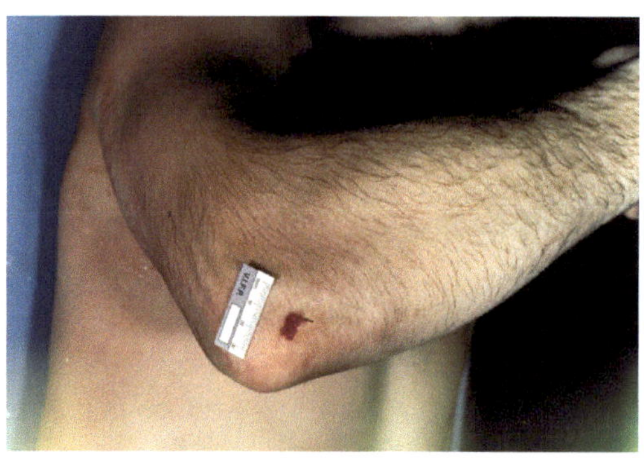

Figure 2.2 Abrasion to the back of the right elbow as seen in a fall backward following an episode of collapse.

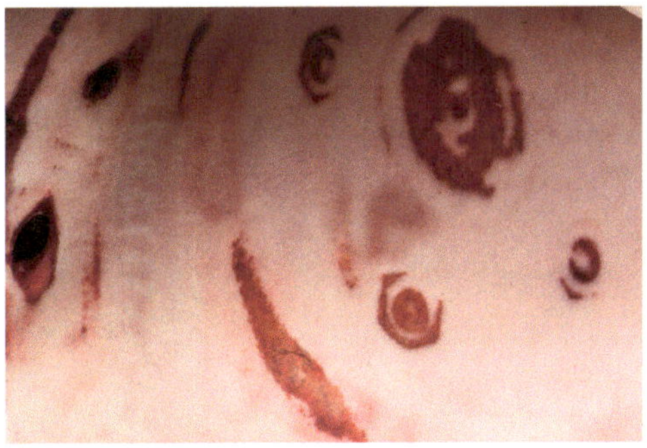

Figure 2.3 A patterned abrasion to the chest. The injury clearly shows the shapes of wheel nuts and central axle that struck the chest of a cyclist.

(a) (b)

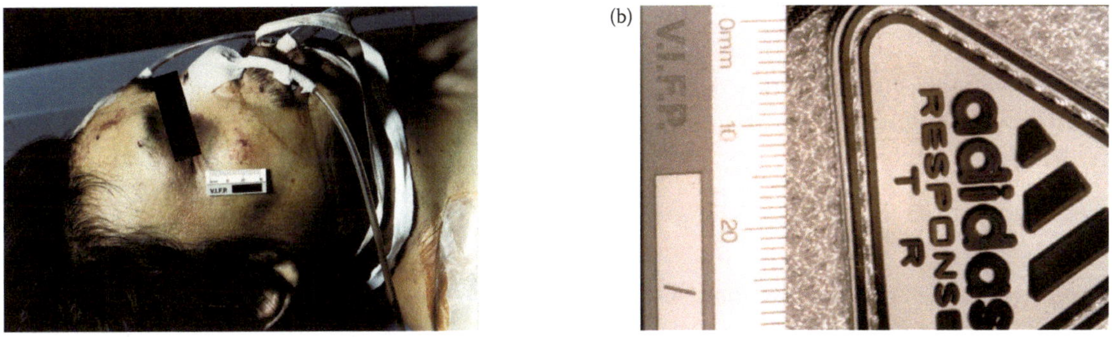

Figure 2.4 (a) An unusual patterned abrasion was noted to the cheek of an adult male found deceased adjacent to a railway line. The pattern suggested an impression from a shoe. An assailant was charged and found guilty of manslaughter. (b) Detail of a shoe similar to the one worn by the assailant who kicked the deceased to the face causing a fatal head injury.

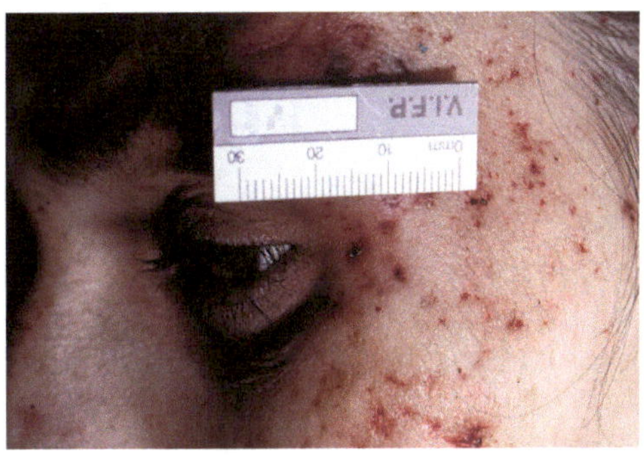

Figure 2.5 Numerous punctate abraded and incised injuries seen to the side of the face adjacent to broken tempered glass in a motor vehicle incident.

(a) (b)

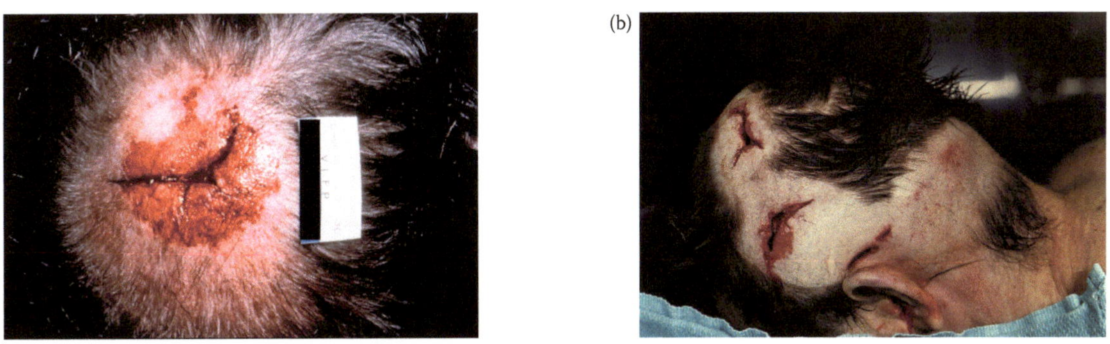

Figure 2.6 (a) A typical laceration to the top of the head. There is a broad abraded injury indicating a minimum width of contact between the weapon and the deceased's head. (b) Multiple lacerations to the head of a victim from blunt force trauma with an iron bar. The injury immediately above the left ear was continuous with an abrasion and bruise across the occiput.

(a) (b)

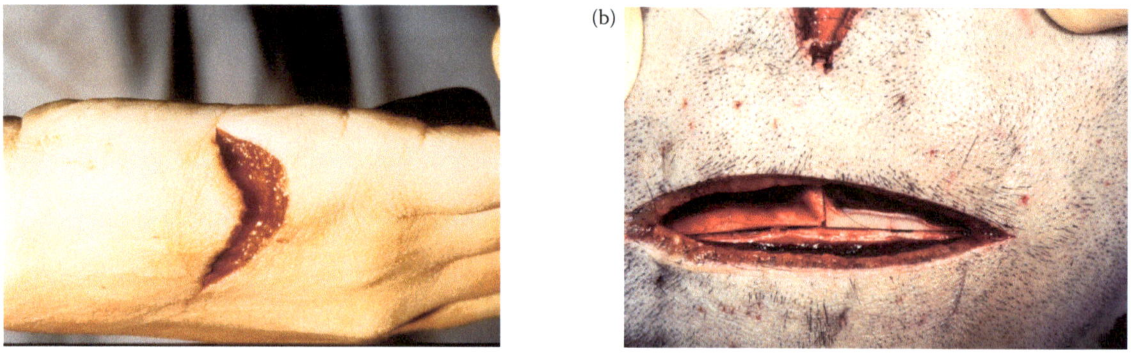

Figure 2.7 (a) An incised injury to the hand of a young woman assaulted with a sharp-edged weapon. The location of the injury suggests the injury may have occurred while she was trying to defend herself. (b) An incised injury to the head of a young woman attacked with a machete. There is an underlying incised injury to the skull. Compared to a laceration, the edges of the wound are clean and straight.

This occurs when the region of damaged skin has been in firm contact with an unyielding surface as the skin is punctured, forming an abrasion around the wound.

Bruises

A bruise may be defined as extravasation of blood from vessels into the surrounding soft tissues. A bruise results from the application of blunt force.

The extent of a bruise will tend to increase with escalating degrees of force. Other factors influence the size of a bruise from a given amount of force. These variables include the age of the victim, the presence of natural disease processes such as liver cirrhosis and chronic renal disease, and the use of various medications, such as aspirin and nonsteroidal anti-inflammatory drugs, anticoagulant medications, and corticosteroids.

The shape of a bruise may have considerable forensic significance. When the body is struck with any rod-shaped object, the blood vessels directly beneath the object will be compressed, whereas the blood vessels along the edge of the rod will be stretched (Figure 2.8). The damage to the blood vessels will be shown by two parallel lines of bruising with a central region of pallor. This is termed tram tracking. A second type of patterned bruise usually associated with opposing crescentic abrasions is the bite mark (Figure 2.9a,b).

Bruises have a tendency to increase in size over time. In the medicolegal investigation of a death where a significant period of time has elapsed between the onset of the injury and the subsequent death of the victim, it is highly likely a bruise would have changed in size and shape. Blood may track along tissue planes some distance from the site of origin. An impact to the nose can lead to bilateral periorbital hematomas, and a fractured base of skull can cause blood to track between the soft tissue planes along the neck. Thus with time bruises can be a poor indicator of the exact site of the application of blunt force.

An exception to this rule is the intradermal bruise. This injury is akin to the patterned abrasion. The intradermal bruise results when small blood vessels within the papillary dermis are damaged, causing bleeding into the superficial layers of the skin. A typical forensic example is the patterned bruise caused by forceful contact with a car tire (Figure 2.10).

In light-skinned individuals most bruises are visible over the surface of the skin. This is not always the case. In

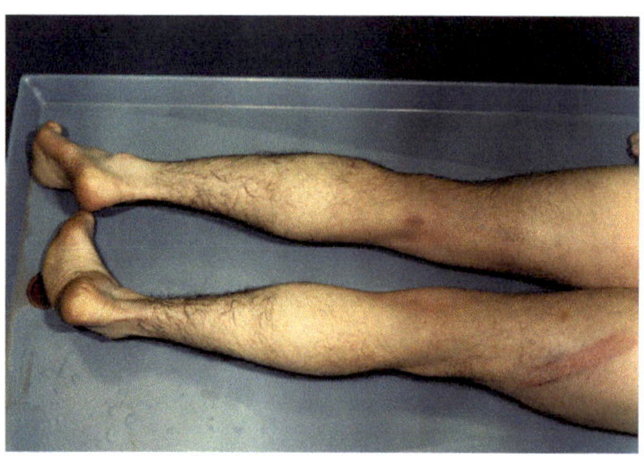

Figure 2.8 The posterior aspect of the right thigh shows a well-defined linear bruise. The bruise has defined parallel edges. The implement that caused the injury was a square-shaped segment of pipe.

(a) (b)

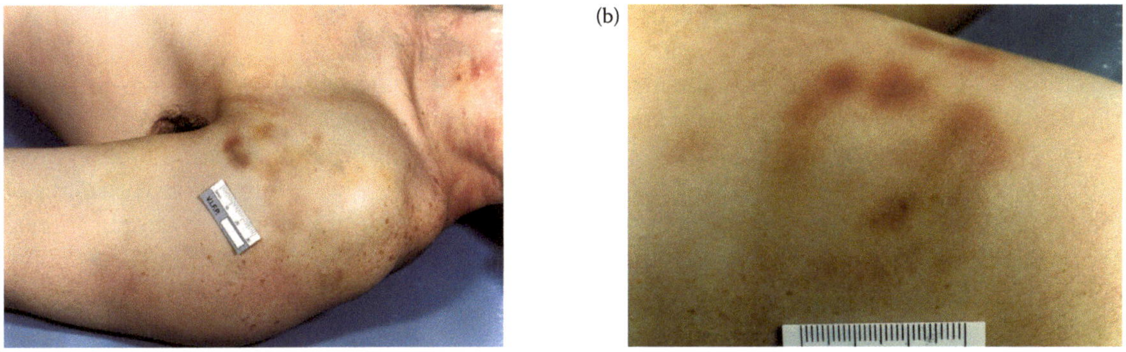

Figure 2.9 (a) Circular bruises to the anterior aspect of the left shoulder in a homicide victim. The brown color of the injuries clearly indicate the bite marks were not associated with the incident that lead to death. (b) Close-up photograph of a bite mark which showed marked changes in color indicating the bite mark is remote to the injury that lead to death.

many instances of deaths associated with significant blunt force a bruise is not visible over the surface of the skin but may be revealed by subcutaneous dissection of the region. In darker-skinned individuals this issue is compounded.

Bruises are more prominent where there is minimal subcutaneous fat over bones. Conversely, a severe blow to the abdomen may not be associated with any discernable changes to the skin even though the blow may cause lethal blood loss from a ruptured liver or spleen.

Bruises are much more pronounced when there is differential movement between the body and the object(s) that come into contact with it. It is the common experience of forensic pathologists that in many cases of suicidal hanging there may be no associated subcutaneous bruise in relation to the position of the ligature. This is due, in part, to the minimal amount of movement between the ligature and the skin of the neck. When there is a substantial difference between the size of an assailant and the victim (e.g., an adult male and a small child) such that there is minimal differential movement between the two individuals, there may be no detectable subcutaneous or submucosal bruising. This phenomenon may also occur when a broad object such as a forearm is applied to the neck of a smaller assault victim.

Other Skin and Soft Tissue Injuries

For completeness, a brief description of gunshot injuries and incised injuries is provided.

Gunshot Injuries

Firearms may be divided into smooth bore and rifled weapons. Shotguns are smooth bore weapons. Rifled weapons include the various handguns and long arm weapons. In simple terms gunshot injuries may be divided into entrance and exit injuries.

Entrance Injuries

The characteristics of entrance injuries vary with respect to the type of weapon used, and the distance between the end of the barrel and the surface of the skin, and the presence of overlying clothing or hair. One can also see additional injuries from the involvement of intermediate targets.

All entrance injuries have the characteristic features of a skin perforation with a surrounding abrasion collar. When the end of the barrel is hard against the skin, there may be a laceration due to stretching of the skin

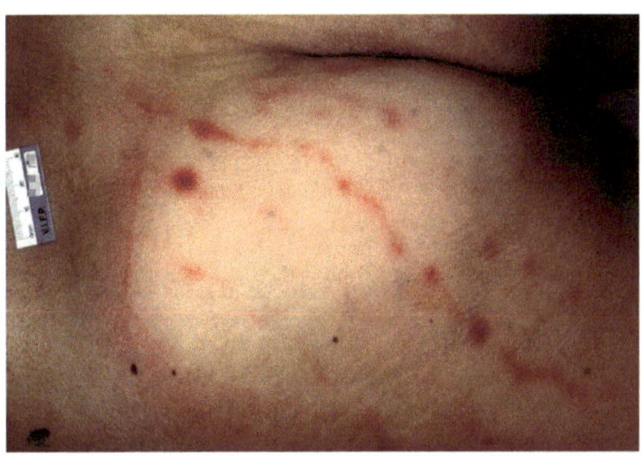

Figure 2.10 Intradermal bruising to the left buttock of a young woman who was struck by a light truck. The tire-mark bruise is less well defined than a patterned abraded injury.

from rapid expansion of the underlying soft tissues by gases emanating from the barrel. The hot gases produced from the explosive chemical reactions may sear the surface of the skin. When the barrel of the weapon is close to the skin soot produced from burning of the propellant may be deposited onto the skin. As the barrel is moved further away from the skin unburnt propellant may be embedded into the skin surrounding the entrance wound. The presence of unburnt propellant in the skin that cannot be removed by gentle washing is termed tattooing or stippling, and is the characteristic feature of a pathological intermediate range of fire. When the barrel is a sufficient distance from the surface of the skin one only sees the skin perforation and abrasion collar.

Apart from contact gunshot injuries the determination of the range of fire is a ballistics question that requires test firing with the weapon in question and identical ammunition.

Exit Wounds

Simple exit injuries do not have an abrasion collar. Shored exit wounds have an associated abrasion around the skin perforation. The shored abrasion is due to compression of the skin between the exiting projectile and the firm object that is against the skin. Sometimes a sliver of the projectile or a piece of the projectile's jacketing may result in an exit injury with characteristics of a sharp force injury.

Sharp Force Injuries

The classical sharp force injuries to the skin are stab and incised injuries. A stab injury is defined as being deeper than it is wide. Conversely an incised injury is defined as being wider than it is deep. Both types of sharp force injuries occur as a result of forceful contact to the skin with a sharp edge such as a knife, machete, glass edge, or scissors. The edge of the skin injury is typically very clearly defined. The connective tissues within the depths of the wound, such as blood vessels and collagen, are cleanly divided.

Inflammation and Artifacts

Acute inflammation is an essential first part in the healing of any injury. There is a sequence of inflammatory events that ultimately lead to repair of the injury. Damaged tissue releases various factors, which in turn cause dilatation of blood vessels, increased permeability of capillaries, and migration of neutrophil polymorphs. One consequence of these processes is swelling of the damaged tissue.

The inflammatory process is arbitrarily divided into acute and chronic phases but is of course a continuous process. The onset of inflammation is often quoted to commence a few minutes after the injury occurred [1]. This statement has significant implications for forensic practice. The presence of swelling in relation to an abrasion or laceration may imply the deceased individual had survived for some time after sustaining the injury.

Inflammatory cell function does not immediately cease with the somatic death of the individual [2]. This activity does not normally extend to margination of neutrophils around the vessel wall, which is generally considered a vital reaction [3]. However, a recent laboratory study on human cadavers investigating postmortem hypostatic hemorrhages in the anterior neck and strap muscles of cadavers showed "buffy coat" sedimentation that closely mimicked acute inflammation [4]. Furthermore, the study demonstrated hemorrhages that were histologically indistinguishable from true antemortem bruises.

On the other hand, the absence of neutrophil margination within blood vessels at the site of an injury is not evidence that the injury occurred in the immediate perimortem period or is a postmortem injury. Although the inflammatory response occurs upon the onset of trauma, the morphological features seen on histological examination can be delayed for a variable but considerable period of time.

A region of the body that is dependent after death can develop swelling. This will be associated with hypostatic lividity and is usually quite obvious. The process of decomposition may make this determination somewhat problematic. A previous case of remarkable facial swelling and bruising arising from infliction of postmortem injuries to an elderly woman has been reported [5]. In this case the corpse of an elderly woman was damaged when it was illegally exhumed from a grave. The body was subsequently returned to the grave in a head down dependent position. The subsequent examination of the body showed considerable extravasations of blood into the soft tissues of the face potentially mimicking true antemortem injuries.

Postmortem Insect Predation

Ants and other insects can cause a surprising degree of damage to the body after death and simulate a true antemortem injury. There is a distinct tendency for ants to follow the border between the edges of clothing and bare skin. This can sometimes mimic a ligature mark when there is a crew-neck-type collar around the neck or cause a postmortem abrasion around the belt line.

Maggot activity occurs around natural body openings and in areas away from direct light. When there is maggot activity in an unusual site there is a strong possibility of an underlying antemortem injury.

The Forensic Importance of Skin Injuries

Site of Application of Blunt Force

In the vast majority of forensic cases the presence of an abrasion, laceration, or bruise to the skin and subcutaneous soft tissues indicates the application of blunt force to that site. In some circumstances secondary effects may lead to skin or soft tissue injuries that are not due to direct overlying force. These include local, soft tissue bruises resulting from a fracture, which in turn was the result of indirect force. In such a case one does not expect a large bruise to the skin. A classical example of such an injury is the fracture to the tibia and fibula adjacent to the top of an ankle-length boot in a pedestrian who is struck by a motor vehicle. In this case the site of the fracture does not directly correlate with the site of primary contact with the vehicle [6]. However there will be a bruise associated with the fracture.

A common example in forensic practice is the relatively localized subgaleal bruise associated with a fracture to the calvarium. Another forensically important example is the scalp laceration caused by protrusion through the skin by the edge of fractured calvarium secondary to a crushing-type head injury. The pathologist could simply count the number of skin injuries, equate this with a number of blows, and potentially mislead the police investigators and the courts. The evaluation of the injury produced from such a mechanism will show an absence of an adjacent abrasion and no bridging by connective tissue within the depths of the lacerated injury.

In such cases during a conventional autopsy examination the lacerations can be aligned with the underlying fractures to the skull. It is usually readily apparent that the fractures and lacerations are the result of compression to the skull with subsequent fractures from a bursting-type mechanism.

Case Study

An adult male was riding a motorcycle along a major metropolitan road. He was said to be riding at a speed greater than the legal speed limit. He swerved abruptly into the inside lane when a truck stopped suddenly in front of him. He collided into the back of a stationary, small, four-wheel-drive motor vehicle. The man suffered a cardiac arrest at the scene but was resuscitated by ambulance personnel. He was taken to the hospital where emergency laparotomy and thoracotomy revealed a massive liver injury with a substantial hemoperitoneum. Despite ongoing fluid and blood replacement and attempts to stop the hemorrhage he died in the operating room.

The external examination showed a patterned abraded injury to the right lower chest (Figure 2.11). The injuries were photographed. The postmortem CT scan showed no evidence of head or cervical spine injury. The police informant was contacted and informed of the patterned abrasion. The officer indicated that there were no charges to be laid in relation to the death.

Individuals who suffer a cardiac arrest outside of the hospital secondary to hypovolemic shock have a dismal prognosis. The pathologist determined that a full autopsy would not progress the medicolegal investigation any further. The coroner ordered that no additional examination of the deceased's body was indicated.

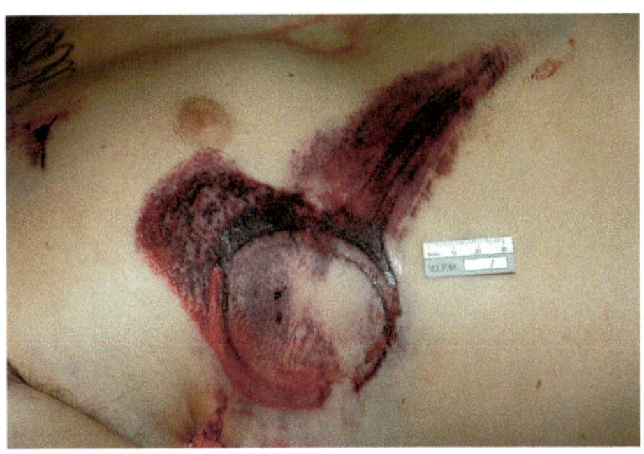

Figure 2.11 A patterned abraded injury to the chest of the motorcyclist. To determine what part of the motorcycle, truck, or other object caused the injury would require the pathologist to either attend the scene of death, or compare the images with the motorcycle and truck at a later date.

The death investigation was able to be managed by a review of the hospital records, which detailed the known injuries in the death; an external examination, which identified and recorded the site of primary impact to the body; and examination of the CT scans, which effectively excluded an occult head or neck injury.

References

1. Kumar V, Abbas AK, Fausto N, Aster JC. *Robbins and Cotran pathologic basis of disease,* 8th ed. Saunders/Elsevier, Philadelphia, PA, 2010.
2. Saukko P, Knight B. *Knight's pathology*, 3rd ed. Arnold, London, 2004.
3. Koszyca B, Gilbert JD, Byard RW. Ante mortem trauma from rodent activity. *Forensic Sci. Med. Pathol.* 2006; 2(4):269–272.
4. Pollanen MS, Perera SD, Clutterbuck DJ. Hemorrhagic lividity of the neck: Controlled induction of postmortem hypostatic hemorrhages. *Am. J. Med. Pathol.* 2009; 30(4):322–326.
5. Burke MP, Olumbe AK, Opeskin K. Postmortem extravasation of blood potentially simulating ante mortem bruising. *Am. J. Forensic Med. Pathol.* 1998; 19(1):46–49.
6. Eisele JW, Bonnell HJ, Reay DT. Boot top fractures in pedestrians. A forensic masquerade. *Am. J. Med. Pathol.* 1983; 4(2):181–184.

Fractures

3

Anatomy of Bone

Composition of Bone

Bone is a complex metabolically active tissue composed of organic and inorganic components. It consists of osteiod and hydroxyapatite [1]. Osteoid is produced by osteoblasts. It is comprised of collagen and ground substance. The predominant type of collagen is type 1. Hydroxyapatite is formed from calcium and phosphate.

There are essentially two structural forms of bone. These are compact bone and cancellous bone. Compact bone is the most abundant type of bone in the human body. It accounts for approximately 80% of the total bone mass and is important in providing bone with its strength. Compact bone is a dense tissue permeated by interconnecting canals called the Haversian system. This provides the bone with its blood supply.

Cancellous bone has a spongy or honeycombed architecture. It is formed from bony processes called trabecullae, which are aligned along lines of stress. The spaces between the trabecullae are filled with bone marrow or fat.

Bones are covered in a dense sheath called the periosteum, which is composed of an outer fibrous layer and an inner cellular layer containing osteoblasts. The periosteum completely invests the bones except at the articular surfaces, which are covered by articular cartilage.

Development of Bone

Ossification occurs through two ossification processes, endochondral and intermembranous. Endochondral ossification is the most common type of ossification in humans. Ossification centers in the cartilaginous "skeleton" of the embryo arise when osteoblasts produce osteoid with rapid deposition of inorganic salts. Long bones usually have three ossification centers, one central ossification center in the diaphysis and one at each epiphysis. Ossification continues until a relatively thin ribbon of cartilage remains in the epiphyseal plate. The epiphyseal plate closes upon cessation of growth and skeletal maturity. Intermembranous ossification occurs in the flat bones including those of the calvarium. The fibrous membranes of these bones undergo ossification from the osteoid secreted into the membranes by osteoblasts.

The microscopic organization of bone tissue largely determines its strength. Immature or woven bone has an irregular interwoven pattern of collagen and hydroxyapatite. Remodeling of woven bone occurs such that the layers of collagen and inorganic salts are subsequently arranged into organized, extremely orientated layers called lamellae. This provides the bone with its great strength.

Remodeling of Bone

As noted earlier, osteoblasts are bone-forming cells. Osteoclasts are multinucleated cells derived from a monocyte stem cell lineage. Osteoclasts break down bone resulting in bone resorption. The process of sculpturing bone during growth and repair of damaged bone requires an interaction of both osteoblasts and osteoclasts [2]. The coordinated action of osteoblasts and osteoclasts has been referred to as the bone-remodeling unit [1].

Classification of Bone

Bones may be classified according to their shape and function into long bones, short bones, flat bones, and irregular bones.

Long bones are longer than they are wide and are comprised of a layer of compact bone overlying a spongy inner layer containing the bone marrow. The bones typically have ends covered and protected by hyaline cartilage. Long bones have a central tubular shaft or diaphysis that extends to the juxta-epiphyseal metaphysis, with proximal and distal epiphyses. The epiphyses contain the epiphyseal or growth discs. Typically one thinks of a long bone as one of the major limb bones such as the femur or humerus, however the metacarpals and phalanges are also long bones.

Short bones are about as long as they are wide. Typical short bones are the carpal and tarsal bones of the hands and feet. The patella and sesamoid bones can also be defined as short bones. Short bones are formed principally from cancellous bone covered by a thin layer of compact bone. Sesamoid bones develop within tendons and are composed chiefly of cancellous bone.

Flat bones describe two layers of compact bone that sandwich a layer of spongy bone. The various bones of the calvarium, the sternum, and the scapula are examples of flat bones.

Irregular bones are those that, by virtue of their shape, do not fit easily into the other categories. The vertebral bodies are examples of irregular bones.

Fractures

Definition

A fracture may be defined as a break or discontinuity in a bone or cartilage. The most common cause of a fracture is the application of blunt trauma. A bone may be predisposed to a fracture by underlying natural disease such as osteoporosis or malignancy, or repetitive small amounts of trauma leading to a stress fracture.

Types of Fracture

A fracture may be classified using clinical and descriptive terms, or by the presumed mechanism of the injury. Descriptive classifications include the compound, or open fracture, where the skin or mucosa adjacent to the broken bone is breached. This may occur from the edge of the fractured bone protruding through the skin or a mucous membrane from the inside, or from an object extending though the skin and fracturing the bone.

Comminuted fractures occur when the bone is broken into many fragments. A chondral fracture occurs when only cartilage is involved. An osteochondral fracture occurs when there is a fracture of articular cartilage and a small segment of underlying bone.

Occult fractures have been described as bone bruises. These can vary from compression-type injuries limited to bony trabecullae to fractures involving the articular or bone surface. These injuries are not usually discernable on computed tomography (CT) examination but are well seen on magnetic resonance imaging (MRI). Bone bruises can be demonstrated at autopsy examination by sawing a segment of bone off the specimen to display the underlying architecture.

Mechanisms of Fracture

A mechanistic approach to fracture classification is attractive to forensic pathologists. The goal of this approach is to provide a reasoned expert opinion on the most likely mechanism of injury based on the physical characteristics of the fracture, scene information, and findings on external examination of the body.

An understanding of the mechanisms involved in bone fractures has been approached from an analysis of experimental work, by computer modeling, and from observational work studying fractures sustained by the living and deceased victims of trauma. Mature bone is a complex biological material often with variously shaped external surfaces and with an internal network of collagen orientated to best deal with physiological stresses. Thus the behavior of uniform homogeneous models of inert material cannot be directly correlated to human bone.

In the forensic setting where information surrounding the incident that led to the injury may be incomplete and the legal consequences of the medicolegal opinion may well be considerable, the reconstruction of the mechanism of injury from an examination of the deceased's body is often extremely difficult. One should always take a conservative approach in suggesting a mechanism of injury based on the examination of the body. Fractures in bone may result from:

- A large force localized to a small area
- A large force applied to a broad area

In the former case one tends to observe a localized or depressed fracture, whereas in the latter situation one tends to see a crushing-type fracture.

Long Bone Fractures

Long bone fractures are a good place to commence a discussion on fractures as they are common and the principles of fracture are somewhat intuitive. Fractures to long bones may be:

- Transverse
- Oblique
- Spiral
- Torus (buckle)

The mechanisms that lead to long bone fracture include:

- Tensile force
- Axial force
- Bending force
- Torsion force

Very often in any particular case there will be a combination of these forces.

Tensile Force Pure tensile force acting on a long bone is extremely unusual. A component of tensile force is

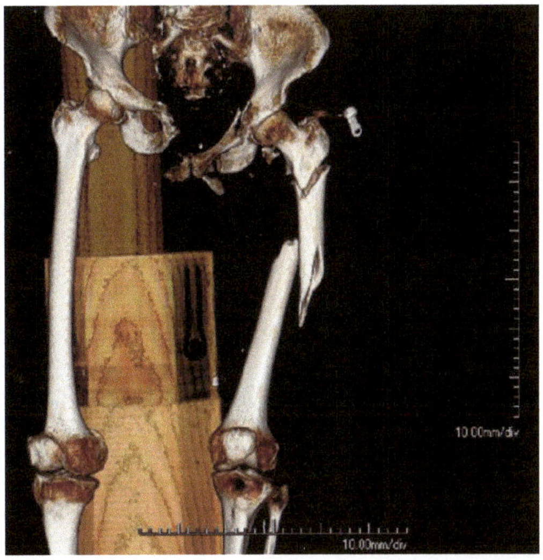

Figure 3.1 Three-dimensional reconstruction image showing a typical oblique fracture to the left femur in a pedestrian struck by a motor vehicle.

applied to bone when a laterally applied force leads to bending of the bone. In these instances there are tensile forces acting on the site opposite to the applied force, with a compressive (axial) ipsilateral component.

Axial Force Because of the relatively large amount of compact cortical bone in the diaphysis of long bones, crush fractures resulting from pure axial loading are unusual. Axial forces are associated with oblique fractures in long bones. According to Alms [3], increasing axial force in a pillar leads to "a linear shear fracture, at an angle slightly steeper than 45 degrees." This is explained by the resolution of forces into a purely compressive force along the axis of the bone and a tangential shearing force that leads to the oblique plane of fracture (Figure 3.1). Axial forces commonly cause compression fractures to the vertebral bodies in those with long-standing osteoporosis (Figure 3.2).

Bending Force Bending forces are by far the most common type of force that leads to fracture in the clinical and forensic setting. Bending forces typically result in transverse fractures (Figure 3.3). A typical fracture from relatively pure bending force would be a fracture to a long bone of the arm that had been held up to ward off an impact by a baseball bat.

When a long bone is bent it develops a convexity on the side opposite the application of force and a concavity adjacent to the application of force. A compression force is generated on the ipsilateral side, whereas tension

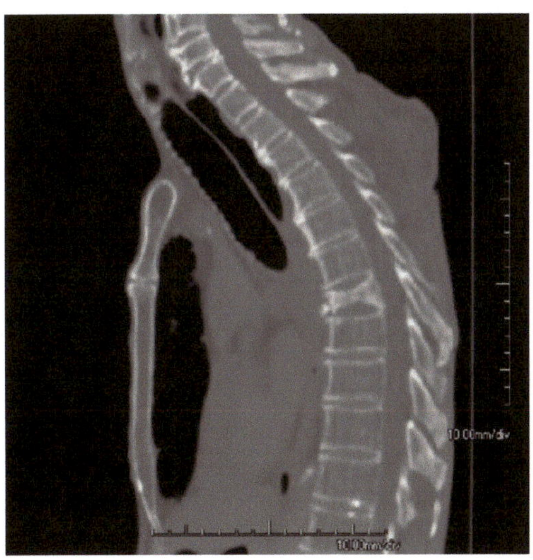

Figure 3.2 Sagittal CT image showing a typical crush fracture associated with osteoporosis.

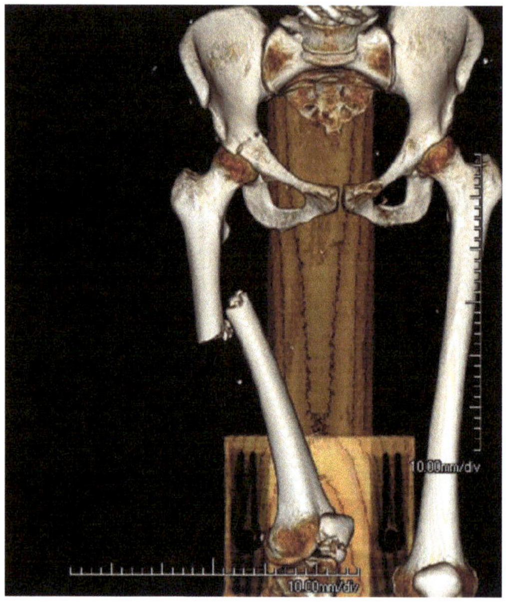

Figure 3.3 Three-dimensional reconstruction image showing a transverse fracture to the right femur of a pedestrian who was struck by a motor vehicle. The fracture is the result of bending forces.

forces are generated on the opposing side. At some point between these points there is a neutral position where neither tension nor compression is exerted.

The vast bulk of experimental work on mechanisms of fractures suggests bones tend to fail in tension as opposed to compression, though recently investigators have questioned whether this finding is universally true, most notably when fractures occur to the adult ribs. It is intuitive that a fracture will originate, all other things being equal, at the point of greatest tension at the surface of the bone, and extends in a transverse plane through the neutral point toward the concave side under compression [3].

In forensic practice it is common for the long bone that is subjected to a bending force to also be subjected to a degree of axial loading. The classical example is the weight-bearing tibia of a pedestrian who is struck by a motor vehicle. It has been reported that on reaching the neutral point within the bone, the fracture forms a triangular splinter as it forks around the neutral point [4]. This then leads to a typical "butterfly" segment in the fracture. Others have criticized this analysis as being too simplistic.

Torsion Pure torsional or twisting force applied to a limb is a relatively uncommon event. The pure mechanism is most commonly seen in babies and infants in the setting of nonaccidental injury. However, importantly, a spiral fracture to the tibia may be seen in a toddler following a rotational fall.

In practice the application of a torsional force is usually seen in association with axial loading. In young adults a severe tortional force may be imparted to the humerus when vigorously throwing a ball. In the older adult population this type of fracture is usually seen in older osteoporotic individuals.

Healing of Fractures

The healing of a fracture is a continuous dynamic process, which is arbitrarily divided into a number of phases. The injury sequentially undergoes inflammation, the creation of soft callus, followed by hard callus, and finally remodeling.

The initial fracture site contains a hematoma, with both viable and necrotic bone and bone marrow, and with adjacent torn periosteum (Figure 3.4). The inflammatory response occurs immediately after the injury and stimulates the accumulation of polymorphonuclear cells, mast cells, and macrophages. Osteoclasts and macrophages are activated to commence removal of necrotic bone and tissue debris. Angiogenesis is stimulated and granulation tissue migrates into the hematoma.

Soft callus formation usually takes about three to four weeks to occur. Soft callus is composed of a matrix of collagen and glycoproteins and contains osteoblasts, fibroblasts, and chondroblasts. Early cellular differentiation results in cartilage formation at the fracture margins. The soft callus extends beyond the margins of the fracture to connect the bone fragments.

Hard callus derives from the conversion of soft callus into woven bone via the action of the bone-remodeling unit. This process evolves over two to three months for an adult long bone (Figure 3.5a,b,c).

Remodeling of the hard callus occurs in concert with hard callus formation. The woven bone is gradually

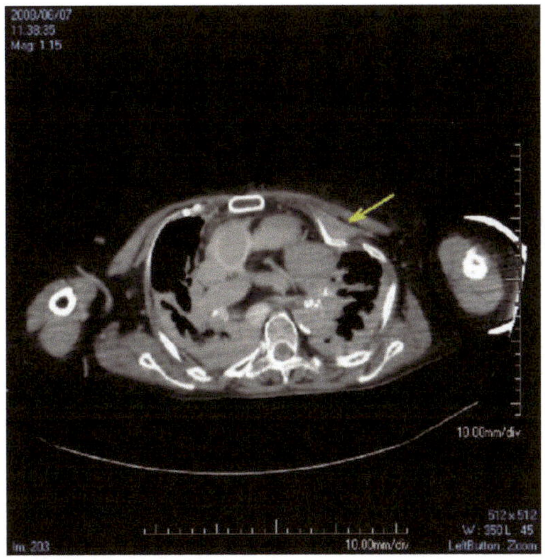

Figure 3.4 Axial CT image showing fractured rib with chest wall hematoma (arrow). The blood has Hounsfield units of ~40.

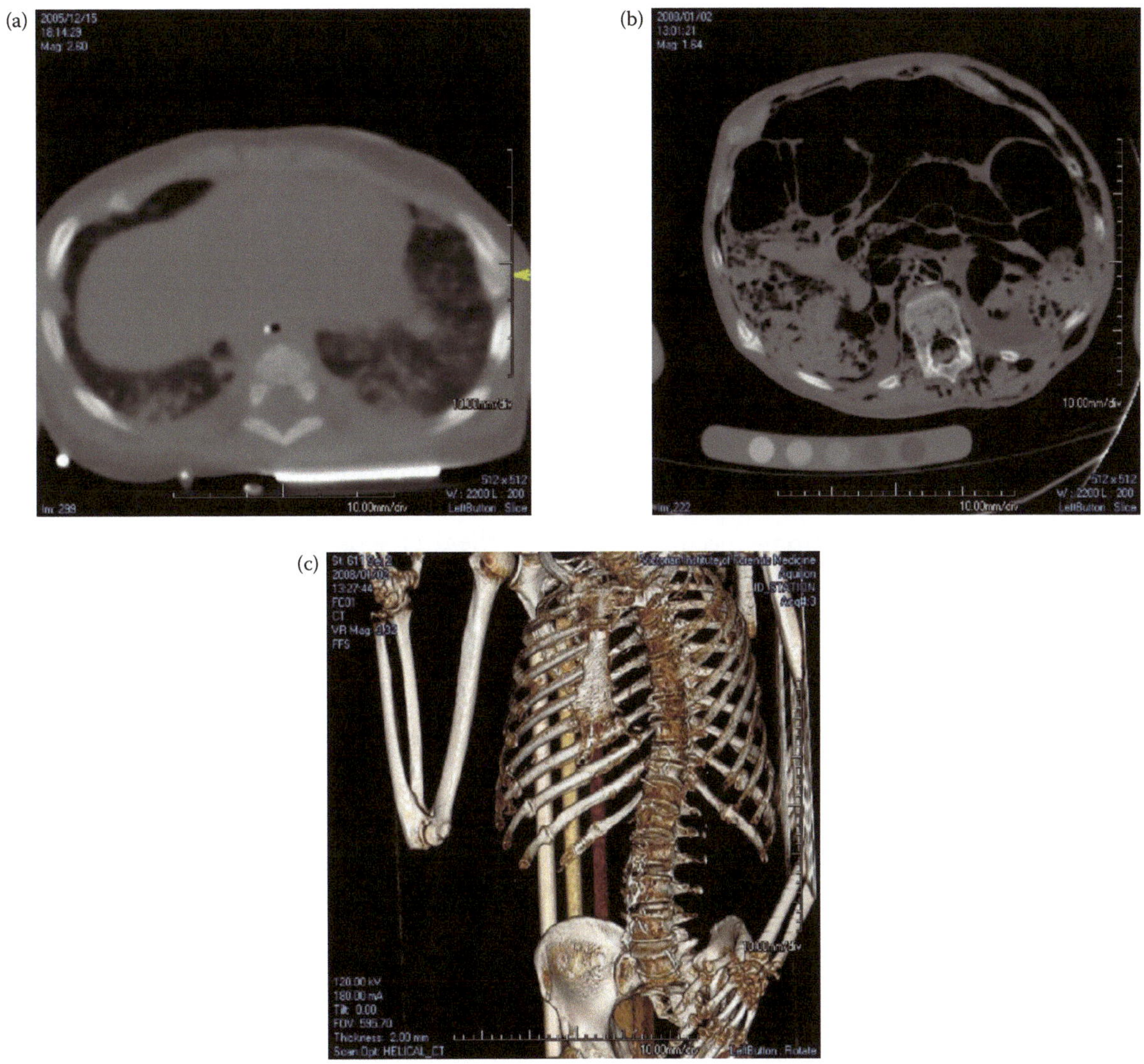

Figure 3.5 (a) Axial CT showing early callus to left rib (arrow). (b) Axial CT image showing more mature callus to right ribs in a decomposed body. Note decomposition gas in soft tissues. (c) Three-dimensional reconstruction image showing well-formed callus in multiple ribs in an alcoholic.

transformed into lamellar bone over a period of months to even years. Remodeling may be complete in children and eventually the fracture may not be visible. This situation is rarely observed in adults (Figure 3.6a,b,c,d,e).

Healing of a fracture is dependent upon a wide variety of factors including the age and overall health of the individual, the proper anatomical alignment of the fracture, maintenance of an immobile fracture site, and the absence of foreign material and infection. In an otherwise fit and healthy person a typical fracture of a long bone takes between six weeks and three months to heal.

Complications of Fractures

Fractures may cause immediate or late complications. The most important immediate complication that can lead to significant morbidity and mortality is hemorrhage. An early complication of major fracture that may cause death is fat embolism syndrome. Later complications include pulmonary thromboembolism and infection.

Catastrophic hemorrhage may be seen with pelvic fractures. Pelvic fractures are associated with significant mortality, especially in the elderly population. The pelvic bleeding can originate from raw fracture surfaces, from rupture of venous plexuses, as well as from lacerated arteries. Fractures of the femur can also cause significant hemorrhage into the thigh.

Fat embolism is not uncommon in victims of trauma. Systemic fat embolism syndrome is a multisystem disorder that is classically associated with fractures but may also be seen in diverse clinical situations such as severe burns, liposuction, liver injury, and bone marrow transplantation [5]. When the syndrome occurs secondary to bony trauma, the bones most commonly injured are the femur, the tibia, and the pelvis.

Systemic fat embolism syndrome occurs when multiple systems are affected by fat droplets within the microvasculature. The origin of the fat is believed to originate from mechanical disruption of marrow fat or activation of lipases. Activated lipases release circulating free fatty acids from the circulation. Systemic fat embolism syndrome has a characteristic petechial rash. The syndrome presents with respiratory failure and central nervous system involvement ranging from disorientation to confusion and coma [6].

Pulmonary thromboembolism occurs in up to 4% of trauma patients [7]. The mortality rate ranges from 20% to 50%. Risk factors for deep venous thrombosis and pulmonary thromboembolism include the severity of the trauma, lower limb fractures, and obesity. The formation of thrombus within peripheral veins and the subsequent onset of symptoms or sudden death usually occur about a week after the incident of trauma. Lethal thromboembolism has been described within a few hours of the injury, though this is highly unusual.

Fractured ribs may lead to pneumothorax through damage to the visceral pleura. A simple pneumothorax can cause significant physiological effects in those with underlying cardiorespiratory compromise. A ball valve effect may cause a tension pneumothorax. The tension pneumothorax leads to acute respiratory embarrassment as the volume of air within the pleural space increases with each inspiration. If the tension is not relieved the patient will develop decreased venous return with subsequent cardiovascular compromise.

The major late life-threatening complication of fractures is sepsis.

Forensic Issues

As is known to all medical practitioners, a fracture per se is not the immediate cause of death. However, the courts and lay population may have considerable misunderstanding about the forensic significance of fractures. This is most likely to be seen when one is dealing with a skull fracture. The courts may mistakenly believe that the CT images are demonstrating the actual cause of death when a skull fracture is identified. To the forensic pathologist the presence of a skull fracture infers the application of significant blunt force to the brain or upper cervical spine. In the appropriate circumstances the assumption can be made that there is a very high likelihood of underlying parenchymal injury to the brain such as diffuse axonal brain injury. To confirm such parenchymal injury, a full internal examination with neuropathological examination is required.

The degree of force required to cause a fracture is a common question in forensic practice. In the absence of pathological processes such as osteoporosis or malignancy one requires a significant degree of force to cause a fracture to any substantial bone. All things being equal, the larger and more robust a bone, the greater amount of force is needed to cause a fracture. There are a number of papers in the biomechanical literature that quantify the range of force that will cause fractures to many different bones. This research is largely intended for the development of safety equipment for motor vehicles.

Although the average layperson will have some understanding of the size and sturdiness of a lower limb long bone, thus understanding the considerable force required to cause a fracture, it can be difficult to convey to the medicolegal system a suitable measure of force when describing other fractures. One can use scientific and descriptive methods.

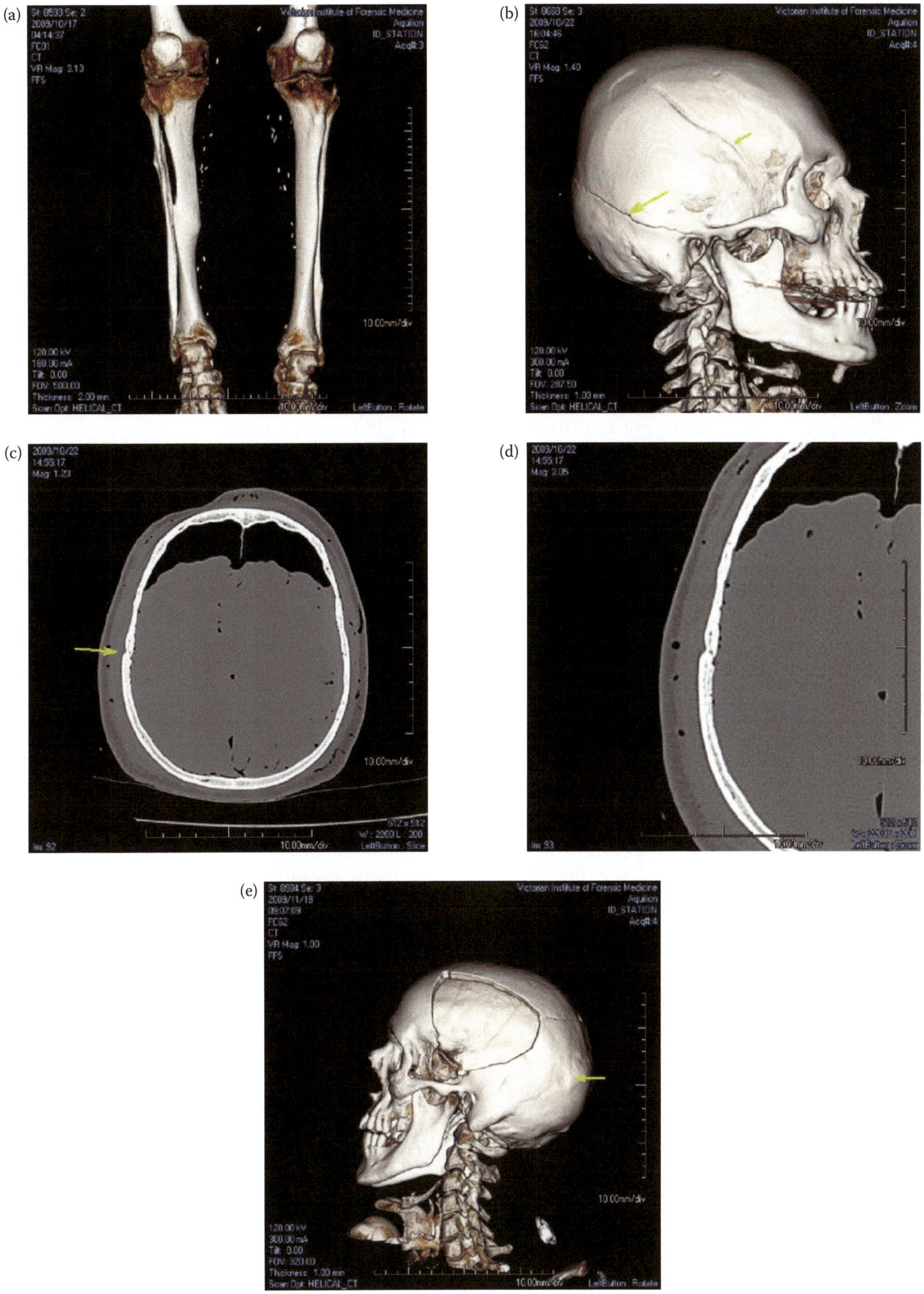

Figure 3.6 (a) Three-dimensional reconstruction image showing residual deformity in the right tibia following a fracture. (b) Three-dimensional reconstruction CT image showing a recent skull fracture (long arrow) and an old, healed skull fracture (short arrow). (c) Axial CT image showing a region of smooth indentation to the outer table of the skull in an old, healed skull fracture. (d) Axial CT close-up image showing indentation of the skull associated with an old, healed fracture. (e) Three-dimensional reconstruction image showing a round smooth region of indentation to the skull from a remote depressed fracture from a blow with a hammer. There is a recent left craniectomy with a recent fracture to the left temporoparietal region.

A scientific approach can use biomechanical data, with comparisons of the force associated with fractures to the bone in question against the force required to cause a fracture to a bone more intuitive to the community, such as the tibia. Most laypersons have some understanding of the force required to cause a fractured tibia.

A descriptive method uses the mechanism of the injury to communicate the force that is necessary to cause a fracture. An example is a simple linear fracture of the occiput. A reasonable description could be the force that would be generated to the back of the head from a fall directly to a hard surface from a standing position.

Comminuted fractures to the skull can be expressed to the courts in terms of "shattering" and the breaking of eggshells, however, these terms are emotive and may be seen as prejudicial. Furthermore, laboratory studies have shown that once a linear fracture to the skull has occurred it requires a relatively minor degree of force to cause comminution.

A similar situation exists with the radius and ulna. To a layperson it may appear instinctive that a much more severe degree of force would be necessary to cause fractures of both bones as opposed to one. However, this is not the case. The ulna and fibula are rigidly tethered to each other by the interosseous membrane, and a fracture of one bone can then be associated with a fracture of the other bone, or dislocation to the wrist or elbow. The identification of the more significant injury certainly infers the injury was the result of a greater degree of force but not a "doubling" of the force.

Individuals with osteoporosis may suffer a fracture from relatively minor trauma. Fractures to the neck of the femur are particularly common in elderly osteoporotic women. Such fractures may occur with a fall from a standing height. Other common fractures associated with osteoporosis include fractures to the radius and ulna, the humeral shaft, the ribs, and vertebral body compression fractures.

Bedridden and chronically ill patients can suffer fractures with minimal force. A retrospective study described 30 nursing home patients who suffered spontaneous long bone fractures [8]. The fractures consisted of closed supracondylar femoral fractures in 23 patients, 6 patients had femoral shaft fractures (five spiral), and 1 patient had a fracture to the distal tibia and fibula. There were no spontaneous upper limb fractures, though these injuries have been described previously in the literature [9]. The authors noted that none of the patients appeared to be a victim of assault, though the presence of a fracture in a bedridden patient should always raise the possibility.

Pediatric Fractures

Pediatric bones are significantly more pliable than adult bones. Pediatric bones also have active growth centers. Pediatric bony trauma is not directly analogous to injuries in adults. Children are not small adults. The physiological differences lead to distinct fracture patterns.

Pediatric fractures may be classified into:

- Plastic deformity without fracture
- Buckle or torus fractures
- Greenstick fractures
- Transverse fractures
- Spiral fractures
- Oblique fractures
- Physeal fractures

In mechanical engineering the application of a sufficient load will deform a metal or other material. Elastic deformation occurs when the material returns to its original shape when the load is removed. Plastic deformation may be defined as a permanent alteration in the shape of the material once the load is removed. At a molecular level elastic deformation results from "stretching" of bonds between atoms whereas plastic deformation occurs when bonds between atoms are broken, allowing movement between planes. Plastic deformation is seen in pediatric long bones. The bone is typically bowed following the application of a significant load, though there is no evidence of cortical disruption.

Buckle or torus fractures are commonly seen in the pediatric population. These fractures are the result of axial loading [10]. The fracture tends to occur at the junction of the diaphysis and the metaphysis. The fracture is characterized by compression of trabeculae across the fracture with either cortical angulation, or unilateral or bilateral cortical bulging. The most common clinical fracture is to the radius following a fall to the outstretched hand.

Greenstick fractures result from bending or tensile forces to a pediatric long bone. Greenstick fractures may be viewed as an extension of a simple buckle fracture, but where there is a break to one side of the cortical bone with a buckle to the opposite cortex. Clinically, greenstick fractures are typically seen in the radius and ulna following a fall to the outstretched hand.

Transverse fractures also result from bending forces. A transverse fracture is the outcome of higher energy events than greenstick fractures. Typical scenarios are a significant fall or a transportation injury such as a motor vehicle incident or a fall from a bicycle.

Spiral fractures occur from the application of torsional force to a long bone. This injury has been cited as a common fracture in cases of child abuse [11]. However, as previously noted, a spiral fracture to a toddler's tibia is most commonly related to a rotational fall. In older children it has been reported that sufficient torsion to cause a spiral fracture may be applied to a long bone following a trip when running [10].

Oblique fractures are similar to adult fractures as they are produced from a combination of axial loading and bending, or rotational forces.

Physeal fractures are common in pediatric trauma. The mechanism in the majority of cases is the application of a shearing force such as may occur with shaking. The fracture involves recently laid down bone from the epiphyseal plate. The literature on nonaccidental injury has consistently associated this fracture with abuse, however, some papers have stated the fracture is either not as indicative of abuse as has been traditionally believed, or the fracture may be explained by an accident in some cases. In any event, the presence of a physeal fracture should stimulate a detailed postmortem examination with the possibility of nonaccidental injury being actively questioned.

Physeal fractures are classified according to the Salter–Harris classification. The classification is summarized as follows:

- Type I—Complete separation of the epiphyseal plate.
- Type II—The most common type. Involves a fracture through the epiphysis and epiphyseal plate with partial separation from the metaphysis.
- Type III—Involves a fracture through the epiphysis, which separates part of the epiphysis and epiphyseal plate from the metaphysis.
- Type IV—Involves a fracture extending through the epiphysis, epiphyseal plate, and into the metaphysis.
- Type V—An uncommon injury where there is crushing of the epiphysis and the associated epiphyseal plate.

The pattern of fractures that involves joints in the pediatric population may well be influenced not only by the presence of an unfused epiphyseal plate but also by partial fusion. A Salter–Harris type III fracture to the knee of three adolescent patients were reported by McKissick and colleagues [12]. They found that a valgus force to the knee during sports activity caused the type III fracture because of partial closure to the medial femoral condyle.

The common pediatric fractures vary with respect to age. From an analysis of the clinical literature it is also readily apparent that the frequency of different pediatric fractures also varies depending upon the location surveyed, that is, general practice or hospital. Commonly fractured bones seen in hospital emergency departments are

- Clavicle (most common)
- Supracondylar humerus
- Skull
- Femoral shaft
- Pelvis

In summary the type of fracture caused by a particular mechanism may be altered by the unique anatomical features of the pediatric skeleton.

Case Study

The remains of a 78-year-old man were exhumed following the receipt of information suggesting his death may have been a case of vehicular homicide. The deceased's body had been found beside a country road 20 years previously. The death was issued as multiple injuries.

The information passed onto police alleged that a conventional passenger motor vehicle had been speeding around a corner and the driver lost control of the vehicle. The car skidded sideways and the passenger door was said to have struck the deceased. As the original postmortem report did not provide sufficient details with respect to the fractures sustained by the deceased, the remains were exhumed.

Examination of the bones showed a localized fracture to the shaft of the left femur with a butterfly fragment (Figure 3.7a,b). There was a comminuted fracture to the proximal left tibia and fibula (Figure 3.7c). There were comminuted fractures to the face and skull (Figure 3.7d).

The distribution of the fractures appeared more in keeping with the front of a conventional passenger car striking the deceased to the lower limbs, with the facial and skull fractures resulting from impact with the windscreen and surrounds, rather than the alleged "sideswipe" incident.

We were able to obtain the original police photographs taken in the mortuary, which showed patterned abraded injuries to the front of the legs, which were highly suggestive of headlights and grill of an older style vehicle.

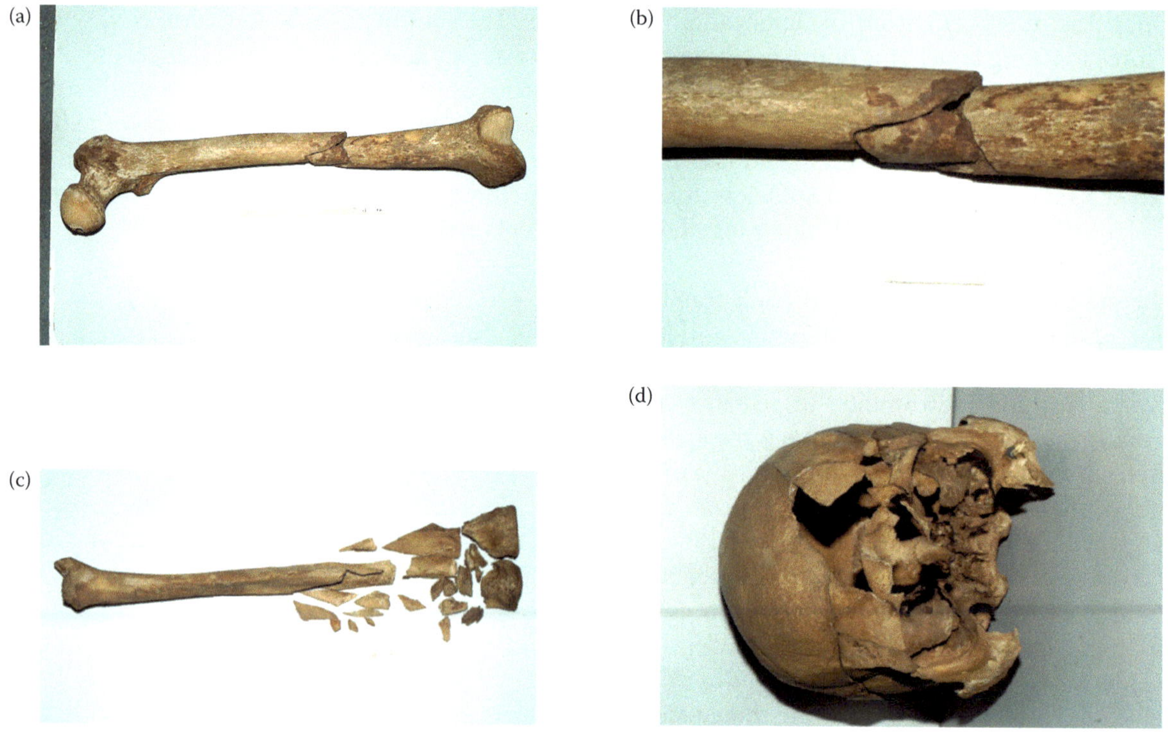

Figure 3.7 (a) Photograph showing localized fracture to the shaft of the left femur. (b) Close-up photograph showing butterfly fragment in femoral shaft fracture. (c) Photograph showing comminuted fracture of the left tibia. (d) Photograph showing comminuted fractures to the face and skull.

References

1. MacMahon P, Eustace SJ. General principles. Semin. *Musculoskelet. Radiol.* 2006; 10(4):243–248.
2. Nakamura M, Udagwara N, Nakamura H. Bone remodeling and mineral homeostasis. *Clin. Calcium.* 2006; 16:46–53.
3. Alms M. Fracture mechanisms. *J. Bone Joint Surg. Br.* 1961; 43-B:162-166.
4. Yankovskii VE, Chernenko ON. Theory of the biomechanism of fractures of the diaphysis of long tubular bones. *Mech. Comp. Mat.* 1971; 7(2):318–322.
5. Taviloglu K, Yanar H. Fat embolism syndrome. *Surg. Today* 2007;37:5–8.
6. Parisi DM, Koval K, Egol K. Fat embolism syndrome. *Am. J. Orthop.* 2002; 31:507–512.
7. Bendinelli C, Balogh Z. Post-injury thromboprophylaxis. *Curr. Opin. Crit. Care* 2008; 14(6):673–678.
8. Wang TC, Wu WC, Cheng HS, Cheng YC, Yam SK. Spontaneous fractures in nursing home residents. *Hong Kong Med. J.* 2007; 13:427–429.
9. Sherman FT. "Transfer" and "turning" fractures in nursing home patients. *Am. J. Med.* 1991; 91:668–669.
10. Pierce MC, Bertocci GE, Vogeley E, Moreland MS. Evaluating long bone fractures in children: A biomechanical approach with illustrative cases. *Child Abuse Negl.* 2004; 28(5):505–524.
11. O'Connor-Read L, Teh J, Willett K. Radiographic evidence to help predict the mechanism of injury of pediatric spiral fractures in nonaccidental injury. *J. Pediatr. Orthop.* 2007; 27(7):754–757.
12. McKissick RC, Gilley JS, DeLee JC. Salter-Harris type III fractures of the medial distal femoral physis—A fracture pattern related to the closure of the growth plate: A report of 3 cases and discussion of the pathogenesis. *Am. J. Sports Med.* 2008; 36(3):572–576.

Computed Tomography

4

Introduction

Computed tomography (CT) is a routine radiological investigation in clinical practice. In the practice of forensic pathology the CT should be viewed as an additional investigative tool with the potential to provide forensic pathologists with important information that may be highly beneficial in the death investigation. However, the introduction of CT into a routine forensic pathology service also brings with it a number of major challenges.

Challenges in Routine CT Analysis by Forensic Pathologists

"Expert Interpretation" of CT Images by Forensic Pathologists

It is self-evident that a forensic pathologist cannot be expected to interpret CT images as would an expert radiologist. At the Victorian Institute of Forensic Medicine (VIFM) the forensic pathologist is required to perform routine evaluation of postmortem CT images for a number of reasons. These include the prohibitive cost of having expert radiological assessment on every routine case (currently ~5000 cases/year), the limited availability of radiologists to report on such material, and the reluctance of many clinical radiologists to be called to provide expert evidence in court.

There are fundamental differences between the interpretation of CT images by an expert radiologist in the clinical setting, an expert radiologist interpreting postmortem CT scans, and the forensic pathologist viewing CT scans.

Clinical radiologists need to gain experience in postmortem CT interpretation to familiarize themselves with the various artifacts that are not seen in clinical practice [1]. Problems of interpretation often relate to postmortem soft tissue changes including alteration in organ shape, lividity, and thrombus and gas formation. That being said, clinical radiologists do understand the various CT patterns of trauma that are common in the forensic environment.

Forensic pathology is a unique branch of medicine that requires a set of skills quite different from clinical practice. Forensic pathologists are able to identify the fundamental issues in a case that are not necessarily apparent to other medical practitioners including clinical radiologists. They are also able to articulate these findings in such a way that is of value to the legal system. It is these abilities that forensic pathologists bring to the evaluation of postmortem CT images.

Clearly the optimum radiology service in a forensic institute is radiological interpretation by an expert radiologist who has additional qualifications, or a particular interest and experience in forensic medicine. A more realistic working situation is one where the consultant (clinical) radiologist has a close working relationship with the institution's forensic pathologists.

Standard of CT Analysis by the "Reasonable" Forensic Pathologist

A fundamental question for various stakeholders involved in the coronial and criminal justice system is what can be reasonably expected of the "nonexpert" forensic pathologist in this process. The pathologist is also faced with issues concerning the different levels of certainty required in the coronial and criminal courts. In Victoria, Australia, the coronial system requires a level of proof based on "the balance of probabilities," whereas in criminal matters the courts require proof "beyond reasonable doubt." The forensic pathologist may be comfortable providing an opinion for the Coroner's Court but not for a higher court. A difficulty arises when a case that was initially deemed not suspicious is later shown to be a criminal case. Although an expert radiologist can review the images, the pathologist's credibility may come into question. It is then quite conceivable that the higher court could find that the cause of death provided by the pathologist, based on nonexpert analysis of the CT, is not acceptable and the case not proceed.

A one-year study of child deaths in Canada that compared the radiological diagnoses in skeletal surveys between forensic pathologists and consultant radiologists showed that forensic pathologists missed an important finding in 3 of 20 cases [2]. The paper alerted forensic pathologists to seek a secondary radiological opinion in designated cases or undertake more extensive radiological training.

One may argue that the "reasonable" expectations of the forensic pathologist are similar to a doctor working in the accident and emergency department of a hospital.

Both the forensic pathologist and emergency physician have completed undergraduate teaching, which includes formal teaching in radiology. However, there are differences between the two specialties. The various images ordered and examined by doctors in hospitals are all subsequently reviewed by radiologists. The images are also interpreted with respect to specific clinical information.

At VIFM an expert radiologist does not routinely review the majority of forensic images. Furthermore, there may be scanty information available on the case at the time of the radiological examination, and the known information may evolve or completely change with time. Thus an issue that was not appreciated at the time of initial CT examination by the pathologist could undergo considerable scrutiny some time later.

Practical Problems Raised by the Introduction of CT into Routine Forensic Practice

A major issue for forensic institutes is the availability of expert radiologists to interpret CT images. Even if an experienced radiologist is available the financial commitment of employing such a person is a concern. It is not uncommon for forensic services to be under substantial financial constraint.

Radiologists in clinical practice provide a professional opinion on a limited number of images in response to specific clinical questions. It is certainly not common clinical practice for a radiologist to provide a report on a total body scan. Moreover clinical radiologists are not always familiar with the requirements of a forensic report where a determination of the manner or mechanism of the death may be as important as the actual cause of death. The courts will become more familiar with the use of CT images in proceedings and direct that the images be presented to the court. In jurisdictions with adversarial systems some radiologists will probably be unwilling to become involved in forensic cases.

A further issue for forensic pathologists is the fact that the image data set is available at a later date for review by an expert radiologist. Under instruction from a lawyer the radiologist may highlight discrepancies between the images and the autopsy report. From a positive point of view this practice could be an important factor in ensuring that justice is served in a particular case. However, it is also possible that a painstaking examination of the CT images in a particular case could reveal an unimportant incidental finding that is not included in the autopsy report. This can then be used by the legal team to undermine the pathologist's credibility, causing embarrassment to the pathologist, damage to his or her reputation, and not serve the interests of justice.

The pathologists at the VIFM have worked with the CT scanner for more than four years. There have been no instances of an attack on a pathologist's competence and diligence during this time. There have been cases where pathology has been detected on the scans that had gone unnoticed at conventional autopsy. Our initial unease and misgivings about having a full body CT record for every case in the archives has been replaced by a more constructive outlook. The CT is considered to be part of a system to maintain standards and improve the quality of evidence presented to the courts.

Basic Principles of CT

X-rays are produced from a vacuum tube with a negatively charged, heated cathode and a positively charged anode composed of a heavy metal such as tungsten, which has a high melting point. When a large voltage is applied across the electrodes, electrons that are boiled off the cathode are accelerated to the positive anode with the release of radiation (x-rays).

X-rays are emitted from the metal in the anode by two means. The electrons may be slowed as they approach the positively charged nucleus of the metal with release of electromagnetic radiation (*bremsstrahlung*, "braking radiation"). Alternatively electromagnetic radiation is produced when outer shell electrons fill inner shell vacancies created when the accelerated electrons displace metallic anode inner shell electrons.

The photons of electromechanical radiation (x-rays) exit the tube through an aperture located over the object of interest. As they pass through the object of interest they are variably attenuated depending on differences in electron density of constituent atoms. The pattern of attenuation is captured on radiographic film or other detector.

Evolution of CT Scanning

The word *tomography* is derived from the Greek word *tomos* meaning "section" or "cut." Conventional or focal plane tomography was first described by Bocage in 1921. It is characterized by synchronous movement of the x-ray tube and film in a plane parallel to the film. The concept of computed tomography scanning was developed by Sir Godfrey Hounsfield and colleagues at Electric and Musical Industries (EMI) in 1967.

The Hounsfield group proposed the concept of a scanned axial slice of a subject being made up of a matrix of small boxes called voxels, each with an attenuation coefficient μ. By acquiring sequential tomographic images of a subject at a given point one could construct an axial slice derived from the relative attenuations of the organs and tissues. Each two-dimensional pixel in a CT image matrix represents the x-ray attenuation within a three-dimensional voxel. The development of computer technology made the massive mathematical calculations necessary for such a process possible.

The first CT images were presented in 1972. Since that time there have been successive improvements in scanner technology. The first-generation scanners used a pencil-width collimated beam of x-rays and a single detector that required both translation across and rotation around the subject for data acquisition. The scan time was long and would take several minutes per slice.

Second-generation scanners used a fan beam of x-rays and had multiple detectors in a linear array thus improving efficiency of x-ray detection. The machine would acquire data at multiple angles in progressive subject positions but still required translation across the subject. Data acquisition was still slow at approximately 20 seconds per rotation.

Third-generation scanners use a fan x-ray beam with multiple detectors that rotate around the subject in unison and require no translation. The x-ray tube and detectors are rigidly linked in a gantry as they rotate around the subject. The tube and detectors rotate 360 degrees around the subject and the gantry high-tension cables require successive respooling to unwind the high-tension cables. The data acquisition was much faster at 0.5 seconds per rotation.

Fourth-generation scanners have static detectors within the gantry and use slip ring technology by means of electrical brushes to allow constant rotation of the x-ray tube within the detector array.

Fifth-generation or electron beam CT scanners use an electron gun (linear accelerator) to create an electron beam that is focused and deflected along a tungsten target to produce a fan-shaped x-ray beam. The machine uses a fixed semicircular multidetector array.

Helical Computed Tomography (HCT) Scanning

Helical HCT scanning is characterized by continuous motion of the x-ray tube combined with continuous forward movement of the subject on the table along the axis of the scanner (*z*-axis). The typical table velocity is in the range of 1 to 10 mm/sec. A complete 360 degree rotation can be achieved in 0.5 seconds and the nominal fan beam thickness is 1 mm or greater.

As the name suggests the HCT scanner traces a spiral around the subject's body, and as such, there is not a one-to-one relationship between the complete rotations around the body and the number of slices obtained. HCT utilizes two positions at which data is obtained. No slice plane contains sufficient data to reconstruct a slice; however, measurements are interpolated through a complex mathematical relationship. Interpolation of data applies throughout all data points in the helix to generate estimates of the axial data.

HCT introduces the concept of pitch. Pitch may be defined as the ratio of the distance that the patient moves in one rotation to the slice thickness. For example, for a subject advance of 10 mm and a nominal slice width of 10 mm, the pitch is 1. Pitch values are typically in the range of 1 to 2. This is dependent on the spatial resolution. Pitch selection is essentially a trade-off between patient coverage and accuracy, that is, a large pitch allows more coverage but slice data must be interpolated between points that are farther apart, allowing more chance for error.

Multidetector Computed Tomography (MDCT) Scanning

MDCT scanning was an important advance in the management of patients in clinical medicine. MDCT is based on third-generation scanners.

As noted earlier, single-slice CT scanning used a large number of detector elements in a single row arranged across the irradiated slice to capture the x-ray beam. In the *z*-direction the detectors were monolithic, that is, single elements long enough to intercept the entire x-ray beam, which were typically approximately 20 mm.

By broadening the fan beam of the scanner along the *z*-axis and using two-dimensional detectors, it is possible to produce a number of slices per rotation. By fashioning the fan beam into a cone, volume imaging and cone beam CT scanning is introduced. Multidetector scanning can then be established. In MDCT scanners, slice thickness is not determined by x-ray collimation but by detector configuration. Data from more than one detector group can be added to reconstruct wider slices. Thin slices provide better *z*-axis resolution and finer detail in multiplanar reformations.

The full benefit of MDCT is gained by isotropic or near isotropic data sets, which require submillimeter-thick axial slices. The axial slice is not directly irradiated but is interpolated and reconstructed. The average linear attenuation coefficient, μ, between tube and detectors reflects the degree to which the x-ray intensity is reduced by the material.

Isotropic imaging is realized when the volume elements, or voxels, have equal dimensions in the *x* and *y* planes (axial scan plan) as well as the *z*, or patient, plane. This allows subsequent resolution in all three directions [3]. Because a volume of data is acquired and interpolation is used, then images can be formed anywhere, that is, slice location is arbitrary and overlapping images can be created (e.g., 10 mm thick, 5 mm apart).

The isotropic data set allows for multiplanar reconstruction and three-dimensional imaging. Thus a major advantage of MDCT in the clinical setting was rapid scanning of patients in the emergency room without the need for specific positioning of the patient. In the forensic setting the deceased can be scanned in the body bag, thus alleviating any possibility of introducing artifacts into the medicolegal investigation.

As noted earlier, in MDCT each of the individual monolithic detectors in single-slice scanners is divided in the *z*-direction into several smaller detector elements, thus forming a two-dimensional array [4]. The initial MDCT scanners had 16 rows of detector elements, each 1.25 mm long in the *z*-direction, and thus covering 20 cm in length. The mathematics of the potential computations is substantial. Each of the 16 detectors could concurrently collect data, and during a single rotation of the detector array this could potentially result in 13 million measurements per 0.5 second rotation. For this reason the early MDCT scanners were limited to data acquisition from four rows.

The four detector rows (or slices) are fed into four parallel data channels. The machines are flexible with respect to their configuration. That is, the machine could link four 1.25 mm elements so that the machine overall had four "5 mm" wide detectors. The machines can be configured such that the two innermost detector elements are overlapping and are partially irradiated so that two slices of 0.625 mm could be obtained. This then leads to essentially isotropic resolution in all three directions.

The introduction of 64-slice, and now 256-slice MDCT scanners has markedly reduced detector times and has allowed dynamic-kinematic imaging of joints [7]. This has important advantages in the clinical situation, most notably in pediatric patients where the need to sedate patients is markedly decreased.

Reconstruction in CT Scanning

The typical MDCT scanner consists of a gantry that contains the generators, x-ray tube, collimators, and detectors. Depending upon the information required of the machine, a whole body scan might produce several thousand images. The CT scanner pushes the images to a picture archive and communication system (PACS) that manages and distributes the images.

The creation of an image on a screen or monitor from scanning a subject involves three processes. The subject is scanned, which provides data; the data is reconstructed into a digital image; and last an analogue picture is produced from conversion of the digital image.

The objective of CT image reconstruction is to determine how much attenuation of the narrow x-ray beam occurs in each voxel of the reconstruction matrix. The calculations are complex and time consuming even for modern computers. The calculated attenuation values are represented as gray levels in a two-dimensional image. Thus the absorption of x-rays in each single volume element, or voxel, represents the darkness on a scale of gray for each corresponding pixel. The attenuation coefficients are stored in an arrangement that corresponds to their position as a pixel value.

A pixel is the smallest item in a graphic image. A graphic monitor displays images by dividing the screen into large numbers of pixels, arranged in arrays of rows and columns. The array of pixel rows and columns is called a matrix. A typical matrix is composed of 512 rows and 512 columns.

The attenuation values are used to calculate CT number values. The CT scanner is calibrated with water having a value of zero Hounsfield units (HUs). Dense tissues and materials have positive HUs and less dense materials have negative HUs. Typical Hounsfield units are

Water	zero HU
Air	−1000 HU
Cancellous bone	400 HU
Cranial bone	2000 HU
Blood	~40 HU
Liver	40 to 60 HU
Brain white matter	20 to 30 HU
Brain grey matter	35 to 45 HU
Muscle	10 to 40 HU
Cerebrospinal fluid	15 HU

The Detection of Foreign Materials by MDCT

Conventional x-rays have been traditionally used to detect foreign bodies such as projectiles. Other foreign material including wood, concrete, and other metals can be present within the body of the deceased following accidents and explosions. MDCT has the distinct advantage over conventional radiography by allowing discrimination of different materials via their radio densities in Hounsfield units [6]. A case report described the appearance of a wooden foreign body on a CT scan in a patient who fell onto a wooden needle [7]. The dry porous wood was shown to have a CT attenuation value of ~400 HU.

An experimental study of MDCT using various foreign materials used a Somaton Emotion Scanner (Siemens Medical Solutions) with 6 × 1 mm collimation at 130 kV and 60 Ma [4]. The maximum HU was 30710 HU. The various materials showed attenuation values of

Gold, lead, brass	up to 30710 HU
Steel, silver, copper	20346, 16949, and 14033 HU, respectively
Limestone	2765 HU
Aluminum, granite, car window glass	2088 to 2329 HU
Cement, pottery	1000 to 1500 HU
Window pane glass	493 HU

Practical Issues in CT Scanning

Following admission to the VIFM, the deceased undergoes a full body CT scan. The institute has a 16-channel MDCT scanner (Aquilion 16, Toshiba, Tokyo). The head and body are scanned separately. The head and body images are reconstructed into overlapping 1 mm and 2 mm slices, respectively. The images are conveyed to the institute's PACS and analyzed on a workstation (Vitrea 2, Vital Images, Minnetonka, Minnesota).

Spatial Resolution

Spatial resolution or the sharpness of an image refers to how well small details are seen in an image. Spatial resolution is lower in CT compared to conventional radiology. CT is limited mainly from the size and spacing of measurements in the data collection, a concept known as spacing [8].

Contrast Resolution

Contrast resolution refers to how clearly different intensities (or shades of gray) can be differentiated. As is the case in conventional radiology, CT subject contrast is fundamentally determined by the differential attenuation of adjacent tissues [Goldman]. CT is able to resolve relatively small differences in soft tissue density.

Conspicuity

Conspicuity may be defined as the ease of finding an image feature during a visual search. Radiological imaging necessitates a three-dimensional object to be represented on a two-dimensional plane. Thus there are overlying and underlying structures superimposed on the object, which has the effect of decreasing conspicuity.

Noise

Noise raining of an image is analogous to poor TV reception. The degree of noise in the image is directly related to the number of photons detected, the matrix size, slice thickness, and the algorithm. Increasing kilovoltage, scan time, and slice thickness will decrease the noise in an image. Low signal-to-noise ratio occurs most commonly with thin slices.

Windowing

A typical display device can display 256 shades of gray, although some medical display devices can resolve up to 1024 shades of gray. These shades of gray can be distributed over a narrow range of HU values (narrow window) centered over the average HU value of a particular structure. This process is called windowing and allows more subtle differences in attenuation to be appreciated.

Artifacts in CT Scanning

The term *artifact* in CT scanning has been defined as "any systemic discrepancy between the CT numbers in the reconstructed image and the true attenuation coefficients of the object" [9]. Thus an artifact is an image that is not representative of a corresponding anatomical structure. Barrett and Keat [9] classified CT artifacts with respect to patient- or subject-based issues, physics-based issues, scanner-based issues, and helical and multisection CT-based issues. The majority of common types of artifacts observed on an image involve shading artifacts, ring artifacts, and streak artifacts.

Physics-Based Issues

Beam Hardening

Beam hardening is the most common type of shading artifact and is frequent in postmortem CT (Figure 4.1). It is essentially due to uneven densities in the scan field, for example, when the deceased's arm or shoulder is adjacent to the head when scanned in the body bag. Beam hardening artifact presents as a dark band between dense objects such as bone.

The physical reason beam hardening occurs is because of the preferential absorption of lower energy photons from the x-ray beam. This is a particular problem in imaging the dense compact bone at the base of the skull.

Manufacturers of CT machines address the problem with metallic filters to remove low energy photons from the beam prior to the beam entering the subject, by using beam hardening software corrections, and specific calibration of the scanners using various phantoms.

Photon Starvation

Photon starvation is a cause of streaking artifact. This typically occurs in highly attenuating regions such as

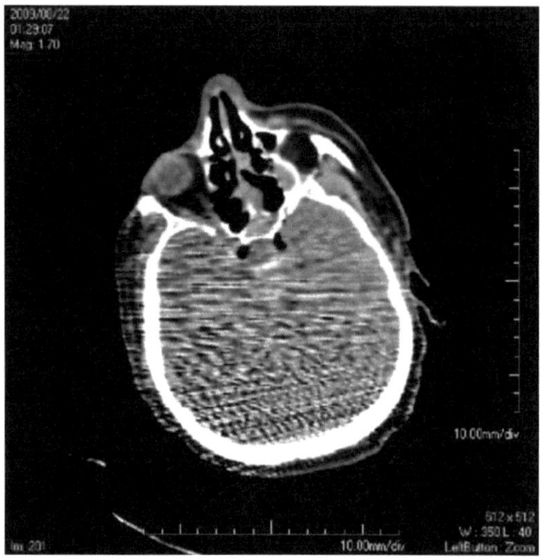

Figure 4.1 Axial CT showing beam hardening artifact.

the shoulders. The problem arises because insufficient photons are able to reach the detectors, resulting in a noisy image. The situation is compounded by the process of reconstructing the images resulting in horizontal streaks. A solution to the problem is to increase the tube current. This is not a viable option in clinical patients who would then be subjected to increased radiation dose, but can be undertaken in the postmortem situation. The long-term consequence of increasing tube current can be to decrease the life of the tube.

Manufacturers have addressed the problem with automatic variation in tube current such that low attenuation regions are not subjected to unnecessary radiation. A further type of software correction called adaptive filtration smoothes the attenuation data prior to the reconstruction process.

Partial Volume Artifact

Partial volume effect results from a lesion of interest being lost when thick slices "average out" the attenuation of a region in which a small lesion such as a metastasis is located. Partial volume artifact can be addressed by using thin slices and a smaller field of view in acquiring attenuation data. This may have the effect of increasing noise. The noise is decreased by combining a number of thin sections to produce thick slices.

Patient- or Subject-Based Issues

Partial Scanning

Because the deceased is scanned within the body bag, a reasonably common problem in postmortem CT is partial scanning of the body. When a part of the body, usually a portion of a limb, is not included in the field of view of the scan, the computer is provided with incomplete information leading to streaking or shading artifact [9].

Metal Artifact

Metal artifact is seen as streaks radiating from the metal object. The type of metal largely determines the severity of the artifact. Metal artifact is seen with amalgam dental fillings; orthopedic hardware; and, in forensic practice, by bullets and other projectiles, knife blades, and other electron-dense foreign bodies within or associated with the deceased (Figure 4.2a,b).

Metal artifact is a problem in the forensic setting as the streak artifact causes a loss of resolution in the adjacent structures, including bone. Such details include the presence of beveling in gunshot injuries and points of interest in orthopedic cases. The use of bone windows can improve the quality of the images even in the presence of metal artifact (Figure 4.2c). Metal-reduction software goes some way to attend to the problem, however, this does not alleviate the issue of reduction in anatomical detail. The CT operator can increase the kilovoltage to enable penetration, and simple angulation of the gantry can be used in selected cases to physically avoid the metal [9].

The forensic technical staff can be trained to identify and address metal artifact while performing admission scans.

Scanner-Based Issues

Ring Artifact

Ring artifacts appear on CT images as an intensely bright or dark circular line within the image. When the

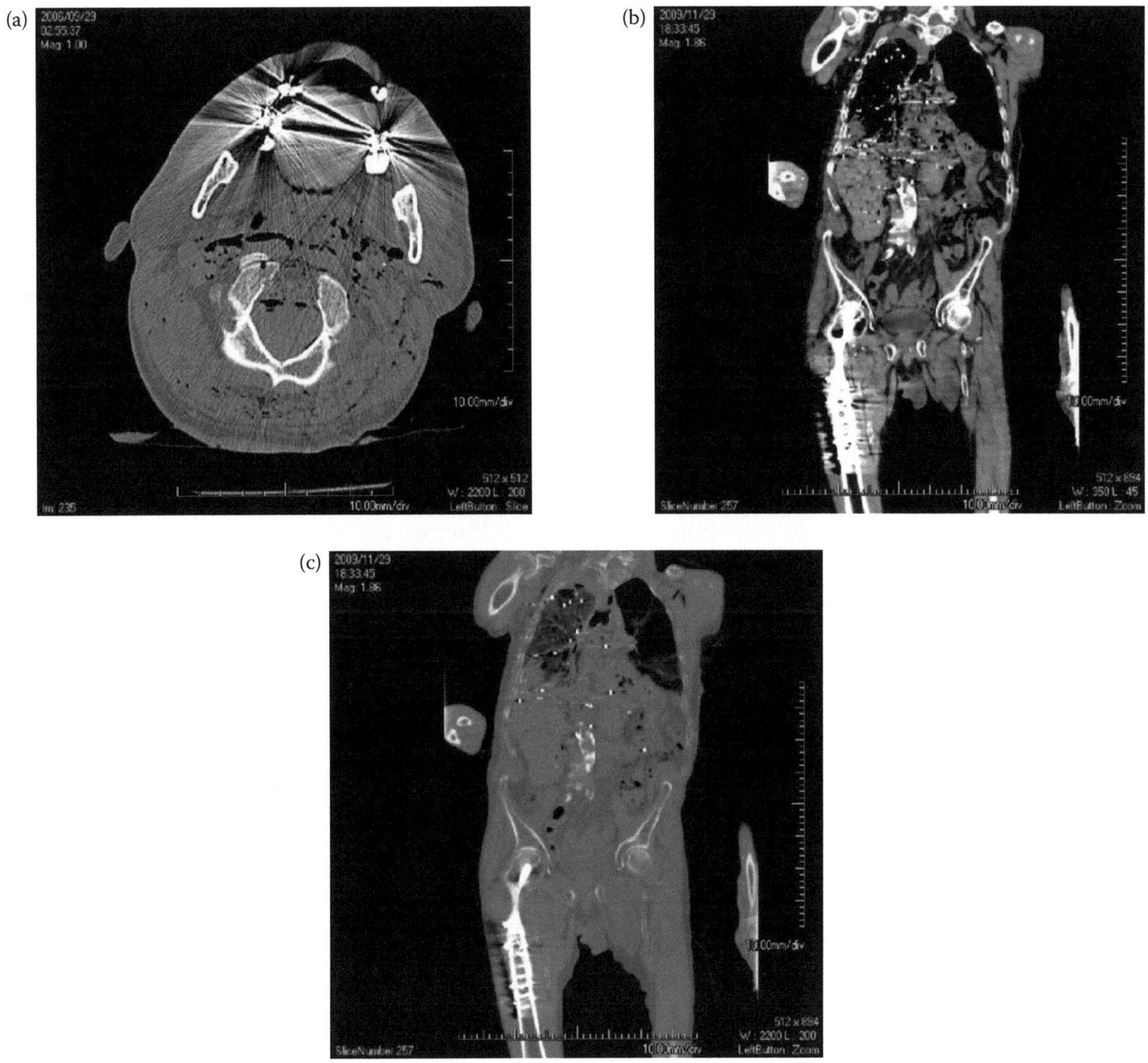

Figure 4.2 (a) Axial CT image showing flare associated with dental amalgam fillings. (b) Coronal CT showing the considerable artifact that can be seen with orthopedic hardware. (c) CT image from panel b using bone window.

artifact is relatively subtle it can occasionally suggest a pathological abnormality. Ring artifact can result from a number of detector issues on third-generation scanners. A problem with the counting accuracy of a detector, errors in individual detector calibration, variations in gain, increased temperatures in the CT room, and radiation damage to a detector are some causes of ring artifact.

Helical Scanning or Reconstruction-Based Issues

Helical scanning introduces additional artifacts as a consequence of the interpolation and reconstruction process. In general the artifacts are most prominent when high pitches are used and in body regions where there is abrupt change in anatomy in the axial axis (z-direction) of the body.

Cone Beam Effects

The cone beam refers to the divergent, or conelike form, of the x-ray beam. As one increases the number of detectors in a machine the x-ray beam must change from a fanlike shape to a cone shape to accommodate the extra detectors in the z or longitudinal axis.

In single-section CT scanners with a 360 degree rotation, the same point is measured twice along the same path as the x-rays travel in opposite directions. In helical scanning, as the tube and detectors rotate around the subject in a helix, the data accumulated by the detectors relate to volumes produced via cones of x-ray beams. This introduces artifacts similar to partial volume artifact as noted earlier.

Because of beam divergence the x-ray beam samples points in question from a slightly different path, which can potentially lead to data inconsistency and streak artifact. Thicker slices lead to the increased divergence and increased chance of data inconsistency. Thus this artifact is more pronounced for machines with increasing numbers of detectors along the *z*-axis.

Cone beam effects are generally ameliorated by cone beam algorithms incorporated into the machines by manufacturers.

Helical Artifacts in Multisection Scanning

Helical artifact appears as a windmill effect in the image. The artifact appears as a result of increased *z*-spacing because anatomy is more likely to change abruptly over increased distance. Increasing pitch can thus lead to increased helical artifact.

Stair-Step Artifacts

Stair-step artifact is uncommon in helical CT reconstructions. It is seen as right-angled "steps" in three-dimensional reformatted images. The artifact is practically eliminated by using thin slices.

Fracture Diagnosis

The clinical diagnosis of a fracture commences with the patient's history of the mechanism of the injury. This "mechanistic" approach enables the clinician to form a differential diagnosis of the most likely injuries (including fractures) in that particular case.

Doctors are taught a basic method that incorporates classical historical features, and signs and symptoms of a fracture. Clinical features that may suggest the presence of an underlying fracture are soft tissue swelling, severe pain at the site of injury, and inability to move the limb. Clinical signs of a fracture include gross deformity, crepitus upon moving the injured limb, and abnormal movement at the point of injury. The radiological examination is used to confirm or refute this clinical diagnosis.

Conventional radiology is still central in managing patients who have suffered uncomplicated fractures in the emergency departments of hospitals [10]. However, CT is used clinically in complex fractures and where the conventional radiographs are negative but the mechanism of injury or clinical findings are highly suggestive of an occult fracture. A recent retrospective study from Finland investigated 38 patients who had suffered a wrist injury and compared MDCT to conventional radiographs. MDCT revealed nine occult fractures of the wrist, mainly involving the small carpal bones [10].

The forensic pathologist does not have the same quality of clinical information or the advantage of typical clinical signs. In the practice of forensic pathology, although there may be witness accounts of the circumstances that lead to an injury, these descriptions may be unreliable or incomplete. For example, the pathologist may not be made aware of the possibility of an injury to the lower limb in a case of death from blunt force head injury until some months after the autopsy is completed. The credibility of a witness may hinge on the identification and documentation of a blunt force injury to the lower limb. In the majority of suspicious deaths the pathologist will perform subcutaneous dissection and thus identify these occult regions of significant blunt force trauma. However, it is possible that a subtle lower limb fracture could go unnoticed. An important feature of routine postmortem CT scanning is that the images can be reviewed at a later date to investigate such an occurrence.

An informal straw poll of forensic pathologists' approach to using the CT revealed that most pathologists examine the CT images once they are acquainted with the known circumstances of the case. A few pathologists view the images blind to the circumstances before reviewing the scans when *au fait* with the circumstances.

Radiological Fractures

Radiological signs of a fracture include

- Identification of adjacent soft tissue changes
- Alteration in the normal contour of the bone
- Recognition of a fracture line

Soft Tissue Changes

Changes to the soft tissues include swelling, the presence of air or hematoma, and changes in fat planes (Figure 4.3). Soft tissue swelling is an important sign in clinical radiology, though in forensic pathology one must be aware of the possible contribution of postmortem dependent edema. This problem is more significant with longer postmortem intervals. Localized swelling in areas not affected by postmortem dependency and decomposition is an important sign.

The presence of air within soft tissues and anatomical spaces can be a very important indicator of a fracture. The presence of pneumocephalus indicates a compound fracture of the skull with communication to the skin or a mucosal surface (Figure 4.4). Air associated with a fractured pelvis can indicate a compound fracture involving the skin surface, or involvement of the vagina or bowel (Figure 4.5).

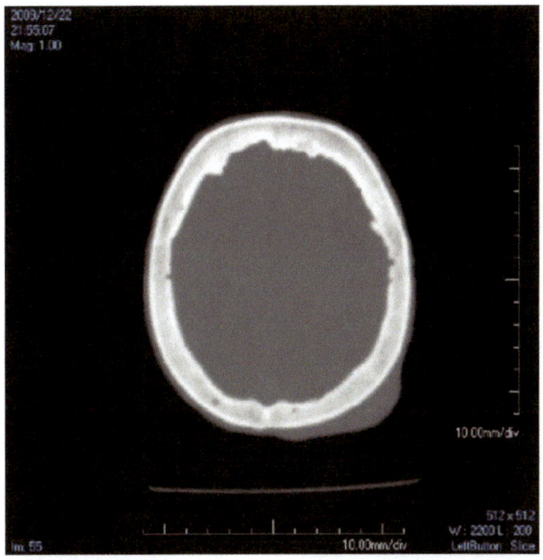

Figure 4.3 Axial CT image of the head showing scalp swelling associated with a skull fracture.

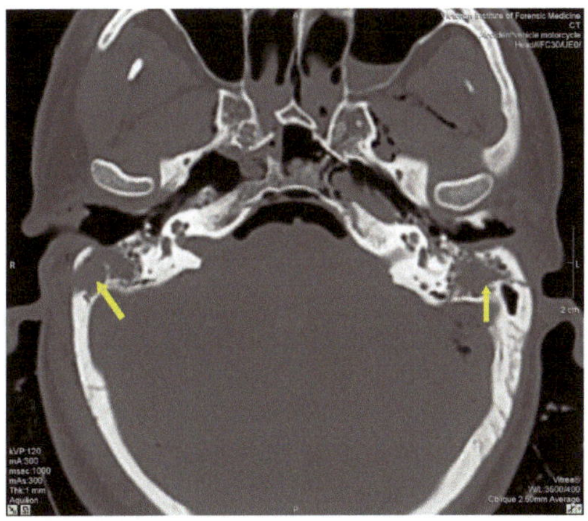

Figure 4.4 Axial CT image showing a subtle base of skull fracture with associated pneumocephalus.

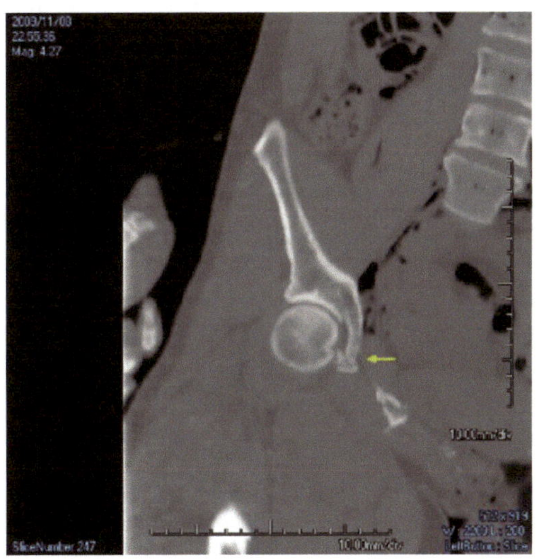

Figure 4.5 Fractured acetabulum showing interruption of the normal cortical contour. There is air within soft tissues indicating involvement of a viscus.

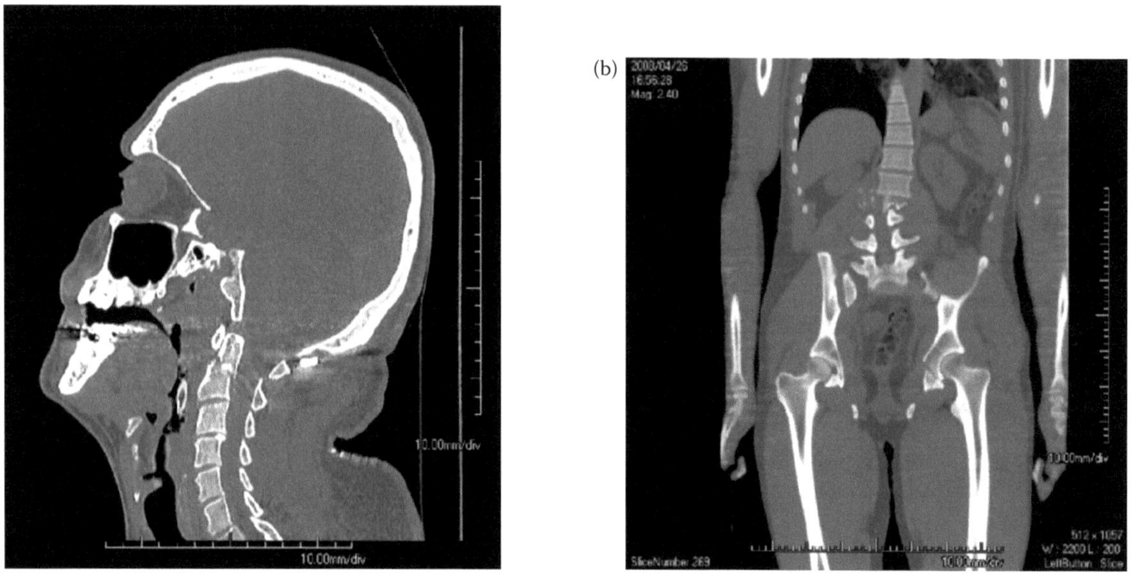

Figure 4.6 (a) Sagittal CT image of the head and neck showing disruption of the normal bony contour of the odontoid. (b) Coronal CT image showing marked displacement of a lumbar fracture. There are bilateral acetabular fractures with differing degrees of displacement.

Alteration in the Normal Contour of the Bone

An alteration in a bone's outline or shape is readily apparent in gross fractures but may be subtle with non-displaced fractures (Figure 4.6a,b). Clearly radiologists are better equipped in recognizing abnormal skeletal radiology, however, forensic pathologists are probably better acquainted with normal and abnormal skeletal morphology than most other medical specialists. The interpretation of conventional radiographs traditionally involves an examination of orthogonal views, that is, two radiographs in perpendicular planes. The postmortem CT allows orthogonal views and three-dimensional reconstructions.

It is good practice to compare the contour of the bone on the uninjured side especially if the suspected fracture is not displaced. In many cases of postmortem top-to-toe CT scans, a fracture may not be seen if not specifically sought. The mechanism of the injury may well allow the pathologist to target an examination of the images. For example, a careful systematic examination of the ribs may be required if resuscitation injuries are suspected in a case (Figure 4.7). The possibility of pericardial tamponade secondary to resuscitation may be raised when rib fractures are identified during the initial inspection of the images.

A subtle fracture to the wrist is unlikely to be identified from the initial examination of the images unless it is known to be an issue and is actively looked for. The expertise of a radiologist is necessary in cases of possible subtle fracture if a conventional autopsy is not going to be performed (Figure 4.8).

The complex nature of some appendicular fractures, and especially those involving a joint, are often best appreciated with three-dimensional reconstructions.

Identification of the Fracture Line

The third radiographic sign of a fracture is the detection of a fracture line (Figure 4.9). Using bone windows the fracture is visible as an abrupt well-defined radiolucent break in the cortex or bony trabeculae. It is essential to examine the fracture perpendicular to the line of the fracture, otherwise when viewed in the same plane one may pass through the fracture without it being identified.

Once a fracture is identified it needs to be confirmed in another plane to ensure one is not seeing a foramina (pseudofracture). As noted below, pseudofractures tend to be symmetrical (Figure 4.10). It is wise to compare the area in question with the contralateral side.

Because the forces that result in a fracture to a long bone may also lead to injury to the adjacent joints, it is usual practice to examine the CT images of joints adjacent to a fracture.

Pathological Fractures

A pathological fracture may be suggested when the mechanism of the injury does not correlate with the type of fracture suffered by the victim. Features that may suggest the presence of a pathological fracture include a fracture within an osteosclerotic region of bone or a fracture involving a lytic area with clear-cut breaks in the cortex.

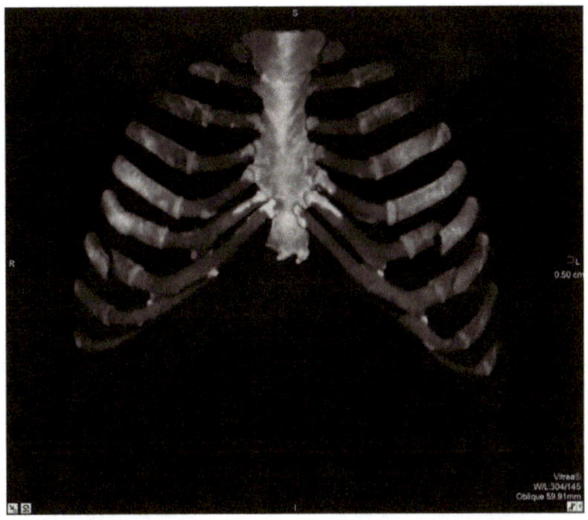

Figure 4.7 Detail of CT image of the anterior chest wall looking for rib fractures.

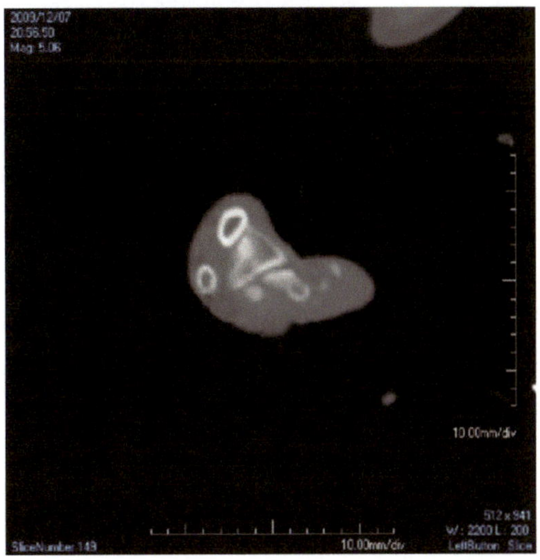

Figure 4.8 CT image of the wrist in the case of a pilot of an ultralight aircraft in order to identify injuries that may have resulted from forceful contact with the joystick.

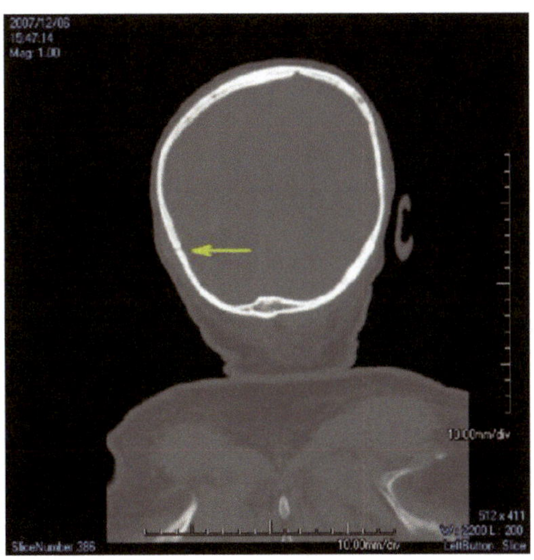

Figure 4.9 Coronal CT showing a fracture line to the right of the occiput.

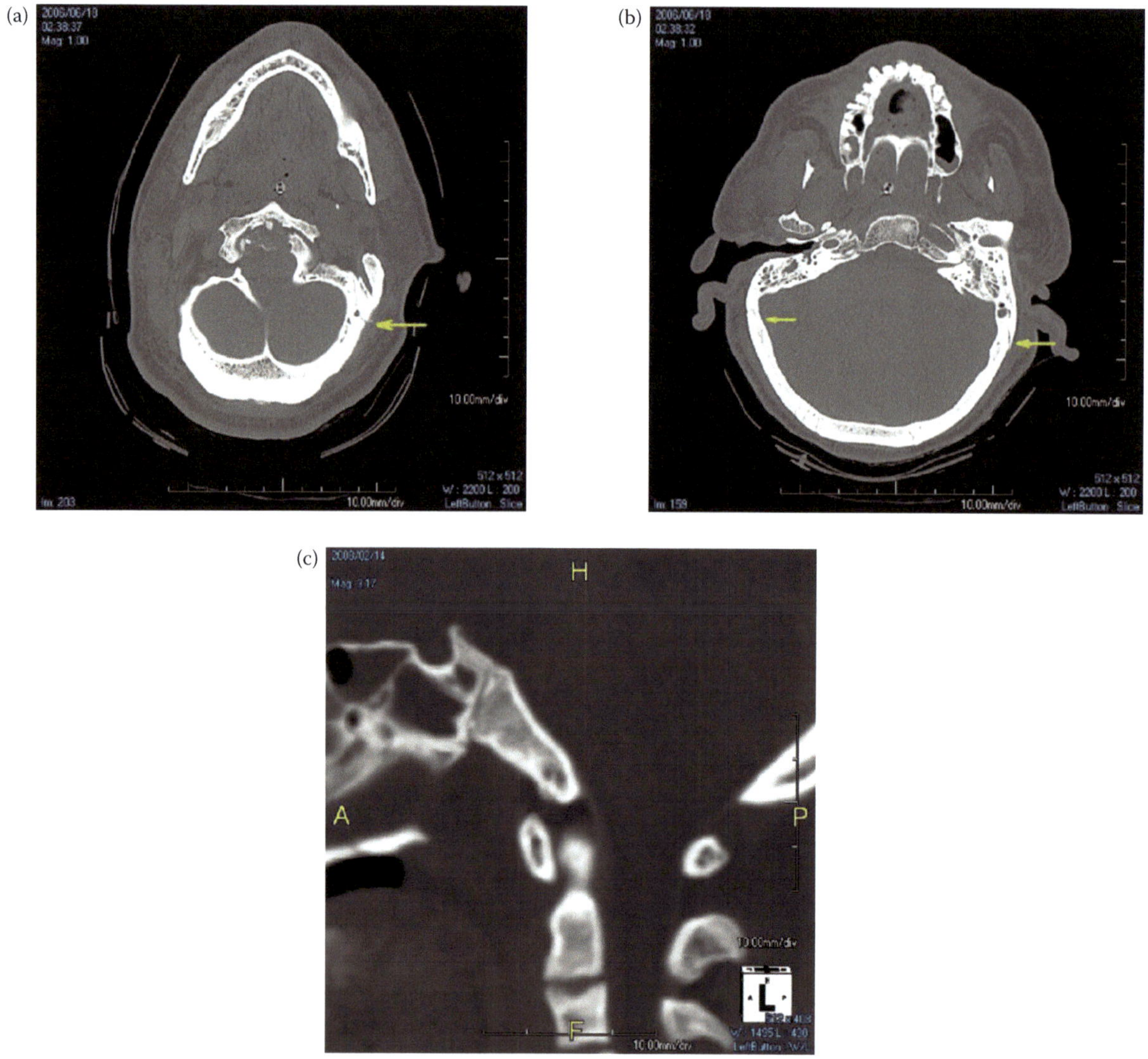

Figure 4.10 (a) Axial CT of the head showing a suture line, which may mimic a basal fracture. The anatomical location of the lucency suggests a suture. The image may be scrolled though to detect a mirror image lucency on the right side (see image b). (b) Axial CT image showing symmetrical lucencies within the skull typical of sutures. (c) Sagittal CT image showing the basiocciput. The longitudinal lucency is a normal anatomical feature and not to be confused with a base of skull fracture.

Pseudofractures

A number of features on conventional radiographs and CT images can be misinterpreted as a fracture. The lucencies caused by sutures in the skull can be a particular problem for pathologists, especially in the base of the skull (Figure 4.10a,b,c).

Nutrient arteries and aberrant sutures can be misdiagnosed as fractures (Figure 4.11). The numerous normal discontinuities within the skull base are an especially difficult region for analysis by nonradiologists [11]. It would seem highly advisable that any forensic diagnosis based solely on CT images involving the skull base should be made by a radiologist. Normal foramina in the facial bones and sinuses may also lead to misdiagnosis by pathologists and require expert review (Figure 4.12).

Basivertebral veins emerge from the posterior aspect of vertebral bodies and can be misdiagnosed as a fracture. They have a tendency to increase in size with age. The isolated nature of this CT finding with no associated soft tissue hemorrhage or bony displacement is a clue to the correct diagnosis.

Pseudofractures may occur in metabolic disorders such as osteomalacia [12]. Developmental changes in children, and being unfamiliar with ossification centers and growth plates in the pediatric population pose a considerable risk for pathologists who examine those images. It is wise practice for the pathologist to refer

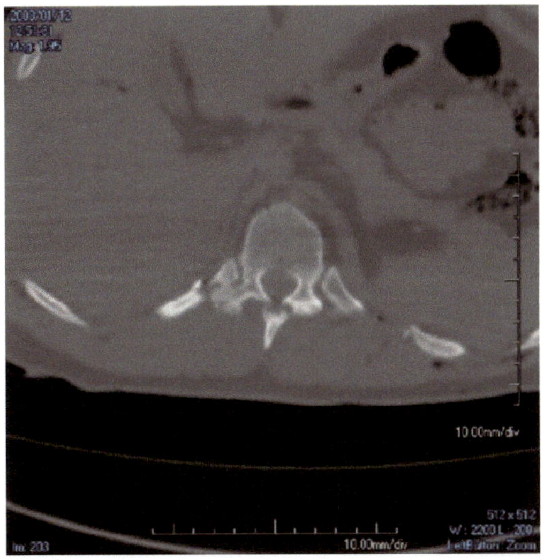

Figure 4.11 Axial CT image of a thoracic vertebra showing a nutrient artery. The lucency may mimic a fracture if taken in isolation.

such cases to an expert radiologist if one is contemplating the diagnosis of a pseudofracture.

Pediatric Fractures and CT

The multitude of ossification centers in the pediatric population means that fractures, and especially those involving the epiphyses, may not always be noticeable to the inexpert observer. Sometimes a joint effusion may be the subtle indicator of an associated fracture. Such fine-print expertise is certainly not going to be able to be achieved by the vast majority of forensic pathologists.

Practical Guidelines for Forensic Pathologists Reading CT Scans

MDCT has significant advantages over conventional radiology in the routine practice of forensic pathology.

- There is no need for special positioning of the deceased or special radiological views.
- Multiplanar reconstructions allow demonstration of anatomy without superimposition.
- Fracture lines are more clearly demonstrated.
- There is better presentation of depressed or distracted articular surfaces.

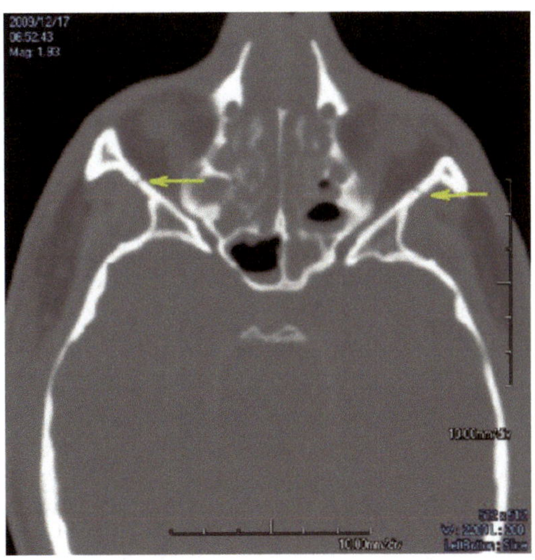

Figure 4.12 Axial CT image of the head showing bilateral symmetrical foramina, which could potentially mimic fractures.

A suggested protocol for examination of a postmortem CT in a routine case is

- A complete examination of the axial views from top to toe for assessment of viscera (see later)
- Sagittal reconstructions with bone windows for preliminary assessment of the spine
- Three-dimensional reconstructions for preliminary assessment of the skull, ribs, pelvis, and long bones
- Skull fractures sought for with a careful inspection of axial, coronal, and sagittal views using bone windows
- Gross rib fractures can be seen on three-dimensional reconstructions; subtle fractures and buckle fractures require careful inspection of axial views with bone windows
- Pelvic fractures are well demonstrated on three-dimensional reconstructions; more subtle fractures can be visualized with axial reconstructions using bone windows

For the majority of cases undergoing either visual inspection or conventional autopsy the described approach is usually sufficient. The individual pathologist will develop his or her own approach to using the CT in routine and suspicious cases.

Common Fracture Complications Seen on CT

The introduction of CT allows some common and important fracture complications to be documented without conventional autopsy.

Head Injury

As previously stated, the presence of a skull fracture indicates the application of significant blunt force trauma to the head. The fracture per se is not lethal. The fracture may be directly associated with lethal intracranial hemorrhage or diffuse brain injury.

An extradural hemorrhage most commonly results from rupture of a middle meningeal artery. The artery may be damaged when a fracture involves the squamous temporal bone. Middle meningeal rupture is more frequently seen in the absence of a fracture.

Extradural hemorrhages have typical CT findings (Figure 4.13). Extradural hematomas are uncommon. The blood strips the dura from the bone, and typically this process takes some considerable time.

- The CT appearance of the hematoma is characteristically biconvex in shape and is well defined.
- The scans may demonstrate midline shift and compression of the ipsilateral lateral ventricle.
- Acute bleeding is recognized by a high attenuation signal (40 HU).

A rare type of extradural hemorrhage is the posterior fossa extradural hematoma. Although extradural hemorrhages are usually from arterial bleeding, posterior fossa extradural hemorrhages result from bleeding from venous sinuses. The lesion is often associated with an occipital fracture. Posterior fossa extradural hemorrhages may be difficult to see on CT as the posterior fossa is often not well visualized.

Subdural hemorrhages are easily seen on noncontrast CT. The blood is seen as a high attenuation density over the surface of the brain with a somewhat crescentic

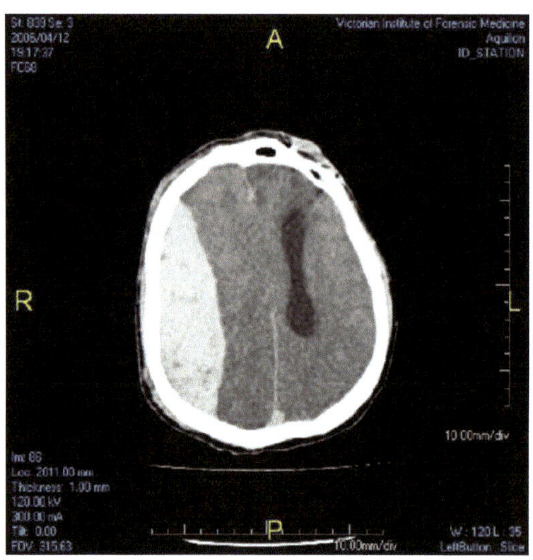

Figure 4.13 Axial CT image of the head showing a right extradural hematoma. The image demonstrates the typical localized biconvex shape of the hematoma. There is marked midline shift.

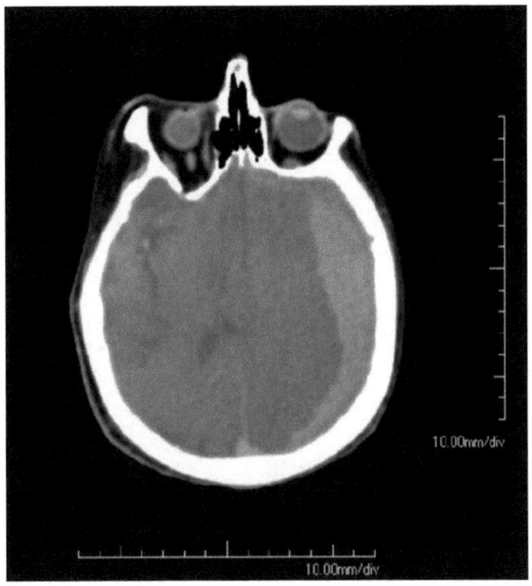

Figure 4.14 Axial CT image showing a left subdural hematoma extending over the entire cerebral hemisphere.

shape. As there is no anatomical structure to limit the spread of blood over the brain, subdural hemorrhages are typically seen over the convexity of the cerebral hemispheres (Figure 4.14). The subdural hemorrhage results from a rotational insult to the head and is not usually associated with a fracture. When a fracture is present it reflects the site of application of blunt force trauma. The side of the fracture does not necessarily correlate with the side of the hematoma.

Acute on chronic subdural hemorrhages are commonly seen in forensic practice. The acute hemorrhage may cause the previously stable individual with a chronic subdural hemorrhage to decompensate.

The CT images will typically show hypodense fluid over the brain admixed with fresh blood and may result in a layering effect (Figure 4.15). Some cases may show a membrane on the noncontrast postmortem scans.

Traumatic subarachnoid hemorrhage over the cerebral hemispheres may be the only positive CT or autopsy finding in cases of blunt force head injury (Figure 4.16).

Traumatic subarachnoid hemorrhage is characteristically seen as foci of high attenuation over the cerebral hemispheres, often best seen in the Sylvian fissure.

Basal subarachnoid hemorrhage associated with traumatic head injury may be problematic. Among other causes, a basal subarachnoid hemorrhage may result from rupture of a berry aneurysm within the circle of Willis or derive from rupture of the basilar artery or a vertebral artery.

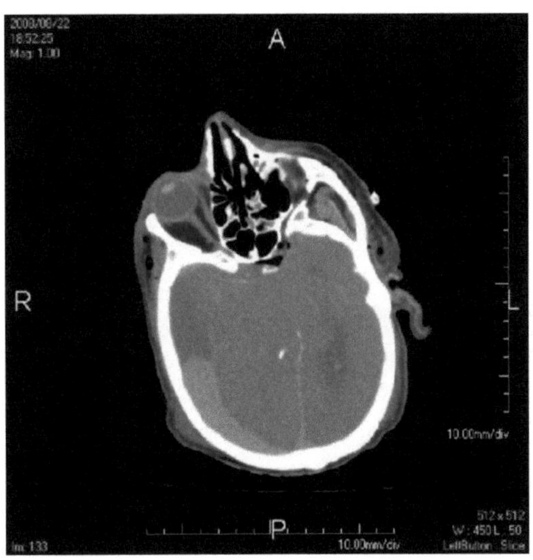

Figure 4.15 Axial CT image of an acute on chronic subdural hematoma showing the layering effect within the hematoma.

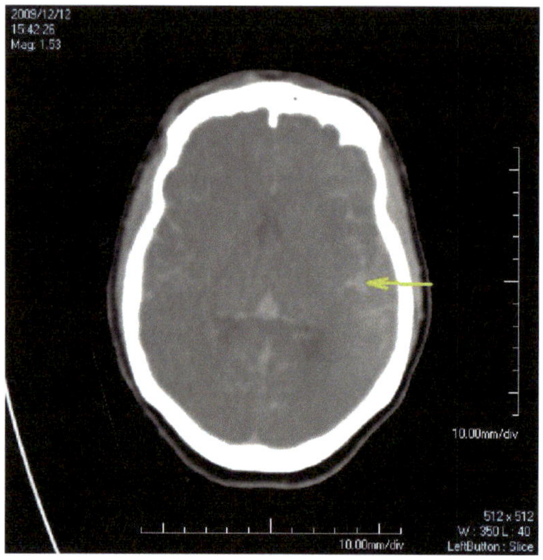

Figure 4.16 Axial CT image showing traumatic subarachnoid hemorrhage with bleeding between gyri over the cerebral hemispheres.

Basal subarachnoid hemorrhage shows high attenuation within the fourth ventricle and prepontine cistern with possible settling effect within the blood. Blood is also seen between the cerebral hemispheres and in the Sylvian fissure (Figure 4.17).

The hematoma is generally centered on the position where the lesion originated. A hematoma centered on the basal ganglia is most probably a primary lesion from a hypertensive-type bleed (Figure 4.18). A localized hematoma within the basal aspect of the frontal lobe in a deceased individual with a longitudinal occipital fracture is usually a secondary contrecoup hemorrhage. A lobar hemorrhage associated with leaky blood vessels in amyloid angiopathy will tend to be more lateral from the basal ganglia within the parietal lobe white matter.

Chest Injury

In the absence of a conventional autopsy, a CT examination can reveal lethal intrathoracic hemorrhage with and without associated fractures (Figure 4.19a,b). Victims of motor vehicle incidents who die rapidly at the scene often succumb to deceleration injury. The classic injury is traumatic rupture of the descending thoracic aorta. In such circumstances one sees a massive hemothorax. The volume of the hemorrhage can be estimated by CT.

Massive hemothorax may of course happen with other major vascular or cardiac injury. Pneumothorax may occur as an acute or delayed complication of a fractured rib [13]. The CT appearance of tension pneumothorax reveals an absence of lung markings and depression

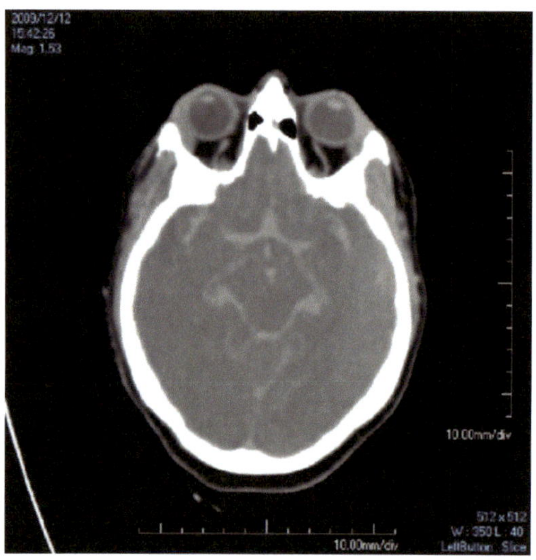

Figure 4.17 Axial CT showing basal subarachnoid hemorrhage with blood within the basal cisterns and between the cerebral gyri.

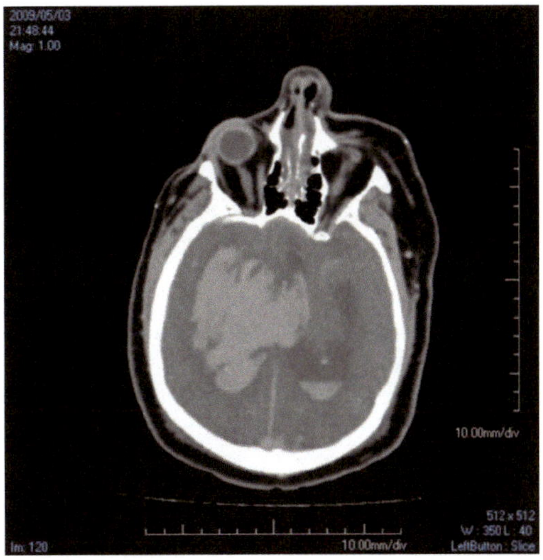

Figure 4.18 Axial CT showing a large hemorrhage centered on the basal ganglia. The image is highly suggestive of a hypertensive hemorrhage. Correlation with the clinical history is important.

of the hemidiaphragm on the affected side and shift of the mediastinum and trachea to the contralateral side (Figure 4.20). The differential diagnosis includes simple pneumothorax where the mediastinum is shifted to the ipsilateral side, and lung collapse where the lung markings are visible on the less attenuated side.

Abdominal and Pelvic Injuries

Hemoperitoneum is the major underlying cause of death in victims of significant abdominal or pelvic trauma. The source of the trauma is most commonly from a ruptured liver or spleen, and the noncontrast postmortem CT shows intraperitoneal blood centered on the origin of the blood and surrounding the abdominal viscera [12]. In the postmortem setting it is not unusual for the blood to change in attenuation from anterior to posterior. Hounsfield units typically range from 10 units anteriorly to 50 units posteriorly.

Lubner described blood originating in the liver flowing along anatomical pathways, principally along the right paracolic gutter into the cul-de-sac, whereas in splenic injury the blood tends to flow along the left paracolic gutter and into the pelvis [14].

The attenuation of blood in the peritoneum is measured at 30 to 45 HU in the acute death. Clotted blood may have an attenuation of up to 70 HU. Other possible fluids that may be seen in the deceased victim following

(a) (b)

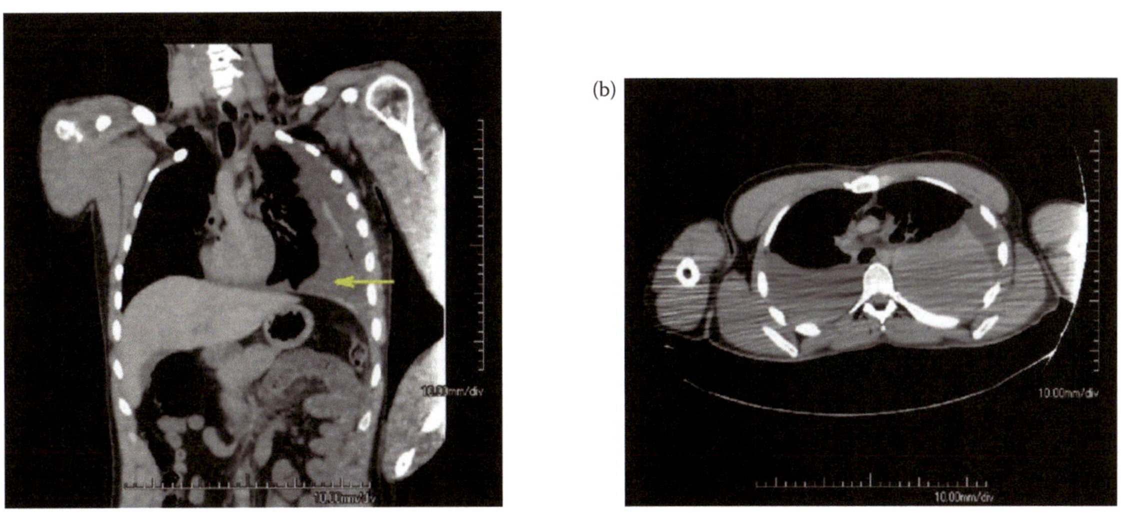

Figure 4.19 (a) Coronal CT showing a massive left hemothorax in a young victim of a motor vehicle collision. The radiopaque fluid within the left chest had Hounsfield units of ~40. The most likely cause of the hemorrhage is a ruptured thoracic aorta. To be certain of the cause of the hemorrhage an internal examination is required. (b) Axial CT showing bilateral hemothoraces.

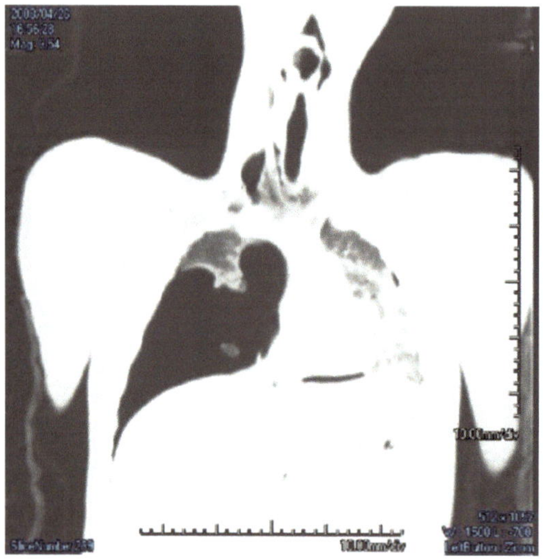

Figure 4.20 Coronal CT using lung windows showing a tension pneumothorax. There is mediastinal shift to the left, flattening of the right hemidiaphragm, and loss of lung markings on the right.

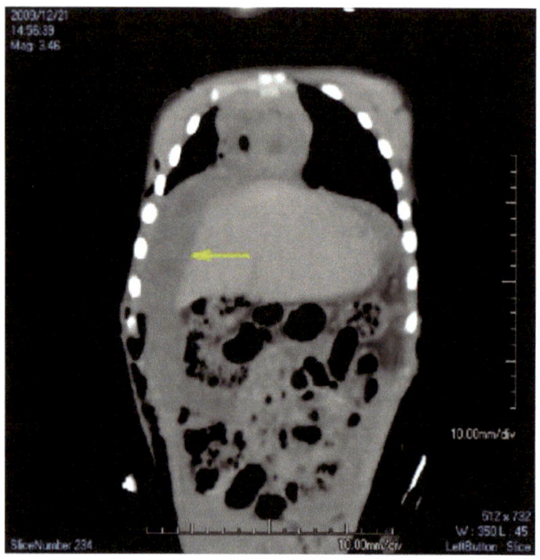

Figure 4.21 Coronal CT image of a child struck by a motor vehicle. The fluid (blood) surrounding the liver had Hounsfield units of approximately 40.

major abdominal trauma include bile, urine, and intestinal contents. The HU of these fluids typically ranges up to 15 HU. Our unpublished analysis of stomach contents has shown that gastric contents can have HU into the 90s when still *in situ* within the stomach.

It would seem reasonable that if abdominal trauma with hemoperitoneum or retroperitoneal hemorrhage is to be designated as the cause of death that the case be referred for expert radiological opinion (Figure 4.21).

Rupture of a hollow viscus will result in a pneumoperitoneum (Figure 4.22). As CT is an excellent modality to demonstrate the presence of air and gas such an abnormality is readily observed using postmortem CT.

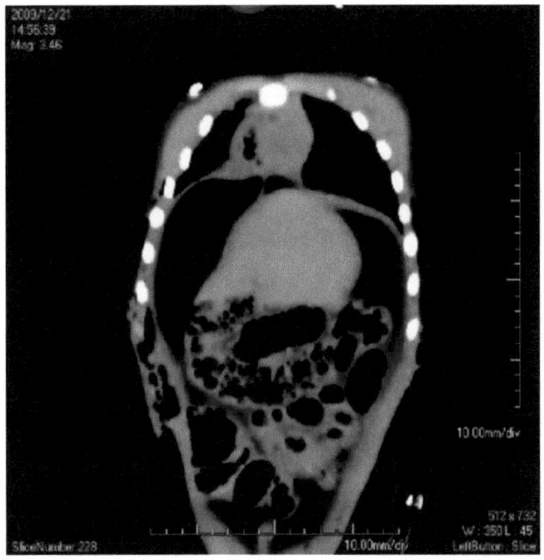

Figure 4.22 Coronal CT image of Figure 4.21 captured at an anterior position. The image clearly shows the presence of gas indicating a ruptured viscus. Figures 4.21 and 4.22 show the importance of scanning through all of the images.

References

1. O'Donnell C, Woodford N. Post-mortem radiology—A new sub-specialty? *Clin. Radiol.* 2008; 63:1189–1194.
2. Kremer C, Racette S, Marton D, Sauvageau A. Radiographs interpretation by forensic pathologists. A word of warning. *Am. J. Forensic Med. Pathol.* 2008; 29:295–296.
3. Geijer M, El-Koury GY. Imaging of the acetabulum in the era of multidetector computed tomography. *Emerg. Radiol.* 2007; 14:271–287.
4. Goldman LW. Principles of CT and CT technology. *J. Nucl. Med. Technol.* 2007; 35:115–128.
5. Kalia V, Obray RW, Filice R, Fayad LM, Murphy K, Carrino JA. Functional joint imaging using 256-MDCT: Technical feasibility. *Am. J. Roentgenol.* 2009; 192(6):W295–W299.
6. Bolliger SA, Oesterhelweg L, Spendlove D, Ross S, Thali M. Is differentiation of frequently encountered foreign bodies in corpses possible by Hounsfield density measurement? *J. Forensic Sci.* 2009; 54(5):1119–1122.
7. Ablett M, Kusumawudjaja D. Appearance of wooden foreign body on CT scan. *Emerg. Med.* 2009; 26:680.
8. Goldman LW. Principles of CT: Multislice CT. *J. Nucl. Med. Technol.* 2008; 36:57–68.
9. Barrett JF, Keat N. Artifacts in CT: Recognition and avoidance. *Radiographics* 2004; 24:1679–1691.
10. Kiuru MT, Haapamaki VV, Koivikko MP, Koskinen SK. Wrist injuries: Diagnosis with multidetector CT. *Emerg. Radiol.* 2004; 10:182–185.
11. Connor SE, Tan G, Fernando R, Chaudhury N. Computed tomography pseudofractures of the mid face and skull base. *Clin. Radiol.* 2005; 60(12):1268–1279.
12. Whyte MP. Atypical femoral fractures, bisphosphonates, and adult hypophosphatasia. *J. Bone Miner. Res.* 2009; 24(6):1132–1134.
13. Lu MS, Huang YK, Liu HP, Kao CL. Delayed pneumothorax complicating minor rib fracture after chest trauma. *Am. J. Emerg. Med.* 2008; 26(5):551–554.
14. Lubner M, Menias C, Rucker C, Bhalla S, Peterson CM, Wang L, Gratz B. Blood in the belly: CT findings of hemoperiteum. *Radiographics* 2007; 27:109–125.

Head
Skull, Face, and Hyoid Bone

5

Skull

Calvarium

Anatomy

The calvarium is formed from the membranous neurocranium, whereas the base of skull forms from the cartilaginous neurocranium [1]. Thus, the cranial vault undergoes intramembranous ossification, whereas the skull base is ossified via endochondral ossification. At birth, the bones of the cranium are separated by fibrous tissue. This fibrous tissue is continuous with both the periosteum externally and the dura mater internally.

The large anterior fontanel closes by the end of the second year by which time the smaller posterior fontanel has been closed for over 18 months.

The calvarium is composed of the frontal bone, and the bilateral parietal and temporal bones. The occipital bone is usually described with the base of the skull. The occipital bone and temporal bone both have regions that share anatomical characteristics of the calvarium and the base of the skull.

The bones of the calvarium are composed of outer and inner tables of compact bone surrounding a central diploe. The longitudinal sagittal suture unites the two parietal bones, which are then joined to the frontal bone through the coronal suture. Posteriorly the lambdoid suture lies between the parietal bones and occipital bone at the posterior aspect of the calvarium. The squamous suture connects the parietal bone and temporal bone on each side.

The temporal bones are situated at the lateral aspects of the cranial vault and the base of the skull. The bone has five parts: the squama, the petrous, the mastoid, the tympanic, and the styloid process. The superior border of the temporal bone is thin and beveled at the expense of the inner table to overlap with the parietal bone at the squamosal suture. This region of the temporal bone is thinner compared to the parietal, occipital, and frontal bones.

The postmortem CT provides excellent images of the skull and facial bones. The axial, coronal, and sagittal images may be more difficult for the forensic pathologist to initially diagnose fractures of the skull or face. The three-dimensional reconstructions are quite intuitive for the pathologist, the police investigators, and the courts (Figure 5.1a,b,c).

Fractures of the Calvarium

Introduction

In Western societies the majority of skull fractures result from blunt force trauma in motor vehicle incidents. Other causes include falls from a height, falls from a standing height, assaults from blunt force trauma, and firearm injury.

The introduction of passive and active safety systems to motor vehicles has decreased the number of skull fractures in collisions. For example, the etiology of temporal bone fractures has recently been determined to be due to motor vehicle accidents in 12% to 47% of cases, assault in 10% to 37% of cases, falls in 16% to 40% of cases, and gunshot injuries in 3% to 33% of cases [2].

Types of Fracture

The fractures to the calvarium may be described as linear, comminuted, and depressed.

Linear Skull Fractures Linear skull fractures are the most frequent skull fractures seen in clinical practice and are the type of skull fracture least likely to be associated with significant brain injury [3]. A linear skull fracture is particularly well depicted on three-dimensional reconstructions (Figure 5.2). The position of the fracture is important with respect to its clinical and forensic importance. Fractures involving the temporal bone carry a risk of middle meningeal artery injury. On the other hand, occipital fractures may cause tears to dural sinuses leading to posterior fossa venous extradural hemorrhage.

In the 1920s, Lecount and Apfelbach reported six areas within the cranial vault where greater thickness of the skull bones resisted bending. These skull buttresses consist of the parietosphenoidal, parietopetrous, midfrontal, and midoccipital buttresses. The presence of the skull buttresses can prevent or modify a linear skull fracture.

Although linear fractures might cross the bony buttresses of the skull, this tends to occur when the path of the fracture is almost perpendicular to the orientation of the buttress. Fractures that meet the buttress at a

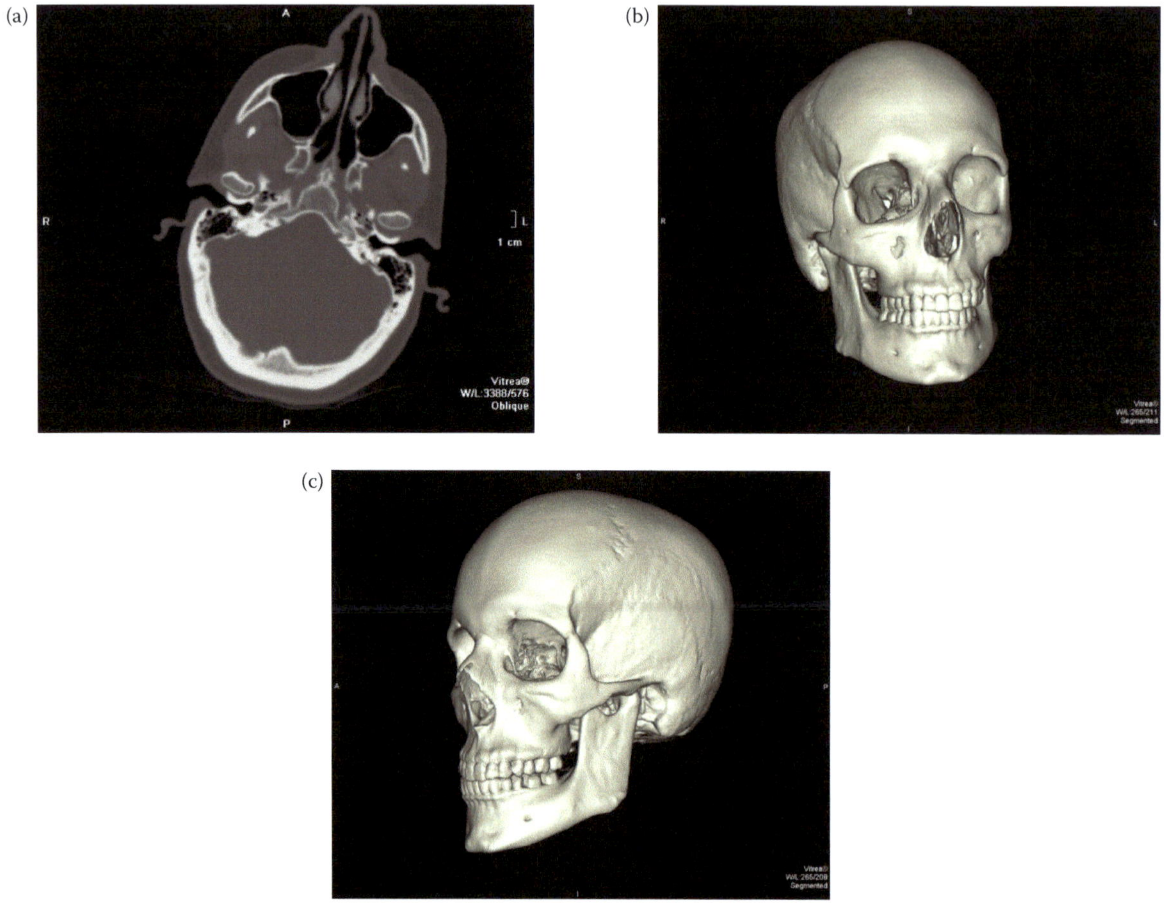

Figure 5.1 (a) Anterior view of three-dimensional reconstruction of the skull and face. (b,c) Lateral view of three-dimensional reconstruction of the skull and face.

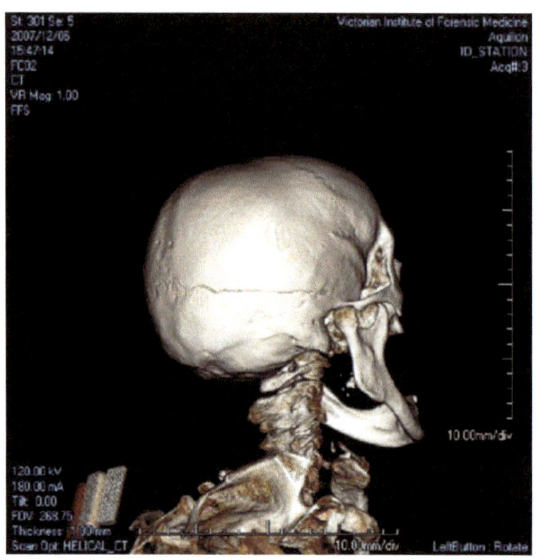

Figure 5.2 Three-dimensional reconstruction of the skull showing a linear parietal fracture extending to the lambdoid suture.

more oblique angle will usually extend along the path of a structurally weaker area.

Although linear fractures can travel in any direction, there is a tendency for impacts to the top of the head to travel in a vertical orientation toward the base of the skull, and for fractures to otherwise follow the path of the application of blunt force. Linear fractures can rarely be discontinuous. In these circumstances a "separate" fracture can be found following a section of uninvolved bone in a continuing line extending a short distance away in the same direction.

Linear fractures in pediatric trauma victims can widen and extend with swelling of the brain in what are termed growing fractures. Linear fractures may extend into and separate unfused sutures, resulting in a diastatic fracture.

Biomechanics Research into the biomechanics of skull fractures have used defleshed, dried, and embalmed skulls; fresh head specimens from postmortem subjects; and complete unembalmed cadavers. More recent studies have highlighted some inadequacies with respect to the choice of some experimental material and the design of some of the earlier studies.

It has been shown that the use of previously dried and rehydrated skulls as experimental material introduces significant effects upon the bone's biomechanical properties [4]. In some early biomechanical studies, multiple impacts were applied to a single specimen. This process may be seen to invalidate the forces required to cause a subsequent fracture in the specimen at a different site. The absence of the normal axial loading of the cervical spine in isolated head specimens has been shown to alter the biomechanical characteristics of the head specimen.

A number of studies have demonstrated that following a blunt force impact to the skull there is maximum in-bending directly beneath the point of impact, and out-bending in areas surrounding the point of impact. The in-bending and out-bending are modified by factors such as the buttresses of the skull, the presence of foramina, and the radius of curvature of the bone in question in different regions.

A series of experimental impact studies using the so-called stresscoat technique investigated the biomechanics of skull fractures. The studies utilized fresh cadaver skulls, which were dried following removal of all soft tissues. The skulls were coated with a thin layer of aluminum lacquer following which they were sprayed with a brittle lacquer. The lacquer would form cracks in relation to strain on the surface of the bone following the application of blunt force [5].

The experimental work showed that linear fractures initiate at a point distant from the point of impact and extend back to the point of impact. The cracks visible to the stresscoat lacquer were always maximal in the direction of the maximum radius of curvature, which corresponds to the flattest portion of the skull. Furthermore, more than one fracture could be initiated from the initial point of impact on either side of impact, resulting in more than one skull fracture.

Comminuted Fractures Laboratory studies investigating the amount of force required to cause linear fractures of the cranial vault showed that the application of a relatively minor increase in the applied force would lead to comminution of the fracture. This was believed to occur as a result of the initial linear fracture causing loss of structural integrity of the cranial vault. Thus a comminuted fracture, of itself, does not necessarily indicate a degree of force far exceeding the blunt head trauma required to cause a simple linear fracture [6].

Comminuted fractures are very well seen on three-dimensional reconstructions (Figure 5.3). These images are sometimes able to demonstrate the point of application of blunt force trauma. These reconstructed images illustrate a common feature of curved fracture edges at the

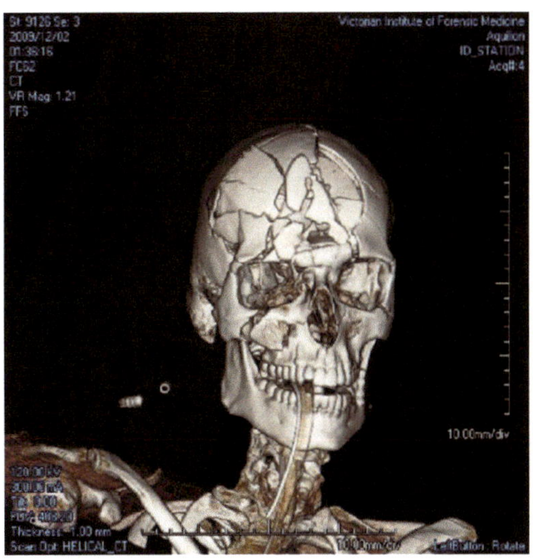

Figure 5.3 Three-dimensional reconstruction of the skull showing a comminuted fracture. The CT images demonstrate the position of the application of blunt force.

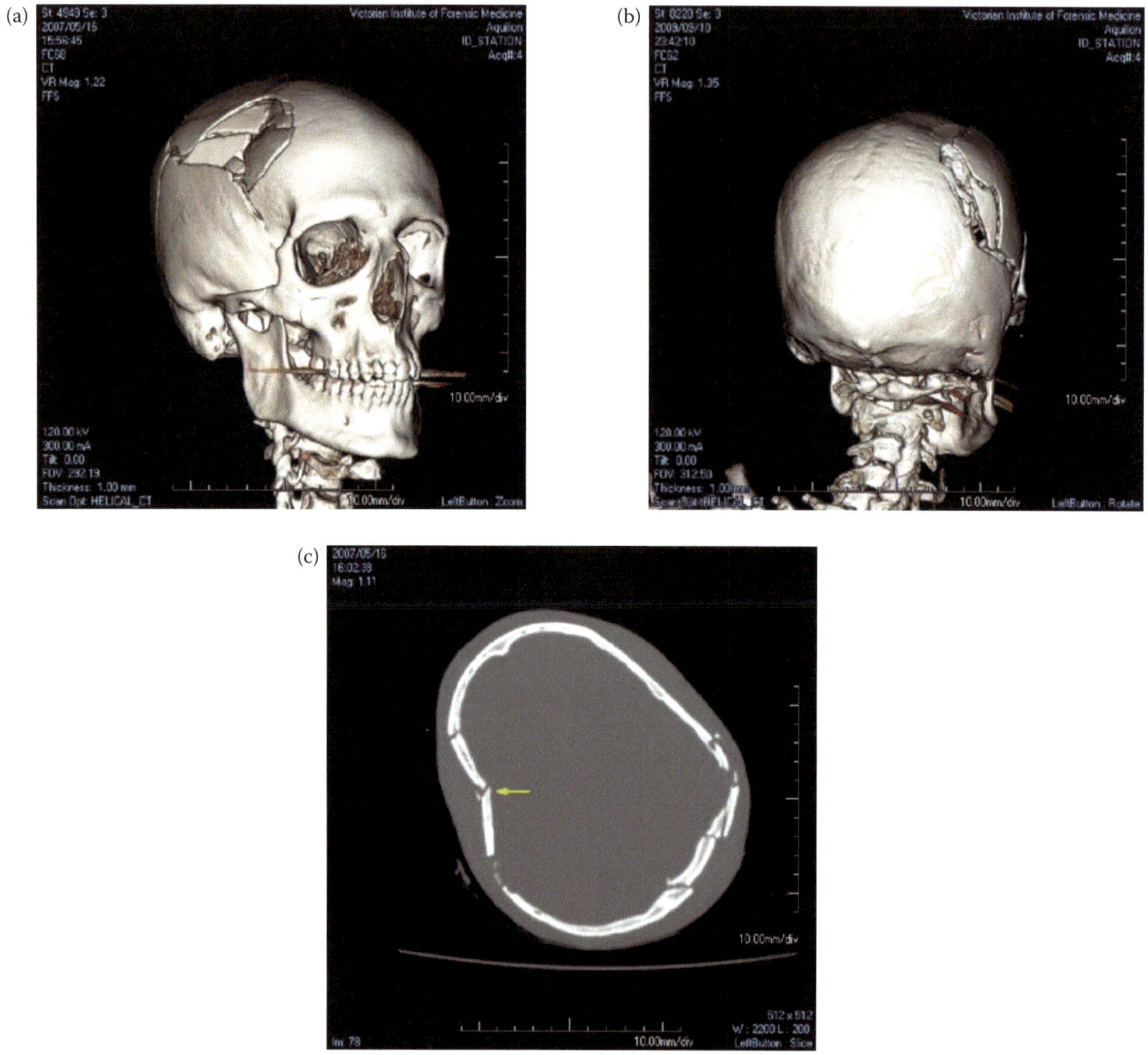

Figure 5.4 (a) Three-dimensional reconstruction showing a right depressed parietal fracture. (b) Three-dimensional reconstruction showing a right depressed parietal fracture. (c) Axial CT image with bone window showing a depressed fracture to the right side of the head indicating a site of application of blunt force trauma. The image reveals the degree of indentation to the skull, a second site of blunt force trauma to the back of the head resulting in a comminuted fracture.

periphery of a comminuted fracture as occurs when the death results from a significant fall to a hard flat surface.

Some comminuted fractures may show tertiary concentric fractures that are perpendicular to, and terminate in, radiating linear fractures. These concentric fractures are typically curved, and as such may be easier to recognize in fragmented material or when the primary site of trauma is not present with skeletal remains.

A study utilizing 79 skulls that had sustained concentric fractures resulting from blunt force trauma showed that the concentric fractures also had established internal beveling. On the other hand the examination of concentric fractures from ballistics trauma revealed external beveling. This difference may allow one to differentiate between blunt force trauma and gunshot injury, especially in cases of skeletal remains [7].

The examination of the edge of a fracture to determine the presence of internal or external beveling cannot only permit one to establish the presence of a gunshot entrance or exit injury, but even in the absence of these latter two features one may be able to express an informed opinion as to whether the case is related to a firearm injury or blunt force trauma.

Depressed Fractures A depressed fracture represents a definite site of the application of blunt force trauma (Figure 5.4a,b,c). The fracture also represents the application of a large amount of force being applied to a relatively small area.

When an object impacts with the skull at sufficient force it may lead to complete fracture of the outer diploe only, or a segment of both the outer and inner diploes. The fracture segments may be displaced inward resulting

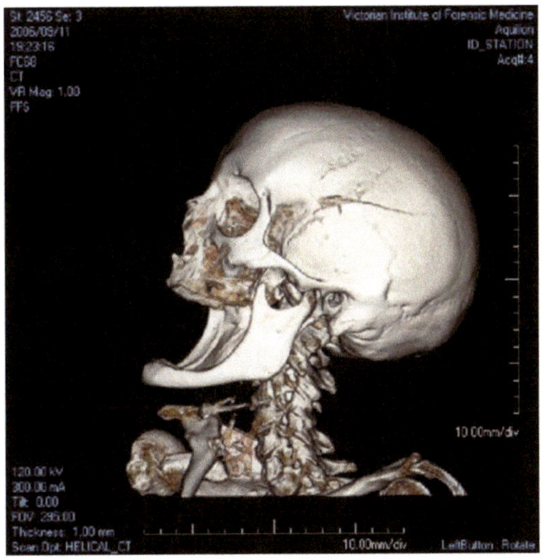

Figure 5.5 Three-dimensional reconstruction of the skull showing a linear left parietal fracture.

in compromise of the dura mater and possible lacerations to the brain or dural sinuses. Depressed fractures tend to occur with localized application of the force, as may occur with the edge of a hard object or with severe force occurring over a larger area.

Sites of Skull Fracture

Parietal Fracture

Two common sites of application of blunt force to the head are impacts to the side of the head and to the vertex (Figure 5.5). Impacts to the vertex may be associated with fractures extending over the lateral aspect of the cranial vault to the base of the skull. Experimental studies have shown the parietal region of the skull fractures in a similar fashion to the frontal, temporal, and occipital bones [8].

Frontal Fracture

The biomechanics of frontal bone fractures have been extensively investigated, as the initial research targeting motor vehicle incidents concentrated on frontal impacts. An experimental study using 18 unembalmed postmortem human specimens showed that frontal bones failed at an energy range between 22 and 24 J for dynamic frontal loading [9]. Interestingly, a further study on 14 cadaver heads using a pendulum technique concluded that the frontal bone fractured before any significant movement of the head [10].

Linear frontal skull fractures tend to be vertically orientated fractures. Secondary zones of stress concentration in midfrontal trauma include the supraorbital notch. The fractures may extend into the frontal sinus and orbital plate (Figure 5.6). Frontal bone fractures were subclassified into five groups by Manolidis depending

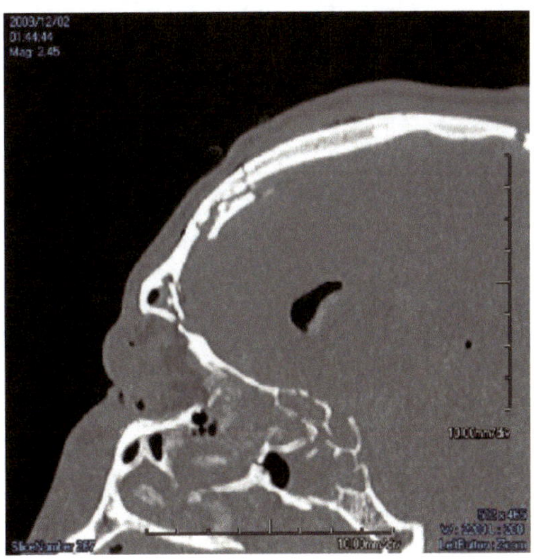

Figure 5.6 Coronal CT image showing involvement of the frontal sinus and the orbital plate. One notes a small amount of fluid (blood) within the frontal sinus.

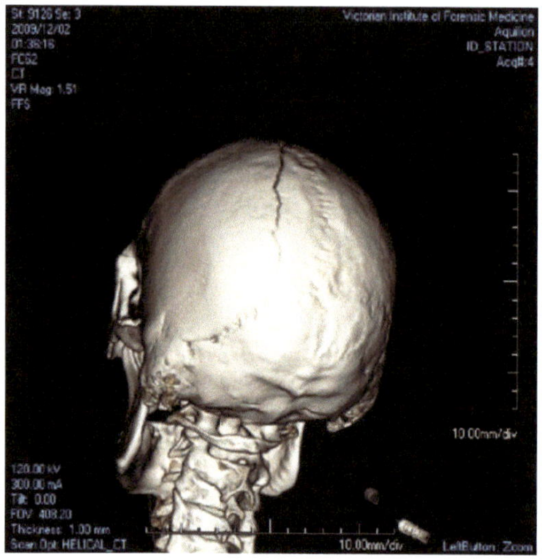

Figure 5.7 Three-dimensional reconstruction of the skull showing a linear fracture extending over the calvarium toward the back of the head.

upon the involvement of the anterior or posterior sinus walls, the degree of comminution of the fracture, and the presence of a cerebrospinal fluid (CSF) leak.

Not infrequently, fractures involving the frontal region will radiate to the temporal region or to the vertex (Figure 5.7). In fractures of considerable force there may be extension of a frontal fracture over the calvarium to the occiput.

Occipital Fracture

The occipital bone has biomechanical characteristics that are common to the other bones of the cranial vault, as well as having other characteristics identical to the base of the skull. Impacts to the occipital bone may lead to fractures extending to the vertex, to the foramen magnum, or lateral to the foramen magnum and involving the middle cranial fossa (Figure 5.8).

Simple linear fractures may be difficult to appreciate on axial, coronal, or sagittal images. A fracture must be differentiated from a suture. The assistance of an expert radiologist is invaluable in this respect. Once a fracture is observed at autopsy or on three-dimensional reconstructions then the fracture is easier to appreciate on the other images (Figure 5.9).

Base of Skull Fractures

Anatomy

The base of the skull is formed from five bones. These are the orbital plate of the frontal bone, the cribriform plate of

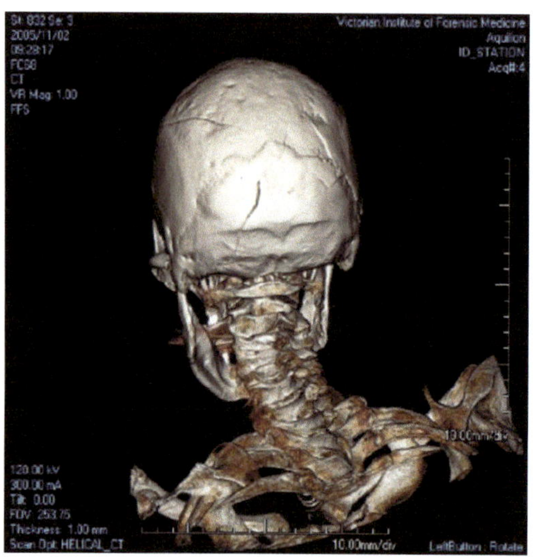

Figure 5.8 Three-dimensional reconstruction showing a linear fracture of the occipital bone just to the left of the midline and extending toward the foramen magnum. An additional fracture to the posterior aspect of the left parietal bone extends to the right lambdoid suture.

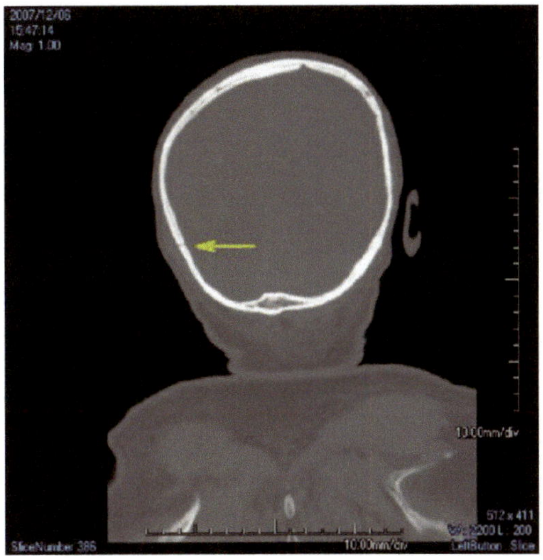

Figure 5.9 Coronal CT image showing a linear fracture to the occipital bone.

the ethmoid bone, the sphenoid bone, occipital bone, and squamous and petrous portions of the temporal bone.

The skull base has been traditionally separated into anterior, middle, and posterior cranial fossae. The anterior cranial fossa comprises the orbital plate of the frontal bone, the cribriform plate, and the anterior aspect of the lesser wing of the sphenoid. The sphenoid is a robust, somewhat butterfly-shaped bone that consists of a body, two greater and lesser wings, and the two pterygoid processes.

The anterior cranial fossa is separated from the middle cranial fossa primarily by the lesser wing of the sphenoid. The middle cranial fossa is comprised of the body and greater wings of the sphenoid and the petrous and squamous parts of the temporal bone. The posterior cranial fossa is bordered anteriorly by the superior border of the petrous temporal bone. The posterior fossa is formed from the occipital bone. The occipital bone is composed of the basiocciput, exocciput, supraocciput, and occipital squamosa.

The occipital condyles are ovoid or bean-shaped lateral prominences of the occipital bone. The condyles form the foramen magnum together with the basioccipital segment anteriorly and the squamosa segment posteriorly. The convex occipital condyles articulate with the concave articulate facets of the underlying first cervical vertebra (atlas).

Numerous canals and fossae are present within the base of the skull with the foramen magnum central within the occipital bone (Figure 5.10). Some of these foramina are constant and some are inconstant. Constant foramina within the middle cranial fossa include the superior

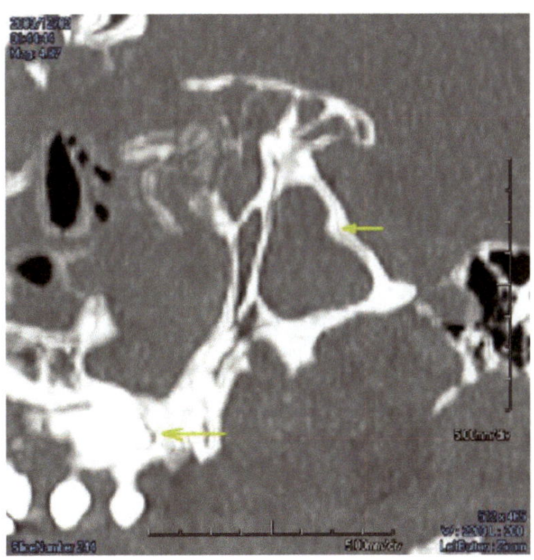

Figure 5.10 Coronal CT at high magnification showing well-defined lucencies within the base of the skull not related to any trauma.

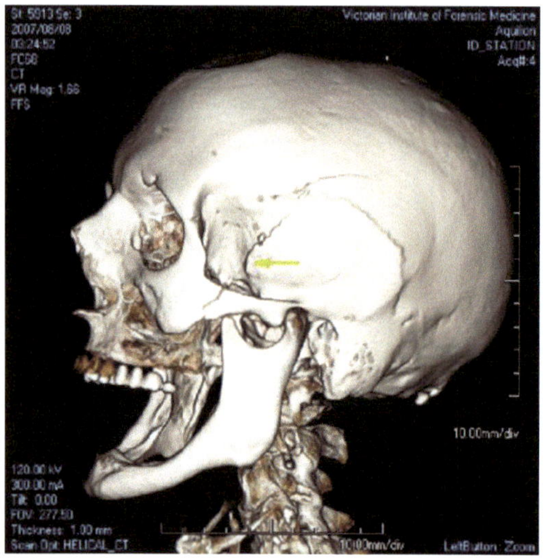

Figure 5.11 Three-dimensional reconstruction showing fractures to the left temporal bone and zygoma. The image indicates the application of blunt force trauma to the left side of the head.

orbital fissure, the foramen rotundum, the foramen ovale, and the foramen spinosum. Inconstant foramina include the anastomotic and emissary foramina, which transmit a branch of the middle meningeal artery and a vein to the pterygoid plexus, respectively.

The importance of these constant and inconstant foramina is the possibility of misinterpreting normal foramina on CT scanning as a base of skull fracture. It is unlikely that the average forensic pathologist will gain enough experience to confidently diagnose such imaging features without expert radiological support.

Etiology

Studies have shown that fractures of the skull base occur in 4% to 30% of head injuries, with up to 40% involving the temporal bone [11]. The most important acute clinical and forensic complication of base of skull fracture is hemorrhage and results from mucosal tears in the nasopharynx. The bleeding can lead to profound hypoxia from upper airway occlusion and is especially significant, as these individuals will often have an associated decreased conscious state due to an associated primary brain injury.

The majority of temporal bone fractures are unilateral (Figure 5.11). Bilateral fractures are reported to occur in 9% to 20% of cases [2]. Squamous temporal bone fractures are important injuries because of the potential intracranial hemorrhagic complications (Figure 5.12). Although middle meningeal artery rupture can occur in the absence of temporal fracture, the occurrence of arterial damage and subsequent extradural hemorrhage is significantly increased when the temporal bone is fractured.

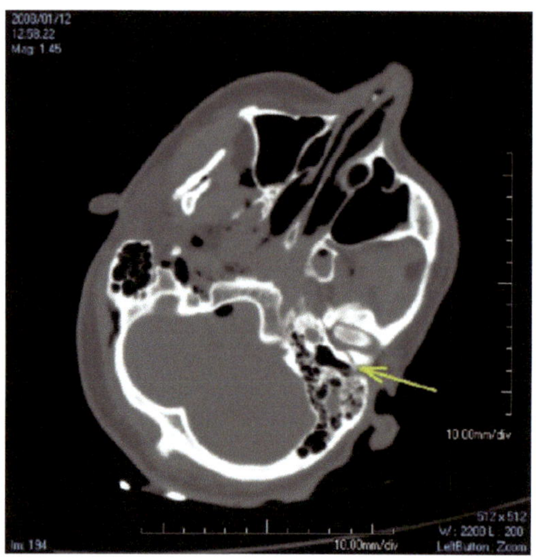

Figure 5.12 Axial CT image showing a fracture to the left temporal bone. Note the fluid (blood) within the sphenoidal sinus.

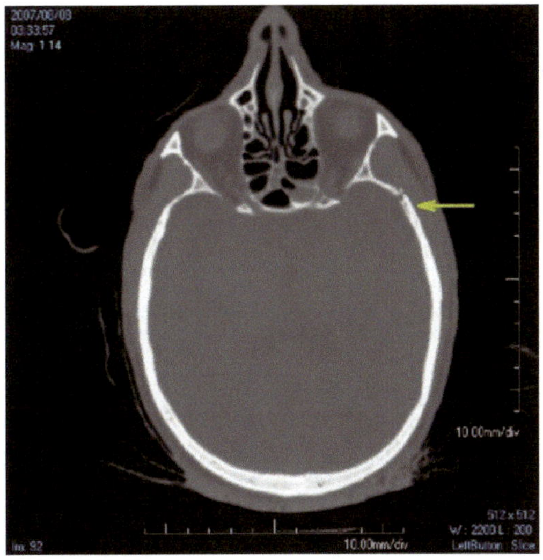

Figure 5.13 Axial CT image showing a fracture to the squamous temporal bone.

Base of skull fractures involving the temporal bone fracture have traditionally been separated into longitudinal and transverse fractures. Longitudinal fractures are more common and occur in approximately 90% of cases. Longitudinal fractures generally result from blunt force trauma to the temporoparietal region. These fractures extend from the squamosa through the external auditory canal to the foramen spinosum of the middle cranial fossa (Figure 5.13).

Transverse fractures can result from frontooccipital forces and course perpendicular to the long axis of the petrous bone from the foramen magnum into the middle cranial fossa [2]. Research has shown that many temporal bone fractures do not fit into either longitudinal or transverse types and have been classified as oblique fractures [12]. In a series of 150 temporal bone fractures, oblique fractures comprised 75% of the cases.

Mechanisms of Basal Skull Fractures

Central and lateral skull base fractures are often the result of lateral or sagittally directed indirect forces [13].

Fractures involving the anterior cranial fossa are often longitudinal extensions from linear and comminuted fractures of the frontal bones at the superior orbital ridge (Figure 5.14a,b). A distinct fracture involving the anterior cranial fossa is the contrecoup fracture to the anterior cranial fossa secondary to occipital bone impact. The mechanism of this fracture is transferred force through the base of the frontal lobes to the orbital roof and cribriform plate.

(a) (b)

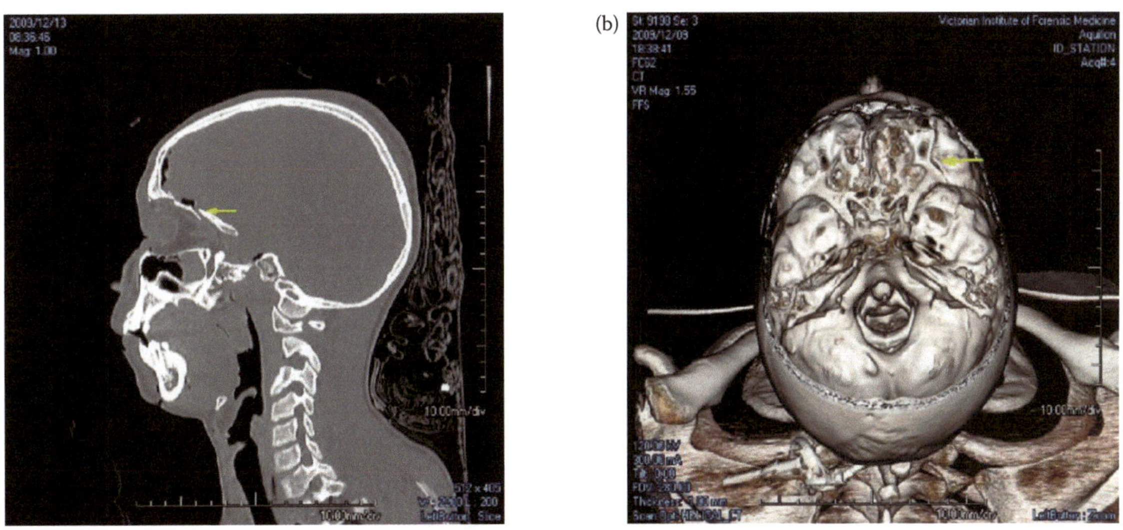

Figure 5.14 (a) Sagittal CT image showing a fracture to the anterior cranial fossa. Note the air within the cranial vault (pneumocephalus). Note the air adjacent to the mental protuberance of the mandible. (b) Three-dimensional reconstruction showing a fracture to the orbital plate (anterior cranial fossa). The fracture suggests the application of blunt force trauma to the forehead.

(a) (b)

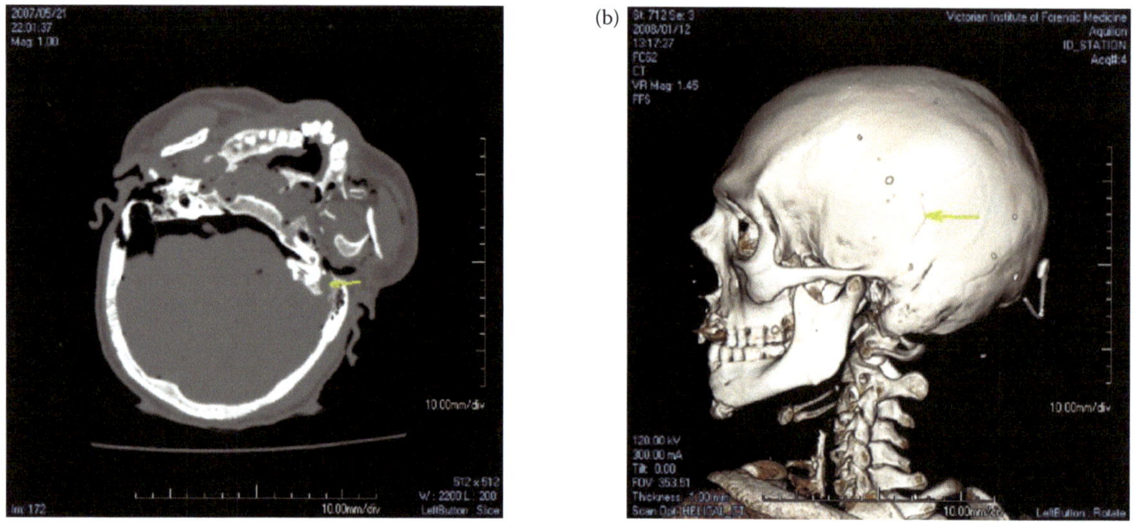

Figure 5.15 (a) Axial CT image showing a fracture involving the middle cranial fracture. Fractures with wide separation of the fracture edges are relatively straightforward diagnoses for the forensic pathologist to make. Nondisplaced fractures are often very problematic. (b) Lateral three-dimensional reconstruction CT image showing a fracture to the left temporoparietal region extending into the base of the skull.

Middle cranial fossa fractures are commonly seen in forensic pathology. Transverse or hinge fractures are seen in cases of significant blunt force head injury as may occur in a motor vehicle incident (Figure 5.15a,b). Although uncommon, the injury may also be seen in cases of severe impact to the head with a heavy object in an assault. Although these fractures are typically associated with impacts to the side of the head, it is well recognized that hinge fractures may occur with impacts to various points along the base of the skull or to the chin [14]. Transmitted force can occur through an impact to the mandible via the temporomandibular joint.

Basal skull fractures that occur when the impact site is at a remote location to the fracture are believed to occur as a consequence of the interaction of various mechanisms including traction forces, torsion, and wedging effects [15]. The presence of the various canals and foramina act as focal points of physical weakness in the skull base. Thus fractures at this site will tend to involve these structures and can be associated with significant clinical and forensic complications such as carotid artery dissection and thrombosis.

A longitudinal occipital skull fracture is commonly seen in individuals who have fallen backward from a standing position to a hard surface onto the back of the head. Posterior basal skull fractures may occur from transmitted forces from impacts to the skull, particularly the vertex, and the mandible. Ring fractures of the occipital bone may occur from hyperextension at the atlantooccipital joint secondary to a fall at the forehead or chin, or from forced flexion of the cervical spine secondary to a fall from a height (Figure 5.16) [16]. The strength

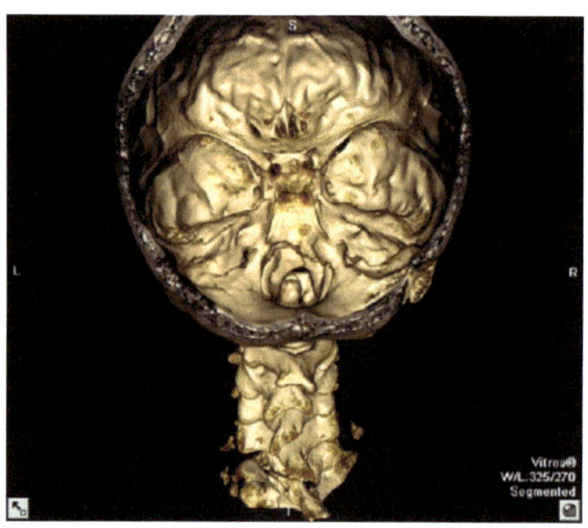

Figure 5.16 Three-dimensional reconstruction CT image with the top of the cranium digitally removed to demonstrate a ring fracture around the foramen magnum.

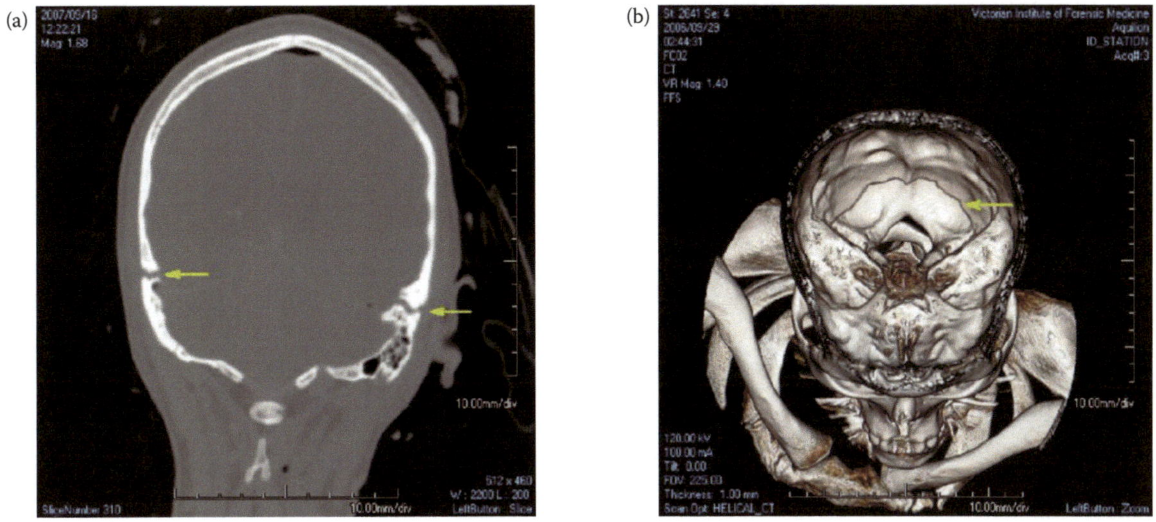

Figure 5.17 (a) Coronal CT image showing symmetrical fractures to the lateral aspects of the skull in a wider ring fracture involving the base of the skull. (b) Three-dimensional reconstruction of the skull demonstrating a ring fracture extending around the occiput.

of the atlantooccipital ligaments can lead to failure of the bone before rupture of the ligament occurs.

Ring fractures may also be seen with axial force resulting from severe blunt force to the vertex or falls from a height onto the feet. These injuries are well recognized in the forensic setting and have often been thought to be universally fatal. However, the use of CT in clinical cases has revealed the injury in survivors of trauma [17].

Other ring fractures may extend more widely around the base of the skull involving the occipital bone around the level of the external occipital protuberance (Figure 5.17a,b).

Occipital condylar fractures were previously believed to be quite rare. However, a study that examined high energy blunt trauma to the head and neck involving axial compression, lateral bending, rotation, or direct trauma showed an incidence of 16% in these cases (Figure 5.18a,b) [18]. The definite mechanism of injury in a given case may well be problematic. In addition to the forces listed earlier other mechanisms involved in condylar fracture include hyperflexion, hyperextension, and the direct application of force to the posterior occiput. Often in real-world situations there can be a combination of forces acting sequentially or in unison.

Occipital fractures are important because of the intimate anatomical relationship between the condyles and the medulla oblongata, the vertebral arteries, and internal vertebral venous plexuses [19]. As such, a displaced fragment from an occipital condyle fracture has

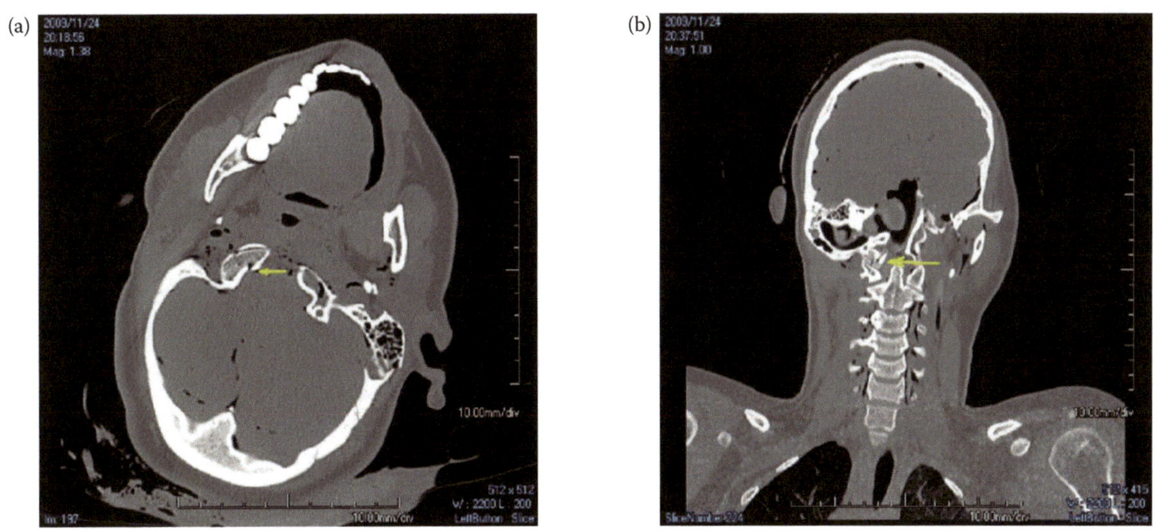

Figure 5.18 (a) Axial CT image showing a fracture to the right occipital condyle. (b) Coronal CT image showing a fracture to the right occipital condyle.

(a)

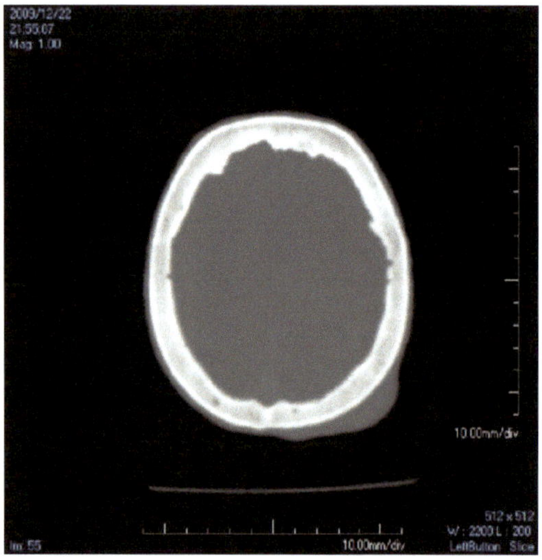

(b)

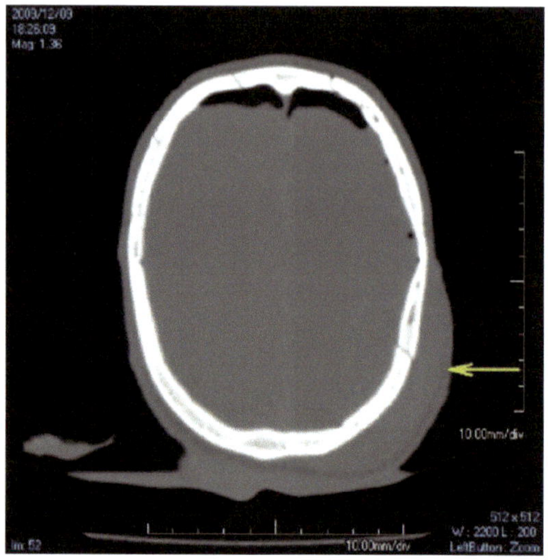

Figure 5.19 (a) Axial CT image showing localized swelling to the left occipital region. The finding should be correlated with the external examination findings. (b) Axial CT image showing more diffuse scalp swelling associated with multiple skull fractures and pneumocephalus.

the potential to injure these vital neural centers and vessels [20].

According to the classification system of Anderson and Montesano, there are three types of occipital condyle fracture. Type I is a comminuted fracture of the condyle with minimal fracture displacement, type II is a basilar skull fracture extending into the condyle, and type III is a fracture with a fracture fragment displaced medially into the foramen magnum [21].

Practical Forensic Issues in CT Scanning of the Head

CT provides more detailed and authoritative evaluation of the skull than conventional radiographs. CT can show soft tissue swelling, though in a forensic setting one needs to be guarded when dealing with parts of a deceased body that may have been in a dependent position after death (Figure 5.19a,b).

A formal analysis of the biomechanics of linear skull fractures and CT scanning showed that CT images identified the skull fracture but did not demonstrate the direction or location of the impact to the skull [22]. The fracture widths were consistently wider some distance from the site of impact. Thus based purely on the CT images, one could not determine with absolute certainty the anatomical region that sustained the primary impact. An autopsy is required.

Depressed skull fractures and comminuted skull fractures indicate the application of significant blunt force trauma to that region of the skull.

CT analysis of temporal bone fractures requires high-resolution CT with thin collimation (0.5–0.75 mm) reformatted into axial and coronal images. CT of the temporal bone must allow for delineation of fracture anatomy and visualization of the canals and middle cranial fossa floor. The axial images are best seen angulated along the tympanic segment of the facial nerve. Images of the skull base should be examined using both bone and soft tissue windows [23].

Base of skull fractures may result in pneumocephalus (Figure 5.20a,b). Pneumocephalus is the presence of air or gas within the cranial cavity. The presence of gas caused by trauma must be differentiated from the effects of decomposition. The CT images of the abdomen should be reviewed to exclude putrefactive gas within the portal veins and liver.

Traumatic pneumocephalus may be extradural, subdural, subarachnoid, parenchymal, or intraventricular, and may be the result of an open skull fracture or fracture involving a sinus or mastoid air cells. Subarachnoid pneumocephalus suggests a basilar skull fracture. Subarachnoid air is seen to outline gyri and may be present within basal cisterns.

The various neurovascular channels (foramina, canals, and channels), sutures, and fissures can cause problems diagnosing fractures to the base of the skull. As previously indicated, for experienced radiologists this does not normally create a major problem, as many of the defects within the skull are well characterized; however, for forensic pathologists reading CT images, these normal structures are highly likely to be problematic [24]. The presence of such defects in a symmetrical pattern, interdigitating margins in sutures, and smooth margins are indicators of a normal anatomical structure.

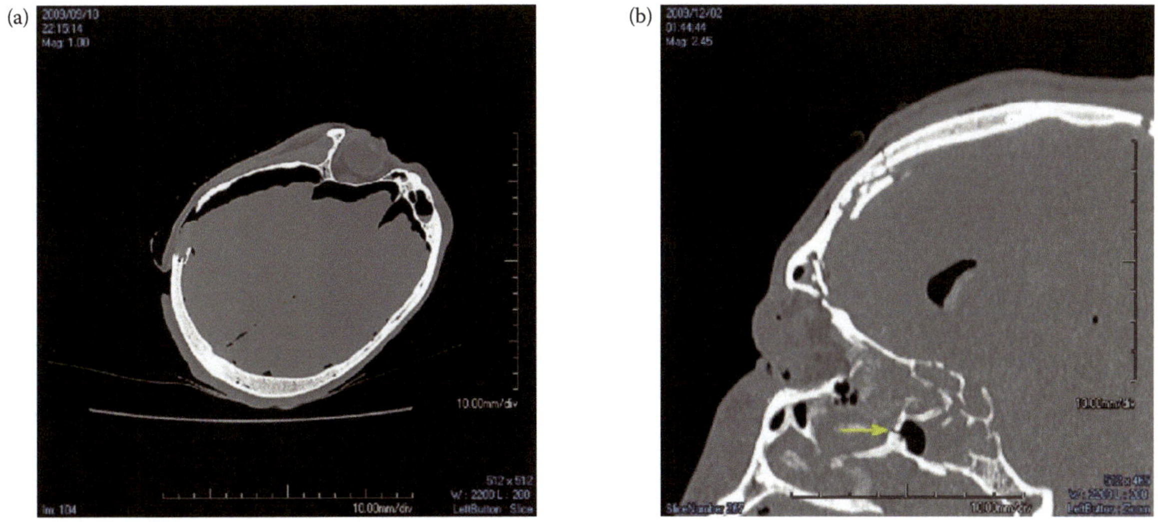

Figure 5.20 (a) Axial CT image showing a gross fracture to the right temporal region with pneumocephalus. Pneumocephalus is illustrated by black (air) under the skull and overlying the intracranial contents. (b) Sagittal CT image showing a fractured base of skull associated with pneumocephalus.

Practical Guidelines for Forensic Pathologists Interpreting CT Scans of the Head

- Localized soft tissue swelling may suggest the site of application of injury to the head.
- Intracranial air suggests the presence of either a penetrating injury or a basal skull fracture communicating with a sinus. One must exclude decomposition/putrefaction as the cause of gas.
- The presence of blood within the sphenoid sinus suggests the presence of an adjacent fracture (Figure 5.21a,b).
- The common hinge-type base of skull fracture is best visualized by using axial and sagittal views (Figure 5.22a,b).
- A fracture detected in one plane should be confirmed using another view.
- Occipital condyle fractures can be seen using axial and coronal views (Figure 5.23a,b).

Case Study

A 27-year-old man was riding a motor scooter on a major metropolitan road at approximately 70 km/h when a motor vehicle turned in front of him. The deceased struck the front panel of the car and was thrown from the scooter to the roadway. He died at the scene.

The deceased was transported to the Victorian Institute of Forensic Medicine (VIFM) for medicolegal

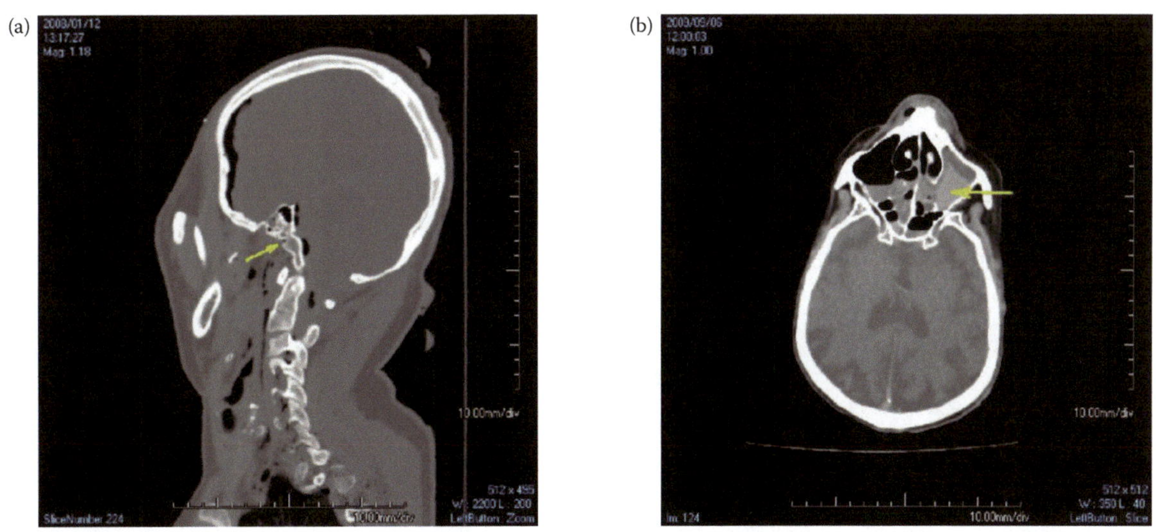

Figure 5.21 (a) Sagittal CT of the head showing a fracture involving the sphenoid sinus. There is an associated pneumocephalus and blood within the sinus. (b) Axial CT image showing fluid in multiple sinuses. There is separation of the fluid into a hematocrit within the left maxillary sinus.

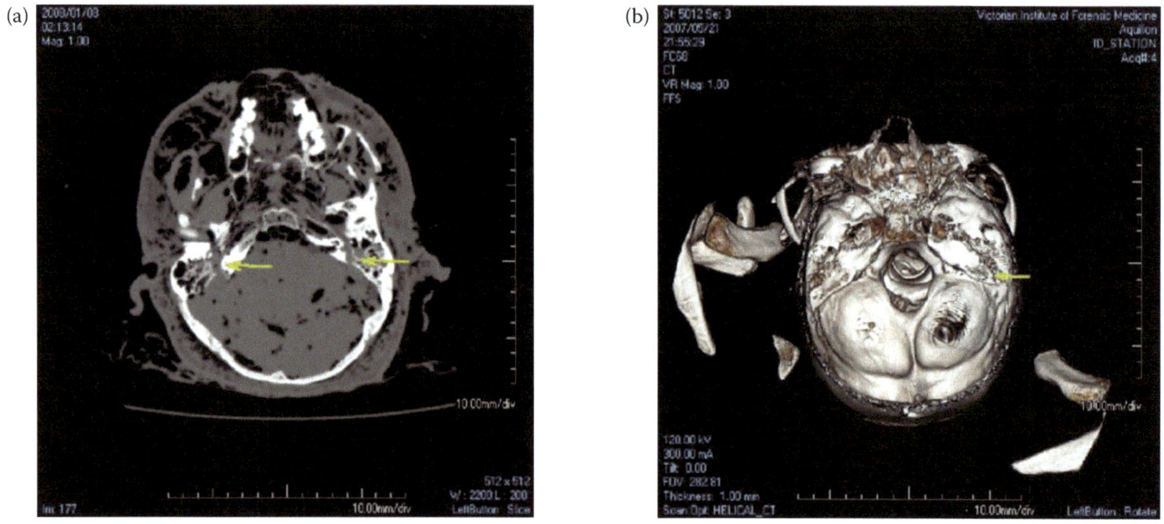

Figure 5.22 (a) Axial CT image showing typical symmetrical fractures involving the middle cranial fossa. (b) Three-dimensional reconstruction looking down to the base of skull in a victim of multiple trauma. The fracture extends across the anterior aspect of the middle cranial fossa in this case.

examination. The senior next of kin lodged a formal objection to autopsy. The deceased had been wearing a helmet during the incident. The helmet showed scuff marks to the left posterior aspect. There was no paint from the motor vehicle seen on the helmet.

The external examination of the deceased showed abrasions over bony prominences of the upper and lower limbs. There was no external evidence of head injury. The postmortem CT scan showed a fractured base of skull (Figure 5.24). There was no evidence of intracranial hemorrhage.

The coroner was informed that there was objective evidence of significant blunt force trauma to the head resulting in a fracture to the base of the skull. The coroner was informed that the base of skull fracture, in these circumstances, reflected a fatal injury to the brain parenchyma. The coroner ordered that no further examination was required and the body was released for burial.

Pediatric CT of the Skull

Mimics of skull fractures include anomalous sutures. Pediatric radiologists are unlikely to misdiagnose an anomalous suture as a fracture; however, a pathologist may well misinterpret such changes on the CT images. A recent case report described an anomalous parietal suture that was misdiagnosed as a fracture in a case of a child who had drowned. The correct diagnosis was made by postmortem histological examination [25].

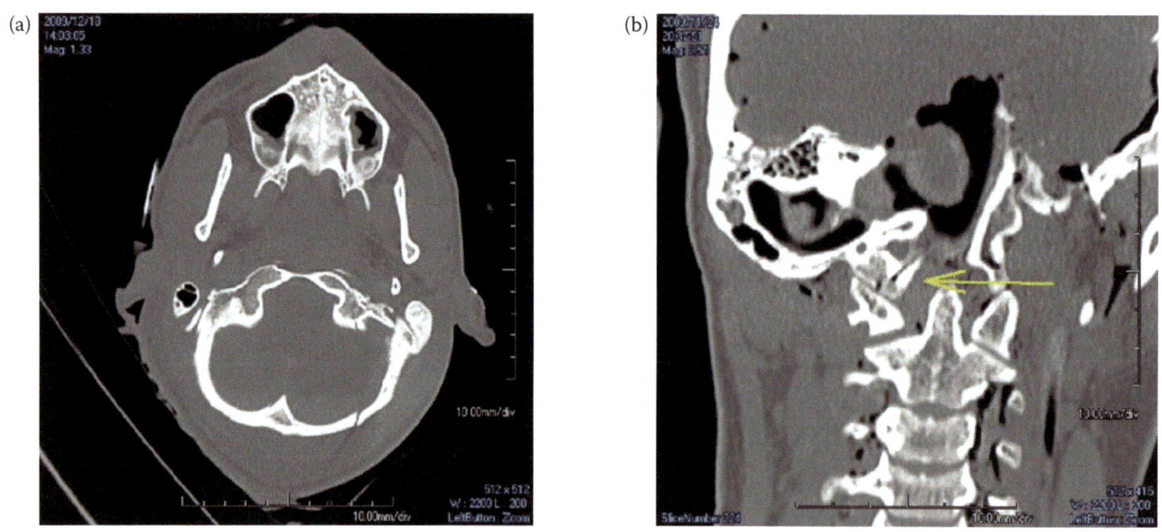

Figure 5.23 (a) Axial CT showing a fracture to the left occipital condyle. There is a fracture to the left aspect of the occiput suggesting an impact to this site. (b) Coronal CT showing a right occipital fracture.

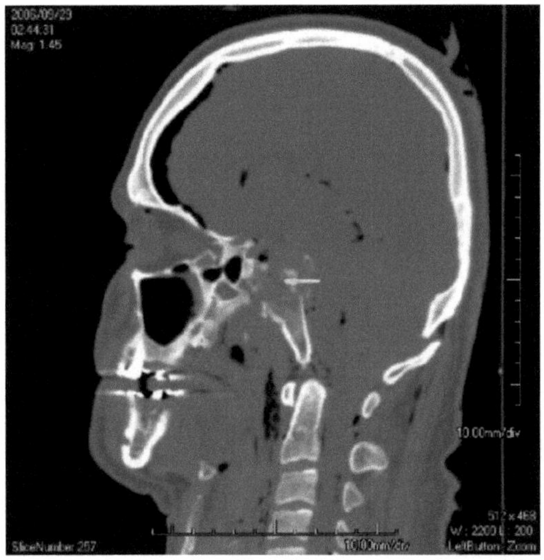

Figure 5.24 Sagittal CT of the head showing a fracture to the base of the skull with pneumocephalus.

Pediatric Aspects of Skull Fractures

Head injury is the most common traumatic cause of death in babies and infants. A retrospective review of pediatric craniofacial trauma in Switzerland showed that the most common causes of injury were falls in 64% of cases, followed by motor vehicle incidents in 22% of cases, and sports-related injury in 9% of cases [26]. One-third of the patients suffered concomitant injuries, mostly cerebral contusions.

Between 15% and 25% of skull fractures in pediatric patients who are admitted to hospital are depressed fractures [27]. Of the 530 patients in the study, a fall was the most common cause of the fracture. Two-thirds of the depressed fractures were compound fractures.

The pediatric skull responds to the application of blunt force differently than the adult skull. In adults the bone and sutures have similar properties, and adult calvaria will deform relatively slightly before fracture occurs. On the other hand, pediatric bone is 35 times stiffer than sutures, and deforms 30 times more before failure. Pediatric bone will deform 243 times more than adult bone, hence the skull of an infant may undergo marked deformation before a fracture occurs. In most of these cases there will be an associated bruise indicating the site of the application of blunt force.

In the extensive review paper Kemp and colleagues stated, "An infant or toddler with a skull fracture has a 1 in 3 chance of being abused" [28]. The most common site of fracture in both abused and accidentally injured pediatric cases is the parietal region. The majority of these fractures are simple linear fractures.

Characteristics of skull fractures that have been described as being features seen in abuse include depressed fractures, complex and multiple fractures, diastatic fractures of at least 3 mm in width, fractures that cross sutures, and bilateral fractures [29].

A review of the radiographic characteristics of skull fractures in cases of abuse compared to accidental injury was published in 1987. The study included 39 cases of documented abused infants and 95 cases of accidental head injury in infants under two years of age [30]. The authors stated that there were no significant differences between the effects of abuse and accidental injury with regard to (1) nonparietal fracture, (2) depressed fracture, (3) diastatic fractures of at least 3 mm, and (4) complex fractures. Three features were identified that were described as more frequent in cases of abuse when compared to accidental injury. These characteristics were (1) multiple fractures, (2) bilateral fractures, and (3) fractures that cross sutures.

A later review by Kemp and colleagues [28] suggested that not all of these features may be entirely reliable discriminators. Their conclusion was that, other than the possible exception of the three characteristics identified in the aforementioned study, no clear difference had been demonstrated for the other types of complex skull fracture.

It should be noted that skeletal dysplasias, such as osteogenesis imperfecta, may present with multiple fractures including skull fracture. On radiological examination, osteogenesis imperfecta shows thin cortices, decreased ossification at the base of the skull, and multiple intersutural Wormian bones along the lambdoid suture [31].

Skull fractures associated with birth trauma are well described. Although the majority of these fractures occur in instrument-assisted deliveries, in rare cases babies delivered by spontaneous, uncomplicated normal vaginal delivery have been reported to have sustained a linear skull fracture [32].

Clearly in cases of skull fracture in a pediatric death a formal expert radiological opinion is required.

Facial Fractures

Introduction

A recent retrospective study on 437 patients with 929 facial fractures showed that the most common cause of facial fracture was assault (36%), followed by motor vehicle trauma (32%), falls (18%), then sports and occupational injuries [33]. The most common fracture site was to the nasal bone. An earlier study on 788 patients collected through 1980 to 1984 showed the zygoma was the most commonly fractured facial bone (23.6%) followed by the orbital floor (21.4%), then the maxilla, mandible, and nasal bone [34]. The most frequent cause of the injury was assault (70.1%) followed by motor vehicle trauma (13.5%) and falls (9.3%).

A 10-year review of over 9500 patients with over 20,000 faciomaxillary injuries admitted to a craniomaxillofacial trauma department showed midfacial fractures accounted for 71.5% of cases, mandibular fractures for 24.3%, and supraorbital and frontobasal fractures for 4.2% of cases respectively [35].

Frontal sinus fractures account for approximately 15% of maxillofacial fractures. As the frontal bone is considered to be a robust bone that requires considerable force to cause a fracture, the presence of a frontal sinus fracture is indicative of the application of significant force to the head. The incidence of faciomaxillary injury is much lower in the pediatric population [36].

Anatomy

The face is formed from the frontal bone, the paired zygomas, lacrimal bones, and nasal bones, portions of the ethmoid bone, the paired inferior nasal conchae, maxillae and palatine bones, the vomer within the nasal cavity, and the mandible.

The bones of the face may be viewed as comprising a series of struts in axial, sagittal, and coronal planes. Between the struts are sinuses, which are surrounded by a thin layer of bone. In the axial plane there are three major bony struts comprised of the orbital roof (cribriform plate and ethmoidalis), the middle horizontal strut consisting of the orbital floor and zygomatic arch, and the inferior strut comprising the hard palate.

The sagittal struts of the face comprise the nasal septum and two parasagittal struts formed from the medial walls of the maxillary sinus and orbit. The lateral facial struts consist of the lateral aspect of the maxillary alveolar ridge and lateral wall of the maxillary sinus and orbit.

Within the coronal plane there are two bony struts. The anterior strut is the frontal bone, zygoma and nasofrontal complex, the anterior wall of the maxillary sinus, and the anterior aspect of the alveolar ridge. Posteriorly the coronal strut is comprised of the posterior wall of the maxillary sinus and the medial and lateral pterygoid plates [37].

There are certain fracture patterns that result from blunt force trauma to the face. A break in one of the buttresses can lead to a weakness in the remainder of the "lattice work," resulting in its collapse [38]. The understanding of these patterns allows the radiologist and the faciomaxillary surgeon to analyze the CT images in a more targeted approach. The common patterns of facial fracture include [38]

- Zygomaxillary complex (ZMC) or "tripod" fracture
- Naso-orbito-ethmoid (NOE) complex fracture
- LeFort fracture

Pediatric Faciomaxillary Fractures

Facial fractures in pediatric patients account for up to 15% of all faciomaxillary injuries [39]. The common causes of injury include falls from bicycles, simple falls, motor vehicle incidents, and assaults.

Nasal fractures are the most common faciomaxillary fracture in the pediatric population. Orbital fractures have been reported to occur in 10% to 30% of cases. Mandibular fractures occur in about 30% of cases and are the most common fractures leading to hospitalization.

Forensic Aspects of Facial Fracture

Facial impacts are commonly seen in a number of circumstances. Uncomplicated falls secondary to an episode of collapse will frequently lead to cutaneous abrasions, bruises, and lacerations to bony prominences such as the eyebrow, cheek, nose, and chin. In the absence of an intermediate object struck during the fall, these injuries should be in the same plane. Not infrequently such simple falls will result in a fractured nose.

It is self-evident that the face is a prime target in cases of assault. The trauma sustained by a victim of an assault can vary from one punch to the face to a sustained assault from a weapon with multiple blows in different planes. The presence of a facial fracture by postmortem dissection or postmortem CT scanning provides objective evidence of the application of significant force to the face. The difficulty arises in trying to apportion a degree of force that is objective, reproducible, and understandable to both colleagues and laypersons.

Experimental biomechanical work has measured fracture tolerances of the various facial bones. This research was designed to assist engineers to design motor vehicles to make them less likely to cause facial injury in a collision. A review of these biomechanical studies was carried out by Hampson in the early 1990s [40]. It was found that the force tolerance of the facial bones could be summarized as follows:

Nose	342 to 450 N
Zygoma	489 to 2401 N
Mandible	685 to 1779 N
Maxilla	668 to 1801 N
Zygomatic arch	890 to 1779 N
Frontal bone	1000 to 6494 N

It is very difficult in the real world to quantify these degrees of force. Although it is probably not a purely scientific approach, one could use such a table to give at least some idea of the forces involved in inflicting a particular fracture, given that most laypersons have some notion of the amount of force to cause a fractured nose. The CT scans may then provide objective information to the investigating police officers and the courts in regard to the degree of force used in the incident.

Facial fractures are a marker of direct force applied to the head and neck. The presence of upper midface injuries have been associated with lower cervical fractures, whereas mandibular fractures are more often associated with upper cervical fractures [41].

CT Diagnosis of Facial Fracture

CT is the principle imaging modality for the clinical evaluation and diagnosis of facial fractures. It is progressively replacing specialized traditional radiographs such as the panoramic radiograph, Waters' view, and axial films. CT removes the issue of superimposition, which is a problem when reading conventional radiographs. Thin collimation of slices (0.75–1 mm) is required for proper analysis of the face as well as the base of the skull.

Axial and coronal multiplanar reconstructions are used in both high resolution bone windows and soft tissue settings, whereas sagittal reconstructions are useful in the examination of central midface structures and the mandibular condyles [42].

Probably more so than in other regions of the body, facial CT has major advantages for the forensic pathologist assessing radiology images. Overlapping lines are seen in normal conventional radiographs of the facial bones, and the special views used are quite foreign to the radiological nonexpert and make any such assessment prone to error. Multidetector computed tomography (MDCT) with reformations and three-dimensional reconstructions allow the pathologist a more intuitive recognition of the anatomy, as opposed to the radiologic anatomy (Figure 5.25).

It should be noted that in just less than 10% of clinical patients with facial fractures there are concomitant cervical spine injuries [43]. This percentage is likely to be higher in the forensic setting where there are generally more severe injuries. The presence of a facial fracture should stimulate an examination of the cervical spine for an occult fracture or other injury.

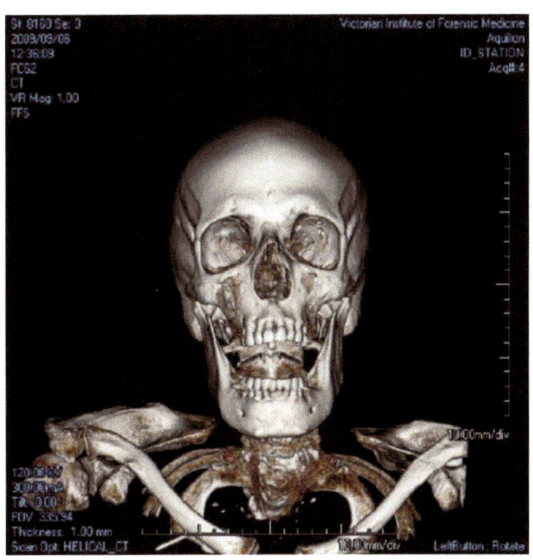

Figure 5.25 Three-dimensional reconstruction of the head. The contours of the facial bones can be sequentially examined, and especially so if one can compare a possible injury to the normal, uninjured side.

Facial CT

Soft Tissue Signs Soft tissue signs are important in recognizing facial trauma and fractures. Valuable soft tissue changes are

Soft tissue swelling—Associated soft tissue swelling and hematoma can assist in identifying the site of primary impact and associated fracture on the CT images.

Orbital emphysema—Air within the orbit is seen as a dark (radiolucent) area within the confines of the orbit. The presence of air within the orbit indicates a breakdown between the orbit and an air-containing space. As previously indicated one must endeavor to exclude the possibility of putrefaction gas.

Opacified maxillary sinus or ethmoid air cells—Opacification of a space that usually contains air in the setting of acute blunt force trauma suggests the presence of blood. The blood is usually associated with an air–fluid level. Blood has Hounsfield units of approximately 40. Blood within a sinus or air cell is usually due to a fracture.

The absence of paranasal sinus hemorrhage has been termed the "clear sinus" sign. The clear sinus sign has been used as an adjunct to exclude the presence of a fracture contiguous with a sinus wall. A sagittal view is useful for confirmation of the fracture in these circumstances.

One must keep in mind that opacification of a sinus may reflect the presence of chronic sinusitis, which is relatively common in many communities.

Bony Contours In the clinical setting one may take a targeted approach to interpret radiological images with respect to the known mechanism of the injury. For example, a case of an assault involving a blow to the side of the face would stimulate a specific search for orbital, zygomaticomaxillary complex, or middle third of face fractures.

The presence of an injury to one side of the deceased's face or the presence of ipsilateral soft tissue swelling allows the pathologist to determine the likely injured side of the face. The uninjured contralateral side may then be used as a control to sequentially examine the CT images for any irregularity in the contours of the bones. Axial CT images are useful in identifying fractures of the zygomatic arch and maxillary sinus.

Three-dimensional reconstructions are often used clinically by faciomaxillary surgeons for planning of surgical repair of facial fractures. These images are also familiar and intuitive to pathologists and are useful in presenting fractures to the courts. As an initial screen of the CT images looking for a facial fracture, the three-dimensional reconstruction images are very useful for the forensic pathologist to examine prior to conducting an examination of the deceased's body.

Fractures of the Orbit

Anatomy

The orbit is a four-sided pyramid. The base is formed by the orbital rim. The orbital rim may be divided into superior, inferior, medial, and lateral margins. The superior margin is formed by the frontal bone. The inferior margin is formed by the maxilla medially and the zygoma laterally. The medial margin is formed by the frontal process of the maxilla, and the lateral rim is formed by the zygoma.

The orbital roof is composed of the frontal bone with about 1 cm toward the apex of the pyramid formed by the lesser wing of the sphenoid. The orbital floor is composed of the orbital plate of the maxilla, with a small proportion provided posteriorly by the orbital plate of the palatine bone. The medial wall is composed primarily by the frontal process of the maxilla anteriorly, with segments formed by the lacrimal and ethmoidal bone, and the lesser wing of the sphenoid. The lateral wall is comprised by the greater wing of the sphenoid with a smaller portion anteriorly by the zygoma (Figure 5.26).

Etiology

The most common cause of injury to the orbit is from a direct blow. The common causes of blunt force orbital trauma are assault, motor vehicle incidents, and sports injuries. The "blowout" fracture of the orbit was coined by Converse and Smith [44] in 1957 and describes an orbital wall fracture with an intact orbital rim.

The introduction of seat belts has markedly reduced the incidence of eye injury in front seat occupants of motor vehicles involved in collisions. There is a relatively small number of eye injuries caused directly from airbag deployment.

Mechanism

The weakest part of the orbit is the floor. The most common area of the orbital floor to be fractured is the posteromedial region [45]. The fracture is believed to occur secondary to hydraulic pressure caused by increased intraorbital pressure secondary to direct impact, although other workers think backward displacement of the orbital rim leads to buckling and comminution of the thin-walled orbit [46,47]. A single case report described a blowout fracture of the orbit secondary due to vigorous nose blowing [48].

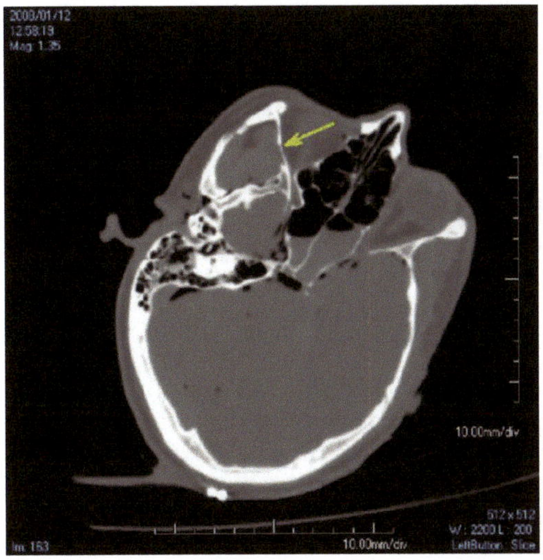

Figure 5.26 Axial CT image of the head showing blood within sphenoid sinuses. There is a probable undisplaced fracture of the right lateral orbital wall (zygoma). The fracture would need to be confirmed using another view.

CT Diagnosis of Orbital Fracture

Following severe trauma to the face there may be considerable swelling and hemorrhage around the eye making an adequate examination of the eye extremely difficult. This issue is a frequent problem in clinical cases and is not uncommonly an issue at postmortem examination even though one is able to use a greater degree of vigor in the examination of the eyes in this situation.

In clinical practice CT is regarded as the best imaging modality to diagnose orbital fractures [49]. Postmortem CT of the orbit has the potential to provide valuable information in some cases. It would seem reasonable to suggest that, without a specific assessment of the CT images in a homicide case where death was caused by blunt head injury, an orbital fracture could easily go undiagnosed. The identification of the injury may indicate an additional blow was struck to the deceased.

In the CT examination of the orbits:

- An axial view is often ideal to illustrate the loss of a regular contour to the orbit (Figure 5.27).
- An orbital blowout fracture can be suggested by the presence of orbital emphysema (intraorbital air) on CT imaging. The air gains access to the orbit via one of the contiguous air-filled sinuses.
- The existence of maxillary sinus opacification in the setting of periorbital soft tissue swelling may reflect the presence of a fractured orbital floor.

A checklist of features to assess a clinical orbital CT scan include examination of the orbital walls for irregularity or discontinuity; identify the position of the lens, which can be detached and displaced following blunt force trauma; identify the presence of a ruptured globe, which may be heralded by an alteration in normal globe contour or discontinuity.

The "flat tire" sign in orbital CT refers to an obvious "deflation" of the globe, which is analogous to a flat tire.

Fractures of the Zygoma

Anatomy

The zygoma is a somewhat rectangular-shaped bone that forms the prominence of the cheek. The zygoma forms the anterior aspect of the zygomatic arch through its temporal process. The zygoma comprises the lateral rim and lateral portion of the inferior rim of the orbit, and the lateral wall of the orbit. It has articulations with the frontal bone, the maxilla, and the sphenoidal and temporal bones.

Etiology

The zygoma forms the prominence of the cheek. As such the zygoma is commonly fractured in cases of assault. Up to 80% of cases of fractures of the zygoma occur in young males, with assault being the cause in 40% of cases. Sports-related injuries and injury from motor vehicle incidents lead to smaller numbers of cases. Alcohol is detected in about one-third of those patients who suffer the injury. In some regions motor vehicle incidents are the most common cause of fractured zygoma [50].

Mechanism

Fractured zygomas may be divided into three categories [51]. Category A refers to isolated fractures of one of the three

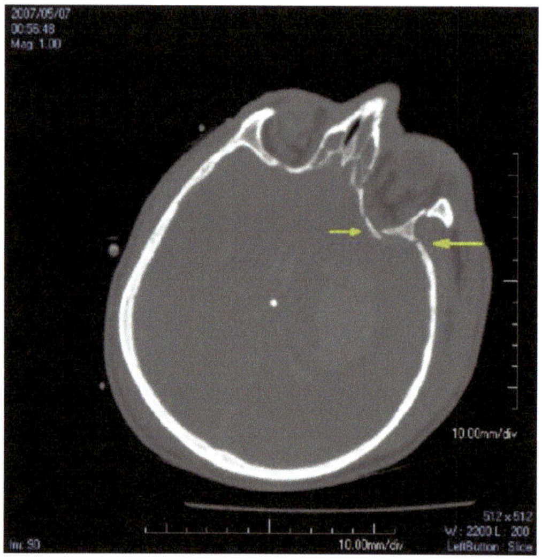

Figure 5.27 Axial CT showing a "blowout" fracture secondary to direct trauma to the orbital rim. There are multiple fractures evident on the axial view with some displacement of the posterior fracture.

extensions or processes of the zygoma. Category B refers to fractures where all three processes are involved (tripod fracture), and category C refers to comminuted fractures.

The majority of zygomatic fractures result from the application of direct blunt force trauma to the zygoma. Some cases of zygomatic fracture can occur from indirect forces as may occur if a blow is struck to the mandible. The force can then be transmitted through the head of the mandible to the temporomandibular joint and to the zygoma (Figure 5.28).

CT Diagnosis of Zygoma Fractures

Zygomatic fractures are best diagnosed on CT imaging using axial views (Figure 5.29) [52]. The contour of the uninvolved and the injured arches are compared with particular regard to any depression or outward bending of the injured side. Of course, one must bear in mind that both sides may have suffered fractures with similar depression to the arches.

Key features for the forensic pathologist in recognizing a ZMC (tripod) fracture are

- Zygomatic arch fracture (compare to contralateral side)
- Fracture to the lateral wall of the maxillary sinus
- Fracture to the lateral orbital rim
- Fracture to the inferior orbital rim and orbital floor

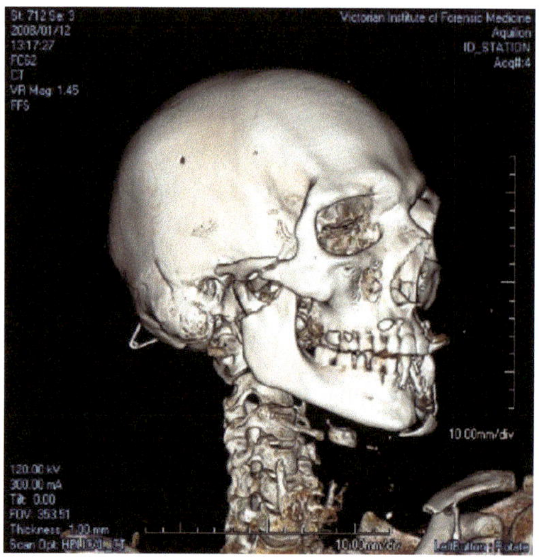

Figure 5.28 Three-dimensional reconstruction showing a fracture to the right zygoma. The deceased had suffered a significant impact to the point of the chin with mandibular fractures to the region of the mental protuberance and the right condylar neck.

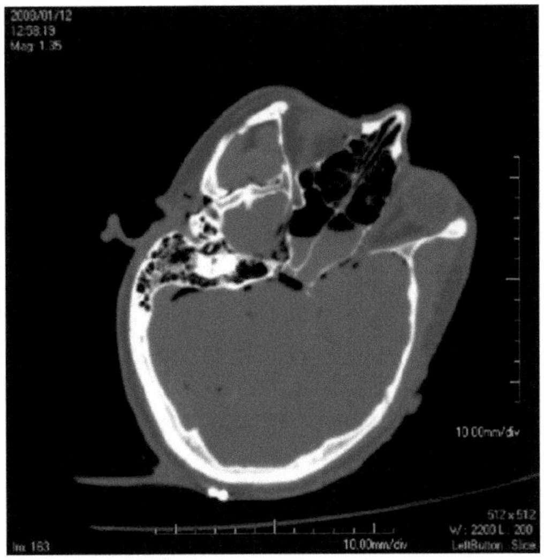

Figure 5.29 Axial CT image showing a fracture to the right zygoma.

Maxillary and Nasal Fractures

Anatomy

The structure and three-dimensional anatomical relationships of the maxilla are complex. The two maxillae fuse in the midline to form the middle third of the face. The maxilla is, to some extent, pyramidal in shape. It contains the large maxillary sinus and has a number of surfaces, projections, and articulations. The maxillae form considerable portions of the floor of the nose and roof of the mouth. The orbital surface contributes to the inferior orbital rim and provides the majority of the floor of the orbit.

The paired nasal bones form the roof of the nasal cavity. The quadrangular-shaped bones articulate superiorly with the frontal bone and inferolaterally with the frontal process of the maxilla.

Within the nasal cavity are the vomer, parts of the ethmoid, inferior nasal conchae, and palatine bones. The vomer is a thin plate of bone that forms the posterior, inferior aspect of the nasal septum. The anterior part of the septum is formed from cartilage. The vomer articulates superiorly with a perpendicular plate that extends downward from the ethmoid. The inferior border articulates with the maxillae and palatine bones.

The palatine bones are situated in the posterior aspect of the nasal cavity. This three-dimensionally complex bone contributes to the walls of the nasal cavity, the mouth, and the floor of the orbit. It has a horizontal part; a vertical part; and pyramidal, orbital, and sphenoidal processes.

The ethmoid is a cuboidal, somewhat spongy bone that has an inferior thin projection called the perpendicular plate and forms part of the nasal septum. It has two lateral masses, which each form the superior lateral aspects of the nasal cavity. The lateral masses provide the paired superior and middle nasal concha.

The inferior nasal concha are paired, scroll-like laminae of spongy bone situated in the lateral wall of the nasal cavity and articulate with the ethmoid, maxilla, lacrimal bone, and palatine bone.

Etiology

The nasal bone is the most commonly fractured midfacial bone [53]. The most common cause of the injury is a direct blow to the face during a sports-related injury or an assault. In forensic practice the fracture is often seen in association with other facial fractures. Multiple fractures are commonly seen in cases of motor vehicle incidents and falls.

An isolated fracture of a nasal bone is rarely, of itself, a major forensic issue. A fracture to the nose is not uncommonly seen in individuals who have suffered a sudden incapacitating natural event leading to death. As such, the presence of the nasal fracture may provide objective support for the diagnosis of a sudden cardiac arrhythmia leading to unconscious collapse and death.

In rare cases transverse fractures of the hard palate can be associated with palatine artery laceration resulting in airway occlusion from anterior cervical hematoma [54].

Fractures to the maxilla are frequently caused by direct blows to the front or sides of the face in blunt force trauma during an assault. Significant falls and direct blunt trauma during a motor vehicle collision are other common causes of the injury. Less commonly the fracture can result from transmitted forces from an impact to the mandible, causing forceful occlusion of the teeth.

Mechanism

In 1901 LeFort classified maxillary fractures from human cadavers. LeFort classified the middle third of face fractures into three basic types. According to Galloway [55], a LeFort I fracture usually occurs as a result of blunt force trauma to the alveolar process of the maxilla on either side of the face. A LeFort II fracture occurs from more central trauma and results in a fracture extending through the maxilla, into the orbits and through the interorbital region. A LeFort III extends behind the orbits and through the bridge of the nose.

CT Diagnosis of Nasomaxillary Fractures

In instances of relatively low impact force to the face, a fracture is often limited to the nasal bone (Figure 5.30a,b). Simple nasal fractures may be associated with blood within the frontal sinus (Figure 5.31). Significant blunt force trauma to the nose may be associated with injury to the ethmoid sinuses [56].

- The forensic diagnosis of a nasal bone fracture is not necessarily made solely on the CT images. The diagnosis of a fracture is based on an irregularity or defect in the contour of a bone in association with the findings on external examination.
- One must exclude the possibility of a natural orifice within the bone (Figure 5.32).
- An isolated irregularity of a nasal bone may well reflect an old injury.
- Axial, coronal, and sagittal images are ideal for the expert radiologist to visualize the maxilla (Figure 5.33).
- Fractures of the maxilla may be very subtle and require an expert radiology opinion (Figure 5.34a,b).
- For forensic pathologists, the three-dimensional reconstruction images are very useful in screening for fractures of the maxilla (Figure 5.35a,b).
- A fracture of the pterygoid process almost always indicates that a fracture in at least one of the LeFort planes is present [57].
  - A LeFort I fracture involves the anterolateral margin of the nasal fossa. This may be seen on coronal, sagittal, or three-dimensional CT images (Figure 5.36).
  - A LeFort II fracture involves the inferior orbital rim. This fracture is best seen on coronal, sagittal, or three-dimensional CT images.
- The LeFort III fracture involves the zygomatic arch. This is best seen on axial or three-dimensional CT images [57].

Mandibular Fractures

Anatomy

The mandible is the largest bone of the face. The mandible consists of paired, roughly horizontal segments (body) that both extend posteriorly at a near right angle to the rami. Each ramus has two projections at its superior border. The anterior, somewhat triangular extension termed the coronoid process provides points of insertion for the temporalis and masseter muscles. Posterior to the coronoid process is the condyloid process. The condyloid process is composed of a neck portion that broadens to the head, which articulates with the mandibular (glenoid) fossa of the temporal bone.

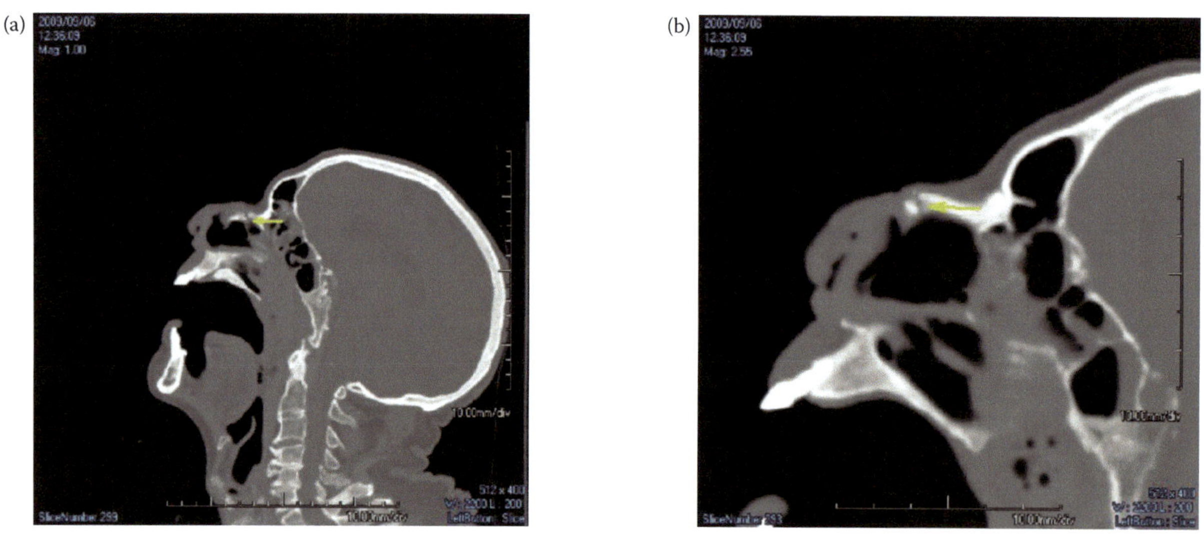

Figure 5.30 (a) Sagittal CT image of a deceased individual who had collapsed face forward to the ground resulting in an abrasion to the nose. (b) Close-up CT image showing irregularity to the nasal bones consistent with a fracture.

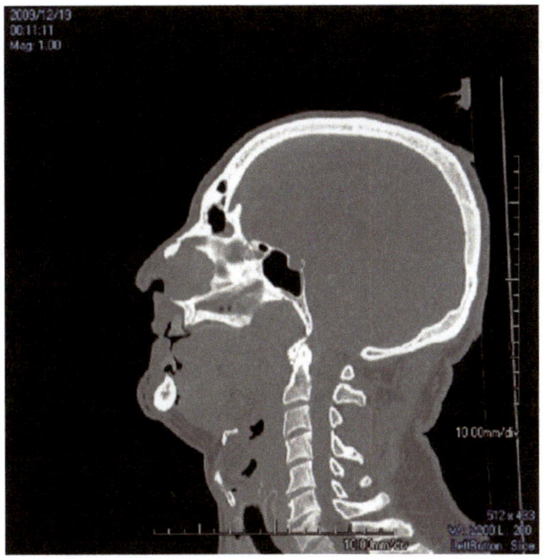

Figure 5.31 Sagittal CT image showing an irregularity to the nasal bone associated with fluid (blood) within the frontal sinus.

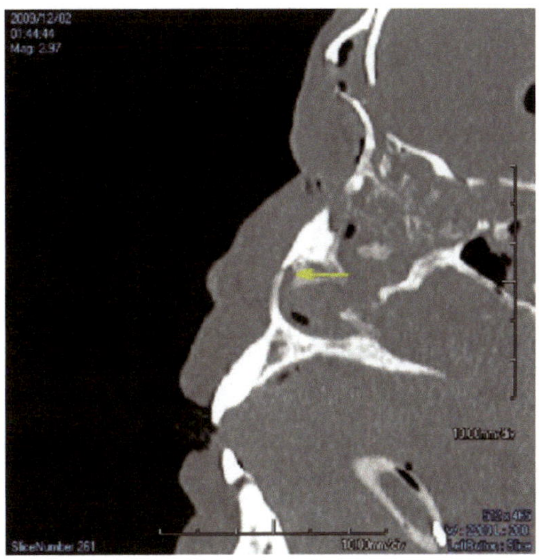

Figure 5.32 Sagittal CT showing a well-defined lucency in the nasal bone. This finding, in isolation, can be seen with a normal blood vessel.

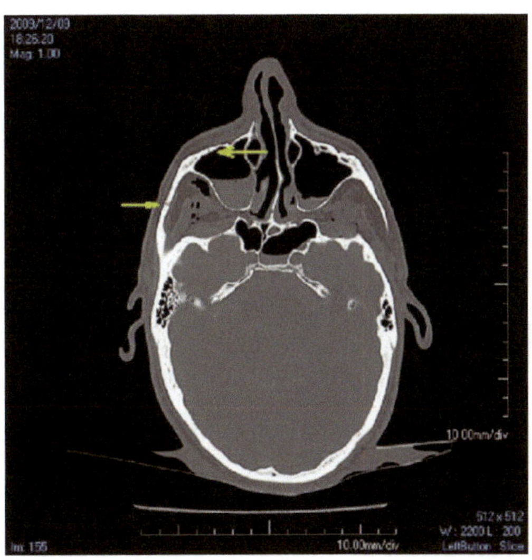

Figure 5.33 Axial CT image of trauma victim with fractures to the right maxilla and zygoma.

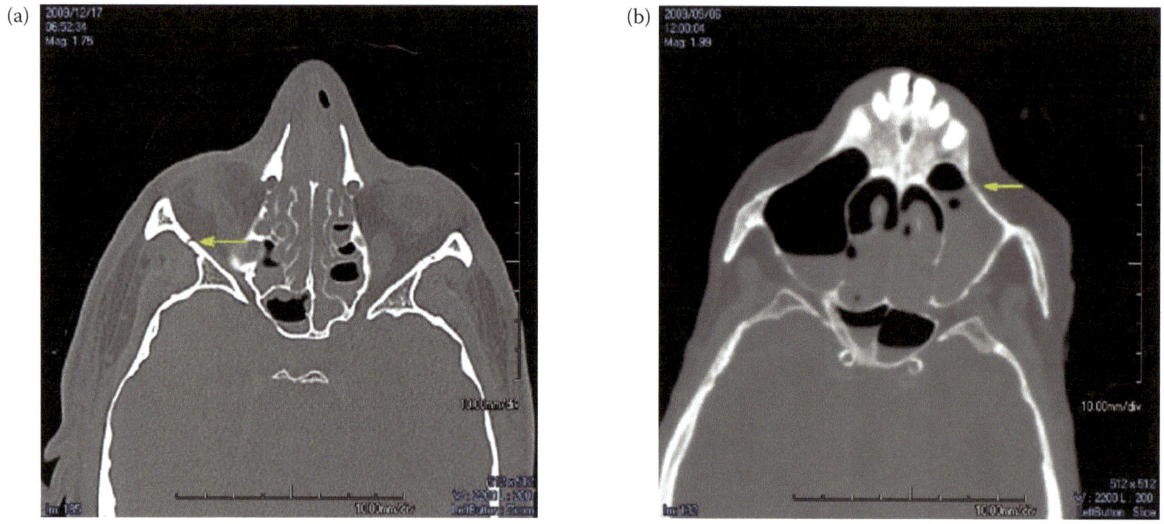

Figure 5.34 (a) Axial CT showing a subtle fracture of the right maxilla. (b) Axial CT showing a subtle fracture of the left maxilla.

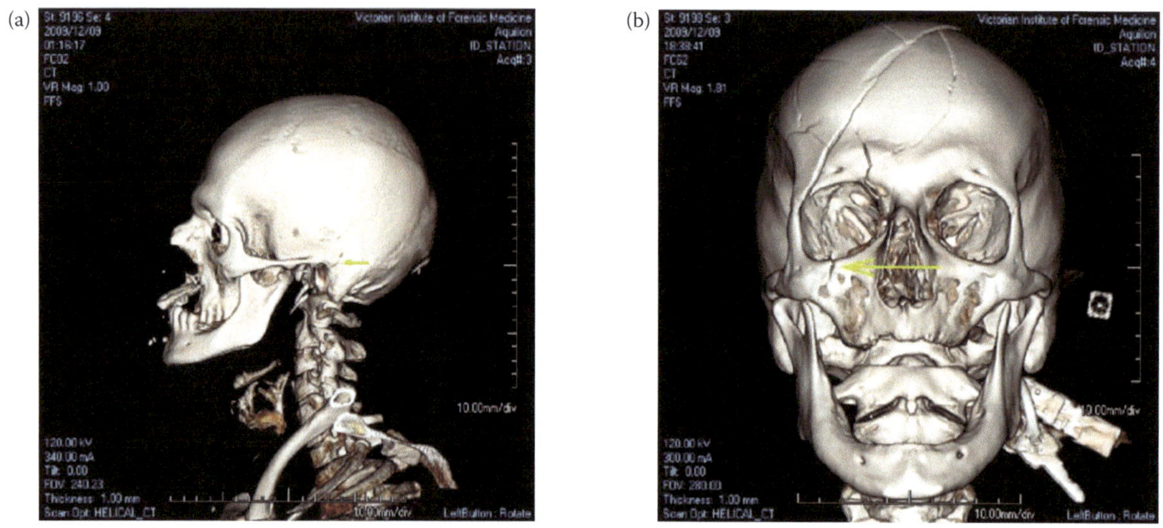

Figure 5.35 (a) Three-dimensional reconstruction showing fracture to the mandible from front-on head trauma. There is an associated base of skull fracture. (b) Three-dimensional reconstruction showing a fracture to the right maxilla and to the cranial vault.

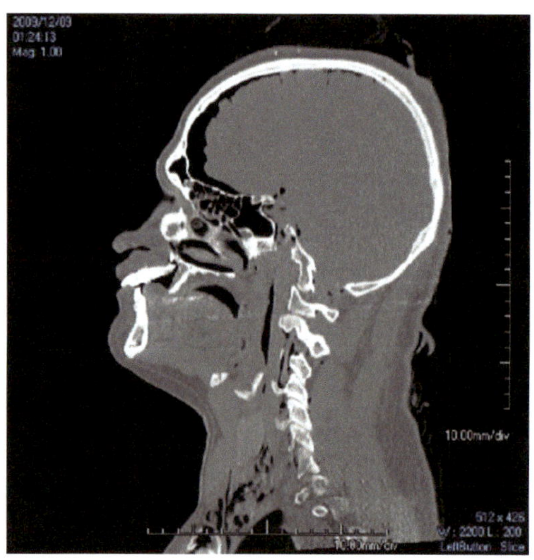

Figure 5.36 Sagittal CT image of LeFort I fracture.

Etiology

Common causes of mandibular fractures include assault, trauma sustained in motor vehicle incidents, falls, sporting injury, and workplace accidents. A review of over 1000 cases of mandibular fracture in the 1980s showed that the major cause of mandibular fractures were from assaults (37.5%), transportation incidents (31.5%), falls (7.1%), sporting injuries (5.4%), work-related incidents (3%), and other causes (5.5%) [65]. The relative incidence of mandibular fractures from various causes will vary principally with the incidence of assault in the community in question.

Over the last three decades the introduction and use of seat belts and the development of airbags has markedly decreased the rate of mandibular fractures in motor vehicle incidents.

Although the majority of mandibular fractures occur in young males aged between 16 and 30 years, fractures of the mandible are not uncommon in the elderly. Fractures of the mandible in the elderly population result frequently from falls, a particular problem for the aging population. Motor vehicle incidents are the major cause of fracture in males over the age of 65, however, falls predominate in females. Loss of teeth leading to atrophy of the bone will predispose one to mandibular fracture [58].

A study on mandibular fracture patterns in Tasmania, Australia, showed fractures to the angle of the mandible were most common (32%), with condylar fractures occurring at a rate of 23.3%, whereas fractures of the body and parasymphysis occurred at rates of 17.7% and 15.6%, respectively. Symphyseal, alveolar, ramus, and coronoid fractures all occurred at rates of less than 4% [59]. Mandibular condyle fractures can be either intra- or extra-articular.

In cases of flail mandible the tongue can be posteriorly displaced leading to occlusion of the airway and is a possible cause of obscure death in circumstances of significant blunt force trauma to the face [54].

Mechanism

The somewhat horseshoe-shaped mandible is commonly fractured in more than one position following a single blow [60]. It had been traditionally thought that the closed-ring structure of the mandible almost invariably had to fracture at two points (Figure 5.37a,b). In fact, in a study population of patients presenting to an emergency department and undergoing conventional x-rays for mandibular fractures, only two-thirds were shown to have multiple sites of fracture [60]. A recent study on 102 patients using CT showed the incidence of unilateral mandibular fractures was 42% [61]. Of these fractures 58% were simple fractures, 26% were comminuted, and 16% had associated condylar subluxation.

It has been recognized for some time that different areas of the mandible are more commonly fractured when blunt force trauma is applied to a particular region [62]. A clinical study demonstrated that more than half of the 319 cases of mandibular fractures resulted from an impact to the chin. The most frequently fractured area of the mandible was the subcondylar region (36.3%). Interestingly the authors showed that all areas of the mandible could be fractured by an impact to the symphysis [62]. A laboratory study showed that the deformation sustained by the mandible from an impact to the symphysis varied with respect to fixation of the condyles [63].

Fracture Patterns in Mandibular Fractures

Fridrich et al. [64], in their extensive review of mandibular fractures in the 1980s, showed that fractures associated with assaults occurred most commonly at the angle (39.1%). Condylar, symphyseal, and alveolar fractures were less common than when they occurred in motor vehicle incidents.

In motor vehicle incidents the condylar region was most commonly fractured (29.8%), symphyseal fractures accounted for 25.9%, whereas angle and body fractures occurred with an incidence of 13.3% and 10.7%, respectively.

An experimental study used seven human mandibles that were struck to breaking point. The specimens were impacted to the frontal or lateral aspects of the bone [65]. The frontal impacts resulted in multiple fractures to the posterior mandible (condyle and collum) with a fracture threshold between 2.5 and 3.1 kN. Lateral impacts led to fractures near the impact zone with a fracture threshold between 0.6 and 0.8 kN.

The presence of mandibular third molars has been shown to decrease the risk of condylar fractures [66]. The presence of third molars increases the risk of angle fracture due to moderate force irrespective of the mechanism of the injury [67]. A moderate degree of force was defined as that which resulted in two fracture sites. In instances of three or more mandibular fractures there is no association of fracture site with third molars.

CT Diagnosis of Mandibular Fractures

- Three-dimensional reconstructions will show the majority of fractures allowing the pathologist to scan the head and neck on the initial inspection (Figure 5.38a,b).
- The body of the mandible is best viewed with axial images.

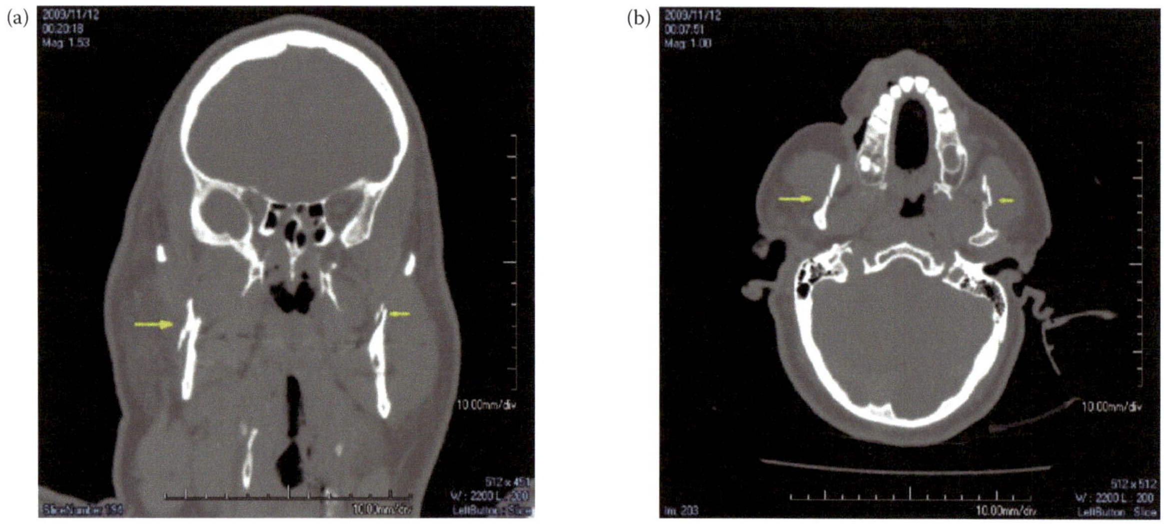

Figure 5.37 (a) Coronal CT image showing bilateral fractures of the mandibular rami. (b) Axial CT image showing bilateral fractures of the mandibular rami.

- The ramus and condyle are best seen with coronal views.
- In clinical practice condylar fractures are usually associated with medial displacement of the fracture due to the action of the masseter muscle (Figure 5.39). This may be seen in the postmortem setting due to the effects of rigor mortis.
- The classical orthopanoramic radiograph can be replaced by CT reconstruction along the alveolar ridge (Figure 5.40) [42].

Hyoid Bone

Introduction

The hyoid bone is a small but anatomically and forensically important bone in the neck. The postmortem CT is an excellent tool to visualize the hyoid bone (Figure 5.41). The hyoid may be fractured in cases of neck compression. Neck compression may occur in cases of homicide, suicide, and occasionally from accidents.

In all cases of deaths due to neck compression, a fundamental objective of the postmortem investigation is to document the presence of fractures to the hyoid bone and the thyroid cartilages. It is a relatively straightforward process in a conventional autopsy examination to identify and document hyoid fractures. With the increasing use of CT scanning in the investigation of nonsuspicious deaths in many institutions, the ability to confidently identify hyoid fractures using CT will probably become a routine part of the initial assessment of a case.

It has been reported, albeit in a relatively small number of cases, that postmortem imaging of laryngohyoid

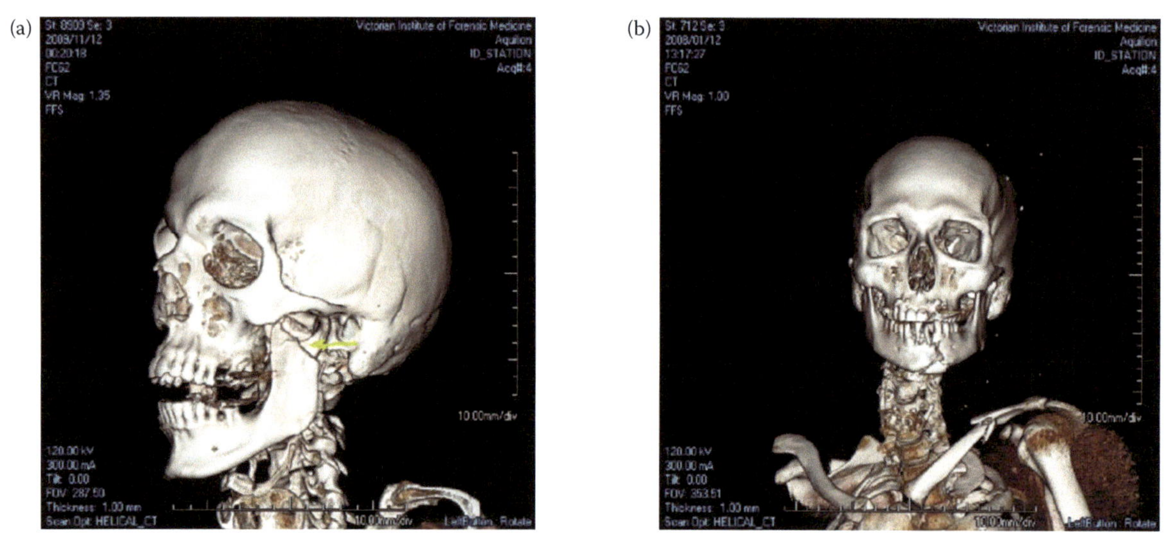

Figure 5.38 (a) Three-dimensional reconstruction showing a fractured mandible (coronoid and condylar processes). (b) Three-dimensional reconstruction showing a fracture to the left anterior mandible.

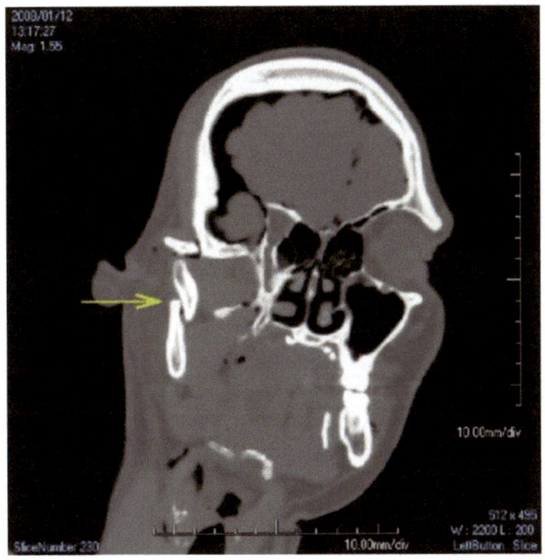

Figure 5.39 Fractured right mandible with medial displacement of the proximal fractured bone (presumably due to rigor).

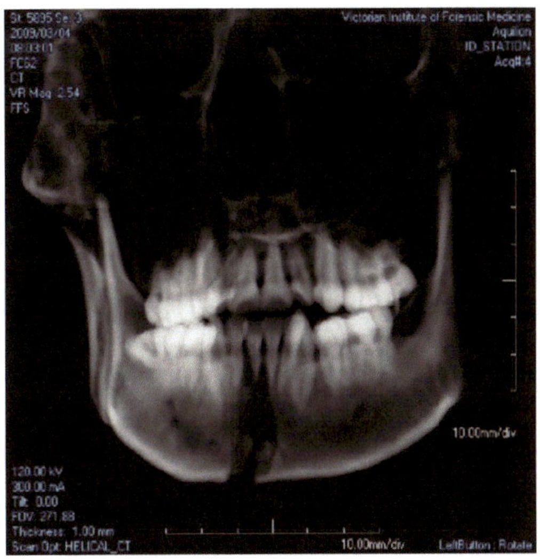

Figure 5.40 Orthopanoramic reconstruction from the CT data showing a fracture to the mandible.

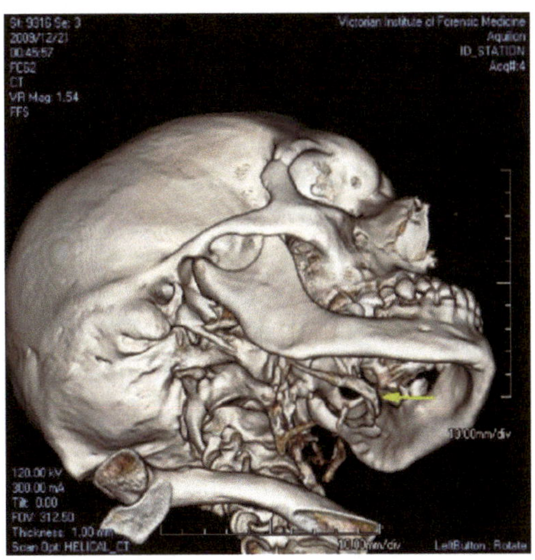

Figure 5.41 Three-dimensional reconstruction image rotated to show normal hyoid appearance.

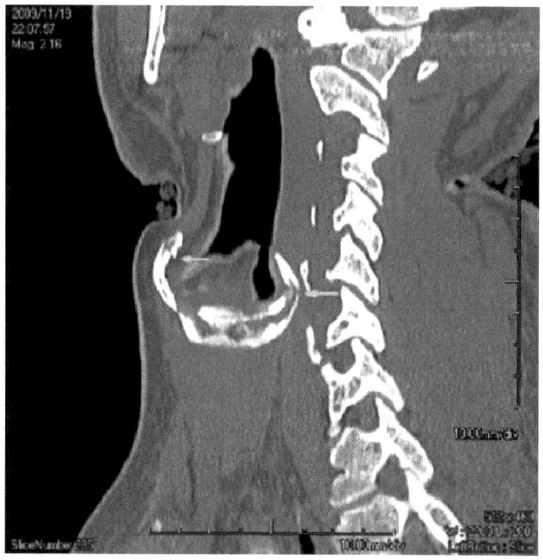

Figure 5.42 CT image showing typical sharp edges of a true fractured hyoid.

fractures may be a viable alternative to conventional autopsy, provided a thorough external examination and incident scene investigation are performed [68].

However, there are practical problems in the evaluation of injuries to the hyoid bone and larynx using postmortem CT scanning. A study by Pollanen and Ubelaker [69] confirmed the anecdotal experience of his colleagues that anatomical variations are not uncommon in cases of death coming to autopsy. For the experienced radiologist the differentiation between an anatomical variant and a true antemortem fracture is generally not particularly difficult. The more acute edges of the fracture can usually be appreciated (Figure 5.42). The recognition of this radiological finding may be more challenging for the forensic pathologist.

Subtle neck compression may occur in cases of concealed homicide or sexual asphyxia. As CT is unable to resolve small skeletal muscle or mucosal hemorrhages these important forensic markers of neck compression may get missed. In young women, who comprise the majority of the deaths from manual and ligature strangulation, the noncalcified hyoid is very pliable and not readily fractured. Although the majority of cases of neck compression from homicide display prominent skin injuries to the neck, in a minority of cases the external examination findings may be subtle.

A study comparing fractured and nonfractured hyoids from victims of strangulation showed that although macroscopic fractures may not always be present, a significant number of cases revealed histological microfractures [70].

Anatomy

The hyoid is a U- or horseshoe-shaped bone composed of a rectangular-shaped central body and paired greater and lesser horns or cornua. The cornua and body of the hyoid articulate by fibrous and chondroid tissue. The hyoid is suspended in the neck by numerous muscular attachments to the tongue and floor of the mouth, the "strap" muscles of the neck, and via the stylohyoid ligament to the styloid process of the temporal bone.

The hyoid has six ossification centers. There are two for the body and one for each of the four cornua. The ossification of the greater cornua occurs in late fetal life, the body commences shortly after birth, and the lesser cornua begin to ossify during infancy. Ossification of the hyoid does not appear in children less than 15 years of age [71]. Ossification of the hyoid is usually complete by 20 years of age [72].

Fusion of the greater cornua with the body occurs with increasing age. The age of fusion may vary in different ethnic groups. Indian authors have reported that fusion of the hyoid occurred after 40 years of age in Indian subjects, whereas fusion occurred in non-Indian subjects around 30 to 40 years of age [73].

Bony fusion is rare before the age of 20 [74]. It should be noted that numerous elderly individuals can have either unilateral fusion or indeed bilateral absence of fusion [75]. The importance of unfused hyoid bones is the potential for this normal anatomical variant to be misdiagnosed as a fracture on CT imaging.

Etiology

In the adult forensic population the majority of hyoid bone fractures occur from hanging. The mode of death is overwhelmingly one of suicide. A prospective study of deaths from neck constriction in India showed that hanging was the cause of 69% of asphyxia deaths [76]. The male to female ratio was 2:1. The hyoid was fractured in 21% of the cases.

An earlier Australian prospective study investigated fractures of the hyoid bone and laryngeal cartilages in 40 cases of suicidal hanging [77]. The age of the victims ranged from 17 to 74 years with an average of 35 years. There was a much higher male predominance in these cases with a ratio of 33:7. Nine of the cases showed only fractures of the thyroid cartilages, six victims had fractures to both thyroid cartilage and hyoid bone, whereas examination of four victims revealed isolated fractures of the hyoid bone.

Although in absolute terms hanging is the most common cause of hyoid fracture, the hyoid is more prone to fracture in cases of manual or ligature strangulation, and especially so in older individuals. Ubelaker [78] reported that 34% of cases of manual strangulation were associated with a fracture of the hyoid.

Fractures to the hyoid bone may also be seen in association with other fractures to the face or soft tissue injury to the neck. Such injuries are often the result of motor vehicle trauma. Isolated fractures to the hyoid bone are uncommon, but may be seen in sporting accidents and other causes of direct trauma to the neck [79].

An uncommon but important cause of isolated hyoid bone fracture is indirect force applied to the neck following impact with the ground after a fall from a height. A retrospective study on falls from a mean height of 15 m to the ground (concrete in 94% of cases) revealed that laryngohyoid fracture occurred in five cases [80]. The fracture mechanisms were explained by a combination of direct force and indirect force caused by high muscle strains from cervical hyperflexion or extension.

It is generally accepted that resuscitation injuries involving the larynx are generally composed of minor bruises. Inexpert resuscitation may lead to more significant injuries. Fractures to the hyoid and thyroid cartilages attributed to expert resuscitation and therapeutic intervention have been described [81].

An interesting large autopsy study involved dissection of the hyoid in a series of 1160 cases. The study revealed healed fractures in 65 (5.6%) cases [82]. Chronic alcoholics comprised 35 of the cases. The paper suggested that falls, which are certainly increased in this group, may account for the presence of healed fractures. It was also possible that this group could well have been involved in a higher incidence of violent assaults than the general population.

Overall it would seem reasonable to suggest that in the absence of the typical features of hanging, an isolated hyoid or thyroid cartilage fracture, although not pathognomonic of an assault, is certainly a worrisome finding in a medicolegal investigation. In all cases other than properly investigated cases of suicide by hanging, where the postmortem CT scan demonstrates the presence of a laryngohyoid fracture, a conventional postmortem should be performed with formal neck dissection.

Mechanism

In forensic practice the classical mechanism of hyoid fracture is a compressive force to the neck leading to "squeezing" of the bone. There are numerous factors at play in determining whether the hyoid bone will fracture in a particular case and in certain circumstances. These factors include the age of the victim, whether the hyoid synchondrosis is fused and ossified, the position of a ligature around the neck, the duration and magnitude of the force applied, and the presence of various anatomical variations in a given case.

A study comparing the anatomical features of the hyoid bone in cases of fracture versus nonfractured specimens showed a number of morphological features of the hyoid bone were more likely to be associated with a fracture [70]. These features included the length of the hyoid in the anterior–posterior plane, the slope of the greater cornu, and the asymmetry of the hyoid.

In clinical practice a direct blow may fracture the hyoid bone. The injury occurs most commonly when the neck is extended. A fracture can also occur as a consequence of an avulsion injury. This is seen in circumstances of sudden hyperextension of the neck and occasionally in cases of forced swallowing.

CT Diagnosis of Hyoid Bone Fractures

Conventional x-rays have been used to document hyoid fractures for some time. In the nonfractured case the inner aspect of the hyoid bone displays a smooth semicircle between the body and the greater cornu. The joint space has a smooth regular edge and measures from 0 to 4.1 mm [74].

An x-ray analysis of the position of the fracture in 19 fractures in 15 hyoid bones resulting from manual strangulation in 13 cases and hanging in 2 cases was performed by Pollanen and colleagues in 1995 [83]. The study divided the hyoid into three segments. The anterior segment was adjacent to the normal fusion point between the body and the greater cornu. The middle and posterior segments were defined as equidistant portions of the greater cornu from the anterior segment to the tip of the greater cornu. The study showed that in 47% of the cases fractures occurred in each of the middle and posterior segments. Anterior fractures were rare. The study also showed that the hyoid bone fractures at specific points of curvature, defined as "the angle of inclination of the fracture from the center of the body of the hyoid." All fractures occurred between 30 and 60 degrees of

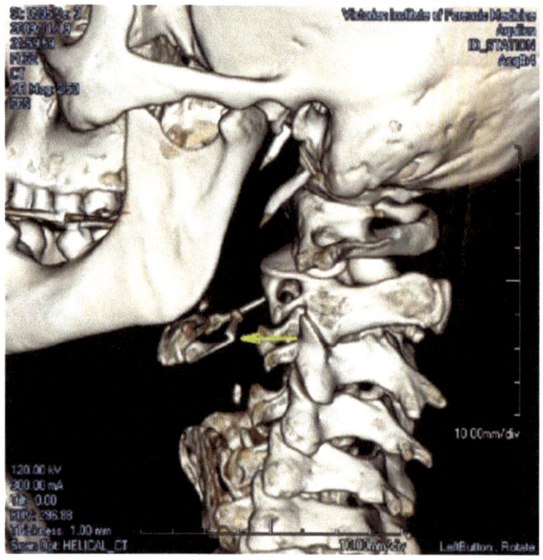

Figure 5.43 Three-dimensional reconstruction showing marked displacement of fractured hyoid.

curvature, suggesting the precise location of the fracture is a function of the shape of the greater curvature.

In a forensic examination of the hyoid by CT a number of valuable features are

- The hyoid is well seen on CT images using thin slices in the axial and coronal planes.
- The hyoid is typically visualized at the level of the third cervical vertebra.
- The scans may reveal marked displacement of the cornua (Figure 5.43).
- The detection of gas within the mediastinum and soft tissues of the neck has been recently reported as a possible vital sign in cases of hanging [84]. The mechanism of gas formation may be from a tear within the upper airway or a Valsalva maneuver.

Case Study

A 42-year-old man with a long history of depression was located deceased in remote parkland. His body was found with a rope around the neck. An identical segment of rope was found tied to a tree branch some 5 to 6 m above the deceased. The death was reported to the coroner. The deceased's senior next of kin lodged an objection to autopsy.

The external examination showed no evidence of injury save for the abrasion and indentation to the neck associated with the ligature. The postmortem CT scan revealed a fracture to the left thyroid cartilage and to the right aspect of the hyoid bone (Figure 5.44). There was no skull fracture. There was no fracture associated with the fall.

The coroner was informed of these findings. The deceased's body was released from the institute.

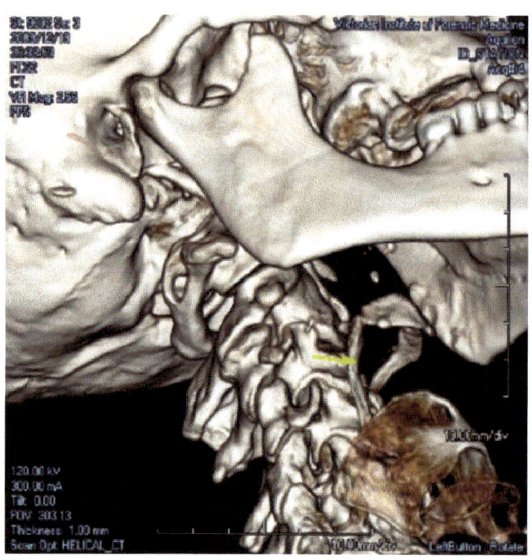

Figure 5.44 Three-dimensional reconstruction showing a fractured hyoid. Review of the whole body CT and the external examination showed no evidence of any suspicious injury.

References

1. Glass RBJ, Fernbach SK, Norton KI, Choi PS, Naidich TP. The infant skull: A vault of information. *Radiographics* 2004; 24:507–522.
2. Johnson F, Semaan MT, Megerian CA. Temporal bone fracture: Evaluation and management in the modern era. *Otolarygol. Clin. N. Am.* 2008; 41:597–618.
3. Provenzale J. CT and MR imaging of acute cranial trauma. *Emerg. Radiol.* 2007; 14:1–12.
4. Amprino R. Investigations on some physical properties of bone tissues. *Acta Anat.* 1958; 34:161–186.
5. Gurdjian ES, Lissner HR. Study of deformations of the skull by the "stresscoat" technique. *Surg. Gynae. Obstet.* 1945; 81:679–687.
6. Gurdjian ES, Webster JE, Lissner HR. Mechanism of skull fracture with particular reference to engineering factors. *Am. J. Surg.* 1949; 78(5):736–742.
7. Hart GO. Fracture pattern interpretation in the skull: Differentiating blunt force from ballistics trauma using concentric fractures. *J. Forensic Sci.* 2005; 50(6):1276–1281.
8. Yoganandan N, Pintar FA. Biomechanics of temporoparietal skull fracture. *Clin. Biomech.* 2004; 19:225–239.
9. Delye H, Verschueren P, Depreitere B, Verpoest I, Berckmans D, Vander Sloten J, Van der Perre G, Goffin J. Biomechanics of frontal skull fracture. *J. Neurotrauma* 2007; 24(10):1576–1586.
10. Verschueren P, Delye H, Depreitere B, Van Lierde C, Haex B, Berckmans D, Verpoest I, Goffin J, Vander Sloten J, Van der Perre G. A new test set-up for skull fracture characterisation. *J. Biomech.* 2007; 40(15):3389–3396.
11. Nosan DK, Benecke JE Jr, Murr AH. Current perspective on temporal bone trauma. *Otolaryngol. Head Neck Surg.* 1997; 117(1):67–71.
12. Ghorayeb BY, Yeakley JW. Temporal bone fractures: Longitudinal or oblique? The case for oblique temporal bone fractures. *Laryngoscope* 1992; 102(2):129–134.
13. Schuknecht B, Graetz K. Radiologic assessment of maxillofacial, mandibular, and skull base trauma. *Eur. Radiol.* 2005; 15(3):560–568.
14. Harvey FH, Jones AM. "Typical" basal skull fracture of both petrous bones: An unreliable indicator of head impact site. *J. Forensic Sci.* 1980; 25(2):280–286.
15. McElhaney JH, Hopper RH, Nightingale RW, Myers BS. Mechanisms of basilar skull fracture. *J. Neurotrauma* 1995; 12(4):669–678.
16. Zhu BL, Quan L, Ishida K, Taniquchi M, Oritani S, Fujida MQ, Maeda H. Longitudinal brainstem laceration associated with complex basilar skull fractures due to a fall: An autopsy case. *Forensic Sci. Int.* 2002; 126(1):40–42.
17. Gan YC, Charkravarty D, Flint G. Ring fracture of the skull base: Case report and review of the literature. *Br. J. Neurosurg.* 2002; 16(3):300–303.
18. Bloom AI, Neeman Z, Slasky BS, Floman Y, Milgrom M, Rivkind A, Bar-Ziv J. Fracture of the occipital condyles and associated craniocervical ligament injury: Incidence, CT imaging and implications. *Clin. Radiol.* 1997; 52(3):198–202.
19. Leone A, Cerase A, Colosimo C, Lauro L, Puca A, Marano P. Occipital condylar fractures: A review. *Radiology* 2000; 216:635–644.
20. Caroli E, Rocchi G, Orlando ER, Delfini R. Occipital condyle fractures: Report of five cases and literature review. *Eur. Spine J.* 2005; 14(5):487–492.
21. Anderson PS, Montesano XP. Morphology and treatment of occipital condyle fractures. *Spine* 1988; 13:731–836.
22. Yoganandan N, Pintar FA, Sanses A Jr., Walsh PR, Ewing CL, Thomas DJ, Snyder RG. Biomechanics of skull fracture. *J. Neurotrauma* 1995; 12(4):659–668.
23. Dolan KD. Temporal bone fractures. *Seminars in Ultrasound, CT, and MR.* 1989; 10(3):262–279.
24. Connor SEJ, Tan G, Fernando R, Chaudhury N. Computed tomography pseudofractures of the midface and skull base. *Clin. Radiol.* 2005; 60:1268–1279.
25. Tharp AM, Jason DR. Anomalous parietal suture mimicking skull fracture. *Am. J. Foren. Med. Pathol.* 2009; 30(1):49–51.
26. Eggensperger Wymann NM, Holzle A, Zacariou Z, Iizuka T. Pediatric craniofacial trauma. *J. Oral Maxillofac. Surg.* 2008; 66(1):58–64.
27. Ersahin Y, Mutluer S, Mirai H, Palali I. Pediatric depressed skull fractures: Analysis of 530 cases. *Childs Nerv. Syst.* 1996; 12(6):323–331.
28. Kemp AM, Dunstan F, Harrison S, Morris S, Mann M, Rolfe K, Datta S, Thomas P, Sibert JR, Maguire S. Patterns of skeletal fractures in child abuse: Systematic review. *BMJ* 2008; 337(21):a1518.
29. Hobbs CJ. Skull fracture and the diagnosis of abuse. *Arch. Dis. Child.* 1984; 59:246–252.
30. Meservy CJ, Towbin R, McLaurin RL, Myers PA, Ball W. Radiographic characteristics of skull fractures resulting from child abuse. *AJR* 1987; 149:173–175.
31. Aplin DS, Greenspan A, Reinhart M, Grix A. Differentiation of child abuse from osteogenesis imperfecta. *AJR* 1990; 154:1035–1046.
32. Heise RH, Srivatsa PJ, Karsell PR. Spontaneous intrauterine linear skull fracture: A rare complication of spontaneous vaginal delivery. *Obstet. Gynaecol.* 1996; 87(5 pt 2):851–854.
33. Erdmann D, Follmar KE, Debruijn M, Bruno AD, Jung SH, Edelman D, Mukundan S, Marcus JR. A retrospective analysis of facial fracture etiologies. *Ann. Plast. Surg.* 2008; 60(4):398–403.
34. Scherer M, Sullivan WG, Smith DJ Jr, Phillips LG, Robson MC. An analysis of 1,423 facial fractures in 788 patients at an urban trauma center. *J. Trauma* 1989; 29(3):388–390.
35. Gassner R, Tuli T, Hachl O, Rudisch A, Ulmer H. Craniomaxillofacial trauma: A 10 year review of 9543 cases with 21,067 injuries. *J. Cranio-Maxillofacial Surg.* 2003; 31:51–61.
36. Zimmermann CE, Troulis MJ, Kaban LB. Pediatric facial fractures: Recent advances in prevention, diagnosis and management. *J. Oral Maxillofac. Surg.* 2006; 35(1):2–13.
37. Gentry LR, Manor WF, Turski PA, Strother CM. High-resolution CT analysis of facial struts in trauma: 1. Normal anatomy. *AJR* 1983; 140:523–532.

38. Linnau KF, Stanley RB Jr, Hallam DK, Gross JA, Mann FA. Imaging of high-energy trauma: What the surgeon needs to know. *Eur. J. Radiol.* 2003; 48:17–32.
39. Chan J, Putnam MA, Feustel PJ, Koltai PJ. The age dependent relationship between facial fractures and skull fractures. *Int. J. Pediatr. Otorhinolaryngol.* 2004; 68:877–881.
40. Hampson D. Facial injury: A review of biomechanical studies and test procedures for facial injury assessment. *J. Biomech.* 1995; 28(1):1–7.
41. Lewis VL, Manson PN, Cerullo LJ, Meyer PR. Facial injuries associated with cervical fractures: Recognition, patterns and management. *J. Trauma* 1985; 25:90–93.
42. Schuknecht B, Graetz K. Radiologic assessment of maxillofacial, mandibular, and skull base trauma. *Eur. Radiol.* 2005; 15:560–568.
43. Dufresne CR, Manson PN. Facial injuries and pediatric facial trauma. In McCarthy JG, editor. *Plastic surgery*, Vol. 2. W.B. Saunders Co., Philadelphia, 1990, pp. 867–1187.
44. Converse JM, Smith G. Enophthalmous and diplopia in fractures of the orbital floor. *Br. J. Plast. Surg.* 1957; 9:265–274.
45. Katzen JT, Jarrahy R, Eby JB, Mathiasen RA, Margulies DR, Shahinian HK. Craniofacial and skull base trauma. *J. Trauma* 2003; 54:1026–1034.
46. Smith B, Regan WF. Blow-out fracture of the orbit, mechanism and correction of internal orbital fracture. *Am. J. Ophthalmol.* 1957; 44:733–739.
47. McCoy FJ, Chandler RA, Magnum CG Jr, Moore JR, Siemsen G. An analysis of facial fractures and the complications. *Plast. Reconstr. Surg.* 1963; 29:381–391.
48. Suzuki H, Furukawa M, Takahashi E, Matsuura K. Barotraumatic blow-out fracture of the orbit. *Auris. Nasus. Larynx* 2001; 28(3):257–259.
49. Kubal WS. Imaging of orbital trauma. *Radiographics* 2008; 28:1729–1739.
50. Tadj A, Kimble FW. Fractured zygomas. *ANZ J. Surg.* 2003; 73:49–54.
51. Zingg M, Chowdhury K, Laedrach K, Vuillemin T, Sutter F, Raveh J. The treatment of 813 zygoma-lateral orbit complex fractures: New aspects. *Arch. Otolaryngol Head Neck Surg.* 1991; 117:611–622.
52. Gruss JS, Van Wyck L, Phillips JH, Antonyshyn O. The importance of the zygomatic arch in complex midfacial fracture repair and correction of posttraumatic orbitozygomatic deformities. *Plast. Reconstr. Surg.* 1990; 85(6):878–890.
53. Hussain K, Wijetunge DB, Jackson IT. A comprehensive analysis of cranio-facial trauma. *J. Trauma* 1994; 34–47.
54. Teichgreaber JF, Rappaport NH, Harris JH Jr. The radiology of upper airway obstruction in maxillo-facial trauma. *Ann. Plast. Surg.* 1991; 27:103–109.
55. Galloway A. *Broken bones: Anthropathological analysis of blunt force trauma.* Charles C. Thomas, Springfield, IL, 1995.
56. Shelton D. Nasal-orbital-ethmoid fractures. In Alling CI, Osbon D, editors. *Maxillofacial trauma.* Lea & Febiger, Philadelphia, 1988, pp. 363–371.
57. Rhea JT, Novelline RA. How to simplify the CT diagnosis of Le Fort fractures. *AJR* 2005; 184:1700–1705.
58. Sidal T, Curtis DA. Fractures of the mandible in the ageing population. *Spec. Care Dentist.* 2006; 26(4):145–149.
59. Dongas P, Hall GM. Mandibular fracture patterns in Tasmania, Australia. *J. Aust. Dent. J.* 2002; 47(2):131–133.
60. King RE, Schianna JM, Petruzzelli GJ. Mandible fracture patterns: A suburban trauma center experience. *Am. J. Otolaryngol.* 2004; 25:301–307.
61. Escott EJ, Branstetter BF. Incidence and characterisation of unilateral mandible fractures on CT. *Am. J. Neuroradiol.* 2008; 29:890–894.
62. Hagan EH, Huelke DF. An analysis of 319 case reports of mandibular fractures. *J. Oral Surg. Anesth. Hosp. Dent. Serv.* 1961; 19:93–104.
63. Huelke DF. Mechanics in the production of mandibular fractures: A study with the “stresscoat” technique: 1. Symphyseal impacts. *J. D. Res.* 1961; 40(5):1042–1056.
64. Fridrich KL, Pena-Velasco G, Olsen RAJ. Changing trends with mandibular fractures: A review of the 1,067 cases. *J. Oral. Maxillofac. Surg.* 1992; 50:586–589.
65. Unnewehr M, Homann C, Schmidt PF, Sotony P, Fisher G, Brinkmann B, Bajanowski T, DuChesne A. Fracture properties of the human mandible. *Int. J. Legal Med.* 2003; 117:326–330.
66. Iida S, Nomura K, Okura M, Kogo M. Influence of the incompletely erupted lower third molar on mandibular angle and condylar fractures. *J. Trauma* 2004; 57:613–617.
67. Duan DH, Zhang Y. Does the presence of mandibular third molars increase the risk of angle fracture and simultaneously decrease the risk of condylar fracture? *Int. J. Oral Maxillofac. Surg.* 2008; 37:25–28.
68. Kempter M, Ross S, Spendlove D, Flach PM, Preiss U, Thali MJ, Bollinger SA. Post-mortem imaging of laryngohyoid fractures in strangulation incidents: First results. *Legal Med. (Tokyo)* 2009; 11(6):267–271.
69. Pollanen MS, Ubelaker DH. Forensic significance of the polymorphism of hyoid bone shape. *J. Forensic Sci.* 1997; 42(5):890–892.
70. Pollanen MS, Chiasson DA. Fracture of the hyoid bone in strangulation: Comparison of fractured and unfractured hyoids from victims of strangulation. *J. Forensic Sci.* 1996; 41(1):110–113.
71. Reed MH. Ossification of the hyoid bone during childhood. *Can. Assoc. Radiol. J.* 1993; 44(4):273–276.
72. Parsons FG. The topography and morphology of the human hyoid bone. *J. Anat. Physiol.* 1909; 43:279–290.
73. Gupta A, Kohli A, Aggarwal NK, Banerjee KK. Study of age of fusion of hyoid bone. *Legal Med. (Tokyo)* 2008; 10(5):253–256.
74. Shimizu Y, Kanetaka H, Kim Y-H, Okayama K, Kano M, Kikuchi M. Age-related morphological changes in the human hyoid bone. *Cells Tissues Organs* 2005; 180:185–192.
75. Miller KWP, Walker PL, O’Halloran RL. Age- and sex-related variation in hyoid bone morphology. *J. Forensic Sci.* 1998; 43:1138–1143.

76. Sharma BR, Harish D, Sharma A, Sharma S, Singh H. Injuries to neck structures in deaths due to constriction of neck, with special reference to hanging. *J. Forensic Leg. Med.* 2008; 15(5):298–305.
77. Green H, James RA, Gilbert JD, Byard RW. Fractures of the hyoid bone and laryngeal cartilages in suicidal hanging. *J. Clin. Forensic Med.* 2000; 7(3):123–126.
78. Ubelaker DH. Hyoid fracture and strangulation. *J. Forensic Sci.* 1992; 37(5):1216–1222.
79. Dalati T. Isolated hyoid bone fracture: Review of an unusual entity. *Int. J. Oral Maxillofac. Surg.* 2005; 34:449–452.
80. de la Grandmaison GL, Krimi S, Durigon M. Frequency of laryngeal and hyoid bone trauma in nonhomicidal cases who died after a fall from a height. *Am. J. Forensic Med. Pathol.* 2006; 27(1):85–86.
81. Gregersen M, Vesterby A. Iatrogenic fractures of the hyoid bone and the thyroid cartilage: A case report. *Forensic Sci. Int.* 1981; 17:41–43.
82. Maxeiner H. Healed fractures of the larynx and the lingual bone in forensic autopsy. *Arch. Kriminol.* 1999; 203(5–6):175–183 (abstract).
83. Pollanen MS, Bulger B, Chiasson DA. The location of hyoid fractures in strangulation revealed by xeroradiography. *J. Forensic Sci.* 1995; 40(2):303–305.
84. Aghayev E, Yen K, Sonnensschein M, Jackowski C, Thali M, Vock P, Dirnhofer R. Pneumomediastinum and soft tissue emphysema of the neck in postmortem CT and MRI: A new vital sign in hanging? *Forensic Sci. Int.* 2005; 153:181–188.

6 Spine

Vertebral Column

Anatomy

The vertebral column consists of 7 cervical vertebrae, 12 thoracic vertebrae, and 5 lumbar vertebrae (Figure 6.1a,b,c). The fifth lumbar vertebra articulates with the sacrum. Because of its functional anatomy the sacrum will be considered with the pelvis.

A typical vertebra consists of an anterior body that extends into a posterior vertebral arch, two lateral transverse processes, a posterior spinous process, and paired superior and inferior articular processes (Figure 6.2a,b,c).

The principle function of the vertebral body is to support weight. The vertebral arch is composed of paired pedicles and laminae. The prime function of the vertebral arch is to mechanically protect the spinal column. The transverse processes and spinous processes provide attachment points for skeletal muscles. The articular processes limit movement to within certain boundaries.

The cervical, thoracic, and lumbar regions all allow varying amounts of flexion or extension and lateral movement. The cervical spine permits considerable rotation. The thoracic vertebrae allow medial and lateral rotation, whereas there is none in the lumbar vertebrae.

The spine's anatomical integrity is maintained by structural anatomical features, such as the synovial facet joints (apophyseal joints). Each vertebra has two sets of facet joints, one pair facing upward (superior facet) and one pair facing downward (inferior facet). The anterior and posterior longitudinal ligaments situated to the anterior and posterior aspects of the vertebral bodies are integral in maintaining vertebral body alignment [1]. Other important ligaments include the supraspinous and interspinous ligaments, and the ligamentum flavum.

Intrinsic skeletal muscles are also very important in static and dynamic loading, and stress to the vertebral column.

Vertebral Fractures

Vertebral fractures typically result from varying combinations of excessive forceful movement or abnormal axial loading. Although a discussion of fracture patterns usually describes the effects of "pure" isolated excessive movement or loading, in real-world incidents, and especially those leading to rapid death, there are often complex insults to the spine.

Different segments of the spine are more liable to undergo certain types of fracture. For example, the upper segments of the thoracic spine (T1–T8) are prone to flexion injuries, whereas the lower lumbar spine and sacrum tend to undergo fractures from excessive axial loading.

Spinous Process and Transverse Process Fractures

Direct blunt force trauma may lead to adjacent fractures of the spinous and transverse processes. Rapid movements around a particular region of the spine may also cause avulsion fractures to spinous and transverse processes.

Typically L3 is the most commonly involved level in cases of direct blunt force trauma. The presence of such a fracture is associated with visceral injury (including renal, pancreatic, and diaphragmatic injury) in up to 25% of cases. Fractures of the transverse process of L5 are associated with a high incidence of pelvic fracture.

Avulsion injury to cervical spinous processes is well described. The clay-shoveler's fracture is a hyperflexion avulsion injury to the lower cervical and upper thoracic spinous processes (C7 > C6 > T1). The injury is the result of sudden flexion causing avulsion of bone from muscular exertion. In a forensic setting the injury may be seen in cases of direct trauma to the occiput leading to rapid forced flexion of the neck.

Cervical Spine

Anatomy

The cervical spine is comprised anatomically and functionally of the first (atlas), second (axis), and third to seventh vertebrae. These different regions have significant differences in their anatomical features, their functions, and particular types of fracture patterns. Anatomically, the axis holds a pivotal position in the cervical spine with the many skeletal muscles radiating from it in different directions. An inspection of the muscle attachments to the posterior neck also illustrates the individual nature of the muscle attachments above the axis as opposed to below it.

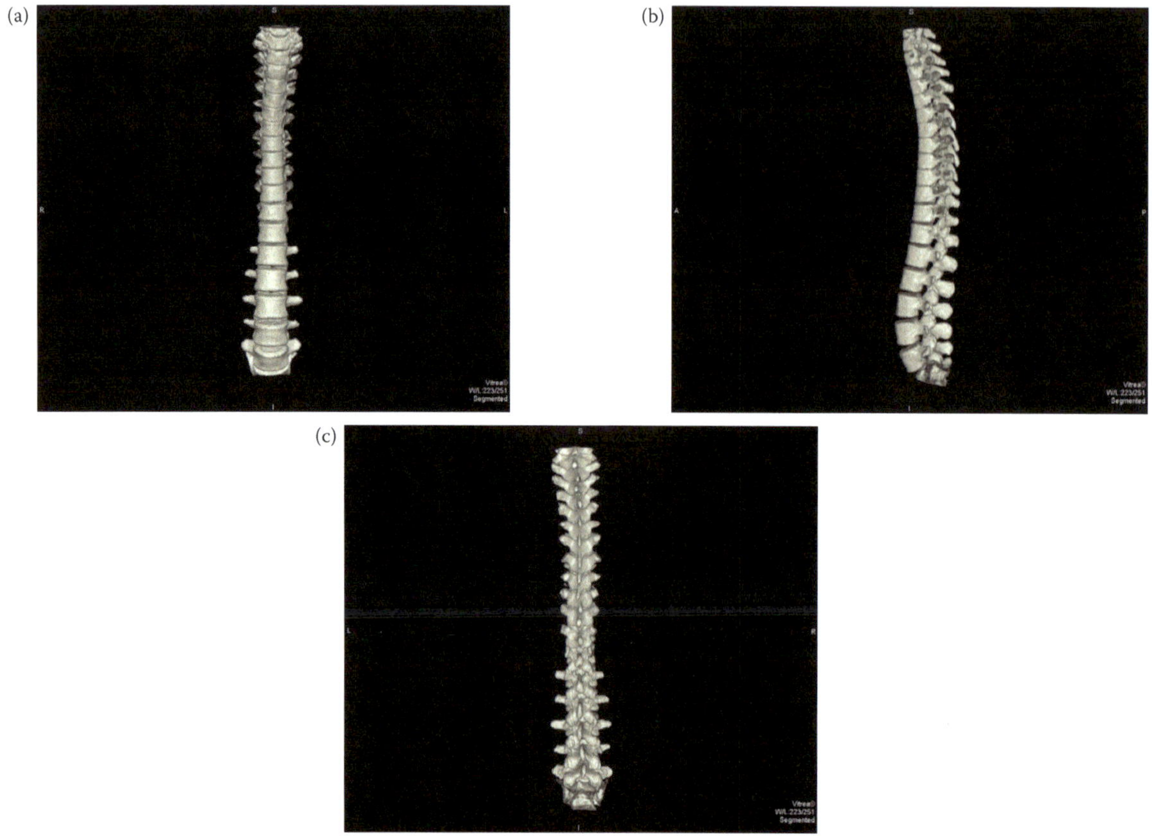

Figure 6.1 (a) Three-dimensional reconstruction of the anterior aspect of the spine. (b) Three-dimensional reconstruction of the lateral aspect of the spine. (c) Three-dimensional reconstruction of the posterior aspect of the spine.

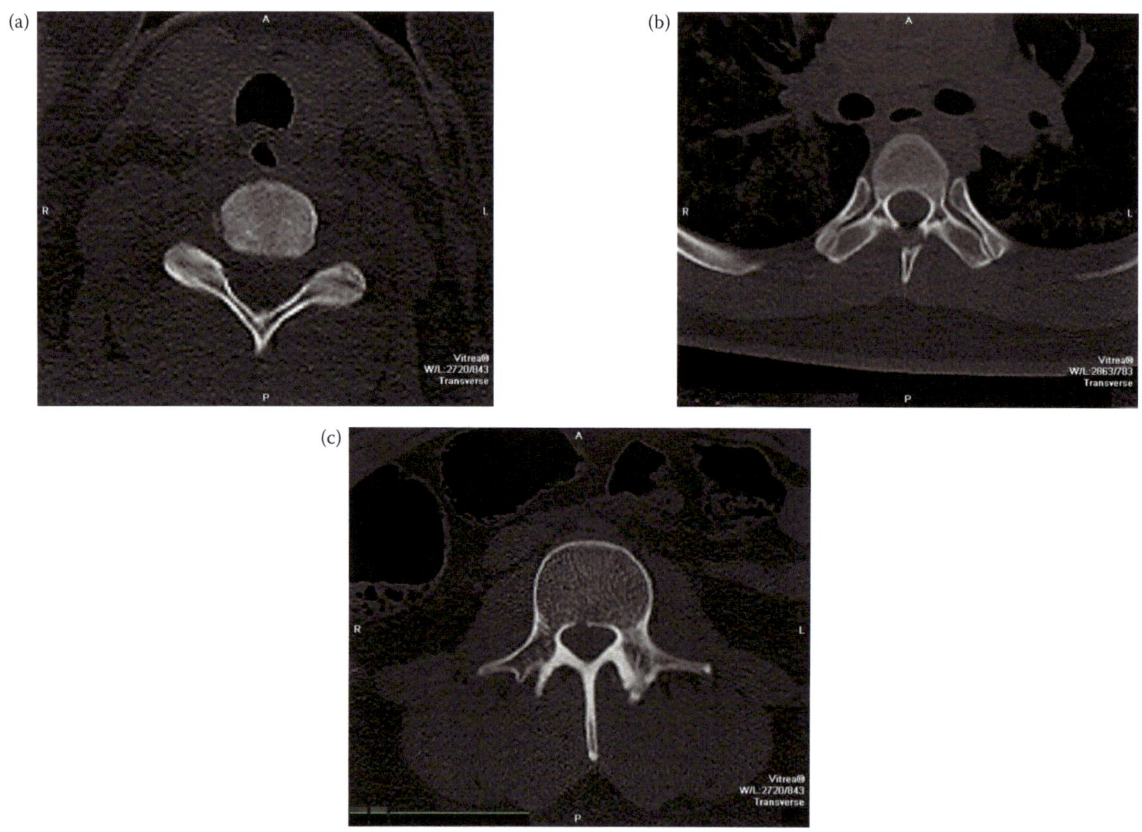

Figure 6.2 (a) Axial Computed tomography (CT) of a cervical vertebra. (b) Axial CT of a thoracic vertebra. (c) Axial CT of a lumbar vertebra.

A distinctive feature of cervical vertebrae is the presence of the paired foramina transversarium, which contain the vertebral arteries. The atlas is unique among the vertebrae in that it has no body. The atlantooccipital and atlantoaxial connections contain joints and ligaments but no intervening discs.

Head rotation occurs around the odontoid of the axis [3]. The atlantooccipital joint allows the movements of flexion, extension, and some lateral bending.

Below C2–C3 the cervical spine allows flexion and extension, and combined lateral bending and rotation [3]. The lower cervical spine, defined as extending from C2–C3 through to C6–C7, is structurally different to the upper cervical spine, which is reflected in its range of movement and injuries that occur at this region.

The combination of the occiput, with the foramen magnum and clivus, the atlas, axis, and associated ligaments is called the craniovertebral or craniocervical junction [2].

Cervical Spine Fractures

Injuries to the cervical spine occur in approximately 2% to 3% of cases of blunt force trauma [4]. Injuries to the cervical spine occur as a consequence of a number of forces that often act in concert or in succession. Many experimental models have used isolated forces to determine the tolerance of the cervical spine to injury and fracture. The mechanisms involved in cervical spine injury include axial compression, distraction, hyperflexion, hyperextension, rotation, and lateral flexion.

A means of conceptualizing injury to the cervical spine is to visualize the consequences of movement in flexion, extension, rotation, and to the left and right lateral planes beyond the normal range of movement. In forced movement beyond the normal range there tends to be compression fractures of the bony structures in the direction of the particular plane of movement. Rupture of ligaments in the opposite plane of the movement will tend to occur. Forced flexion beyond the normal range of movement can lead to locking of facet joints, especially if associated with a rotational component.

As noted earlier, real-world incidents usually involve a combination of forces, though one particular type of force may predominate. By an examination of the pattern of cervical spine injuries one may be able to provide a reasoned opinion on the likely directions of significant force acting upon a victim of trauma.

First Cervical Vertebra (Atlas)

Anatomy

The atlas articulates with the occiput through the paired occipital condyles at the anterolateral aspect of the foramen magnum via paired synovial joints. An array of ligaments stabilizes the atlantooccipital joint. These ligaments are both intrinsic to the atlantooccipital joint and also common to the vertebral column.

The principle stabilizing ligaments between the occiput and the upper cervical spine are the tectorial membrane and the dual alar ligaments. The tectorial membrane connects the posterior body of the atlas and the anterior aspect of the foramen magnum, and the alar ligaments attach the occipital condyles to the odontoid process.

The range of motion at the atlantooccipital joint is 25 degrees in flexion or extension, and only 5% in the lateral bending and rotation.

Etiology

Fractures of the atlas comprise approximately 10% of cervical spine injuries and are highly associated with other significant cervical spine fractures and ligament disruptions [5].

The most common cause of atlantooccipital joint injury is transportation injuries. These injuries are frequently seen in motor vehicle occupants involved in various types of collisions but especially in victims of rollover incidents and those ejected from the vehicle. Other common causes include motorcycle riders and pedestrians struck by motor vehicles. Less frequent causes are shallow diving accidents and falls.

Vertical fractures of the body of the axis are caused by forced flexion injury. When compared to the other cervical vertebrae, horizontal fractures of the body of the axis are rare. A review of 674 consecutive patients with cervical spine fractures admitted to hospital showed only 0.3% (two cases) with a horizontal Chance-type fracture of the body of the axis [6].

Craniocervical distraction injury (CCD) is common at the atlantooccipital joint. Differential movement between the head and trunk can lead to rotational shearing forces acting upon the ligamentous structures with partial or complete rupture. CCD is often associated with major lower brainstem and upper cervical cord injury leading to rapid death.

Movement beyond the normal range of movement at the joint can lead to compression force to the atlas and occipital condyles, whereas rotational forces are particularly prone to cause severe ligament disruption. The injury is a common rapid cause of death in motor vehicle incidents.

Mechanism

The most common fracture of the atlas occurs from hyperextension. This movement results in compression of the posterior aspect of C1 between the occiput and

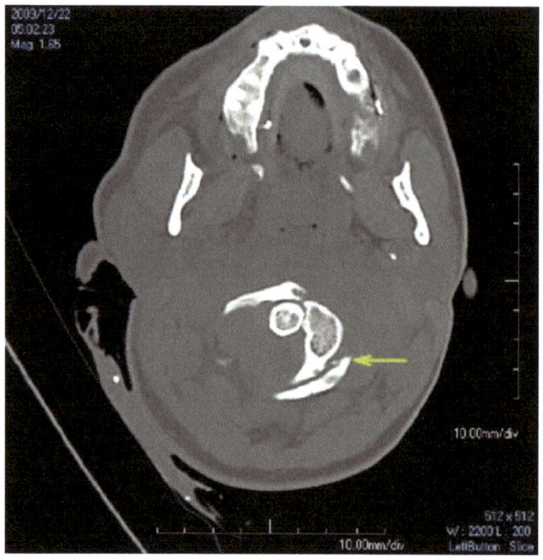

Figure 6.3 Axial CT showing a fracture to the posterior aspect of the neural arch of the atlas.

neural arch of C2. The resultant fracture most commonly manifests as a bilateral fracture through the neural arch of C1 (Figure 6.3) [7].

An anterior fracture is usually caused by compression force with associated flexion (Figure 6.4). Less commonly an anterior arch fracture may occur with hyperextension. These fractures have a tendency to involve the transverse foramina and may be associated with vertebral artery injury. Lacerations or rupture to the vertebral artery may result in death from massive basal subarachnoid hemorrhage or brainstem infarction secondary to arterial thrombosis. A hyperextension injury at the craniocervical junction has also been reported to shear the anterior arch of the atlas [8].

Compressive force can lead to fracture of the atlas. The Jefferson fracture is a burst-type fracture of the atlas resulting from compressive force and is characterized by bilateral fractures in the anterior and posterior arches (Figure 6.5). A classical Jefferson fracture produces an anterior fragment, a posterior fragment, and two lateral fragments. As there is a relatively large amount of space around the cord in the upper cervical spine, this injury is not particularly associated with neurological deficit.

The genesis of an atlas fracture may well be more complex than simply involving the direction of blunt force that is applied to the head and neck. A laboratory study on 40 isolated specimens subjected to pure axial force showed slow force impact (0.5 mm/s) lead to different types of atlas fractures than fast force impact (300 mm/s) [9].

Another biomechanical study of Jefferson fractures was performed using 15 specimens tested with pure tensile force to failure. The results showed that fractures

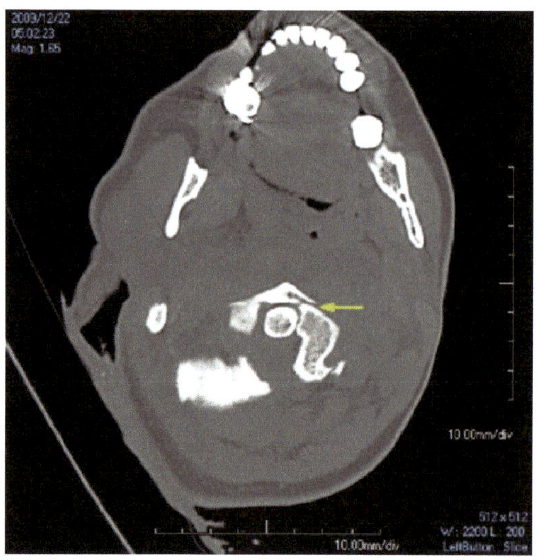

Figure 6.4 Axial CT showing a fracture to the anterior aspect of the atlas. The injury is most often associated with compressive forces with flexion.

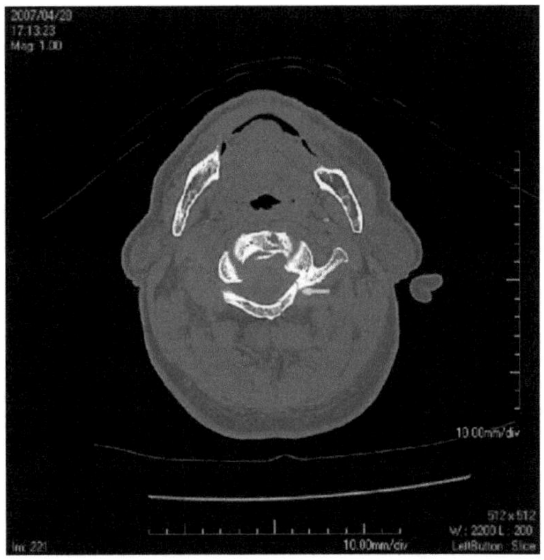

Figure 6.5 Axial CT showing a Jefferson fracture.

of greater than two parts of the C1 ring can occur with purely tensile loading rather than compressive force in isolated specimens and with as little as 1 mm of deformation [10].

Thus one should be wary of dogmatic statements regarding the type of force applied to the neck in a case of Jefferson fracture, though one may suggest that it is generally caused by compressive force.

Craniocervical Distraction Injury A craniocervical distraction (CCD) injury is a cause of rapid demise at the scene of a traumatic death. For the medicolegal system, when the circumstances of the death are not a particular issue, the correct identification of CCD by computed tomography (CT) scanning can mean an internal examination of the deceased's body may not be necessary. The expert radiologist is often able to make the diagnosis on postmortem CT scans (Figure 6.6). As will be indicated later, formal measurements can be performed with the images in orthogonal planes to confirm radiological abnormal separation of various anatomical markers. Furthermore, using different views can verify the diagnosis when the initial screening views are problematic (Figure 6.7a,b)

Interestingly, a recent study showed that the diagnosis of CCD was one of the diagnoses most frequently overlooked by radiology residents [11]. It is thus not surprising that forensic pathologists have considerable difficulty in making the diagnosis in these cases. In cases where the pathologist can detect abnormal mobility of the head in a deceased person following a major impact to the head and neck, the pathologist can usually confirm the suspicion of atlantooccipital injury on examination of the CT images.

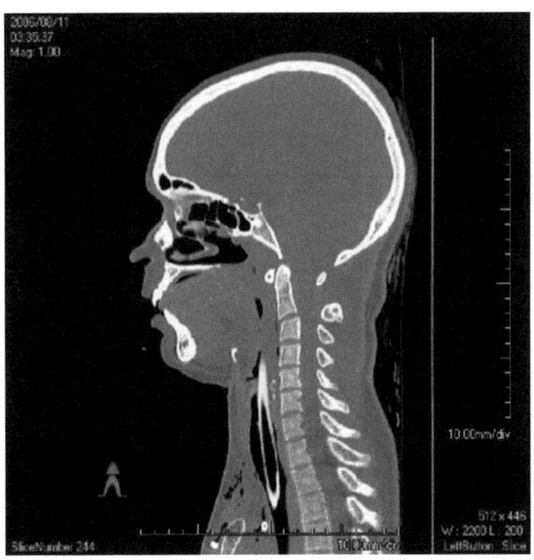

Figure 6.6 Sagittal CT showing subtle avulsion of atlantooccipital ligaments with caudal displacement of the atlas and axis.

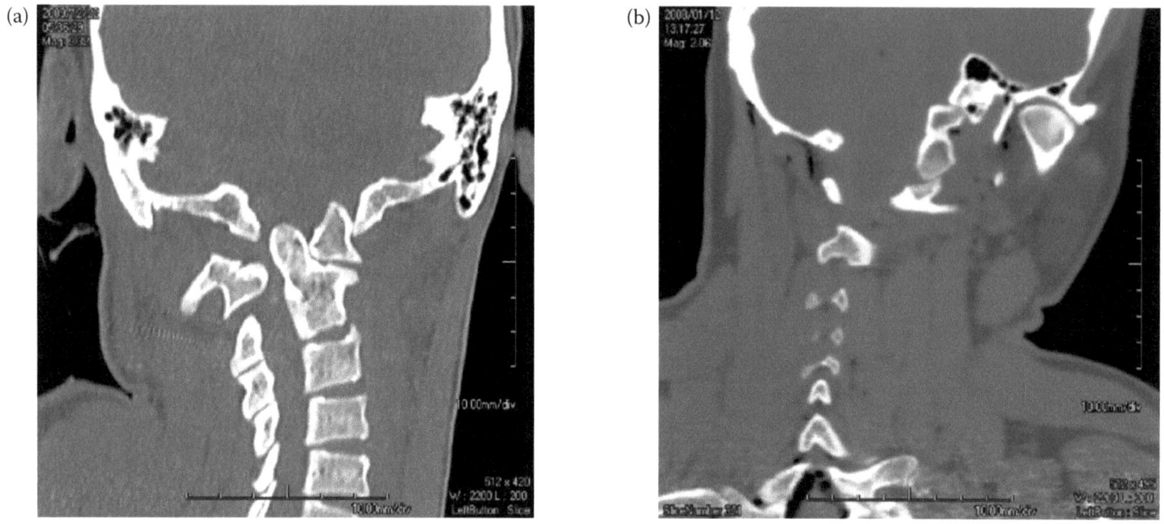

Figure 6.7 (a) Oblique CT image showing dislocation of the atlantooccipital joint. There is marked displacement especially seen to the left side. (b) Detail showing dislocation of an atlantooccipital joint.

Distraction injuries are usually associated with anterior displacement of the skull base with respect to the atlas. Posterior displacement is uncommon. A retrospective review of 35 patients with craniocervical dissociation showed "a sum of the bilateral distances between the midpoint of the occipital condyle and the C1 condylar fossa exceeding 4 mm had a sensitivity of 100%" [12]. Furthermore, the data suggested an upper limit of 4.2 mm for the summed intercondylar distance or an upper limit of 7.8 mm for the C1–C2 spinolaminar line length detected more than 95% of cases with injury.

Flexion force often leads to rupture of the transverse atlantal ligament, and ala and apical ligaments. Displacement of greater than 7 mm (normal 3 mm) of the atlantodens interval (ADI) is associated with loss of integrity of the alar ligament and tectorial membrane [13].

Dislocations may be associated with various fractures of the atlas and occipital condyles (Figure 6.8).

Second Cervical Vertebra (Axis)

Anatomy

The axis is the pivot on which the atlas, and thus the head, rotates. The odontoid process, or dens, is a unique elongation of the body of the axis that articulates with the anterior arch of the atlas. The odontoid process is held against the anterior arch of the atlas by the thick transverse ligament, which attaches to the lateral masses of the atlas. The odontoid is attached to the medial aspects of the occipital condyles via the alar ligaments. The alar ligament serves to limit rotation.

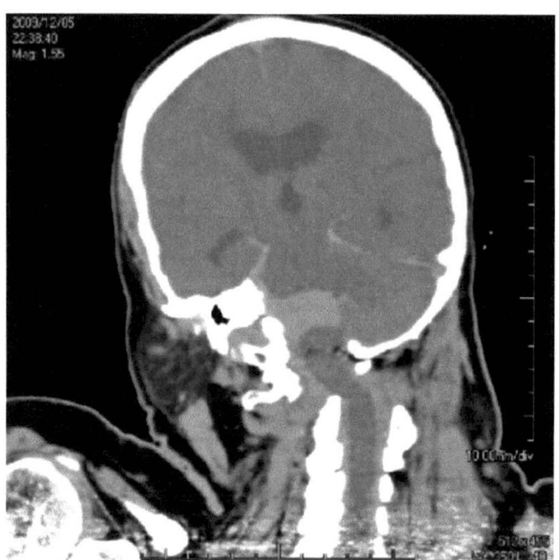

Figure 6.8 Coronal CT showing a fracture dislocation of the atlantooccipital joint. This CT image shows marked displacement of the cord.

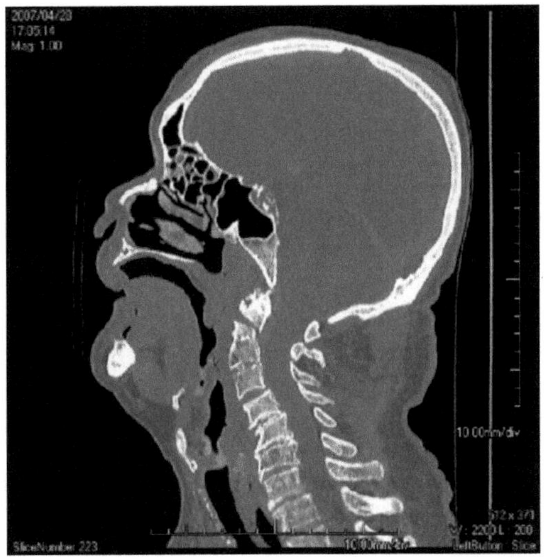

Figure 6.9 Sagittal CT image showing typical interruption to the bony contour from a fractured odontoid process.

The superior articular facets lie on the lateral masses of the vertebra.

Although uncommon, the odontoid process may rarely be congenitally absent or may be hypoplastic. The most common anomaly of the odontoid process is os odontoideum [13]. Os odontoideum refers to an ossicle with a smooth circumferential cortical margin with no bony continuity with the vertebral body of C2. The lesion may be associated with neck pain or myelopathy.

A forensic case of a death in a patient with os odontoideum who suffered an upper cervical cord injury in a motor vehicle incident has been described [14]. The CT findings that suggest the diagnosis of os odontoideum are [2]

- The line of separation is below rather than above the articular facet.
- The line is smooth and corticated rather than irregular and not corticated in a fracture.
- The anterior arch of the atlas is hypertrophic and round as opposed to half-moon shaped.

Etiology

Fractures of the odontoid process constitute approximately 7% to 13% of all cervical spine fractures [15]. Odontoid fractures are associated with high velocity trauma such as may occur in motor vehicle incidents. Low velocity injuries, such as what may occur in a fall, usually account for the majority of such fractures in the elderly and in children.

Mechanism

Odontoid Fractures Fractures of the odontoid process are most commonly associated with forced flexion. Forced flexion leads to anterior fracture or dislocation with anterior displacement of the dens. Less commonly forced extension applied to the upper cervical spine, as may occur with a fall onto the forehead, can cause a fracture of the odontoid with posterior displacement [16]. The fracture may be subtle on examination of the sagittal views, however, it is seen reasonably easily by an interruption in the cortical contour associated with an irregular lucency extending through the odontoid (Figure 6.9).

Anderson and D'Alonzo proposed a classification system of odontoid fractures that was based on the anatomical site of the fracture [17]. A type 1 fracture is an oblique fracture through the upper odontoid process (Figure 6.10). This fracture may be associated with loss of alar ligament integrity and is thus an unstable injury [18]. A fracture to the base of the dens is most common (65%). A fracture below the dentate occurs in approximately 30% of cases. Fractures to the tip of the dens are relatively rare (5%). Type 1 odontoid fractures are typically associated with impacts to the head leading to forced extension and lateral shear or compression. A type 2 fracture occurs at the base of the odontoid process (Figure 6.11). The fracture can be the result of either forced flexion or extension. Type 2 fractures are associated with axial rotation and lateral shear [15]. A type 3 fracture involves the vertebral body (Figure 6.12). As this fracture permits the occiput and atlas to move as a single unit, it is mechanically unstable.

Spondylolisthesis of the Axis Traumatic spondylolisthesis is the fracture classically associated with judicial hanging (hangman's fracture). The hangman's fracture is the most common fracture of the second cervical vertebra. The mechanism of the injury is forced hyperextension and compression. Nowadays this fracture is most commonly associated with motor vehicle incidents

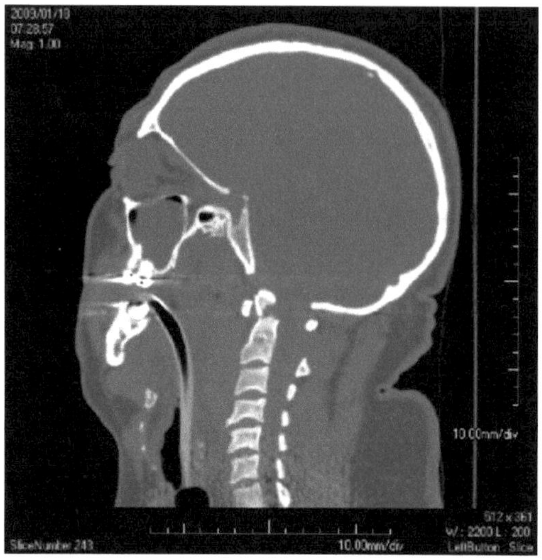

Figure 6.10 Sagittal CT showing a type 1 fracture of the odontoid process.

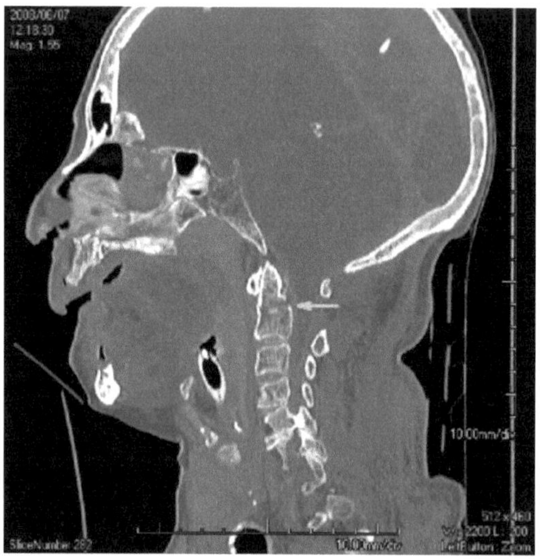

Figure 6.11 Sagittal CT showing a type 2 fracture of the odontoid process.

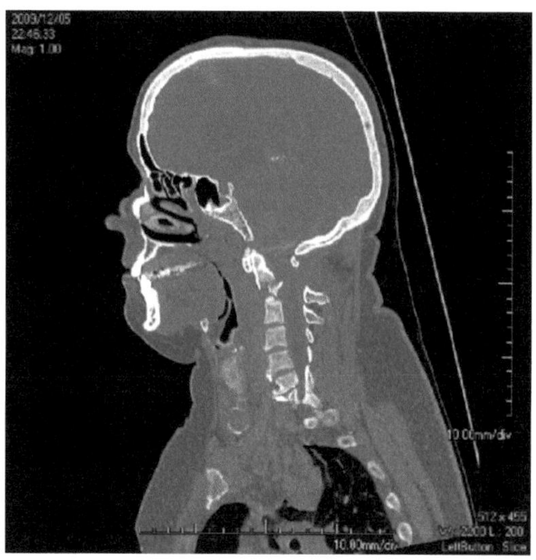

Figure 6.12 Sagittal CT showing a type 3 fracture of the odontoid process. There is anterior displacement associated with the fracture.

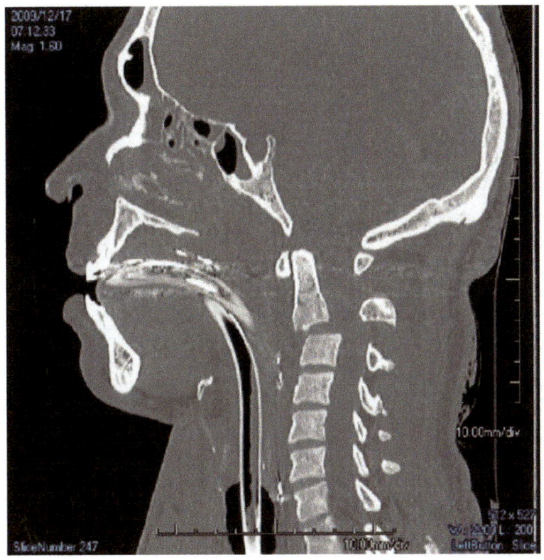

Figure 6.13 Sagittal CT showing forward displacement of C2 on C3. The hangman's fracture is not visible in this image.

or falls and represents approximately 15% to 20% of cervical spine fractures.

The fracture occurs through the pedicles of the axis resulting in anterior movement of C3 on C2. The anterior displacement is usually best seen using sagittal views (Figure 6.13). When such abnormal anatomy is appreciated on a screening examination of the scans, one can slowly scroll through the images and one may then see the fracture (Figure 6.14).

Traumatic spondylolisthesis is classified into three types according to the Levine classification system. A type 1 fracture involves the neural arch with intact C2–3 disc and ligaments, minimal displacement (<3 mm), and no angulation. A type 1A fracture is of forensic importance as the fracture involves extension into the foramen transversarium, which may result in involvement of the vertebral artery.

Type 2 fractures are the most common subtype. These fractures are associated with posterior longitudinal ligament disruption and significant angulation (>10 degrees). Type 2 fractures are the result of hyperflexion and are unstable injuries. Type 3 fractures have the features of a type 2 fracture in addition to dislocation of the C2–C3 facet joints. This fracture is unstable with free-floating articular processes.

For the forensic pathologist the fractures are best appreciated when, in the circumstances of a fall to the forehead or motor vehicle trauma with no obvious head injury or hemorrhage, one scans slowly through the axial views of the cervical spine using bone windows (Figure 6.15).

Extension Teardrop Fracture of the Axis Extreme hyperextension of the neck can result in an avulsion

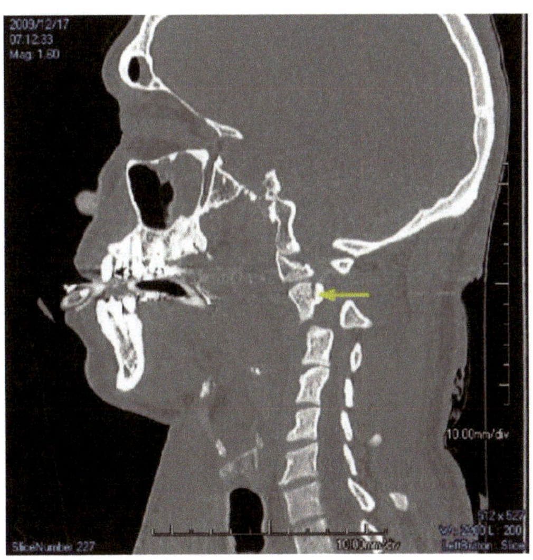

Figure 6.14 Sagittal CT image showing a fracture through the neural arch.

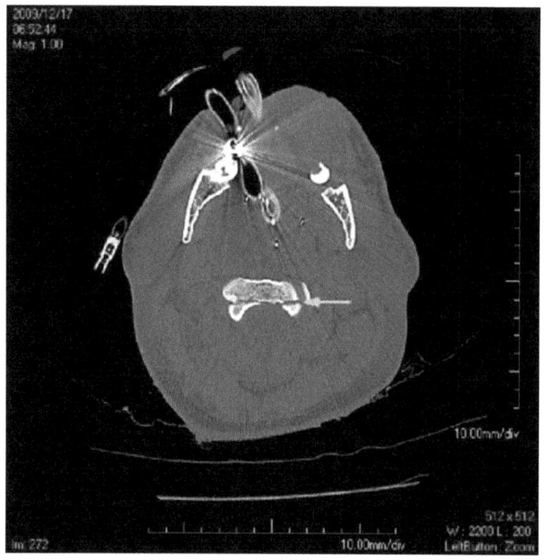

Figure 6.15 Axial CT showing bilateral fractures to the neural arches.

fracture of the anterior inferior aspect of the C2 vertebral body associated with the anterior longitudinal ligament. Typically the avulsed fragment of bone is greater in its horizontal width. The fracture is unstable in extension.

Subaxial Cervical Spine Injury (C3–C7) It has been shown that approximately two-thirds of cervical spine fractures and three-quarters of all cervical spine dislocations occur in the subaxial spine [19]. Furthermore, about 17% of all injuries to the cervical spine are accounted by fractures to C7 or to dislocation of C7–T1 [20].

Subaxial cervical spine injury has a bimodal distribution. Young males are most frequently injured in motor vehicle incidents, motorcycle incidents, sporting accidents, and assaults with weapons (Figure 6.16). In older individuals the injury is associated with a low energy insult. This population may have an underlying disease process such as cervical spondylosis or ankylosing spondylitis. In these victims the cause is usually a fall from a standing position, and there is a tendency for the fracture to occur at the level of the maximum pathology.

As may occur in upper cervical spine injury, fracture or dislocation of the subaxial cervical spine can be associated with rapid death from rupture of the vertebral artery (Figure 6.17a,b).

The fractured lower cervical spine more frequently leads to neurological deficit ranging up to quadriplegia. In older patients there is a significant risk of death in the postoperative period from pulmonary thromboembolism and bronchopneumonia. Acute death from hyperextension injury to the lower cervical spine from falls in 14 victims has been reported in the

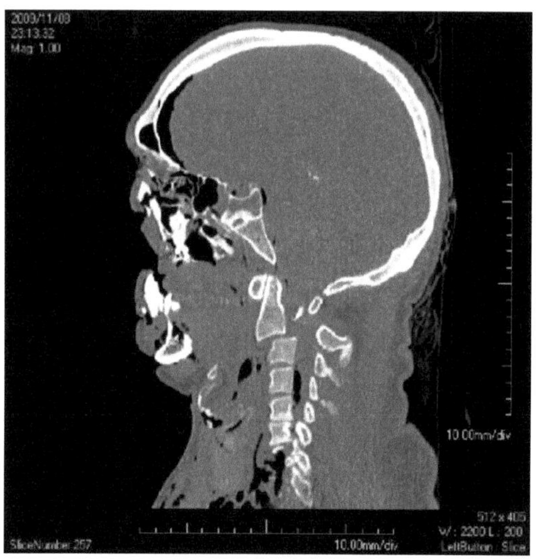

Figure 6.16 Sagittal CT showing a fracture/subluxation at C2/C3. There is subluxation through the disc between C2 and C3. There is a fracture fragment within the spinal canal that probably originates from a facet. The injury is likely to have resulted predominantly from a forced flexion mechanism.

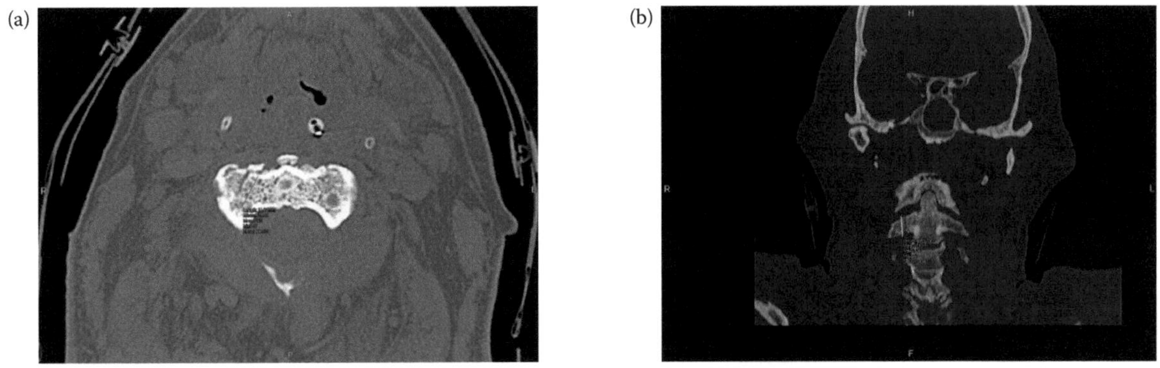

Figure 6.17 (a) Axial CT showing a fracture to the right lateral mass of C2 extending to the foramen transversarium. (b) Coronal CT showing a fracture to the right lateral mass of C2.

forensic literature [21]. The deceased showed central hemorrhage in the spinal cord. Clearly, cases of rapid death at the scene where the CT images show an injury to the subaxial cervical spine must undergo full conventional autopsy examination with neuropathological evaluation of the cervical spine.

CT Diagnosis of Cervical Spine Injury

The introduction of CT has greatly improved the precision of cervical spine examination, which is used in clinical practice to clear the cervical spine of serious injury [22]. CT has been shown to be superior to conventional radiographs in detecting cervical spine fractures.

The basic approach to screen for a cervical spine injury includes

- The diagnosis of a cervical spine injury may be determined by a systematic examination of the edges and contours of the spine or a targeted approach taking into account the known mechanism of the injury.
- The presence of one cervical spine injury should stimulate a search for noncontiguous spinal column injuries. Such injuries are seen in 10% to 15% of these cases [23].

Analysis of conventional cervical radiographs, and research and experience with the various CT modalities has introduced a number of anatomical measurements that can be used to diagnose a cervical spine injury. It should always be remembered that such measurements are only valid in the correct anatomical plane. Reformatted CT images may not always be in the true sagittal or coronal axis, and have the potential to introduce error into such measurements.

Forensic pathologists may be expected to be proficient in identifying fractures with large separation of the fracture edges or those injuries with marked displacement. As subtle fractures are known to be misdiagnosed by radiology residents and occasionally by radiology consultants, it is to be expected that pathologists will miss some of these diagnoses. The pathologist does have the distinct advantage of the knowledge he or she is dealing with a lethal injury of some description, which may provide impetus for a more careful examination of the cervical spine images or referral to an expert radiologist.

Following are CT findings that suggest the presence of a major ligamentous injury.

- Loss of the normal contours to the spine. For the forensic pathologist a useful first screening tool is the examination of the sagittal images for the normal contours of the anterior aspects of the vertebral bodies (Figure 6.18).
- Soft tissue retropharyngeal swelling greater than 5 mm at a level of C3 raises suspicion of an underlying anterior arch fracture.
- The clivus on a sagittal view should point toward the tip of the odontoid process with the tip of the clivus within 5 mm of the odontoid.
- A separation of greater than 2 mm between the atlas and occiput is also considered abnormal [24].

Chamberlain's, McGregor's, and McRae's skull-base lines are standard reference lines that were established using conventional lateral cervical spine radiographs over 50 years ago. These measurements can be used with reformatted midline sagittal CT images.

- Chamberlain's line is defined as a line from the posterior margin of the hard palate to the posterior margin of the foramen magnum. The odontoid process should be approximately 3.3 mm from this line.

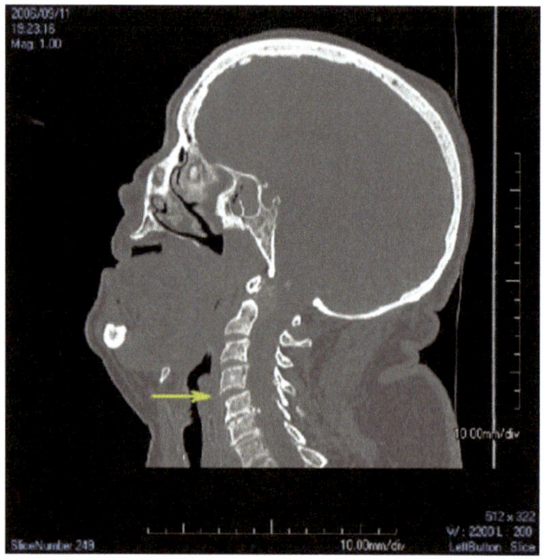

Figure 6.18 Sagittal CT image showing a subluxation between C2 and C3.

- McGregor's line is defined as a line from the posterior–superior margin of the hard palate to the lowest point on the midline occipital curve. The tip of the dens does not project more than 4.5 mm above this line.
- McRae's line is defined as a line from the basion of the foramen magnum to the posterior border. The dens should not project above the line.

Practical Points for Pathologists

- Flexion force often leads to rupture of the transverse atlantal ligament, and alar and apical ligaments (Figure 6.19).
- Displacement of greater than 7 mm (normal 3 mm) of the atlantoodontoid interval is associated with loss of integrity of the alar ligament and tentorial membrane (Figure 6.20) [13].
- Odontoid process fracture is best appreciated using images in a coronal or sagittal plane.
- The typical "hangman's fracture" of C2 can show a teardrop fracture of the inferior aspect of C2 or C3.
- Hyperflexion injury on sagittal reformations shows wedge fractures of the anterior superior vertebral bodies, widened disc spaces posteriorly, and with separation of the spinous processes.
- As CT does not show ligamentous injury, CT will miss atlantooccipital injury if there is no displacement.
- Axial views are particularly useful in a targeted approach with respect to the known mechanism of injury, for example, a Jefferson fracture.

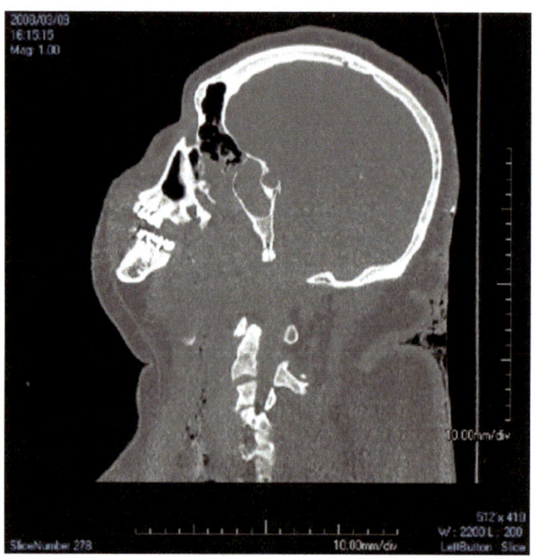

Figure 6.19 Sagittal CT showing marked separation between the base of the skull and the atlas.

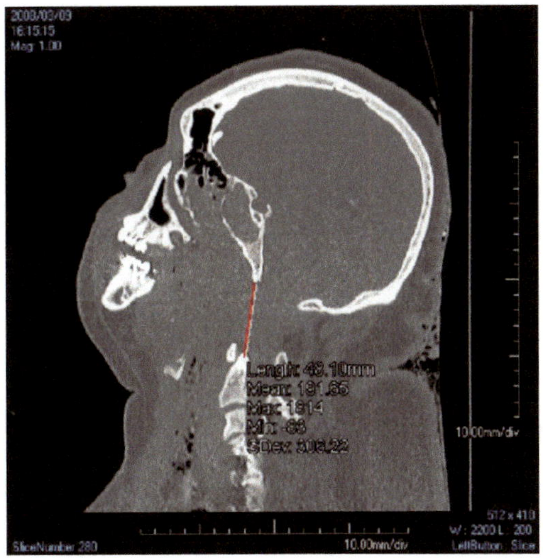

Figure 6.20 Sagittal CT image with formal measurement of the interval between the basion and tip of the odontoid process confirming atlantooccipital dissociation.

- A line drawn along the basiocciput should extend to the tip of the dens.
- A simple compression fracture is a flexion injury. If there is anterior wedging of 3 mm or more, a fracture is suggested. The fracture typically involves the superior endplate of the vertebral body.

Pediatric Issues

Compared to adults the pediatric population has a higher frequency of ligamentous injury as opposed to fractures [25]. The pediatric head is relatively larger than the adult head with respect to the body. The occipital condyles are relatively flatter and the intrinsic and extrinsic neck musculature is less developed. These anatomical features result in a comparatively higher incidence of upper cervical spine injury in infants as opposed to older children and adults. Older children tend to suffer lower cervical injury. Craniocervical dissociation is also more common in infants and toddlers. As in adults, the mechanism of the injury is forced hyperextension and is usually fatal.

A retrospective analysis of cervical spine injuries in 103 consecutive pediatric patients treated at a level 1 trauma center showed a mean age of 10.3±5.2 years with a predominance of males to females (1.6:1) [26]. The most common cause of cervical spine injury was motor vehicle incidents, which caused 52% of cases, especially vehicle versus pedestrian incidents. Sporting injuries caused 27% of cervical spine injury. Of these cases 68% occurred from C1–C4, 25% from C5–C7, and 7% involved both regions of the cervical spine. The overall mortality rate was 18.5% and was most commonly secondary to pedestrian incidents. Dislocations to the upper cervical spine were mainly seen in younger children (mean age 6.6 years). In this subset of patients fractures were most frequently associated with falls and dives.

A review of the National Pediatric Trauma Registry between 1994 and 1999 demonstrated a high proportion of motor vehicle accidents (44%) compared to sports injuries (16%). Pedestrian incidents were involved in 16% of cases. Those aged 10 years or less more often sustained higher cervical spine injury. The mortality rate was 17% and was higher in the younger individuals and most often due to associated head injury [27].

Spinal cord injury without radiological abnormality (SCIWORA) is an uncommon but well-described neurological entity that occurs more frequently in the pediatric population. As the name suggests, SCIWORA refers to a clinical spinal cord injury with no x-ray or CT evidence of cervical spine injury [28]. Magnetic resonance imaging demonstrates a high signal in the T2-weighted image.

Case Study 1

A 46-year-old woman was walking across a well-lit road when startled by an oncoming car traveling at 60 km/h, flashed its lights. Independent witnesses stated she moved into the outside lane where she was struck by a second vehicle. She died at the scene. A cask of red wine was found in her bag. The police indicated there were no charges to be brought against the driver of the motor vehicle.

The investigating police officers stated there was an area of impact to the motor vehicle's windscreen surround with deposition of hair and blood.

The external examination of the deceased showed nonpatterned abrasions to the lateral aspect of her right knee, a compound fracture of her right humerus, and

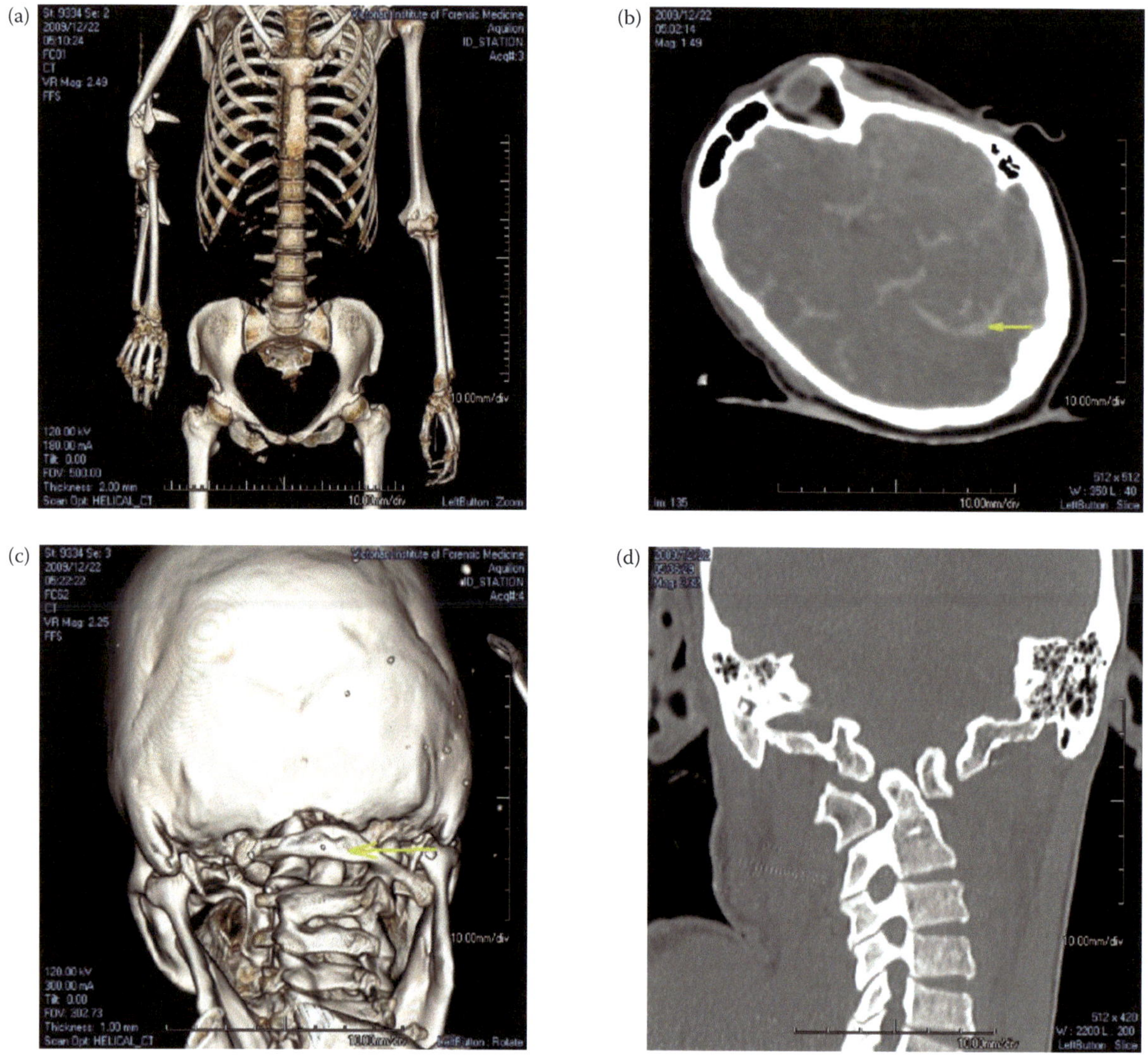

Figure 6.21 (a) Three-dimensional reconstruction of the skeleton showing fractures to the right arm and pelvis. (b) Axial CT showing basal subarachnoid hemorrhage. (c) Posterior view of a three-dimensional reconstruction of the skull and upper cervical spine showing dislocation of the atlantooccipital joint. (d) Lateral CT showing dislocation of the atlantooccipital joint.

closed fracture of her right forearm. There was a 1 cm bruise to the left side of her chin. The head appeared distracted to the left.

Postmortem CT scan showed fractures to the right humeral shaft, right ulnar shaft, and dislocation of the head of the radius (Figure 6.21a). There were fractures to the right superior and inferior pubic rami. CT of the brain showed florid basal subarachnoid hemorrhage (Figure 6.21b). There was no fracture seen to the base of skull or cervical vertebrae. The postmortem CT also showed atlantooccipital dissociation (Figure 6.21c,d).

The cause of death was issued as atlantooccipital disruption in a woman struck by a motor vehicle. The analysis of the case suggested the deceased was struck to her right side, with distraction and dislocation of her atlantooccipital joint to the left, resulting in rupture of vertebral arteries and basal subarachnoid hemorrhage.

Case Study 2

An 82-year-old man with known dilated cariomyopathy was found deceased lying face down on the tiled floor of his bathroom. From the examination of the scene he appeared to have collapsed face forward onto the floor.

The external examination showed a bruise and abrasion to the forehead.

The postmortem CT scan showed gross cord compression at the craniocervical junction incompatible with life (unventilated) (Figure 6.22a,b).

A full postmortem examination was performed. The examination confirmed a markedly enlarged and

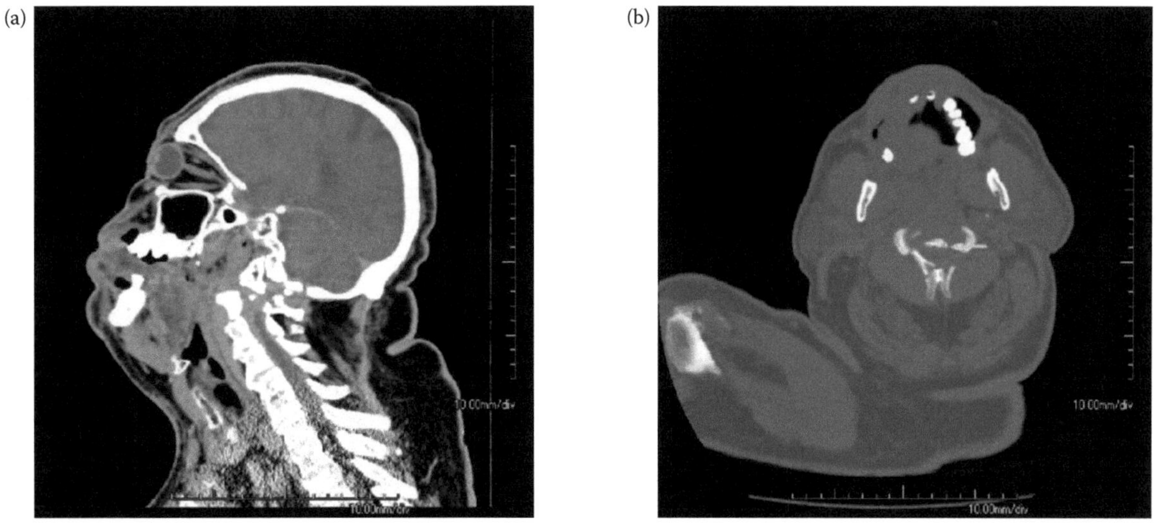

Figure 6.22 (a) Sagittal CT image showing fractured base of odontoid process with gross compression of the cord. (b) Axial CT image showing compression of cord by displaced odontoid.

dilated heart weighing 900 g. There was no evidence of acute infarction or acute coronary lesion. There was hemorrhage noted to the prevertebral soft tissues suggesting an active circulation for a period following the spinal injury.

The cause of death was issued as upper cervical spine injury in a man with dilated cardiomyopathy. The coroner was informed that the death was a direct result of the spinal injury, but one could not determine with certainty whether a cardiac event had caused the initial collapse.

Thoracolumbar Spine

Anatomy

The 12 thoracic vertebrae have articular facets for the ribs. The bodies of the thoracic vertebrae have an upper facet for the rib of its thoracic vertebral number and a smaller inferior facet for the immediately inferior rib. The first to the tenth vertebrae also have rib facets to the transverse processes.

The spinous processes of the thoracic vertebrae vary considerably. The fifth to the eighth vertebrae have lengthy processes with considerable overlap. The first, second, eleventh, and twelfth have shortish, horizontal processes. The remaining four vertebrae have somewhat oblique processes. The lateral extension of the transverse processes decreases progressively from the first to the twelfth vertebrae.

The lumbar vertebrae are robust bones with large, long transverse processes most notably at L3. The superior articular processes face medially to articulate with the lateral facing inferior facet of the higher vertebra.

The lumbar vertebrae are more mobile than the thoracic vertebrae, however the presence of the facet joints oriented in the coronal plane is apt to decrease movement in the sagittal plane.

The Concept of the Three Spinal Columns

There have been a variety of models used to explain the stability of the spine. The three-column concept of thoracolumbar spinal stability was described by Denis in 1983 [29]. This system divides the spine into anterior, middle, and posterior columns.

The anterior column comprises the anterior longitudinal ligament and the anterior portion of the vertebral body. The middle column extends from the middle of the vertebral body and includes the posterior longitudinal ligament. The posterior column extends posteriorly from the posterior longitudinal ligament and includes the pedicles, facets, spinous processes, and associated ligaments.

Cervicothoracic Junction

The cervicothoracic junction (CTJ) may be defined as the segment of spine including C7 and T1 with the intervening disc and associated ligaments. Some workers also include one or more of the adjacent cervical and thoracic vertebrae. The CTJ can be considered to be a distinctive region within the spine with particular biomechanics given its position between the relatively mobile cervical spine and the relatively more inflexible thoracic spine. The cervicothoracic junction is more mobile and thus more prone to fracture dislocation with extreme flexion and extension than other segments of the spine.

Injuries involving the CTJ are not uncommon. They have been reported to comprise about 2% to 5% of spinal trauma in clinical cases [30]. The injuries commonly involve dislocations with ligament injury, facet fractures, and burst vertebral body fractures.

Thoracolumbar Spine

In the thoracic and lumbar spine the majority of fractures occur at the pivoting point between T11 and L2 [31]. The upper thoracic spine is relatively rigid due, in part, from the presence of the ribcage. In the upper and midthoracic spine there is a tendency for flexion injuries.

Although the lumbar region does not have ribs that provide a degree of stability to the thoracic vertebrae, fractures and dislocations below the second lumbar vertebra are uncommon. Such injuries account for 10% to 20% of spinal fractures [32]. Axial load injuries are frequent.

Etiology

Victims of multiple traumas have a high incidence of thoracic and lumbar fractures. Compression (wedge) fractures are the most common type of thoracolumbar fracture. Fractures and dislocations involving the thoracolumbar spine are most commonly seen in pedestrian deaths, motorcycle crashes, and victims of significant falls. Due to the relatively large forces involved in these incidents there are often severe thoracic and abdominal visceral injuries.

Mechanism

There are a number of classification systems to classify thoracic and lumbar spinal fractures. A classification system that uses the mechanism of injury and fracture morphology to categorize fractures is the McAfee classification [33].

The majority of vertebral fractures are vertical or oblique in orientation. Horizontal fractures, including Chance fractures, comprise around 5% of thoracolumbar fractures. The fracture types can be separated into five broad groups. These are [34]:

- Forced flexion fractures (Chance fracture)
- Compression wedge fracture
- Burst fracture
- Flexion-distraction fracture
- Translational injury

The forced flexion or Chance fracture was originally seen in motor vehicle occupants wearing lap seat belts who were involved in front-on motor vehicle collisions. A horizontal vertebral injury results from flexion about an axis positioned in front of the anterior longitudinal ligament. The characteristic features of the injury include disruption of the vertebral bodies and pedicles, spinous processes, transverse processes, and laminae (Figure 6.23).

A compression wedge fracture occurs from hyperflexion with axial loading. The vertebral body tends to fail in compression at the anterior aspect of the vertebral body (Figure 6.24a,b,c).

The burst fracture involves the anterior and middle columns. This injury may occur with or without a posterior column fracture. The biomechanics of the burst fracture involve hyperflexion and axial loading (Figure 6.25). This fracture is differentiated from a wedge fracture by way of the herniation of the intervertebral

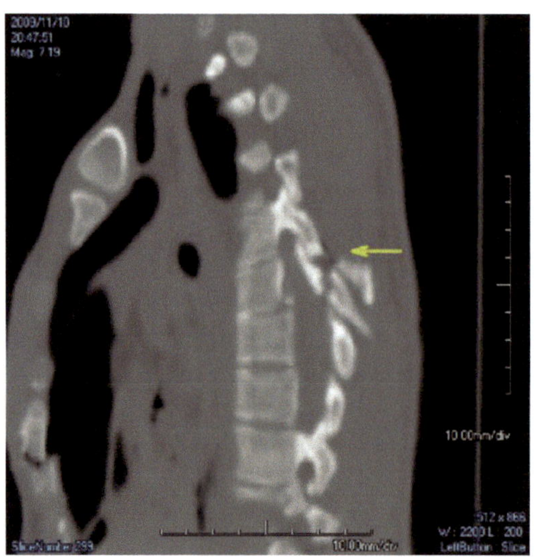

Figure 6.23 Sagittal CT showing fractures to the spinous processes and vertebral body. Primary impact site to the chest with associated fracture to the sternum.

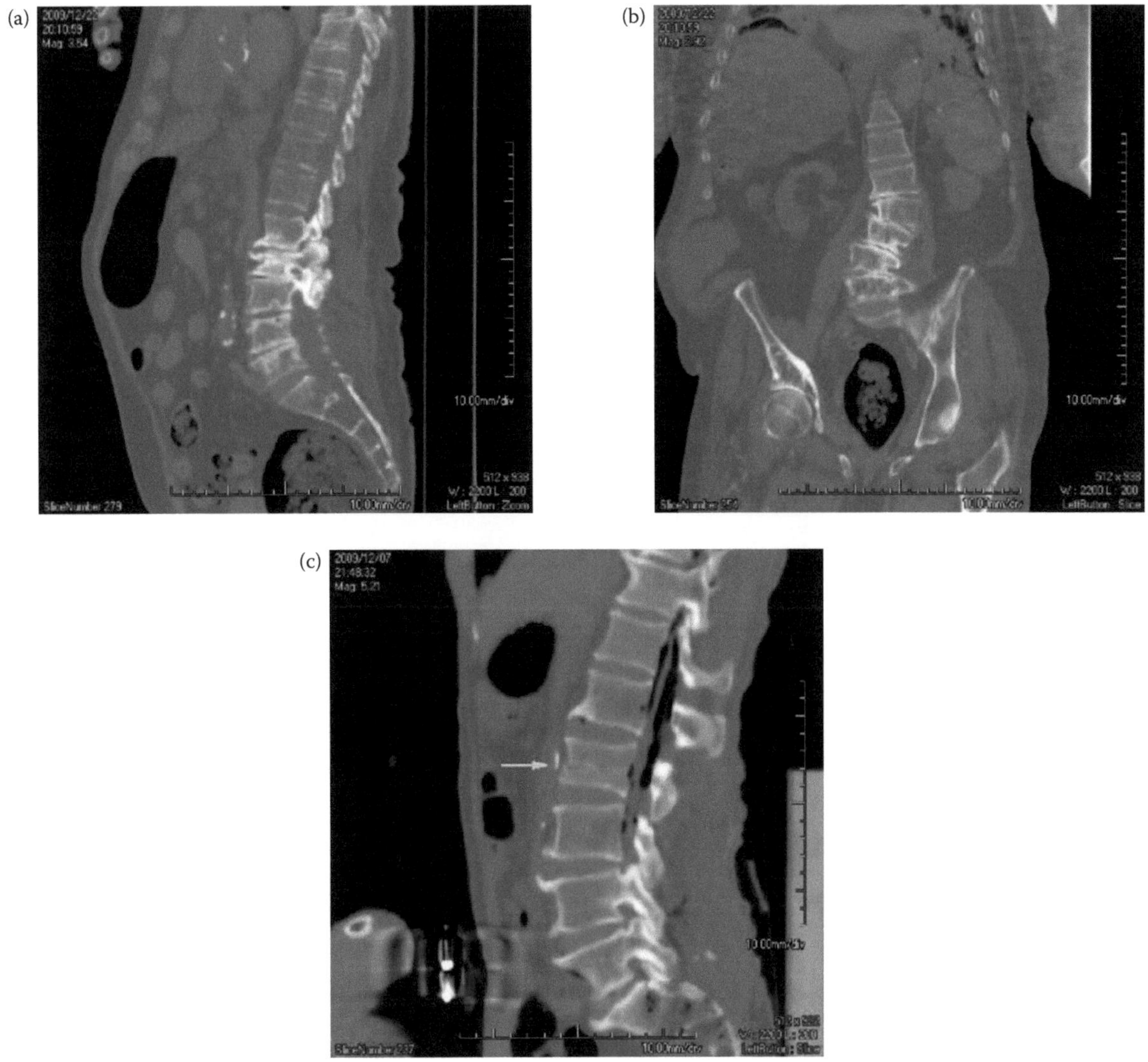

Figure 6.24 (a) Sagittal CT showing a crush fracture to L2 in an osteoporotic spine with osteophytes and adjacent minor crush fracture. (b) Coronal CT showing a crush fracture and osteoporotic spine. (c) Sagittal CT showing a crush fracture to the vertebral body from axial loading secondary to a fall onto the feet from a considerable height.

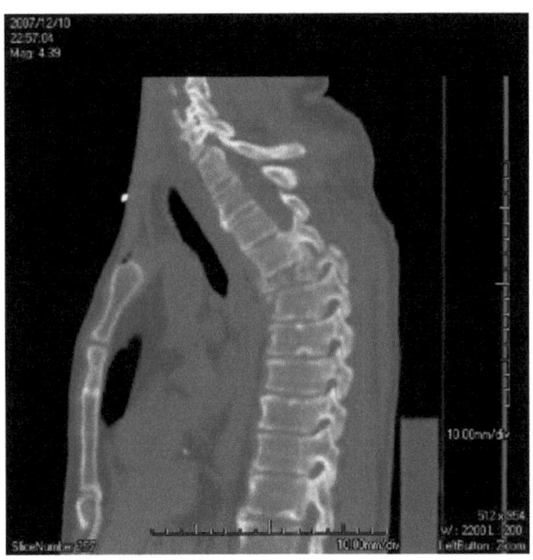

Figure 6.25 Sagittal CT showing a burst fracture to the thoracic spine.

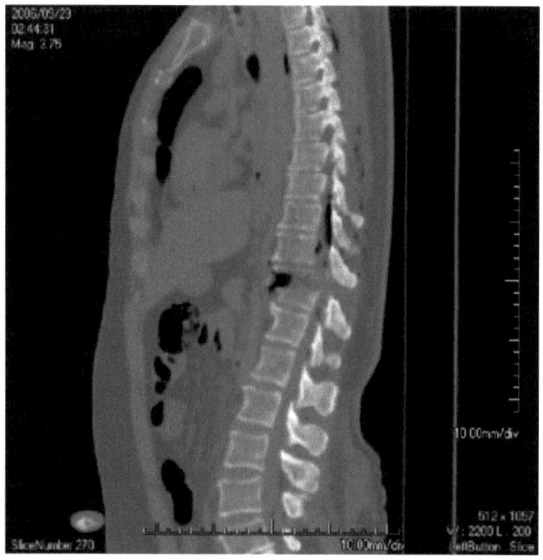

Figure 6.26 Sagittal CT showing a flexion distraction injury to the thoracic spine.

disc into the affected vertebral body. This leads to an increase in interpeduncular distance, which can be seen on the CT scans.

The flexion distraction injury occurs when the axis of the flexion is posterior to the anterior longitudinal ligament. This leads to a compression-type fracture of the anterior column (Figure 6.26). Destructive forces are applied to the middle and posterior columns with an associated tear of the posterior longitudinal ligament.

Translational injury is the result of shearing forces. There is often disruption of all three columns with ruptures of multiple ligaments.

CT Diagnosis of Thoracolumbar Fractures

A specific visualization of the thoracic and lumbar spine in axial, sagittal, and coronal planes in addition to three-dimensional reconstructions is required if all fractures are to be documented. The expected fractures from the specific mechanisms of the injury may be sought using targeted views of the images.

Following are general suggestions for pathologists reviewing thoracolumbar images.

- The height of vertebral bodies and discs should be equal and uniform.
- One should trace the anterior, posterior, and spinolaminar lines. Sagittal multiplanar reformations are obligatory to evaluate fractures in the plane of the x-ray beam as these may be overlooked on axial views.
- The visualization of a Chance fracture is enhanced with a sagittal view. Subtle changes include an increased space between the adjacent spinous processes above and below the injury. The images may demonstrate a tear in the vertebral body and posterior arch. Axial images alone may not reveal the fracture.
- The compression wedge fracture is best seen with sagittal views.
- The flexion distraction injury classically displays posterior distraction with separation of the spinous processes and anterior vertebral body compression.
- Translational injury shows anterior translation of the upper vertebral body on sagittal views. Coronal images show widening of the interspinous distance. There may be "naked facets" or "double vertebrae" reflecting rotational malalignment. Naked facets are seen when the articulating processes are exposed secondary to anterior subluxation of the vertebrae with widening of the facet joints [1].
- Multidetector computed tomography (MDCT) in flexion-distraction injury showed posterior cortical buckling or retropulsion in 48% of cases. Serial transaxial CT shows gradual loss of definition of the pedicles, which has been termed the "dissolving pedicle sign." This was evident in 76% of cases [35].

Forensic Issues in Thoracolumbar Fractures

A recent study on flexion-distraction injuries of the thoracolumbar spine showed that thoracolumbar injuries are often associated with significant intra-abdominal injuries.

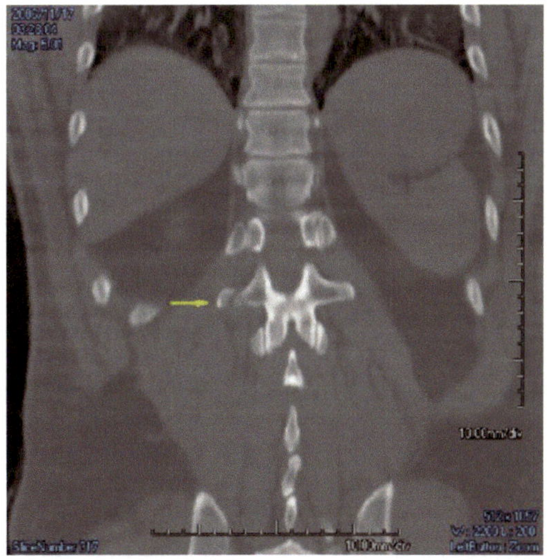

Figure 6.27 Coronal CT showing a fracture to the right second lumbar transverse process.

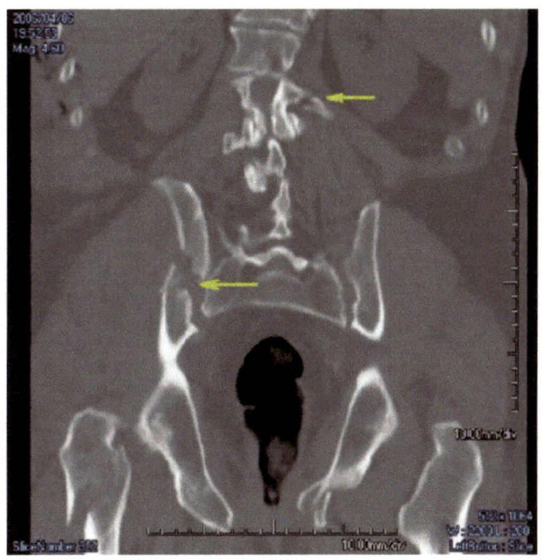

Figure 6.28 Coronal CT showing fractures to the pelvis and lumbar transverse process.

Individuals who suffer a seizure may sustain a compression fracture of a vertebral body through contraction of the paraspinal muscles. These fractures are more frequently seen in the thoracic spine but have also been described in lumbar vertebrae [36].

Fractures to the thoracolumbar spinous and transverse process fractures usually indicate the application of direct blunt force trauma.

Fractured lumbar spinous and transverse processes usually indicate the application of direct blunt force trauma (Figure 6.27). In some reports transverse process fracture has been associated with such visceral injury in up to 25% of cases. Lower lumbar transverse process fracture is frequently seen in association with pelvic fractures (Figure 6.28).

References

1. Lingawi SS. The naked facet sign. *Radiology* 2001; 219:366–367.
2. Chen Y-F, Liu H-M. Imaging of craniovertebral junction. *Neuroimag. Clin. N. Am.* 2009; 19:483–510.
3. Penning L. Normal movements of the cervical spine. *Am. J. Roentgenol.* 1978; 130:317–327.
4. Lowery DW, Wald MM, Browne BJ, Tigges S, Hoffman JR, Mower WR. Epidemiology of cervical spine injury victims. *Ann. Emerg. Med.* 2001; 38:12–16.
5. Levine AM, Edwards CC. Fractures of the atlas. *J. Bone Joint Surg. Am.* 1991; 73:680–691.
6. Korres DS, Papagelopoulous PJ, Mavrogenis AF, Benetos IS, Kyriazopoulos P, Psycharis I. Chance-type fractures of the axis. *Spine* 2005; 30(17):E517–E520.

7. Landells CD, Van Peteghem PK. Fractures of the atlas: Classification, treatment and morbidity. *Spine* 1988; 13:450–452.
8. Mohit AA, Schuster JA, Mirza SK, Mann FA. "Plough" fracture: Shear fracture of the anterior arch of the atlas. *AJR* 2003; 181:770.
9. Gebauer M, Goetzen N, Barvencik F, Beil FT, Rupprecht M, Rueger JM, Puschel K, Morlock M, Amling N. Biomechanical analysis of atlas fractures: A study on 40 human atlas specimens. *Spine* 2008; 33(9):766–770.
10. Beckner MA, Heggeness MH, Doherty BJ. A biomechanical study of Jefferson fractures. *Spine* 1998; 23(17):1832–1836.
11. Goradia D, Blackmore CC, Talner LB, Bittles M, Meshberg E. Predicting radiology resident's errors in diagnosis of cervical spine fractures. *Acad. Radiol.* 2005; 12:888–893.
12. Chang W, Alexander MT, Mirvis SE. Diagnostic determinants of craniocervical distraction injury in adults. *AJR* 2009; 192:52–58.
13. Fielding JW, Cochran GV, Lawsing JF III, Hohl M. Tears of the transverse ligament of the atlas: A clinical and biomechanical study. *J. Bone Joint Surg. Am.* 1974; 56:1683–1691.
14. Dempster AG, Heap SW. Fatal high cervical spinal cord injury in an automobile accident complicating os odontoideum. *Am. J. Forensic Pathol.* 1990; 11(3):252–256.
15. Puttlitz CM, Goel VK, Clarke CR, Traynelis VC. Pathomechanisms of failures of the odontoid. *Spine* 2000; 25(22):2868–2876.
16. Cusick JF, Yoganandan N, Pintar F, Gardon M. Cervical spine injuries and high-velocity forces: A pathoanatomic and radiologic study. *J. Spin. Disord.* 1996; 9(1):1–7.
17. Anderson LD, D'Alonzo RT. Fractures of the odontoid process of the axis. *J. Bone Joint Surg. Am.* 1974; 56:1663–1674.
18. Hadley MN, Dickman CA, Browner CM, Sonntag VK. Acute axis fractures: A review of 229 cases. *Neurosurgery* 1989; 71(5):642–647.
19. Goldberg W, Mueller C, Panacek E, Tigges S, Hoffman JR, Mower WR. Distribution and patterns of blunt traumatic cervical spine injury. *Ann. Emerg. Med.* 2001; 38:17–21.
20. Kwon BK, Vaccaro AR, Grauer JN, Fisher CG, Dvorak MF. Subaxial cervical spine trauma. *J. Am. Acad. Orthop. Surg.* 2006; 14:78–89.
21. Osawa M, Satoh F, Hasegawa I. Acute death due to hyperextension injury of the cervical spine caused by falling and slipping onto the face. *J. Forensic Leg. Med.* 2008; 15(7):457–461.
22. Widder S, Doig C, Burrows P, Larsen G, Hurlbert RG, Kortbeck JB. Prospective evaluation of computed tomographic scanning for spinal clearance of obtunded trauma patients. *J. Trauma* 2004; 56:1179–1184.
23. Vaccaro AR, An HS, Lin S, Sun S, Balderston RA, Cotler JM. Noncontiguous injuries of the spine. *J. Spinal Disord.* 1992; 5:320–329.
24. Jackson RS, Banit DM, Rhyne AL III, Dardn BV II. Upper cervical spine injuries. *J. Am. Acad. Orthop. Surg.* 2002; 10:271–280.
25. McCall T, Fassett D, Brockmeyer D. Cervical spine trauma in children: A review. *Neurosurg. Focus* 2006; 20(2):E7.
26. Brown RL, Brunn MA, Garcia VF. Cervical spine injuries in children: A review of 103 patients treated consecutively at a level 1 pediatric trauma centre. *J. Pediatr. Surg.* 2001; 36(8):1107–1114.
27. Kokoska ER, Keller MS, Rallo MC, Weber TR. Characteristics of pediatric cervical spine injuries. *J. Pediatr. Surg.* 2001; 36(1):100–105.
28. Kim SH, Yoon SH, Cho KH, Kim SH. Spinal cord injury without radiological abnormality in an infant with delayed presentation of symptoms after a minor injury. *Spine* 2008; 33(21):E792–E794.
29. Denis F. The three column spine and its significance in the classification of acute thoracolumbar spinal injuries. *Spine* 1983; 8:817–831.
30. Wang VY, Chou D. The cervicothoracic junction. *Neurosurg. Clin. N. Am.* 2007; 18(2):365–371.
31. Bohlman HH. Treatment of fractures and dislocations of the thoracic and lumbar spine. *J. Bone Joint Surg. Am.* 1985; 67(1):165–169.
32. Ohashi K, El-Khoury GY. Musculoskeletal CT: Recent advances and current clinical applications. *Radiol. Clin. North Am.* 2009; 47(3):387–409.
33. McAfee PC, Yuan HA, Fredricksen BE, Lubicky JP. The value of computed tomography in thoracolumbar fractures: An analysis of one hundred consecutive cases and a new classification. *J. Bone Joint Surg. Am.* 1983; 65:461–473.
34. Roos JE, Hilfiker P, Platz A, Desbiolles T, Marincek B, Weishaupt D. MDCT in emergency radiology: Is a standardized chest or abdominal protocol sufficient for evaluation of thoracic and lumbar spine trauma? *AJR* 2004; 183:959–968.
35. Bernstein MP, Mirvis SE, Shanmuganathan K. Chance-type fractures of the thoracolumbar spine: Imaging analysis in 53 patients. *AJR* 2006; 187:859–868.
36. Mehlhorn AT, Strohm PC, Hausschildt O, Schmal H, Südkamp NP. Seizure-induced muscle force can cause lumbar spine fracture. *Acta Chir. Orthop. Traumatol. Cech.* 2007; 74(3):202–205.

Chest

7

Ribs

Anatomy

The 12 ribs vary in shape from the costovertebral junction to the costochondral junction but are basically wedge shaped on cross-section. The ribs are divided into the head, which articulates with the vertebral body; the somewhat flattened neck, which extends laterally from the head; the shaft or body of the rib; and the sternal aspect.

The third to tenth ribs can be regarded as typical. The head of the ribs have two facets. The larger, lower facet articulates with its own vertebral body. The smaller, upper facet articulates with the immediately superior vertebral body. The tubercle situated at the lower aspect of the neck of the rib articulates with its own vertebral body's transverse process. At the anatomical angle of the rib, the immediately posterior aspect of the bone is bent medially toward the vertebral body.

The first rib articulates with the manubrium. The second to seventh ribs articulate with the sternum, and the eighth, ninth, and tenth ribs articulate with the cartilages of the immediately superior rib at their costal cartilage. The eleventh and twelfth ribs are unusual in that they have only one articulation, which is from the head of the rib to their own vertebral body.

Etiology

The ribs form a protective cage around the thoracic viscera, yet are pliable enough to allow expansion during respiration. Ribs in young children are extremely pliable and fractures may not be seen despite considerable compressive force. The thin cortex of the ribs in adults makes them susceptible to fracture. With the development of osteoporosis, rib fractures may occur with relatively minor blunt force trauma.

Rib fractures are a common injury in cases of chest trauma and comprise 50% of skeletal fractures. Common causes of rib fractures in Western societies are motor vehicle incidents, falls, and other accidents. Fractures of the first, second, and third ribs are associated with an increased incidence of significant thoracic visceral trauma [1]. Rib fractures in the elderly, or in those with significant pulmonary or cardiac disease, are a significant independent risk factor for increased morbidity and mortality.

A flail chest results from rib fractures involving at least two separate sites on two or three consecutive ribs. Flail segments have been shown to occur in about 10% of clinical patients with chest trauma. A flail chest results in paradoxical movement of the fractured segment with respect to the remainder of the chest and may lead to atelectasis, pneumonia, and respiratory failure.

Mechanisms

It is currently accepted that bones tend to fail more readily in tension rather than compression. However, at least two studies have cast doubt on the primary role of tension forces in causing rib fracture. A study of 43 blunt force trauma cases involving 492 ribs with 733 individual fractures showed a total of 195 incomplete and 63 buckle fractures [2]. Buckle fractures refer to failure of cortical bone secondary to compression forces and are classically seen in the long bones of the forearm following a fall to the outstretched hand in adolescents. Incomplete or partial fractures had previously been considered to be uncommon in adults.

The occurrence of buckle fractures was confirmed in a later experimental study [3]. Although this study was based on a sample of only eight ribs, it did demonstrate a variety of fracture types with transverse, buckle, spiral, and butterfly-type fractures observed following the application of a specified compression force to the isolated rib specimen. The authors indicated that "human ribs may undergo considerable plastic deformation prior to complete structural failure." The experiment also demonstrated variation in the stiffness within ribs with the anterior rib shafts that are not as stiff and weaker than the posterior regions [3].

Clinical observations suggest that anterior chest compression leads to anterolateral rib fractures (Figure 7.1a,b). Anterior chest loading from blunt force trauma such as may occur in a motor vehicle accident results in a fracture pattern similar to those seen in attempted cardiopulmonary resuscitation. A laboratory study using human cadavers investigated injury patterns with respect to three-point seat-belt combinations and airbags. This study showed that there was a distinct

(a)

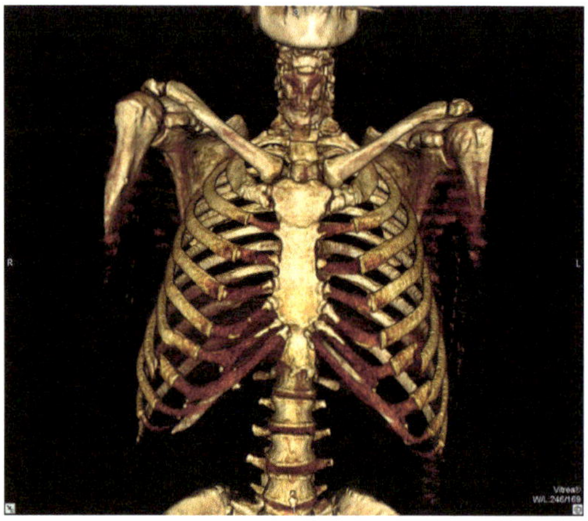

(b)

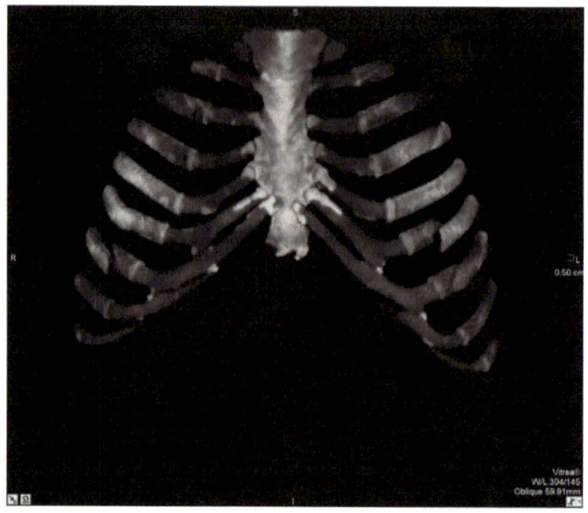

Figure 7.1 (a) Three-dimensional reconstruction of the chest showing multiple, somewhat symmetrical fractures to the anterior aspects of the ribs. (b) Detail of typical anterior rib fractures as seen in cardiopulmonary resuscitation.

tendency for rib fractures to follow the line of the shoulder belt in airbag–three-point belt tests, whereas bilateral symmetrical lower rib fractures were seen in association with the use of an airbag alone [4].

The study showed a similar pattern of rib trauma to a previous study that compared the effects of a seat belt alone with a steering-wheel-mounted airbag. This study revealed that the force to the anterior chest resulted in an increase in the radius of curvature at the lateral aspect of the rib and thus initiated fractures from bending.

Pediatric Rib Fractures

Etiology and Significance of Pediatric Rib Fractures

Rib fractures in children are an independent marker of severe trauma. A study that addressed the clinical importance of multiple rib fractures in children showed that when compared to traumatized children without rib fractures, those children who had rib fractures had a statistically higher mortality rate [5]. Furthermore, the risk of mortality in these children increased with the number of ribs fractured.

Pediatric chest injury from blunt force trauma is generally the result of falls, motor-vehicle-related trauma, and falls from bicycles [7]. In a clinical review from Turkey comprising 137 cases of blunt thoracic trauma in children aged from 1 to 16 years, only three cases (2.2%) were the result of abuse [7].

A study on chest injuries in 100 children resulting from motor vehicle incidents was performed in a clinical study from South Africa [6]. Ninety-one of the children were pedestrians struck by motor vehicles. In this clinical study eight of the patients died. The most common injuries seen were pulmonary contusions ($n = 73$). Rib fractures were seen in 62 of the 100 cases.

Rib fractures are not common injuries in infants, and when diagnosed apart from the typical clinical situation of motor vehicle incident or independently witnessed fall, the possibility of nonaccidental injury must be raised. A study on rib fractures in infants <12 months of age was performed at two tertiary children's hospitals [8]. Thirty-nine infants with rib fractures were identified over a 3-year period. Thirty-two cases (82%) were determined to be due to abuse, three cases (7.7%) from accidents, one case (2.6%) from birth trauma, and three (7.7%) were deemed to be due to bone fragility.

As noted earlier, pediatric ribs can absorb a considerable amount of force without sustaining a fracture. It is the anecdotal experience of many forensic pathologists who have examined pediatric victims of severe blunt chest trauma that one may observe virtual pulping of the thoracic viscera yet with no associated rib fracture. This is an interesting observation as it may reflect the way forces are delivered to the chest in nonaccidental injury (NAI) rather than simply the magnitude of the force. It has been suggested that posterior rib fractures caused by abuse arise from the posterior rib being forced against the transverse process of the vertebra by a fulcrum action.

Nonaccidental Injury (NAI)

Rib fractures are the most common fracture seen in cases of child abuse. When a rib fracture is found in an infant in the absence of a history of significant trauma, the most likely cause is NAI (Figure 7.2) [9]. A rib fracture resulting from NAI is most frequently seen in those less than one year of age [10].

The mechanism of NAI causing rib fracture can be anterior–posterior or lateral compression of the chest. The insult may be from relatively slow compression from a squeezing action, or an abrupt impact from a direct

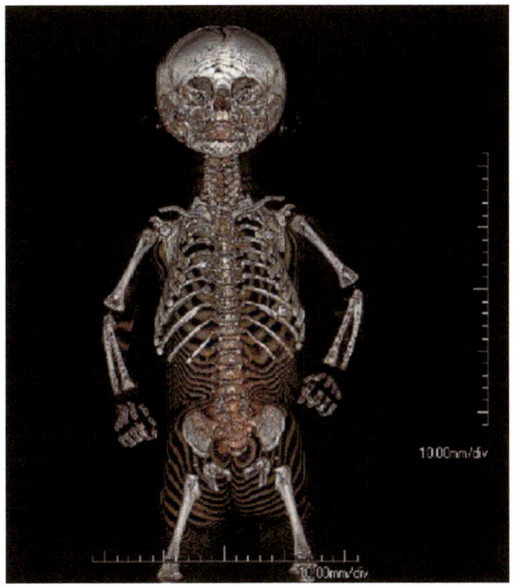

Figure 7.2 Overall three-dimensional reconstruction showing multiple posterior rib fractures in an abused infant. Expansion of the ribs adjacent to the vertebral bodies is clearly evident in the right ribs when compared to the left side.

blow or being thrown against a hard object. The common sites of fractures resulting from NAI in pediatric ribs are the posterior aspects of the rib in the region of the costovertebral process articulation and the head of the rib.

The position of a fracture may provide information regarding the mechanism of rib fracture. Unfortunately the literature is somewhat complicated by the use of different terms to describe anatomical regions of the ribs in the different papers. Even so, a number of generalizations can still be reached. In their comprehensive literature review of rib fractures in the pediatric population, Worn and Jones suggested that anterior–posterior compression of the chest was the likely mode of injury in fractures caused by abuse [9].

A study by Kleinman et al. analyzed the site of pediatric rib fractures with respect to the underlying cause. About 32% of 84 fractures in 31 infants at the costotransverse process articulation were the result of abuse [11]. The mechanism of this injury was believed to be from a levering action of the rib against the transverse process of the vertebral body (Figure 7.3). Fractures in the region of the head of the rib occurred in approximately 33% of the abuse cases. Anteriorly and laterally positioned fractures are relatively uncommon, and fractures of the costochondral junctions are rare in nonaccidental injury [12].

The presence of old healing fractures is of crucial importance in the differentiation between accidental and nonaccidental injury. Healing fractures can be documented by the presence of callus in computed tomography (CT) scans. Although radiologists may offer a view on the age of a fracture, it is unlikely that a radiologist is going to be able to provide an opinion of the age of a fracture that has the accuracy implicit in the histological examination of a section of bone.

Cardiopulmonary Resuscitation

Rib fractures are commonly seen following cardiopulmonary resuscitation (CPR) in adults. In children, recent rib fractures in those receiving CPR are decidedly uncommon. It can be a crucial issue in such cases to determine whether the rib fractures are due to resuscitation or are associated with abuse. In a paper by Feldman and Brewer 113 children were studied. It was found that "in spite of prolonged resuscitation performed with variable degrees of skill, no fractures could be identified" [13].

A previous retrospective paper reported injuries sustained in CPR on a population of deceased children with no history of preceding trauma [14]. There were 211 cases. Fifteen children had at least one injury that was considered to be medically significant. However, there was only one case of rib fracture. Laypersons and emergency personnel performed the prolonged CPR. There were bilateral fractures of the eighth and ninth ribs at the sternochondral junction.

A recent literature review also concluded that rib fractures after cardiopulmonary resuscitation are rare [15]. The review involved 427 studies from which, after an appraisal process, 6 were included. The collective data was on a total of 923 children who underwent CPR. Three children were found to have suffered rib fracture from CPR. All three cases had anterior fractures.

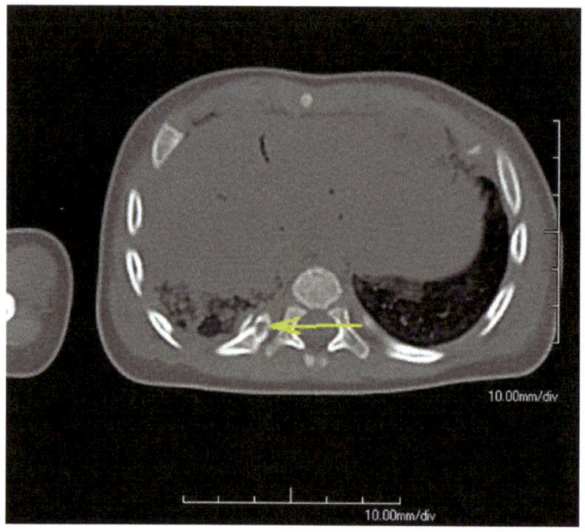

Figure 7.3 Axial CT of an infant showing a recent posterior fracture to a left rib. There were multiple other recent and old fractures.

The traditional two-finger technique to perform CPR in young pediatric patients is believed to be biomechanically incapable of causing rib fractures [9]. A two-thumb technique, where the infant's thorax is grasped between both hands with the thumbs over the sternum and with the fingers oriented to the back of the chest, has been introduced as a recommended method of resuscitation in infants.

It has been suggested that the two-thumb technique may lead to an increased incidence of rib fractures to the head of the rib or costotransverse process articulation. This would occur from a "levering" effect as occurs when an abused infant is grasped between the hands and shaken. Further studies will be required to determine if the alteration in resuscitation technique is a possible cause of rib fracture.

Reports of pediatric homicide from intentional anteroposterior manual chest compression have been published in the forensic literature [16]. It has been reported that some child abusers may punish children by inflicting manual chest compression. Ensuing injuries that are identified at postmortem examination may be explained by inexpert CPR. Two deaths were described that had fractures of multiple ribs, rupture of viscera, and hemorrhage extending from the mediastinum to regions far from the site of the blunt force trauma. Hemorrhage into the adrenal medulla from pressure effects through the adrenal veins may also be seen.

CT Diagnosis of Rib Fractures

Early studies comparing conventional chest radiographs and autopsy have shown that autopsy examinations reveal fractures that are not seen on the x-ray films. However, other studies suggested results to the contrary.

CT is an excellent tool in demonstrating rib injury (Figure 7.4). The technique is able to demonstrate rib

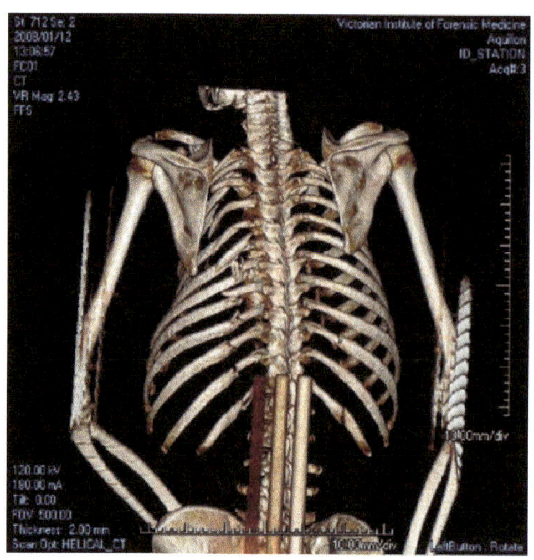

Figure 7.4 Three-dimensional reconstruction CT showing that all of the left ribs and the tenth and twelfth right ribs are fractured.

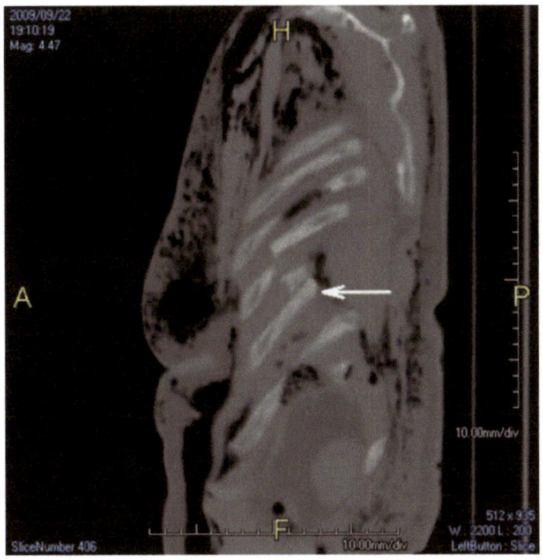

Figure 7.5 Sagittal CT demonstrating fractured ribs in a decomposed body.

fractures in difficult cases such as decomposed or markedly burnt bodies (Figure 7.5).

A retrospective study compared the ability of conventional chest x-ray and helical CT scan to diagnose rib fractures and the presence of pulmonary contusions, and endeavored to predict respiratory failure and mortality [17]. The chest x-rays and CT scans of 388 patients admitted to the hospital with at least one rib fracture during the period from January 2003 to December 2005 were systematically reviewed. The study showed that screening chest x-rays missed rib fractures in more than half of the cases. Interestingly, the initial CT report was shown to incorrectly underdiagnose the number of rib fractures in 43% (179 of 388) of cases. A scanning view of the three-dimensional reconstruction images may result in the pathologist overlooking subtle rib fractures (Figure 7.6).

- The presence of subcutaneous emphysema may suggest an associated rib fracture (Figure 7.7).
- The presence of a pneumothorax may suggest an associated rib fracture.
- CT can demonstrate more subtle subtypes of fracture including bending or buckle fractures, which may not be evident on the routine autopsy examination.
- The clinical reporting of CT rib images has been shown to underdiagnose rib fractures. Thus it is likely forensic pathologists will probably underdiagnose rib fractures on CT.
- The forensic pathologist can use a combination of axial views using bone windows and three-dimensional reconstructions for the initial screening of the images.

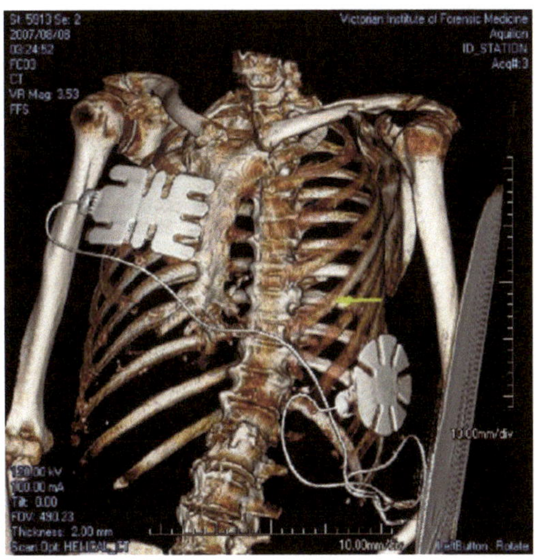

Figure 7.6 Three-dimensional reconstruction showing multiple fractured ribs. The fractures are not easily seen on this image and could easily be overlooked by a pathologist.

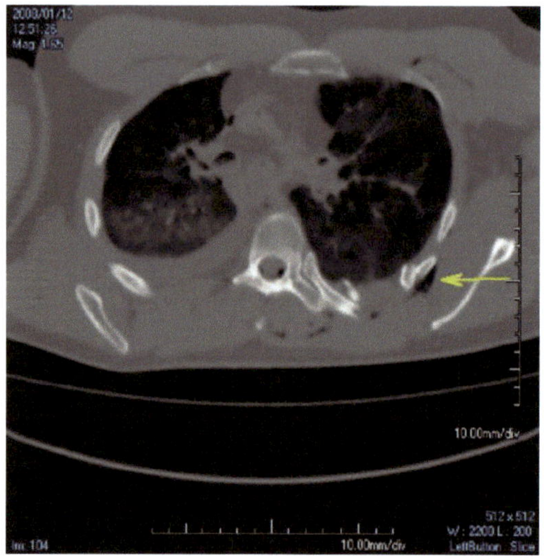

Figure 7.7 Axial CT showing a fractured left rib with adjacent subcutaneous emphysema.

Pediatric CT Scanning

Chest radiographs have been the standard way to detect rib fractures in the pediatric population [18]. The classical appearance of rib fractures on a conventional radiograph is the so-called string of beads indicating healing posterior rib fractures. There are a number of reasons why a fracture may not be visible on a traditional x-ray image. The fracture may be nondisplaced, incomplete, or superimposed over other structures.

Postmortem CT scanning does not have the issue of radiation dose that is clearly of major concern in living patients. A preliminary retrospective clinical study compared the detection rates of CT and conventional radiology in 12 abused infants [19]. Although the study group was small, CT demonstrated 131 fractures, whereas only 79 fractures were seen with conventional x-rays. In one patient, fractures were apparent only with CT. The study concluded that CT was superior in detecting early subacute, subacute, and old fractures. No significant differences were seen in acute fractures.

At this point in time at the Victorian Institute of Forensic Medicine (VIFM) we have examined a relatively small number of pediatric deaths. It is our practice to obtain a traditional skeletal survey and a full body CT that are then reported by an expert radiologist in every case.

Forensic Issues in Rib Fractures

Rib fractures are important injuries in all age groups. The presence of fractures of the first through to the third ribs is a marker of significant force applied to the chest and the high likelihood of intrathoracic visceral injury. Fractures of the eighth through to the eleventh ribs are associated with an increased incidence of intra-abdominal visceral injury.

The number of fractured ribs is associated with increased mortality rates following blunt force chest trauma. The presence of a flail segment also affords a statistically higher risk of death. A research paper examined data from the National Trauma Data Bank in the United States and collected over 64,000 cases with at least one fractured rib. The study showed that with increasing numbers of fractured ribs there was a direct correlation with increasing pulmonary morbidity and overall mortality [20].

Individuals with six or more fractured ribs were at increased risk of death from causes not directly related to rib fracture. Hence the presence of more than six rib fractures may be viewed as a marker for the presence of a remote potentially lethal injury.

The heightened mortality and morbidity risks are especially significant for the very young and the elderly. Interestingly it has also been shown that middle-aged victims of blunt force chest trauma are at risk of adverse outcomes when they sustain four or more rib fractures [21]. Elderly patients who suffer blunt force injury to the chest with rib fractures have double the mortality of younger patients with similar injuries [22].

Sternum

Anatomy

The sternum is an elongated, flattened bone consisting of three parts: the manubrium, the body of the sternum, and the xiphoid process. The manubrium is a somewhat quadrangular bone that has articulations at its upper aspect with the clavicle and first rib, and articulates with the second rib at its lower portion. The body of the sternum is slightly convex anteriorly. The body of the sternum has articulations with the second through to the seventh ribs.

A sternal foramen is not an uncommon congenital anomaly arising from a defect in ossification. Its forensic importance is that it may be misinterpreted as a bullet wound.

Etiology

In clinical practice sternal fractures are not common injuries. The incidence of sternal fracture has been reported to range between 0.64% and 3.7% of all injuries [23]. The mortality rate in those admitted to hospital with a fractured sternum is reported to be up to 2.6% [23]. Once usually associated with multiple rib fractures, isolated sternal fractures have been seen with increasing regularity since the introduction of seat belts [24].

A retrospective review involving 10 of years experience at a trauma center in Los Angeles, California, investigated the incidence of sternal fracture in victims of trauma. It was shown that in a total of 37,087 patients, 125 (0.33%) had a sternal fracture [25]. Occupants of cars in motor vehicle collisions resulted in 68% of the cases and pedestrians comprised 18% of cases. Associated rib fractures occurred in just under one-half of the cases.

A fractured sternum is an indicator of the application of severe force to the chest. As such, the injury is associated with a high frequency of other thoracic bony and visceral injuries. These injuries include multiple fractured ribs, cardiac and pulmonary injury, and aortic tears. Sternal fractures are also associated with extrathoracic injuries including craniocerebral injury [26].

The traditional view of sternal fractures has been that the injury represents a significant marker for cardiac contusions. This view has been questioned in cases of sternal fracture with negligible displacement [27]. In a study of 100 consecutive patients admitted to the hospital with sternal fracture, 4 patients succumbed to their injuries [24]. There were cases of respiratory failure, myocardial infarction, and pulmonary contusion, with a single case of cardiac contusion. A recent retrospective review of sternal fracture and associated bony and visceral injuries showed that thoracic aortic injuries were seen in 4% of cases, heart lacerations in 2.4%, and cardiac contusions in 8.0% of cases [25].

Motor vehicle collisions are a significant cause of sternal fractures in adults. Sternal fractures have been reported to be particularly common in front-seat occupants wearing seat belts in older vehicles not equipped with airbags. It has been reported that 262 of 42,055 victims of motor vehicle collisions who suffered a sternal fracture were in vehicles where there was no airbag or there was airbag malfunction [23]. Sternal fractures are rare in vehicle crash victims when an airbag deploys in the incident. Sternal fractures occur in collisions where a seat belt is not worn, or an airbag is either not fitted or does not deploy.

A literature review of rib and sternal fractures associated with cardiopulmonary resuscitation showed a very wide reported range of sternal fractures with incidences varying from 1% to 43% [28]. No reports of sternal fractures were found in pediatric patients.

Mechanism

The majority of sternal fractures are the result of direct anterior blunt force trauma resulting in anterior–posterior compression of the chest. The overwhelming majority of sternal fractures are transverse, involve the body of the sternum, and occur directly at the point of impact [29]. Isolated fractures of the manubrium are uncommon (Figure 7.8).

Occasionally indirect forces can lead to a sternal fracture. The proposed mechanism is severe hyperflexion of the spine. As suggested initially by De Tarnowsky at the turn of the preceding century, and recently reviewed by Raghunathan and Porter [30], such hyperflexion may occur with falls onto the head or shoulder leading to forward and upward pressure on the ribs and, in turn, the sternum.

Sternal fractures are usually not displaced (Figure 7.9) [31]. When displacement occurs, the degree of displacement is proportional to the increasing amount of force, and thus allied to increasing risk of intrathoracic injury (Figure 7.10). In cases of displaced fracture the lower fractured segment tends to be displaced posteriorly when caused by direct force, but when the fracture is due to indirect forces there is usually forward buckling of the sternum with outward movement of the fracture edges.

CT Diagnosis of Sternal Fractures

- Sagittal reformatting is the ideal modality to identify sternal fractures with CT.
- Soft tissue windows can reveal the presence of a hematoma deep to the fracture.
- Postmortem noncontrast CT images are not able to distinguish whether the hematoma arises from the fracture or from a mediastinal hematoma.

Pediatric Sternal Fractures

Sternal fractures are distinctly uncommon in the pediatric population. There are few reports of isolated sternal

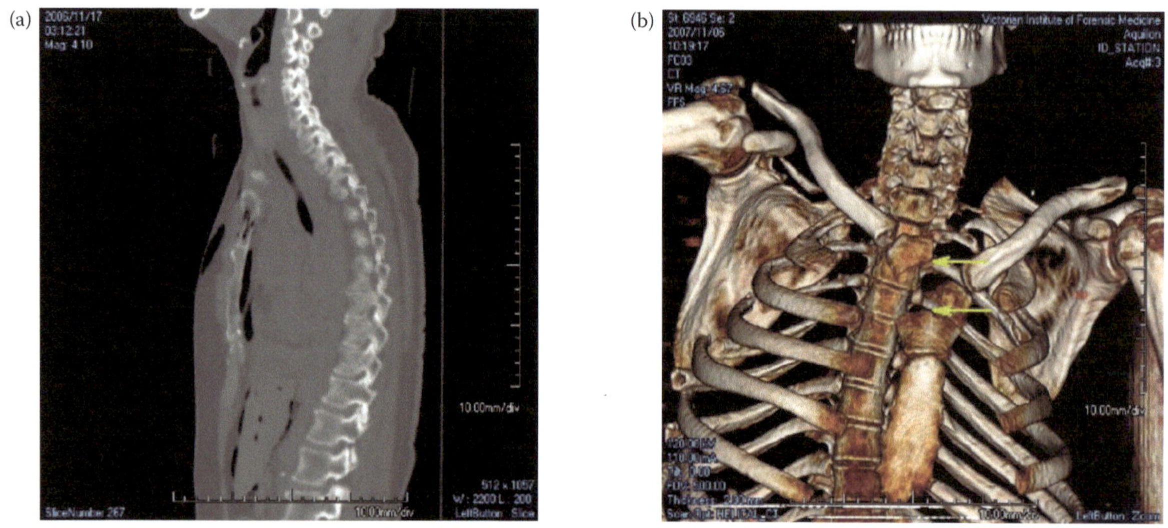

Figure 7.8 (a) Sagittal CT showing a fracture to the manubrium. (b) Three-dimensional reconstruction showing a fracture to the manubrium. There are multiple fractured ribs.

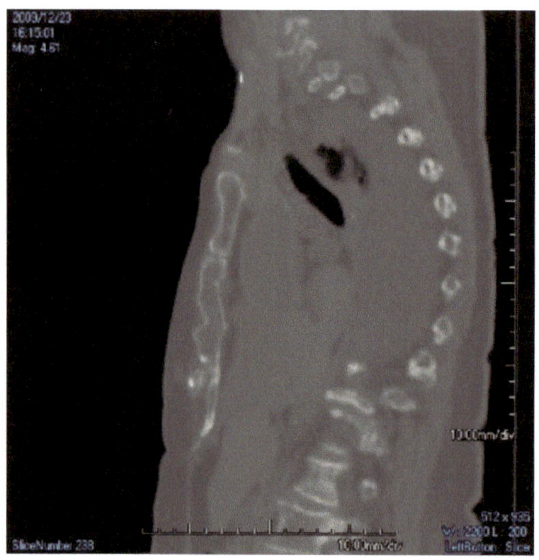

Figure 7.9 Sagittal CT image showing a fracture to the sternum with buckling of the cortices.

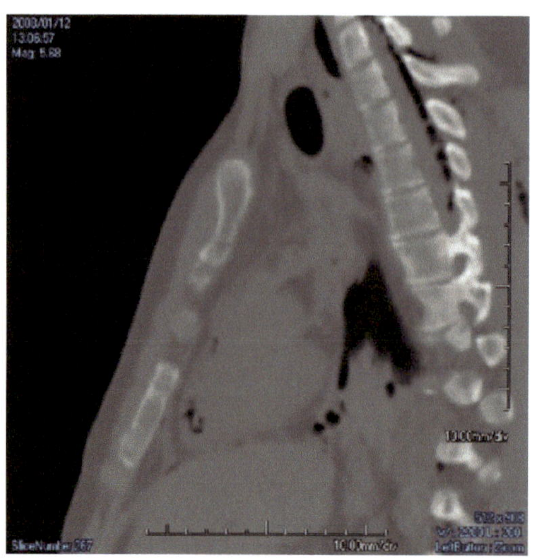

Figure 7.10 Sagittal CT showing a wide separation of the fractured ends of the bone. This injury is associated with severe forces.

fractures [32]. The common causes of sternal fracture are falls, especially from bicycles, and sports injury. Motor vehicle incidents are not reported as a common cause of sternal fracture in the clinical literature. This may be the consequence of sternal fracture in these circumstances being usually associated with other lethal injuries.

Analogous to the situation with adult sternal fractures, the injury in children may be the result of direct or indirect forces [29].

When a fracture of the sternum is present in a child it has been customary to infer significant trauma was applied to the chest. A recent study investigated isolated sternal fracture in 12 children aged between 5 and 12 years [33]. The fractures resulted from a mixture of direct blows and indirect forces. Somewhat surprising, the study showed that relatively minor trauma can result in sternal fracture in pediatric patients.

Sternal fracture has been considered an injury with high specificity for abuse in infants [34]. However, a retrospective study, albeit on only 12 children, suggested that "sternal fractures are unusual injuries, yet they, in themselves, are not highly specific for abusive injury" [35].

Sternoclavicular Dislocation

Sternoclavicular dislocation is a very uncommon injury. The injury results from blunt force trauma. The dislocation is most commonly anterior. Posterior dislocation is rare but has clinical and forensic importance as the injury can be associated with obstruction of the upper airway and major vessels [36].

On CT, axial views clearly demonstrate the relationship between the clavicle and sternum (Figure 7.11a). Three-dimensional reconstruction images can provide the pathologist with early recognition of the abnormality (Figure 7.11b).

Manubriosternal Fracture Dislocation

Manubriosternal dislocation is a rare injury. Two subtypes have been described. In type I dislocation the body of the sternum is displaced posteriorly, whereas in type II dislocation the body of the sternum is displaced anteriorly. Type I dislocation occurs from direct trauma and is usually seen in the context of a motor vehicle incident [37]. Type II manubriosternal dislocations occur from direct or indirect trauma from a flexion compression mechanism. On CT, sagittal views will usually demonstrate the fracture and show any bony displacement.

Scapula

Anatomy

The scapula is a flat, triangular bone with thickened borders. The scapula has ventral and dorsal surfaces, and medial (vertebral), lateral (axillary), and superior borders. The spine of the scapula is a prominent ridge of bone that extends obliquely across the superior dorsal aspect of the bone and separates the supraspinatous and infraspinatous fossae. The lateral aspect of the spine is expanded into the acromion, a flattened, robust portion of the bone that projects over the glenoid fossa.

At the junction of the lateral and superior borders, the scapula is at its thickest and contains a shallow articular surface, the glenoid fossa. The coracoid process is a broad protuberance that derives from the upper part of the neck

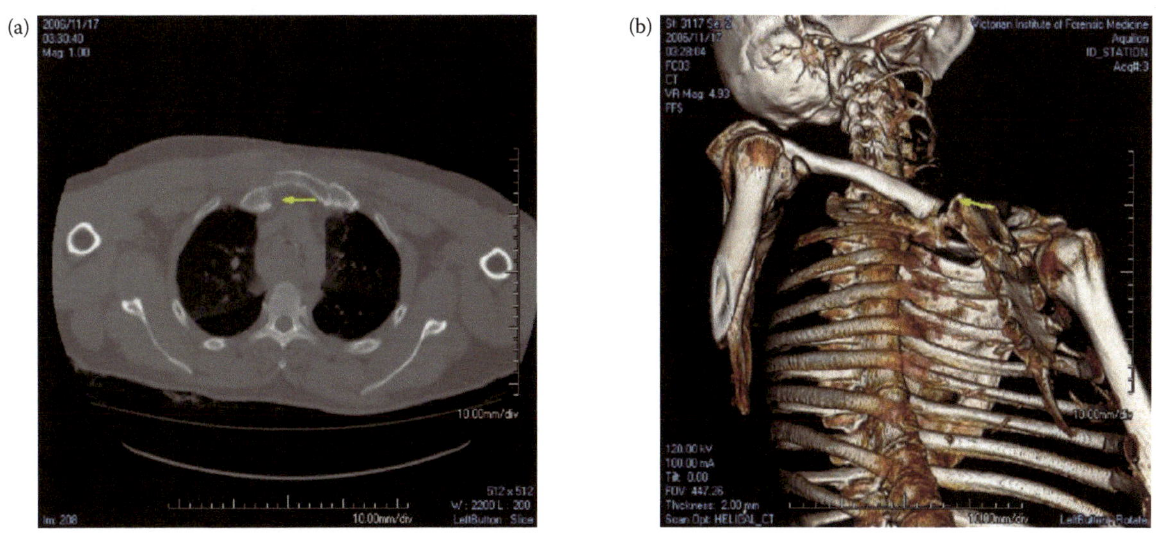

Figure 7.11 (a) Axial CT showing a dislocation of the right sternoclavicular joint. (b) Three-dimensional reconstruction image showing posterior displacement of the right clavicle in sternoclavicular dislocation.

(a) (b)

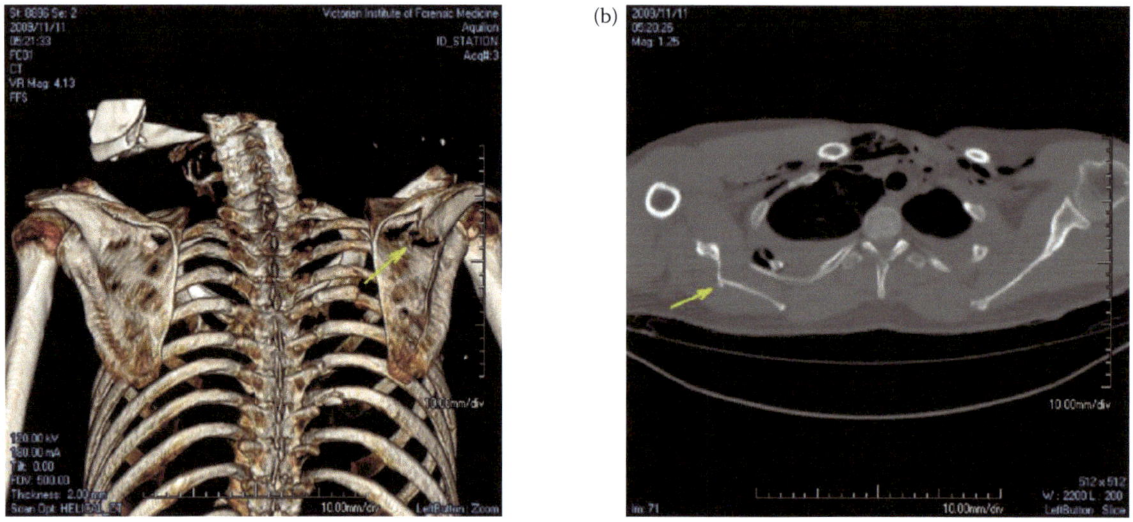

Figure 7.12 (a) Three-dimensional reconstruction CT showing fractures to the right scapula and right ribs. (b) Axial CT showing a fracture to the right scapula. There is extensive subcutaneous air within the anterior chest reflecting multiple fractured ribs.

of the scapula. The coracoid process projects forward and laterally over the glenoid fossa, anterior to the acromion.

Etiology

Fractures of the scapula are uncommon injuries. They comprise about 1% of all fractures. Scapular fractures tend to occur most frequently in the 20 to 50 age group and are the result of significant blunt force trauma. These fractures most commonly result from motor vehicle incidents or falls from a significant height. Road traffic accidents caused 78% of 41 scapular fractures that were diagnosed in a study from Tehran [38]. Of these cases, almost one-half were the result of pedestrian incidents. Fractures of the body of the scapula may occasionally be seen in significant blunt force trauma in contact sports.

Because fractures of the scapula are caused by significant blunt force trauma, they are associated with a high incidence of ipsilateral chest wall, lung, and shoulder girdle injury (Figure 7.12a,b) [39]. In 56 patients with a total of 58 scapular fractures, rib fractures and lung contusions were present in 53.6% of cases; clavicular fracture in 26.8% of cases; and subclavian, brachial, or axillary artery were noted in 10.7% of cases [39].

Interestingly, in a separate study it was shown that although patients with scapula fractures do tend to have more serious chest injuries, there was no difference in the mortality rate [38].

Mechanism

Fractures of the scapula are divided into glenoid neck fractures (both extra-articular and intra-articular), scapular body fractures, scapular neck fractures, and scapulothoracic dissociation.

Fractures of the body of the scapula are the most common type of fracture, being seen in up to 80% of cases. These fractures are associated with the application of significant direct blunt force to the lateral or superior–posterior aspect of the forequarter.

Significant blunt force directed from above the shoulder can lead to fractures of the acromion or the scapular neck (Figure 7.13).

Fractures of the glenoid fossa may occur when significant force is applied laterally to the shoulder forcing the humeral head against the glenoid fossa and resulting in a transverse glenoid fossa fracture (Figure 7.14). These fractures may then propagate in various directions. The particular fracture in any given case depends upon the direction of the applied force [40]. Falls to the ground onto the outstretched hand or cases of dislocation of the shoulder may also lead to glenoid rim fractures [41].

Traction forces may occasionally cause avulsion fractures of the scapula processes. Rarely a scapular fracture may result from intense muscular activity secondary to seizures or electric shock [42].

Scapulothoracic dissociation occurs with severe traction mechanisms. The majority of injuries results from motor vehicle crashes and commonly involve pedestrians. The other major causes of scapular fracture are falls from a substantial height.

Axial, coronal, and sagittal CT views may all be useful in demonstrating scapular fractures and show comminution and displacement of fractures (Figure 7.15).

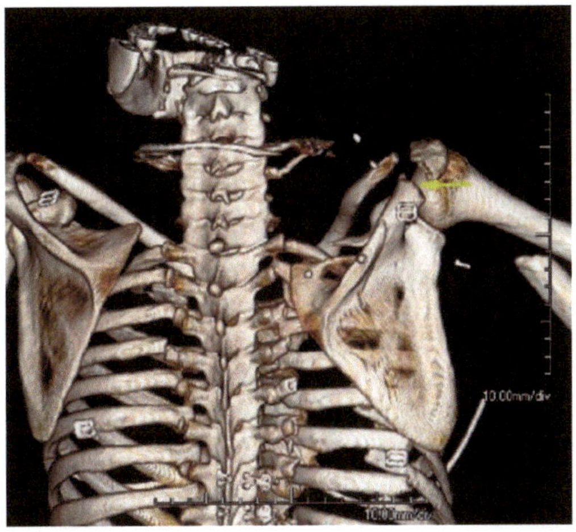

Figure 7.13 Three-dimensional reconstruction image showing a fracture to the right acromion.

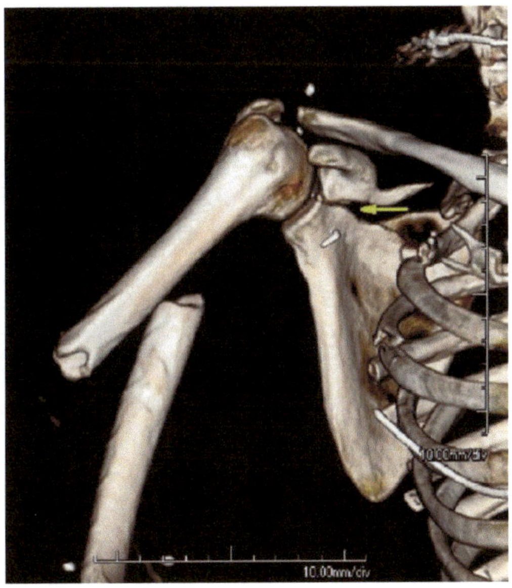

Figure 7.14 Fracture to the right shaft of the humerus and right glenoid fossa from impact to the right shoulder in a motor vehicle incident. Note also the multiple fractured ribs.

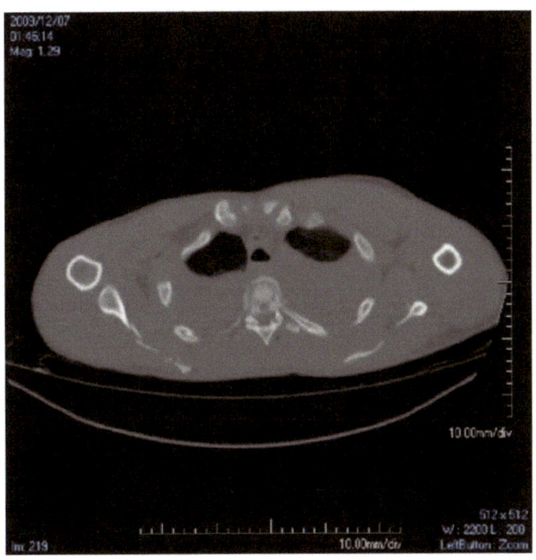

Figure 7.15 Axial CT showing a comminuted fracture of the right scapula. There are bilateral hemothoraces.

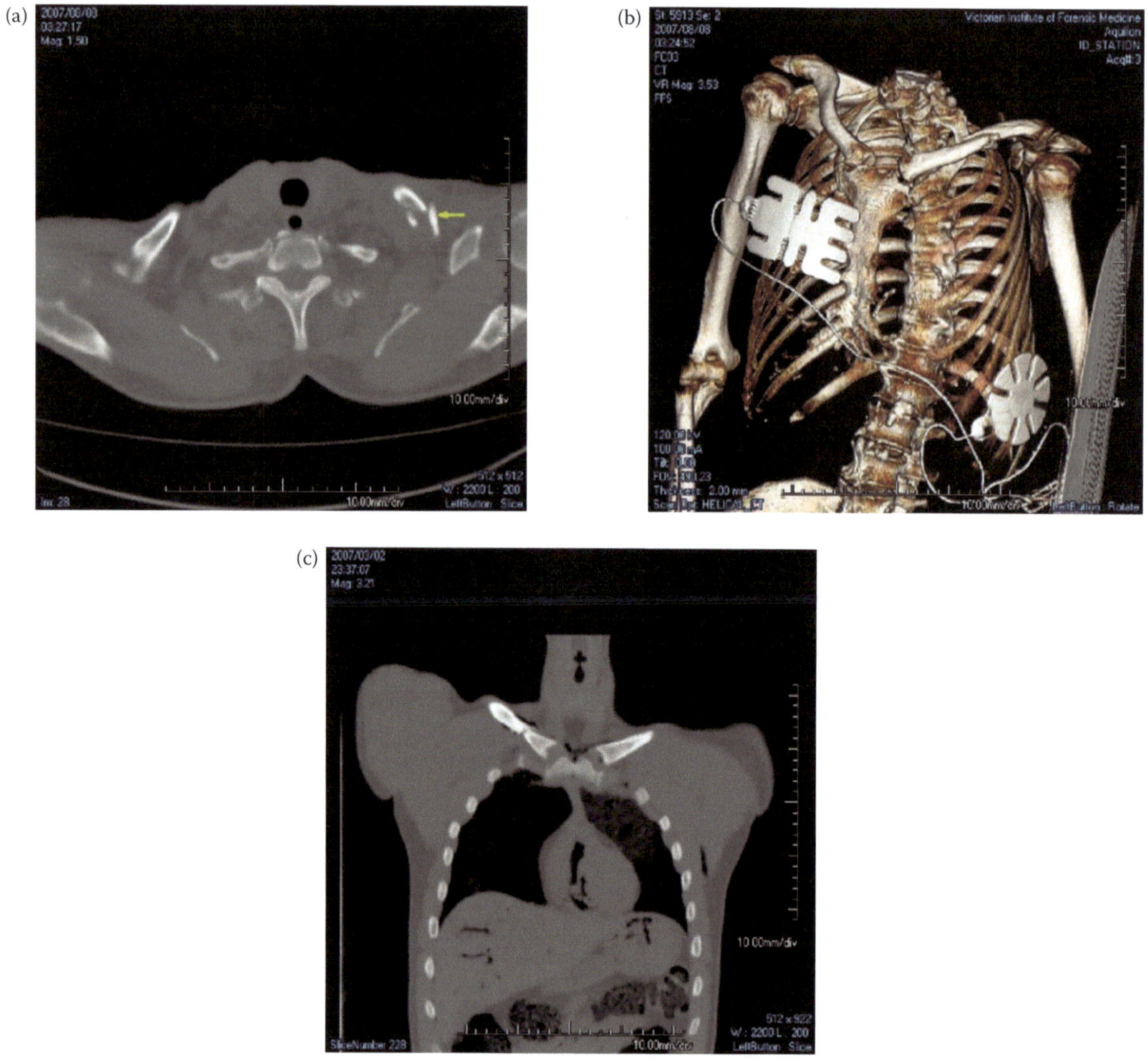

Figure 7.16 (a) Axial CT showing a fracture to the middle third of the right clavicle. (b) Three-dimensional reconstruction CT showing a fracture of the middle third of the left clavicle. (c) Coronal CT showing a fractured middle third of the left clavicle.

Clavicle

Anatomy

The clavicle is an S-shaped bone that may be thought of as a strut connecting the upper limb to the trunk. The clavicle articulates medially with the manubrium (sternum) and laterally with two processes of the scapula. The medial portion of the clavicle has secure soft tissue attachments to the first rib. The lateral attachments to the acromion and coracoid process of the scapula are via the acromioclavicular and coracoclavicular ligaments, respectively.

Etiology

Clavicular fractures are common injuries. They comprise approximately 4% of all fractures in adults [43]. The middle third of the clavicle accounts for at least two-thirds of such injuries (Figure 7.16a,b,c).

Fractures of the medial end (inner third) of the clavicle are more uncommon (Figure 7.17). A recent retrospective study of medial clavicular fractures over a five-year period was reported from the United States. A total of 57 fractures were identified. The patients were typically male and the injuries usually occurred in motor vehicle collisions. The study showed that most patients with medial fractures had associated multiple system traumas, and approximately

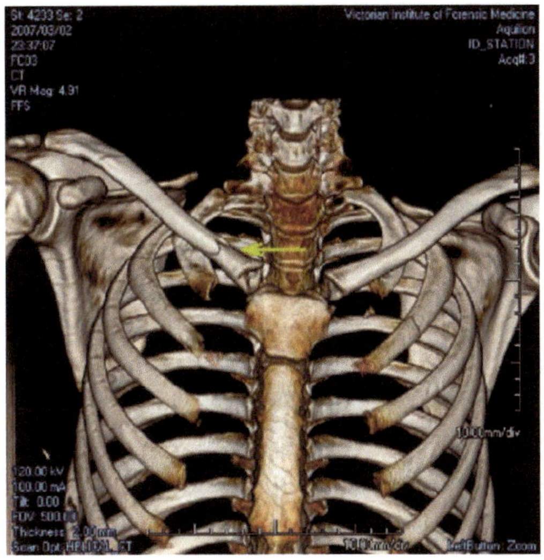

Figure 7.17 Three-dimensional reconstruction CT showing an undisplaced fracture to the medial aspect of the right clavicle.

20% succumbed to the injuries sustained in the incident. The fractures were always visible on CT scanning.

Mechanism

The clavicle may be injured by direct or indirect trauma. The most common mechanism of injury is a fall to the lateral aspect of the shoulder causing an axial load to the bone. This accounts for just over 90% of fractures [44]. It was previously believed that a fall onto the outstretched hand was the most common cause of clavicle fracture, however, it is now known that only 2% to 5% of midshaft fractures occur in this fashion.

A further common mechanism of clavicular fracture is direct trauma from a blow. This has been described as causing around 10% of midshaft fractures. The junction between the outer and middle thirds is the most vulnerable part of the bone. The bone is relatively thin at this point and there is no protection afforded by any surrounding musculature.

Acromioclavicular joint injuries are particularly frequent in the sporting environment. The mechanism of injury in such cases is often a fall onto the tip of the shoulder with the arm in adduction [45]. In heavy contact sports a further common mechanism of injury is solid lateral impact to the shoulder, often with the hands raised above the head.

CT Diagnosis of Clavicular Fractures

Fractures of the clavicle are easily visible on CT scanning. CT imaging is often used clinically to demonstrate medial clavicular fractures. This is especially so for fractures that extend to the sternoclavicular joint [46]. In the forensic setting the diagnosis will be readily made by an inspection of the bone on axial or three-dimensional formatted views.

Case Study

A 30-year-old man was intoxicated at a party. He was witnessed falling approximately 5 m from a balcony onto a concrete car parking area. He was deceased on arrival of ambulance personnel.

The deceased's body was conveyed to the VIFM for medicolegal examination. The external examination showed a laceration to the occiput, and abrasions over the right upper back and right lumbar region. There were no injuries to suggest an assault.

The postmortem CT showed no fractured skull, intracranial hemorrhage, or cervical spine injury. The CT examination of the chest showed a fracture to the right scapula, right ribs, and massive right hemothorax (Figure 7.18). The coroner was informed of these findings. No further examination of the deceased was ordered and the body was released from the VIFM.

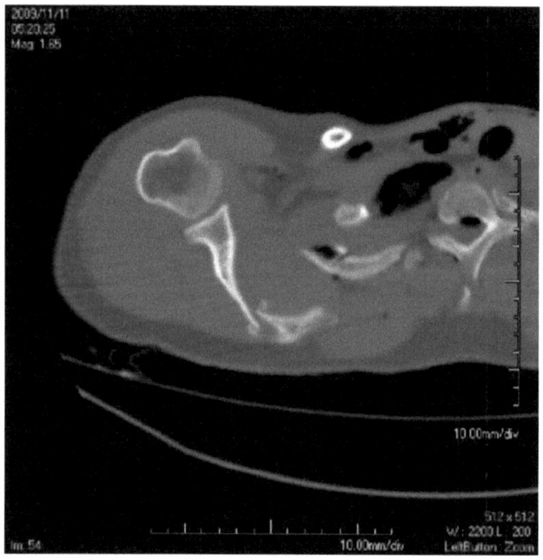

Figure 7.18 Axial CT showing adjacent fractures to the right scapula and right ribs consistent with a significant fall to the back.

The presence of the fractured right scapula and immediately adjacent ribs would indicate a point of application of significant force to the body and suggests the man fell to his back. Although one cannot exclude the presence of a significant head injury, such as a pontomedullary tear, it would seem reasonable to suggest the fall lead to a major intrathoracic visceral injury.

References

1. Fermanis GG, Deane SA, Fitzgerald PM. The significance of first and second rib fractures. *Aust. NZ J. Surg.* 1985; 55:383–386.
2. Love JC, Symes SA. Understanding rib fracture patterns: Incomplete and buccal fractures. *J. Forensic Sci.* 2004; 49(6):1153–1158.
3. Daegling DJ, Warren MW, Hotzman JL, Self CJ. structural analysis of human rib fracture and implications for forensic interpretation. *J. Forensic Sci.* 2008; 53(6):1301–1307.
4. Yoganandan N, Morgan RM, Eppinger RH, Pintar FA, Sances A Jr, Williams A. Mechanisms of thoracic injury in frontal impact. *J. Biomech. Eng.* 1996; 118:595–597.
5. Garcia VF, Gotschall CS, Eichelberger MR, Bowman LM. Rib fractures in children: A marker of severe trauma. *J. Trauma* 1990; 30(6):695–700.
6. Roux P, Fisher RM. Chest injuries in children: An analysis of 100 cases of blunt force trauma from motor vehicle accidents. *J. Pediatr. Surg.* 1992; 27(5):551–555.
7. Balci AE, Kazez A, Eren S, Ayan E, Özalp K, Eren MN. Blunt thoracic trauma in children: Review of 137 cases. *Eur. J. Cardiothorac. Surg.* 2004; 26:387–392.
8. Bulloch B, Schubert CJ, Brophy PD, Johnson N, Reed MH, Shapiro RA. Cause and clinical characteristics of rib fractures in infants. *Pediatrics* 2000; 105(4):E48.
9. Worn MJ, Jones MD. Rib fractures in infancy: Establishing the mechanisms of cause from the injuries—A literature review. *Med. Sci. Law* 2007; 47(3):200–212.
10. Schweich P, Fleisher G. Rib fractures in children. *Pediatric Emerg. Care* 1985; 1:187–189.
11. Kleinman PK, Marks Jr. SC, Nimkin K, Rayder SM, Kessler SC. Rib fractures in 31 abused infants: Post mortem radiologic-histopathologic study. *Radiology* 1996; 200:647–650.
12. Ng CS, Hall CM. Costochondral junction fractures and intra-abdominal trauma in non-accidental injury (child abuse). *Pediatr. Radiol.* 1998; 28:671–676.
13. Feldman KW, Brewer DK. Child abuse, cardiopulmonary resuscitation, and rib fractures. *Pediatrics* 1984; 73(3):339–342.
14. Bush CM, Jones JS, Cohle SD, Johnson H. Pediatric injuries from cardiopulmonary resuscitation. *Ann. Emerg. Med.* 1996; 28(1):40–44.
15. Maguire S, Mann M, John N, Ellaway B, Sibert JR, Kemp AM. Does cardiopulmonary resuscitation cause rib fractures in children? A systematic review. *Child Abuse Negl.* 2006; 30(7):739–751.
16. Gunther WM, Symes SA, Berryman HE. Characteristics of child abuse by anteroposterior manual compression versus cardiopulmonary resuscitation. *Am. J. Forensic Med. Pathol.* 2000; 21(1):5–10.
17. Livingston DH, Shogan B, John P, Lavery RF. CT diagnosis of rib fractures and the prediction of acute respiratory failure. *J. Trauma* 2008; 64(4):905–911.
18. Kemp AM, Butler A, Morris S, Mann M, Kemp KW, Rolfe K, Silbert JR, Maguire S. Which radiological investigations should be performed to identify fractures in suspected child abuse? *Clin. Radiol.* 2006; 61:723–736.
19. Wootton-Gorges SL, Stein-Wexler R, Walton JW, Rosas AJ, Coulter KP, Rogers KK. Comparison of computed tomography and chest radiography in the detection of rib fractures in abused infants. *Child Abuse Negl.* 2008; 32:659–663.

20. Flagel BT, Luchette FA, Reed RL, Esposito TJ, Davis KA, Santaniello JM, Gamelli RL. Half-a-dozen ribs: The breakpoint for mortality. *Surgery* 2005; 138(4):717–723.
21. Testerman GM. Adverse outcomes in younger rib fracture patients. *South Med. J.* 2006; 99(4):335–339.
22. Bulger EM, Arneson MA, Mock CN, Jurkovich GJ. Rib fractures in the elderly. *J. Trauma* 2000; 48(6):1040–1046.
23. Knobloch K, Wagner S, Haasper C, Probst C, Krettek C, Otte D, Richter M. Sternal fractures occur often in old cars to seat-belted drivers without any airbag often with concomitant spinal injuries: Clinical findings and technical collision variables among 42,055 crash victims. *Ann. Thorac. Surg.* 2006; 82:444–450.
24. Athanassiadi K, Gerazounis M, Moustardas M, Metaxas E. Sternal fractures: Retrospective analysis of 100 cases. *World J. Surg.* 2002; 26(10):1243–1246.
25. Recinos G, Inaba K, Dubose J, Barmparas G, Teixeira PG, Talving P, Plurad D, Green D, Demetriadis D. Epidemiology of sternal fractures. *Am. Surg.* 2009; 75(5):401–404.
26. Restrepo CS, Martinez S, Lemos DF, Washington L, McAdams HP, Vargus D, Lemos JA, Carrillo JA, Diethelm L. Imaging appearances of the sternum and sternoclavicular joints. *Radiographics* 2009; 29:839–859.
27. Sadaba JR, Oswal D, Munsch CM. Management of isolated sternal fractures: Determining the risk of blunt cardiac injury. *Ann. R. Coll. Surg. Engl.* 2000; 82(3):162–166.
28. Hoke RS, Chamberlain D. Skeletal injuries secondary to cardiopulmonary resuscitation. *Resuscitation* 2004; 63(3):327–338.
29. De Tarnowshy G. Vii. Contrecoup fracture of the sternum. *Ann. Surg.* 1905; 41(2):252–264.
30. Raghunathan R, Porter K. Sternal fractures. *Trauma* 2009; 11:77–92.
31. von Garrel, Ince A, Junge A, Schnabel M, Bahrs C. The sternal fracture: Radiographic analysis of 200 fractures with special reference to concomitant injuries. *J. Trauma* 2004; 57:837–844.
32. Peek GJ, Firmin RK. Isolated sternal fracture: An audit of 10 years' experience. *Injury* 1995; 26:385–388.
33. Ferguson LP, Wilkinson AG, Beattie TF. Fracture of the sternum in children. *Emerg. Med.* 2003; 20:518–520.
34. Kleinman PK. Diagnostic imaging in infant abuse. *AJR* 1990; 155:703–712.
35. Hecter S, Huyer D, Manson D. Sternal fractures as a manifestation of abusive injury in children. *Pediatr. Radiol.* 2002; 32(12):902–906.
36. Salgado RA, Ghysen D. Post-traumatic posterior sternoclavicular dislocation: Case report and review of the literature. *Emerg. Radiol.* 2002; 9:323–325.
37. Kalicke T, Frangen T.M, Muller E.J, Muhr G, Hopf F. Traumatic manubriosternal dislocation. *Arch. Orthop. Trauma Surg.* 2006; 126(6):411–416.
38. Salimi J, Khaji A, Karbakhsh M, Saadat S, Eftekhar B. Scapular fracture: Lower severity and mortality. *Sao Paulo Med. J.* 2008; 126(3):186–189.
39. Thompson DA, Flynn TC, Miller PW, Fischer RP. The significance of scapular fractures. *J. Trauma* 1985; 25(10):974–977.
40. McGahan JP, Rab GT, Dublin A. Fractures of the scapula. *J. Trauma* 1980; 20(10):880–883.
41. Lapner PC, Uhthoff HK, Papp S. Scapular fractures. *Orthop. Clin. N. Am.* 2008; 39:459–474.
42. Kotak B, Harddo O, Iqbal M, Chissell H. Bilateral scapular fractures after electrocution. *J. Royal Soc. Med.* 2000; 93(3):143–144.
43. Nowak J, Mallmin H, Larsson S. The etiology and epidemiology of clavicular fractures: A prospective study during a two-year period in Uppsala, Sweden. *Injury* 2000; 31(5):353–358.
44. Stanley D, Trowbridge EA, Norris SH. The mechanism of clavicular fracture: A clinical and biomechanical analysis. *J. Bone Joint Surg. Br.* 1988; 70(3):461–464.
45. Simovitch R, Sanders B, Ozbaydar M, Lavery K, Warner JJ. Acromioclavicular joint injuries: Diagnosis and management. *J. Am. Acad. Orthop. Surg.* 2009; 17(4):207–219.
46. Khan LA, Bradnock TJ, Scott C, Robinson CM. Fractures of the clavicle. *J. Bone Joint Surg. Am.* 2009; 91(2):447–460.

Upper Limbs

8

Humerus

Anatomy

The humerus is the longest tubular bone of the upper limb. The proximal humerus is divided into four major anatomical sections: (1) the head, (2) the greater and (3) lesser tuberosities, and (4) the surgical neck extending into the humeral shaft.

The head of the humerus is almost hemispherical and articulates with the glenoid fossa of the scapula at the shoulder joint. The greater tuberosity is lateral to the head of the humerus. The greater tuberosity has insertions for the supraspinatus, infraspinatus, and teres major muscles. The lesser tuberosity is medial to the head of the humerus. Although smaller than the greater tuberosity, it is actually more prominent. It provides a muscle insertion for the subscapularis.

The surgical neck of the humerus is described as the constricted region of the humerus just below the tuberosities. The surgical neck is a common site of fracture. The surgical neck extends into the humeral shaft. The body or shaft of the humerus is roughly triangular on cross-section.

The distal humerus articulates with the ulna and radius at the elbow joint. The spool-shaped trochlea of the distal humerus articulates with the olecranon of the ulna. The lateral extension of the trochlea is the capitulum, which articulates with the head of the radius.

Etiology

Fractures of the humerus are most frequent in the young and the aged. Fractures of the humerus comprise approximately 4% to 5% of all fractures in the United States. The surgical neck of the humerus is a common site of fracture in the elderly. Most fractures involve the midshaft and result primarily from falls and motor vehicle incidents.

Fractures to the humeral shaft have a distinctly bimodal distribution. A peak in incidence occurs in the third decade in males as a result of moderate to severe trauma in motor vehicle incidents and falls from a height, and a larger peak in women in their seventh decade as a consequence of simple falls. Other causes of humeral shaft fracture include sports injuries, pathological fractures, assaults, being struck by a falling object, and industrial incidents. Supracondylar fractures are common injuries in the pediatric population.

Mechanisms

Tuberosity Fractures

Fractures of the greater tuberosity of the humerus are commonly seen in association with comminuted fractures to the proximal humerus. Isolated fractures of the greater tuberosity are much less common [1]. Isolated lesser tuberosity fractures are exceedingly rare. Isolated greater tuberosity fractures comprise approximately one-fifth of proximal humeral fractures. The exact mechanism of the greater tuberosity fracture is somewhat controversial, though in general the underlying factors are believed to be due to shear or impaction forces.

The cause of the shear injury is most often from an anterior shoulder dislocation where the tuberosity is avulsed by the action of rotator cuff muscles. An impaction injury results from a fall directly to the shoulder, which in turn forces the greater tuberosity onto the acromion or superior aspect of the glenoid [1]. An alternative impaction injury can result from forceful contact between the greater tuberosity and glenoid during anterior shoulder dislocation.

A recent retrospective study from Germany on 103 patients showed that 59 cases of greater tuberosity fracture were sustained during traumatic shoulder dislocation. A direct injury was responsible for the injury in 47.6% of fractures, whereas 32% of patients reported indirect force. There was only one abduction-external rotation injury. Just over a fifth of the patients could not recall the mechanism of injury [2]. This data is in contradiction to the theory of avulsion injury from rotator cuff muscular contraction.

Proximal Humeral Fractures

Proximal humeral fractures commonly occur in falls to the outstretched hand or elbow (Figure 8.1a,b). The classification of proximal humeral fractures is somewhat complex. The most frequently used classification system for proximal humeral fractures is the Neer system. This system is based on the displacement of the four major anatomical segments of the proximal humerus, which

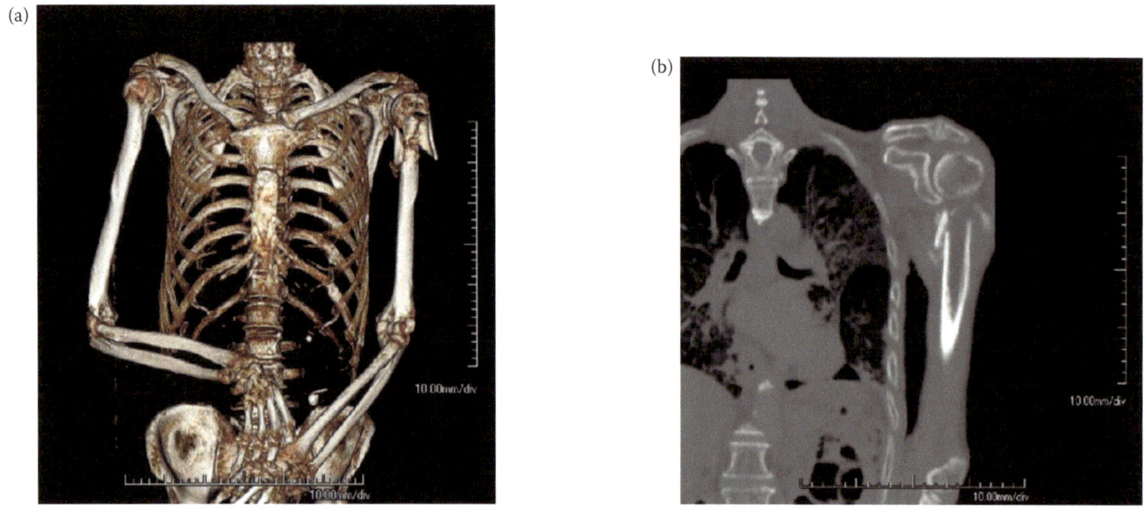

Figure 8.1 (a) Three-dimensional reconstruction of a complex proximal humeral fracture that occurred secondary to a fall. (b) Coronal CT showing a fracture to the proximal left humerus.

occurs from the action of the associated muscles on the fracture fragments following the injury.

In essence a type I fracture can involve any of the fragments but has minimal angulation, a type II fracture has one displaced fragment, a type III has two displaced fragments with involvement of a tuberosity, and a type IV involves three fragments. The effect of postmortem rigidity on the muscle pull on the fracture fragments would suggest such a classification system may not be directly transferable to the forensic situation.

Humeral Shaft Fractures

Direct bending forces to the humeral shaft tend to lead to transverse fractures, whereas rotational forces during the injury may cause oblique or spiral fracture. The middle third of the humeral shaft is fractured in approximately 60% of cases (Figure 8.2). Fractures to the proximal third accounted for 30% of the cases, and 10% occur in the distal third [3].

Fractures of the humerus while throwing can occur during sporting activities such as baseball and cricket. A study of 90 patients with humeral shaft fractures sustained during throwing activity was performed by Ogawa and Yoshida [4]. An interesting observation in the study was that all of the cases showed external rotation spiral fractures. It was suggested that the direction of the spiral fracture line directly reflected the direction of the rotational force applied to the bone.

Condylar and Supracondylar Fractures

Fractures involving the condyles and supracondylar regions are common in children. Supracondylar fractures

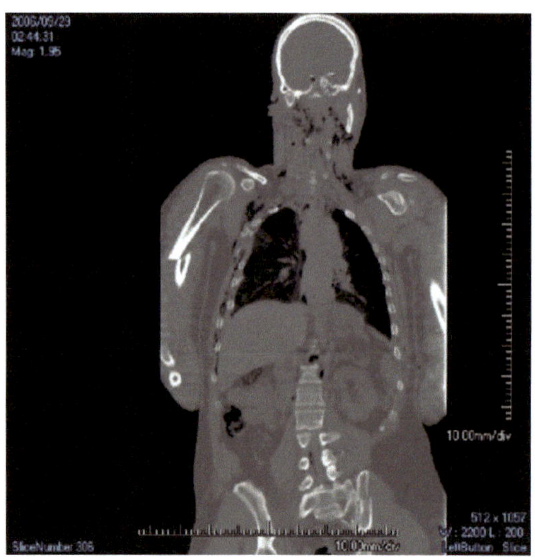

Figure 8.2 Fractured humeral shaft (coronal view).

are also frequent in the older, osteoporotic female population. The classical mechanism is a fall from a standing height onto the outstretched hand. This leads to indirect force extending from the hand, through the forearm, and the humerus. The fracture may be T- or Y-shaped and can extend to the articular surface.

Supracondylar humeral fractures are the most frequent elbow fractures in the pediatric population resulting in over 50% of such cases. The fracture is most commonly the result of a fall onto the outstretched hand leading to forced hyperextension of the distal humerus. In less than 5% of cases the injury may be the result of the application of blunt force directly to the humerus when the elbow is flexed.

Lateral condyle and avulsion fractures of the medial epicondyle are very common injuries to the elbow. The fractures can result from direct force or from an axial load. The medial epicondyle tends to be fractured with valgus stress and axial loading, whereas lateral condyle fractures are associated with varus stress and axial loading. The fracture may have very little displacement making the diagnosis on computed tomography (CT) particularly difficult.

Distal Articular Fractures

Distal articular fractures are apt to involve both the capitulum and the trochlea. They result from shearing forces and occasionally from a wedging force. The fracture is usually associated with axial loading through the radius and ulna.

A specific and rare subtype of distal articular fracture is the Kocher fracture. The Kocher fracture always occurs in conjunction with a radial head injury and is due to a fall onto the flexed arm. The anterior aspect tends to fracture when the elbow is injured in extension, whereas the posterior surface is fractured when the elbow is flexed.

Pediatric Humeral Fractures

Different age groups within the pediatric population tend to suffer different types of fractures to the humerus, and are also different from adult injuries.

Fractures of the proximal humerus and the humeral shaft are relatively rare in the pediatric population. Proximal humerus fractures account for less than 3% of all pediatric fractures [5]. Fractures to the elbow comprise about 15% of all pediatric fractures. The distal humerus is most commonly involved in these fractures and causes approximately 85% of fractures to the elbow in children. The most frequent pediatric fractures are the supracondylar humeral fracture, the lateral condyle fracture, the medial epicondyle fracture, and the transphyseal fracture [5].

The common mechanism of injury in supracondylar fractures in the pediatric population is forced hyperextension. The fracture occurs secondary to a fulcrum effect of the olecranon into the olecranon fossa. Supracondylar fractures are more likely than not to be caused by accidental trauma. Epicondyle fractures are an uncommon injury in children and usually the result of an avulsion injury. A medial epicondyle fracture may occur in direct trauma.

Medial epicondyle fractures account for approximately 10% of pediatric elbow fractures. The mechanism of the injury is usually a valgus force leading to an avulsion fracture via the action of both flexion and pronation musculature [5]. The fracture is most often related to falls or a sports injury.

Transphyseal elbow fractures are relatively uncommon but have significant forensic implications. The fracture usually occurs in children less than two years of age and has been said to be caused by nonaccidental injury in over 50% of cases. The mechanism of transphyseal elbow fractures in accidental cases is generally a fall to the outstretched arm, whereas in nonaccidental injury a twisting rotational element is the usual mechanism.

It has been suggested that in absolute numbers midshaft fractures of the humerus are more common in cases of nonaccidental than accidental injury. However, a retrospective study on humeral shaft fractures in 38 children less than three years of age showed that only 18% were classified as due to abuse [6]. The authors determined that the history of the incident and findings other than the fracture itself were vital in establishing the correct mechanism of injury.

Fractures of the humerus have been described in pediatric patients during the use of restraints [7]. Five cases were described in a report following the use of handcuffs on skeletally immature patients each resulting in Salter–Harris type I or type II injuries involving the epiphyseal plate.

CT Diagnosis of Humeral Fractures

CT has been a huge advance in the clinical diagnosis and management of proximal humeral fractures [8]. This is partly because the complexities of the fractures that have been diagnosed on two-dimensional radiographs are much more easily conceptualized and diagnosed using CT with three-dimensional reconstructions.

The clinical classification systems are designed to allow comparisons in clinical management and are not directly transferable to the forensic setting.

For the forensic pathologist the three-dimensional reconstruction images are intuitive and understood. These images are also more readily recognizable by laypeople.

Pediatric CT of Humeral Fractures

The CT diagnosis of pediatric elbow fractures is difficult because of the presence of nonossified cartilage in this population. The absence of ossified bone in a complex joint such as the elbow means that one cannot simply follow the bony contours as one would do when examining the radiograph of an adult individual.

The correct anatomical orientation of the capitellum, the head of the radius, the medial epicondyle, the olecranon, the trochlea, and the lateral epicondyle are crucial to interpreting images of the pediatric elbow. The sequence of ossification in the elbow is as follows. The capitellum first ossifies at about 1 year of age in both males and females. The radial head and the medial epicondyle follow at approximately 5 to 6 years of age. The olecranon ossifies between 8 and 10 years of age. The trochlea and the lateral epicondyle are the last two centers to ossify.

The anterior humeral line and the capitellum are important features in the diagnosis of elbow injury.

- The anterior humeral line should bisect the capitellum on lateral views.
- The radial head points toward the capitellum on all views in the normal pediatric elbow.
- On a true anterior–posterior image of the elbow the intersection of a line along the physis of the capitellum with a line perpendicular to the humerus is between 8 and 28 degrees.

The demonstration of abnormal alignments of the long bones in the joint is of crucial significance in making the correct diagnosis. Although pathologists are interested in improving their diagnostic skills in image interpretation, this area would seem to be the realm of the expert pediatric radiologist.

Ulna

Anatomy

The ulna is a tubular long bone located at the medial aspect of the forearm. The cortical compact bone of the shaft of the ulna is somewhat thinner than the proximal segment and more susceptible to injury.

The coronoid process articulates with the spool-shaped trochlea of the humerus. The olecranon of the proximal aspect of the ulna extends into the olecranon fossa of the distal humerus during extension at the elbow. The ulna also has an articulation proximally with the head of the radius at the radial notch. The radial head is secured by the annular ligament. The distal aspect of the ulna has a further articulation with the distal radius with a ligamentous attachment through the articular disc.

The interosseous membrane attaches the interosseous borders of the ulna and radius. The interosseous membrane is a significant biomechanical factor in many upper limb fractures. The fibers of the membrane are orientated such that an axial force applied to the radius is transferred to the ulna.

The ulna does not articulate directly with the carpus.

Etiology

The ulna is susceptible to fracture because of the stability of the hinge joint of the elbow. As the ulna does not have direct articulation with the carpal bones, it is less likely to be injured in falls onto the outstretched hand. Other causes of ulnar fracture include falls, motor vehicle trauma, and workplace incidents. Fractures of the olecranon are second only to the head of the radius in fractures involving the elbow in adults.

Mechanisms

Olecranon

The olecranon is usually fractured from a direct blow. With smaller degrees of force there are often transverse fractures to the olecranon, whereas larger amounts of force tend to result in a comminuted fracture to the bone. A simple oblique fracture of the olecranon can result from hyperextension at the elbow. Powerful contraction of the triceps and brachialis muscles can cause a transverse avulsion fracture of the olecranon.

Coronoid Process Fracture

The coronoid process may be fractured from axial impact. The mechanism underlying the injury is primarily radial displacement, which causes the coronoid process to be forced against the trochlea.

Ulna Shaft Fracture

The ulna is typically fractured by direct blows (Figure 8.3a). Falls to the hand are usually associated with radial fractures though ulnar shaft fractures may be seen (Figure 8.3b).

The eponym, Monteggia fracture, describes a fracture to the ulna with an associated dislocation of the radial head. The injury is uncommon. It comprises

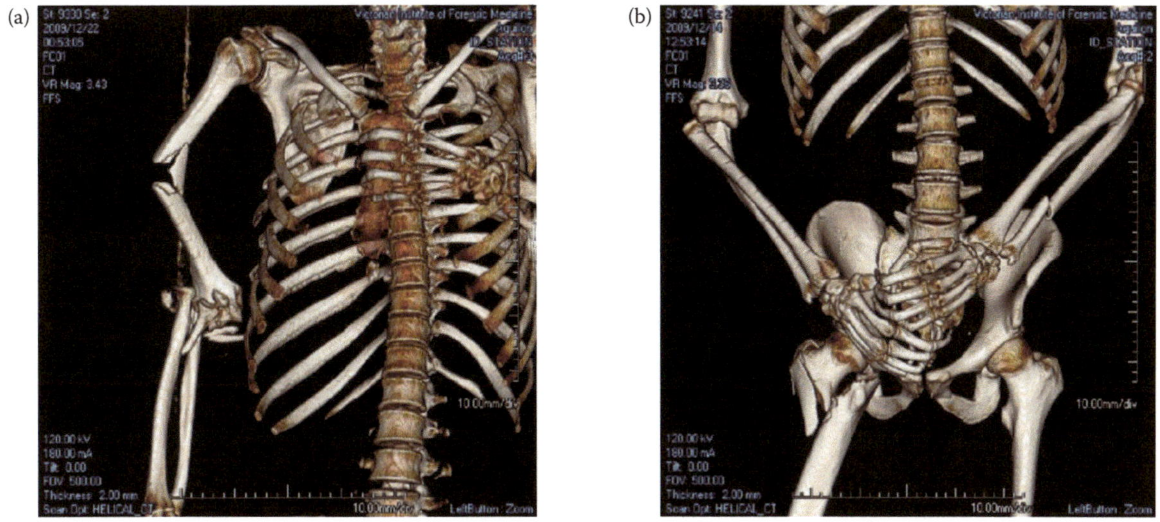

Figure 8.3 (a) Fractured proximal right ulna in direct trauma from a motor vehicle collision. Also note the fractured shaft of the right humerus and fractured right ribs. (b) Three-dimensional reconstruction image showing a fracture to the distal left ulna and a fractured right femur in a deceased motorcyclist.

approximately 5% of forearm fractures in adults and about 2% to 3% of elbow injuries in children [9]. The mechanism of the fracture is usually due to a fall to the ground with the hand held in dorsiflexion and pronation. Cadaver studies have shown the arm needs to be flexed at the elbow with the forearm neutral or moderately pronated.

Three subtypes of Monteggia fracture have been identified. The type I injury results from rotation of the body upon the fixed hand during a fall such that the radius acts like a fulcrum and fractures the ulna. The type II injury is associated with a posterior dislocation and occurs with supination of the arm. The type III injury involves lateral dislocation at the elbow joint due to an acute adduction of the forearm.

Distal Ulna Fractures

Distal ulna fractures typically involve the styloid process. These injuries are the result of severe axial loading and are typically seen in motor vehicle incidents and falls.

Radius

Anatomy

The radius is a long tubular bone situated at the lateral aspect of the forearm in the standard anatomical position. The radius has a proximal and distal articulation with the ulna. The disc-shaped head of the radius articulates with the capitulum of the humerus at the elbow.

The radiocarpal joint (wrist joint) is formed by the distal radius and the scaphoid and lunate. The distal articular surface of the radius is somewhat biconcave and triangular in shape. The apex of the triangle is formed by the radial styloid process. The triangular fibrocartilage complex is a concave, elliptical articular disc between the ulna and radius, which is a key stabilizer of the wrist.

The interosseous membrane also connects the forearm long bones. The interosseous membrane is composed of a proximal flexible segment, which merges with the more rigid and thicker distal segment.

Etiology

Fractures of the radius are common injuries. The radius is the most frequently fractured bone in the upper limb. There is a bimodal distribution to the fractures with peaks occurring in ages 5 to 15, and a second peak in those between 60 and 70 years of age. The site of fracture varies according to age. Young children tend to suffer metaphyseal injuries, teenagers sustain physeal injuries, and middle-aged and older adults suffer distal radial (and ulna) fractures.

Mechanism

The mechanisms of radial fracture include direct blunt force trauma and axial loading as occurs in a fall to the outstretched hand.

Radial Head

Radial head fractures are particularly common in elbow injuries. The mechanism is often from transmission of axial force from a fall, especially when the elbow is flexed and the forearm pronated. The radial head is then driven into the capitulum. With increasing force there is usually pronounced comminution.

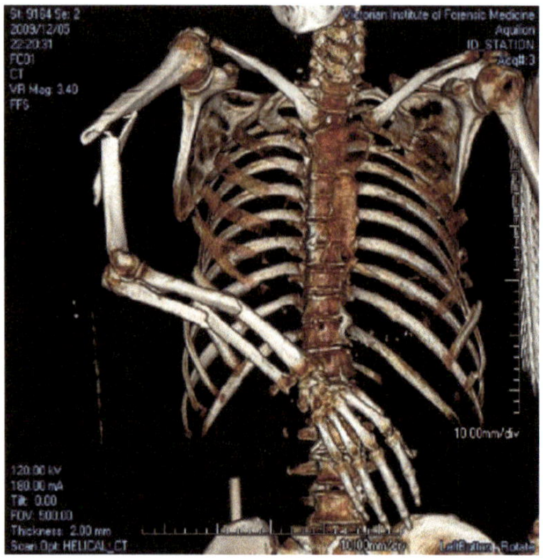

Figure 8.4 Fractures to the shafts of the right radius and ulna in a motor vehicle occupant. Note also the fractured shaft of the right humerus.

Radial Shaft Fractures

An isolated fracture of the radius from a direct blow is relatively uncommon. Most fractures occur from an axial load secondary to a fall onto the outstretched hand. The force is transmitted through the metacarpals, and the scaphoid and lunate to the distal radius. Direct blows to the radius commonly result in an associated fracture to the ulna (Figure 8.4). The morphology of the elbow joint predisposes the radial head to dislocation and protects it somewhat from an adjacent proximal fracture.

In adults radial shaft fractures tend to be transverse or oblique, complete, and involve the middle third of the bone. A butterfly or wedge fragment is seen in about 15% of cases. Spiral fractures in adults are distinctly uncommon. Distal radial shaft fractures most commonly occur from falls from a standing height. The radial fracture is usually seen in association with dislocation of adjacent bones.

A number of eponymous names are associated with fractures of the shaft of the radius:

The *Colles' fracture* is a frequent injury in older women with osteoporosis who suffer a fall. The typical mechanism is a fall onto an outstretched pronated forearm. The fracture is a bending-type injury. The fracture to the distal radius is usually within a few centimeters of the wrist joint.

The *Smith's fracture* (or reverse Colles' fracture) is a bending-type injury. The mechanism is commonly a fall onto the forearm with the limb in supination, rotating into pronation, and with a fixed dorsiflexed hand. The injury has also been seen in victims of direct force to the metacarpophalangeal joints in motor vehicle incidents.

The *Barton's fracture* occurs from falls to the hand when there is dorsiflexion and pronation of the wrist causing shearing forces at the wrist joint. This results in a fracture that involves the articular surface and extends to the dorsal aspect of the metaphysis.

The *Galeazzi fracture* is not common. It is defined as a fracture of the distal aspect or middle third of the radial shaft allied with disruption of the distal radioulna joint. The mechanism of the injury is axial loading, as would occur with a fall onto the hand with the forearm in forced pronation.

Fractures of the radial styloid have been described in four patients through the use of handcuffs [10].

Radiocarpal Fractures and Dislocations

Radiocarpal dislocations are very uncommon injuries [11]. Radiocarpal fracture–dislocations are usually the result of the application of significant force. The pathology involves rupture of the radiocarpal ligaments and generally involves both the radius and ulna styloid [12]. The dislocations can be anterior or posterior. Posterior dislocation is more common. Radiocarpal dislocation is often associated with disruption of the triangular fibrocartilage complex. The mechanism of radiocarpal dislocation is one of rotational force in addition to shear force with angulation [13].

Pediatric Forearm Fractures

Fractures of the forearm are the most common type of fracture in children [14]. The majority of forearm fractures are to the distal aspect of the forearm (Figure 8.5).

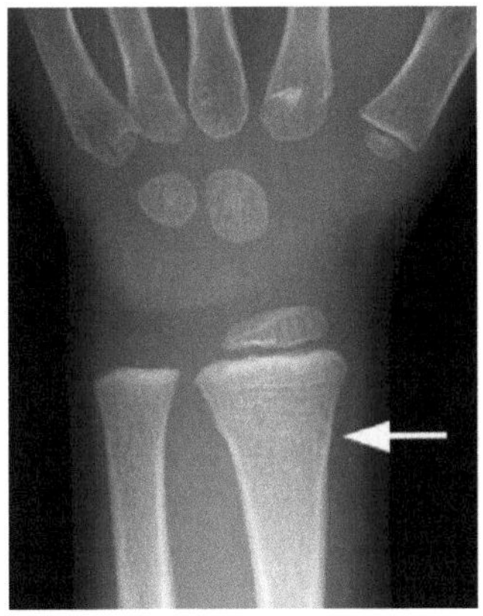

Figure 8.5 Torus fracture of the distal radius.

The common causes of forearm fractures in the pediatric population include falls and sports or play injuries. Falls from bicycles and skateboards are particularly common. When the cause of the fracture is a fall, the injury tends to involve the radius and ulna. Pediatric fractures involving the unfused epiphysis may cause separation of the disc.

Carpal Bones

Fractures of the carpal bones are very common injuries in the clinical setting but are rarely seen as an issue in forensic casework. The CT allows noninvasive demonstration of the carpal bones in every case. If forensic pathologists routinely examine the CT images, we may find that additional information may be gleaned on selected cases.

Scaphoid

The scaphoid is the largest bone in the proximal row of the carpus. It lies between the lunate proximally and the trapezoid and the trapezium distally. The scaphoid is the most commonly fractured bone of the wrist. These fractures account for approximately 75% of clinical cases [15]. A scaphoid fracture is most commonly seen in men in their second and third decades.

The common clinical situation causing a fractured scaphoid is a fall onto the hyperextended hand resulting in forced dorsiflexion. The biomechanical basis of the fracture appears to be from forced extension of the wrist. This action leads to compression of the scaphoid and subsequent failure of the bone.

From a forensic point of view, the use of rigid handcuffs has been reported as a cause of scaphoid fracture [16]. The mechanism of injury was believed to have occurred as a consequence of incorrect positioning of the handcuffs. The alleged offender was prevented from falling forward by pulling back on the handcuff bar. This resulted in his body weight being supported by the handcuffs and causing a fracture to the waist of the scaphoid.

The scapho-capitate fracture (Fenton's syndrome) is a rare lesion with an uncertain causal mechanism.

Capitate

The capitate is the largest bone in the carpometacarpal complex. The capitate is situated into the concavity formed by its proximal carpal neighbors. The capitate articulates with seven bones. These are the scaphoid and lunate proximally; the second, third, and fourth metacarpals distally; the trapezoid on the radial side; and the hamate on the ulna side. The capitate has a keystone position in the wrist. It functions in the maintenance of the transverse and longitudinal palmar arches of the hand [17].

A fall onto the outstretched hand transmits force principally to the capitate, then to the other bones of the carpus, and finally to the radius. Despite its crucial position in the hand the capitate is not often fractured. A fall onto the hand is a common occurrence and is the most common cause of fracture when the capitate is forced against the radius.

Hyperextension of the wrist allows contact between the capitate and the posterior aspect of the radius, which can in turn lead to a fracture.

Navicular

A fall onto the hand may also result in what has been termed the navicular–capitate fracture syndrome. This syndrome is caused by a fall to the hand when the wrist is in dorsiflexion and radial deviation. The transmitted forces cause the radial styloid to impact with the waist of the navicular.

A fracture to the navicular may dissipate the force that has been applied, however, if the application of force continues, a fracture can also occur through the waist of the capitate. Another mechanism of injury is direct force over the dorsum of the wrist. When this occurs there are usually other associated carpal bone fractures. The last mechanism that may lead to fracture is direct force to the heads of the second and third metacarpals, or dorsal aspect of the hand with the wrist dorsiflexed.

A study of 91 cases of capitate fracture showed that 44 were due to falls onto the hand, with only 8 cases the result of direct trauma.

Trapezoid

Isolated trapezoid fractures are rare. The mechanism of injury is generally accepted to result from an axial load transmitted through the second metacarpal. However, a case report described an isolated trapezoid fracture that was caused by direct trauma [18].

Metacarpals and Phalanges

Anatomy

The hand contains five metacarpals. Each metacarpal has a base, a shaft, a neck, and a head. The first metacarpal is the shortest, functionally the most mobile, and articulates at its base with the trapezium. The second metacarpal articulates proximally with the trapezoid and capitate. The third metacarpal articulates proximally with the capitate. The fourth metacarpal articulates proximally with the capitate and hamate. The fifth metacarpal articulates proximally with the hamate. Each metacarpal articulates distally with the base of the proximal phalanx. The thumb has only two phalanges, whereas each of the four fingers has a proximal, a middle, and a distal phalanx.

Etiology

Fractures involving the metacarpals are among the most common of all fractures. Fractures of the fifth metacarpal are the most frequent of all hand fractures. They have been estimated to involve almost a third of all hand fractures.

Striking a hard object with a closed fist is widely held to be a common etiological factor. Interestingly, the most common cause of a fractured fifth metacarpal in a study of all hand fractures in a hospital in Norway was in fact a fall. The fractures were found to be more common in women. Other less common causes included a sports injury, squeezing of the hand, and work-related injury [19]. Of 130 aggression-related fractures, 84 involved the subcapital region, 31 were diaphyseal, and 15 were basal.

Mechanism

The cause of metacarpal and phalangeal fractures will vary with respect to the level of interpersonal violence and the use of firearms in a particular community. A retrospective clinical study from Miami, Florida, in the late 1980s involving 53 consecutive patients with 68 fractures showed that gunshot injury was the most common cause of fracture [20]. Blunt force assault was the cause of injury in six cases, machine and power tool accident in five cases, sports injury in four cases, and motor vehicle incident in five cases.

A study published in 1979 analyzing 150 phalangeal fractures showed that the shaft of the proximal phalanx was involved in over 50% of the cases [21]. A later study of 40 unselected patients with 50 phalangeal fractures from the Natalspruit Hospital Hand Unit in South Africa included 34 males and 6 females [22]. There was no difference in hand dominance. Of the 38 extra-articular fractures, 50% were transverse fractures and approximately 30% were oblique fractures. The middle finger was injured in 16 cases, the index finger in 12 cases, and the ring and fifth fingers were injured in 9 and 8 cases, respectively. The thumb was injured in 5 cases. The cause of the fractures was assault in 80% of the cases with 22 caused by blunt force trauma.

Fractures of the fifth metacarpal have traditionally been referred to as "boxer's fractures." In circumstances where an individual strikes a hard object with a closed fist, the subcapital region is most commonly fractured. The fracture has a reported frequency of 60%. Diaphyseal and basal fractures occur in 6% and 34% of cases, respectively [23]. Interestingly, fractures to the subcapital region of the fifth metacarpal are an unusual injury in professional boxers, presumably because of the use of boxing gloves [24].

CT Diagnosis of Upper Limb Fractures

Humerus

CT has been a huge advance in the clinical diagnosis and management of proximal humeral fractures [8]. This is partly because the complexities of the fractures that have previously been diagnosed on two-dimensional radiographs are much more easily conceptualized and diagnosed using CT with three-dimensional reconstructions.

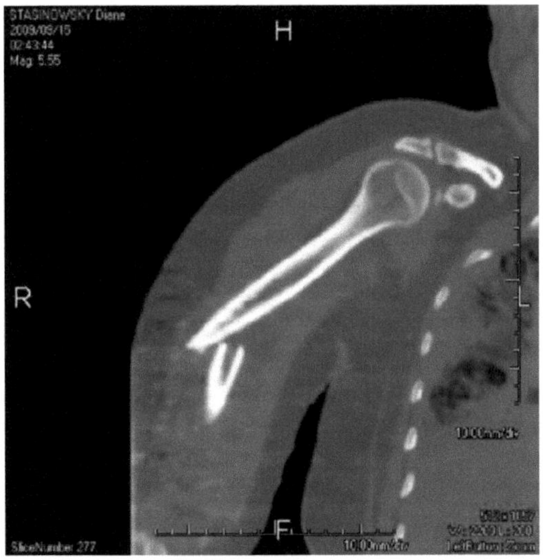

Figure 8.6 Coronal CT of a displaced fracture to the shaft of the right humerus.

CT features useful for the diagnosis of humeral fractures include:

- A linear lucency through the shaft or distal humerus is the feature observed in a simple fracture.
- An elbow effusion with displacement of a fat pad is a sign of fracture that may be recognized with more experience by pathologists and is a routine observation for radiologists.
- Olecranon fractures are generally easily seen on sagittal reformations.
- In forensic cases, a humeral fracture associated with multiple injuries is often obvious (Figure 8.6).

Forearm

The shaft of the ulna is more frequently fractured than the shaft of the radius. Because the ulna and radius are rigidly bound by the interosseous membrane, in injuries involving considerable force there are often fractures of both bones, and frequently associated with a dislocation of the wrist or elbow.

When examining CT images of the forearm:

- If a fracture of one forearm long bone is present, the other bone should be carefully evaluated.
- If a fracture of a long bone is identified, the wrist and elbow should be carefully examined.

Wrist Injuries

Multidetector computed tomography (MDCT) is particularly useful in the examination of the carpal bones, because the reformatted images remove the problem of bone overlap, which makes evaluation on conventional radiographs so difficult. On MDCT imaging a scaphoid fracture is diagnosed by the presence of a sharp lucent line or discontinuity with the bone's trabecular pattern, or a step in the contour of the cortex [25].

Shoulder Dislocation

Anatomy

The glenohumeral joint is a shallow ball in a socket-type joint, which allows complex combinations of abduction, adduction, internal rotation, and external rotation. The articular surface of the head of the humerus articulates with the glenoid fossa of the scapula.

The joint is stabilized through a combination of static and dynamic restraints [26]. The principal static components are the cartilaginous glenoid labrum, the joint capsule, and associated glenohumeral ligaments. The principal dynamic component leading to joint stability is the four muscles and tendons around the shoulder joint, which comprise the rotator cuff muscles.

Etiology

The great mobility of the shoulder joint also leads to it being the joint in the body that is most frequently dislocated. In more than 95% of cases of shoulder dislocation the humerus is displaced anteriorly [27]. The majority of shoulder dislocations result from a simple fall. In active youths, shoulder dislocation is often related to sports injury. The mean age of victims at the time of first dislocation is 37±17 years for men and 59±19 years for women [28]. Shoulder dislocation occurs in a bimodal pattern with peaks in adolescence and in the sixth decade, the latter especially in women.

Posterior shoulder dislocation is associated with seizures and may be seen in cases of electrocution. Bilateral posterior dislocation is a rare entity and is almost always associated with seizure activity [29]. Seizures have been described to be associated with posterior dislocation in 78% of reported cases [30].

Mechanism

Anterior dislocation of the shoulder classically occurs from a position of abduction, extension, and external rotation. The position formed when an athlete spikes a volleyball characterizes the position when the shoulder is at greatest risk for anterior dislocation. Other shoulder movements associated with heightened chance of anterior dislocation include throwing a ball and, in older individuals, a fall onto the outstretched hand. Of forensic interest is the mechanism of forceful pulling of the arm, as may occur in a struggle.

Posterior dislocation of the shoulder is uncommon, occurring in about 1% to 3% of cases of shoulder dislocation. Posterior dislocation is characterized by displacement of the articular surface of the humerus posterior to the glenoid fossa. The mechanism of the injury is usually from a direct blow to the anterior aspect of the shoulder, or a fall to the outstretched hand or elbow with the arm adducted and internally rotated. As noted earlier, posterior dislocation may be related to seizure activity. In these cases there may also be a compression defect to the articular surface of the head of the humerus from continual pressure against the glenoid fossa [30]. It may be useful in selected cases to directly inspect the articular surface of the glenoid fossa during the autopsy examination.

Superior dislocation of the humerus is rare. The injury occurs from the application of force to the arm that is extended overhead, and often with the forearm in pronation. Superior shoulder dislocation is characterized by upward displacement of the humerus. The shaft of the humerus is parallel to the spine of the scapula. The injury is often associated with a fracture of the clavicle, acromion, coracoid, or greater tuberosity of the humerus [31].

Another rare type of shoulder dislocation is inferior dislocation [31]. Inferior shoulder dislocation (or luxatio erecta) has an incidence of 0.5% of all shoulder dislocations [32]. The clinical presentation is unique. The arm is typically elevated and fixed, with the forearm resting on the head. The injury most commonly occurs during a fall.

The most common mechanism of the injury is a severe forward and upward displacement of the adducted arm such as may occur when a motorcycle rider is vaulted over the handlebars. The injury can result from indirect forces when the neck of the humerus is levered against the acromion, tearing the inferior aspect of the capsule as the humeral head is dislocated inferiorly.

CT Diagnosis of Shoulder Dislocation

- On conventional radiographs the medial part of the head of the humerus normally overlaps the glenoid fossa to form a shadow shaped like a half moon, which reaches the inferior border of the glenoid fossa. The absence of this radiological feature is an indicator of posterior shoulder dislocation.
- Shoulder dislocation is usually easily seen on axial CT images (Figure 8.7a).

(a)

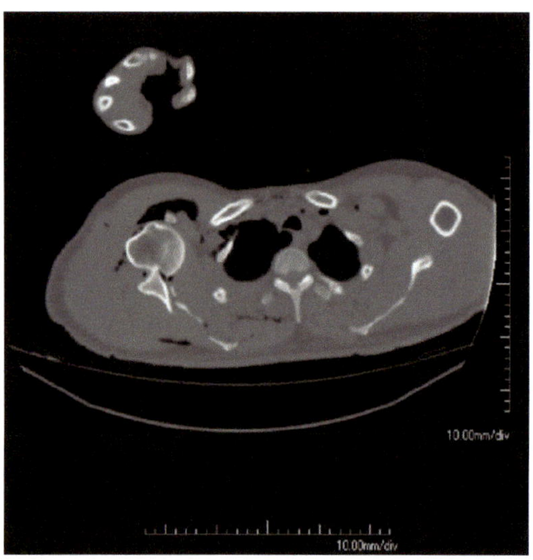

(b)

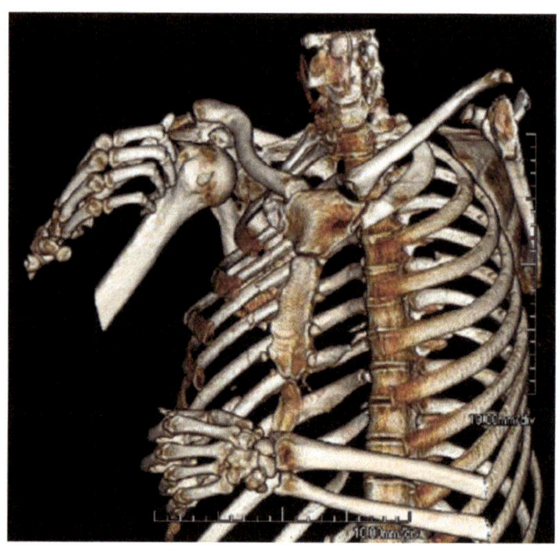

Figure 8.7 (a) Axial CT image showing an anterior dislocation of the right shoulder. (b) Three-dimensional reconstruction image showing an anterior shoulder dislocation.

- Three-dimensional reconstruction images will demonstrate most cases of significant dislocations (Figure 8.7b).
- Anterior dislocation is associated with greater tuberosity fracture, whereas posterior dislocation is associated with lesser tuberosity fracture.
- In superior dislocation of the humerus, the CT images show the head of the humerus to be subcoracoid in abduction.

Elbow Fracture Dislocation

Anatomy

The elbow is described as a trochoginglymoid joint, which has two major actions: flexion–extension and pronation–supination. A hinge joint is formed between the trochlea of the humerus and the trochlea notch of the ulna, and the radial head and capitulum of the humerus. A ridge in the trochlear notch articulates with the groove in the trochlea of the humerus. The coronoid process of the ulna is an important stabilizer of the elbow in extension. Rotation at the elbow joint is afforded between the head of the radius and the radial notch of the ulna.

The annular ligament of the radius applies the radial head to the radial notch of the ulna, and is attached to the humerus by the radial collateral ligament of the elbow. The medial (ulna) collateral ligament and lateral (radial) collateral ligaments provide further stability against valgus and varus movement.

The joint capsule is lined with synovium. Displacement of intra-articular anterior and posterior fat pads is used in radiographic examinations in the diagnosis of intracapsular fractures.

Etiology

Elbow fractures occur in approximately 7% of all adult fractures [33]. In young adults the common causes of elbow fracture include motor vehicle incidents, falls from a height, and sports-related injuries [34]. In elderly patients almost two-thirds of cases occur from falls from a standing height.

Although the complementary shapes of the distal humerus and proximal ulna and radius afford considerable inherent stability, the elbow is the second most commonly dislocated joint in the adult and the most commonly dislocated joint in children [35]. Approximately 80% to 90% of elbow dislocations result in the ulna being displaced posteriorly.

Elbow dislocations may be classified into simple or complex dislocations. A simple dislocation is defined as an elbow dislocation without an elbow fracture, whereas a complex elbow dislocation is defined as an elbow dislocation with an associated elbow fracture.

Surgical examination of completely dislocated joints has demonstrated ruptures of the joint capsule and the lateral and medial collateral ligaments. Subluxation of the elbow joint has been shown to result in rupture of the lateral collateral ligament and joint capsule, however, the medial collateral ligament remained intact [36].

Mechanism

The majority of elbow dislocations are the result of a fall onto the outstretched hand resulting in a combination of axial loading, valgus stress, and rotation force to the joint. Biomechanical studies have shown that elbow stability decreases with progressive loss of the olecranon process of the ulna [25].

The coronoid process acts as a buttress to prevent posterior dislocation and is a major stabilizer to varus stress in extension. Coronoid fractures are usually associated with elbow dislocation. The mechanisms of coronoid fractures are varied and include hyperextension, twisting, and flexion.

CT Diagnosis of Elbow Fracture Dislocation

The use of CT in the clinical management of complex elbow fractures has been reported to aid in determining the underlying mechanism of injury [37]. The use of three-dimensional multiplanar reformatted images is especially important when reviewing elbow fractures.

- The fat pad sign is an indicator of intra-articular injury to the elbow. Fat is normally present within the joint capsule but outside the synovium. Typically fat is hidden within the concavity of the olecranon and coronoid fossa such that it is not visible on a conventional lateral radiograph. Injuries that produce intra-articular hemorrhage cause distension of the synovium and forces the fat out of the fossa, producing triangular radiolucent shadows anterior and posterior to the distal end of the humerus.
- A positive fat pad sign indicates intra-articular hemorrhage and intra-articular skeletal injury. Of note is the fact that the great majority of elbow injuries associated with a positive fat pad sign are due to a fractured head of radius.

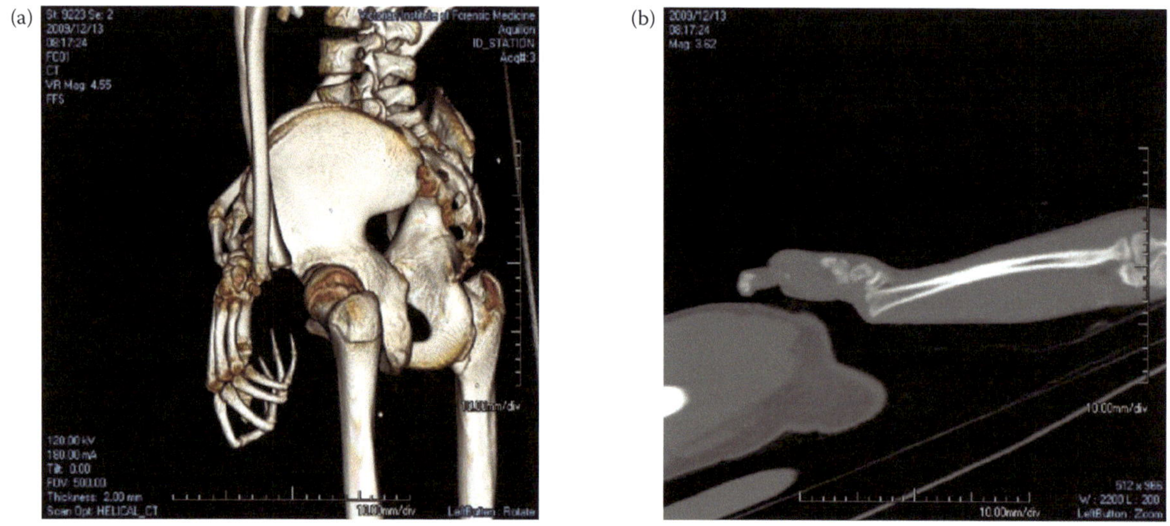

Figure 8.8 (a) Skeletal overview showing a dislocation to the left wrist. (b) Sagittal CT showing dorsal displacement of the carpus in a dislocation of the wrist seen in a motorcycle rider.

Wrist Fracture Dislocation

In adults, wrist injuries most commonly involve the distal forearm. The radius is most frequently involved and then the ulna. The mechanism of injury is usually a fall to the hand (Figure 8.8a,b). Carpal dislocations most commonly result from a fall onto the outstretched hand. This leads to axial loading with hyperextension. The majority of metacarpal dislocations are multiple lesions that result most frequently from direct force, as may occur when striking a hard object with a closed fist. Coronal and sagittal reformatted views are best to diagnose wrist, carpal, and metacarpal fractures.

Forensic Aspects of Upper Limb Injury

Assault

One may argue that it is not the responsibility of the forensic pathologist to opine as to whether an injury or fracture resulted from an offensive action by an assailant or a defensive reaction by a victim of assault. Indeed in many instances two individuals involved in an altercation may be both aggressor and defender.

However, even if it is not one's practice to volunteer an opinion on the mechanism of an injury, it is inevitable that investigating police officers and the courts will request such an opinion in certain cases. Although the pathologist is usually conservative in assigning causation to a particular injury, there are patterns of fracture that are regularly seen in certain circumstances. The "offensive" fracture is usually caused by an assailant striking another individual or object with a closed fist. A "defensive" fracture is usually caused when the victim's upper limb is raised to ward off a blow from a weapon.

Offensive-Type Fractures

A fracture to the fifth metacarpal is traditionally viewed as a fracture classically associated with an offensive-type injury. It would be everyday anecdotal experience of those working in emergency departments to see fractures of the metacarpals in young (usually) males who had struck a wall or other object with a closed fist. The subcapital region of the bone is fractured most frequently in these situations. However, the report from a series of cases in Norway certainly indicates that the injury may occur in other circumstances.

Damage to the articular surface of a metacarpal has been described in clenched-fist injuries, where the assailant's hand comes into hard contact with a tooth [38]. The third metacarpal was the most frequently involved region with 53 of 91 such cases. Eight of 139 patients were shown to have loose intra-articular fragments of articular cartilage, whereas tooth indentations were found in 23 of these patients. These features can be explored during conventional autopsy examination by opening the metacarpal joints and inspecting the articular surface.

An interesting single case report of a fracture to the hand of a 31-year-old woman who punched an assailant's shoulder was reported by Christodoulou et al. [39]. The mechanism was axial loading with the wrist in hyperextension, radial deviation, and the forearm in pronation. Investigations revealed she had sustained an oblique transverse fracture of the proximal pole of the scaphoid and a coronal plane fracture of the lunate and triquetrum.

An individual who strikes another person with a closed fist with the thumb held across the thenar eminence and the fingers folded over the thumb, may suffer a fracture of the trapezium by way of transmitted force through the first metacarpal.

In a wrestling-type struggle the aggressor or victim may suffer a dislocation of the shoulder. There may be a discernable alteration in contour to the affected shoulder with respect to the contralateral normal side on external examination, however, these changes may be subtle and easily overlooked.

Defensive-Type Injuries

The ulna is injured more commonly than the radius in direct blows involving the forearm. This is probably not related to any difference between the relative strengths of the ulna and radius, but due to the usual position of the arm and forearm a victim of assault will adopt to ward off a blow with a weapon. The fracture has traditionally been termed a "nightstick" injury. Whilst an altercation is clearly a dynamic process with numerous variables, the forearm is typically pronated so the medial aspect of the forearm is vulnerable in a defensive pose.

A study on blunt force assault using baseball bats in Washington, DC, between 1987 and 1990 described the 146 fractures and 7 dislocations resulting from nonlethal assaults [39]. The upper limbs were involved in 112 of the cases and the lower limb was targeted in 41 cases. The ulna was the bone most commonly fractured with 61 such injuries. Fractures to the hand occurred in 27 injuries and there were 14 fractures to the radius. The left side of the body was injured in 67% of the cases and the right side was injured in 23% of cases. The average age of the trauma victims was 30 years. There were 108 males and 8 females included in the study. Of the 146 fractures, 29% were significantly displaced.

Documentation of upper (and lower) limb fractures and dislocations by CT may provide important information to investigating police and the courts with respect to the totality of injuries sustained in the altercation.

Motor Vehicle–Related Injury

Airbag use is associated with injury to the upper limb. Most of these injuries are minor soft tissue injuries. Early studies reported a frequency of 4.4% of upper limb fractures from airbag deployment [41]. A number of factors have been purported to be important in causing airbag-related upper limb fractures. Osteoporosis has been suggested to be a major factor, although the position of the arm at the moment of impact is believed the most important. Having the forearm extending across the steering wheel at the time of the collision over the airbag module maximizes the risk of forearm injury and fracture [42].

Injuries to the hand and elbow are relatively rare in airbag deployment, though open dislocations of the thumbs may be seen. The thumbs are believed to be injured when forcefully pushed back by the airbag module cover [42].

The region of the upper limb most commonly fractured during airbag deployment is the distal third. Distal comminuted, and often compound fractures of the distal radius and ulna have been described [43]. Radial metaphyseal and diaphyseal fractures are typical injuries, whereas the distal radial articular region is also sometimes involved.

Trauma Associated with Seizures

The risk of accidental injury is marginally increased in patients with epilepsy compared to control patients without seizures. The risk of fracture is roughly doubled, resulting directly from injury or made susceptible by drug-induced decrease in bone density [44]. Fractures may occur from a fall or other accident subsequent to a seizure, or can result from the forces generated from the muscle contractions during the seizure. The most common injuries sustained in such a fall are minor soft tissue injuries.

As noted earlier, seizures are the most common cause of posterior fracture–dislocation of the shoulder, and when the injury is bilateral, seizures are almost always the underlying cause [45]. The considerable forces generated by the sustained contraction of the infraspinatus, teres minor and major, deltoid, and latissimus dorsi can culminate in fractures and dislocation at the shoulder. Other typical fractures associated with seizures include compression fractures of the thoracic spine and acetabular fractures [46,47].

References

1. George MS. Fractures of the greater tuberosity of the humerus. *J. Am. Acad. Orthop. Surg.* 2007; 15(10):607–613.
2. Bahrs C, Lingenfelter E, Fischer F, Walters EM, Schnabel M. Mechanism of injury and morphology of the greater tuberosity fracture. *J. Shoulder Elbow Surg.* 2006; 15(2):140–147.
3. Tytherfield-Strong G, Walls N, McQueen MM. The epidemiology of humeral shaft fractures. *J. Bone Joint Surg. Br.* 1998; 80(2):249–263.
4. Ogawa K, Yoshida A. Throwing fracture of the humeral shaft. *Am. J. Sports Med.* 1998; 26:242–246.
5. Shrader MW. Pediatric supracondylar fractures and pediatric physeal elbow fractures. *Orthop. Clin. N. Am.* 2008; 39:163–171.
6. Shaw BA, Murphy KM, Shaw A, Oppenheim WL, Myracle MR. Humerus shaft fractures in young children: Accident or abuse? *J. Pediatr. Orthop.* 1997; 17(3):293–297.

7. Hilton M, Yngve DA, Carmichael KD. Proximal humerus fractures sustained during the use of restraints in adolescents. *J. Pediatr. Orthop.* 2006; 26(1):50–52.
8. Sanchez-Sotelo J. Proximal humerus fractures. *Clin. Anat.* 2006; 19:588–598.
9. Sanjay P, Abdunabi M, Shah R. Type 1 Monteggia dislocation (open) associated with ipsilateral distal radial epiphyseal injury. *Injury Extra* 2005; 36(11):489–491.
10. Richmond PW, Fligelstone LJ, Lewis E. Injuries caused by handcuffs. *BMJ* 1988; 297:111–112.
11. Dunn AW. Fractures and dislocations of the carpus. *Surg. Clin. North Am.* 1972; 52:1513–1538.
12. Ilyas AM, Mudgal CS. Radiocarpal fracture-dislocations. *J. Am. Acad. Orthop. Surg.* 2008; 16(11):647–655.
13. Mayfield JK, Johnson RP, Kilcoyne RF. Carpal dislocations: Pathomechanics and progressive perilunar instability. *J. Hand Surg. (Am.)* 1980; 5:226–241.
14. Bochang C, Katz K, Weigl D, Jie Y, Zhigang W, Bar-ON E. Are frequent radiographs necessary in the management of closed forearm fractures in children. *J. Child Orthop.* 2008; 2(3):217–220.
15. Greenspan A. Part II: Trauma. In Greenspan A, editor. *Orthopaedic radiology: A practical approach*, 3rd ed. Lippincott, Williams & Wilkins, Philadelphia, 2000, pp. 45–326.
16. Ball L, Ferran NA, Barton CR. Scaphoid fracture due to rigid handcuffs. *J. Hand Surg. (European Volume).* 2008; 33E(4):484–487.
17. Adler JB, Shaftan GW. Fractures of the capitate. *J. Bone Joint Surg. Am.* 1962; 44:1537–1547.
18. Gruson KI, Kaplan KM, Paksima N. Isolated trapezoid fractures: A case report with compilation of the literature. *Bull. NYU Hosp. Jt. Dis.* 2008; 66(1):57–60.
19. Gudmundsen TE, Borgen L. Fractures of the fifth metacarpal. *Acta Radiol.* 2009; 50(3):296–300.
20. Oullette EA, Freeland AE. Use of the minicondylar plate in metacarpal and phalangeal fractures. *Clin. Orthop. Relat. Res.* 1996; 327:38–46.
21. Barton NJ. Fractures of the shafts of the phalanges of the hand. *Hand* 1979; 2:119–133.
22. Widgerow AD, Edinburg M, Biddulph SL. An analysis of proximal phalangeal fractures. *J. Hand Surg.* 1987; 12A:134–139.
23. Hunter JM, Cowen NJ. Fifth metacarpal fractures in a compensation clinic population. A report on one hundred and thirty-three cases. *J. Bone Joint Surg. Am.* 1970; 52:1159–1165.
24. Bansky R, Racz N. The use of titanium miniplates in arthrodesis of the interphalangeal joints and a metacarpal neck fracture. *Bratisl. Lek. Listy.* 2005; 106(8–9):287–290.
25. Ahn JM, El-Khoury GY. Occult fractures of extremities. *Radiol. Clin. N. Am.* 2007; 45(3):561–579.
26. Dodson CC, Cordasco FA. Anterior glenohumeral joint dislocations. *Orthop. Clin. N. Am.* 2008; 39:507–518.
27. Smith T. Immobilisation following traumatic anterior glenohumeral joint dislocation. A literature review. *Injury* 2006; 37(3):228–337.
28. Chalidis B, Sachinis N, Dimitriou C, Papadopoulos P, Samoladas E, Pournara J. Has the management of shoulder dislocation changed over time? *Int. Orthop.* 2007; 31:385–389.
29. Betz ME, Traub SJ. Bilateral posterior shoulder dislocation following seizure. *Intern. Emerg. Med.* 2007; 2(1):63–65.
30. Tellisi NK, Abusitta GR, Fernandes RJ. Bilateral posterior fracture dislocation of the shoulders following seizure. *Saudi Med. J.* 2004; 25(11):1727–1729.
31. Downey EF, Curtis DJ, Brower AC. Unusual dislocations of the shoulder. *AJR* 1983; 140:1207–1210.
32. Taskin RS, Sedlin ED. Luxatio erecta in infancy. *Clin. Orthop.* 1971; 80:126–129.
33. Anglen J. Distal humerus fractures [review]. *J. Am. Acad. Orthop. Surg.* 2005; 13:291–297.
34. Pollock JW, Faber KJ, Athwal GS. Distal humerus fractures. *Orthop. Clin. N. Am.* 2008; 39:187–200.
35. Hildebrand KA, Patterson SD, King GJW. Elbow trauma and reconstruction. *Orthop. Clin. N. Am.* 1999; 30(1):63–79.
36. O'Driscoll SW, Morrey BF, Korinek S, An KN. Elbow subluxation and dislocation. A spectrum of instability. *Clin. Orthop. Relat. Res.* 1992; 280:186–197.
37. Ohashi K, El-Khoury GY. Musculoskeletal CT: Recent advances and current clinical applications. *Radiol. Clin. N. Am.* 2009; 47:387–409.
38. Patzakis MJ, Wilkins J, Bassett RL. Surgical findings in clenched-fist injuries. *Clin. Orthop.* 1987; 220:237–240.
39. Christodoulou L, Palou CH, Chamberlain ST. Proximal row transcarpal fracture from a punching injury. *J. Hand Surg. (Br.)* 1999; 24(6):744–746.
40. Bryant DD III, Greenfield R, Martin E. Musculoskeletal trauma: The baseball bat. *J. Natl. Med. Assoc.* 1992; 84:957–960.
41. Huebner CJ, Reed MP. Airbag-induced fracture in a patient with osteoporosis. *J. Trauma* 1998; 45:416–418.
42. Danne P. Serious injuries from airbags. *ANZ J. Surg.* 2001; 71:507–508.
43. Nabarro M, Myers S. Airbag injuries: Upper limb fractures due to airbag deployment. *Aust. N Z J Surg.* 2000; 70(5):377–379.
44. Serra C, Delattre O, Despeignes R, Cousins A. Upper limb traumatic lesions related to airbag deployment: A case report and review of literature. *J. Trauma* 2008; 65(3):704–707.
45. Wirrell EC. Epilepsy-related injuries. *Epilepsia* 2006; 47 Supp. 1:79–86.
46. Shaw JL, Topeka K. Bilateral posterior fracture-dislocation of the shoulder and other trauma caused by convulsive seizures. *J. Bone Joint Surg.* 1971; 53-A:1437–1440.
47. Takahashi T, Tominaga T, Shamoto H, Shimizu H, Yoshimoto T, Fabinyi G. Seizure-induced thoracic spine compression fracture: Case report. *Surg. Neurol.* 2002; 58(3–4):214–217.
48. Friedberg R, Buras J. Bilateral acetabular fractures associated with a seizure: A case report. *Ann. Emerg. Med.* 2005; 46(3):260–262.

Pelvis

9

Anatomy

The pelvis is a stable ring of bones and ligaments that encloses the pelvic viscera (Figure 9.1a,b,c,d). The pelvis is formed by the paired innominate bones and the sacrum. The innominate consists of the ilium, ischium, and pubis. The sacrum is a wedge-shaped bone formed from the fusion of the five sacral vertebrae.

The pelvis articulates with the lower limb through the hip joint and with the lumbar spine via the sacrum through the left and right sacroiliac joints. The superior and inferior pubic rami join at the symphysis pubis forming the pubic arch. The pubic arch is acute in males and more obtuse in females. The iliac wing of the ilium comprises the superior two-thirds of the lateral pelvis and top two-fifths of the acetabulum. The ilium articulates with the sacrum at the sacroiliac joint.

The integrity of the pelvis is highly dependent upon its ligaments. There are posterior, anterior, and pelvic floor ligaments. The posterior ligaments are more important than the anterior ligaments in maintaining the integrity of the pelvis [1]. The symphysis is a cartilaginous disc with anterior and dorsal ligamentous supports.

The sacroiliac joint is stabilized anteriorly by the interosseous sacroiliac ligaments, and the posterior short and long sacroiliac ligaments. The sacrospinous ligament fastens the coccyx and ischial spine. The sacrotuberous ligament joins the sacrum and ischial tuberosity.

The hip joint is a ball and socket joint. A thick capsule called the acetabular labrum extends almost circumferentially around acetabulum and deepens the socket. Capsular ligaments attach the acetabulum to the femoral neck and intertrochanteric region. Anterior to the joint is the iliofemoral ligament. Posterior to the joint is the ischiofemoral ligament.

Etiology

Pelvic fractures in adults are associated with significant morbidity and mortality. In otherwise active and healthy individuals, pelvic fractures are an indicator of severe trauma and a marker of potential major pelvic and abdominal visceral damage [2]. Exsanguination can result from disruption of major arteries, venous plexuses, and from the fracture itself, with certain fractures being related to specific vessel trauma. Pelvic fractures lead to early death from associated damage to major arteries and veins. Delayed deaths are more often the result of the systemic effects of visceral injury or multiple system dysfunction and fat embolism syndrome.

The causes of pelvic fractures vary with respect to age. In young adults the most common cause of pelvic fracture is trauma from motor vehicle incidents. Other causes are falls from a height and industrial accidents. Older individuals may also suffer a pelvic fracture from a motor vehicle incident. These crashes may be of lesser force than those causing injury in younger individuals. Other common causes are intermediate falls such as a fall from a ladder. Elderly individuals with osteoporosis may sustain pelvic trauma from relatively minor trauma such as a fall from a standing height. Less commonly, bed-bound or wheel chair–confined persons can suffer a pelvic fracture from very minor trauma such as turning the patient in bed. Rarely an acetabular fracture, fracture of the neck of the femur, or hip dislocation may result from a seizure [3].

Mechanisms

Forces brought to bear on the pelvis may be directed from anterior–posterior, lateral, or vertical.

Pelvic fractures may be divided into simple, stable fractures and complex unstable fractures. Low energy incidents, such as simple falls from a standing height, tend to cause stable simple fractures, whereas high energy trauma, such as motor vehicle incidents, are more likely to cause unstable, more complex fractures.

Stable pelvic fractures are characterized clinically and on internal autopsy examination by preservation of resistance to anterior–posterior, lateral, or vertical movement in the pelvic ring. Higher energy forces will tend to cause more severe injuries, and may involve both the anterior and posterior aspects of the pelvis resulting in an unstable pelvic ring.

Anterior forces have a propensity to cause separation of the symphysis pubis, or fractures to the pubic rami and a second posterior fracture in the vicinity of the ipsilateral sacroiliac joint (Figure 9.2). Posteriorly directed forces tend to cause iliac or sacral fracture with

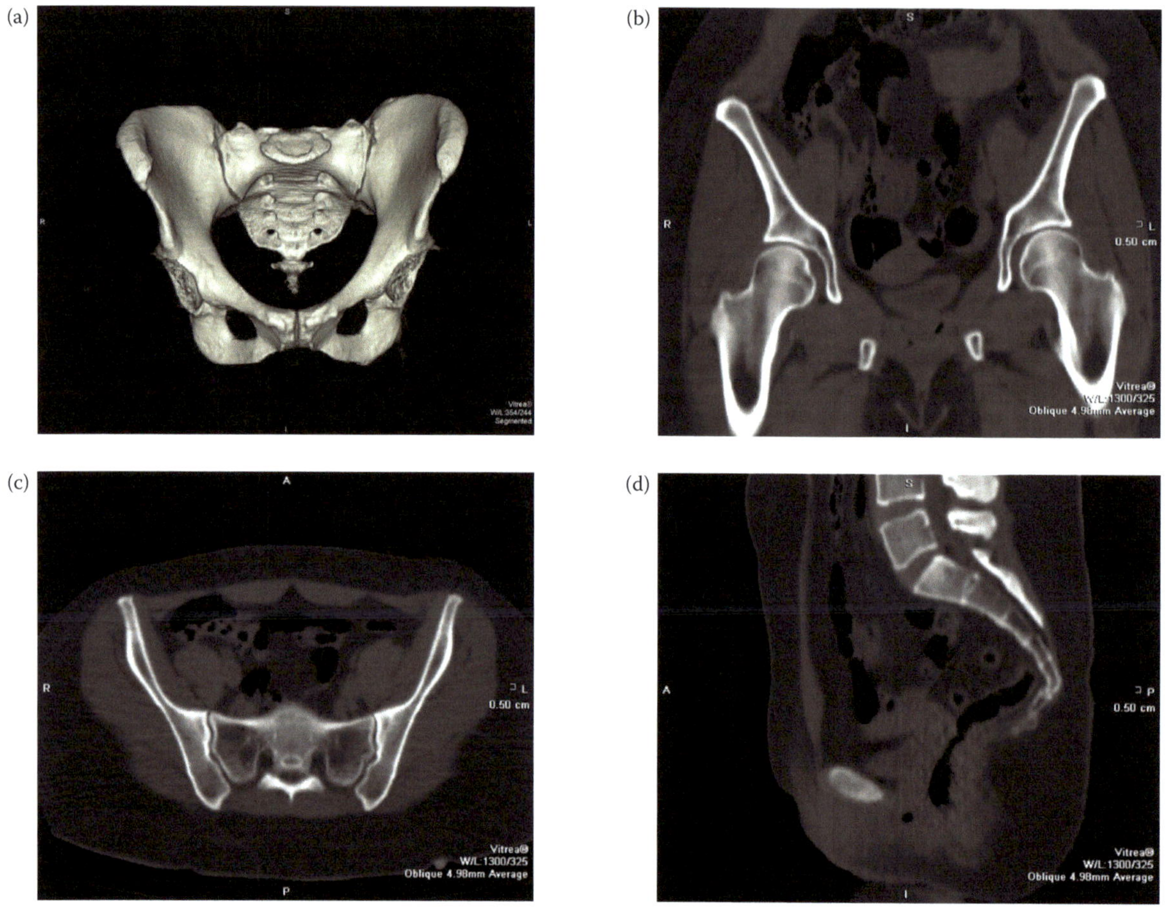

Figure 9.1 (a) Three-dimensional reconstruction of a normal pelvis. (b) Coronal CT of a normal pelvis. (c) Axial CT of a normal pelvis. (d) Coronal CT of a normal pelvis.

secondary anterior fractures (Figure 9.3). There is a tendency for the bones closest to the point of the application of the force to show a greater degree of injury. Laterally directed forces tend to cause injury to the sacroiliac joint and fractures to the pubic rami (Figure 9.4). Laterally directed forces over the region of the greater trochanter of the femur can lead to central acetabular fractures.

Increasing degrees of force may be associated with a sacral fracture. With more posteriorly directed force there may be a fracture of the iliac crest. A further rise in degree of force can lead to corresponding fractures to the contralateral aspect of the pelvis.

Vertically directed forces through the femur or directly to the ischium tend to produce fractures to the ipsilateral superior and inferior pubic rami, and vertical fractures to the ilium or sacrum (Figure 9.5a,b) [4]. Vertical shear injuries are virtually always clinically unstable.

The mechanism of pelvic fracture has implications for the occurrence of pelvic hemorrhage. Fractures that involve shearing injury, with posterior fractures involving the ilium or anterior sacroiliac disruption can cause damage to the iliolumbar artery, which is in close proximity to the anterior sacroiliac joint [5].

Fractures through the sacrum may lead to injury to the lateral sacral arteries. This is most often seen with lateral compression or vertical shear injury.

The superior gluteal artery may be lacerated from severe blunt force applied to the posterior aspect of the pelvis in a posterior–anterior compression-type injury [6]. The superior gluteal artery may be lacerated by the fascia of piriformis or via direct trauma through the gluteal muscles [7]. The superior and inferior gluteal artery may be involved in fractures to the region of the greater sciatic foramen, the upper part of the ischial tuberosity, and the ischial spine.

The internal pudendal artery may be damaged in open book fractures. Fractures around the acetabulum can lead to rupture of branches of the obturator artery [7].

Avulsion Fractures

Avulsion fractures are generally a clinical issue rather than a forensic problem. Avulsion fractures typically occur around the pelvis in children and sudden stress associated with various sporting activities. The action of

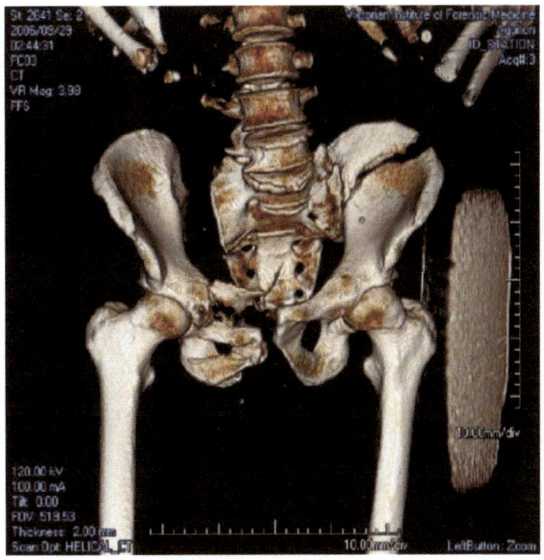

Figure 9.2 Three-dimensional reconstruction showing a complex pelvic fracture. There are fractures to the superior and inferior pubic rami and sacroiliac joint on the right, and a left iliac wing fracture.

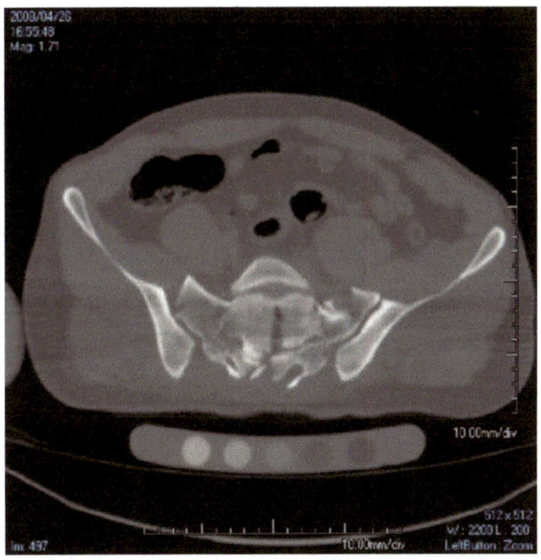

Figure 9.3 Axial CT showing the consequences of posterior force with a fractured sacrum and fracture/dislocation of the right sacroiliac joint.

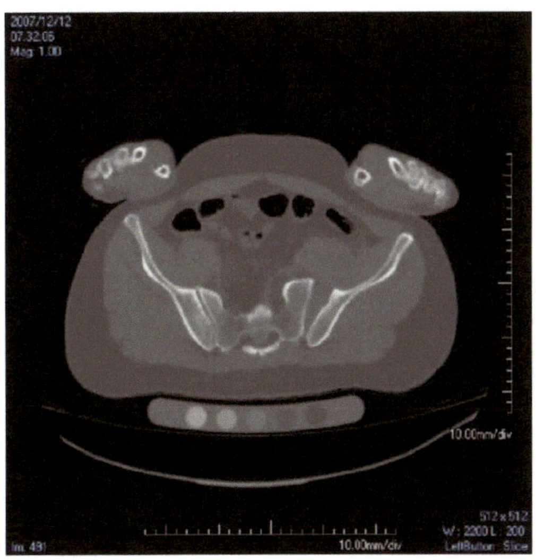

Figure 9.4 Axial CT showing the consequence of lateral applied force with left sacroiliac joint disruption.

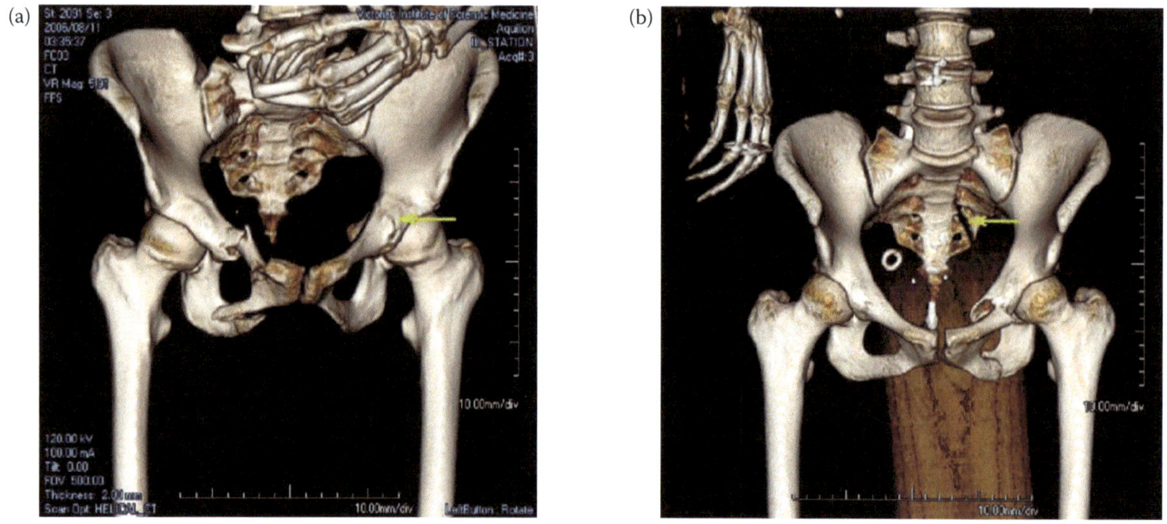

Figure 9.5 (a) Three-dimensional reconstruction CT image showing the consequences of vertically directed force. Fractures are seen to the left acetabulum and bilateral pubic rami. (b) Three-dimensional reconstruction showing a vertical force injury through the left pubic rami and a longitudinal fracture to the sacrum.

sudden muscle contraction avulses a segment of bone at the tendonous insertion. Typical sites of avulsion fracture in the pelvis include the anterior and inferior superior iliac crest, ischial tuberosity, and syphysis pubis.

In a forensic setting, an avulsion fracture to the pelvis may be seen with sudden extreme movement of the lower limb beyond the normal range of movement. This mechanism is likely to involve significant forces, and as such, it is highly probable that other fractures and associated injuries will be present (Figure 9.6).

Simple Pelvic Fractures

A common simple fracture of the pelvis is the isolated pubic ramus fracture (Figure 9.7a,b,c). This fracture comprises approximately 40% of pelvic fractures and is commonly seen in older, female individuals with osteoporosis. Pubic ramus fractures may result from anterior–posterior, lateral, or vertical compression. A study investigating the biomechanics of the pelvis in lateral impact showed that ramus fractures were correlated to

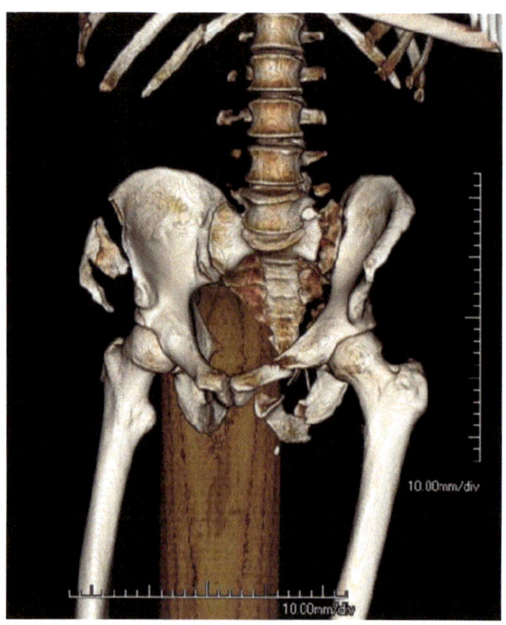

Figure 9.6 Three-dimensional reconstruction image showing avulsion of the right anterior superior iliac crest. In this case there are multiple other fractures. The mechanism of fracture was determined to be blunt force trauma to the posterior lateral aspect of the right hip region.

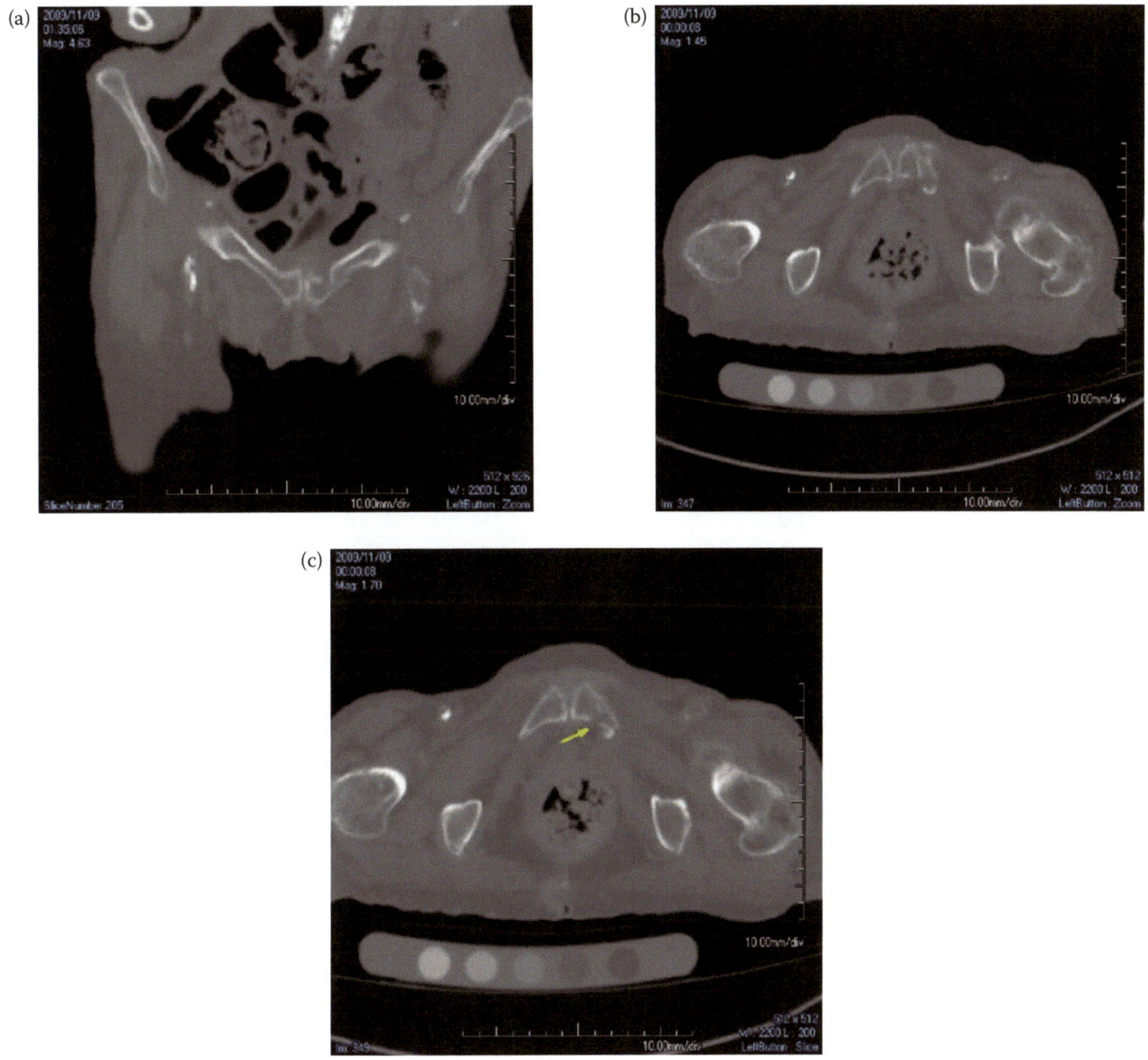

Figure 9.7 (a) Coronal CT showing a right superior ramus fracture. (b) Axial CT showing a fractured left superior ramus. (c) Axial CT showing a fractured left inferior ramus.

the degree of compression of the pelvis, rather than the impact force or pelvic acceleration [8].

A pubic symphyseal injury is typically caused by traction forces and scissorlike movements [9]. The anterior ligament is stronger than the dorsal ligament, hence the dorsal ligament will tend to rupture irrespective of whether the injurious force is directed from the front or the back.

The straddle fracture results from direct trauma to the pelvic arch, inferior to the symphysis pubis (Figure 9.8). The fracture may involve all four pubic rami, or two pubic rami and the symphysis pubis. A common situation where the straddle fracture occurs is when a motorcycle rider's pelvis sustains forceful contact with the fuel tank of the motorcycle following a head-on collision. More recently this fracture has been reported in riders of recreation jet skis. Rarely this fracture may also be seen as a stress fracture [10].

The Duverney fracture is an isolated fracture of the iliac wing (Figure 9.9a,b). The fracture results from direct impact or lateral compression [11]. It is caused by high energy impact. The fracture is rotationally and vertically stable [12]. It may rarely be associated with significant vascular injury.

Sacral Fractures

The majority of sacral fractures occur in motor vehicle occupants who are involved in crashes. Victims of motor vehicle trauma account for 57% of cases, pedestrian victims in 18% of cases, and with 9% of cases occurring in falls from a height. Approximately 9% of cases result from workplace incidents [13,14].

Sacral fractures have been classified with respect to the direction, location, and the anatomical level of the injury [13]. The Denis classification of sacral fractures divides the sacrum into three sections with respect to neural foramina. Type I fractures are lateral to the neural foramina, type II fractures are present through the foramina, and type III fractures occur through the spinal canal.

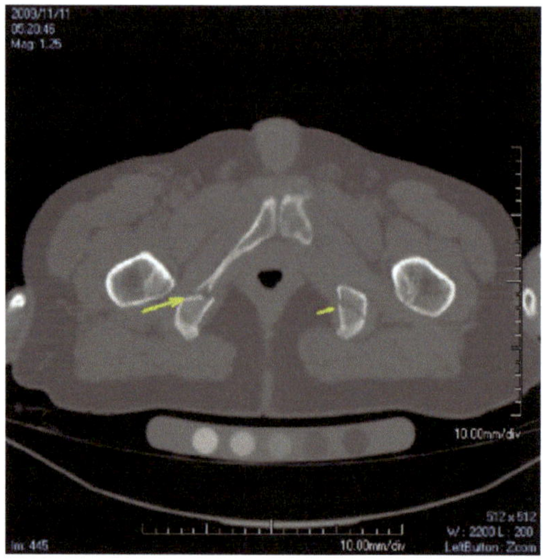

Figure 9.8 Axial CT showing bilateral fractures of the pubic rami in a straddle fracture.

Pure isolated fractures of the sacrum occur in less than 5% of cases, are usually transverse, and are associated with high energy trauma [15]. Such fractures are often seen in connection with significant falls and involve direct force to the posterior aspect of the pelvis. Sacral fractures occur in association with other pelvic fractures in 45% of cases and are usually vertically orientated (Figure 9.10a,b) [16].

Complex Pelvic Fractures

Pelvic fractures are often complex injuries. The two common classification systems are the Young–Burgess system and the Tile system. These two systems are based on the mechanism of the injury and the stability of the pelvis. The direction of the force delivered to the pelvis may involve anterior–posterior compression, lateral compression, or vertical compression [17].

The Young–Burgess system describes pelvic fractures as follows:

Lateral compression
- Type I—Sacral compression fracture on the side of the impact
- Type II—Iliac wing fracture on the side of the impact
- Type III—Either of the above fractures with a contralateral open book fracture

Anterior–posterior compression
- Type I—Slight widening of the pubic symphysis or anterior aspect of the sacroiliac joint with intact anterior and posterior sacroiliac ligaments

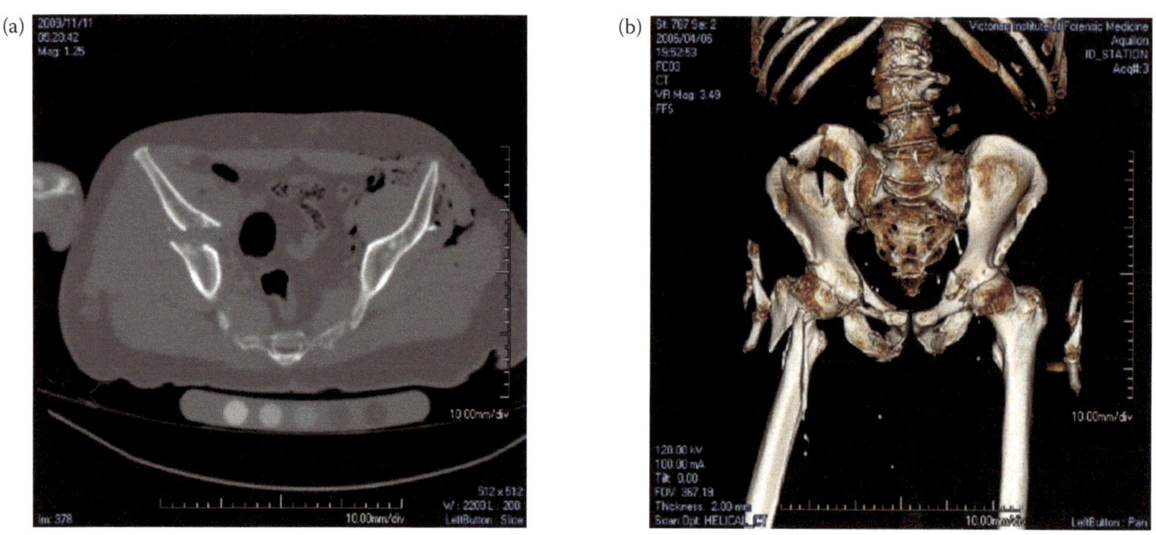

Figure 9.9 (a) Axial CT showing a right fractured ilium. (b) Three-dimensional reconstruction showing a fractured right ilium.

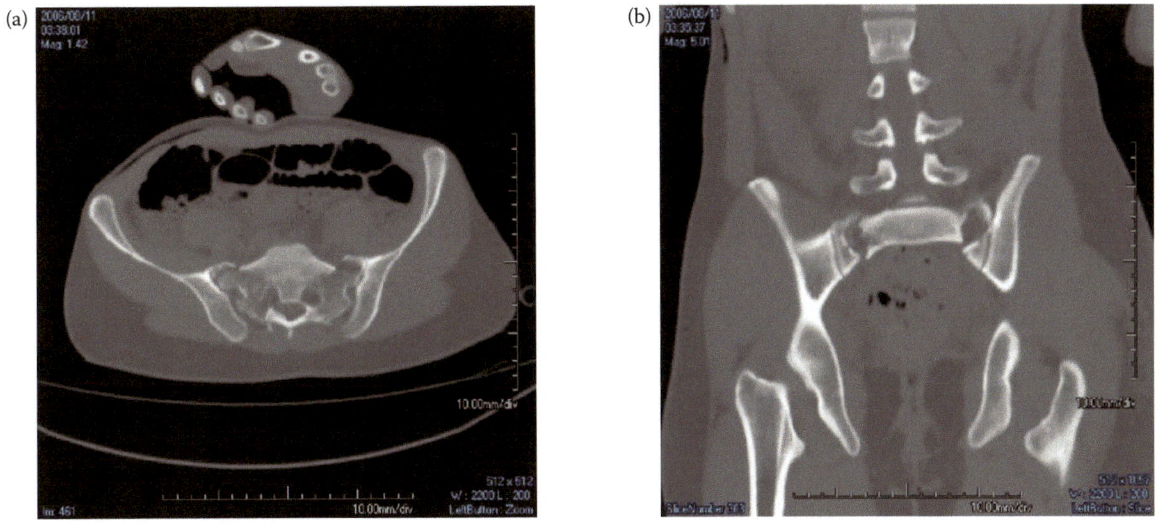

Figure 9.10 (a) Axial CT showing bilateral sacral ala fractures. (b) Coronal CT showing bilateral sacral ala fractures.

Type II—Widening anterior aspect of the sacroiliac joint with disruption of the anterior ligament and intact posterior sacroiliac ligaments

Type III—Complete disruption of the sacroiliac joint

Vertical shear

Vertical displacement anteriorly and posteriorly

Combined mechanism

Combination of both mechanisms

The Tile classification describes pelvic fractures as follows:

Type A—Stable
- A1—Without involvement of the pelvic ring
- A2—With involvement of the pelvic ring

Type B—Rotationally unstable
- B1—Open book
- B2—Ipsilateral lateral compression
- B3—Contralateral lateral compression

Type C—Rotationally and vertically unstable
- C1—Rotationally and vertically unstable
- C2—Bilateral fractures
- C3—Acetabular fractures

Open Book Fracture

An open book fracture of the pelvis is classically caused by severe anterior–posterior compression. The injury complex encompasses disruption of the symphysis pubis, with intact posterior sacroiliac joint ligaments such that the pelvis can open as a hinge (Figure 9.11). The injury is stable in the vertical direction but unstable in rotation.

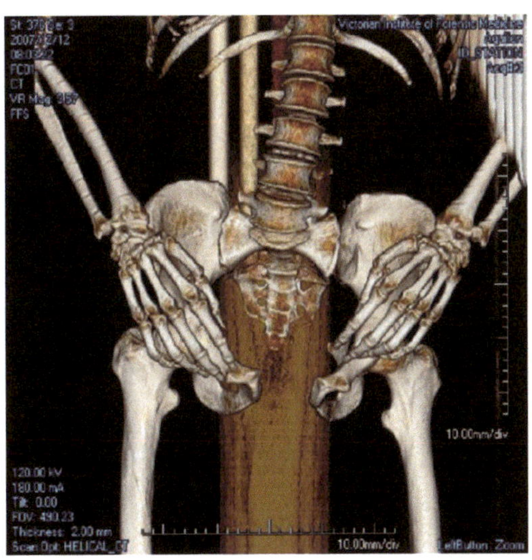

Figure 9.11 Three-dimensional reconstruction showing a separation of the symphysis pubis and separation of the left sacroiliac joint (open book fracture).

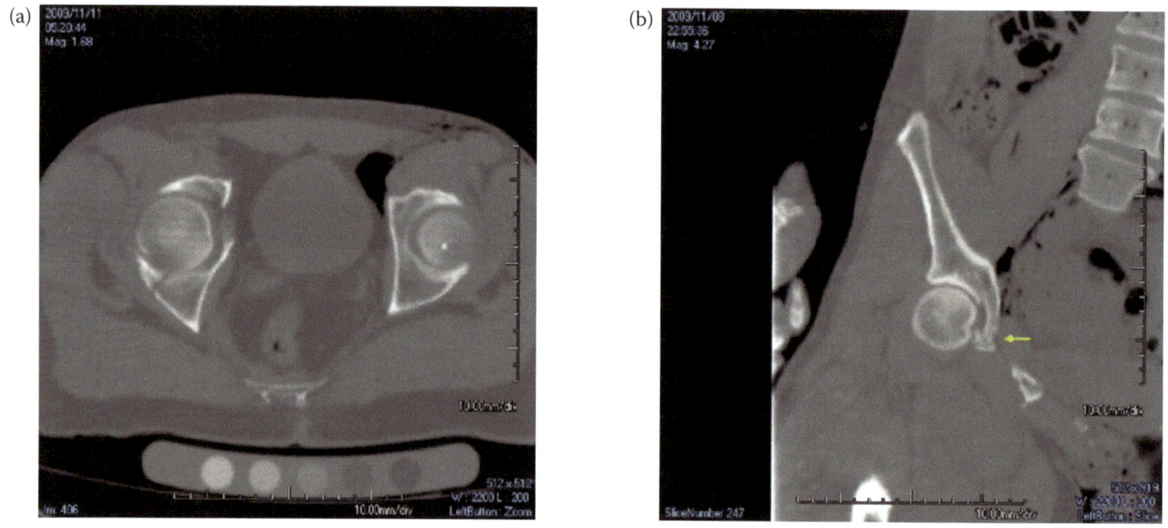

Figure 9.12 (a) Axial CT showing a fracture to the right acetabulum. (b) Coronal CT showing a fracture to the right acetabulum.

Acetabular Fracture

An acetabular fracture occurs in about one-third of all pelvic fractures (Figure 9.12a,b). Acetabular fractures have been classified with respect to the different anatomical regions of the acetabulum. These fractures are typically associated with significant trauma as occurs with motor vehicle incidents [18]. Motor vehicle incidents have been shown to cause approximately 75% of acetabular fractures. A major cause of acetabular fracture in younger individuals is falls from a considerable height.

The mechanism of acetabular fracture in occupants of motor vehicles in head-on impacts is axial loading through the femur by direct impact to the knee from the dashboard or force directed through the extended knee from the vehicle's floor pan associated with vehicle intrusion (Figure 9.13). A major mechanism of injury in side impacts is lateral force to the acetabulum via the femoral head from force applied to the greater trochanter of the femur (Figure 9.14).

Off-set or angled impacts to the front quarter panel area of the vehicle can lead to rotation of the occupant's body such that an element of abduction/adduction or internal/external rotation may occur prior to axial loading [18].

With an incidence of ~33% posterior rim fractures are the most common type of fracture to the acetabulum. Posterior rim fractures occur primarily in motor vehicle incidents from axial transmission of force through the extended femur. The injury may be seen with posterior dislocation of the femoral head.

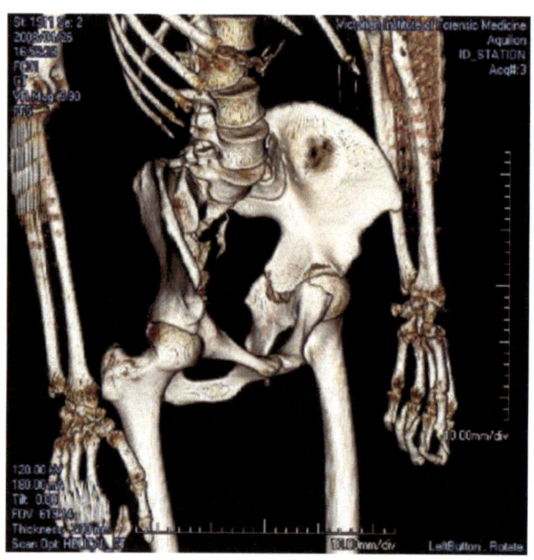

Figure 9.13 Three-dimensional reconstruction showing an acetabular fracture associated with axial loading through the femoral shaft.

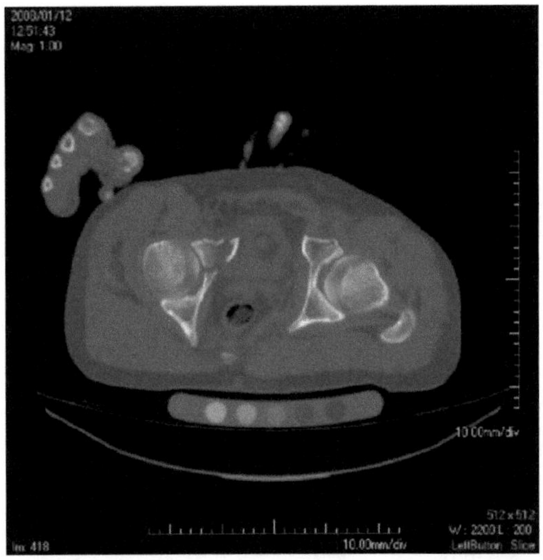

Figure 9.14 Axial CT image showing a central acetabular fracture resulting from lateral force applied to the region of the greater trochanter of the femur.

A transverse fracture is classically associated with a force directed to the lateral aspect of the hip through the greater trochanter of the femur. The fracture may be associated with central dislocation of the femoral head through the acetabulum into the true pelvis and can result in separation of the innominate into two parts. The fracture is associated with breaks in both iliopubic and ilioischial radiological lines.

An anterior column fracture indicates a fracture through the iliopubic line and may be associated with central dislocation of the femoral head. A posterior column fracture involves a fracture through the ilioischial line and may be associated with central dislocation of the femoral head.

Malgaigne Fracture

The Malgaigne fracture is a common unstable pelvic fracture. It occurs in up to 15% of such cases. A Malgaigne fracture typically results from the application of axial force through the femur, as may occur through extended knees when a motor vehicle occupant is bracing during a frontal collision or from direct impact to the knees from the dashboard.

The vertical shearing forces lead to fractures of both anterior and posterior arches. One may also see two fractures on one side of the pelvis, anterior fractures through the symphysis and unilateral superior and inferior rami fractures, with posterior fractures of the ipsilateral ilium, sacrum, or sacroilial joint. As such, this fracture is unstable in both rotational and vertical axes [19].

Bucket Handle Fracture

A bucket handle fracture refers to ipsilateral fractures of the pelvis and femur. This uncommon injury may occur from axial force through the femur resulting in a posterior acetabular fracture and femoral shaft fracture, or from lateral force to the greater trochanter leading to a central acetabular fracture and proximal femoral fracture [20].

Hip Dislocations

Hip dislocations are caused by severe forces as may occur in motor vehicle collisions. Approximately 90% of hip dislocations are posterior [21]. The mechanism is axial loading through the femoral shaft and is often associated with a posterior acetabular fracture (Figure 9.15a,b,c). The uncommon anterior dislocation occurs when the hip is abducted and in external rotation at the point of impact [22].

Pediatric Pelvic Fractures

Compared to pelvic injury in adults, pediatric pelvic fractures are associated with significantly lower mortality rates [23]. Children most commonly sustain pelvic fractures from motor vehicle incidents and pedestrian incidents, and are often the result of lateral compression. The injury is often seen in association with other significant head or abdominal injury. Pelvic fracture in the setting of nonaccidental injury is uncommon but described in the literature [24]. The presence of a pelvic fracture outside the situation of a motor vehicle incident or other significant accident is suggestive of nonaccidental injury.

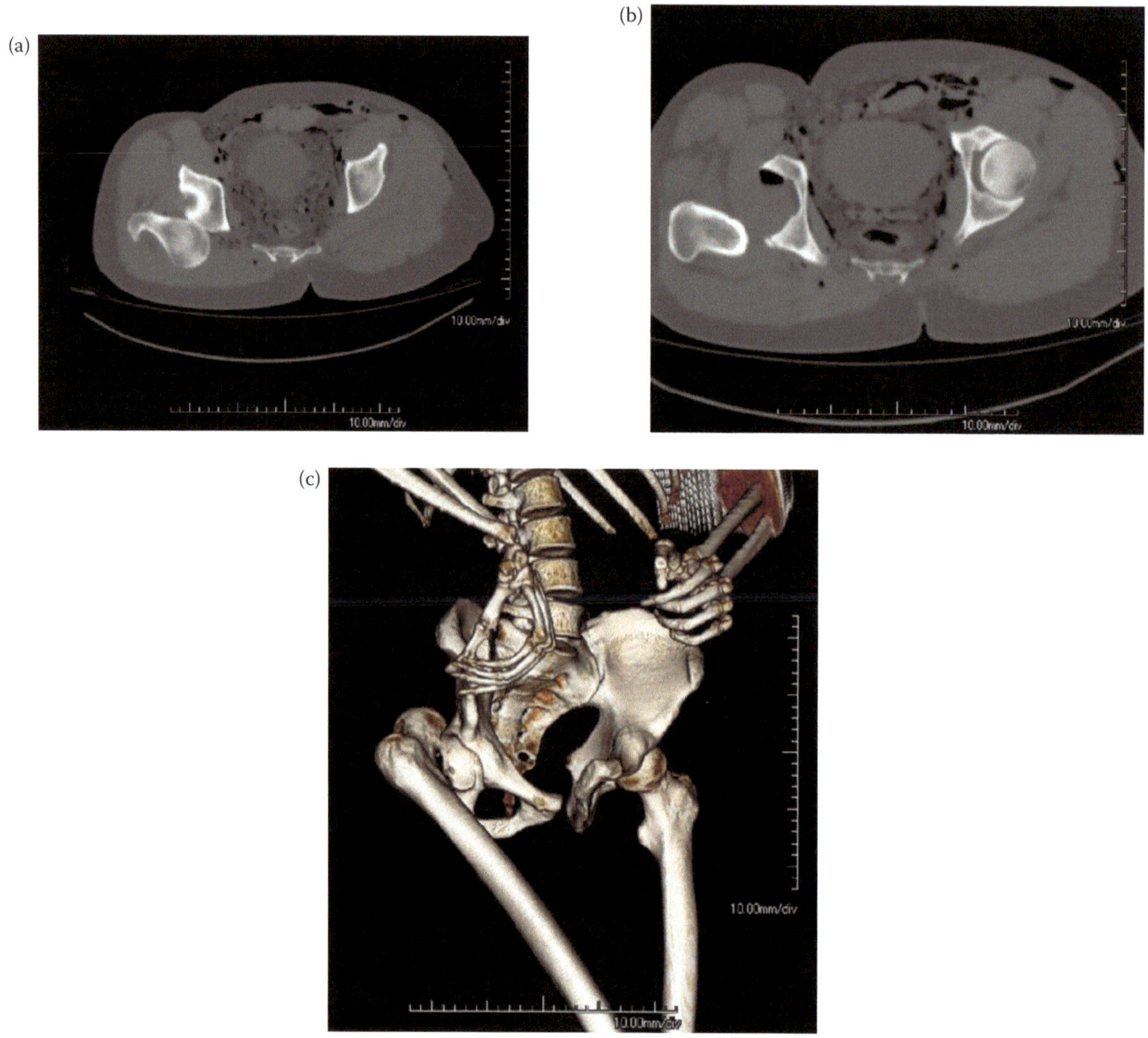

Figure 9.15 (a) Axial CT showing a posterior dislocation of the right hip. This injury is most commonly seen in frontal motor vehicle collisions with axial loading along fixed limb. (b) Axial CT showing a common fracture to the posterior aspect of the acetabulum. One may also see a shaving fracture of the head of the femur. (c) Three-dimensional reconstruction image clearly demonstrates the hip dislocation. Associated open book fracture to the pelvis.

CT Diagnosis of Pelvic Fractures

Postmortem noncontrast CT imaging of pelvic fractures has major advantages for the diagnosis of pelvic fractures when compared to conventional radiology. There is an absence of bowel gas, one may be able to appreciate an associated pelvic hematoma, and the three-dimensional reconstructions are intuitive to the pathologist.

A practical approach to diagnosis of pelvic fractures can commence with the determination as to whether the fracture is a simple or complex fracture.

- If the posterior pelvic arch appears intact the fracture is highly likely to be a simple and stable pelvic fracture.
- As the pelvis is a ring structure, if there is an anterior fracture of the ring one should look carefully for an associated posterior fracture (Figure 9.16).
- Axial, coronal, and sagittal reconstruction views are used in the diagnosis of sacral fractures (Figure 9.16a,b).
- Pelvic ring fractures
    - Reformatted images are central to the diagnosis of pelvic fractures [25].

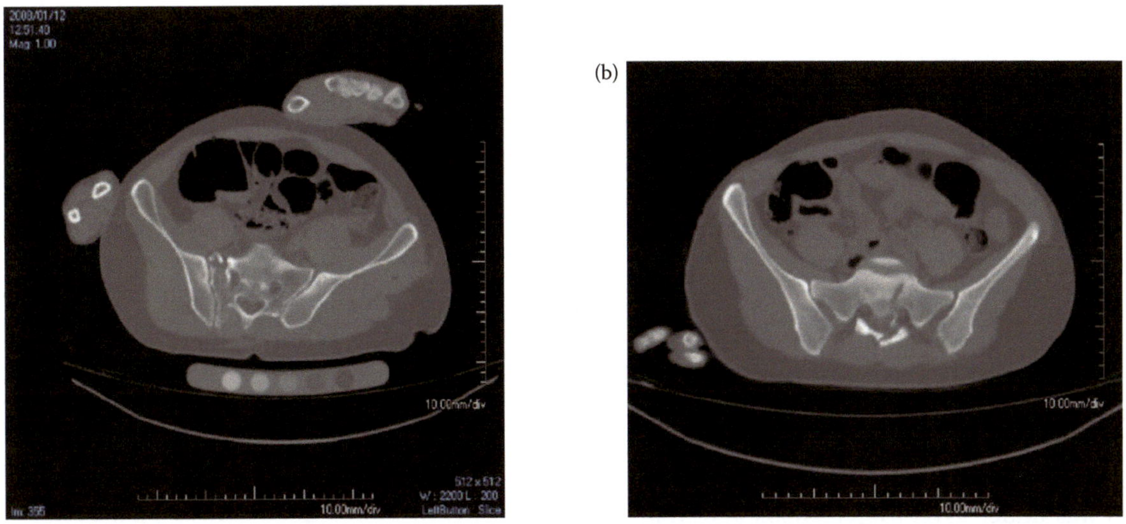

Figure 9.16 (a) Axial CT showing a right-sided sacral fracture. (b) Axial CT showing a left longitudinal sacral fracture.

- Multiplanar reconstruction along the coronal and sagittal planes and three-dimensional imaging are especially valuable [26]. The images facilitate the diagnosis of minimally displaced fractures. However, one must not have blind faith in any test or technique. It should be remembered that an autopsy-confirmed fracture to the pubic rami might not always be seen on an examination of the three-dimensional reconstruction images (Figure 9.17).
- The images can be manipulated to allow tangential or inlet views of the pelvis.
- Obscuring features such as the femur can be subtracted from the image to reveal underlying fractures.

For forensic pathologists acetabular fractures are especially amenable to identification through multidetector computed tomography (MDCT). Multiplanar reformation along the anterior column (a line that extends through the anterior aspect of the acetabulum from the ilium to the pubis), the posterior column (a line that extends through the posterior aspect of the acetabulum from the ilium to the pubis), and the inferior ramus, and

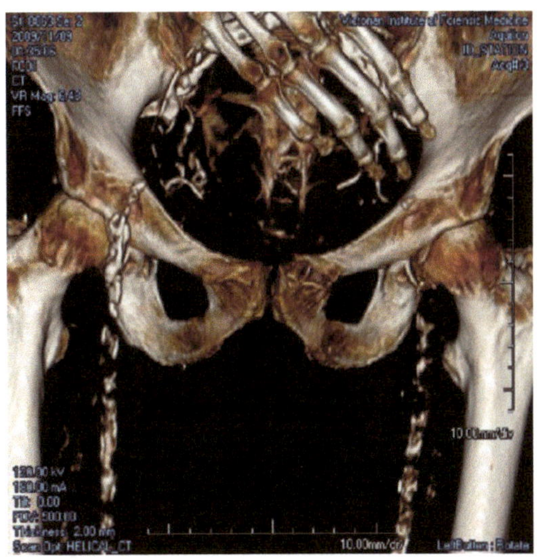

Figure 9.17 Three-dimensional reconstruction of the pelvis that did not show a pubic ramus fracture detected at autopsy.

en face view of the acetabulum and medial cranial views are necessary for diagnosis.

Forensic Aspects of Pelvic Fractures

Pelvic fractures are associated with severe trauma in young adults, but may be seen with minor to moderate trauma in the elderly. In young adults, motor vehicle incidents and falls from a height are the predominant cause of fractures, whereas a fall from a standing height can cause a pelvic fracture in the elderly.

A study of pelvic and hip joint injuries in 371 pedestrian victims as reconstructive factors in car–pedestrian injuries was undertaken by Teresinski and Madro [27]. They examined trauma victims who had been struck both in the upright position as well as run-over victims. The conclusions from the study were that direct impact to the lateral pelvis in the upright pedestrian generally showed unilateral ipsilateral sacroiliac joint injury, and superior ramus fractures, which were seen on the same side as the trauma compared to the contralateral side in a ratio of 2:1. Run-over injuries were suggested by bilateral injuries to the sacroiliac joints, and external dislocation of the hip joints.

Case Study 1

A 70-year-old man was walking along a railroad line when a train struck him from behind. He was thrown a considerable distance and barely conscious when ambulance personnel arrived on the scene. The patient was taken to a major metropolitan hospital where he was resuscitated. It was clinically apparent that the victim had severe pelvic injuries with active bleeding. He was taken to the interventional radiology suite for embolization of severed pelvic vessels, however, the patient suffered a cardiac arrest and could not be revived. The death was referred to the coroner and an autopsy was ordered.

The external examination showed multiple bruises and abrasions in keeping with the circumstances of the incident. A complex fracture of the pelvis with associated pelvic and retroperitoneal hemorrhage was identified. Because the deceased died while waiting to undergo interventional radiology to the pelvic vessels, a postmortem angiography was performed. The distal abdominal aorta was cannulated and contrast medium was injected. CT scans of the pelvis were obtained (Figure 9.18). The images showed extravasation of contrast medium in the radiological anatomical location of the right superior gluteal artery. The reformatted, three-dimensional images clearly show the location of the damaged artery.

The man was deemed to have succumbed to multiple injuries. The clinical diagnosis of hemorrhage from a pelvic artery associated with the pelvic fracture was confirmed.

Case Study 2

A 20-year-old man ran from between two parked cars onto the roadway and was struck to the left of his body by a sports utility vehicle. He struck his head on the ground and suffered a lethal head injury. His body was taken to the Victorian Institute of Forensic Medicine (VIFM) for medicolegal examination. The police investigators indicated there were no charges to be levied against the vehicle's driver.

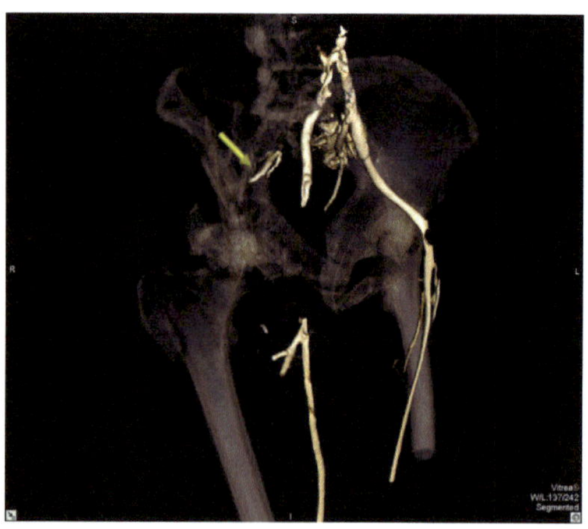

Figure 9.18 Postmortem CT angiogram showing a blush of contrast associated with a pelvic fracture localizing the site of an antemortem hemorrhage.

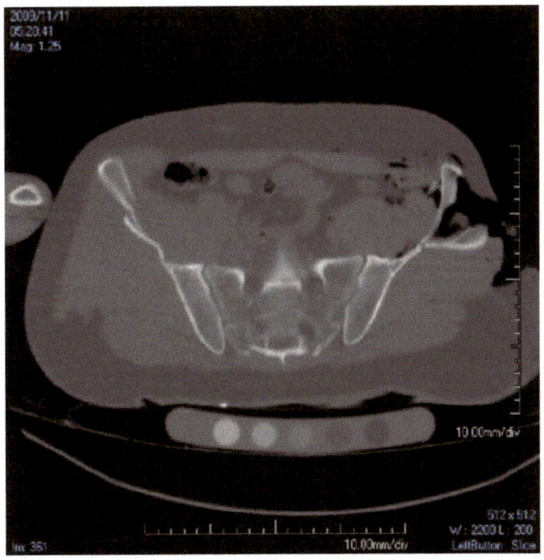

Figure 9.19 Axial CT showing a major soft tissue injury to the left lateral hip region with associated pelvic fractures.

The external examination showed multiple abrasions over bony prominences and a laceration over the left lateral aspect of the pelvis. There was blood noted in the external auditory canal.

The postmortem CT scan showed a fractured base of skull. The images of the pelvis confirmed a gaping laceration with an underlying fracture of the left iliac wing and a second fracture to the right iliac wing (Figure 9.19).

The external examination and CT findings were consistent with the known circumstances of the death, which suggested the deceased had been struck to his left side, with a primary impact to the left lateral hip, before suffering a fatal head injury when his head struck the road.

Case Study 3

A 30-year-old man was at work when he was crushed between two large pieces of concrete. It took some time to remove the slab of concrete and he was dead at the scene. The deceased's body was taken to the VIFM for medicolegal examination.

The external examination showed marked plethora of the upper body associated with petecheal hemorrhages within the conjunctivae. The postmortem CT scans showed no skull fracture or intracranial hemorrhage. There was no evidence of cervical spine injury. There were bilateral fractured ribs but no hemothorax. The CT images of the pelvis showed bilateral iliac crest fractures and pubic rami fractures (Figure 9.20). The

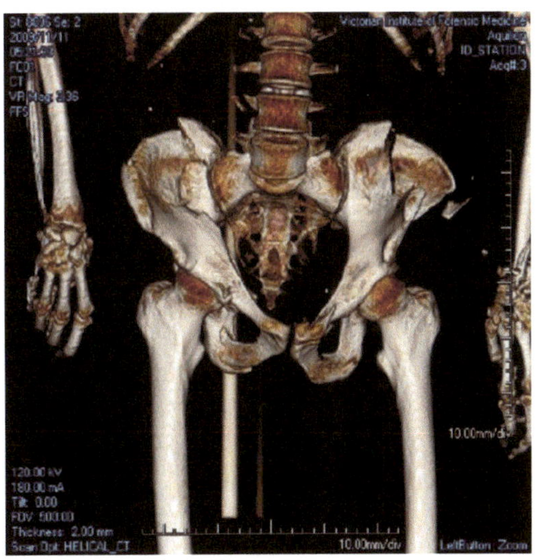

Figure 9.20 Three-dimensional reconstruction showing bilateral iliac wing and pubic rami fractures resulting from a lateral pelvic compression.

external examination and CT findings were suggestive of mechanical asphyxia and lateral compressive trauma to the body (pelvis).

References

1. Vrahas M, Hearn TC, Diangelo D. Ligamentous contributions to pelvic stability. *Orthopaedics* 1995; 18:271–274.
2. Biffl WL, Smith WR, Moore EE, Gonzales RF, Morgan ST, Hennessey T, Offner PT, Ray CE Jr, Fraciose R, Burch JM. Evolution of a multidisciplinary clinical pathway for the management of unstable patients with pelvic fractures. *Ann. Surg.* 2001; 233:843–850.
3. Ribacoba-Montero R, Salas-Puig J. Simultaneous bilateral fractures of the hip following a grand mal seizure. An unusual complication. *Seizure* 1997; 6(5):403–404.
4. Galloway A. *Broken bones: Anthropological analysis of blunt force trauma*. Charles C Thomas, Springfield IL, 1999.
5. Yiming A, Baque P, Rahili A, Mayer J, Braccini AL, Fontaine A, Leplatois A, Clave A, de Peretti F. Anatomical study of the blood supply of the coxal bone: Radiological and clinical application. *Surg. Radiol. Anat.* 2002; 24:81–86.
6. Ben-Menachem Y, Coldwell DM, Young JW, Burgess AR. Hemorrhage associated with pelvic fractures: Causes, diagnosis, and emergency management. *AJR Am. J. Roentgenol.* 1991; 157:1005–1014.
7. Yoon W, Kim JK, Jeong YY, Seo JJ, Park JG, Kang HK. Pelvic arterial haemorrhage in patients with pelvic fractures: Detection with contrast-enhanced CT. *Radiographics* 2004; 24:1591–1606.
8. Viano DC, Lau IV, King AI, Begman P. Biomechanics of the human chest, abdomen and pelvis in lateral impact. *Accid. Anal. Prev.* 1989; 21(6):553–574.
9. Kernbach-Wighton G, Salamat B, Gotz W, Saternus KS. Some medicolegally important aspects of symphyseal injuries due to trauma. *Am. J. Forensic Med. Pathol.* 2006; 27(2):145–150.
10. Osman TE, Holtby R. Straddle pelvic stress fractures in a female marathon runner. *Am. J. Sports Med.* 1998; 26:850–851.
11. Yacoub B, Collier WS. Duverney fracture: Distinguishing scintigraphic features. *Clin. Nucl. Med.* 2007; 32(7):538–539.
12. Abrassart S, Stern R, Peter R. Morbidity associated with isolated iliac wing fractures. *J. Trauma* 2009; 66(1):200–203.
13. Denis F, Davis S, Comfort T. Sacral fractures: An important problem. A retrospective analysis of 236 cases. *Clin. Orthop. Relat. Res.* 1988; 227:67–81.
14. Vaccaro AR, Kim DH, Brodke DS. Diagnosis and management of sacral spine fractures. *Instr. Cours. Lect.* 2004; 53:375–385.
15. Robles LA. Transverse sacral fractures. *Spine* 2009; 9(1):60–69.
16. Mehta S, Auerbach JD, Born CT, Chin KR. Sacral fractures. *J. Am. Acad. Orthop. Surg.* 2006; 14:656–665.
17. Burgess AR, Eastridge BJ, Young JN, Ellison TS, Ellison PS Jr, Poka A, Bathen GH, Brumback RJ. Pelvic ring disruptions: Effective classification system and treatment protocols. *J. Trauma* 1990; 30:848–856.
18. Dakin GJ, Eberhardt AW, Alonso JE, Stannard JP, Mann KA. Acetabular fracture patterns: Associations with motor vehicle crash information. *J. Trauma* 1999; 47(6):1063–1071.
19. Frakes MA, Evans T. Major pelvic fractures. *Crit. Care Nurse* 2004; 24:18–30.
20. Liebergall M, Mosheiff R, Safran O, Peyser A, Segal D. The floating hip injury: Patterns of injury. *Injury* 2002; 33(8):717–722.
21. Sanders S, Tejwani NC. Asymmetric bilateral hip dislocation after motor vehicle accident: A case study and review of the literature. *Bull. NYU Hosp. Jt. Dis.* 2008; 66(4):320–326.
22. DeLee JC. Fractures and dislocations of the hip. In Rockwood CA Jr, Green DP, Bucholz R, editors. *Fractures in adults*, 4th ed., Vol. 2. Lippincott-Raven, Philadelphia, 1996, pp. 1756–1803.
23. Holden CP, Holman J, Herman MJ. Pediatric pelvic fractures. *J. Am. Acad. Orthop. Surg.* 2007; 15:172–177.
24. Starling S, Heller RM, Jenny C. Pelvic fractures in infants as a sign of physical abuse. *Child Abuse Negl.* 2002; 26:475–480.
25. Falchi M, Rollandi GA. CT of pelvic fractures. *Eur. J. Radiol.* 2004; 50:96–105.
26. Magid D, Fishman EK, Ney, DR, Kuhlman JE, Frantz KM, Sponseller PD. Acetabular and pelvic fractures in the pediatric patient: Value of two- and three-dimensional imaging. *J. Pediatr. Orthop.* 1992; 12:621–625.
27. Teresinski G, Madro R. Pelvis and hip joint injuries as a reconstructive factor in car-to-pedestrian accidents. *Forensic Sci. Int.* 2001; 124:68–73.

Lower Limbs

10

Femur

Anatomy

The femur is a robust tubular bone that articulates with the innominate at the ball-and-socket hip joint, and to the tibia via the hinge joint of the knee. The proximal and distal metaphyseal aspects of the femur are considerably less robust than the diaphysis. The femoral neck extends from the intertrochanteric region of the femur to the femoral head. The distal femoral condyles articulate with the broad tibial plateau.

Etiology

The femoral shaft is typically fractured in the middle third. In young adults the femoral shaft is fractured from episodes of significant trauma as may occur in motor vehicle incidents and falls from a considerable height. In elderly victims a femoral shaft fracture may be caused by low to moderate force.

Fractures of the femoral neck in elderly osteoporotic women are typically the result of a fall. The fracture can occur with minor trauma. Fractures to the femoral neck in young adults are associated with significant trauma such as falls from a height and motor vehicle incidents.

Subtrochanteric fractures have a bimodal age distribution with peaks in young adults and in the elderly [1]. In the young, subtrochanteric fractures result from high-energy trauma and are usually seen in association with other injuries. In the older individual with osteoporosis, the fracture may be seen in isolation in the circumstances of a fall from a standing height.

Intercondylar fractures are seen in occupants of motor vehicle incidents by way of an anvil effect when the patella is forced against the flexed knee.

Mechanism

Femoral Shaft Fractures

The femoral shaft is fractured by the application of considerable force (Figure 10.1). Experimental work on isolated femur specimens using the "stresscoat" technique has shown that lateral loading to the midpoint of the femoral shaft leads to deformation patterns at the opposing point of the shaft which is under tensile strain. The application of increasing force beyond the failure point of the bone can lead to a fracture occurring to the opposing area of bone, which then extends toward the point of application of force [2]. Investigators have applied a torsion force to the femur and produced a spiral pattern to the stresscoat lacquer, which was then followed by a typical spiral fracture [2].

Femoral shaft fractures have been classified by Winquist:

- Type 0—Simple transverse fracture
- Type I—Small butterfly fragment
- Type II—Large butterfly fragment
- Type III—Large butterfly fragment >50% of the shaft circumference
- Type IV—Segmental comminution

Although it is generally true that a significant degree of force is required to cause fractures to the shaft of the femur, such fractures have been shown to occasionally occur in specific situations with relatively minor trauma. A report of 20 comparatively low-speed frontal motor vehicle collisions described femoral shaft fractures in collisions involving forces that were believed to be insufficient to cause a fracture to the femur [3]. The authors concluded that the compressive force applied to the bone from muscle contraction prior to vehicle impact contributed to the formation of the fracture. A fall to the knee may result in a fracture to the shaft of the femur in older, osteoporotic individuals (Figure 10.2).

Neck of Femur Fractures

A fractured neck of femur may be defined as a fracture that is present between the femoral head and the greater and lesser trochanter (Figure 10.3a,b,c). In clinical practice an important distinction is made between intracapsular fractures (subcapital, transcervical, and basal fractures) and extracapsular fractures (trochanteric fractures). The difference is important because intracapsular fractures have a propensity to lose the blood supply to the head of the femur with issues in healing. The reversed obliquity intertrochanteric fracture extends through the intertrochanteric region in a more perpendicular plane than the usual intertrochanteric fractures (Figure 10.4a,b).

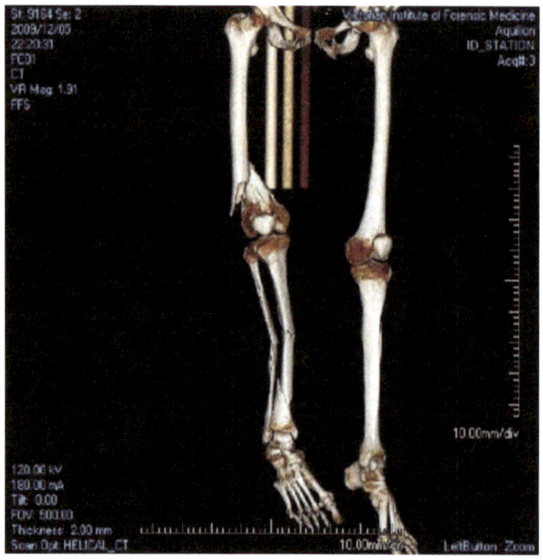

Figure 10.1 Overall three-dimensional reconstruction image of the lower limbs. Note the fracture to the right femur and right tibia and fibula resulting from a vehicle intrusion to the deceased's right side.

Fractures of the femoral neck occur in a 4:1 ratio between women and men, and between the femoral neck and the intertrochanteric region in a ratio of 2:1.

The classical mechanisms of action in fractures of the neck of the femur are

- Direct trauma to the greater trochanter
- Torsion to the anterior aspect of the femoral neck extending posteriorly
- Cyclical loading leading to a stress fracture with a complete fracture resulting from relatively minor torsion injury

Experimental work using the stresscoat technique involved axial loading on isolated femur specimens. The axial load was applied to the femoral head. Examination of the specimens showed deformation cracks in the lacquer to the superior aspect of the neck of the femur and anterolateral part of the shaft. Increasing the static load resulted in fractures to the neck of the femur [2].

In other specimens the loading was applied to the greater trochanter. This approach lead to cracks in the stresscoat lacquer in the inferior aspect of the femoral neck and then to the medial aspect of the bone. Increasing the static and dynamic loads to the greater trochanter would eventually lead to typical subcapital, intertrochanteric, and femoral neck fractures [2]. In these experiments no torsion was required to cause a fractured neck of femur.

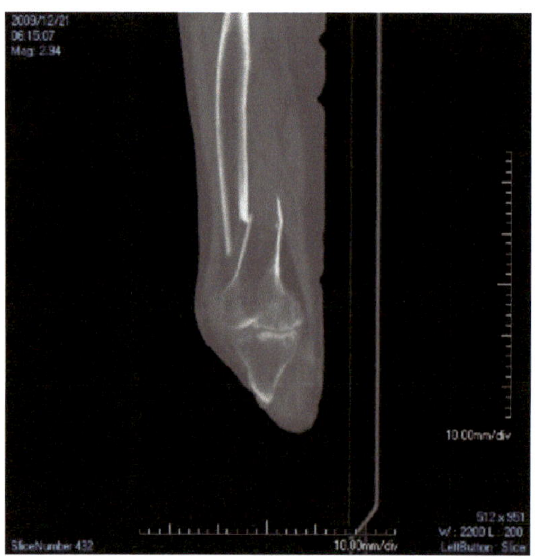

Figure 10.2 Fractured femoral shaft from a fall to the knee in an elderly woman. One notes the presence of osteoporosis.

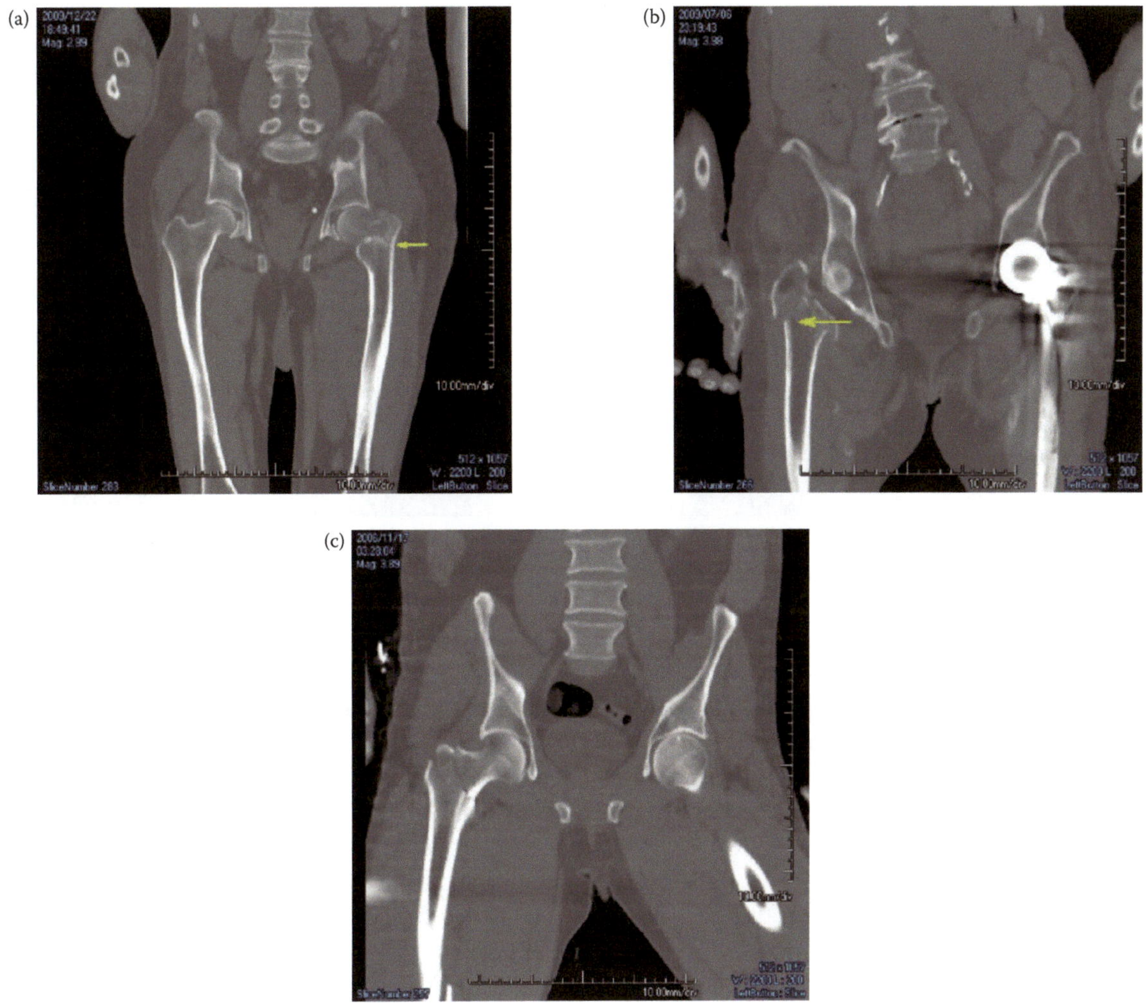

Figure 10.3 (a) Coronal CT showing a left pertrochanteric fractured neck of a femur. (b) Coronal CT showing fractured right interochanteric neck of a femur. One notes the prior left hip replacement, osteoporosis, and osteophytes in the vertebrae. (c) Coronal CT image showing a right intertrochanteric and greater trochanter fracture. The mechanism of the injury was a fall on to the hip.

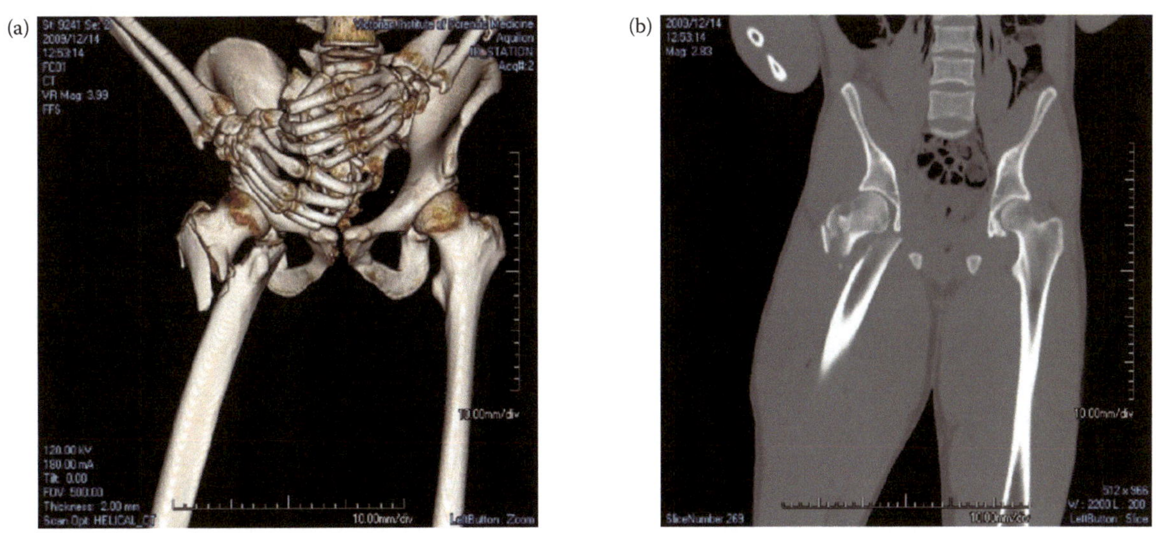

Figure 10.4 (a) Three-dimensional reconstruction CT image of a motorcyclist struck on his right. There is an intertrochanteric fracture to the right side. (b) Coronal CT showing the reversed obliquity intertrochanteric fracture from blunt force trauma to the region of the right lateral hip.

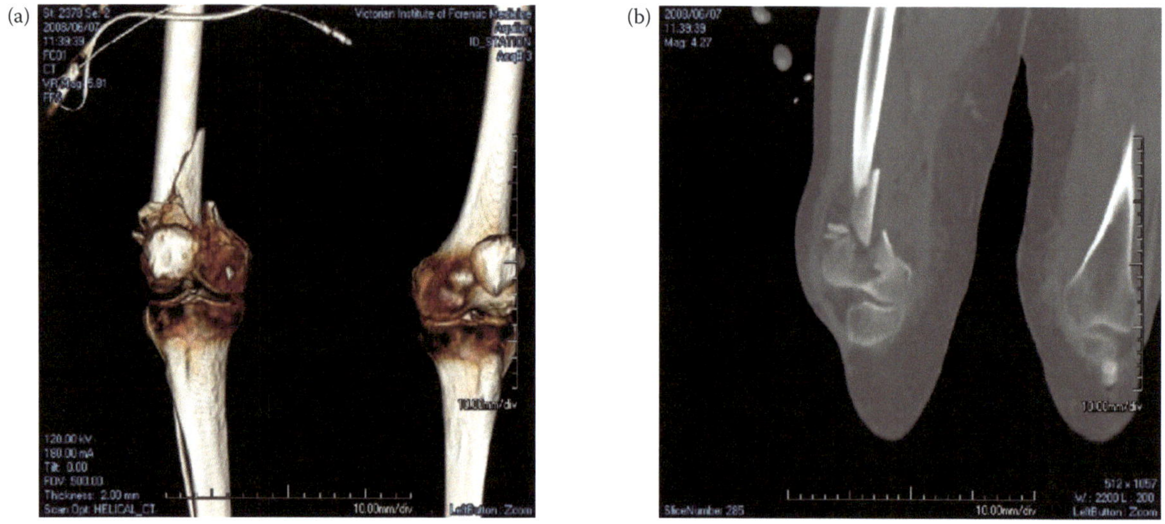

Figure 10.5 (a) Right femoral supracondylar fracture following a fall to the knee in an elderly person. (b) Right supracondylar fracture of the femur extending to the articular cartilage. There is osteoporosis in the distal femur.

An uncommon subtype of femoral neck fracture is the ipsilateral femoral neck and shaft fracture [4]. This injury pattern is seen in victims of high energy trauma and mainly affects individuals in the fourth decade of life. The combined fracture is seen in up to 6% of femoral shaft fractures [5].

A classical mechanism of injury that results in a fractured neck of femur in all ages is axial loading of the lower limb through the knee or plantar aspect of the foot in frontal motor vehicle collisions. Significant force to the region of the greater trochanter may also cause a fractured neck of femur in individuals of any age. A fracture of the neck of the femur is more likely when the force is directed to the knee when the thigh is in an abducted position [6].

Femoral Head Fractures

Fractures of the femoral head are uncommon and are typically associated with traumatic posterior dislocation of the hip [7]. Most femoral head fractures occur secondary to motor vehicle incidents, falls from a height, and industrial injuries.

Subtrochanteric Femoral Fractures

Subtrochanteric fractures extend from the femoral neck or intertrochanteric region to the lesser trochanter [8]. The fractures are extracapsular. Subtrochanteric fractures are classified in the Russell–Taylor system [9].

Supracondylar and Condylar Fractures

Supracondylar fractures may occur in healthy young individuals who suffer significant blunt force trauma just above the knee. The fracture may extend distally to involve the articular cartilage. The injury is most commonly associated with road trauma. Supracondylar fractures may also be seen in elderly osteoporotic individuals following a fall onto the knee (Figure 10.5a,b).

Intercondylar fractures generally result from significant blunt force trauma to the patella when the knee is flexed. The classical example is severe contact to the flexed knee from the dashboard of a motor vehicle in a front- on collision (Figure 10.6). The injury may also be seen in significant falls with direct impact to the flexed knee.

The Hoffa fracture is defined as an intra-articular lateral condyle or bicondylar fracture of the distal femur in the coronal plane [10]. These fractures are distinctly uncommon injuries. The fracture is typically seen in young adults and is the result of severe direct trauma. The mechanism of injury is often from direct trauma to the knee or axial compression to the flexed knee. A further cause is a fall from a significant height.

Pediatric Femoral Fractures

Femoral shaft fractures follow diaphyseal fractures of the radius, ulna, and tibia in the frequency of common fractures in pediatric patients. The mechanism of fracture most frequently involves falls from playground equipment, sporting injuries, and motor vehicle incidents [11]. In infants nonaccidental injury can cause a fractured femur. Clearly a fractured femur that occurs in a nonambulatory infant is highly suggestive of nonaccidental injury. An isolated femoral fracture in an infant who is walking is probably accidental in origin [12].

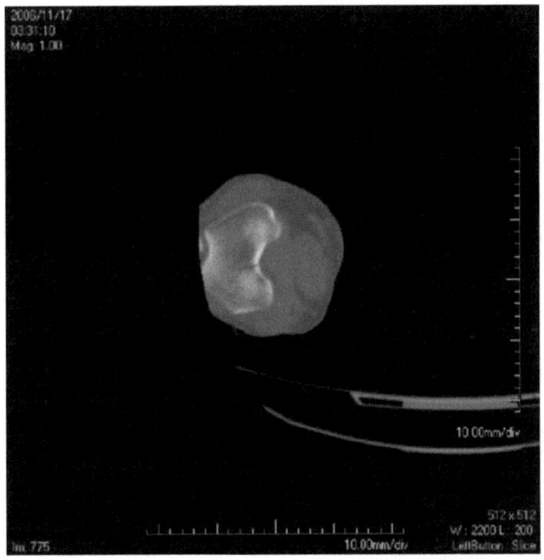

Figure 10.6 Coronal CT image showing a right intercondylar fracture, which occurred in a motor vehicle collision.

CT Diagnosis of Femoral Fracture

Gross displacement of fracture fragments are readily identified on the three-dimensional reformatted computed tomography (CT) images.

- Subtle fractures, including nondisplaced spiral fractures, require review in two orthogonal planes using bone windows.
- As femoral fractures are often associated with posterior dislocation, the femoral head is displaced superiorly with overlapping of the acetabular roof (disruption of Shelton's line).
- Condylar fractures are best seen with sagittal reformatted images.

Patella

Anatomy

The patella is a triangular, flat sesamoid bone within the tendon of the quadriceps femoris located in front of the knee joint. The posterior cartilaginous part of the bone is involved in the patellofemoral joint.

Etiology

Common causes of patella fracture are the application of significant direct blunt force as may occur in motor vehicle incidents and major falls. Avulsion injuries are relatively uncommon.

Mechanism

Fractures to the patella most commonly result from direct blunt force trauma and may be vertical, transverse, or comminuted (Figure 10.7). The transverse fracture comprises about 60% of these injuries. The relatively exposed character of the bone means that compound fractures are not uncommon.

The patella sleeve fracture is an avulsion fracture involving the cartilaginous aspect of the lower patella in young individuals [13]. The injury classically occurs with rapid contraction of the quadriceps in a partially flexed knee.

Tibia

Anatomy

The tibia is a robust, tubular, long bone. The tibia is second to the femur in absolute strength. The bone is situated at the medial aspect of the lower limb and forms part of the knee and ankle joints.

The proximal aspect of the tibia forms the tibial plateau that articulates with the femoral condyles. The tibial spine (intercondylar eminence) is a rough depression to the central aspect of the medial and lateral tibial condyles for attachment of the anterior and posterior cruciate ligaments, and menisci. The tibial tuberosity provides attachment to the ligamentum patellae.

The tibial shaft has three borders. These are the anterior, medial, and lateral borders. The anterior border begins just below the tibial tuberosity and ends at the medial malleolus. The medial border commences at the posterior aspect of the medial condyle and extends to the posterior portion of the medial malleolus. The lateral border gives attachment to the interosseous membrane between the tibia and the fibula.

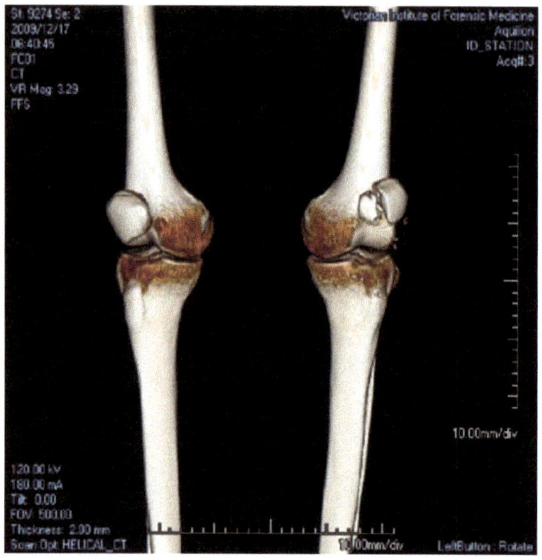

Figure 10.7 Three-dimensional reconstruction image showing a longitudinal fracture to the left patella.

A dense fibrous interosseous membrane connects the interosseous borders of the tibia (medial border) and the fibula. The upper portion of the interosseous membrane forms the tibiofibular syndesmosis.

Etiology

The tibia is a major weight-bearing bone that is involved in two major joints and has a relatively large area that is comparatively exposed. The tibia is thus associated with a high likelihood of compound fractures. As the bone is quite robust, fractures are caused by significant trauma.

The tibial shaft is involved in 15% of fractures in children. When compared to adults, minor falls are associated with tibial shaft fractures in young children [14].

The tibia is commonly fractured in motor vehicle occupant trauma victims, and is frequently fractured in pedestrians who are struck by motor vehicles. Other common causes of tibial fracture include falls and sports-related injuries.

Distal tibial fractures involving the medial malleolus are often seen in relation to other ankle and foot fractures.

Mechanism

Tibial Shaft

A literature review of nine clinical studies involving 2055 tibial shaft fractures from a variety of causes showed the distal shaft was most commonly fractured in 45.2% of cases, the middle third was fractured in 43.7% of cases, and the proximal third was fractured least commonly in 11.1% of cases [15].

Tibial shaft fractures in adults are caused by a variety of mechanisms, all of which involve significant energy. The classical mechanism is a bending-type force applied to a border of the shaft of the bone as may occur in a pedestrian who is struck by a motor vehicle, or axial force applied to the tibia such as may occur with front seat occupants of motor vehicles secondary to floor pan intrusion (Figure 10.8a,b).

A spiral fracture can occur in adults in circumstances of considerable trauma involving twisting and axial loading. A spiral fracture can happen with an apparently benign fall in young children.

Tibial Plateau Fractures

Tibial plateau fractures involve the articular surface of the proximal tibia (Figure 10.9). The medial plateau is larger and concave, whereas the lateral side is smaller and convex [16]. The medial plateau is stronger.

Tibial plateau fractures may be caused by high or low energy trauma [16]. High energy trauma is generally associated with motor vehicle incidents or falls, whereas low energy trauma is due to twisting mechanisms about the knee. Lower energy forces directed to the knee tend to result in compression fractures of the lateral condyle in the older individual, whereas high energy forces lead to split- or wedge-type fractures.

Nonarticular Proximal Tibial Fractures

The most common cause of nonarticular proximal tibia fracture is direct trauma as may occur in a pedestrian struck by a motor vehicle (Figure 10.10a,b).

Distal Tibial Fractures

The pilon fracture is defined as a comminuted fracture of the distal tibia resulting from axial loading leading to impaction of the talus to the tibial plafond as may occur in a fall from a height.

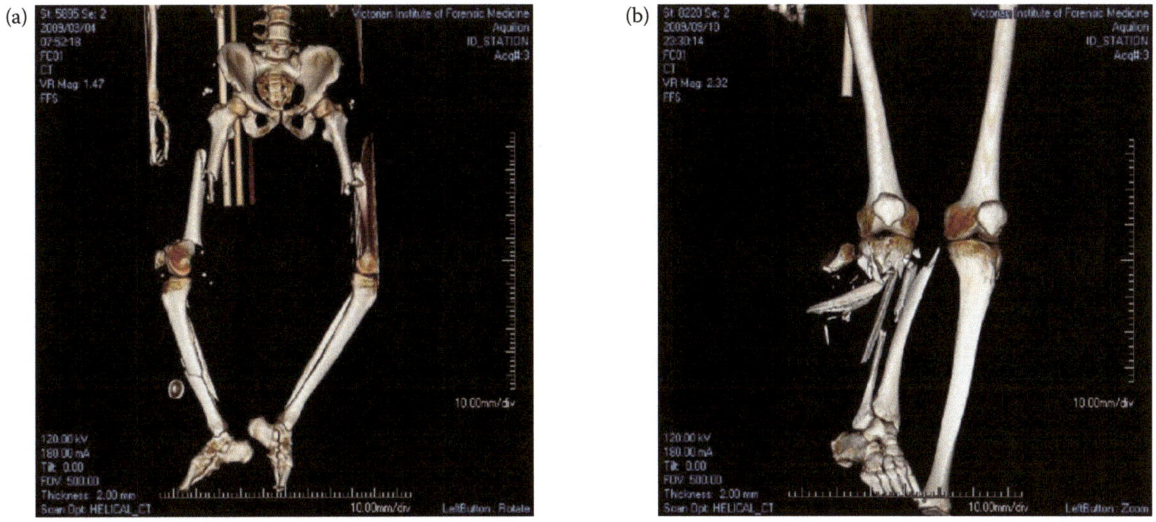

Figure 10.8 (a) Three-dimensional reconstruction image showing complex bilateral femoral fractures and a right tibial fracture. The primary impact site was believed to be to the thighs with a secondary bending/axial force applied to the right lower leg. (b) Three-dimensional reconstruction CT image from a pedestrian killed in a high-speed motor vehicle incident. The CT image provides an objective record of the comminuted fractures of the right tibia and fibula.

Pediatric Fractures

Tibial shaft fractures are common in children and adolescents. Twisting injuries that occur in sports activities are a common mechanism in spiral fractures of the tibia in adolescents. Minor falls can lead to transverse fractures to the middle or distal tibial shaft in younger children.

Nonaccidental injury is a common cause of tibial fracture in abused children [17]. Shaft fractures are not commonly associated with abuse. Apophyseal or metaphyseal corner fractures have been traditionally related to nonaccidental injury.

CT Diagnosis of Tibial Fracture

- CT scans with sagittal and coronal reconstruction provide excellent visualization of fracture patterns in plateau fractures.
- The CT examination of tibial plateau fractures displays the degree of articular compression better than conventional radiology [18].
- Three-dimensional reconstruction images are very useful to pathologists in identifying tibial shaft fractures.
- The CT may demonstrate the presence of air within the fracture indicating a compound fracture (Figure 10.11).

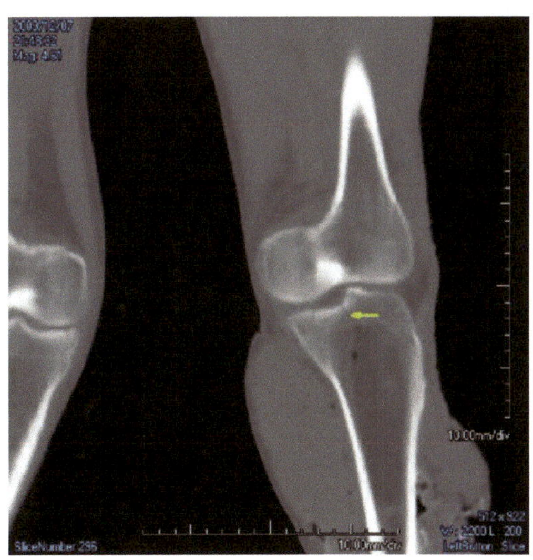

Figure 10.9 Coronal CT image of the left tibia in a victim of an ultralight aircraft that crashed. There is a depressed fracture of the medial tibial plateau.

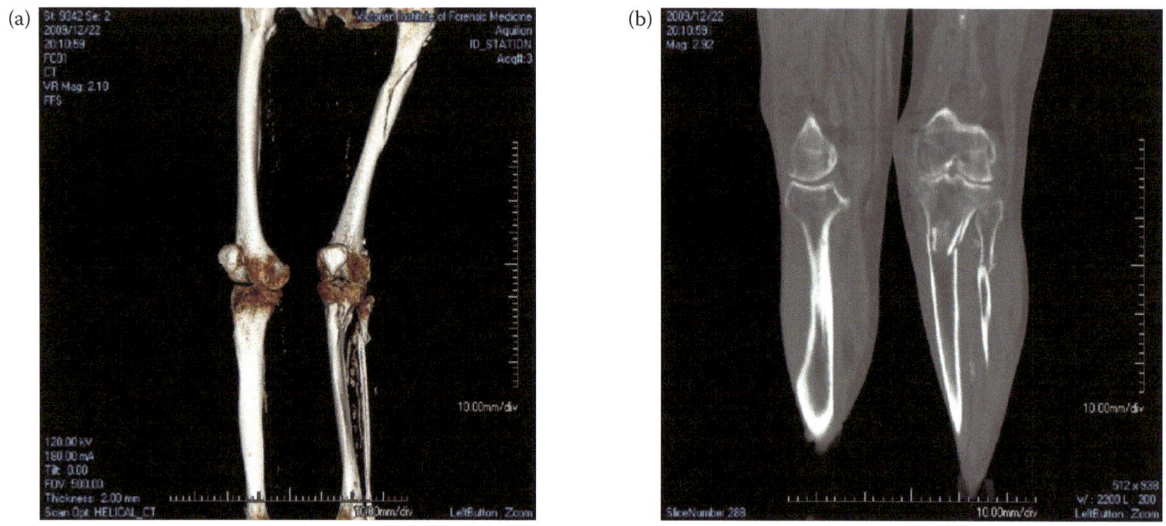

Figure 10.10 (a) Three-dimensional reconstruction image showing extra-articular tibial and fibular fractures in a pedestrian. One notes a fracture to the left femoral shaft and left femoral shaft malalignment from a prior injury. (b) Coronal CT showing extra-articular tibial and fibular fractures and osteoporosis.

Fibula

Anatomy

The fibula is a long tubular bone situated at the lateral aspect of the lower leg and has a significant role in the ankle joint. The proximal part of the bone articulates with the tibia but has a minimal functional role in the knee joint save for ligamentous attachments.

Etiology

The presence of the tough interosseous membrane between the tibia and fibula means that general fractures of the tibia are also associated with fractures to the fibula. Isolated fractures of the fibula may be seen with direct blunt force trauma, often directed to the lateral aspect of the lower leg. Fractures of the fibula are frequently associated with injuries to the ankle or knee.

Mechanism

Fibula shaft fractures occur most commonly from direct trauma and are often seen in relation to associated ipsilateral tibial fractures (Figure 10.12). Less commonly, rotational forces centered on the ankle joint can lead to indirect torsion forces to the fibula with a subsequent spiral fracture.

Isolated fractures to the lateral malleolus are caused by forced inversion of the ankle. Such fractures are particularly common in older females.

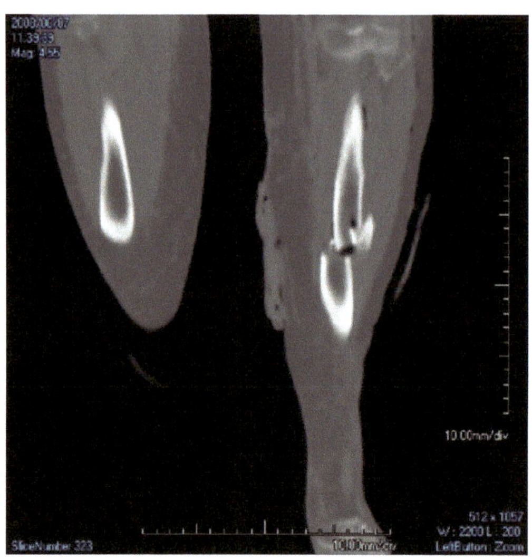

Figure 10.11 Coronal CT image showing air within a fracture to the left tibia confirming the clinical impression of a compound fracture.

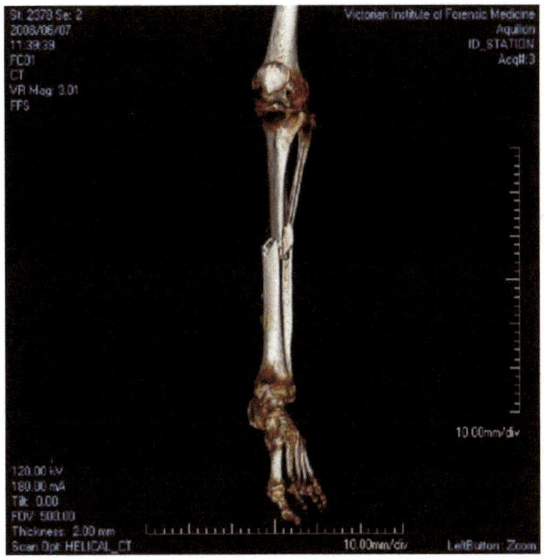

Figure 10.12 Three-dimensional reconstruction CT image showing typical fracture of the fibula associated with a fracture to the tibia in a pedestrian death.

Maisonneuve described a fracture of the proximal fibula with an associated rupture of the syndesmotic ligament and an injury to the medial ankle [19]. The injury is uncommon. The generally accepted mechanism of the injury is an external rotation force to the ankle that is either in pronation or supination. An experimental study on cadavers demonstrated the injury initially is due to rupture of the deltoid ligament, followed by disruption of the syndesmosis and finally a fracture of the proximal fibula.

Forensic Issues in Fractures to the Lower Leg

Pedestrians

In the upright pedestrian who is struck by a motor vehicle, there are often lower limb fractures caused by the primary direct blunt force trauma (Figure 10.13). The forensic interpretation of lower limb fractures in pedestrians has traditionally included the direction of the application of force and whether a motor vehicle was braking at the time of the incident.

The classical bumper bar injury to the lower leg has traditionally been used as an indicator of the site of impact to the leg. The early descriptions of the injury were in the context of the classical passenger sedan with a projecting bumper bar. The evolution of motor vehicle design has led to more molded bumpers in conventional passenger vehicles. Furthermore, there has been a marked increase in the number of sports utility vehicles on the roads. More molded bumpers leads to a more dispersed application of the force to the body of the trauma victim, and sports utility vehicles are usually associated with a higher primary impact site to the victim's body.

Primary direct blunt force injury to a bone may cause a depressed fracture to the cortical bone. This could be identified with conventional autopsy examination and subcutaneous dissection. Unless the depressed area of bone was quite sizeable, it is unlikely to be identified on CT scanning. Interestingly in a laboratory study of isolated tibia specimens impacted with a 1 cm steel loading stamp causing a fracture, no localized depressed fractures were seen [20].

The direction of the application of blunt force in a motor vehicle to pedestrian incident has traditionally been deduced following the recognition of the wedge-shaped Messerer fracture [21]. The tip of the wedge shape is said to correspond with the direction of the force. Others have challenged this view [22]. It has been shown that the presence of these fractures occurs when the limb was weight bearing at the time of the incident [22]. Depending upon the dynamics of the incident, a trauma victim may not be struck on the presenting weight-bearing leg but on the outside leg.

The conventional knowledge of fracture mechanism in tubular long bones suggests that bone fails in tension as opposed to compression. It would appear intuitive that a perpendicular force applied to a long bone, which leads to a transverse fracture originating on the opposite side of the bone, would propagate through the bone to the site of application of force. In a laboratory experiment using an isolated human tibial specimen, this was shown to occur in the isolated tibia with force applied to

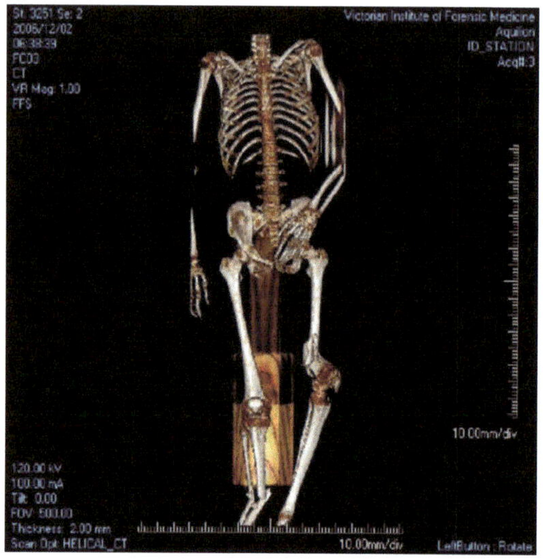

Figure 10.13 Overall skeletal survey demonstrating the presence of fractures to the lower limb in a pedestrian death. In cases where there are no apparent legal issues and the deceased's family objects to conventional autopsy, the CT images may suffice in recording the injuries without further dissection. In this case, in isolation, the CT cannot differentiate between the left thigh or right lower leg as primary contact points.

the dorsal, medial, and lateral aspects of the bone [20]. However, force applied to the ventral aspect resulted in a direct transverse fracture in less than 50% of cases [20].

The forensic examination of a pedestrian victim of trauma often includes measuring the distance of the fracture of the lower limb to the heel. This distance may then be compared to the height of the bumper of the offending vehicle. If the measurement of the fracture length is less than the bumper height it is then inferred that the vehicle was braking at the time of the incident. However other factors can contribute to the position of a fracture to the lower leg. The presence of ankle-high boots has been associated with fractures at the top level of the boot in a case report of two pedestrians, an injury that is analogous to boot top fractures in skiers [24].

CT in Pedestrian Deaths

The CT will usually provide a reasonable cause of death in pedestrian deaths. The common causes of death include ruptured aorta with massive hemothorax, atlantooccipital dissociation, upper cervical spine fracture with associated cord injury, and severe head injury. All of the these injuries can be seen, or directly implied, on the CT images.

Other concerns such as the primary contact point to the deceased's body may well be an issue.

In selected cases the medicolegal investigation may comprise an assessment of the circumstances of the death, the CT images, and appropriate forensic photography. This practice may be especially attractive when the deceased's family objects strongly to autopsy, and there are no medicolegal issues surrounding the death at the time of compiling the report. There will be occasional cases where questions such as the primary contact point may not be able to be addressed in the absence of conventional autopsy with extensive subcutaneous dissection.

It may be argued that the directions of the wedge-shaped fragments in a fractured long bone or the position of fractured bones within the tissues adequately reflects the action of the severe forces applied to the bone. However, cases such as that depicted in Figure 10.13, which shows opposite angulation of the fractures to the left femur, right tibia, and fibula, illustrate the limitation of CT in these cases. One cannot be sure of what other forces were applied to the right thigh and left lower leg during the entire incident that led to death. Nor can we be certain that movement of the body by bystanders at the scene, ambulance officers, those removing the body from the scene, and even mortuary staff has not altered the position of fracture fragments before the CT is performed.

It would seem a reasonable position that until there is considerable experience with routine CT in pedestrian deaths, a conservative position is generally adopted and most cases undergo conventional autopsy.

Fractures Involving the Foot

Calcaneus

Anatomy

The calcaneus is a robust weight-bearing bone that forms the heel, supports the talus, and indeed the weight of the

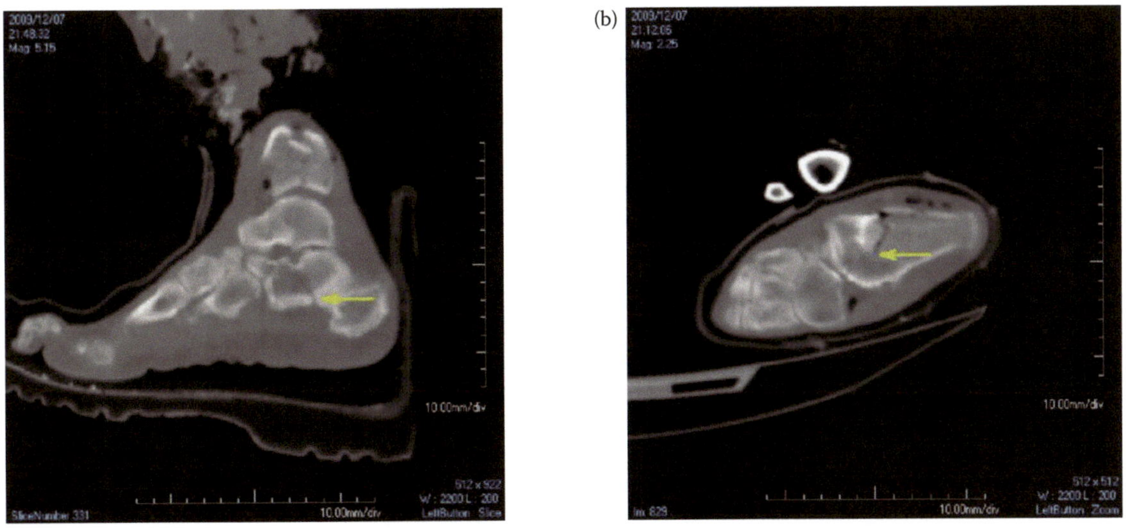

Figure 10.14 (a) Sagittal CT showing a fracture to the calcaneus in the pilot of an ultralight aircraft. The fracture suggests the application of a significant axial load. (b) Axial CT showing detail of the calcaneal fracture of an ultralight aircraft pilot. In these circumstances the fracture suggests significant axial loading.

body. The calcaneus articulates superiorly with the talus via the anterior, superior, and middle facets, and anteriorly with the cuboid [25]. The calcaneus has a relatively thin cortex but has inferior, superior, and posterior trabecullae to support articular facets. The region between these trabecullae contains relatively sparse trabecullar bone and is prone to fracture.

Etiology

Excluding simple fractures involving the toes, foot fractures are not particularly common traumatic injuries. The calcaneus is the most frequently fractured tarsal bone [26]. Calcaneal fractures account for about 1% to 2% of all fractures.

The most commonly injured group is adult men who have suffered significant axial loading to the foot. A fracture of the calcaneus is associated with high velocity trauma such as may occur with a fall from a height or a motor vehicle incident (Figure 10.14a,b).

Mechanism

Calcaneal fractures have distinctive features depending upon the mechanism of the injury. The fractures are classically divided into intra-articular and extra-articular injuries. Up to three-quarters of the fractures are intra-articular. Axial loading produces shear and compression forces within the calcaneus.

Shear forces lead to fractures that usually extend in a sagittal plane through the posterior facet. The plane of the fracture can vary depending upon the position of the foot at the moment of impact. Compression forces result in a fracture that usually extends in a coronal plane dividing the middle facet and adjacent ligaments.

Extra-articular fractures occur in about one-quarter of calcaneal fractures. The fractures are defined as not involving the posterior facet. The injuries are divided into fractures of the anterior process, fractures of the mid-calcaneus (including the body), and fractures of the posterior calcaneus. The injury mechanism varies between the different subgroups and includes forced inversion, forced abduction of the forefoot, and exaggerated dorsiflexion.

Talus

Anatomy

The talus is a resilient bone comprising a head, neck, and body, with approximately two-thirds covered by cartilage. The talus acts as a junction between the lower leg and the foot, and has complex joints and ligamentous connections [27].

Epidemiology

Fractures of the talus are not common. Talar fractures comprise only 0.32% of all fractures and 3.4% of fractures involving the foot. However, the talus is the second most frequently fractured tarsal bone. A retrospective analysis of 388 patients who underwent multidetector computed tomography (MDCT) of the foot and ankle secondary to acute trauma showed that fractures of the talus comprised 14% of foot fractures [28]. The robust nature of the talus means that significant forces are required to cause a talar fracture. The neck of the talus is relatively weak compared to the rest of the bone and is fractured in approximately 50% of cases.

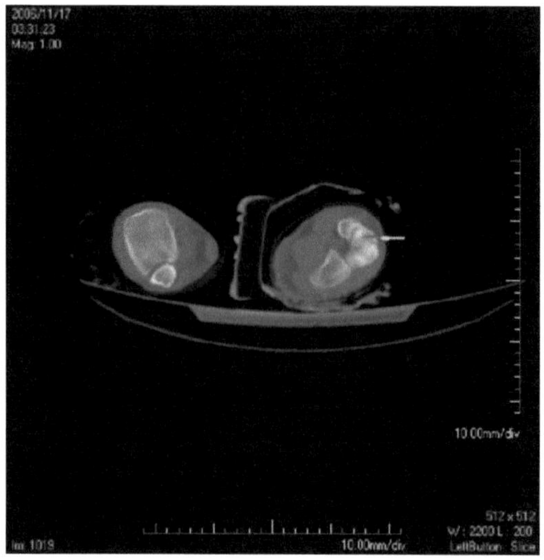

Figure 10.15 Axial CT showing a fractured left talus. The fracture is easily missed on routine screening of the CT images. The fracture is often recognized when actively sought in the typical circumstances, such as falls from a height or certain motor vehicle incidents.

Mechanism

Falls from a height and motor vehicle incidents are the classical causes of a fracture to the talus. Such mechanisms have been shown to lead to approximately 50% of talar fractures, with the remainder being caused by indirect force [29]. Axial compression forces can produce fractures of the neck of the talus (Figure 10.15). Biomechanical studies have shown that during dorsiflexion the lateral projection of the talus (sustentaculum tali) acts a cantilever against the calcaneus, and contributes to fracture [30]. Shearing forces can also lead to fractures of the body of the talus [31].

Cuboid

Anatomy

The cuboid is located at the lateral aspect of the midfoot [32]. The cuboid articulates proximally with the calcaneus, medially with the navicular and third cuneiform, and distally with the base of the fourth and fifth metatarsals.

Epidemiology

Fractures of the cuboid are uncommon injuries.

Mechanism

The cuboid may be fractured by direct injury, from a crushing-type injury, and by indirect twisting injuries. Forced eversion of the cuboid on the hind foot is a classical form of indirect injury. The fracture is often displaced. Forced plantar flexion–inversion leads to compression of the cuboid.

Cuboid dislocation may occur with a fall from a significant height onto an everted forefoot. This causes a force directed to the lateral and dorsal aspect of the foot. The ensuing injury is cuboid dislocation in a plantar-medial direction as the bone is pushed up by the heads of the fourth and fifth metatarsals [33].

The nutcracker fracture was described by Hermel in the 1950s. The mechanism of the fracture is forced abduction of the midfoot or forefoot, usually in combination with an axial force [34]. This leads to a compression fracture of the cuboid between the fourth and fifth metatarsals and the calcaneus, and an avulsion fracture of the navicular at its tuberosity medially. The presence of the fracture should prompt a search for a fracture of the navicular, cuboid, and calcaneus.

Plantar dislocation may also rarely occur from secondary rotation of the cuboid on the navicular secondary to severe twisting upon the weight-bearing foot [35].

Navicular

Anatomy

The navicular is a medial midfoot tarsal bone which articulates with the talus posteriorly, the cuboid medially, and the first, second, and third cuneiform bones distally.

Etiology

Fractures of the body of the navicular are uncommon. Navicular injuries can vary from mild to severe. The navicular is crucial for maintaining medial longitudinal arch and Chopart's joint of the foot. Nutcracker injuries indicate the application of severe forces to the foot as may occur with contact with the floor pan of a car in a head-on collision or a fall from horseback.

Mechanism

The most common injuries to the navicular bone are avulsion fractures [36]. The mechanism of the injury is often an indirect axial load. A case report of a cuboidal fracture that occurred in a motor vehicle collision described a mechanism involving forced plantar flexion at the moment of impact and showed an associated dorsal dislocation of the navicular [37].

Cuneiform Bones

Anatomy

The three cuneiform bones articulate proximally with the navicular and distally with the first, second, and third metatarsals. The third cuneiform also articulates laterally with the cuboid.

Epidemiology

Fractures of the cuneiform bones are uncommon injuries. Although isolated fractures of the cuneiforms have been reported in the literature, usually such fractures are associated with fractures of other midfoot bones.

Mechanism

Cuneiform fractures may be the result of direct or indirect force. The first cuneiform is the most commonly injured, may be injured in isolation, and is usually the result of direct blunt force.

Metatarsals and Tarsometatarsal Complex (TMC)

Anatomy

The tarsometatarsal complex (TMC) comprises the first, second, and third (or medial, middle, and lateral) cuneiforms, and the cuboid with the distal heads of the first to the fifth metatarsals. The stability of the joint results from the bony architecture and complex ligaments, which include dorsal, plantar, and interosseous ligaments. The most important of the ligaments is between the lateral surfaces of the first cuneiform and inserts to the medial aspect of the base of the second metatarsal [38]. This ligament has been given the eponymous name of the Lisfranc ligament.

Etiology

Injuries to the TMC are distinctly uncommon. The majority of reported injuries have occurred in motor vehicle incidents, which comprise about 40% of the injuries.

Mechanism

The mechanism of metatarsal fractures is from direct or indirect forces. A heavy object falling upon the foot most commonly results in transverse or comminuted fractures. Indirect trauma occurs when the body is twisted upon the fixed foot. This will usually result in an oblique fracture.

The Jones fracture is defined as a fracture of the fifth metatarsal ranging from 1.5 to 2.0 cm from the distal aspect of the tip of the tuberosity at the metaphyseal–diaphyseal junction. The mechanism of a Jones fracture is forceful adduction with the foot in plantar flexion. This results in the foot undergoing sudden dorsiflexion with the fourth and fifth articulations providing a fulcrum.

Metatarsophalangeal (MTP) joint injuries are common. Dislocation of the first MTP requires high energy trauma as may be seen in motor vehicle trauma and is frequently seen in association with other injuries to the lower leg.

Falls from a height onto the plantar flexed foot or "bracing" of the foot at the time of impact in a motor vehicle collision are typical mechanisms involved in fractures involving the tarsometatarsal complex. The resultant injury is typically dorsal or dorsolateral dislocation of the metatarsals [39].

The fifth metatarsal is the most commonly injured metatarsal. The common cause of fracture is forced inversion [40]. The first metatarsal is a relatively robust bone and is not commonly fractured. The fourth metatarsal is the least commonly fractured. This is generally held to be due to it being more freely mobile and its somewhat protected position.

CT Diagnosis in Foot Fractures

The radiological anatomy of the tarsal bones is complex. Axial and coronal views of both feet aid in diagnosis. CT scanning is more sensitive than plain radiographs in the detection of fractures of the TMC [41].

- Calcaneal fractures are well visualized on axial, sagittal, and coronal planes.
- Acute metatarsal fractures typically show a well-defined fracture, which is often unicortical.

The use of CT will become more important and routine in cases of a fall from a height if the conventional autopsy is not performed. During the autopsy one can make simple incisions into the skin of the heel to demonstrate subcutaneous bruises in cases where the victim landed on his or her feet. In the absence of this dissection one needs to be able to recognize overt and subtle fractures to the calcaneus and other foot bones on the CT images.

Joint Injury to the Lower Leg

Knee

Anatomy

The knee is a large complex hinge joint with two articulations. The foremost joint is between the femoral and tibial condyles. The femoropatellar articulation occurs between the patella and the patellar groove of the femur. The joint has an articular capsule composed of a fibrous and synovial membrane. There are extracapsular and intracapsular ligaments, medial and lateral menisci, and numerous bursae.

The major extracapsular ligaments consist of the patella ligament, the cordlike lateral collateral ligament connecting the lateral epicondyle of the femur to the head of the fibula, and the medial (tibial) collateral ligament, which extends from the medial epicondyle of the femur to the medial tibial condyle.

The major intracapsular ligaments are the anterior and posterior cruciate ligaments. The cruciate ligaments extend from the intercondylar region of the tibia to the intercondylar region of the femur. The anterior cruciate ligament extends from the anterior intercondylar region of the tibia to the medial aspect of the lateral condyle of the femur. The posterior cruciate ligament extends from the posterior intercondylar region of the tibia to the medial aspect of the lateral femoral condyle.

The medial knee ligaments prevent excessive valgus movement at the knee. The lateral knee ligaments prevent excessive varus movement at the knee. The posterior cruciate ligament prevents the forward movement of the femur on the tibia. This action is particularly so when the knee is in a flexed position. The anterior cruciate ligament prevents backward sliding of the femur on the tibia, thus averting hyperextension of the joint. The anterior cruciate ligament also limits medial rotation of the femur upon the tibia when the limb is weight bearing.

Etiology

Knee injuries are seen as a consequence of direct contact as well as noncontact insults to the joint. Sports-related injuries are especially common in young individuals. Direct trauma is a particular cause of knee injury in pedestrians and motor vehicle occupants.

Mechanism

An injury to a knee ligament can be predicted from the mechanism of injury. An injury that results in forced valgus movement may tear the medial collateral ligament. Forced varus movements may result in a lateral collateral tear. Forced hyperextension may tear the anterior cruciate ligament, whereas a fall to the flexed knee may rupture the posterior cruciate ligament.

The medial collateral ligament is more prone to rupture than the lateral collateral ligament and the anterior cruciate ligament is ruptured more often than the posterior cruciate ligament in a ratio of approximately 10:1.

The effect of impact velocity on the type of lower limb injury has been addressed in a number of clinical and laboratory studies. An experimental study on intact cadavers showed that blunt force trauma applied to the lower legs by a ram caused different patterns of injury depending upon the impact velocity [42]. It was shown that an impact velocity of 20 km/h caused ligament injury to the knee, whereas an impact velocity of 40 km/h caused ligament injury and bone fractures.

A further study on intact cadavers with lateral thigh impacts at constant velocity but different impact energies showed that knee ligament injuries occurred with an impact energy of 450 J, whereas a femoral fracture resulted from an impact energy of 600 J [41]. Thus the type of injury sustained by a victim of trauma is dependent on more than just a review of the side and anatomical position the individual was struck.

The typical dashboard injury to the knee occurs from forceful contact between the knee and the dashboard in frontal motor vehicle collisions and can result in hemorrhage or edema to the anterior aspect of the tibia and also to the posterior aspect of the patella [44]. These changes can be visualized on magnetic resonance images. The bone bruises and subcutaneous bruises can, of course, be revealed by conventional autopsy dissection.

Reconstruction of Mechanism of Injury

An article by Teresinski and Madro described bone contusions and ligament injury to the knee joint in 357 pedestrians who were killed following impact with conventional passenger vehicles and from light trucks or sports utility vehicles [45]. Knee injuries were found in 60% of cases. Following autopsy examination of the subarticular tibial and femoral epiphyses for bone contusions this percentage of injury increased to 80%. In cases deemed to be due to lateral impact to the pedestrian the percentage of injuries to the knee was 94%. Of particular interest was their finding that bone contusions were only seen in pedestrians who were upright and weight bearing at the moment of impact.

Rather than being an effect of direct blunt force trauma the epiphyses showed contusions secondary to

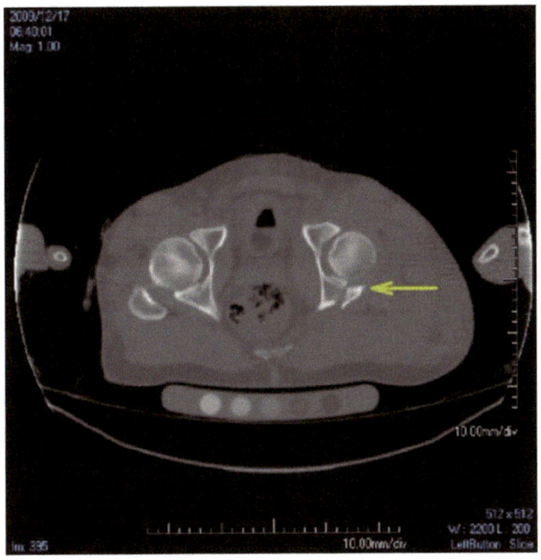

Figure 10.16 Axial CT showing a posterior fracture to the left acetabulum indicating severe axial loading through the femur.

axial compression forces to bone or avulsion forces to ligament. The exact positions of the bone contusions and ligament injury reflected the forced movement to the femur and tibia beyond the normal range of movement.

Examination of the other CT images can provide information to explain fractures (and ligament tears) involving the knee joints. A fractured patella or posterior fracture to the acetabulum in a motor vehicle occupant can suggest axial loading in the initial collision as the cause of a distal femoral fracture, rather than secondary vehicle intrusion in a multi-impact, complex crash (Figure 10.16).

Pediatric Injuries

Injuries to the knee in children are quite common and tend to differ from those in adults.

Femoral epiphyseal fractures are classified according to the Salter and Harris system [46]. The classification system describes whether the fracture involves the articular surface, involves the metaphysis or epiphysis, or whether a crushing-type injury to the growth plate is present. A type II fracture, where the fracture passes through the physis before exiting across the corner of the metaphysis, is most common [47].

Fractures of the tibial tubercle involve avulsion of the tubercle and may have associated extension of the fracture to the tibial articular surface. The injuries are classified according to the degree of fracture fragment displacement and the presence of comminution [48]. The mechanism of tibial tuberosity injury is either avulsion through contraction of the quadriceps group of muscles, or acute passive flexion. As such these injuries tend to occur on the sporting field.

Tibial spine injuries typically occur with a fall onto the knee. The classical situation follows a fall from a bicycle. The degree of displacement ranges from minor displacement to total avulsion [49].

Nonaccidental injury is associated with fractures of the proximal tibial metaphysis. These are otherwise highly unusual injuries in the pediatric population. The common type is a valgus greenstick injury. The fracture may occasionally extend all the way across the proximal metaphysis but usually involves less than two-thirds of the bone.

CT Diagnosis of Pediatric Knee Injuries

Because of the comparatively large amount of cartilage around the knee joint in children, the radiological diagnosis can be difficult, and the expertise of a radiologist is required for complete analysis of the CT images.

- Sagittal and coronal reconstructions are used to visualize fractures of the tibial spine.
- Proximal metaphyseal fractures are best visualized on coronal and sagittal planes.

Ankle

Anatomy

The ankle joint is a hinge joint allowing flexion and extension with a small degree of rotation and translation of the talar dome [50]. There are three groups of ligaments within the ankle joint: the medial collateral ligaments, the lateral collateral ligaments, and the syndesmotic ligament. The syndesmotic ligament stabilizes the normal anatomical relationship between the distal tibia and fibula. The fibula carries about 16% of the normal axial load.

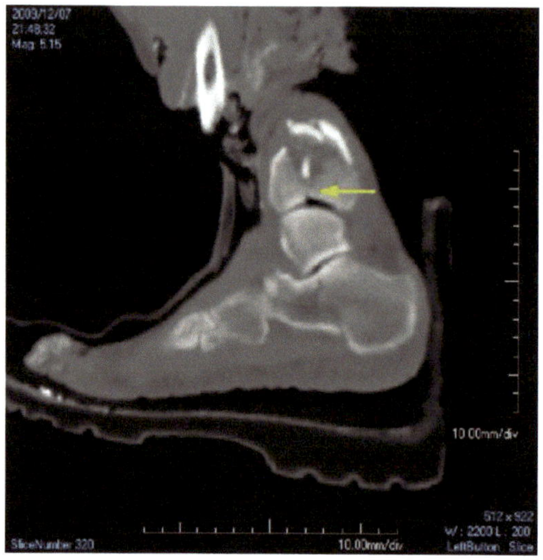

Figure 10.17 Sagittal CT showing a fracture involving the distal tibial articular surface through severe axial loading.

Etiology

Ankle fractures are common injuries. In the clinical situation, an ankle fracture is the most common fracture to be managed by orthopedic surgeons [23]. Ankle fractures are usually defined as an injury involving the distal tibia (medial malleolus), the distal fibula (lateral malleolus), or the talus.

Ankle fractures occur frequently in all age groups. In younger individuals the injury is usually sustained in falls and recreational and sports activities. In older patients an ankle fracture is most often seen in an osteoporotic individual in the setting of a twisting fall. Direct blunt force trauma, most commonly in relation to motor vehicle trauma, is seen in all age groups.

Mechanism

Ankle fractures occur with axial force through the foot with abnormal movements leading to compression and tensile stresses (Figure 10.17). These forces lead to bending, avulsion fractures, and ligament rupture.

Five types of force applied to the ankle joint may cause an ankle fracture. They are

Supination–adduction
Supination–external rotation
Pronation–abduction
Pronation–external rotation
Severe axial loading

Supination–adduction is the most common mechanism of injury and occurs from adduction of the inverted foot. This can lead to a transverse horizontal fracture through the middle of the lateral malleolus and a vertical fracture through the medial malleolus.

Ankle fractures that involve the talus usually occur to the talar neck or talar dome. Injuries to the talar neck are most frequently the result of forced dorsiflexion, whereas fractures of the talar dome are usually the result of inversion of the ankle.

CT Diagnosis of Ankle Injuries

The classical radiographs obtained to examine the ankle joint include the anterior–posterior, lateral, and mortise views. The mortise view is obtained by internally rotating the joint approximately 15% to 20% to provide a clear view of the talar dome and the tibial plafond. CT is an excellent modality to show ankle fracture.

- Axial images alone are often insufficient to adequately determine the boundaries of a complex ankle fracture.
- Multiple views may be required and three-dimensional reconstructions to visualize complex fracture patterns.

References

1. Waddell JP. Subtrochanteric fractures of the femur: A review of 130 patients. *J. Trauma* 1979; 19:582–592.
2. Evans FG, Pederson HE, Lissner HR. The role of tensile stress in the mechanism of femoral fractures. *J. Bone Joint Surg. Am.* 1951; 33:485-501.
3. Tencer AF, Kaufman R, Ryan K, Grossman DC, Henley MB, Mann F, Mock C, Rivara F, Wang S, Augenstein J, Hoyt D, Eastman B. Crash Injury Research and Engineering Network (CIREN). Femur fractures in relatively low speed frontal crashes: The possible role of muscle forces. *Accid. Anal. Prev.* 2002; 34(1):1–11.

4. Peljovich AE, Patterson BM. Ipsilateral femoral neck and shaft fractures. *J. Am. Acad. Orthop. Surg.* 1998; 6:106–113.
5. Zettas JP, Zettas P. Ipsilateral fractures of the femoral neck and shaft. *Clin. Orthop.* 1981; 160:63–73.
6. Ritchey SJ, Schonholtz GJ, Thompson MS. The dashboard femoral fracture: Pathomechanics, treatment, and prevention. *J. Bone Joint Surg. Am.* 1958; 40:1347–1358.
7. Droll KP, Broekhuyse H, O'Brien P. Fracture of the femoral head. *J. Am. Acad. Orthop. Surg.* 2007; 15:716–727.
8. Lundy DW. Subtrochanteric femoral fractures. *J. Am. Acad. Orthop. Surg.* 2007; 15:663–671.
9. Russell TA, Taylor JC. Subtrochanteric fractures of the femur. In Browner BD, Jupiter JB, Levine AM, Trafton PG, editors. *Skeletal trauma,* Vol. 2. Saunders, Philadelphia, 1992, pp. 1490–1492.
10. Kumar R, Malhotra R. The Hoffa fracture: Three case reports. *J. Orthop. Surg.* 2001; 9(2):47–51.
11. Hunter JB. Femoral shaft fractures in children. *Injury, Int. J. Care Injured* 2005; 36:S-A86–S-A93.
12. Schwend RM, Werth C, Johnson A. Femur shaft fractures in toddlers and young children: Rarely from child abuse. *J. Pediatr. Orthop.* 200; 20(4):475–481.
13. Strahan R. Non-contact paediatric knee injuries, including patellar sleeve fractures. *J. Med. Imaging Radiat. Oncol.* 2008; 52(6):544–549.
14. Mashru RP, Herman MJ, Pizzutillo PD. Tibial shaft fractures in children and adolescents. *J. Am. Acad. Orthop. Surg.* 2005;13:345–352.
15. Ivarsson BJ, Manaswi A, Genovese D, Crandall JR, Hurwitz SR, Burke C, Fakhry S. Site, type, and local mechanism of tibial shaft fractures in drivers in frontal automobile crashes. *Forens. Sci. Int.* 2008; 175(2–3):186–192.
16. Berkson EM, Virkus WW. High-energy tibial plateau fractures. *J. Am. Acad. Orthop. Surg.* 2006; 14:20–31.
17. King J, Diefendorf D, Aptorp J, Negrete VF, Carslon M. Analysis of 429 fractures in 189 battered children. *J. Pediatr. Orthop.* 1988; 8:585–589.
18. Liow RY, Birdsall PD, Mucci B, Greiss ME. Spiral computed tomography with two- and three-dimensional reconstruction in the management of tibial plateau fractures. *Orthopaedics* 199; 22:929–932.
19. Kalyani BS, Roberts CS, Giannoudis PV. The Maisonneuve injury: A comprehensive review. *Orthopaedics* 2010; 33(3):196–197.
20. Rabl W, Haid C, Krismer M. Biomechanical properties of the human tibia: Fracture behavior and morphology. *Forensic Sci. Int.* 1996; 83:39–49.
21. Messerer O. Ueber die gerichtlich-medicinische Bedeutung verschiedener Knochenbruchformen. Friedreichs Blatter F. *Gerichtl. Med.* 1885; 36:81–104.
22. Patscheider H. Ueber Anprallverletzungun der unteren Gliedmassen bei Strassenverkehrs-unfallen. *Dtsch. Z. Ges. Gerichtl. Med.* 1963; 54:336–366.
23. Yukawa N, Kojimahara M, Green MA, Saito T, Osawa M, Takeichi S. A Messerer fracture. Letter to the editor. *Forensic Sci. Int.* 1997; 88:231–232.
24. Eisele JW, Bonnell HJ, Reay DT. Boot top fractures in pedestrians. A forensic masquerade. *Am. J. Forens. Med. Pathol.* 1983; 4(2):181–184.
25. Daftary A, Haims AH, Baumgaertner MR. Fractures of the calcaneus: A review with emphasis on CT. *Radiographics* 2005; 25(5):1215–1226.
26. Heckman J. Fractures of the talus. In Bucholz R, Heckman J, editors. *Rockwood and Green's fractures in adults*, ed. 5, Vol. 2. Lippincott Williams and Wilkins, Philadelphia, 2001, pp. 2091–2132.
27. Rammelt S, Zwipp H. Talar neck and body fractures. *Injury* 2009; 40:120–135.
28. Haapamaki VV, Kiuru MJ, Mustonen AO, Koskinen SK. Multidetector computed tomography in acute joint fractures. *Acta Radiol.* 2005; 46:587–598.
29. Zwipp H. Severe foot trauma in combination with talar injuries. In Tscherne H, Schatzker L, editors. *Major fractures of the pilon, the talus, and the calcaneus.* Springer-Verlag, Berlin, 1993, pp. 123–135.
30. Peterson L, Romanus B, Dahlberg E. Fracture of the collum tali—An experimental study. *J. Biomech.* 1976; 9(4): 277–279.
31. Sneppen O, Christensen SB, Krogsoe O, Lorentzen J. Fracture of the body of the talus. *Acta Orthop. Scad.* 1977; 48:317–324.
32. Pinney SJ, Sangeorzan BJ. Fractures of the tarsal bones. *Orthop. Clin. N. Am.* 2001; 32(1):21–33.
33. Drummond DS, Hastings DE. Total dislocation of the cuboid. *J. Bone Joint Surg. Br.* 1969; 51:716–718.
34. Ceroni D, De Rosa V, De Coulon G, Kaelin A. Cuboid nutcracker fracture due to horseback riding in children: Case series and review of the literature. *J. Pediatr. Orthop.* 2007; 27(5):557–561.
35. Buscemi MJ, Page BJ. Transcuneiform fracture-cuboid dislocation of midfoot. *J. Trauma* 1986; 26:290–292.
36. Eichenholtz SN, Levine DB. Fractures of the tarsal navicular bone. *Clin. Orthop.* 1964; 34:42–57.
37. Rymaszewski LA, Robb JE. Mechanism of fracture-dislocation of the navicular. Brief report. *J. Bone Joint Surg. Br.* 1988; 70:492.
38. de Palma L, Santucci A, Sabetta SP, Rapali S. Anatomy of the Lisfranc joint complex. *Foot Ankle Int.* 1997; 18:356–364.
39. Thompson MC, Mormino MA. Injury to the tarsometatarsal complex. *J. Am. Acad. Orthop. Surg.* 2003; 11:260-267.
40. Armagan OE, Shereff MJ. Injuries to the toes and metatarsals. *Orthop. Clin. N. Am.* 2001; 32(1):1–10.
41. Goiney RC, Connell DG, Nichols DM. CT evaluation of tarsometatarsal fracture-dislocation injuries. *AJR Am. J. Roentgenol.* 1985;144:985–990.
42. Kajzer J, Schroeder G, Ishikawa H, Matsui Y, Bosch U. Shearing and bending effect at the knee joint at high speed lateral loading. *SAE Trans. J. Passenger Cars* 1997; 106:3682–3696.
43. Kajzer J, Matsui Y, Ishikawa H, Schroeder G, Bosch U. Shearing and bending effect at the knee joint at low speed lateral loading. *SAE Trans. J. Passenger Cars* 1999; 108:1159–1170.

44. Sanders TG, Medynski MA, Feller JF, Lawhorn KW. Bone contusion patterns of the knee at MR imaging: Footprint of the mechanism of injury. *Radiographics* 200; 20:S135–S151.
45. Teresinski G, Madro R. Knee injuries as a reconstructive factor in car-to-pedestrian accidents. *Forensic Sci. Int.* 2001; 124(1):74–82.
46. Salter RB, Harris WR. Injuries involving the epiphyseal plate. *J. Bone Joint Surg. Am.* 1963; 45:587–622.
47. Zionts LE. Fractures around the knee in children. *J. Am. Orthop. Surg.* 2002; 10:345–355.
48. Ogden JA, Tross RB, Murphy MJ. Fractures of the tibial tuberosity in adolescents. *J. Bone Joint Surg. Am.* 1980; 62:205–215.
49. Meyers MH, McKeever FM. Fracture of the intercondylar eminence of the tibia. *J. Bone Joint Surg. Am.* 1970; 52:1677–1684.
50. Donatto KC. Ankle fractures and syndesmosis injuries. *Orthop. Clin. North Am.* 2001; 32(1):79–90.

11 The Use of CT in Difficult Forensic Cases

There are certain types of cases that are apt to create problems for forensic pathologists. These cases include but are not limited to the following:

- Decomposed and burnt remains
- Deaths associated with falls
- Child abuse
- Transportation deaths

Decomposed and Burnt Remains

Decomposed and burnt remains are a routine part of forensic casework. Skeletonized remains are relatively uncommon. The forensic pathologist is most comfortable when examining well-preserved deceased bodies where injuries to the skin and soft tissues provide important information on the blunt force trauma that lead to death. As previously noted, the presence of an injury to the skin usually indicates a site of the application of trauma. The fractures that are identified by routine postmortem examination or computed tomography (CT) scanning can then be interpreted with respect to the location of the blunt force trauma.

The resolution of CT is such that one cannot totally exclude that presence of a minute stab or incised injury to a bone in a case with marked decomposition or burning artifact. A small injury to a bone that is identified on routine conventional autopsy may indeed be present on the full body CT images, but unless there is some concern surrounding the case when the images are initially reviewed, the abnormality could be easily overlooked.

In essence, CT does not provide all the information required for a safe evaluation of decomposed and burnt cases. The decision for complete autopsy examination is guided by classic forensic factors, such as the circumstances of the death and the scene findings. A careful external examination of the remains by a forensic pathologist is crucial to resolve the majority of cases.

Decomposition

The processes of autolysis and putrefaction cause various changes in color to the skin, subcutaneous fat, skeletal muscles, and other soft tissues. Postmortem predation by insects, rodents, and other animals may further alter the appearance of the remains. The degree of decomposition can vary from mild discoloration, through varying degrees of soft tissue destruction, to completely skeletonized remains. The requirement for a full conventional autopsy examination will vary depending upon the degree of decomposition, the scene findings, the results of the postmortem CT, and the medical history.

The production of gases from decomposition introduces a practical issue in performing postmortem CT scans. The proportion of deceased bodies that do not physically fit through the gantry is much higher in bloated decomposed cases. Such cases should proceed to autopsy.

The production of gas through putrefaction means that one may be unable to diagnose air embolism in such cases. However, the images can still provide important information (Figure 11.1).

In a conventional autopsy, and depending upon the degree of decomposition in a given case, the pathologist may need to deflesh either certain regions or even the entire remains to ascertain the presence of any bony injury. In these instances the use of postmortem CT provides an objective, ongoing record of a fracture. The CT may also reveal the presence of projectiles or other foreign bodies shortly after formal admission to the forensic department. Timely review of the CT images in such cases ensures that the investigating police officers can immediately arrange a forensic scientific assessment of the scene in cases where there had been no initial suspicions surrounding the case.

The decision to perform a complete autopsy examination also relies on any unusual findings on the external examination. Maggot infestation commences in and around normal body orifices. Masses of maggots also tend to be in regions that are shielded from direct light. The presence of maggots in a body region away from a normal orifice suggests the presence of preexisting antemortem injury.

The CT can demonstrate significant soft tissue findings in decomposed cases. Intracerebral hemorrhages are often easier to appreciate on the CT images than in the autopsy room where the liquefied brain may only allow a passing moment to view the parenchyma before it is collected in the container.

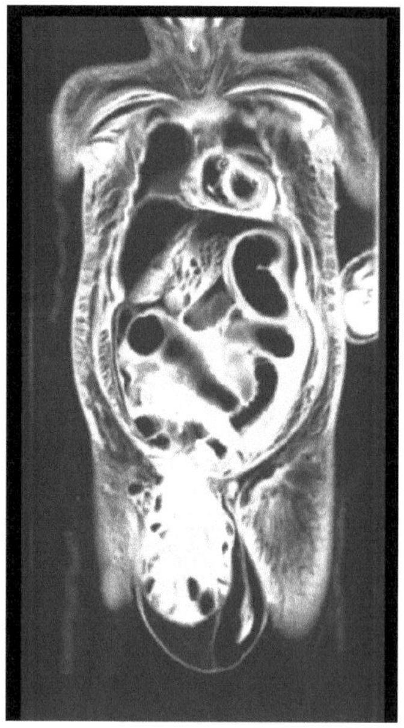

Figure 11.1 Coronal CT showing marked gas within soft tissues. The CT image demonstrates a right inguinal hernia with the bowel extending into the scrotum.

Burnt Remains

The process of burning results in destruction of the skin, soft tissues, and eventually bone. The internal organs, and bones some distance from the seat of the fire, are usually remarkably preserved. Burning can cause marked brittleness of the neighboring residual bone and lead to considerable artifacts. The postmortem collapse of a brittle skull can mask the presence of a skull defect and associated fractures.

Fire causes heat-related artifacts such as mosaic fractures to the calvarium, heat extradural heat hematoma, and blood to emanate from the nares. The mosaic postmortem artifactual skull fractures occur primarily to the external table of the calvarium and are most prominent adjacent to areas most affected by fire. These postmortem fractures do not extend into the base of the skull. A paper described the sequence of changes that occur to a human body throughout a cremation [1]. The authors observed that fractures to the calvarium began after 20 minutes. Fractures to the base of the skull were not seen in any of the cases.

The heat hematoma is a classical postmortem artifact caused by the boiling of blood within the diploe of the skull. The extradural hematoma is readily differentiated from a subdural hematoma by correlating the external examination findings with the CT images. Loss of the external table of the calvarium close to the seat of the fire is well seen on CT images.

Blood around the external nares may be due to the boiling of fluids within the chest during a fire. When the fluid cools it can have the appearance of blood around the nose. The CT provides an objective visualization of the nasal bones to exclude or document a fracture.

Case Study

The markedly burnt remains of a middle-aged woman were found in the bedroom of a house that was extensively burnt following a fire. At the time of the incident there was a report of a threat having been recently made against the deceased by an adult male.

The remains were transported to the Victorian Institute of Forensic Medicine (VIFM) where a postmortem CT was performed (Figure 11.2a). The CT revealed a massive volume of fluid within the right chest with Hounsfield units of 40 consistent with a hemothorax (Figure 11.2b,c). The homicide squad was informed of the findings.

The external examination showed total destruction of the skin with charring of the subcutaneous fat and skeletal muscle. Internal examination revealed a stab defect involving the right common carotid artery that then extended to the apex of the right hemothorax with a stab injury noted to the apex of the right lung. Review of the CT images by the radiologist revealed a track extending through the neck and into the right chest consistent with a stab injury.

At the time of the internal examination, information gleaned by the police raised the possibility the deceased had been struck a number of times across her anterior thighs with an iron bar. Following dissection of the heat-affected skeletal muscles and inspection of the

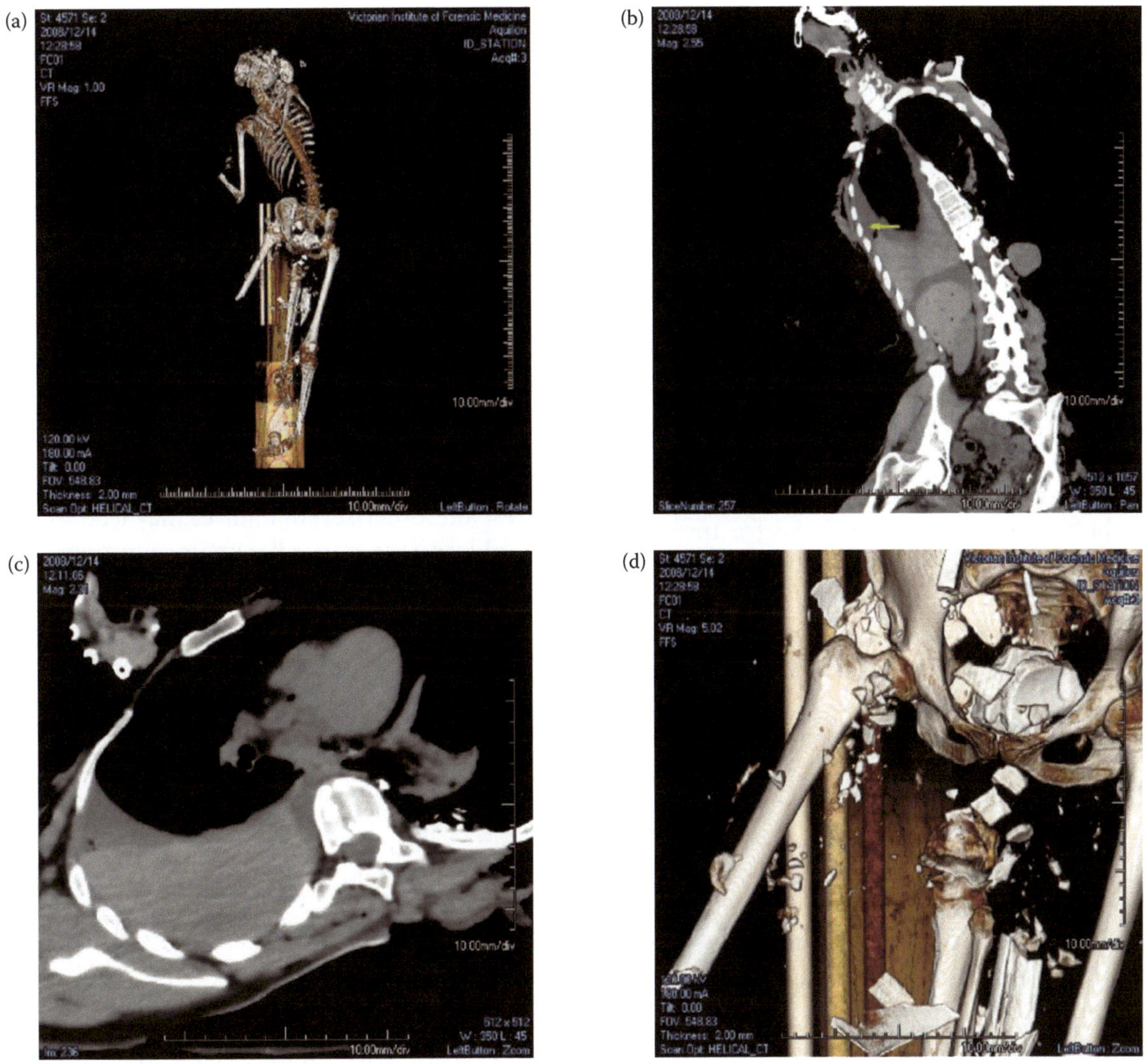

Figure 11.2 (a) Overall three-dimensional reconstruction CT of the burnt remains. (b) Coronal CT of overall image of burnt remains. (c) Axial CT showing the right hemothorax. (d) Detail of three-dimensional reconstruction image showing heat effect and debris related to the fire. There was no suggestion of blunt force trauma seen to the femori.

femur, no injury could be seen. The CT allowed further digital inspection of the femori prior to any manipulation in the autopsy room (Figure 11.2d).

Falls

Falls may occur from a standing height, from a relatively low height (such as from ladders or horses), down stairs, from a significant height (such as from a building), and may occur in the context of a struggle or altercation. The manner of death from a fall may be accidental, suicidal, occasionally homicidal, and may be a consequence of underlying natural disease. These cases can have a large variety of pathological findings. Often determining the cause of death is not particularly difficult as there are often severe head, neck, and chest injuries. As will be detailed in the following, the different types of falls are often, but certainly not universally, associated with a particular pattern of injuries.

Natural Deaths

An individual who suddenly collapses secondary to a cardiac arrhythmia or catastrophic primary brain hemorrhage will not attempt to break his or her fall. The victim may fall forward, backward, or to the side. The victim may fall from a seated position, from an elevated position such as a ladder, or in any number of scenarios. The common forensic case involves an episode of collapse to the ground from a standing position.

The skin and soft tissue injuries most frequently encountered in such cases are abrasions, bruises, and lacerations to areas of bony prominence. The major bony prominences of the face and head are the nose, the forehead and eyebrows (supraorbital ridge), the prominence of the cheek, the chin, the external ear, and the posterior aspect of the occiput. In a simple fall the soft tissue injuries will be in a single plane. In complex falls, which include intermediate targets, or falls down steps, there can be secondary impacts to more than one site and more than one plane. In these scenarios there may be injuries beyond the typical bony prominences.

The skull fracture that results from an episode of collapse in association with natural disease depends upon the direction of the fall. A fall to the back of the head from a standing position often leads to a longitudinal linear fracture of the occiput. The fracture may extend to the foramen magnum. The fall to the back of the head from a standing height is also often associated with contrecoup fractures to the orbital roofs. Forward falls to the forehead may cause facial fractures. These fractures are most commonly to the nose, frontal bone (sinus), zygoma, and maxilla.

In the majority of institutions one suspects it is not routine practice to perform subcutaneous dissection of the face or obtain conventional radiographs of the face in such cases. Interestingly, a retrospective clinical analysis of 437 patients with facial fractures showed that falls comprised 18% of the cases [2]. Patients with fractures involving the frontal sinus who presented to a level 1 trauma center had sustained a fall in 54% of cases [3]. It would seem highly likely that facial and frontal bone fractures are underdiagnosed in the forensic autopsy. The use of CT scanning has the promise of increasing the accuracy of facial fracture diagnosis postmortem in these cases.

An episode of collapse from a standing height is an uncommon cause of middle cranial fossa fracture.

Suicidal Deaths

Suicidal falls are usually in the context of a fall from a considerable height, for example, a high-rise building or bridge. This issue will be addressed at length in a later section. In the majority of cases where an individual jumps from a building, bridge, or other elevated fixed structure, there are usually other clinical indicators of suicide including prior suicide attempts, the presence of a suicide note, or history of depression.

Although a note at the scene of the death is a very strong indicator of suicide as the manner of death, it is not absolute proof of suicide. We have investigated a case that was initially presented as a case of hanging. A suicide note at the scene was later found to be false. The case showed numerous facial injuries and was resolved as a case of homicide. If there is doubt in such cases, a formal forensic document examination of the suicide note should be performed and a full conventional autopsy performed.

Accidental Deaths

Deaths from accidental falls can occur in domestic and workplace environments, and occasionally from sporting or recreational activities such as rock climbing. Deaths from falls in the workplace are often associated with significant falls at building sites onto concrete. In the domestic situation, falls leading to death usually occur in falls from ladders or roofs. Not uncommonly the victims are middle-aged and elderly males. The frequent cause of death in these situations is a head injury, often seen in association with a fractured skull. Less commonly a fracture or dislocation to the atlantooccipital joint or upper cervical spine may be the direct cause of death. In older individuals pelvic fractures, rib fractures, and other severe injuries may lead to death from blood loss, systemic inflammatory response syndrome, and multiple organ dysfunction and failure.

One of the major causes of death in the elderly in developed countries is an accidental fall leading to a fractured neck of femur. In this population, who often has significant medical issues, the fracture regularly leads to death due to complications of bronchopneumonia, fat embolism, and pulmonary thromboembolism.

Homicidal Deaths

Cases of homicide from falls are rare. Although also very uncommon, the more common scenario is disposal of a body of a homicide victim by throwing the body from a bridge, cliff, or building.

The difficult issue for the pathologist is to identify injuries that are inconsistent with damage to the deceased's body from the fall. It is self-evident that anatomical dissection will not progress an investigation where the allegation is that the victim was pushed from a height.

A small female or child may be grappled and thrown from a balcony or other point without observable skin injury. It would be extremely unusual for an adult male to be thrown from a height without sustaining associated injuries unless he is severely incapacitated before or during the incident. The external examination, analysis of the CT scans, and any subsequent internal examination is directed toward recognizing restraint injuries and evidence of assault.

Restraint injuries are suggested by groups of discoid bruises to the upper arms, the wrists, or the legs reflecting the victim being grasped by a group of assailants. Bruises, abrasions, and lacerations in multiple planes are suggestive but are not definitive of assault. Bruises, and especially grouped bruises around the neck, are particularly concerning. In these cases the hyoid and thyroid cartilages should be carefully examined using CT or conventional autopsy.

Bruises, abrasions, and lacerations may be seen in a second plane due to effects of underlying fractures. Secondary bruises from an underlying fracture may evolve with time in the postmortem period. Lacerations may result from an edge of a fracture protruding momentarily through the skin. Shored abrasions can occur when the edges of fractured bone force the overlying skin against a hard object.

In suspicious cases where a death is associated with a fall from a relatively low height, the presence of more than one skull fracture is concerning. Simple falls from a standing height from whatever cause almost always result in a single, simple linear fracture. Although it is intuitive and usual for a single impact to result in a single fracture, early experimental work proved the skull bends outward in more than one direction from the point of blunt force trauma to the calvarium. Thus it is theoretically possible for more than one fracture to be produced from a single application of blunt force to the skull. However, it must be said that although multiple skull fractures resulting from a simple low elevation fall are possible, they are highly unusual.

Impacts around the vertex can cause fractures that may radiate in a number of directions. Such an impact may also lead to transmitted forces to the base of the skull causing a ring fracture around the foramen magnum.

A depressed skull fracture is highly unlikely in a fall from a standing height onto a flat surface and raises the possibility of an assault. In such cases a full conventional autopsy is indicated. A death from head injury caused by a fall from a standing height may be deemed to be a case of homicide if the victim was first struck by an assailant. The most common scenario is a fall to the back of the head following a punch to the face, which in turn leads to a fractured occiput. Death may follow as a consequence of primary or secondary brain injury or tear to a major vessel. It has been demonstrated experimentally that impacts to the brain can lead to respiratory center dysfunction (commotio medullaris). This functional abnormality was shown to be increased if the victim is intoxicated with alcohol. A less frequent injury that may be sustained in the course of an assault is a lethal upper cervical spine injury.

Falls from Standing Heights and Relatively Low Heights

Seventy-five deaths associated with ground-level falls were investigated in a study reported by Hartsthorne and colleagues [4]. Eighty-seven percent of the cases underwent full autopsy examination. Of the deceased persons, 61% were least 70 years of age, with only 12% aged less than 50 years. Cardiovascular disease was found in 70% of the cases. It was found that 48% of those tested had alcohol in their system. The primary cause of death was head injury, with 37% having a base of skull fracture and 85% sustaining a subdural hemorrhage.

A retrospective analysis of 14 victims of acute deaths from cervical spine injury due to falls onto the face from a variety of mechanisms and ranging up to a height of 3 m was reported by Osawa and colleagues in 2008 [5]. The authors found that the most frequently damaged region of the cervical spine was the C4-C5 level. Injuries were noted from C2-3 to C6-7. In 12 of the 14 cases there were transverse clefts between a vertebra and the intervertebral disc space at the site of a tear to the anterior longitudinal ligament [5]. Complete dissociation was seen to the injured endplates of the discs with separation of a small bone fragment from the margin of the vertebra. The bone and ligament injuries were seen in association with central cord hemorrhage.

An experimental study used intact cadavers, eight of which had their heads restrained to mimic the presence and effects of the neck musculature. The cadavers were dropped a distance of 0.9 to 1.5 m toward the vertex. Strain gauges showed that the forces applied to the cervical spine in the restrained group were higher than in the nonrestrained group. Examination of the specimens revealed there was an increased number of cervical and upper thoracic fractures in the restrained group. Furthermore, despite the relatively controlled nature of the experiment, a fairly large spread of injuries was identified within the skull, vertebrae, and ligaments of the cervical and thoracic spine [6]. The study was performed in the laboratory situation with a number of parameters controlled and recorded. Even so, the laboratory situation led to a range of documented injuries from the same type of blunt force trauma. These experiments serve to highlight the variation that can occur in the dynamic situations where these injuries occur.

A common injury in conscious individuals who fall from a standing height involves impact to an outstretched hand. The common injuries seen in this mechanism of injury include fractures to the long bones of the upper limb and the clavicle, and dislocation to the shoulder. The presence of these injuries in an unwitnessed forensic case may suggest the victim was conscious at the time of the fall. With the introduction of routine CT there is an opportunity for such peripheral injuries to be documented and the circumstances of such events may be better understood.

Case Study

An 80-year-old man had been at a family function where he had consumed a number of alcoholic beverages. He went outside to have a cigarette. A short time later a family member went outside and found him collapsed face down on the ground. An ambulance was called. The ambulance officer found the man in cardiac arrest. He was resuscitated and taken to a major teaching hospital where he was found to have suffered a severe upper cervical spine injury. The patient regained consciousness a week following the incident but had complete quadriparesis and died from bronchopneumonia the following week. The death was reported to the coroner and a conventional autopsy was performed.

The autopsy showed triple vessel coronary artery atherosclerosis but no histological evidence of acute myocardial infarction. Severe bronchopneumonia was confirmed. The cervical spine was excised and the longitudinal section showed hemorrhage into the dura at the second cervical vertebra. No fracture was seen. The cord was removed and histological examination revealed infarction with foamy macrophages and adjacent axonal retraction spheroids.

The postmortem CT scans were referred to the radiologist. The radiologist diagnosed a subtle oblique fracture to the lateral mass of the second cervical vertebra (Figure 11.3).

No definite cause of the collapse was determined but was most probably related to a cardiac arrhythmia associated with the ischemic heart disease. The conventional autopsy technique of cutting the excised cervical spine specimen longitudinally with a band saw did not show the fractures to the cervical spine even though they were known clinically and there was residual focal hemorrhage at the site of trauma. The CT is superior to routine autopsy dissection in demonstrating nonaxial cervical spine fractures.

Falls Down Stairs

Falls down stairs are a common occurrence. They are especially frequent in the elderly population and those affected by alcohol and other drugs. Falls down stairs may be simple or complex. A fall may be backward due to slipping on a step and lead to injuries akin to a backward fall from a standing height. A fall forward down the stairs can cause multiple primary and secondary impact points. If the individual is carrying something there may be injuries resulting from forceful contact with the item.

Because of the potentially complex nature of a fall down stairs, there may be skin abrasions and bruises in more than one plane. In addition, whereas most simple falls result in skin injury over bony prominences falls down stairs can cause skin and soft tissue injuries away from typical bony prominences. A particularly problematic issue for police investigators and forensic pathologists can be to determine whether the head injuries sustained by a deceased individual found at the bottom of a flight of stairs are accidental or due to inflicted injury. Although it is common for individuals who fall down stairs to sustain soft tissue injuries to their limbs, documented limb fractures are relatively uncommon.

Deaths that occur directly from the primary injury in a fall down stairs are usually the result of a head injury. A retrospective analysis of 92 cases of death from an accidental fall down stairs showed the causes of death were head injury in 80% of cases, hemorrhagic shock from abdominal or thoracic visceral injury in fewer than 10% of cases, and neck injury in 4% of cases [7]. The majority of the deaths occurred at home (97.8%) and alcohol was detected in almost a fifth of the cases. The parietal and temporal bones were fractured in 26 and 24 of the cases, respectively. A base of skull fracture was seen in

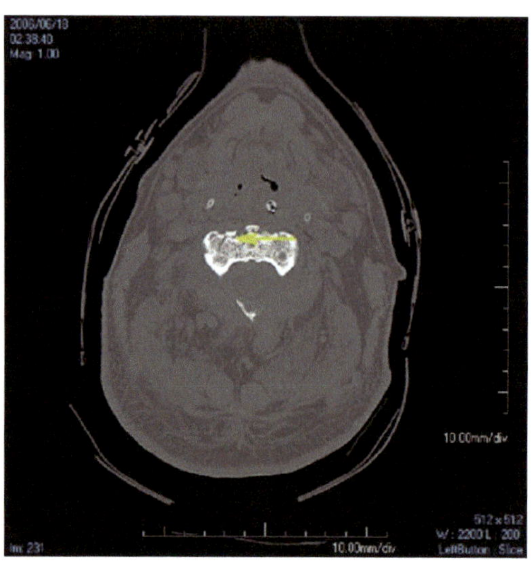

Figure 11.3 Axial CT of the second cervical vertebra showing a fracture extending to the vicinity of the right foramen transversarium.

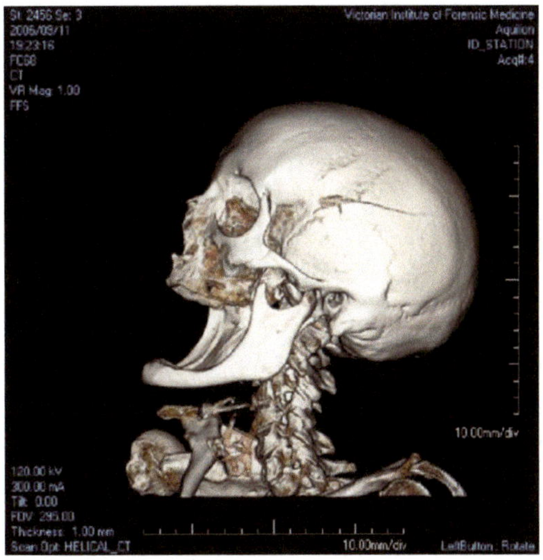

Figure 11.4 Three-dimensional reconstruction of the skull showing a linear fracture to the left temporoparietal region, which occurred in a fall down a flight of stairs. As is often the case, the fracture extends through the hat brim zone.

12 cases. Occipital and frontal fractures were identified in six and four other cases. In 38 cases no skull fracture was seen.

The "hat brim rule" for skull fractures has been used as a tool for determining whether a fall or assault caused head injury with associated skull fracture (Figure 11.4). The hat brim line referred loosely to an area extending around the skull, which would correspond to the brim of a hat. The traditional interpretation of head injuries around the hat brim line is that injuries above the line are suggestive of inflicted injury, whereas injuries below the line favor an accident. The hat brim rule was originally used in falls from a standing position but has been investigated in a number of studies examining injuries sustained in falls down stairs.

A recent retrospective study investigated skull fractures and the hat brim rule, and incorporated an anatomical definition of the hat brim line [8]. The definition allows more accurate documentation to be made in these cases and permits comparisons between different studies. The superior hat brim line is a horizontal plane passing through the glabella, a margin based on an earlier border that was suggested by Ehrlich and Maxeiner [9]. The inferior parallel line passes through the right and left porion (essentially the central aspect of the upper margin of the external auditory meatus), and the left orbitale.

The study examined autopsy data on scalp lacerations and skull fractures resulting from falls and homicide over a five-year period. Eighty cases were retrieved. Thirteen deaths were caused by falls down stairs, 23 deaths resulted from a fall from a standing height, and there were 44 cases of homicide from blunt force head injury. The analysis of the injuries suggested that injuries above the hat brim line zone were more in favor of blows from an assault, whereas in cases where fractures were within the hat brim line zone the manner of death was not able to be determined [8]. Fractures localized to the left were deemed to be more in favor of blows whereas fractures on the right were more in favor of falls. These studies would seem to illustrate that using the hat brim rule to determine the manner of death in a particular case should be preceded with caution.

Case Study

An 85-year-old woman with a past medical history including insulin-dependent diabetes mellitus, congestive cardiac failure, and permanent pacemaker had an unwitnessed fall down three steps at her residence. She was unconscious when found by a neighbor. She was taken to the hospital where a CT scan showed a fractured left parietal bone, associated small extradural hematoma, thin subdural hemorrhages, and a minor subarachnoid hemorrhage. The neurology team reviewed the patient. Following a family meeting the decision was made to institute palliative care. She died two days later.

An inspection and report examination was performed with expert review of the CT scans. The CT showed a left parietal fracture, small left extradural hematoma, small subdural hemorrhages, and a patchy subarachnoid hemorrhage. There was associated left cerebral edema. There was anterior subluxation of C4 on C5 (Figure 11.5).

The coroner was informed of the external examination findings and documented changes on postmortem CT scans. The coroner ordered that no further examination of the deceased was required and her body was released from the VIFM.

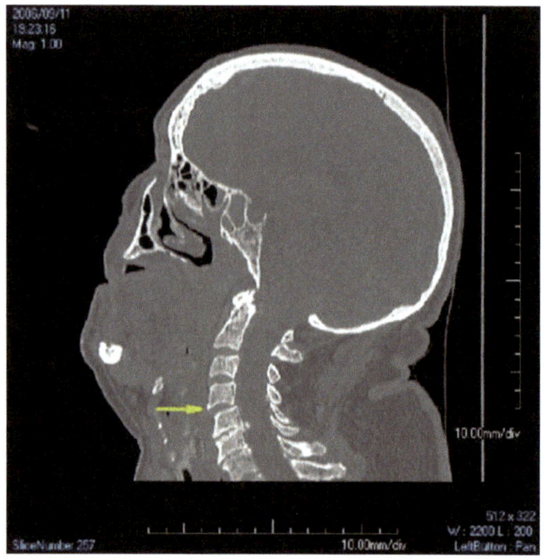

Figure 11.5 Sagittal CT showing subluxation of C4 on C5.

Falls from a Significant Height

Falls from a significant height are not uncommon cases in forensic pathology. The manner of death in the vast majority of cases is suicide, with a smaller number of accidental deaths and occasional cases of homicide.

In general terms, up to a certain height, the higher the distance a body falls before impacting with the ground, the greater the severity of the injuries sustained. Under the effects of gravity a body will accelerate at a rate of ~9.8 m/s^2 until the velocity is matched by the air resistance. The terminal velocity of a falling body is approximately 120 mph. The time taken for a body to reach terminal velocity will vary with respect to the attitude of the body during the fall. A body falling in a vertical orientation will reach terminal velocity faster than a body falling in a horizontal orientation. For practical purposes the average time to reach a terminal velocity of 120 mph is 13 to 14 seconds. This equates to a fall of about 550 m. Thus one does not see more severe injuries in a fall of 1000 m as opposed to a fall of ~550 m.

The determination of manner of death in a case of a fall from a significant height requires the integration of all of the available information. This information includes the past medical and psychiatric history of the deceased, witness accounts of the circumstances leading up to the death, a thorough examination of the scenes related to the death, and a careful forensic examination of the body. The past medical and psychiatric history may reveal the presence of a debilitating medical condition, a diagnosis of depression, or other significant psychiatric illness. Witnesses, family, and friends may provide a history to suggest suicidal ideation or emerging psychosis. The scene analysis will most commonly involve the immediate area from where the jump or fall occurred but can of course include other areas in more complex cases.

The pathological assessment of a death from a suicidal or accidental fall from a significant height that is corroborated by independent witnesses usually only requires an external examination and a review of the CT findings. The discovery of a body at the bottom of a building or in other unusual circumstances is more challenging.

The location of the incident has been said to have relevance to the manner of death. In a study on deaths resulting from falls from height in New York City, it was found that in 69% of suicides and 19% of accidents the site of the fatality was the deceased's residence. Of course this reflects, at least in part, the proportion of citizens who reside in high-rise apartments in a major city. The report also indicated that the incident occurred at the deceased's workplace in only 3% of suicides but 42% of accidents [10].

The distance a body is located from a building or other fixed structure has been suggested as an indicator of the manner of death. This issue was explored in a biomechanical study of running and standing jumps with respect to the reconstructed trajectory of a fall from a building [11]. The study used 13 volunteers to perform a series of running jumps, and standing or swimmer's jumps. The acquired data was then incorporated into a mathematical formula. The mathematical model used a number of hypothetical angles of jumping, which then provided a range of proposed points of impact for a given height.

A further experimental study examined two cases of death from falls with regard to the possible mechanisms of the incident [12]. One case involved a fall from a balcony and the second concerned a fall from a cliff.

(a)

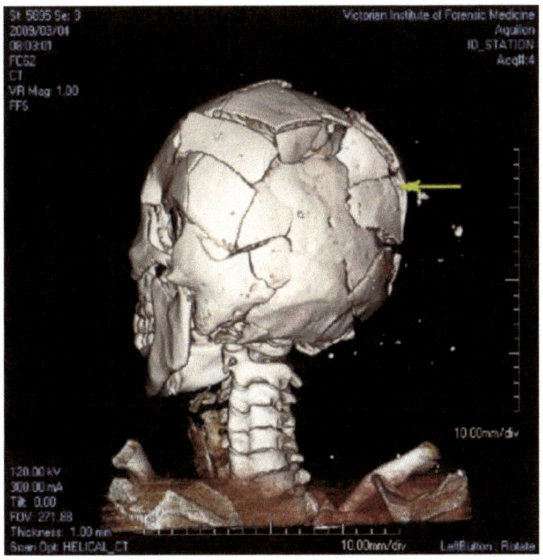

(a)

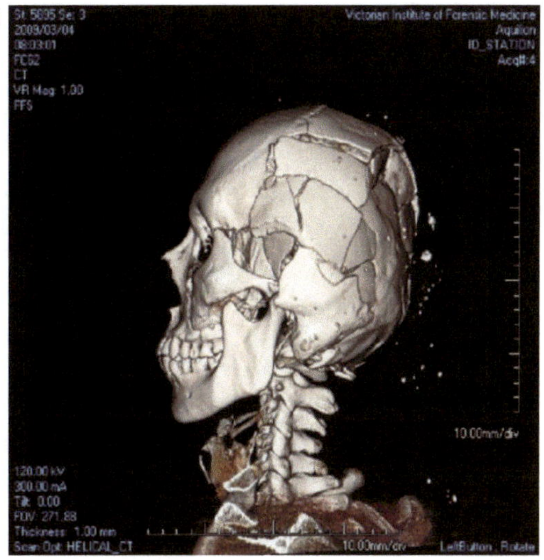

Figure 11.6 (a) Three-dimensional reconstruction showing comminuted fractures to the back of the head. (b) Three-dimensional reconstruction showing marked flattening to the back of the head indicating a point of severe primary impact.

The study employed mathematical formulae and experimental data using male and female cadets from a police academy to test a number of possible scenarios gleaned from the scene examination. The scenarios included standing or running jumps from a "cliff" edge and various throws of the deceased off the "cliff" by one or two assailants. Such studies allow investigators to present the courts with objective information on the likely physical limits there are for different scenarios in a given case.

Distribution of Injuries in Significant Falls

Abrasions and bruises are seen in virtually all cases involving falls from a significant height. In many different types of forensic cases the presence of clothing or hair will provide some protection to the skin from an injury. A report on cases of falls from a height described abrasions to the trunk despite the presence of overlying clothing. The abrasions were noted to the trunk in 47% of cases and always to one plane of the body [13]. In general, if the primary impact point is not to the trunk, one still expects a single plane of impact injuries to the body.

Skin injuries to recessed areas are a concern. Intuitively one does not expect recessed areas such as the neck to be injured when a fall culminates in impact onto a flat surface. However, "stretching"-type abraded injuries to the neck are occasionally observed in extreme falls. These skin injuries are analogous to inguinal skin tears seen with excessive extension at the ipsilateral hip or open book fracture of the pelvis. The etiology of the injuries is due to severe whiplash-type movements of the neck following impact with the ground. One may observe hemorrhage within the "strap muscles" of the anterior neck, which are usually more pronounced toward the muscles' insertion points.

In cases where there had been no contact with an intermediate target during the fall, an investigator can reasonably identify the orientation of the body at the moment of impact to the ground (Figure 11.6a,b).

The pattern of injuries sustained to victims who fall and land on their feet (i.e., "vertical trauma") is reported in the literature as being readily recognizable. The axial load is transmitted through the calcaneus, the tibia and femur, through the pelvis, and vertebral column to the skull. Thus in feet-first impacts one expects fractures to the calcaneus and neck of femur, central acetabular fractures, compression fractures of the vertebral bodies, and a ring fracture to the base of the skull (Figure 11.7a,b,c,d,e). The spinal injuries tend to be seen to the junctions between the relatively mobile and immobile segments of the spine. These are principally the lower cervical spine, the cervicothoracic junction, and the thoracolumbar junction.

One clinical study described 12 individuals who had jumped or fallen through a distance of 20 to 100 feet and landed primarily on their feet [14]. Fractures were the most frequent severe injuries. There were 15 lower extremity fractures, 4 pelvic fractures, and 9 spinal fractures. Thoracic injuries included rib fractures, pneumothoraces, and hemothorax. Secondary impact was believed to have caused severe upper extremity injury and craniofacial injury. One patient died; however, a patient who fell ~100 feet survived.

A concentration of injuries (including fractures) to one side of the body reflects the orientation of the body at the time of impact with the ground (Figure 11.8).

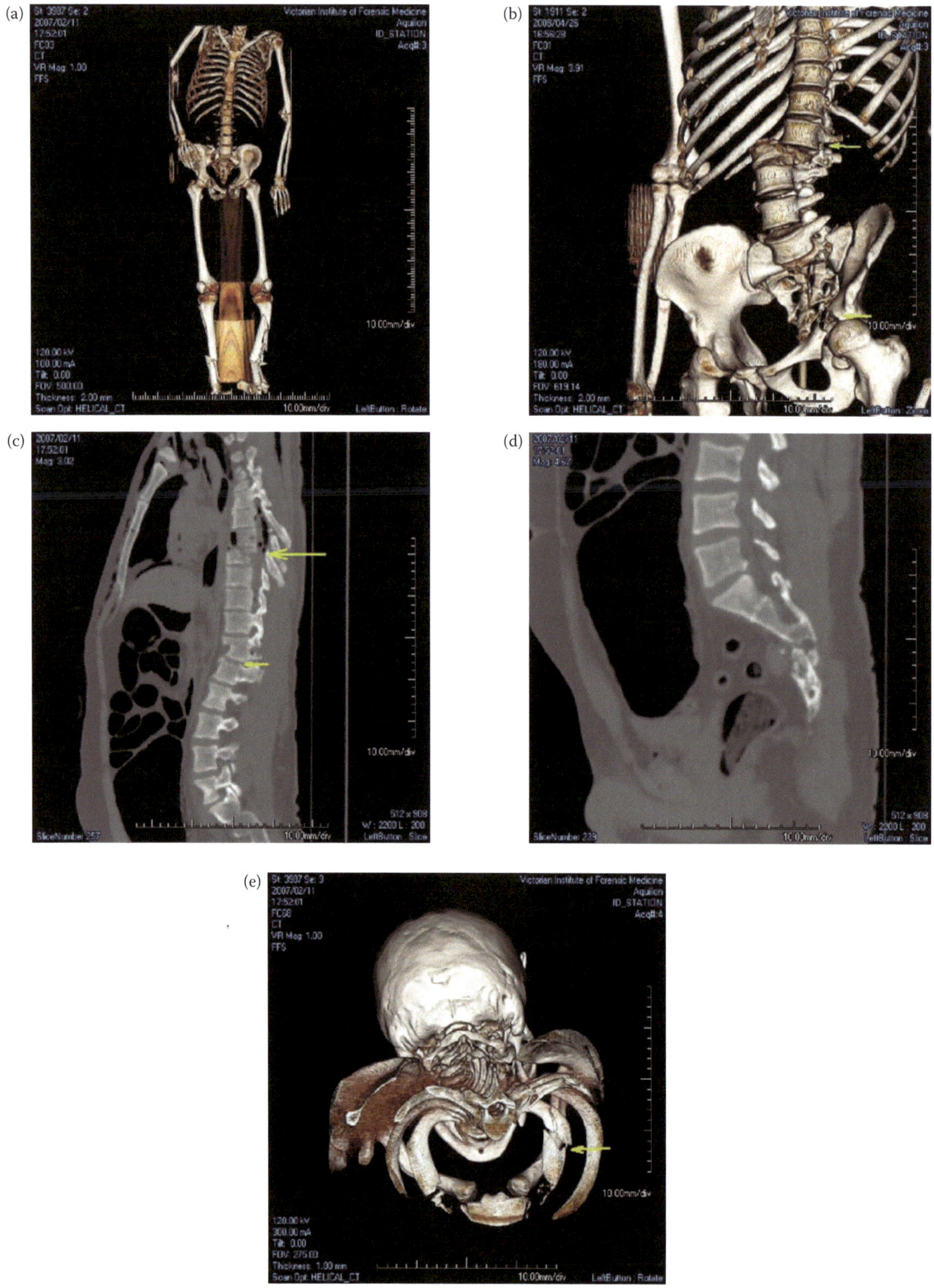

Figure 11.7 (a) Three-dimensional reconstruction showing fractures associated with a fall onto the feet from a significant height. There are bilateral fractures to the lower limbs and pelvis. (b) Three-dimensional reconstruction showing a fracture to the superior aspect of the left acetabulum and the lumbar spine in a fall. There was severe axial loading through the left lower limb. (c) Sagittal CT showing fractures to the thoracic vertebrae. (d) Sagittal CT showing a fracture to the sacrum associated with a vertical fall. (e) Three-dimensional reconstruction showing a fracture to the right first rib.

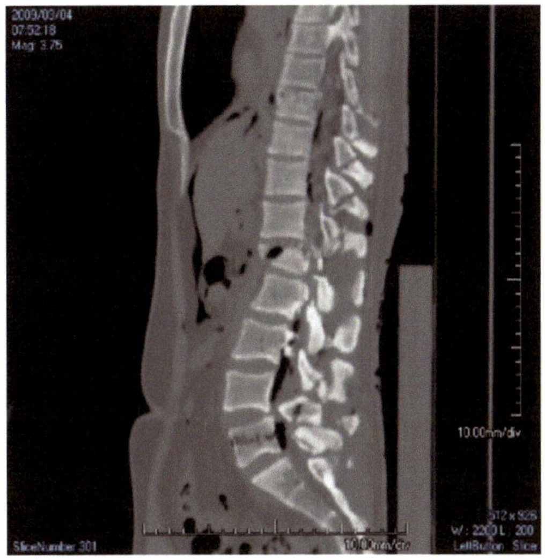

Figure 11.8 Sagittal CT image showing multiple spinous process fractures in a man who had a significant fall onto his back.

The situation is complicated by secondary injuries, including fractures, from extreme hyperflexion or hyperextension of the trunk, and secondary impacts to the limbs and head. This may lead to the formation of somewhat unexpected injuries and raise the possibility of assault. In their study of 68 deaths from falls, Turk and Tsokos [13] described skeletal muscle hemorrhage in the neck and fractures of the hyoid bone in 33% of cases in falls greater than 10 m in height. They were not seen in cases occurring below 10 m. Fractures involving both the sternum and the mandible have been reported. The fracture is a result of forceful contact between the sternum and mandible following forced flexion of the neck secondary to impact to the occiput (Figure 11.9).

The issue of abrasions in more than one plane of the body may raise the question of the body bouncing on impact. Although this is raised as a possibility in courts, and cases anecdotally recounted by pathologists and laypersons alike, we were unable to find documented evidence of the phenomenon in the English-speaking forensic literature. In the absence of documented cases it would seem a reasonable position to state that if bodies do bounce after a significant fall, it is not very far and does not lead to significant injury.

As stated earlier, intuitively one expects the severity of injuries, including fractures, will increase with the distance fallen. One group of workers in Singapore attempted to relate the severity and pattern of injuries in falls from high-rise apartments with the height of the

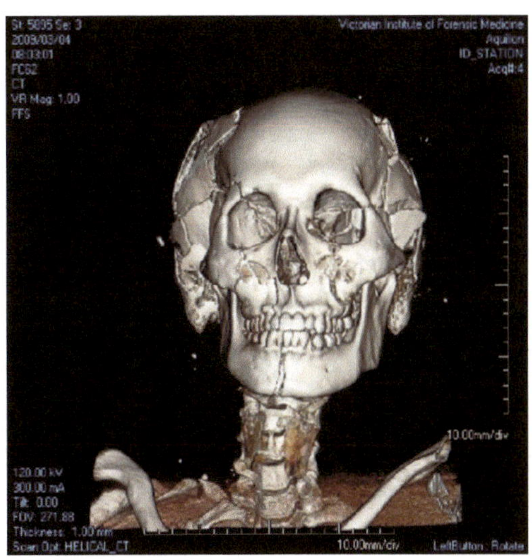

Figure 11.9 Three-dimensional reconstruction CT image showing a secondary fracture to the mandible resulting from forceful contact with the sternum due to impact with the ground following a considerable fall.

fall [15]. A relationship was demonstrated between the Injury Severity Score (ISS) and the distance fallen, providing an objective measure of presumed height fallen given a particular set of injuries in the case. The authors concluded that further research was needed to refine the model using a more precise method of scoring the injuries compared to the rather blunt system of the ISS.

What is somewhat surprising is that a number of papers in the literature have described unusual patterns of injury with respect to the distance fallen. A number of papers have described a bimodal distribution of skull fractures with respect to increasing height. Turk noted that severe head injuries occurred mostly in falls from heights of less than 10 m and greater than 25 m [13]. Atanaseijevic found that head injuries were a feature of falls below 7 m and above 30 m [16]. The type of skull fracture was statistically correlated with the height of the fall in the latter study, with comminuted skull fractures associated with falls of greater than 7 m. Both authors raised the question as to whether the reduction in head injury seen in cases of falls between the upper and lower heights could be explained by the position of the falling body changing during the various stages of a fall.

A recent retrospective autopsy-based study detailing the pattern of skeletal injuries in falls ranging from 2 feet to 75 feet showed that skull fractures were the most common injury sustained in the cases [17]. In 52 of the 80 cases, fractures of the skull were seen. The most common fractures were vault fractures (23 cases), and vault and basal fractures (22 cases). Interestingly, pure basal skull fractures and ring fractures only occurred in four and three cases, respectively. The ring fractures were seen in victims who fell from a lower height (Figure 11.10). In the series of cases the next most frequently fractured bones were the ribs (41 cases), the sternum (18 cases), and the femur (12 cases).

Fractures of the extremities in falls from less than six stories were seen in 53% of 120 cases in one series [10]. This increased to 90% in falls between 11 and 20 stories. All cases involving falls over 20 stories high had extremity fractures.

Not surprisingly the severity of external and internal injuries sustained depends upon whether the fall is over hard ground or water. Fractures are far less common when a fall is into water. A clear difference in the nature and distribution of the injuries sustained in falls into water and a hard surface was seen in a study that investigated falls and jumps in a large city in the United States [18]. Fourteen cases of suicidal jumps into water ranging from heights of 21 m to 112.5 m resulted in a high proportion of abdominal visceral injury. Five of these cases were shown to have suffered relatively minor injuries and subsequently died by drowning.

A study involving 100 consecutive cases where individuals had jumped from the Golden Gate Bridge in San Francisco, California, was reported by Lukas and colleagues in 1981 [19]. The cause of death was issued as multiple injuries in 77 cases, laceration of the aorta in 2 cases, drowning in 12 cases, and a combination of multiple injuries and drowning in the remaining 9 cases. Postmortem examination showed the presence of hemothorax and hemoperitoneum in 82 and 84 cases, respectively. The underlying source of the blood varied, with the more common origins being pulmonary lacerations, great vessel and cardiac lacerations, and liver or splenic lacerations.

Skeletal injuries were less common. Forty-two victims displayed a variety of fractures. Fractures of the humerus were the most common injury (14 cases). There

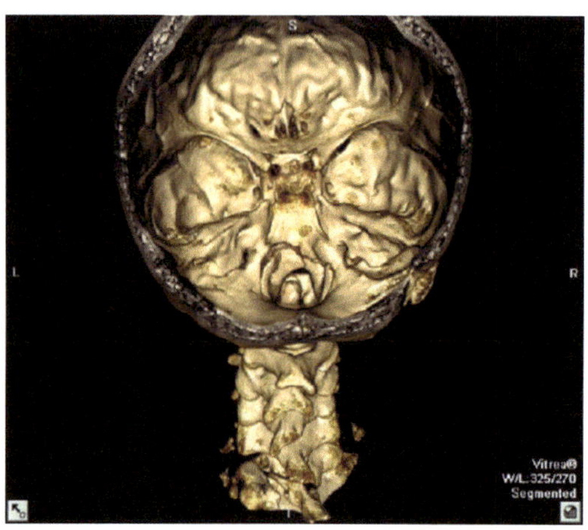

Figure 11.10 Three-dimensional reconstruction image showing a typical ring fracture surrounding the foramen magnum.

were 13 fractures to the femur and 11 tibial/fibular fractures. Compression fractures to the spine were seen in eight patients. The distribution of visceral injuries and fractures and the probability of survival appeared to be associated with the mode of entry into the water. Entering the water feet first allows a longer time for deceleration and thus decreased the deceleration forces applied to the thoracic and abdominal viscera. Skull fractures are an uncommon injury in falls from a significant height into water. A single case of base of skull fracture and a second case of depressed skull fracture were seen in a group of 65 individuals who jumped from the Bosphorus Bridge in Istanbul, Turkey [20]. Interestingly there were two cases of hyoid bone fracture also noted in the cases.

Clearly, the CT is an excellent tool to demonstrate the pattern of fractures in medicolegal cases in deaths from a fall. However, one should have a very low threshold to perform a conventional autopsy examination in a case of death from an unwitnessed fall from a height into water.

Case Study 1

A 63-year-old man was witnessed driving his car to a multilevel suburban parking lot, exiting his vehicle, then jumping approximately 20 m to the concrete footpath below. He had previously stated to his wife he would kill himself at that site. The deceased's body was taken to the VIFM for medicolegal examination.

The external examination showed an abrasion and laceration to the occiput, a parchment-like abrasion to the left lateral chest, an abrasion to the posterior aspect of the left elbow, and multiple bruises and abrasions to the lower limbs.

The postmortem CT images showed fluid within the left and right hemothoraces with Hounsfield units consistent with blood (Figure 11.11a). The images of the lower limbs showed fractures consistent with severe axial loading. (Figure 11.11b,c,d). Axial CT images of the chest showed a fracture to the left scapula (Figure 11.11e). The CT scans of the head showed a flattened, depressed, comminuted fracture to the occiput (Figure 11.11f,g).

The cause of death was issued as multiple injuries in a fall. The manner of death was deemed to be suicide. The combination of the external examination and CT findings suggested the deceased had landed onto his legs and subsequently onto the left aspect of his back and to the back of his head. The coroner accepted the cause of death and did not direct any further examination of the deceased's body.

Case Study 2

A 33-year-old man was witnessed to be pacing around levels nine and ten of a city parking lot. A witness notified police. When the police attended a short time later the man was discovered deceased on the ground at the rear of the parking lot. An examination of the scene indicated the deceased had struck an adjacent fence before hitting the ground. A suicide note was located in a backpack that was found on the ninth floor of the parking lot. The deceased's body was taken to the VIFM for medicolegal examination.

The external examination showed flattening of the forehead with underlying palpable fractures. There were associated abrasions and splitting-type lacerations to the skin of the forehead. There was a fractured nose and fractured middle third of face. A laceration measuring 15 cm was noted to the left abdomen and left flank. There was an extensive abrasion seen to the lower chest with a well-defined upper margin. There was a fracture dislocation to the left wrist.

The CT images showed a severe comminuted fracture involving the face and head (Figure 11.12a). The images clearly showed there was no evidence of primary impact to the back of the head (Figure 11.12b). The sagittal images of the body showed a fractured sternum with wide separation of the fractured edges (Figure 11.12c). There were multiple spinous process fractures (Figure 11.12d).

The cause of death was issued as multiple injuries in a fall. The manner of death was deemed to be suicide. The coroner accepted the cause of death and did not direct any further examination of the deceased's body.

Taking the scene information, the external examination findings, and the CT findings into account it seemed reasonable to suggest that the deceased had struck the fence to his left abdomen/flank, resulting in extreme and rapid flexion around this point, and causing an indirect fracture to the sternum and avulsion fractures to the spinous processes. He then struck the ground face first resulting in severe facial and skull fractures.

Can the Distribution of Injuries Be an Indicator of the Manner of Death?

The distribution of injuries sustained in a fall has been suggested as a means to differentiate between cases of accident, suicide, and homicide. It has been reported that those who jump from a high building tend to fall feet first, whereas accidental falls result in a slightly higher incidence of head injuries. An experiment that studied the alignment of a body during a fall was performed to provide some insight into the influence of behavior on freefalls [21]. The premise of the paper was based on the idea that conscious falling victims will attempt to right themselves prior to impact. If one can establish the final orientation of a motionless body during a fall

(a) (b) (c) (d)

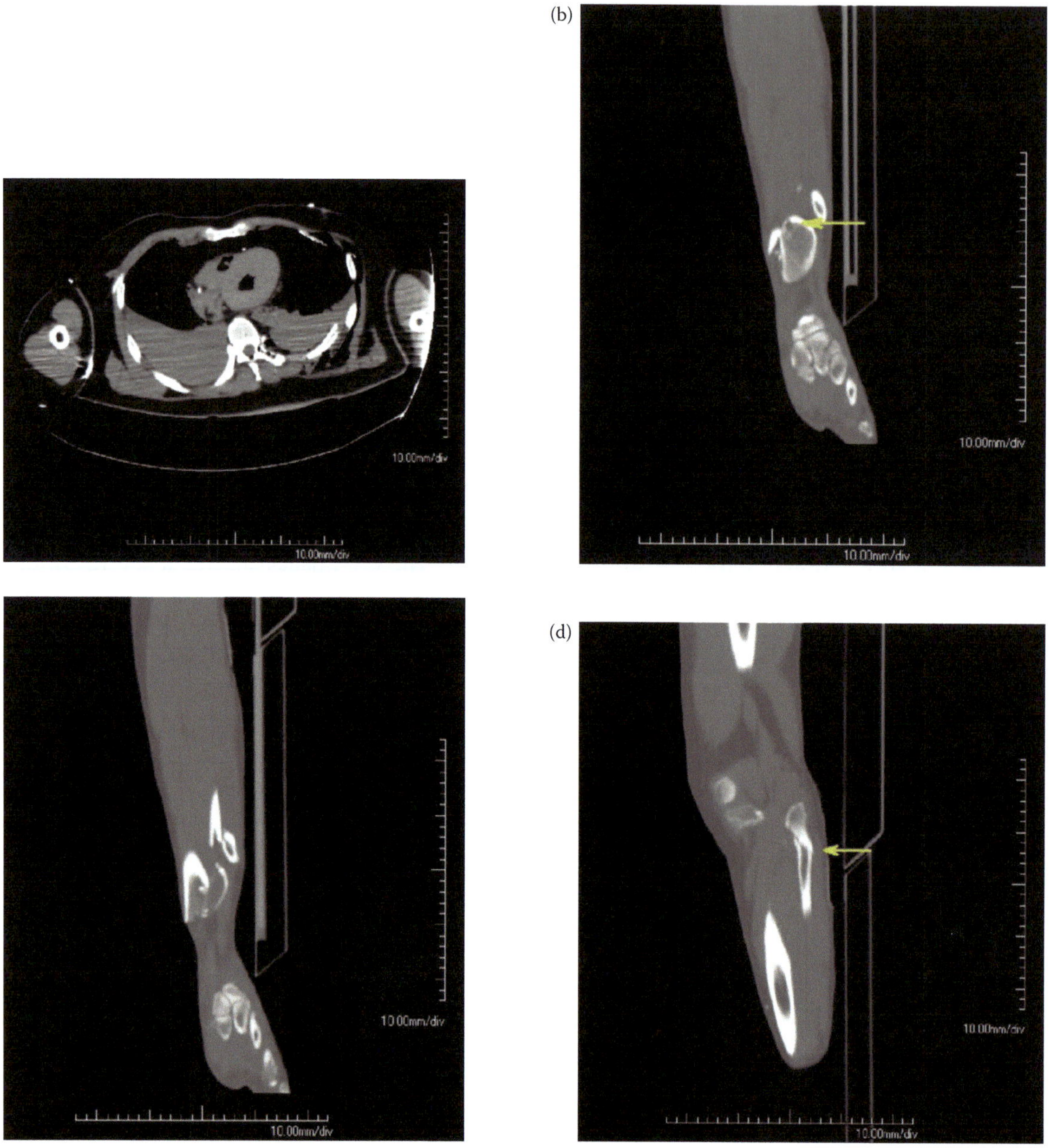

Figure 11.11 (a) Axial CT of the chest showing bilateral hemothoraces. (b) Coronal CT showing a longitudinal fracture to the left tibia. (c) Coronal CT showing fractures to the distal left tibia and fibula. (d) Coronal CT showing a fracture to the neck of the fibula.

from various starting positions, then one may be able to ascertain whether an active falling person can influence his or her falling orientation. It was suggested that this information may shed light on whether a victim was deceased before being thrown form a building or even the mental state of a suicide victim.

The study was carried out using an anthropomorphic dummy that was dropped nine times from a height of 22.62 m in three distinct initial positions. The positions were feet first, prone, and head first. From each of the three starting positions the final impact was in a prone position. The dummy attained a horizontal position approximately 15.24 m into the fall [21]. As noted by the author, although the findings are interesting, one cannot extrapolate this data directly to individual cases due to the small number of the experiments, undoubted differences between the dummy model and actual victims, and the presence of initial angular velocities during the vast majority of real-life falls from a height.

The pattern of injuries seen in those who jump from buildings as opposed to those who suffered a fall was investigated in a recent clinical study [22]. The study population

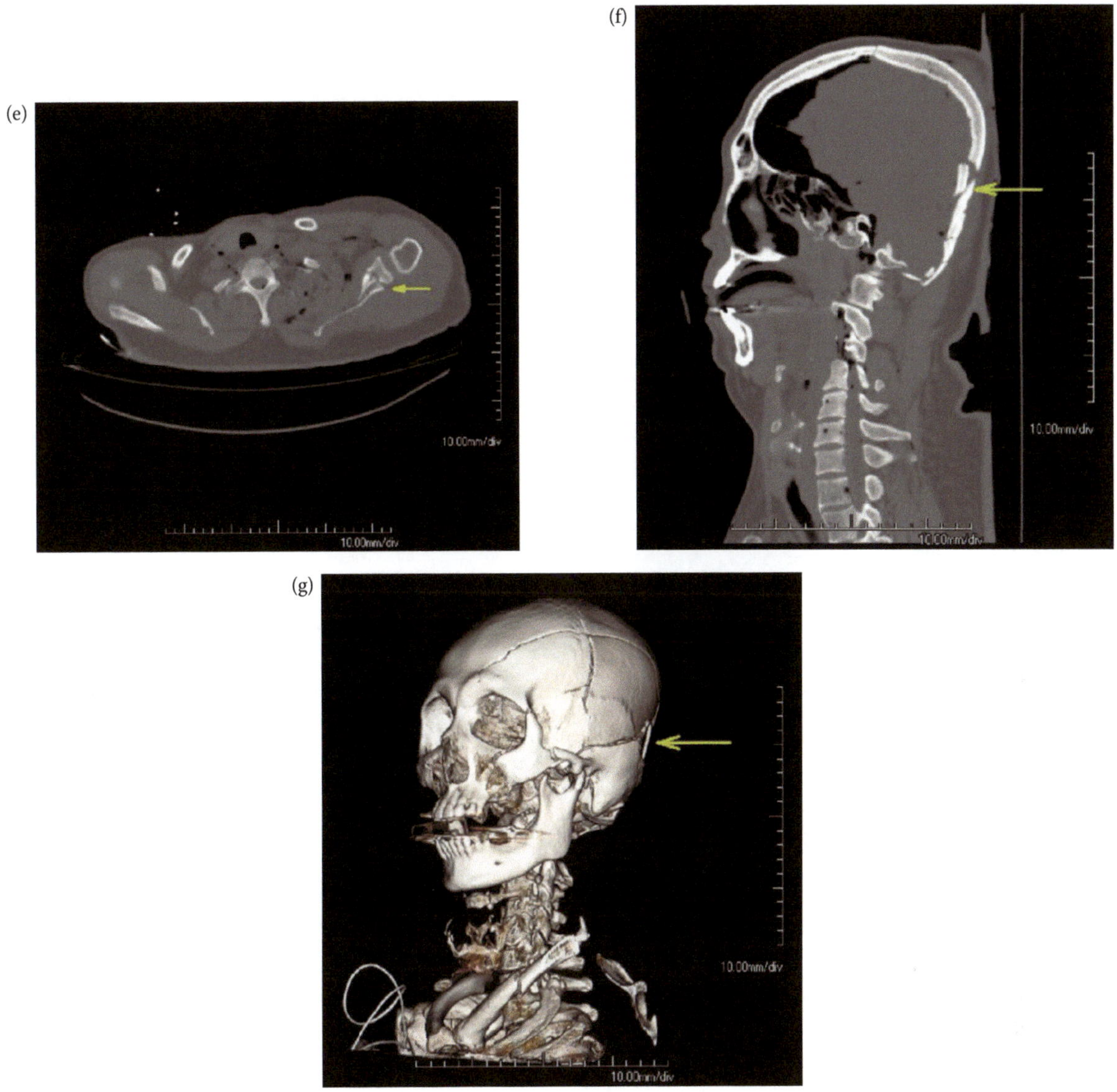

Figure 11.11 (Continued) (e) Axial CT of the chest showing a fracture to the left scapula. (f) Sagittal CT of the head showing a comminuted fracture to the occiput. A fractured segment of bone showing beveling is internally displaced. (g) Three-dimensional reconstruction image of the head showing flattening to the left posterior aspect of the skull. There is an associated zygomaticomaxillary (tripod) fracture.

comprised 342 patients who suffered injuries in falls and 57 who sustained injuries in suicide attempts and were admitted via helicopter emergency medical service to a major teaching hospital. The study showed that those who sustained injuries from jumping had a higher ISS and death rate, and larger number of fractures per person. The mean height of the fall was almost doubled in jumpers as opposed to fallers. Significantly more cervical spine injuries were seen in fallers as opposed to jumpers. Spinal cord injuries were common in the lumbar region among jumpers, whereas those who had fallen had a predominance of thoracolumbar fractures and cervical fractures. Significantly more jumpers had compression or burst thoracic vertebral fractures as opposed to fallers. Pelvic fractures occurred more frequently in those who had jumped.

A further clinical study of 101 individuals who had fallen from a significant height and survived to the hospital was performed by Richter et al. [23]. The patients included 62 accidental falls and 39 falls from a suicide attempt. The average height of the fall was 7.2 m. The most common site of injury was to the thoracic and lumbar spine (83%) and especially the thoracolumbar region. Injuries to the limbs mainly involved the metaphyseal and epiphyseal parts of long bones and distal joints. Fractures of the diaphysis and proximal joints such as the shoulder, humerus, hip, and femur were rare. Fractures of the calcaneus, ankles, and shafts of long bones were all seen more frequently in those who had jumped from a height as opposed to those who had fallen. Only 5% of those who had fallen had a calcaneal fracture. Overall,

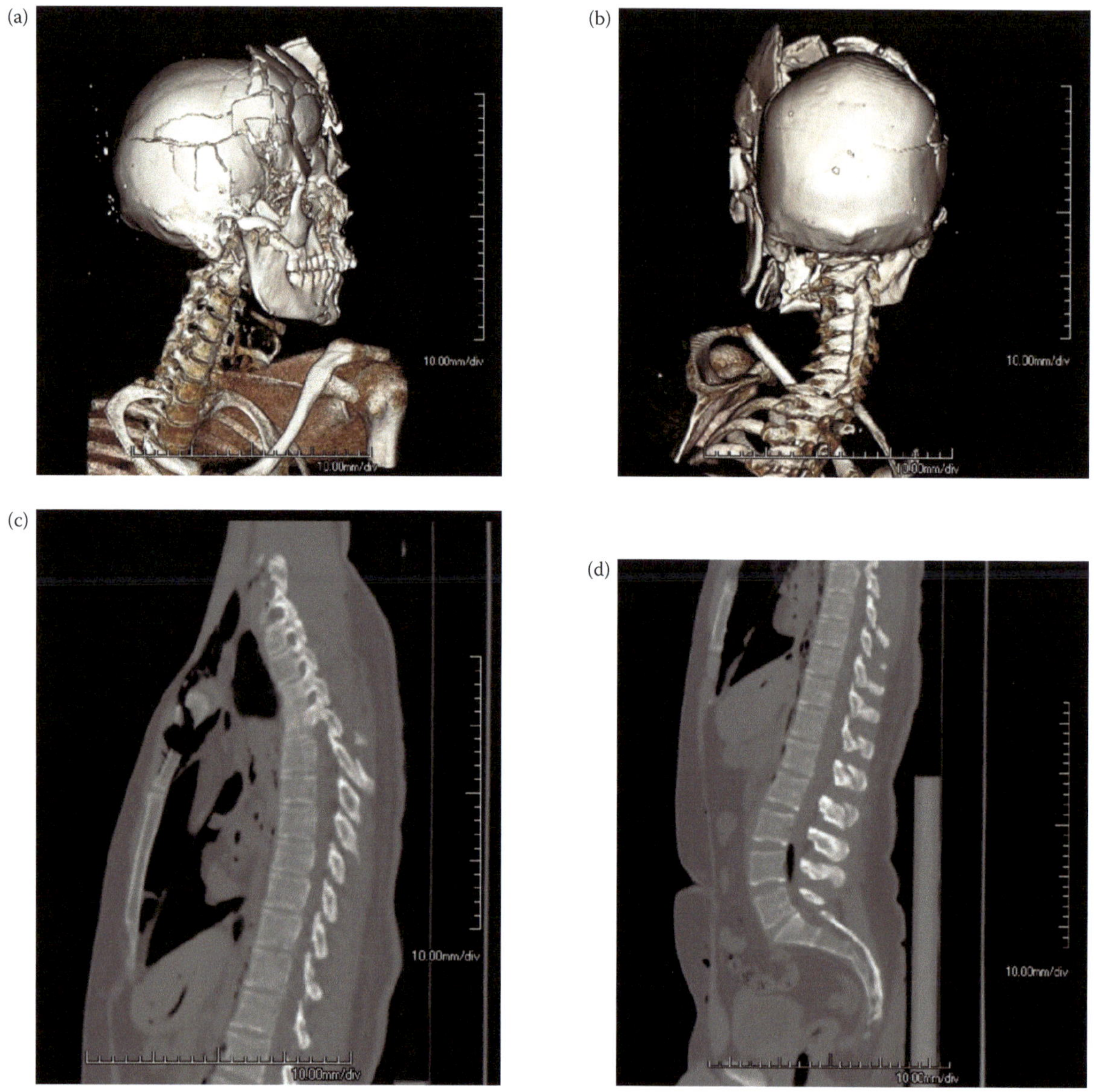

Figure 11.12 (a) Three-dimensional reconstruction image of the head showing a severe comminuted fracture to the face and skull. (b) Three-dimensional reconstruction image shows no suggestion of primary occipital impact in the fall. (c) Sagittal CT image of the chest showing a fractured sternum. (d) Sagittal CT image showing multiple fractures to the vertebral spinous processes.

this finding is consistent with the commonly held view that those who jump from a height tend to land on their feet.

A study using multidetector computed tomography (MDCT) imaging of facial trauma to investigate accidental falls from a height showed that LeFort II and III fractures, frontal bone fractures, and fractures of the base of the skull occur more frequently with increasing distance fallen [24]. An interesting observation was that zygomatic and nasal bone fractures rarely occurred in isolation. The presence of an isolated fracture to the zygoma or nose in such circumstances should raise the possibility of an assault associated with the incident. These cases should proceed to full autopsy examination.

Although such studies are of interest and provide an insight to the types of injuries to be expected in such cases, the medicolegal management of a given case is more dependent on the complete circumstances of the death, an accurate scene examination, and careful external examination by a forensic pathologist.

Pediatric Falls

Falls are a major cause of injury in the pediatric population. Babies may fall from the arms of parents and carers, or from changing tables and beds. Toddler falls primarily occur while walking. In older children fall-related injuries are particularly associated with recreational and sporting activities. It is generally accepted that short distance falls in the pediatric population do not result in a life-threatening injury in the vast majority of cases. The definition of a short fall varies among different studies, though 10 feet appears to be an average height.

Studies on Pediatric Falls

A prospective clinical study of children aged 24 months or younger who had suffered a fall and were presented to an emergency department in 2003 was reported in the emergency medicine literature [25]. Sixty-three cases were identified. The median height of the fall was 48 cm. Not surprisingly a significant correlation was found between the height of the fall and the incidence of injury. A fracture requiring manipulation under anesthesia or admission to the hospital occurred in falls over 56 cm. The authors stated that "significant injury presenting with falls of less than 50 cm should be critically evaluated."

Accidental falls resulting in head injuries were investigated in a clinical study on children under five years of age who were presented to an accident and emergency department over an 18-month period [26]. Seventy-two cases were identified. In these cases there were three instances of linear parietal fracture. Two of the cases involved falls of just over 1 m and the third was from 80 to 90 cm to a hard-edged surface. A single base of skull fracture resulted from a 3 m fall from a balcony. There were no deaths described in the series of cases.

Falls resulting in pediatric cervical spine fractures were investigated in a retrospective review of children six years of age or less and involving falls of less than 5 feet [27]. Eight children aged between 9 and 68 months were found to have suffered cervical spine injury. There were three cases with rotary subluxation of C1, three cases of subluxation between C1 and C2 (one with a fractured odontoid), and two cases of a fractured C2. No deaths were found among the cases.

A literature review study investigated the risk of death in short falls (<1.5 m) in children less than five years of age [28]. A wide range of book chapters, databases, peer-reviewed papers, and medical society papers were reviewed. It was estimated that "the current mortality rate for short falls affecting infants and young children is <0.48 deaths per one million young children per year." A further retrospective study on falls in the pediatric population described 336 high level falls and 393 low level falls [29]. A low level fall was defined as below 15 feet. The mortality rates were 2.4% for high falls and 1.0% for low falls. All four deceased patients suffered head injuries.

A review of the United States Consumer Product Safety Commission database for head injury between January 1, 1988, and June 30, 1999, was also reported, in part, to determine the potential lethality of a short distance fall in infants and young children [30]. The youngest child was 12 months old and the oldest was 13 years old. Of 18 cases of falls from 0.6 to 3 m, 12 were witnessed by noncaregivers. The author concluded that an infant or child might suffer a lethal head injury from a fall of less than 3 m. This view was challenged in a number of letters to the journal.

There would appear to be little doubt that short distance falls are relatively common events and the overwhelming majority of the cases result in nonlethal injuries. A death from a short distance fall is a rare occurrence. However, relatively recent forensic experience has shown that providing the courts with estimates of the probability of death is injudicious. The issue is not the frequency of an injury or death in the population, but the particular injury or the death of the child in question.

Pediatric Falls Down Stairs

Falls down stairs are a common cause of injury in toddlers and young children. Falls down stairs are also used frequently as an explanation for serious nonaccidental injuries and deaths in the pediatric population.

It is generally accepted that simple falls down stairs rarely cause serious injury in children. A prospective study on 69 children with a median age of two years showed injuries to the head and neck occurred in 90% of the cases, injuries to the trunk occurred in 4% of cases, and injuries to the extremities occurred in 6% of the cases [31]. The majority of the injuries comprised abrasions and bruises. However, there were five skull fractures and two fractures of the axis. Importantly, there were no fatalities and injuries did not occur to more than one body region in any case.

A further study on 363 consecutive patients presenting to a pediatric emergency department showed that the most common injuries in stairway falls were head and neck injuries [32]. These occurred in 73% of cases. Extremity injuries were found in 28% of cases, whereas injury to the trunk was very uncommon and occurred in only 2% of cases. Extremity injuries were predominantly to the distal aspect of the limbs. Further important observations included the fact that children were no more likely to suffer significant injury if their fall was more than four steps, and that injury to more than one body part occurred in only 2.7% of cases. Only 3% of the children required admission to hospital. No child was admitted to the intensive care unit and there were no deaths.

Baby Walker–Related Falls

Baby walker–related falls are very common. It has been estimated that over 20,000 children are treated annually in United States hospital emergency departments because of baby walker–related incidents. The majority of these injuries comprise minor bruises and abrasions.

In a retrospective study of 271 children treated at a children's hospital emergency department for baby walker–related injury, the overwhelming majority of the injuries occurred because of falls down stairs (95.9%) [33]. There were 26 patients with skull fractures. There were 17 parietal fractures, 8 frontal fractures, and 1 occipital fracture. There were three children who suffered a depressed skull fracture. Two of these children had a second nondepressed fracture. Three of the children had intracranial hemorrhage. Although a number of the children required admission to the intensive care unit, there were no deaths. The other fractures described in the report were three clavicular fractures, and a single child with a fracture of the ulna and radius.

Falls down stairs that occur with the child in a carer's arms can markedly increase the amount of force applied to the child. As these scenarios may well be quite complex, there is a greater possibility of fracture and significant injury.

Child Abuse

The examination of a deceased child, infant, or baby is one of the most difficult challenges for the forensic pathologist. These cases can show a paucity of findings; may generate considerable media interest; and the report is likely to be carefully scrutinized by other pathologists, legal teams involved in the case, and the courts. The postmortem CT is used in conjunction with a skeletal radiographic survey to identify and document any fractures. The CT may also reveal the presence of suspicious intracranial hemorrhage or hemoperitoneum, which may stimulate an early homicide investigation (Figure 11.13a,b,c,d).

Cause of Death

The most common cause of pediatric nonaccidental death is head injury. Less common causes of death include abdominal and chest injury. Occult causes of death such as smothering may leave no discernable injury, though a close inspection of the mouth may reveal subtle injuries to the buccal mucosa [34].

The mechanism of death in cases of head injury is controversial. In 1962 Kempe and colleagues published an article titled "The Battered-Child Syndrome" [35]. In 1974 Caffey published a paper describing the "whiplash shaken infant syndrome" [36]. The classic triad used in the diagnosis of the (whiplash) shaken baby syndrome is subdural hemorrhage, retinal hemorrhage, and encephalopathy. The subdural hemorrhage is typically a thin film of blood over the cerebral hemispheres, which does not represent a significant space-occupying lesion.

Since this time there has been considerable discussion in the literature with respect to the specificity of the triad of clinical and pathological signs, and the mechanism of the injury. A particular issue in the pathogenesis of the injury is whether the application of blunt force is required to produce the intracranial injuries. The term "shaken impact syndrome" was coined to denote the involvement of blunt force injury to the head in such cases [37].

The core of the controversy resides in the absence of objective autopsy evidence of impact injury to the head. Although an extra-axial collection or brain injury is usually associated with a cutaneous or subcutaneous scalp bruise, most forensic pathologists have practical experience of cases with significant intracranial pathology and no objective evidence of a primary impact site. Gilliland and Folberg's paper describing 80 cases of fatal pediatric head injury found no scalp or skull injuries in 11% of the cases [38].

The conventional autopsy examination may require detailed examination of the cervical spine and subcutaneous dissection of the face to reveal subtle bruising to ligaments, muscles, and the buccal mucosa from "violent" shaking or smothering.

Fractures

Following soft tissue injuries such as bruises, the next most frequent injuries leading to presentation for medical care in abused children are fractures [39]. Fractures are diagnosed in up to a third of children who are clinically investigated for abuse. Of the fractures in children less than 12 years of age caused by abuse, 80% occur in those less than 18 months of age [40]. The vast majority of fractures sustained by children over 5 years of age are the result of accidents due to falls, motor vehicle incidents, and sporting injuries.

The clinical circumstances with regard to the causation of the injury are very important in the correct resolution of the case. A parent or other carer who is present at the time of an assault that leads to a fracture or death may either deny any knowledge of the event or attempt to cloud the facts of the incident. Not uncommonly the reported circumstances of the incident contain some element of truth though the severity of the incident is downplayed. Common false histories include falls from couches, beds, and carer's arms, and falls down stairs.

It is vitally important to have an open mind when comparing the type of pediatric fracture with the

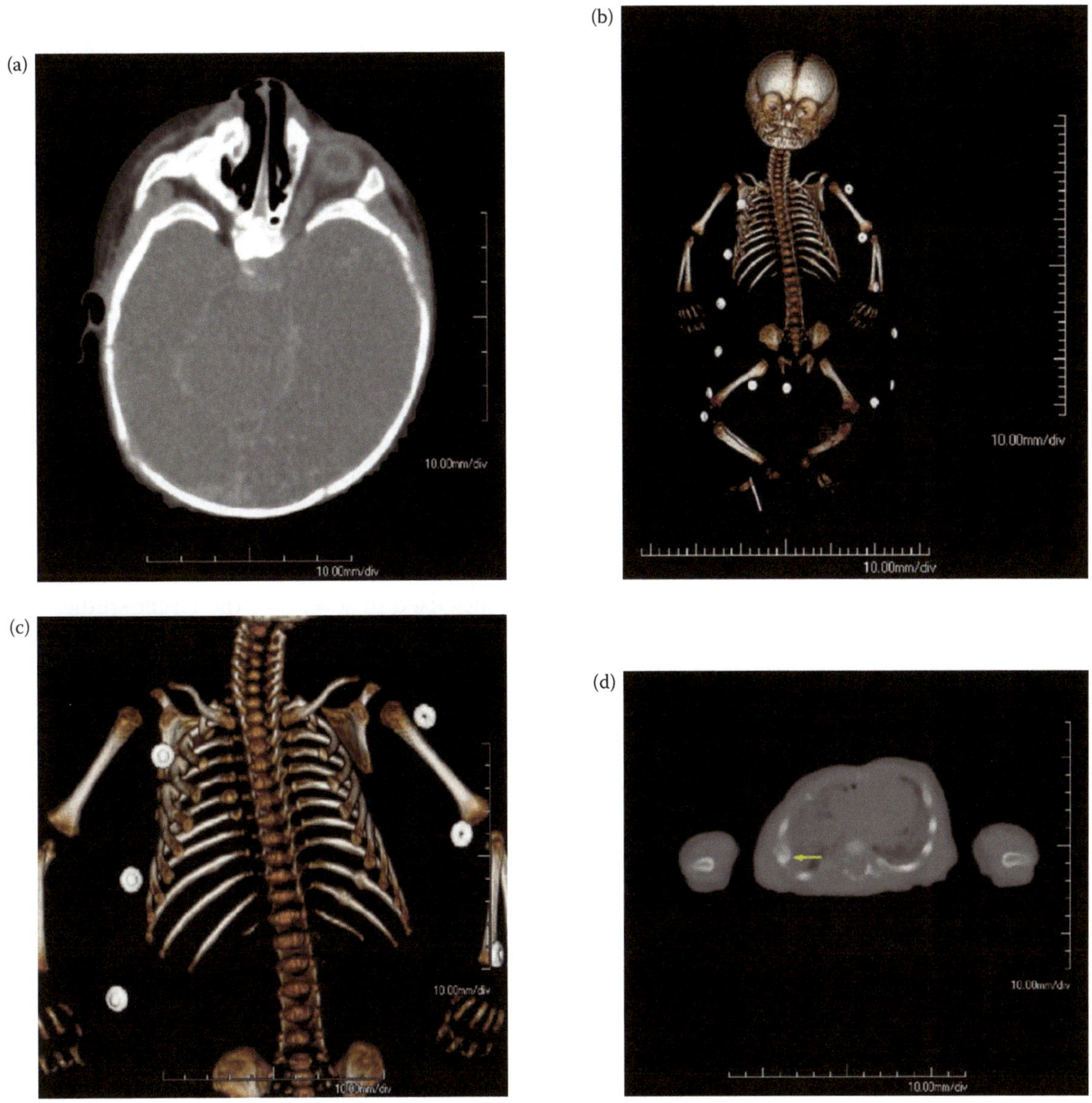

Figure 11.13 (a) Axial CT showing mild patchy subarachnoid hemorrhage in a baby found "collapsed" in his cot. (b) Overall skeletal view showing multiple healing fractured ribs. (c) Close-up of healing fractured ribs. (d) Axial CT showing healing fractured rib.

suggested mechanism of injury. This was illustrated in a case report that described a spiral fracture of the humerus in an infant [41]. The fracture was said to have occurred when an older sibling rolled the infant over. One can imagine a significant proportion of the forensic medical community, police, and laypersons to be extremely skeptical of this scenario. However, the incident was in fact captured on a family video and shown to be true.

Forensic Significance of Fractures

Fractures are a concrete, objective indication of the application of force to a bone. Although some fractures are seen commonly in child abuse, the presence of any particular fracture is not pathognomonic of nonaccidental injury. In the setting of a particular fracture(s) the question to be asked is whether the mechanism of the fracture as put forward by the caregiver is consistent with the known biomechanics of the injury. The issue was summarized by Pierce et al., who declared that the particular fracture must be interpreted with respect to "that specific bone and location in that age-specific child" [42].

The buckle (torus) fracture is typically caused by axial loading. The proposed mechanism of the injury should reflect this. A fracture to the metaphyseal region of a long bone is not generally associated with direct trauma to the bone but from abnormal movement around a joint typically caused by a whiplash-like movement. This is most commonly caused by a shaking or pulling action [43]. A spiral fracture in a long bone raises the possibility of a twisting force to the lower limb of a nonambulatory infant but may be explained by a fall (with rotation) in a toddler. A fracture to the diaphysis of a long bone requires a significant amount of force and the suggested mechanism of the fracture must reflect this. The presence of fractures to the costovertebral aspect of the ribs suggests a fulcrum movement over the transverse process of the vertebral body and is not explained by a simple fall.

Kleinman et al., when dealing with possible clinical cases of child abuse, stated that there are three crucial issues to be addressed [45]:

- How many injuries (fractures) are present?
- What is the specificity of the fracture for abuse?
- How old are the fractures?

Number of Fractures The number of fractures that are present should be recorded using appropriate pediatric skeletal surveys. The use of CT in the diagnosis of child abuse has not been confirmed in the peer-reviewed clinical or forensic literature. Conventional radiographic skeletal surveys are established and there is currently no literature to support a proposition to change to routine CT. Interestingly though, a preliminary study on pediatric rib fractures has suggested CT may be superior to conventional radiology in the detection of rib fractures [44].

The most commonly fractured bones resulting from abuse are the ribs, skull, and long bones. It should be remembered that fractures of the skull are the most common type of fracture leading to hospital admission in babies, and the majority of these cases are accidental in origin.

An interesting issue for forensic pathologists is highlighted in a clinical paper that detailed follow-up skeletal surveys in cases of suspected child abuse [45]. Twenty-three infants and toddlers who were strongly suspected of child abuse were reexamined about two weeks after their initial radiological examination. The number of definite fractures increased from 70 to 89. Thirteen of these additional fractures had not been detected on the first examination. Eight of these involved the ribs.

A recent paper described an autopsy technique for the demonstration of skeletal fractures in infants [46]. It was noted that skeletal injuries might be occult to both radiologic and standard autopsy examination. The technique requires extensive reflection of skeletal muscles to expose bones and joints *in situ*, and was recommended for cases where there is suspicion of nonaccidental injury.

Specificity of Fractures The issue of specificity can be the most difficult question for the pathologist to answer. The case of a pediatric death involving multiple cutaneous bruises, with multiple fractures of varying age, subdural hemorrhage, and retinal hemorrhages is not a major diagnostic challenge. However, the case of a fatal head injury associated with a linear skull, which is said to have occurred when a baby was accidentally dropped onto an uncarpeted floor from the arms of a carer who was in a standing position, is a problem.

Kemp et al. reviewed 32 published studies on pediatric fractures caused by accidental and nonaccidental injury to calculate a probability of nonaccidental injury for individual fracture types [54]. Not surprisingly the authors were challenged by a number of issues in comparing the studies including "a high degree of heterogeneity between studies," the retrospective nature of the reports, and absence of detail on the radiological techniques used in several of the larger studies. The review found that multiple fractures were more common in cases of abuse and, once major trauma is excluded, rib fractures have the highest probability for abuse. It was concluded that "when infants and toddlers present with a fracture in the absence of a confirmed cause, physical abuse must be considered as a potential cause," but "no fracture, on its own, can distinguish an abusive from a non-abusive cause."

Skull Fractures A simple childhood fall that causes a skull fracture will generally result in a simple linear fracture that is usually to the temporoparietal region (Figure 11.14). It has been estimated that in 2% to 3% of childhood falls that result in significant blunt trauma to the head, there will be a simple linear fracture. In the majority of these cases there is no intracranial hemorrhage or neurological deficit [47].

A clinical study reported an increased percentage of skull fractures in an abused group compared to the accidental group with "a tendency toward more diastatic and multiple skull fractures" in the abused group [48]. Conversely, two other studies did not demonstrate any significant difference in the prevalence of these fractures in abused or nonabused children [49,50].

Other features that may raise the possibility of nonaccidental injury to the head include depressed fractures and fractures to the base of the skull. Although more than one skull fracture is highly suggestive of nonaccidental injury, the experimental work on the mechanism of skull fractures by Lissner and Gurdjian and others, albeit using adult skulls, raises the possibility that a single impact results in in-bending and out-bending of the calvarium could theoretically lead to two separate fractures in a single skull bone. However, we know that

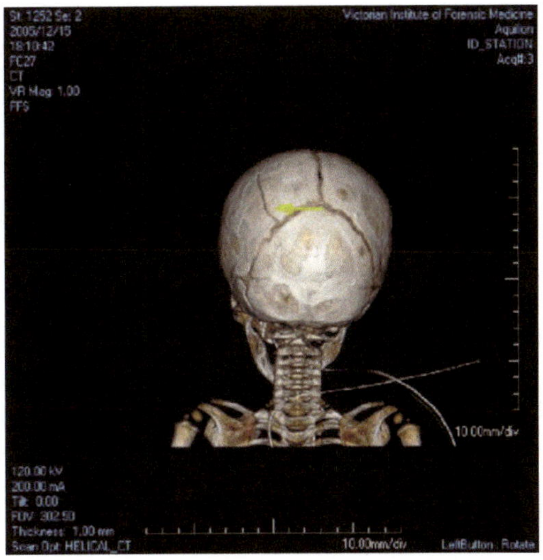

Figure 11.14 Three-dimensional reconstruction image showing a healing linear fracture to the left parietal bone in an infant.

the pediatric skull does not behave biomechanically in an identical manner to the adult skull. This difference in behavior would be increased by the presence of fontanels and unfused sutures.

The conventional autopsy examination allows for inspection of the scalp and subgaleal soft tissues, which can provide objective evidence of two or more separate sites of blunt force trauma.

Rib Fractures Fractures to the ribs are commonly seen in nonaccidental pediatric deaths. These are typically located within the posterior aspect of the ribs adjacent to the costovertebral junction (Figure 11.15). The classical mechanism of this nonaccidental injury is from grasping the infant between both hands, with the thumbs over the sternum and fingers over the posterior aspect of the chest. There may be pure squeezing of the chest or the chest compression may be combined with shaking.

It may be suggested that acute rib fractures have resulted from cardiopulmonary resuscitation. The weight of opinion in the pediatric and forensic literature is that rib fractures from resuscitation are rare, and when they occur they tend to involve the anterior aspect of the ribs [51].

Long Bone Fractures Metaphyseal (bucket handle) fractures are traditionally viewed as being highly suggestive of nonaccidental injury. These and spiral fractures of long bones are suggestive of a twisting mechanism to the limb. Dislocation of the radial head is suspicious of nonaccidental mechanism if a grasping, pulling-type injury to the arm is not volunteered by the parent or carer.

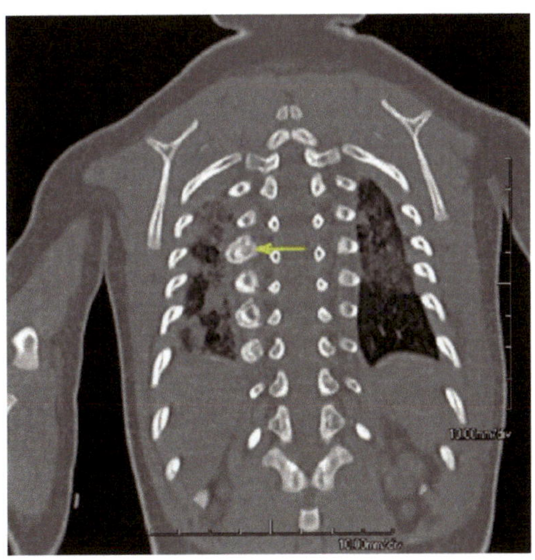

Figure 11.15 Coronal CT showing multiple healing fractures to the posterior aspect of the ribs in a case of abuse.

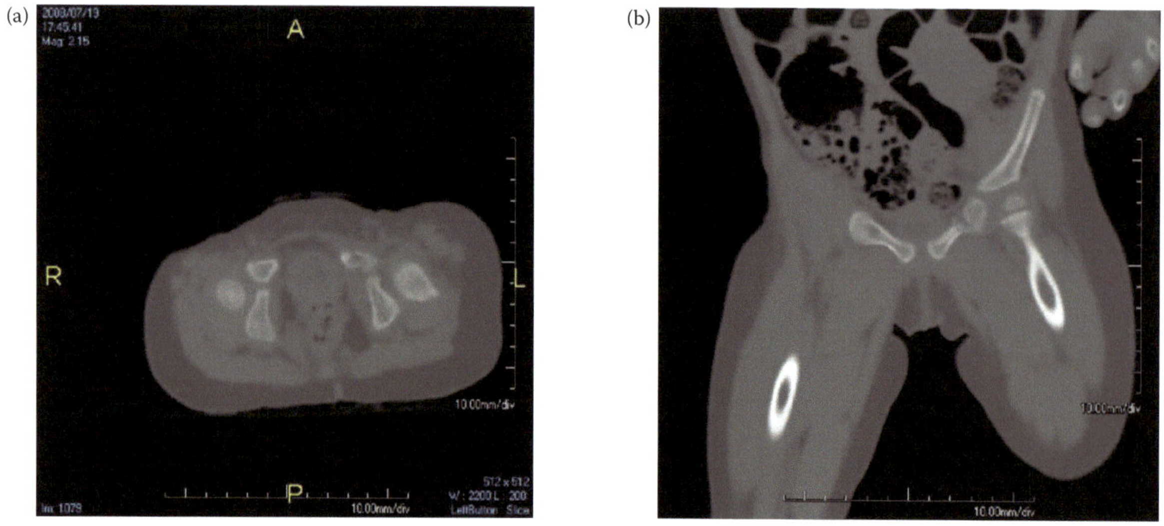

Figure 11.16 (a) Axial CT showing a fracture to the left superior pubic ramus. The fracture was not palpable beneath an overlying hematoma. (b) Coronal CT showing a left superior pubic ramus fracture.

Spinal and Pelvic Fractures Thoracolumbar fracture with listhesis is an uncommon but important sign that is suggestive of nonaccidental injury [52]. The degree of forward slippage of one vertebra over another can range from slight up to frank dislocation.

Pelvic fractures are rare in the pediatric population outside of motor vehicle incidents or sporting injuries in adolescence. Pelvic fractures have been described in cases of abuse (Figure 11.16a,b) [53].

Subtle Fractures in Child Abuse Fractures to the hands and feet, in the absence of a clear history of suitable trauma, are said to be strongly associated with abuse [55]. In some cases fractures to the hands and feet may be the only sign of nonaccidental injury. A retrospective study of radiographs of the hands and feet of 11 abused infants showed 6 infants with fractures of the hand and 5 infants with fractures of the feet [55]. Seven of the patients also had fractures involving long bones of the upper or lower limb. Separate oblique radiographs of the hands and feet were performed in each case. The fractures involved the proximal phalanges and metacarpals of the hands, and one fracture to a proximal phalanx and six metatarsal fractures. Torus fractures predominated in the series of cases. Other subtle fractures that may need to be specifically looked for in assessing skeletal survey or CT images involve the spinous processes and the sacrum [56,57].

Aging of Fractures A crucial issue in the medicolegal investigation of deaths from child abuse is the demonstration that injuries have occurred at different times. There may be issues concerning a suspect's access to the deceased during a certain period of time. Histological examination of tissue taken at postmortem examination is the gold standard technique used in this process. Evidence of the healing process is relatively straightforward and a range of time from the infliction of the injury to death can be offered. This time range is by necessity quite broad.

Can Radiology Assist in Aging Fractures? A paper addressing the issue of dating fractures using radiology studied 141 children aged from 1 to 17 years. The study involved 707 radiographs collected over a four-year period [58]. There were 131 radial fractures and 74 ulna fractures that were immobilized in a plaster cast upon diagnosis of the injury. Over half of the fractures were diaphyseal. It was determined that a periosteal reaction could be seen at 4 weeks, and calcification of the callus was such that it had at least the same density as the cortex 10 weeks after the onset of the injury. However, the authors cautioned that "a wide variation exists in the appearance and duration of the radiographic signs of healing." Furthermore, as was mentioned by the authors, abused pediatric victims invariably do not have their fractures immobilized, which in turn would change the radiological signs of healing.

Differential Diagnosis of Multiple Fractures

Although quite uncommon, a number of natural disease processes may mimic child abuse. It is important that these conditions are diagnosed so that the family of a deceased child with multiple fractures is not falsely accused. Of course one must keep in mind that a child with a metabolic condition that predisposes to fracture can also be subjected to abuse. The conditions of interest include osteogenesis imperfecta, prematurity, rickets, copper deficiency, and other rare metabolic conditions.

Osteogenesis imperfecta is a diverse bony dysplasia that results from mutations in the genes that code for type 1 collagen [59]. The phenotypic expression of the disease can be quite varied. The classical blue sclera may not be present and this finding may also be seen in normal children. The diagnosis can be suggested on CT by the presence of Wormian bones in the cranium. Wormian bones are extra pieces of bone that are present within sutures, most commonly the lambdoid suture. A research paper compared the incidence of Wormian bones in 81 cases of osteogenesis imperfecta and 500 skull radiographs from normal children [60]. All of the cases of osteogenesis imperfecta showed Wormian bones, whereas none of the normal children were found to have a Wormian bone on their skull radiograph.

The diagnosis of osteogenesis imperfecta may be made on fibroblast culture following skin biopsy. The diagnosis can be confirmed in most, but not all cases. Severely affected individuals will have a mutation sequenced to the *COLA1A* and *COLA2A* genes. Mildly affected individuals may not have a demonstrable abnormality, and about 5% of normal children can be shown to have a genetic sequence variation [61].

Osteopenia of prematurity is a well-recognized disorder that appears to have multiple underlying factors. Fractures, when they occur, are often seen in the first year of life, and most are seen below the age of three years [62]. The abnormality does not extend into childhood.

Rickets is caused by vitamin D deficiency, and rarely from abnormal metabolism of vitamin D or inorganic phosphate with resultant decreased mineralization at the growth plate. Solely breast-fed infants are at higher risk. Features on radiological examination that suggest the diagnosis are cupping and fraying of the metaphyseal regions of the bones. Involvement of the costochondral junction causes the classic rachitic rosary. The long bones show osteomalacia with associated greenstick fractures and bowing. A clinical serum test can be performed for vitamin D metabolites that are decreased in affected patients.

Copper deficiency is rare. It may be seen in preterm infants as a functional problem associated with rapid growth. There are usually allied radiographic abnormalities including osteopenia, symmetrical sickle-shaped cupping and fraying of the metaphyses, and subperiosteal new bone formation [63].

Other rare conditions that can present with multiple fractures include Menkes syndrome (kinky hair syndrome), chronic kidney disease, and prolonged use of certain therapeutic medications [59].

A controversial hypothesized condition that has been reported in the pediatric literature is "temporary brittle bone disease." This condition has been suggested as a cause of transient vulnerability to fracture in infants' bones. Most pediatricians and forensic pathologists would be wary of a condition that is presented to explain fractures in babies and infants when there is no defined pathology. A report on five infants where at least some fractures occurred in the hospital has been suggested as evidence of the existence of the disorder [64].

Birth Injury

The incidence of skull fractures have been reported to occur in 2.9% of birth-injured babies [65]. These fractures are usually simple linear fractures involving the parietal bone and are generally asymptomatic [66]. These injuries are typically seen in association with instrumentation, but have been reported following otherwise routine vaginal deliveries [67]. Although depressed skull fractures are also usually seen in association with forceps deliveries, some have also been described in normal vaginal delivery. A study on 68 newborns with depressed skull fractures revealed that 18 of the cases were not associated with instrumentation [68].

Occipital osteodiastasis refers to disconnection of the squamous and lateral parts of the occipital bone [69]. Anterior and superior displacement of the squamous portion of the occipital bone, as may occur during a breech delivery, can lead to fatal brainstem and dural injury.

Healing of a birth-related skull fracture is seen as calcification on radiological studies by 7 days of life [70]. It has been reported that if healing is not demonstrable radiographically by 11 days of life then an injury that occurred after birth must be considered.

Transportation Incidents

The medicolegal investigation of transportation incidents covers a wide range of situations including deaths associated with various motor vehicles, motorcycles, and various types of aircraft. Disasters resulting from a large airplane crash are naturally high profile incidents requiring complex investigation, the need for disaster victim identification, and specialized aviation medicine expertise. The majority of transportation deaths occur from collisions involving motor vehicles on metropolitan and country roads.

Transportation incidents result in the application of severe blunt force to the body, and fractures are common. The patterns of soft tissue injuries and fractures can be used to try to reconstruct the circumstances of the incident. Typical questions asked of pathologists in these cases include, but are certainly not limited to:

- The crucial issue of the cause of death.
- An opinion as to the location of a deceased individual within a motor vehicle at the time of the incident.
- An opinion as to whether an individual was incapacitated at the time of the incident.
- An opinion as to the type of vehicle that struck a pedestrian in a hit-and-run incident.
- An opinion as to the position of a pedestrian at the moment of impact by a motor vehicle.
- An opinion as to whether a pedestrian may have been assaulted prior to a motor vehicle incident.

As is regularly the case in the day-to-day practice of forensic pathology, the external examination is vital in addressing issues that are apparent at the time of the examination. The external examination should also be detailed enough so that questions that are asked some time after the incident can also be adequately addressed. The external examination should include forensic photography in cases where medicolegal issues have been raised at the initial stages of the investigation, and in those cases when it is apparent that further questions may arise in the future.

Cause of Death

It has been the general experience at the Victorian Institute of Forensic Medicine that an external examination and assessment of the CT images, when viewed in conjunction with all of the available information from police investigators, will realize a reasonable cause of death in the majority of deaths associated with motor vehicle incidents.

Deceased victims of motor vehicle trauma typically die as a consequence of blunt trauma to the body or deceleration injury. Blunt head trauma is common in deaths involving motor vehicle occupants and pedestrians. In those who succumb rapidly at the scene of an incident, the ultimate cause of death can be diffuse (axonal) brain injury, pontomedullary rent, reflex cardiac arrest secondary to impact to the medulla oblongata, and atlantooccipital dissociation. Victims of blunt head trauma in a motor vehicle incident who are initially alive at the scene but die later in the hospital before definitive treatment can be instituted may show subdural hemorrhage with mass effect, extradural hemorrhage or subarachnoid hemorrhage, and secondary hypoxic/ischemic injury to the brain. In these cases the postmortem CT scans can provide evidence that blunt trauma to the head (brain) has occurred by showing and documenting a skull fracture.

Though the presence of a skull fracture is not a cause of death per se, for the purposes of the courts the proven existence of a skull fracture in circumstances where the deceased has died as a consequence of head impact has been sufficient evidence for the courts to accept the cause of death. The cause of death is simply issued as head injury secondary to the motor vehicle collision. Although pathologists might recoil at the lack of intellectual rigor in ascribing a cause of death largely on the basis of external examination evidence of head impact and postmortem CT demonstration of a skull fracture, we have found that the prevailing attitude of the court and the community is that a full conventional autopsy is not always indicated in these circumstances.

A similar situation is seen with cases where the postmortem CT examination reveals a massive intrathoracic hemorrhage in a motor vehicle passenger involved in a collision. Following an otherwise unremarkable external examination one may infer that the most likely cause of the death is an aortic tear caused by a deceleration injury. It must be accepted that these inferences are not always going to be correct, and other causes of massive hemothorax will go undetected. The presence of this postmortem CT finding in the driver is more problematic as the hemothorax could well have resulted from rupture of a dissecting thoracic aortic aneurysm.

Each case must be assessed on its own merits. The hemothorax in a driver whose car is struck head-on by a car that was on the wrong side of the road has entirely different connotations to the same CT findings in the driver in a single-vehicle incident. There may be insurance issues resulting from the reported cause of death, and there may be significant psychological and social issues for family members.

The postmortem CT images may alter the pathologist's recommendations to the coroner in regard to the need for a full autopsy examination. For example, the presence of an atlantooccipital dissociation or fracture to the transverse process of a cervical vertebra may suggest that the origin of subarachnoid hemorrhage is most likely to be secondary to trauma. A fracture involving the vertebral foramen would be highly suggestive of a vertebral artery injury. A fracture dislocation of the atlantooccipital joint would be consistent with associated rupture of the intracranial vertebral artery. Although it is conceivable that these injuries could have occurred "perimortem" in an individual already unconscious from a primary subarachnoid bleed from a ruptured berry aneurysm, the latter scenario would seem extremely unlikely.

The demonstration of pericardial blood on the postmortem CT images of a 50-year-old man involved in a relatively low speed collision into a parked car is a good example of the issues facing the pathologist when using CT. The possible causes of the pericardial blood include, but are not limited to, aortic dissection and rupture, ruptured recent myocardial infarct, traumatic intrapericardial aortic rupture, traumatic rupture of an atrial appendage, airbag injury, and even traumatic rupture of the heart from cardiopulmonary resuscitation following collapse due to massive pulmonary thromboembolism.

In this example the requirement of the forensic pathologist to determine a reasonable cause of death is somewhat disingenuous. To issue a cause of death as simply "pericardial tamponade" does not serve the community or the practice of forensic pathology. Many of the reasons as to why an autopsy is carried out are encompassed by such a case. The decision as to whether the death is natural or accidental, the presence of a natural disease that may have caused a fatal collision, the presence of a natural disease process such as Marfan's syndrome that may have been the cause of the collision, and information that could be of vital importance to the deceased's family can all be addressed by a complete autopsy.

These types of decisions are going to become increasingly common as the use of CT imaging becomes an accepted, and expected, part of the postmortem examination. It is the duty of the forensic pathologist to lead the way in the use of postmortem CT in such cases and recommend a conventional autopsy to address issues other than simply the cause of death.

Case Study

A six-year-old boy was playing in the front yard of his home when he was struck by a motor vehicle. The driver of the vehicle was reported to have been performing burnouts in the street immediately prior to the incident. The victim was taken to the emergency department of a provincial hospital but could not be resuscitated. The death was reported to the coroner.

The external examination showed a well-nourished male child with transverse parallel linear abrasions to the left chest. A complete set of forensic photographs was taken. The pathologist reviewed the CT images and identified the presence of a hemopericardium, hemothoraces, a large hemoperitoneum, a left-sided pneumothorax, multiple fractured ribs, increased lung markings suggesting pulmonary contusions, and the endotracheal tube *in situ* within the right main bronchus (Figure 11.17a,b,c,d,e,f,g,h). There was no skull fracture, no intracranial collection, and no evidence of a cervical spine injury.

The case was discussed with the coroner with input from the police informant in charge of the criminal investigation of the case. The deceased's senior next of kin had requested that no internal examination of her son take place. As it was extremely likely that criminal charges would be laid against the driver of the motor vehicle that struck the deceased, the coroner requested the radiologist examine the CT images and prepare a formal report.

The radiologist confirmed the absence of skull fracture or cervical spine injury. Chest injuries included a total of nine fractured ribs, bilateral hemopneumothoraces greater on the left, nonspecific bilateral lung consolidation with no specific features of a contusion, that is, no traumatic pneumatoceles, and a mediastinal hematoma. The endotracheal tube was within the right main bronchus. The abdominal findings included a large hemoperitoneum, extensive free gas within the peritoneum suggesting perforation of a gas-filled viscus, that is, bowel, and marked disruption to the spleen with surrounding hematoma. In addition there were bilateral superior pubic rami fractures with disruption and displacement of the pubic symphysis.

Both the coroner and the investigating police officers accepted the cause of death as multiple injuries to a pedestrian in a motor vehicle incident. The pathologist also believed that further examination such as subcutaneous dissection would not provide the police investigators or the courts with any further substantial information. The deceased's body was released for burial.

Position of the Deceased in a Motor Vehicle at the Moment of the Collision

The pathologist can sometimes provide important information to assist police investigators when a major issue in the case is the position of a trauma victim within a vehicle at the time of a collision. The pathologist should always remember that the forensic scientists and vehicle examiners are often far more important in aiding the courts in making this assessment.

The forensic scientist or crime scene examiner can inspect the webbing of a seat belt, looking for stretching of the fabric to determine whether the seat belt was worn, and search for the presence and distribution of blood, hairs, and fibers. The scientist can take swabs of deployed airbags for DNA analysis. It has been shown that swabs taken of the steering wheel of a motor vehicle will preferentially show DNA from the person who was most recently in contact with the steering wheel [71].

The postmortem examination endeavors to determine the position of the crash victim by means of correlating the soft tissue injuries and fractures with the forces acting on the vehicle and the occupants during

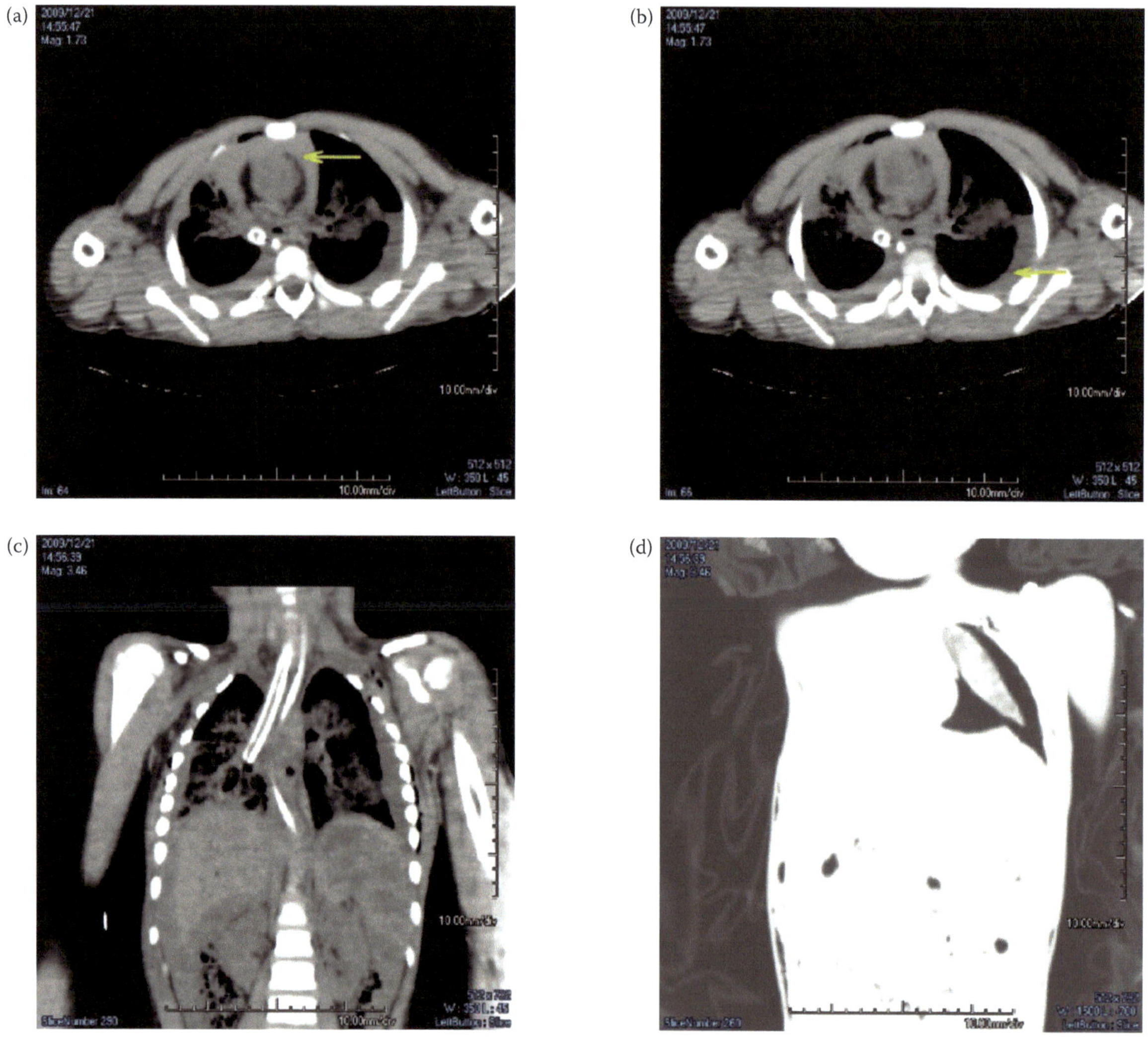

Figure 11.17 (a) Axial CT showing a hemopericardium. (b) Axial CT showing hemothoraces. (c) Coronal CT showing left pneumothorax. The endotracheal tube is seen within the right main bronchus. (d) Coronal CT using the lung window showing the left pneumothorax.

the collision. These forces may be relatively straightforward in a head-on collision, but can be extremely complex in rollovers and crashes involving multiple impacts with rapid changes in direction.

The physical consequences to an occupant of a motor vehicle in a collision result from the application of basic laws of physics. The occupant will move toward the point of contact between the vehicle and other objects(s). The use of an active restraint device such as a seat belt protects the occupant by preventing movement to the point of contact. Modern motor vehicles have crumple zones that absorb significant forces in a major collision and slow deceleration. Seat belts and airbags also have the effect of slowing the occupant's deceleration in frontal collisions by approximating the occupant's deceleration to that of the vehicle. Side impacts lead to soft tissue and bony injury from forceful contact with the side pillars and the doors. Seat belts and airbags do not protect from injury from vehicle intrusion.

The motor vehicle occupant may suffer various skin injuries, visceral injuries, and fractures. The skin injuries are generally individually nonspecific. Occasionally one may see burns and abrasions associated with airbag deployment, patterned abrasion from forceful contact from the seat belt, and, rarely, patterned abrasions from objects within the cabin. The typical seat-belt abrasion is by far the most frequently seen injury noted on external examination, which can place a victim on one side of a car.

Deployment of an airbag results in very high velocities to the module's cover. These speeds can reach up to 200 km/h. Up to two-thirds of injuries sustained directly from airbag deployment are abrasions [72]. There is a risk of minor injury, and a very small risk of lethal injury. Lethal injuries are most commonly associated with occupants of small stature who are sitting too close to the airbag or are out of normal position at the moment of impact.

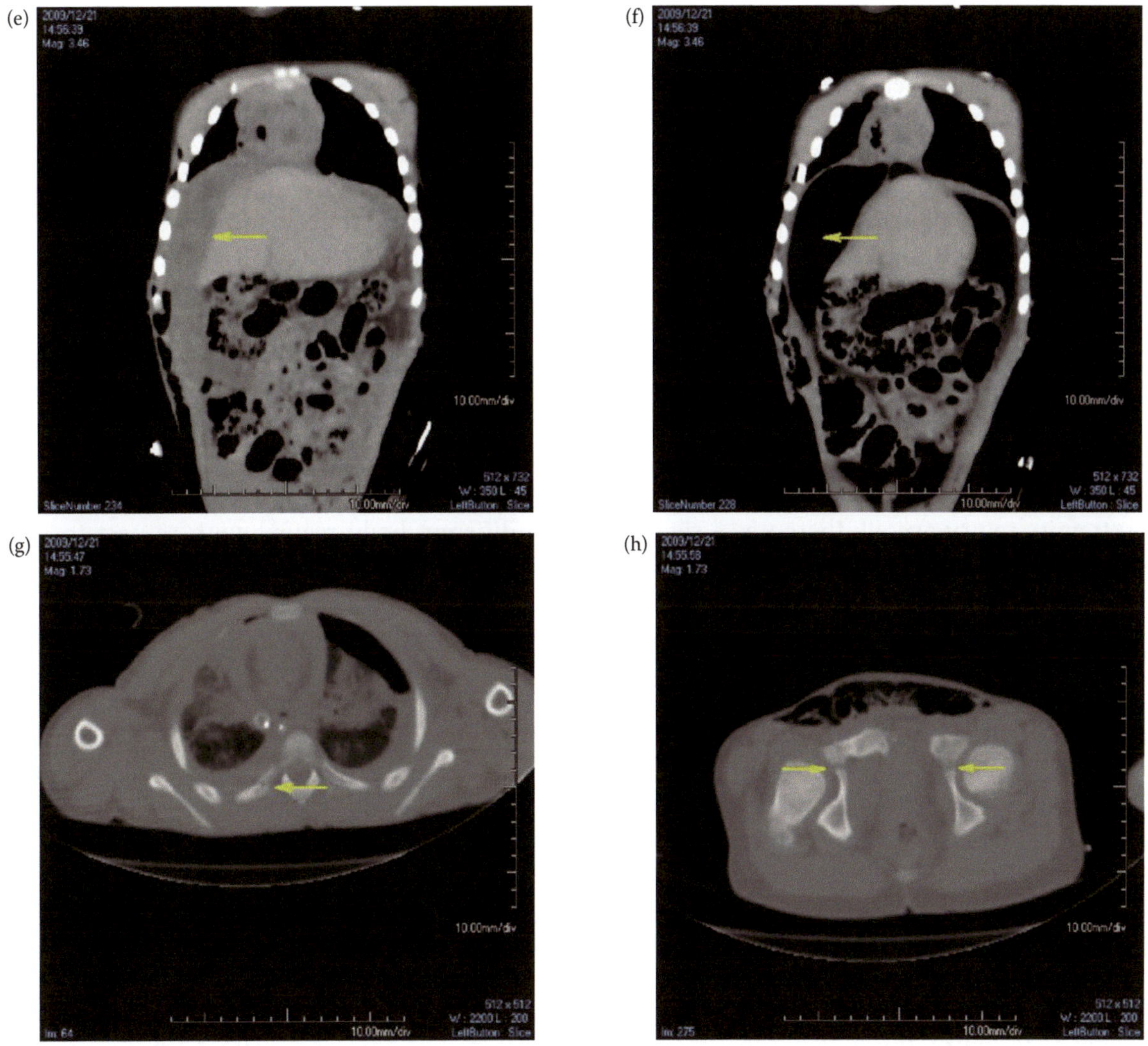

Figure 11.17 (Continued) (e) Coronal CT showing a large hemoperitoneum. Blood (with Hounsfield units of ~40) is often well seen around the liver. (f) Coronal CT showing a pneumoperitoneum. (g) Axial CT showing nonspecific pulmonary opacities. In the context of severe blunt force trauma to the chest, the findings most probably represent pulmonary contusions. (h) Axial CT of the pelvis showing bilateral central acetabular fractures suggesting a crushing mechanism of injury.

Fractures may be associated with the use of seat belts and airbags. It has been suggested that fractures associated with the wearing of seat belts tend to follow the line of the belt (i.e., from shoulder diagonally across the chest toward the contralateral hip). Airbags on the other hand tend to cause symmetrical fractures over the anterolateral aspect of the chest. A current study at the VIFM using postmortem CT to examine rib fractures associated with cardiopulmonary resuscitation has shown buckle fractures caused by the anterior–posterior chest compression (Dr. Kyung-Moo Yang, personal communication, 2009). Further studies using postmortem CT on chest injury associated with loading from seat belts or airbags may provide information on vehicle occupant seating position in the future.

The deployment of an airbag uses a vigorous chemical reaction that leads to the extremely rapid production of hot gases up to 600°C. The external examination of the deceased in a motor vehicle incident may reveal thermal injury from the release of hot gases from an airbag following deployment subsequent to a collision. Burns account for between 5% and 10% of injuries resulting from airbag deployment. The airbag vents are usually toward the back of the bag. Burns to a vehicle occupant can occur from direct contact with the hot gases, contact with the hot airbag, and from melted clothing. In addition to thermal burns, chemical burns may result from direct contact with alkaline corrosives, most commonly sodium hydroxide. Such burns mainly involve the eyes. Burns to an injured party following a motor vehicle crash tend to involve the hands or forearms. One study showed that 1.53% of front seat occupants suffered an airbag-related burn [73].

The airbag deflates primarily by the venting of the hot gases through vents in the bag. Some gases may also leak out through stitching seams in the bag. As the stitching seams are different in the driver and front passenger airbags, a singe pattern on the occupants' clothing could be different and may provide discriminating evidence [74]. The use of cornstarch as a lubricant in some airbags may also be deposited on the clothing of the driver and passenger in different patterns and thus serve as a pointer to position in the vehicle in question.

Airbags may also cause significant injuries to the upper limbs. The association between upper extremity injury and side airbag availability was investigated in a study that examined motor vehicle crashes involving vehicles with and without side airbags in the years between 1995 and 2004 [75]. Although there was no association between side airbag availability and risk of upper extremity injury overall, there was a significant increase in moderate or serious upper extremity injury and the risk of dislocation.

A separate study looked at upper extremity fractures from side airbag deployment using six, small, female cadavers and an anthropomorphic dummy [76]. The resultant fractures included a comminuted midshaft fracture of the humerus, an osteochondral fracture to the elbow, a transverse fracture of the distal radius, and a lunate fracture. A further study examined the association between side airbag deployment and the potential for wrist injuries from the hand becoming entrapped in the handgrip [76]. The experimental study used 17 small, female cadaver upper extremity specimens and a pneumatic impactor to provide a conservative estimate of the wrist tolerance to injury. It was found that 9 of the 17 tests resulted in wrist injury. The injuries included scaphoid, lunate, distal radius, and distal ulna fracture.

From a forensic point of view, although one would not suggest these injuries are going to be common, the studies provide a possible avenue of investigation when using CT to determine the driver or front seat passenger in a collision.

Contact with the peddles of a motor vehicle has been suggested as a cause of ankle fractures in motor vehicle incidents. The hypothesis that drivers would suffer a higher incidence of foot fractures from contact with the vehicle's pedals was investigated in a biomechanical and crash investigation study [77]. It was postulated that drivers would suffer more fractures to the right foot compared to the left due to dorsiflexion and eversion of the right foot on the brake pedal. The study used data from 17 cases from the Crash Injury Research and Engineering Network (CIREN) database and, in addition, involved a biomechanical study on 15 paired cadaver lower leg specimens. The study showed that drivers were more likely to suffer foot or ankle injury than passengers. The difference was almost exclusively due to an increased incidence of right foot injury to drivers.

This study contradicted an earlier retrospective study over 23 years on foot fractures in restrained front seat occupants from 15,559 crashes [78]. A total of 261 front seat occupants sustained foot fractures. Of these cases, 41% of fractures involved the ankle, 29% involved the forefoot, 20% involved the midfoot, whereas 10% involved the hindfoot. The authors concluded that the incidence, location, and Abbreviated Injury Scale (AIS) were similar between drivers and passengers. The probability of foot fracture was deemed to be mainly caused by foot compartment deformation secondary to intrusion during frontal motor vehicle collisions.

Other papers have examined the frequency of injury to different body regions with respect to the victim's position in the vehicle and the mechanics of the collision. These parameters include the type of collision (i.e., frontal, offset frontal, side-on, rollover. etc.), the change in velocity during the collision (delta v), and the type of vehicle involved in the crash (conventional passenger vehicle versus sports utility vehicle). Investigators have used various databases such as the CIREN database, and the results of imaging and postmortem documentation of the injuries sustained.

An issue with data from older studies is that the introduction of seat belts with pretensioners, multiple variably deploying airbags, new brake technology, stability control systems, and frontal crumple zones and enhanced side protection engineering means that injury patterns sustained by current vehicle occupants in a particular crash are likely to be different from those suffered in older vehicles.

A retrospective study from Scotland published in 2004, examined 4189 drivers and 954 front seat passengers [79]. It was found that mortality was higher in the front seat passenger group (6.6% compared to 5.3%). Injuries to designated body regions were coded with the AIS. Front seat passengers were shown to have significantly more injuries to the cervical spine (6.6% compared to 3.3%), chest (41.4% compared to 29%), and lumbar spine (7.4% compared to 5.2%). The information provided by these studies is of limited use when dealing with the practical situation of a particular death resulting from a particular collision.

Side-impact collisions and rollover incidents have consistently been shown to be associated with higher morbidity and mortality rates than frontal collisions. Side-impact collisions tend to cause head, neck, trunk, and extremity injury on the side of the impact. The motor vehicle occupant who is adjacent to the point of impact in a side-on collision will generally suffer injuries of greater severity than the occupant who is far side to the impact.

Moreover, the injuries to their body tend to be more severe on the side of the impact. Thus, a side-impact collision to the left side of a motor vehicle will tend to be associated with left-sided injuries such as left-sided fractured ribs and ruptured spleen, whereas a right-sided impact will tend to cause right-sided fractured ribs and ruptured liver.

Of course, such patterns of injury in a crash with particular parameters will be markedly altered if the car occupant is not wearing a seat belt and when the crash involves multiple impacts with rapid changes in direction.

A recent retrospective paper from Australia endeavored to distinguish drivers and front seat passengers solely from an analysis of the pattern of injuries sustained in the motor vehicle collision [80]. Rather than examining the physical details of the crash, the authors focused on the injury patterns of the deceased as identified by a conventional autopsy. The study period was between January 1996 and December 2000 and comprised 206 drivers and 91 front seat passengers. Three variables were examined. These were the areas of the body that were injured, the severity of the injury (including fractures), and the plane of the injury.

The study was conducted in Australia where cars drive on the left side of the road. The authors found that drivers were more likely to sustain injuries to the brain, fractures to the right femur, right posterior ribs, and the base of skull, right humerus, and right shoulder. Front seat passengers were more likely to sustain a splenic injury and fractures to the left shoulder, the left femur, and the anterior and posterior aspects of the ribs. The authors developed a model for "predicting seating position based on the presence of injury to certain regions of the body." The study had an overall predictive accuracy of 69.3%. As a number of the significant injuries can be assessed using postmortem CT, there may be a place for using CT in follow-up studies and perhaps then in routine cases.

It would seem reasonable to suggest that, as of the present time, a conventional autopsy examination or external examination and CT scanning cannot in isolation determine the position of an injured motor vehicle occupant in a crash. As is the usual case in forensic pathology, the best way one can provide useful information to police investigators and the courts is when one has all the relevant information on hand.

CT and External Examination

In conjunction with the external examination, the CT images reveal and document fractures and also internal collections of blood. The distribution of the fractures can allow one to make a general statement such as, "The majority of the fractures were to the right side of the body suggesting the impact was to this side." A comparison of the fractures seen on CT from one deceased individual compared to another, and following inspection of the vehicle may allow one to say, "The fractures seen to deceased A were on the same side but more severe than deceased B. The vehicle damage was much more extensive on one side of the vehicle. These findings suggest that deceased A was on the side of the impact" (Figure 11.18).

One may take the example of a T-bone collision to the side of a vehicle resulting in major cabin intrusion where both the driver and front seat passenger had been removed from the vehicle prior to the arrival of emergency personnel. If the CT images showed both occupants had suffered multiple fractured ribs and intrathoracic hemorrhage,

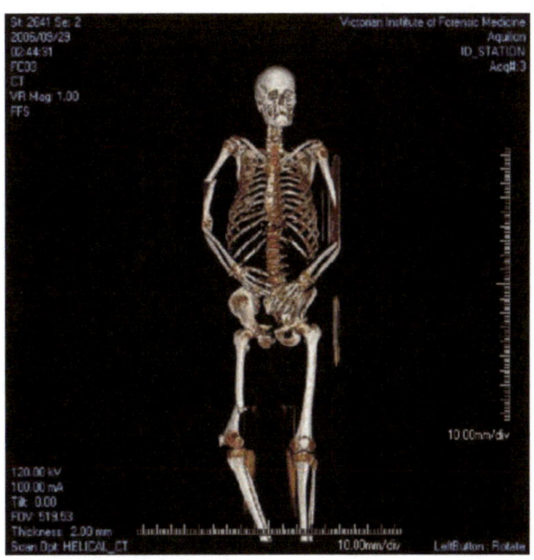

Figure 11.18 Overall skeletal survey showing multiple fractures to the right side of the body. These findings can be correlated with the scene findings, injuries to any other occupants, and damage to the motor vehicle so that one may provide an opinion on the seating position of the deceased.

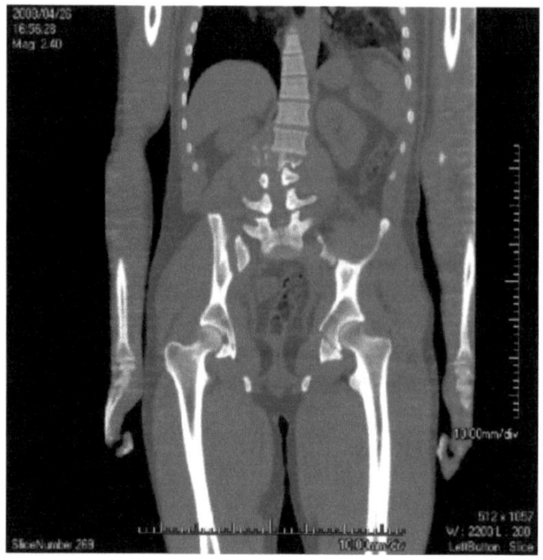

Figure 11.19 Coronal CT showing displaced left acetabular and spinal fractures. If the images are compared to the injuries sustained by other occupants of a vehicle, and interpreted in context with the damage to the vehicle, one may be able to provide an opinion on the likely seating position of the deceased.

but a central acetabular fracture to the pelvis and a spinal fracture in only one of the occupants, it would appear likely, though not certain, that that individual was on the side of the impact (Figure 11.19).

Although one can argue that a full conventional autopsy is required in such a case, it would seem unlikely that internal dissection would provide any more information which would allow a more definitive opinion.

Case Study

A 55-year-old man was riding his motorcycle when he lost control while slowing down to perform a left turn. He fell from the bike and slid along the road. He was run over by a second motorcycle, which had been traveling behind him. The rider of the second bike believed the contact point may have been to the man's neck. He was said to have died instantly in the incident. The death was reported to the coroner. The deceased's wife lodged an objection to autopsy.

Examination of the deceased's helmet revealed longitudinal scrape marks along the right lateral aspect. The external examination of the deceased showed a 16 × 6 cm region of distinct brown discoloration to the posterior aspect of the deceased's neck. The injury was photographed.

The postmortem CT scan showed multiple fractured ribs and a hemothorax. There was a fracture to the fifth cervical vertebrae. There was a fracture to the base of the skull and extensive subarachnoid hemorrhage noted to the base of the brain (Figure 11.20.). The images were referred to the radiologist. He identified a ring fracture to the base of the skull and avulsion of the medulla oblongata from the pons (Figure 11.20).

The coroner was informed of these findings. The pathologist was asked whether a conventional autopsy

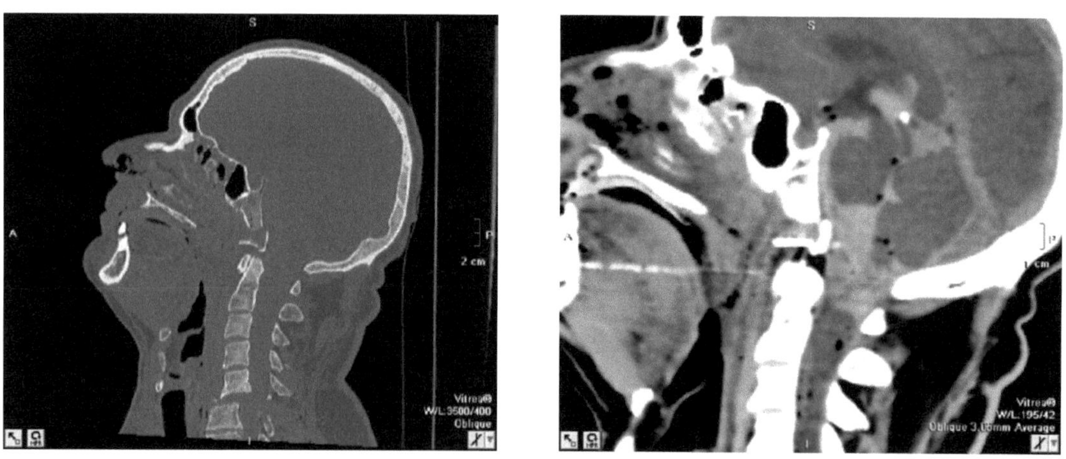

Figure 11.20 Left: Sagittal CT showing a fracture to the base of the skull. Right: Axial CT showing disruption of the medulla oblongata.

examination would determine whether the head injury was the result of the fall from the motorcycle to the road or due to contact from the second bike.

A ring fracture of the base of the skull is believed to typically arise from the application of axial force as may occur from a fall from a height to the feet or buttocks, or to the vertex of the skull. In this case, examination of the helmet showed scraping over its right lateral aspect as occurs when sliding along the roadway. There were no changes seen to the top of the helmet. On review of the CT, there was no fracture to the calcaneus, to the tibial plateau, to the neck of femur, or to the acetabulum. Furthermore, the external examination showed an abrasion to the back of the deceased's neck in a somewhat recessed area, which suggested contact from the second motorcycle.

The pathologist's opinion was that the weight of evidence suggested the lethal injury was the result of trauma from the second motorcycle as it ran over the victim's neck. The deceased's body was released from the VIFM with no internal examination.

Was the Driver of a Vehicle Conscious at the Time of the Collision?

The question as to whether an individual was conscious at the moment of a collision is somewhat surprisingly not often asked of pathologists by the courts. The external examination of the deceased's body can occasionally show dicing-type punctate incised injuries to the palm or forearms from forceful impact from shattered tempered glass. This finding may reflect victims placing their arms in front of their face just prior to a collision involving a motor vehicle.

The postmortem CT can reveal the presence of axial loading in the lower limb. The occurrence of fractures to the tibial plateau, posterior acetabular fractures, and evidence of vertical application of force to the pelvis with fracture dislocation of the sacroiliac joints is evidence of axial loading through the lower limb (Figure 11.21a,b,c). Calcaneal fractures can also reflect axial loading, though isolated calcaneal fractures may be seen in floor pan intrusion with no other evidence of loading through the tibia or femur.

Does the existence of fractures from axial loading provide unequivocal evidence that a car occupant was conscious and bracing immediately prior to the collision? In the author's opinion, probably not. Although it is certainly persuasive, one cannot exclude the possibility that through pure chance the victim's knee was in a fully extended position at the moment of impact leading to axial loading through the limb. There are numerous documented cases of individuals who have been incapacitated through natural disease, yet have caused their motor vehicle to travel at high speed by maintaining pressure on the accelerator peddle before crashing the vehicle.

An Opinion as to the Type of Vehicle That Struck a Pedestrian

The investigation of the death of an individual whose body is found beside a road is a particularly challenging case for the forensic pathologist and police investigators. The examination of a deceased individual found in these circumstances begins with an analysis of the scene by those trained in crime scene analysis. The scene examination includes a search for a possible point of primary impact (e.g., glass from head lights and indicators, and pieces of plastic from body work of the vehicle), tire marks, and associated blood spatter and presence of body tissues.

The external examination may show transfer of paint on items of clothing and deposition of grease. The external examination of the deceased's body may show patterned intradermal abrasions and bruises from contact with a tire (tire mark). Protruding and distinct parts of a motor vehicle are distinctly less common than in the past; however, there may still be a patterned abraded injury or intradermal bruise that can indicate the site of primary impact from a motor vehicle. Nonspecific abrasions are particularly common in pedestrian deaths. They are seen as a consequence of the primary impact by the car, secondary impacts to the road or windshield surrounds, and tertiary impact from other vehicles. It is extremely difficult to match a patterned abraded injury to a specific object.

Depending upon the relative heights of the deceased and the offending vehicle, there may be fractures to the lower limb (tibia or fibula), femur, or pelvis. There may be disruption to the ankle, knee, or hip joint. In general terms, when an upright adult is struck by a conventional passenger motor vehicle with a defined hood, the first impact is to the lower limb around the level of the knee. Depending upon the speed of the vehicle, its shape, and whether it is braking at the time of impact, the victim may be scooped onto the hood, and against the windshield. This typically results in head and neck injury. If the vehicle is traveling at a high speed at the moment of impact, the pedestrian may be vaulted over the cabin.

Larger passenger vehicles, such as four-wheel-drive cars, sports utility vehicles, vans, trucks, and buses, strike pedestrians above their center of gravity and push the victim forward onto the roadway. A study comparing the distribution of injuries to pedestrians struck by passenger vehicles compared to light truck vehicles showed that 62% of adults were "carried" by the passenger vehicle whereas this interaction was seen in only 28% of those

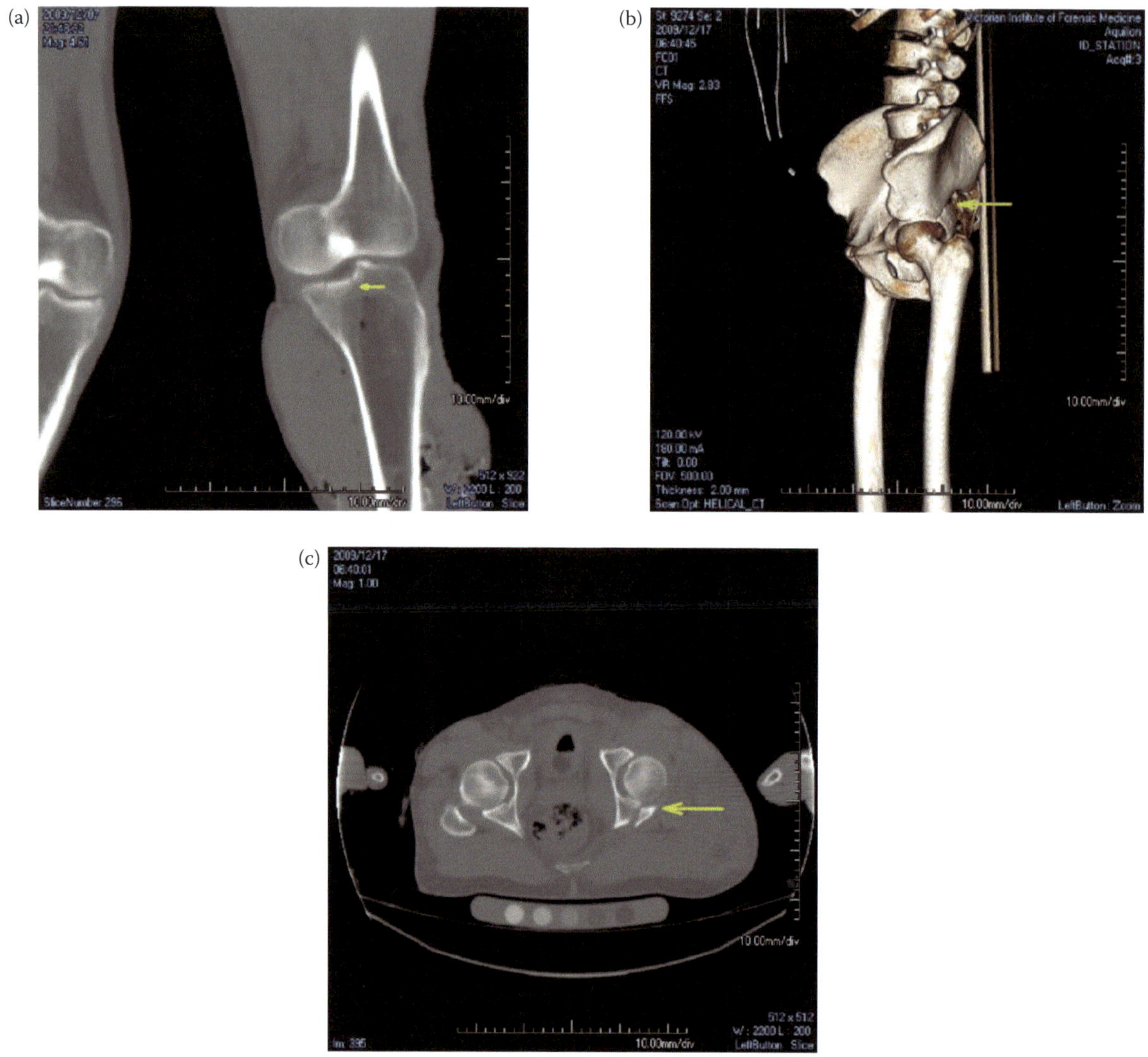

Figure 11.21 (a) Coronal CT showing a left medial tibial plateau fracture reflecting axial loading through the limb. (b) Three-dimensional reconstruction showing a posterior acetabular fracture as seen with severe axial loading. (c) Axial CT showing a fracture to the posterior aspect of the left acetabulum consistent with axial loading.

struck by light trucks [81]. In crashes involving light trucks and adults, the most common interaction (65%) was for the pedestrian to be thrown forward or knocked down. Children struck by motor vehicles of either shape tend to be thrown forward. A study by Roudsari et al. showed that 93% and 46% of children were either thrown forward or knocked down when struck by light trucks or passenger vehicles [81]. When light trucks strike adult pedestrians, light trucks tend to cause increased thoracic injury (37% to 20%) and abdominal injury (33% to 18%) compared to passenger vehicles.

In adult pedestrians struck by a conventional motor vehicle, the primary source of injury to the head is the windshield in 63% of cases. Impact from the hood surface causes 67% of thoracic injury, 58% of abdominal injury, and 36% of upper limb injuries. The bumper causes lower limb injury in 45% of cases. In comparison, the leading causes of injury from light truck versus adult pedestrian incidents were the ground for head injury (37%) and upper limb injury (39%), and the hood edge for thoracic injury (48%) and abdominal injury (56%). The bumper was the most common cause of lower limb injury (45%).

The height of the bumper bar has been shown to influence the type of lower limb injury [82]. Higher bumper heights tend to lead to fractures of the femur. The wearing of ankle-high boots can lead to fractures at the top edge of the boot, despite this not being the primary site of impact.

Forensic pathologists are familiar with the surprisingly extensive subcutaneous bruising that can be seen with relatively minor visible external injury. During a conventional autopsy examination, the side to which the body was struck by a motor vehicle can usually be shown by the presence of large bruises on subcutaneous dissection. In the future, dual energy CT (DECT) may allow the pathologist to identify and document subcutaneous bruises without extensive subcutaneous dissection.

The postmortem CT identifies the number and overall pattern of fractures. In many cases, with the aid of the scene information from the police investigators and a detailed external examination, the information provided by the CT is sufficient to allow one to provide a reasonable opinion on whether the vehicle involved in the incident was a conventional car. In cases where the pathologist is not confident that a reasonable conclusion can be reached the case can proceed to full autopsy examination.

An Opinion as to the Position of the Pedestrian When Struck

The distribution of the fractures as seen on CT can provide the pathologist with valuable information regarding the likely position of a pedestrian (Figure 11.22a,b,c). In the case illustrated in Figure 11.22, the upright pedestrian was witnessed to be struck to the right side of the body by a conventional motor vehicle with a defined hood. One may

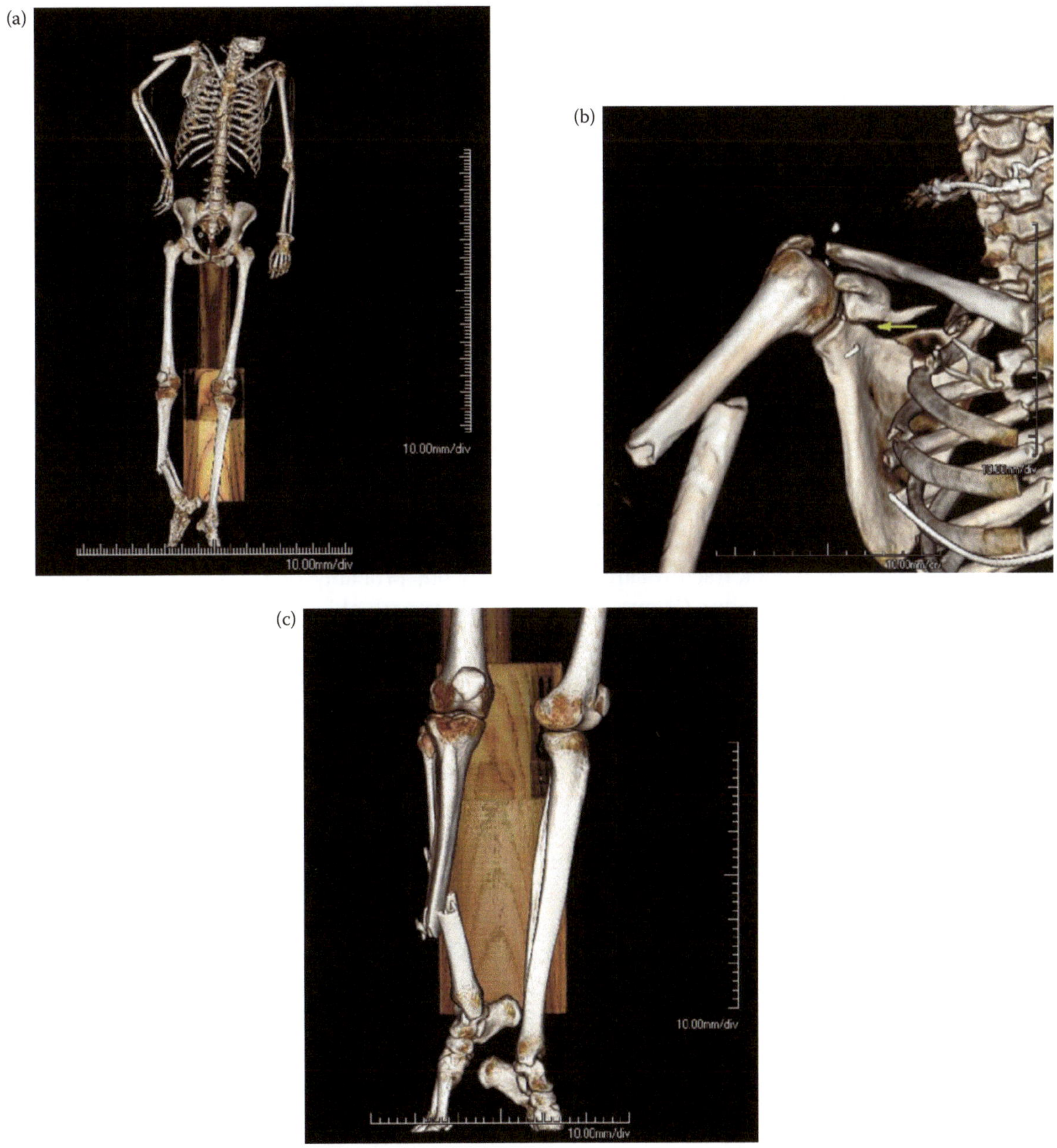

Figure 11.22 (a) Overall skeletal survey showing fractures predominating on the right side of the body. (b) Detail of fractured right tibia and fibula. (c) Detail of right humerus and adjacent fractured right ribs.

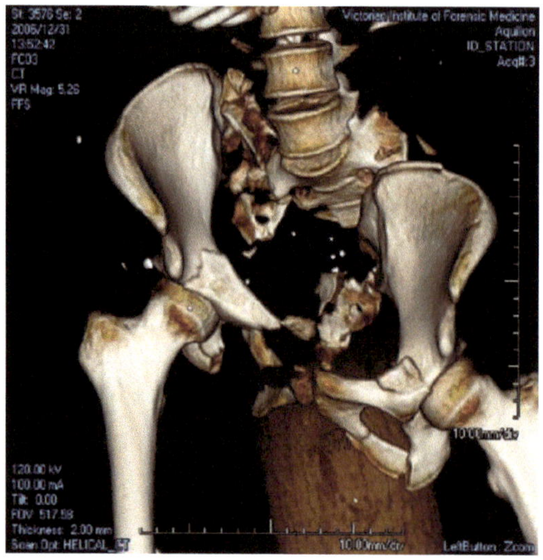

Figure 11.23 Multiple fractures to the pelvis typical of a run-over incident.

suggest the fractures to the right lower limb reflect impact from the front of the vehicle, whereas the fractured humerus and adjacent ribs could have occurred from impact with the hood. The demonstration of subarticular contusions to the femoral condyles or tibial plateau during the autopsy examination indicates the affected limb was weight bearing at the time of the impact. Magnetic resonance imaging (MRI) would allow one to identify such bone bruises without a conventional internal examination.

Teresinski and Madro have analyzed the differences in fractures and associated bony injuries in those that are struck while upright as opposed to those succumbing to run-over injury [83]. Their study showed that lateral sacroiliac joint disruption and open book fractures are particularly suggestive of pure run-over injury (Figure 11.23).

Multiple fractures of the ribs in multiple planes are classically seen with run-over injuries to the chest. More subtle injuries include fractures of the spinous processes and transverse processes at the same anatomical level as the chest injury.

Upper cervical spine injuries are common in pedestrians struck by motor vehicles. These injuries most commonly reflect a whiplash-type insult with subsequent atlantooccipital dissociation. CT can demonstrate atlantooccipital dissociation or facet injury dislocation in whiplash-type scenarios. More subtle injuries include hemorrhages into the various ligaments and strap muscles in the neck caused by rapid flexion and extension of the head. The demonstration of these features requires conventional autopsy examination.

CT and External Examination of Deceased Pedestrians

The management of a pedestrian death is highly dependent upon the known circumstances of the death at the time of the initial medicolegal evaluation. The case of a hit-and-run death or a deceased person found beside a road in unknown circumstances should undergo a conventional autopsy examination in addition to CT scanning.

The internal examination and subcutaneous dissection may provide important objective information such as localized subcutaneous bruising, which suggests the region of the body struck by a vehicle. The internal dissection of a deceased pedestrian who was struck in a sideswipe manner may reveal degloving-type shear injuries along tissue planes. Often these injuries lead to the formation of pockets that may contain blood or fat. The latter injury may well be seen on the postmortem CT, but probably requires a specific inspection of the images with this issue in mind, rather than the usual top-to-toe examination of the CT images.

The conventional autopsy can more thoroughly address issues such as possible prior assault and an examination for trace evidence within lacerations and associated with fractures.

Aircraft Incidents

The investigation of aircraft crashes requires specific expertise in the forensic and medical examination of the incident. The forensic pathology input into the investigation includes the disaster victim identification process, underlying natural disease contributing to the incident, and evidence that may suggest whether the pilot was in control of the aircraft during the incident.

In the majority of aircraft crashes the anatomical cause of death is not an issue. Interestingly, a study that compared conventional autopsy and postmortem CT in detecting injuries in military aircraft showed autopsy to be superior to CT in the overall recognition of injury

[84]. The autopsy revealed 85% of injuries compared to 53.9% for postmortem CT. Not surprisingly, CT was far superior in the detection of abnormal air. The comparison of musculoskeletal injuries was unexpectedly almost identical (91.3% autopsy, 90.3% CT).

The CT scanner can provide valuable information for occupational health and safety such as the presence of metal and glass within the remains. The CT scanner can also aid in the process of identification. The forensic pathology analysis of two victims of a small aircraft crash was recently published [85]. The crash lead to extensive fragmentation of the deceased with a total of 162 segments of human material collected in 41 bags. The CT images provided initial identification of recognizable human material in the body bags, and demonstrated and recorded identifying features such as surgical implants.

The examination of the deceased may reveal injuries that can suggest the pilot was in control of the aircraft during the incident. A report of a plane crash resulting in two fatalities using CT showed different fractures between the two individuals with one case showing injuries to the hand and lower extremities [86]. These "control surface injuries" have been attributed to the pilot's hand and feet for contact with the controls of the aircraft. However, a study that compared injuries to the pilot and passengers in 100 crash decedents showed a high incidence of these injuries to passengers as well as to pilots [87].

References

1. Bohnert M, Rost T, Faller-Marquardt M, Ropohl D, Pollack S. Fracture of the base of the skull in charred bodies—Post-mortem heat injuries or signs of mechanical traumatisation? *Forensic Sci. Int.* 1997; 87(1):55–62.
2. Erdmann D, Follmar KE, Debruijn M, Bruno AD, Jung SH, Edelman D, Mukundan S, Marcus JR. A retrospective analysis of facial fracture etiologies. *Ann. Plast. Surg.* 2008; 60(4):398–403.
3. McRae M, Momeni R, Narayan D. Frontal sinus fractures: A review of trends, diagnosis, treatment, and outcomes at a level 1 trauma center in Connecticut. *Conn. Med.* 2008; 72(3):133–138.
4. Hartsthorne NJ, Harruff RC, Alvord EC Jr. Fatal head injuries in ground level falls. *Am. J. Forensic Pathol.* 1997; 18:258–264.
5. Osawa M, Satoh F, Hasegawa I. Acute death due to hyperextension injury of the cervical spine caused by falling and slipping onto the face. *J. Forensic Leg. Med.* 2008; 15(7):457–461.
6. Yoganandan N, Sances A, Maiman D, Myklebust JB, Pech P, Larson SJ. Experimental spinal injuries with vertical impact. *Spine* 1986; 11(9):855–860.
7. Behera C, Rautji R, Dogra TD. Patterns of injury seen in deaths from accidental falls down a staircase: A study from South Delhi. *Med. Sci. Law* 2009; 49(2):127–131.
8. Kremer C, Racette S, Dionne C-A, Sauvageau A. Discrimination of falls and blows in blunt head trauma: Systematic study of the hat brim rule in relation to skull fractures. *J. Forensic Sci.* 2008; 53(3):716–719.
9. Ehrlich E, Maxeiner H. External injury marks (wound) on the head in different types of blunt trauma in an autopsy series. *Med. Law* 2002; 21(4):773–782.
10. Gill JR. Fatal descent from height in New York City. *J. Forensic Sci.* 2001; 46(5):1132–1137.
11. Shaw K-P, Hsu SY. Horizontal distance and height determining falling pattern. *J. Forensic Sci.* 1998; 43(4):765–771.
12. Cross R. Fatal falls from a height: Two case studies. *J. Forensic Sci.* 2006; 51(1):93–99.
13. Turk EE, Tsokos M. Pathologic features of fatal falls from height. *Am. J. Forensic Med. Pathol.* 2004; 25(3):194–199.
14. Lowenstein SR, Yaron M, Carrero R, Devereux D, Jacobs LM. Vertical trauma: Injuries to patients who fall and land on their feet. *Ann. Emerg. Med.* 1989; 18:161–165.
15. Lau G, Ooi PL, Phoon B. Fatal falls from a height: The use of mathematical models to estimate the height of falls from the injuries sustained. *Forensic Sci. Int.* 1998; 93(1):33–44.
16. Atanasijevic TC, Savic SD, Nikolic SD, Djokic VM. Frequency and severity of injuries in correlation with the height of fall. *J. Forensic Sci.* 2005; 50(3):608–612.
17. Venkatesh VT, Pradeep Kumar MV, Jagannatha SR, Radhika RH, Pushpalatha K. Pattern of skeletal injuries in cases of falls from a height. *Med. Sci. Law* 2007; 47(4):330–334.
18. Li L, Smialek JK. The investigation of fatal falls and jumps in Maryland (1978–1992). *Am. J. Forensic Pathol.* 1994; 15(4):295–299.
19. Lukas GM, Hutton JE Jr, Lim RC, Mathewson C Jr. Injuries sustained from high velocity impact with water: An experience from the Golden Gate Bridge. *J. Trauma* 1981; 21(8):612–618.
20. Çetin G, Günay Y, Fincanci SK, Özdemir Kolusayin R. Suicides by jumping from Bosphorus Bridge in Istanbul. *Forensic Sci. Int.* 2001; 116:157–162.
21. Christensen AM. The influence of behaviour on free-fall injury patterns: Possible implications for forensic anthropological investigations. *J. Forensic Sci.* 2004; 49(1):5–10.
22. Teh J, Firth M, Sharma A, Wilson A, Reznek R, Chan O. Jumpers and fallers: A comparison of the distribution of skeletal injury. *Clin. Radiol.* 2003; 58(6):482–486.
23. Richter D, Hahn MP, Ostermann PA, Ekkernkamp A, Muhr G. Vertical deceleration injuries: A comparative study of the injury patterns of 101 patients after accidental and intentional high falls. *Injury* 1996; 27(9):655–659.
24. Salonen EM, Koivikko MP, Koskinen SK. Multidetector computed tomography imaging of facial trauma in accidental falls from heights. *Acta Radiol.* 2007; 48(4):449–455.
25. Hansoti B, Beattie T. Can the height of a fall predict long bone fracture in children under 24 months. *Eur. J. Emerg. Med.* 2005; 12(6):285–286.

26. Johnson K, Fischer T, Chapman S, Wilson B. Accidental head injuries in children under 5 years of age. *Clin. Radiol.* 2005; 60(4):464–468.
27. Schwartz GR, Wright SW, Fein JA, Sugarman J, Pasternack J, Salhanicks S. Pediatric cervical spine injury sustained in falls from low heights. *Ann. Emerg. Med.* 1997; 30(3):249–252.
28. Chadwick DL, Bertocci G, Castillo E, Frasier L, Guenther E, Hansen K, Herman B, Krouss H. Annual risk of death resulting from short falls among young children: Less than 1 in 1 million. *Pediatrics* 2008; 121(6):1213–1224.
29. Wang MY, Kim KA, Griffith PM, Summers S, McComb JG, Levy ML, Mahour GH. Injuries from falls in the pediatric population: An analysis of 729 cases. *J. Pediatr. Surg.* 2001; 36(10):1528–1534.
30. Plunkett J. Fatal pediatric head injuries caused by short-distance falls. *Am. J. Forensic Med. Pathol.* 2001; 22(1):1–12.
31. Chiaviello CT, Christoph RA, Bond GR. Stairway-related injuries in children. *Pediatrics* 1994; 94:679–681.
32. Joffe M, Ludwig S. Stairway injuries in children. Pediatrics 1988; 82(3 Pt 2):457–461.
33. Smith GA, Bowman MJ, Luria JW, Shields BJ. Baby walker–related injuries continue despite warning labels and public education. *Pediatrics* 1997; 100(2):E1.
34. Burke MP, Path DF, Alamad S, Dip G, Opeskin K. Death by smothering following forced quetiapine administration in an infant. *Am J. Forensic Med. Pathol.* 2004; 25(3):243–245.
35. Kempe CH, Silverman FN, Steele BF, Droegemueller W, Silver HK. The battered-child syndrome. *JAMA* 1962; 180:680.
36. Caffey J. The whiplash shaken infant syndrome: Manual shaking by the extremities with whiplash-induced intracranial and intraocular bleedings, linked with permanent brain damage and mental retardation. *Pediatrics* 1974; 54(4):396–403.
37. Duhaime AC, Gennarelli TA, Thibault LE, Bruce DA, Margulies SS, Wiser R. The shaken baby syndrome: A clinical, pathological, and biomechanical study. *J. Neurosurg.* 1987; 66:409–415.
38. Gilliland M, Folberg R. Shaken babies—Some have no impact injuries. *J. Forensic Sci.* 1996; 41(1):114–116.
39. McMahon P, Grossman W, Gaffney M, Stanitski C. Soft-tissue injury as an indication of child abuse. *J. Bone Joint Surg. Am.* 1995; 77(8):1179–1183.
40. Worlock P, Stower M, Barbor P. Patterns of fractures in accidental and non-accidental injury in children: A comparative study. *Br. Med. J. (Clin. Res. Ed.)* 1986; 293(6539):100–102.
41. Hymel KP, Jenny C. Abusive spiral fracture of the humerus: a videotaped exception. *Arch. Pediatr. Adolesc. Med.* 1996; 150(2):226–227.
42. Pierce MC, Bertocci GE, Vogeley E, Moreland MS. Evaluating long bone fractures in children: A biomechanical approach with illustrative cases. *Child Abuse Negl.* 2004; 28:505–524.
43. Johnson K. Skeletal aspects of non-accidental injury. *Endocr. Dev.* 2009; 16:233–245.
44. Wootton-Gorges SL, Stein-Wexler R, Walton JW, Rosas AJ, Coulter KP, Rogers KK. Comparison of computed tomography and chest radiography in the detection of rib fractures in abused infants. *Child Abuse Negl.* 2008; 32:659–663.
45. Kleinman PK, Nimkin K, Spevak MR, Rayder SM, Madansky DL, Shelton YA, Patterson MM. Follow-up skeletal surveys in suspected child abuse. *AJR* 1996; 167:893–896.
46. Love JC, Sanchez LA. Recognition of skeletal fractures in infants: An autopsy technique. *J. Forensic Sci.* 2009; 54(6):1443–1446.
47. Case ME. Accidental traumatic head injury in infants and young children. *Brain Pathol.* 2008; 18(4):583–589.
48. Stewart G, Meert K, Rosenberg N. Trauma in infants less than three months of age. *Pediatr. Emerg. Care* 1993; 9(4):199–201.
49. Reece RM, Sege R. Childhood head injuries: Accidental or inflicted? *Arch. Pediatr. Adolesc. Med.* 2000; 154(1):11–15.
50. Leventhal JM, Thomas SA, Rosenfield NS, Markowitz RI. Fractures in young children: Distinguishing child abuse from unintentional injuries. *Am. J. Dis. Child.* 1993; 147(1):87–92.
51. Bush CM, Jones JS, Cohle SD, Johnston H. Pediatric injuries from cardiopulmonary resuscitation. *Ann. Emerg. Med.* 1996; 28(1):40–44.
52. Levin TL, Berdon WE, Cassell I, Blitman NM. Thoracolumbar fracture with listhesis—An uncommon manifestation of child abuse. *Pediatr. Radiol.* 2003; 33(5):305-310.
53. Starling SP, Heller RM, Jenny C. Pelvic fractures in infants as a sign of physical abuse. *Child Abuse Negl.* 2002; 26(5):475-480.
54. Kemp AM, Dunstan F, Harrison S, Morris S, Mann M, Rolfe K, Datta S, Thomas P, Sibert JR, Maguire S. Patterns of skeletal fractures in child abuse: Systematic review. *BMJ* 2008; 337:a1518.
55. Nimkin K, Spevak MR, Kleinman PK. Fractures of the hands and feet in child abuse: Imaging and pathologic features. *Radiology* 1997; 203:233–236.
56. Kleinman PK, Zito JL. Avulsion of the spinous processes caused by infant abuse. *Radiology* 1984; 151:389–391.
57. Dorst JP. Child abuse. *Radiologe* 1982; 22:335–341.
58. Islam O, Soboleski D, Symons S, Davidson LK, Ashworth MA, Babyn P. Development and duration of radiographic signs of bone healing in children. *AJR* 2000; 175:75–78.
59. Jenny C. Committee on Child Abuse and Neglect: Evaluating infants and young children with multiple fractures. *Pediatrics* 2006; 118;(3):1299–1303.
60. Cremin B, Goodman H, Spranger J, Beighton P. Wormian bones in osteogenesis imperfecta and other disorders. *Skeletal Radiol.* 1982; 8(1):35–38.
61. Korkko J, Ala-Kokko L, De Paepe A, Nuytinck L, Earley J, Prokop DJ. Analysis of the COL1A1 and COL1A2 genes by PCR amplification and scanning by conformation-sensitive gel electrophoresis identifies only COL1A1 mutations in 15 patients with osteogenesis imperfecta type 1: Identification of common sequences of null-allele mutations. *Am. J. Hum. Genet.* 1998; 62:98–110.

62. Carroll DM, Dorian AS, Paul BS. Clinical-pathological features of fractures in preterm infants—A review. *J. Perinat. Med.* 2007; 35(5):366–375.
63. Grünebaum M, Horodniceanu C, Steinherz R. The radiographic manifestations of bone changes in copper deficiency. *Pediatr. Radiol.* 1980; 9(2):101–104.
64. Paterson CR. Temporary brittle bone disease: Fractures in medical care. *Acta Paediatr.* 2009; 98(12):1935–1938.
65. Hughes CA, Harley EH, Milmoe G, Bala R, Martonella A. Birth trauma in the head and neck. *Arch. Otolaryngol. Head Neck Surg.* 1999; 125:193–199.
66. Zelson C, Lee SJ, Pearl M. The incidence of skull fractures underlying cephalhaematomas in newborn infants. *J. Pediatr.* 1974; 85:371–373.
67. Heise RH, Srivatsa PJ, Karsell PR. Spontaneous intrauterine linear skull fracture: A rare complication of spontaneous vaginal delivery. *Obstet. Gynaecol.* 1996; 87:851–854.
68. Dupuis O, Silveira R, Dupont C, Mottolese C, Kahn P, Dittmar A, Rudigoz RC. Comparison of "instrument-associated" and "spontaneous" obstetric depressed skull fractures in a cohort of 68 neonates. *Am. J. Obstet. Gynaecol.* 2005; 192:165–170.
69. Reichard R. Birth injury of the cranium and central nervous system. *Brain Pathol.* 2008; 18:565–570.
70. Cumming WA. Neonatal skeletal fractures. Birth trauma or child abuse? *J. Can. Assoc. Radiol.* 1979; 30:30–33.
71. Ishiko A, Tsuji A, Yamaguchi H, Hayashiba Y, Inoue H, Ikeda N. Experimental studies on identification of the driver based on STR analysis. *Leg. Med. (Tokyo)* 2008; 10(3):115–118.
72. Willis LA, Greaves I. Injuries associated with airbag deployment. *Emerg. Med.* 2002; 19:490–493.
73. Jernigan MV, Rath AL, Duma SM. Analysis of burn injuries in frontal automotive crashes. *J. Burn Care Rehabil.* 2004; 24:357–362.
74. Schubert GD. Forensic value of pattern and particle transfer from deployed automotive airbag contact. *J. Forensic Sci.* 2005; 50(6):1411–1416.
75. McGwin G Jr, Modjarrad K, Duma S, Rue LN. Association between upper extremity injuries and side airbag availability. *J. Trauma—Injury Infect. Crit. Care* 2008; 64(5):1297–1301.
76. Duma SM, Boggess BM, Crandall JR, Hurwitz SR, Seki K, Aoki T. Upper extremity interaction with a deploying side airbag: a characterization of elbow joint loading. *Accid. Anal. Prev.* 2003; 35(3):417–425.
77. Assal M, Huber P, Tencer AF, Rohr E, Mock C, Kaufmann R. Are drivers more likely to injure their right or left foot in a frontal crash: A crash and biomechanical investigation. *Annu. Proc. Assoc. Adv. Automot. Med.* 2002; 46:273–288.
78. Richter M, Thermann H, Wippermann B, Otte D, Schratt HE, Tschererne H. Foot fractures in restrained front seat occupants: A long-term study over twenty-three years. *J. Orthop. Trauma* 2001; 15(4):287–293.
79. Pedley DK, Thakore S. Difference in injury pattern between drivers and front seat passengers involved in road traffic accidents in Scotland. *Emerg. Med. J.* 2004; 21:197–198.
80. Curtin E, Langlois NEI. Predicting driver from front passenger using only the post-mortem pattern of injury following a motor vehicle collision. *Med. Sci. Law* 2007; 47(4):299–310.
81. Roudsari BS, Mock CN, Kaufman R. An evaluation of the association between vehicle type and the source and severity of pedestrian injuries. *Traffic Inj. Prev.* 2005; 6(2):185–192.
82. Matsui Y. Effects of vehicle bumper height and impact velocity on the type of lower extremity injury in vehicle–pedestrian accidents. *Accid. Anal. Prev.* 2005; 37(4):633–640.
83. Teresinski G, Madro R. Evidential value of injuries useful for reconstruction of the pedestrian–vehicle location at the moment of collision. *Forensic Sci. Int.* 2002; 128(3):127–135.
84. Levy G, Goldstein L, Blachar A, Apter S, Baronboim E, Bar-Dayan Y, Shamis A, Atar E. Postmortem computed tomography in victims of military air mishaps: Radiology–pathological correlation of CT findings. *Isr. Med. Assoc. J.* 2007; 9(10):699–702.
85. Blau S, Robertson S, Johnston M. Disaster victim identification: New applications for post mortem CT. *J. Forensic Sci.* 2008; 53(4):956–961.
86. Folio RL, Harcke HT, Luzi SA. Aircraft mishap investigation with radiology-associated autopsy: Helicopter crash with control injury. *Avia. Space Environ. Med.* 2009; 80(4):400–404.
87. Campman SC, Luzi SA. The sensitivity and specificity of control surface injuries in aircraft accident fatalities. *Am. J. Forensic Med. Pathol.* 2007; 28(2):111–115.

Concluding Remarks

The introduction of postmortem computed tomography (CT) into routine forensic pathology practice is a positive experience for forensic pathologists. It presents an opportunity to educate oneself in a new and interesting field of medicine, and provides an alternative to conventional autopsy examination in selected cases. Most important, the likely shift to fewer full autopsy examinations means the overall skills of the forensic pathologist are absolutely essential to identify which cases require a complete autopsy examination.

However, working in a medicolegal environment does raise some issues. It would appear clear that the average forensic pathologist will not attain the expertise of an expert clinical radiologist in the interpretation of CT images. Nevertheless, we know that consultants in many fields of medicine develop considerable expertise in the interpretation of the various imaging modalities in their particular specialty. There is no reason why forensic pathologists cannot develop expertise in the specific discipline of forensic radiology.

Through a process of ongoing education, sharing, and reviewing our interesting cases; keeping abreast of the literature; and eventually from the successful completion of postfellowship diplomas in forensic radiology, it may be stated that forensic pathologists are experts in postmortem CT.

Index

D

E

F

G

H

I

K

L

T

V

W

X